THE AMERICAN STAGE

THE AMERICAN STAGE

WRITING ON THEATER
FROM WASHINGTON IRVING
TO TONY KUSHNER

Laurence Senelick, editor

THE LIBRARY OF AMERICA

Some of the material in this volume is reprinted with the
permission of holders of copyright and publishing rights.
Acknowledgments are on page 831.

The paper used in this publication meets the
minimum requirements of the American National Standard for
Information Sciences—Permanence of Paper for Printed
Library Materials, ANSI z39.48—1984.

Distributed to the trade in the United States
by Penguin Group (USA) Inc.
and in Canada by Penguin Books Canada Ltd.

Library of Congress Control Number: 2009941636
ISBN 978–1–59853–069–8

First Printing
The Library of America—203s

Manufactured in the United States of America

Contents

Foreword

by John Lithgow

Live theatre is evanescent. It's like a flash of light whose after-image slowly fades. Its impact is most potent at the moment of contact between performer and audience. The moment lives on in memory for a while, and then it is gone. Even the memories die. Theatre is created to be remembered, but also to be forgotten. Every actor, singer, and dancer must make peace with this harsh truth. In fact, they should savor it. The evanescence of theatre is what gives it its electric charge and sets it apart from every other entertainment medium. Everything on television and in the movies can be re-run unchanged, *ad infinitum, ad nauseam*. But if you miss a memorable event on-stage, you have missed it forever.

This lightning-in-a-bottle aspect of theatre is what makes a passionate theatergoer swagger and gloat when he has seen something remarkable and you haven't. He can't contain himself! He will recreate in minute detail the astonishing scene where some histrionic Olympian flung thunderbolts from the stage and throttled him in his seat. And this breathless recitation always carries an unspoken note of withering pity: *I saw it and you didn't*. Everyone who has been at the receiving end of such an effusion has felt the same sensation of gnawing regret. Each of us who loves the theatre has a secret list of the great shows we never got to see. That list keeps growing, no matter how diligent our theatergoing. So does our maddening sense of wistfulness and loss.

This delectable volume offers comfort. Fortunately for us, great writers have always been on hand, sitting in the audience, to capture the best of those fleeting moments. Better yet, theatre has often fired their imaginations, stirring wide-ranging reflections on the world outside the playhouse. Scholar Laurence Senelick, the volume's judicious and tireless editor, has sifted through two centuries of the best writing about American theatre and put these literary riches on display.

In so doing, he and The Library of America have performed an invaluable service. A more diversely entertaining collection is impossible to imagine.

And what writers! There is no greater evidence of the important role theatre has played in our national story than this list of men and women who have written so expansively about it. They come from all walks of literary life but they have one great passion in common: each of them loved going to the theatre. Among them are critics, of course (Clurman, Kerr, Atkinson, Simon, Lahr, and Frank Rich). But we find fiction writers as well (Irving, Poe, Henry James, Willa Cather, and Thomas Wolfe); and humorists (Twain, Benchley, Perelman, Lardner, and Dorothy Parker); and poets (Whitman, Pound, and Langston Hughes). Best of all, there are the theatre artists themselves (Kazan, Miller, Williams, Wilder, Hansberry, Albee, Houseman, Mamet, Kushner, and even an actor, William Gillette), whose writing has the sizzle and pop of dispatches from the front.

If the writers come in all varieties, so too do their subjects. Here are pieces on vaudeville and burlesque; minstrel shows and the Chitlin Circuit; Yiddish theatre, Chicano street theatre, and gay theatre; Brechtian theatre, WPA Theatre, The Living Theatre, Theatre of Cruelty, and The Method; Edwin Booth, David Belasco, George S. Kaufman, Bert Lahr, and Carol Channing; Broadway comedy, Broadway musicals, and the greatly exaggerated reports of the Death of Broadway. These essays, reviews, diary entries, parodies, and playlets are presented chronologically, beginning in 1802 and proceeding up to the present day. Because of the volume's bounty and diversity, there are many ways to approach it. Read it front to back and you have a lively portrait of the American stage, told in many voices. Read it back to front and you travel a unique journey back in time, revisiting American history through the prism of theatre. The playwrights and players become progressively ghostly. You pass from the very familiar, to the vaguely remembered, to the totally forgotten. But fear not: the subject of each and every piece will come to life with equal vividness through the wit and incisiveness of these exuberant chroniclers.

Or, of course, you can just dip in anywhere—although with

such a scattershot abundance of rumination, fulmination, description, opinion, and fun, it's hard to decide what to pick and where to start.

I suggest four journal entries by a 19th-century New Yorker named Philip Hone. In his diary, Hone meticulously describes an unfolding crisis inside two theatres and on the downtown streets of New York City in the month of May, 1849. What became know as the "Astor Place Riots" was one of the most alarming episodes of street violence in the history of New York. Thousands rioted, hundreds of soldiers and police were called in, and 31 people were killed. All of this was fueled by the passionate loyalty of the fans of rival actors William Charles Macready and Edwin Forrest, who were both playing the role of Macbeth in two playhouses only blocks apart. For New York theatergoers of that day, it was not their finest hour. From Hone's description, they behaved abominably, hurling "a shower of missiles, rotten eggs, and other unsavory objects, with shouts and yells of the most abusive epithets."

But what can you expect? Theatre does that to us as nothing else can. Ordinarily we do not riot. But at its best, theatre can make us act crazy. It can make us sob, guffaw, leap to our feet, shout, stamp, and clap until our hands are sore. We are all hungry for theatre that can make us respond that way. And that hunger is the reason you are holding this book in your lap. It is a hunger shared by all the writers collected herein. Open up the book to any page and their writing will help you experience the glories of American theatre from the recent and not-so-recent past. You may feel a pang of remorse that you weren't sitting beside them in the audience. In each case, stunning things happened onstage and you missed out. But the words of these writers will bring these moments back to life. They will almost, *almost* make you feel that you were there.

Introduction

OBSERVING American society in the 1830s, the touring Irish comedian Tyrone Power described its citizens as a theatrical race. Americans seemed always to be on stage, as the New World showed off for the critical Old World. Theatricality was, in his view, the native mode of self-expression. When Constance Rourke quoted Power's observation in her ground-breaking study of 1931, *American Humor: A Study of the National Character*, she made a useful distinction between the theatrical and the dramatic. The theatrical she saw as "full of experiment, finding its way to audiences by their quick responses and rejections. On the stage the shimmer and glow, the minor appurtenances, the jokes and dances and songs, the stretching and changes of plots, are arranged and altered almost literally by the audience or in their close company: its measure is human, not literary. The American theater then . . . was a composite of native feeling. It had significance, not because it might at some later time evolve into great national art, but because it was closely interwoven with the American character and the American experience."

Rourke's differentiation between a theatre that spontaneously incarnates national character and a drama that consciously seeks to be art seems to me more valid and useful than such later proposed dichotomies as highbrow/lowbrow, amateur/professional, mainstream/tributary, or commercial/avant-garde. A popular medium even when it is not populist, the American theatre is improvisatory, regularly reinventing its definitions of both "American" and "theatre." Attempts to institutionalize it usually fail. Its traditions are preserved, not by a conservatory or museum staging, but in an ongoing dialogue with its public.

The absence of such constraints as official censorship, state patronage of the arts, or centralized professional training allowed the early American stage free range. Even so, it had from the outset two substantial handicaps to overcome.

The first was its colonial past: theatre was an importation from the mother country, with English actors and repertoire.

Homespun efforts at dramatic writing and the playing of tragedy were inevitably measured against British models. This has proved to be an enduring tendency. With London society the pattern of gentility, members of refined stock companies affected English accents. At least until the supremacy of the musical, the transatlantic traffic of hit plays was mainly one-way. Even today, a "think play" from the West End is transferred to Broadway each season as the theatrical equivalent of the coffee-table book.

Seekers after a national identity strove vigorously to free the drama from foreign fashions. American topics and characters appeared in the plays of native-born writers even before the Revolution; in the first decades of independence, many works were appreciated as much for their patriotism as their literary qualities. Opening-night prologues and addresses celebrated the triumph of New World enlightenment over Old World superstition; competitions for plays on indigenous themes and the warm reception awarded the winners revealed an urgent desire for a distinctly American theatre.

The playhouse came to be regarded as a site of democratic interaction. Foreign travelers regularly complained that there were no codes of conduct for the audience, no clear class divisions, other than cost, in the seating. (Street urchins and African-Americans, however, were relegated to upper balconies, known as "the peanut gallery" or "nigger heaven.") When, in 1820, the Chestnut Street Theatre in Philadelphia tried to establish a separate entrance for the occupants of the pit, they rebelled and demanded to use the same front door as those who paid for higher-priced seats. The management had to give in. The American theatre was not, at least in principle, to be stratified by class.

The agitation for an identifiably national theatre was kept on the boil by nativist support for Edwin Forrest in his feud with the English actor-manager W. C. Macready and frothed over into the murderous Astor Place Riot of 1849. Less personal animus and more local pride prompted the periodic call for a great American playwright. Faced with a repertoire overloaded with adaptations of European works, at the end of 19th century critics hailed James A. Herne as the "American Ibsen" and Clyde Fitch as "the American Sardou," while the next generation invested its hopes in Eugene O'Neill as the man who would win American drama an international standing.

The other major handicap hobbling the nascent American theatre was a deep-seated anti-theatrical prejudice. The godly disdained actors as the "rogues and vagabonds" of Elizabethan edicts, and equated a woman's going on the stage with going on the streets. This antipathy was not exclusively a Puritan attribute; other sects, the Quakers, Methodists, Presbyterians, and Baptists among them, likewise distrusted the theatre as "the Devil's chapel." The prejudice was not universal, by any means: from the start, the theatre had been welcomed in New York and the Southern colonies. As it traveled westward with frontier settlements, it was greeted enthusiastically, not least by the Mormons.

Playhouses were off-limits to the pious not only because of what took place on stage but because of their profit-taking from the sale of drink and a third tier where prostitutes trawled for trade. Even regular church-goers might, however, turn a blind eye if the entertainment on offer was housed in a "museum," a "mechanics' institute," or a Chatauqua. Shakespeare (bowdlerized) might be revered next to the Bible but he was best heard recited by a reader in street clothes on a bare platform. Many believed that the righteous could be brought to tolerate the theatre so long as it inculcated morality or taught an edifying lesson. This attitude persists. Funding organizations in the United States still prefer to bestow their largess on institutions that profess social betterment; "art for art's sake" or "mere" entertainment is insufficient inducement to open their purses.

Avoidance of playhouse fare meant that non-dramatic amusements played to a wider public than did conventional tragedies and comedies. For three decades, the favorite performers in the nation were not actors, but the Ravels, a troupe of Franco-Danish clowns whose pantomimes, enhanced by feats of dexterity, enchanted Henry James and Ulysses S. Grant in their youth. Blackface minstrelsy became the most widely attended type of antebellum entertainment in part because there were no women in its troupes, and its high spirits could easily be contained by a town hall or assembly room. The show most Americans were likely to see in a lifetime was not an original play, but one of the many dramatizations of *Uncle Tom's Cabin*. Its most famous lines—"I 'spect I jes' growed," "How shiftless!," "My soul ain't yours, massa! It's been bought and paid for by one that is able to keep it and you can't have it!"— became household words. Audiences thrilled to Eliza crossing the ice with the bloodhounds snapping at her heels, the death of Little Eva wafted aloft by angels, and the unredeemed sadism of Simon Legree. Even the South, which long resisted Mrs. Stowe's abolitionist message, succumbed after the Civil War, framing the plays as idylls of bygone plantation life. The pervasiveness of blackface minstrelsy and the Tom show imprinted stereotypes that promoters of an authentic African-American theatre would struggle to efface.

Uncle Tom's Cabin the play was a melodrama, and melodrama —originally devised during the French Revolution for a new semi-literate audience—became the favorite American dramatic genre. Extolling virtue and downplaying dialogue in favor of expressive mime and climactic tableaux, dividing the world into good vs. evil and holding out an optimistic outcome, the reward of virtue achieved by vigorous action, melodrama was congenial to the American temperament. Despite its formulaic nature, melodrama was able to evolve with the society that relished it. The standard conventions could be varied by a coating of surface realism; melodrama readily exploited technological innovations for plot climaxes (railroad trains, the telegraph, sawmills, steam yachts) and special effects (treadmills, revolves, electricity). Stripped of the once obligatory happy ending, melodrama has maintained its primacy on the American stage. Heightened emotions, hidden motives, and over-heated conflicts are characteristic of the works of the most honored American playwrights, from O'Neill, Maxwell Anderson, and Elmer Rice to Lillian Hellman and Tennessee Williams to Sam Shepard and David Mamet.

Comedy ran a close second to melodrama in popularity. Constance Rourke identified three indigenous comic types, the laconic Yankee, the blustering frontiersman, and the rollicking blackface minstrel, as fomenters of rebellion. That may be too strong; they are not so much rebels with a cause as mischief-makers. Shunting between the poker-faced and the loud-mouthed, such "rugged individualists" as the Down-East farmer among city slickers or even the eccentric Sycamore family of *You Can't Take It with You* tease the system without threatening it. The subversion can be as understated as the wisecracks of a gum-chewing Will Rogers. Only occasionally, as with the anarchic antics of the Marx Brothers, does it swell to what Gilbert Seldes would call "the daemonic."

After the Civil War, stage comedy became less text-bound and more spectacular. Pantomime, personified by the clown George L. Fox, exulted in physical horseplay and hyperbolic violence; expanded with variety acts, it catered to short attention spans and unsophisticated tastes. Burlesque, in the form of scantily-clad chorines such as Lydia Thompson's British Blondes, evolved from travestied mythology into a display alternating female pulchritude and male buffoonery. Comic opera, first as laundered Offenbach, then an acclimatized Gilbert and Sullivan and Victor Herbert, eventually triumphed as musical comedy. The most durable hits of the Grant era, *Humpty Dumpty*, *The Black Crook*, and *La Grande Duchesse de Gérolstein*, were seen by far more Americans than competing Shakespearean revivals and adaptations of French sensation drama. Edwin Booth's grand new theatre, built in 1869 as a temple of the muses, went bankrupt in five years. The only "legitimate" play to enjoy the popularity of the musical genres was Joseph Jefferson's ever-green version of *Rip Van Winkle*.

The perennial appeal of *Rip* benefited from the ascendancy of the star player and the efficacy of touring. Theatrical celebrity was not unique to the United States, but here it was abetted by aggressive publicity, the product of Yankee ingenuity. Promoting foreign talent and native oddity, P. T. Barnum and the Chevalier Henry Wikoff were shameless in devising lures for audiences. The newspaper interview, the gossip column, the advance agent, the advertising parade, the color-lithograph poster (known in France as "*l'affiche américaine*") were all native inventions. A rash of new magazines and newspapers kept the profession alert to job opportunities and the public agog about the doings of their favorites. The hyperbole of hoopla became the norm in American theatrical discourse.

Strolling had always been the actor's means of enlarging his audience and earning extra money, especially between seasons. The ever-expanding network of railways now facilitated tours as a prime source of income. Producers fitted up companies to travel from coast to coast for months; plays too crude or too stale to work in New York or Boston might have the longevity of the Wandering Jew on the road. Joseph Murphy, who rarely appeared in Manhattan, became the richest actor in America from years of touring the same four comedy-melodramas of the Ould Sod.

Touring was made easier by the existence in even the smallest towns of an "opera house." Whatever appeared on its stage, from tabloid opera to trained poodles, was deemed "theayter" by its omnivorous public. Second-rate troupers could bill themselves as "stars," even if they were eclipsed when the genuine article, a Henry Irving or Sarah Bernhardt, took to the road to replenish their finances.

The trend to industrial monopoly that characterized America in the Gilded Age extended to "the show business" (a term that goes back as far back as 1850). What Rockefeller was doing in oil and Armour and Swift in pork, the Frohmans, Shuberts, Loews, and their competitors set out to do in the world of entertainment. By controlling the theatres, the booking agencies, and various organs of publicity, they tried to impose pay scales, working hours, itineraries, and codes of conduct on an unruly profession, to make it yield maximum profit. As with all such efforts, the boon of security and organization was counterbalanced by the bane of uniformity and pressure. Many found playing continuous vaudeville as arduous as piecework in a sweat shop. The long run, then as now viewed as an outcome devoutly to be wished, undermined the repertory ideal and caused the demise of the stock company. Ultimately, abuses led to the same calls for unionization and reform that were heard in the other industries, and Actors' Equity and similar associations came into being. It was at this time that New York playhouses moved uptown to Times Square and "Broadway" became a metonym for American theatre.

While performers were signing contracts binding them to ever stricter conditions, the working class was enjoying its few hard-won hours of leisure in new ways. The theatrical syndicates and burlesque wheels could not expand fast enough to regulate the proliferation of commercial diversions "for the million": fun fairs and amusement parks, roller rinks, dance halls, nickelodeons, low-priced melodrama, and, of course, music halls and vaudeville houses. The level of the performance was pitched at fun-seekers of limited education, often recent immigrants still shaky in English. Their own communities sponsored performances in their native languages, feeding the mainstream theatre with talent from the tributaries.

At the other end of the cultural spectrum, the "entertainment industry" was challenged by ideas from an "abroad" that had little in common with that of the huddled masses. The New Stagecraft of Adolphe Appia, Gordon Craig, and Jacques Copeau rejected "realism" in staging and design for more ingenious, elegantly simple solutions. Psychology and atmosphere, already acclimatized in modernist fiction, began to infiltrate the drama, abetted by electric lighting and non-naturalistic scenery. The Provincetown Players and the Washington Square Players, free-spirited collectives of bohemians and college graduates, paved the way for the enterprising Theatre Guild and Playwright's Company, which tried to preserve literary values while making a profit. The Little Theatre movement thrived in small towns and communities.

These idealistic enterprises had to compete (and sometimes partner) with an invigorated commercial stage. Broadway offered dozens of new plays every month, reaching its peak in the 1927–28 season, with 264 productions in 70 theatres; vaudeville, revue, and musical comedy played to full houses. Fortunes were made not just by producers but by playwrights. The period between the wars was a golden age of theatrical journalism, dominated by the wits of the Algonquin Round Table, who moved easily between the press-room and the rehearsal hall, romanticizing the reporter and the actor as symbiotic celebrities.

The theatre as a surefire investment ended with the Wall Street crash of 1929. As the Depression deepened, audiences sought diversion in the cheaper picture show, now enhanced by dialogue spoken by actors from "the legit," and programs emanating for free from the radio in their own parlors. Hard times drove the theatre to become more politically engaged: actors with leftist sympathies formed collectives, among them the Group Theatre, the New Theatre League, and Theatre Union. They were radical in their idealism, evangelical in their agendas. Social progress and artistic edification also motivated the Federal Theatre Project, under the guidance of Hallie Flanagan. As part of the national relief effort, it used government subsidies to support artists and writers across the continent. For four packed years it fostered creativity on a number of fronts, hoping to attract workers, immigrants, and children to theatre as a wholesome mass entertainment and a remedy for social inequities. Bowing to pressure from the right, which suspected Communist subversion, Congress pulled the plug on this promising effort and thwarted the growth of a national theatre.

By the 1950s, an audience troubled by Cold War paranoia and the threat of atomic destruction preferred a theatre leached of politics. Arthur Miller was the only playwright of stature to buck the trend, with messages that aspired to universal application. Tennessee Williams' lyrical treatment of personal trauma was perhaps a clearer symptom of the nation's mood. The Actors Studio, unlike its predecessors the Group and the Los Angeles Actors Laboratory, steered clear of public affairs; its house brand, the Method, encouraged actors to dig deep into personal psyches. The American way of acting became known not for rhetorical finesse or high style, but for the powerful exposure of raw emotions and psychic sores.

As Broadway settled into predictable patterns, its hegemony was challenged from without. Regional theatres, dedicated to staging the classics and local dramatists, replaced "the road"; university theatres, unconcerned with profit margins, freely experimented. Even New York underwent decentralization in the move to smaller houses Off-Broadway and the rise of revues and café theatres. Brechtian notions of "epic acting" and non-Aristotelian dramaturgy, introduced in the 1940s, had by the 1960s been put into practice, if mostly on the margins. Other importations—the so-called "absurdist" playwrights, Antonin Artaud's Theatre of Cruelty, and the "Poor Theatre" of the Polish director Jerzy Grotowski—proved to be heady stimulants, eagerly and uncritically absorbed by enthusiasts. The director displaced the leading actor and often the playwright as the demiurge of the production.

However, the European influence on homegrown movements was more superficial than might appear. Political protest and social unrest more often generated the "alternative theatre," residing in coffee-houses and church halls, spilling out into the streets, creating happenings rather than plays, liberating actors from texts and turning them into "participants," inciting young audiences and infuriating older ones. Censors bristled as nudity, four-letter words, drug-taking, sex acts both simulated and actual invaded the stage. A profusion of manifestos, theories, calls to arms, incoherent scenarios, environmental settings refreshed every aspect of performance. Voices once muffled or silent became loud and strident. Before long the margins moved to the center. Stanley Kauffman pointed out that Sam Shepard was the first American playwright to become world famous without ever having been produced on Broadway.

Local organs of repression were quick to respond, but it took another two decades before the lumbering apparatus of federal disapproval was put into forward gear. During the Reagan administration, Congress again declared art to be subversive, this time not politically but morally. Fearful that the arts might serve as a form of expression and a source for income for sexual minorities, now branded by the AIDS epidemic, conservatives launched a full-throated attack. The NEA Four, a quartet of performance artists, three of them gay, were stripped of their grants. By the time the smoke had cleared, the American theatre was more fragmented than ever. The eager acceptance of Tony Kushner's *Angels in America* as the representative play of the 1990s was due, in part, to its effort at drawing together various threads of national identity and weaving the contradictions of past and present into a persuasive dramatic structure.

Real estate interests had their way and turned Times Square into a theme park. On Broadway, lavish musical spectacles and revivals of classic plays titivated with movie stars targeted an audience of tourists and visitors. The resurgence of the star system has not only displaced the primacy of the director (who still remains dominant in the non-commercial theatre); the need felt by Hollywood celebrities to validate their acting credentials suggests that the theatre has not lost its prestige in the artistic hierarchy. At the same time, it validated its credentials as a "popular" art form when in 2009 Broadway broke all box-office records. The term "corporate theatre" has been coined to describe the blockbuster, based on a pre-existing, tried-and-true money-spinner, promoted by multiple producers, and transported in cloned versions throughout the country. Some speculate that the capital of live entertainment has shifted to Las Vegas, a venue more congenial to showgirls and magicians than to any presentation that runs over an hour. Meanwhile, regional theatres rack their brains to lure audiences, their houses so empty that they can offer "anytime tickets" that allow the playgoer to drop in whenever he feels like it.

At the present time, no common audience, style, or approach can be identified. Playing it safe vies with going over the top. Grass-roots phenomena such as the Chitlin Circuit appeal to audiences that have never heard of the Great White Way; plays are aimed at coteries of the like-minded. The spectrum runs from dinner-theatre patrons, watching abbreviated versions of proven hits, to aficionados of the avant-garde, gathered in a warehouse to cheer on a ceremony of self-mutilation. There is no overlap in these diverse publics, even if their very diversity seems typically American.

Once again, the American theatre has had to reinvent itself or, at the very least, repackage itself. Some of its most exciting work is hybrid, combining movement, music, words, and imagery and punctuating live performance with electronic media. Directors draw on such rival attractions as the rock concert, the sports competition, and the "reality show" to galvanize their *mise en scène*; playwrights reassemble their dialogue as rap lyrics or film scenarios. Flesh-and-blood actors share the stage with puppets, mannequins, and laser projections. What has been gained by this blurring of boundaries is an assertion of theatricality over that "realism" that was for so long the fetish of the American stage.

Precisely because it heightens and condenses reality into forms that lure our senses and tickle our brains, "the give-and-take of real theatrical experience" (in Norris Houghton's expression) continues to exercise an attraction. The primal need of Americans to perform for their fellows and experience reaction on the spot is evident from the current popularity of high-school dramatics and amateur competitions. In the land of opportunity, every spectator is potentially a performer and every performer is potentially a star.

The theatre enables the audience at one unrepeatable moment to be transported by an idea, an image, a phrase, an allure, a virtuosic rendition—or an irresistible combination thereof. The experience may seem ephemeral, but it has a vivid after-life. Once imprinted on the consciousness, it can be summoned up and refashioned in the memory. The potency of the theatre resides in this double action: the immediate call-and-response and the "recollection in tranquility."

To write about the theatre well one has to distill both the immediate experience and the recollected impression, to draw the reader into the charmed circle and conjure up what has already vanished. Consequently, the best writing on American theatre is almost always a personal reaction. Whether it is a playgoer complaining of the hardness of the seats or a critic comparing interpretations of Hamlet, the most vital accounts are by eyewitnesses. As early as William Dunlap's *History of the American Theatre*, the chronicle of events is interwoven with an aggrieved account of the author's own managerial tribulations.

Not that early Americans felt an urgency to record what went on in the theatre. Most were content to regard playgoing as a slightly guilty diversion that required no parsing. Newspaper notices of performances were more announcements than critiques. When Washington Irving invented the lay-figure "Jonathan Oldstyle" to ghost his criticism of the Park Theatre in 1801, he also devised one Andrew Quoz to play devil's advocate. Quoth Quoz: "The critics, my dear Jonathan, are the very pests of society; they rob the actor of his reputation, the public of their amusement; they open the eyes of their readers to a full perception of the faults of our performers; they reduce our feelings to a state of miserable refinement, and destroy entirely all the enjoyment in which our coarser sensations delight." In other words, the theatre appeals to the emotions, not the intellect, so why tax it to be more than it is?

With the proliferation of periodical literature, coverage of the theatre helped to fill columns. Once again, the British acceptance of theatre-going as part of the social calendar provided a model. American criticism sometimes had a mercenary motive: managers and lessees who paid for advertisements expected their offerings to be reported, and, in some cases, the journalists themselves were feed to provide favorable notices. Often the theatrical event was considered newsworthy for extraneous reasons: the opening of a new playhouse, the debut of a foreign star, the premiere of an anticipated play. As readership broadened, reviewers felt an obligation to describe a performance in detail and convey, for the benefit of those who might never see it, something of the effect it had not just on them but on its audience. Writers of fiction found in the theatre a picturesque milieu full of high-flown sentiments and extravagant behavior not met with in everyday life. The acting profession, in its contingent and despised state, could be championed as a downtrodden caste, worthy of respect.

Commentators on national character and behavior held up the theatre as a glass to magnify American virtues and vices in sharp detail. As calls came for polishing American manners, critics conceived their mission as improving the theatre so that it might assist the process of civilization. Alan L. Ackerman Jr. has pointed out that such romantic terms of praise as "awful," "raging," "wild" in the Jacksonian period came to be replaced by "dignified," "stately," "intellectually adequate." The school of William Winter urged the stage to maintain a lofty level of thought and morality. (His concerns live on in the writing of James Huneker, Stark Young, and even Eric Bentley, although there the moral precepts get transformed into ideas of cultural advancement.) Such appeals to dignify the theatre ran up against its expansive evolution into "show business" meant to entertain an ever wider, less discriminating populace.

As part of that evolution, the press enlarged the space devoted to theatrical activities, for in most cities the reporters' Bohemia and the thespians' Bohemia lived cheek by jowl. A considerable number of periodicals devoted exclusively to theatre and drama found an avid readership. By the 1920s, however, a good deal of space was given over to the movies, reflecting a shift in the audience's attendance. In reaction, writing about theatre vaunted its urbanity and sophistication, aware that it was trading in luxury goods for a more select public. Most of the pieces in this book first appeared in weekly and monthly journals aimed at the ostensible "common reader"; their contributors had more time than their colleagues on the dailies in which to ponder their impressions and more space in which to express them. Some of these periodicals, such as *The New Republic*, *The Atlantic*, and *The New Yorker*, are happily still with us, while the dailies, struggling to survive, continue to retrench their arts coverage. Newspaper reviews, once displays of terse wit or compact analysis, have in recent years grown rushed and formulaic, limited to plot summary or tips to consumers. What has fallen by the wayside has been the detailed analysis of a performer's interpretation of a role. Perhaps because they think this obligation has been assumed by electronic documentation, writers no longer feel called upon to record what a performer does or to understand how he does it. In John Mason Brown's words, "the actor has tended to become a last paragraph figure."

Today, reflecting its perceived marginality, few of our "public intellectuals" choose to analyze the theatrical experience in depth. Many of the academics who take the theatre as their field of interest are content to address fellow specialists in an argot impenetrable to the uninitiated. At the other end of the spectrum, print has lost much of its authority to the Internet, where every kibitzer can post an opinion, even during a production's gestation period. Amid this welter of instant estimates, the rich hoard of past writing stands as an articulate testament to the importance of playgoing, play-acting, and playwriting to past generations and to the thinking present.

This book is not a documentary history of the American theatre; there are good ones edited by Barry Witham and William C. Young. Neither is it a survey of the American drama as viewed by its critics (a classic collection edited by Montrose J. Moses and John Mason Brown was published in 1934) nor an anthology of playwrights on playwriting, although playwrights can be found here in abundance.

My intention was to put together an assortment of firsthand written responses to the theatrical experience that display insight, wit, or strong feeling. To this end, I have included samples of various genres: dramatic criticism, reviews, essays, memoirs, novels, poetry, parody, diary entries, manifestoes. The contributors are drawn from both sides of the footlights; playgoers and critics share the stage with dramatists, actors, directors, and designers. If playwrights and critics appear in greater number than actors, directors, and designers, it is simply because their medium is the written word. Most actor biographies are ghost-written or "as told to" and many recent memoirs even of playwrights sound dictated into a tape recorder with a minimum of editing.

With very few exceptions, all the pieces in this book originate as an expression of what happens on a stage and not in a study. What they share is an intense engagement with the theatre, pro or con. From those who believe the stage contributes to the welfare of the nation to those who deplore its corrupting influence, from those who praise its efforts at sublimity to those who revel in the absurdity of its pretensions, each writer believes that theatre matters. Even the most negative of critics, jaded by a long term of servitude to daily reviewing, seems never to lose the utopian belief that, sooner or later, the theatre will live up to its potential. Disappointment when the ideal is not attained is balanced by jubilation when it is; and both states of mind are expressed energetically.

The pieces are arranged in chronological order to evoke a sense of the theatre's protean convolutions (I hesitate to say progress) over time. However, all pieces by a single author are grouped together: this enables us to compare the immediate reactions of a young Walt Whitman, Mark Twain, or Henry James with their older selves indulging in rosy retrospection. For those of the entries that come from memoirs, nostalgia inevitably colors the event: Fred Allen rhapsodizes about vaudeville after its best qualities have already been appropriated and distorted by mass media; John Houseman makes epic the vicissitudes of a Federal Theatre Project for a later generation needful of inspiration.

A favorite refrain of readers of anthologies is "How come you left out (fill in the blank)?" Here I rely on John Mason Brown, apologizing for similar omissions in his anthology: "In seeking to give in one volume a sense of the emerging American theatre that contemporary playgoers have seen, it has committed many sins of omission, which, though they may be unpardonable, have in reality been unavoidable. No library shelf is large enough to hold the books that would be needed to do proper justice to all the dramatists and producers, the actors and playhouses, the productions and designers—yes, and the critics, too—that in their days have figured prominently in the annals of the American stage." Sixty-six years later, the number of phenomena that deserve attention has swollen far beyond what could be encompassed between these covers. The first selection for this book ran to over twice the present number of pages, with double the number of authors and topics. Spatial limitations called for drastic cutting. I would like to think that what remains is superior to what was deleted, but it cannot be denied that a number of distinctive voices go unheard and important works and individuals remain offstage. While certain pieces may be familiar, there are, I hope, some surprises in store.

A number of friends and colleagues made valuable suggestions for inclusions. My heartfelt thanks go to the late Doris Abramson, Noreen Barnes, David Brownell, Connie Congdon, Tom Connolly, Annette Fern, Adrienne Mackie, Monica White Ndounou, Martin Puchner, Lloyd Schwartz, Matthew W. Smith, Amanda Vaill, Arnold Wengrow, Gary J. Williams, Don B. Wilmeth, and Barry Witham. The editorial staff of The Library of America deserves to take a separate bow for its perspicacity and patience.

Now take your seats—the curtain rises!

Laurence Senelick

WASHINGTON IRVING

From his earliest youth, Washington Irving (1783–1859) felt a "persistant passion for the stage." His family of Scottish Covenanters set their face against such diversions, so the boy crawled out onto the roofs by night to make his way to New York's red wooden John Street Theatre. Its deterioration led to the building of a new theatre on Park Row, an elegant playhouse with three tiers of boxes and a gallery overhanging a pink and gold pit. Irving was a regular hanger-on at its stage door and greenroom and frequented "The Shakespeare," a large box in the second tier. Behind the mask of a crusty patrician, Jonathan Oldstyle, Irving contributed a number of columns to *The Morning Chronicle*, which his brother edited, between 1801 and 1803. Seven of them dealt with the Park Street Theatre, mocking its makeshift production values and the taste of the public who preferred chauvinistic battle scenes to Shakespeare and Sheridan. The closing injunction of the last paper was:

> To the actors—less etiquette—less fustian—less buckram.
> To the orchestra—new music and more of it.
> To the pit—patience—clean benches and umbrellas.
> To the boxes—less affectation—less noise—less coxcombs.
> To the gallery—less grog and better constables—and,
> To the whole house—inside and out, a total reformation.

Ultimately Irving's greatest contribution to the American stage may be his tale of Rip Van Winkle, which, frequently dramatized, eventually became the great vehicle for Joseph Jefferson.

FROM
Letters of Jonathan Oldstyle, Gent.

LETTER III

Mr. Editor,
    There is no place of public amusement of which I am so fond as the theatre. To enjoy this with the greater relish I go but seldom; and I find there is no play, however poor or ridiculous from which I cannot derive some entertainment.

I was very much taken with a play-bill of last week, announcing in large capitals

THE BATTLE OF HEXHAM, *or days of old.*

Here said I to myself will be something grand—*days of old!*—my fancy fired at the words. I pictured to myself all the gallantry of chivalry; here, thought I, will be a display of court manners and true politeness; the play will no doubt be garnished with tilts and tournaments: and as to those *banditti* whose names make such a formidable appearance on the bills, they will be hung up, every mother's son, for the edification of the gallery.

With such impressions I took my seat in the pit, and was so impatient that I could hardly attend to the music, though I found it very good.

The curtain rose. Out walked the queen with great majesty, she answered my ideas, she was dressed well, she looked well, and she acted well. The queen was followed by a pretty gentleman, who from his winking and grinning I took to be the court fool. I soon found out my mistake. He was a courtier "*high in trust,*" and either general, colonel, or something of martial dignity.

They talked for some time, though I could not understand the drift of their discourse, so I amused myself with eating pea-nuts.

In one of the scenes I was diverted with the stupidity of a corporal and his men, who sung a dull song, and talked a great deal about nothing: though I found by their laughing, there was a great deal of fun in the corporal's remarks.

What this scene had to do with the rest of the piece, I could not comprehend: I suspect it was a part of some other play thrust in here *by accident.*

I was then introduced to a cavern where there were several hard looking fellows, sitting round a table carousing. They told the audience they were banditti. They then sung a *gallery song,* of which I could understand nothing but two lines:

"The Welchman had lik'd to've been chok'd by a mouse,
"But he pulled him out by the tail!"

Just as they had ended this elegant song their banquet was disturbed by the *melodious sound* of a horn, and in march'd a *portly gentleman*, who I found was their captain. After this worthy gentleman had fumed his hour out: after he had slapped his breast and drawn his sword half a dozen times, the act ended.

In the course of the play I learnt that there had been, or was, or would be, a battle; but how, or when, or where I could not understand. The banditti once more made their appearance, and frighted the wife of the portly gentleman, who was dressed in man's clothes, and was seeking her husband. I could not enough admire the dignity of her deportment, the sweetness of her countenance, and the unaffected gracefulness of her action; but who the captain really was, or why he ran away from his spouse, I could not understand. However, they seemed very glad to find one another again; and so at last the play ended by the falling of the curtain.

I wish the manager would use a *drop scene* at the close of the acts: we might then always ascertain the termination of the piece by the *green* curtain. On this occasion I was indebted to the polite bows of the actors for this pleasing information. I cannot say that I was entirely satisfied with the play, but I promised myself ample entertainment in the after-piece, which was called *The Tripolitan Prize*. Now, thought I, we shall have some *sport* for our money: we will no doubt see a few of those Tripolitan scoundrels spitted like turkeys for our amusement. Well, sir, the curtain rose—the trees waved in front of the stage, and the sea rolled in the rear. All things looked very pleasant and smiling. Presently I heard a bustling behind the scenes—here thought I comes a fierce band of Tripolitans with whiskers as long as my arm.—No such thing—they were only a party of village masters and misses taking a walk for exercise, and very pretty behaved young gentry they were, I assure you; but it was cruel in the manager to dress them in *buckram*, as it deprived them entirely of the use of their limbs. They arranged themselves very orderly on each side of the stage; and sang something doubtless very affecting, for they all looked pitiful enough. By and by came up a most tremenduous storm: the lightning flash'd, the thunder roar'd, the rain descended in torrents; however, our pretty rustics stood gaping quietly at one another, till they must have been wet to the skin. I was surprised at their torpidity, till I found they were each one afraid to move first, through fear of being laughed at for their aukwardness. How they got off I do not recollect, but I advise the manager, in a similar case, to furnish every one with a *trap door*, through which to make his exit. Yet this would deprive the audience of much amusement: for nothing can be more laughable than to see a body of guards with their spears, or courtiers with their long robes *get* across the stage at our theatre.

Scene pass'd after scene. In vain I strained my eyes to catch a glimpse of a Mahometan phiz. I once heard a great bellowing behind the scenes, and expected to see a strapping Musselman come bouncing in; but was miserably disappointed, on distinguishing his voice, to find out by his *swearing*, that he was only a *Christian*. In he came—an American navy officer. Worsted stockings—olive velvet small clothes—scarlet vest—pea-jacket, and *gold laced hat*—dressed quite in *character*. I soon found out by his talk, that he was an American prize master: that, returning thro' the *Mediterranean* with his Tripolitan prize, he was driven by a storm on the *coast of England!*

The honest gentleman seemed from his actions to be rather intoxicated: which I could account for in no other way than his having drank a great deal of salt water as he swam ashore.

Several following scenes were taken up with hallooing and huzzaing between the captain, his crew, and the gallery:—with several amusing tricks of the captain and his son, a very funny, mischievous little fellow. Then came the cream of the joke: the captain wanted to put to sea, and the young fellow, who had fallen desperately in love, to stay ashore. Here was a contest between love and honor—such piping of eyes, such blowing of noses, such slapping of pocket holes! But *old Junk* was inflexible.—What! an American tar desert his duty! (three cheers from the gallery) impossible!—American tars forever!! True blue will never stain!! &c. &c. (a continual thundering among the gods).

Here was a scene of distress—here was bathos. The author seemed as much puzzled how to dispose of the young tar as old Junk was. It would not do to leave an American seaman on foreign ground; nor would it do to separate him from his mistress.

Scene the last opened—it seems that another Tripolitan cruiser had bore down on the prize as she lay about a mile off shore.—How a Barbary corsair had got in this part of the world—whether she had been driven there by the same storm, or whether she was cruising about to pick up a few English first rates, I could not learn. However, here she was—again were we conducted to the sea shore, where we found all the village gentry, in their buckram suits, ready assembled to be entertained with the rare show, of an American and Tripolitan engaged yard arm and yard arm. The battle was conducted with proper decency and decorum, and the Tripolitan very politely gave in—as it would be indecent to conquer in the face of an American audience.

After the engagement, the crew came ashore, joined with the captain and gallery in a few more huzzas, and the curtain fell. How old Junk, his son, and his son's sweetheart settled it, I could not discover.

I was somewhat puzzled to understand the meaning and necessity of this engagement between the ships, till an honest old countryman at my elbow, said he supposed *this* was the *battle of Hexham*; as he recollected no fighting in the first piece.— With this explanation I was perfectly satisfied.

My remarks upon the audience I shall postpone to another opportunity.

JONATHAN OLDSTYLE.

LETTER IV

Mr. Editor,

My last communication mentioned my visit to the theatre; the remarks it contained were chiefly confined to the play and the actors: I shall now extend them to the audience, who, I assure you, furnish no inconsiderable part of the entertainment.

As I entered the house, some time before the curtain rose, I had sufficient leisure to make some observations. I was much amused with the waggery and humor of the gallery, which, by the way, is kept in *excellent* order by the constables who are stationed there. The noise in this part of the house is somewhat similar to that which prevailed in Noah's ark; for we have an imitation of the whistles and yells of every kind of animal.— This, in some measure, compensates for the want of music, (as the gentlemen of our orchestra are very economic of their favors). Some how or another the anger of the gods seemed to be aroused all of a sudden, and they commenced a discharge of apples, nuts & ginger-bread, on the heads of the honest folks in the pit, who had no possibility of retreating from this new kind of thunder-bolts. I can't say but I was a little irritated at being saluted aside of my head with a rotten pippin, and was going to shake my cane at them; but was prevented by a decent looking man behind me, who informed me it was useless to threaten or expostulate. They are only *amusing themselves* a little at our expence, said he, sit down quietly and bend your back to it. My kind neighbor was interrupted by a hard green apple that hit him between the shoulders—he made a wry face, but knowing it was all in joke, bore the blow like a philosopher. I soon saw the wisdom of this determination,—a stray thunder-bolt happened to light on the head of a little sharp-faced Frenchman, dress'd in a white coat and small cock'd hat, who sat two or three benches ahead of me, and seemed to be an irritable little animal: Monsieur was terribly exasperated; he jumped upon his seat, shook his fist at the gallery, and swore violently in bad English. This was all nuts to his merry persecutors, their attention was wholly turned on him, and he formed their *target* for the rest of the evening.

I found the ladies in the boxes, as usual, studious to please; their charms were set off to the greatest advantage; each box was a little battery in itself, and they all seemed eager to out do each other in the havoc they spread around. An arch glance in one box was rivalled by a smile in another, that smile by a simper in a third, and in a fourth, a most bewitching languish carried all before it.

I was surprised to see some persons reconnoitering the company through spy-glasses; and was in doubt whether these machines were used to remedy deficiencies of vision, or whether this was another of the eccentricities of fashion. Jack Stylish has since informed me that glasses were lately all *the go*; though hang it, says Jack, it is quite *out* at present; we used to mount glasses in *great snuff*, but since so many *tough jockies* have followed the lead, the bucks have all *cut* the custom. I give you, Mr. Editor, the account in my dashing cousin's own language. It is from a vocabulary I don't well understand.

I was considerably amused by the queries of the countryman mentioned in my last, who was now making his first visit to the theatre. He kept constantly applying to me for information, and I readily communicated, as far as my own ignorance would permit.

As this honest man was casting his eye round the house, his attention was suddenly arrested. And pray, who are these? said he, pointing to a cluster of young fellows. These I suppose are the critics, of whom I have heard so much. They have, no doubt, got together to communicate their remarks, and compare notes; these are the persons through whom the audience exercise their judgments, and by whom they are told, when they are to applaud or to hiss. Critics! ha, ha, my dear sir, they trouble themselves as little about the elements of criticism as they do about other departments of science or belles lettres. These are the beaus of the present day, who meet here to lounge away an idle hour, and play off their little impertinencies for the entertainment of the public. They no more regard the merits of a play, or of the actors, than my cane. They even *strive* to appear inattentive; and I have seen one of them perch'd upon the front of the box with his back to the stage, sucking the head of his stick, and staring vacantly at the audience, insensible to the most interesting specimens of scenic representation: though the tear of sensibility was trembling in every eye around him.

I have heard that some have even gone so far in search of amusement, as to propose a game or two of cards, in the theatre, during the performance: the eyes of my neighbor sparkled at this information; his cane shook in his hand; the word, *puppies*, burst from his lips. Nay, said I, I don't give this for absolute fact: my cousin Jack was, I believe, *quizzing* me (as he terms it) when he gave me the information. But you seem quite indignant, said I to the decent looking man in my rear. It was from him the exclamation came; the honest *countryman* was gazing in gaping wonder on some new attraction. Believe me, said I, if you had them daily before your eyes, you would get quite used to them. Used to them! replied he, how is it possible for people of sense to relish such conduct. Bless you, my friend, people of sense have nothing to do with it; they merely endure it in silence. These young gentlemen live in an indulgent age. When I was a young man, such tricks and fopperies were held in proper contempt. Here I went a little too far; for upon better recollection I must own that a lapse of years has produced but little alteration in this department of folly and impertinence. But do the ladies admire these manners? truly I am not as conversant in female circles as formerly; but I should think it a poor compliment to my fair country women, to suppose them pleased with the stupid stare and cant phrases with which these votaries of fashion, add affected to real ignorance.

Our conversation was here interrupted by the ringing of a bell. Now for the play, said my companion. No, said I, it is only for the musicians. Those worthy gentlemen then came crawling out of their holes, and began with very solemn and important phizes, strumming and tuning their instruments in the usual style of discordance, to the great *entertainment* of the audience. What tune is that? asked my neighbor, covering his ears. This, said I, is no tune; it is only a pleasing *symphony*, with which we are regaled as a preparative. For my part, though I admire the effect of contrast, I think they might as well play it in their cavern under the stage. The bell rung a second time; and then began the tune in reality; but I could not help observing that the countryman was more diverted with the queer grimaces, and contortions of countenance exhibited by the musicians, than their melody.

What I heard of the music, I liked very well (though I was told by one of my neighbors that the same pieces have been played every night for these three years;) but it was often overpowered by the gentry in the gallery, who vociferated loudly for *Moll in the wad*, *Tally ho the grinders*, and several other *airs* more suited to their tastes.

I observed that every part of the house has its different department. The good folks of the gallery have all the trouble of ordering the music (their directions, however, are not more frequently followed than they deserve.) The mode by which they issue their mandates is stamping, hissing, roaring, whistling, and, when the musicians are refractory, groaning in cadence. They also have the privilege of demanding a *bow* from *John* (by which name they designate every servant at the theatre, who enters to move a table or snuff a candle;) and of detecting those cunning dogs who peep from behind the curtain.

By the bye, my honest country friend was much puzzled about the curtain itself. He wanted to know why that *carpet* was hung up in the theatre. I assured him it was no carpet, but a very fine curtain. And what, pray, may be the meaning of that gold head with the nose cut off that I see in front of it? The meaning—why really I can't tell exactly—tho' my cousin Jack Stylish says there is a great deal of meaning in it. But surely you like the *design* of the curtain? The design—why really I can see no design about it, unless it is to be brought down about our ears by the weight of those gold heads and that heavy *cornice* with which it is garnished. I began now to be uneasy for the credit of our curtain, and was afraid he would perceive the mistake of the painter in putting a *harp* in the middle of the curtain, and calling it a *mirror*; but his attention was *happily* called away by the *candle-grease* from the chandelier, over the centre of the pit, dropping on his clothes. This he loudly complained of, and declared his coat was *bran-new*. How, my friend, said I, we must put up with a few trifling inconveniencies when in the pursuit of pleasure. True said he:—but I think I pay pretty dear for it:—first to give six shillings at the door, and then to have my head battered with rotten apples, and my coat spoiled by candle-grease: by and by I shall have my other clothes dirtied by sitting down, as I perceive every body mounted on the benches. I wonder if they could not see as well if they were all to stand upon the floor.

Here I could no longer defend our customs, for I could scarcely breathe while thus surmounted by a host of strapping fellows standing with their dirty boots on the seats of the benches. The little Frenchman who thus found a temporary shelter from the missive compliments of his gallery friends, was the only person benefited. At last the bell again rung, and the cry of down, down—hats off, was the signal for the commencement of the play.

If, Mr. Editor, the garrulity of an old fellow is not tiresome, and you chuse to give this *view of a New-York theatre*, a place in your paper, you may, perhaps, hear further from your friend,

JONATHAN OLDSTYLE.

1802

CHARLES SPRAGUE

Prologues commissioned for the openings of theatres and plays have a long history. In the new Republic, with its taste for public oratory, such occasions were often open to competition, and Charles Sprague (1791–1875) made a name for himself as a public poetaster. A Boston bank teller, he took first prize in an 1821 competition for a poem on the re-opening of the Park Street Theatre after a fire. In an age of wooden playhouses, theatre fires were common occurrences. The Chestnut Street Theatre in Philadelphia suffered a similar fate; when it re-opened in 1822 the advertisements stressed, "The avenues are large, the doors all open outwards, and the means of egress such [that] any audience that the house might contain might walk out in five minutes."

The Chestnut Street competition for a prologue and a silver cup attracted 60 entries. Sprague's winning poem iterated his favorite themes: the progress of civilization and the stage from benighted Roman Catholicism to enlightened reason, and the value of the theatre as a teacher of morality, whose "every scene" provides "a lecture or a law," an insistence meant to combat widespread anti-theatrical prejudice.

Prologue for the Opening of
the Chestnut Street Theatre, Philadelphia

When learning slumbered in the convent's shade,
And holy craft the groping nations swayed,
By dulness banned, the Muses wandered long,
Each lyre neglected, and forgot each song,
Till Heaven's bright halo wreathed the Drama's dome,
And great Apollo called the pilgrims home!
Then their glad harps, that charmed old Greece, they swept,
Their altars thronged, and joy's high sabbath kept;
Young Genius there his glorious banners reared,
To float for ever loved, for ever feared.
The mystic legions of the cloister known,
Old Superstition tumbled from his throne;
Back to his cell the king of gloom retired,
The buskin triumphed, and the world admired!
Since that proud hour, through each unfettered age,

The sons of light have clustered round the stage.
From fiction's realm her richest spoils they bring,
And pleasure's walls with rapture's echoes ring.
Here hermit Wisdom lays his mantle down,
To win with smiles the heart that fears his frown.
In mirth's gay robe he talks to wandering youth,
And Grandeur listens to the stranger, Truth.
Here beauty's daughters bend with tingling ear,
When lore repeats the tale to love so dear;
Their sacred bowers the sons of learning quit,
To rove with fancy, and to feast with wit.
All come to gaze, the valiant and the vain,
Virtue's bright troop, and fashion's glittering train.
Here Labour rests, pale Grief forgets her wo;
And Vice, that prints his slime on all below,
Even Vice looks on!—For this the stage was reared,
To scourge the fiend, so scorned and yet so feared.
The halls of judgment, as the moral school,
His foot defiles, the bronzed and reckless fool;
God's lovely temple shall behold him there,
With eye upturned, and aspect false as fair.
Then hither let th' unblushing villain roam,
Satire shall knot its whip and strike it home.
The stage one groan from his dark soul shall draw,
That mocks religion, and that laughs at law!
To grace the stage, the bard's careering mind
Seeks other worlds, and leaves his own behind:
He lures from air its bright, unprisoned forms,
Breaks through the tomb, and death's dull regions storms;
O'er ruined realms he pours creative day,
And slumbering kings his mighty voice obey.
From its damp shroud the long-laid spirit walks,
And round the murderer's bed in vengeance stalks.
Poor maniac Beauty brings her cypress wreath,
Her smile a moonbeam o'er a blasted heath;
Round some cold grave sweet flowers she comes to strew,
And, lost to reason, still to love is true.
Hate shuts his soul when dove-eyed mercy pleads,
Power lifts the axe, and truth's bold servant bleeds.
Remorse drops anguish from his burning eyes.

Feels hell's eternal worm, and shudd'ring, dies.
War's trophied minion, too, forsakes the dust,
Grasps his worn shield, and waves his sword of rust;
Springs to the slaughter at the trumpet's call,
Again to conquer, or again to fall.

　　With heads to censure, yet with souls to feel,
Friends of the stage! receive our frank appeal.
No suppliant lay we frame; acquit your trust!
The Drama guard; be gentle, but be just!
Within her courts, unbribed, unslumbering, stand,
Scourge lawless wit, and leaden dulness brand;
Lash pert pretence, but bashful merit spare,
His firstlings hail, and speak the trembler fair.
Yet shall he cast his cloud, and proudly claim
The loftiest station, and the brightest fame.
So from his mountain-perch, through seas of light,
Our untamed eagle takes his glorious flight.
To heaven the monarch-bird exulting springs,
And shakes the night-fog from his mighty wings.
Bards all our own shall yet enchant their age,
And pour redeeming splendour o'er the stage.
For them, for you, Truth hoards a nobler theme
Than ever blest young fancy's sweetest dream.
Bold hearts shall kindle, and bright eyes shall gaze,
When genius wakes the tale of other days,
Sheds life's own lustre o'er each hold deed
Of him who planted, and of him who freed.

　　And now, fair pile, thou chaste and glorious shrine,
Our fondest wish, our warmest smile, be thine.
The home of genius and the court of taste,
In beauty raised, be thou by beauty graced.
Within thy walls may wit's gay bevy throng,
To drink the magic of the poet's song.
Within thy walls may youth and goodness draw
From every scene a lecture or a law.
So bright thy fane, be priest and offering pure,
And friends shall bless, and bigot foes endure.
Long, long be spared to echo truths sublime,
And lift thy pillars through the storms of time.

1822

WILLIAM DUNLAP

North America before and after the Revolution was fertile in polymaths such as Benjamin Franklin and Charles Willson Peale. William
Dunlap (1766–1839) began as a portrait painter and wound up a director of the American Academy of Fine Arts and founder of the National Academy of Design. He also wrote a temperance novel, a
voluminous diary, and a school history of the United States. Dunlap,
however, is most memorable for his position as "Father of the American drama." Over the course of his career, he wrote 53 plays, 29 of
them partially or almost wholly original, thus qualifying him as America's first professional dramatist. Besides satires and history plays, he
popularized "Dutch stuff," the sentimental melodramas of German
playwright August von Kotzebue. In 1823 the *New York Mirror* praised
his pieces as "invariably performed with applause, and free as they are
from false taste and extravagance, show the power of fixing attention
and exciting interest by legitimate means—of touching the true
springs of mirth and pity and terror."

Success led Dunlap to become proprietor and manager of the John
Street Theatre and the Park Street Theatre in New York (1796–1805),
where his fortunes seesawed between financial subsistence and bank-
ruptcy due to unreliable colleagues, temperamental actors, and a
fickle public. His *History of the American Theatre* (1833) weaves personal reminiscence into a detailed chronicle. In the words of the historian Arthur Hobson Quinn, it is "not only a mine of information
about the beginnings of our theatre and our drama, it is a fascinating
autobiography of a man who accomplished much through more than
one failure." Dunlap's chapter on Boston is a typical record of the difficulties of a nascent theatre in overcoming restrictive legislation and
local narrow-mindedness. Dunlap believed that the theatre's salvation
had to be suppression of the star system as well as "governmental patronage." This early call for federal subsidy would go unheeded until
the mid-20th century.

FROM
History of the American Theatre

MASSACHUSETTS, both as a colony of Great Britain and as an
independent state, had been forbidden ground to all Thespians.

13

As early as the year 1750, before any of that dangerous class of people had ventured over the Atlantic, the General Court of Massachusetts, that is, in the language of other parts of our country, the House of Assembly or Representatives, passed an act to prevent stage-plays and other theatrical entertainments. The historian of Massachusetts says, that the cause of "this moral regulation" was, that two young Englishmen, assisted by some townsmen, tried to represent Otway's tragedy of *The Orphan*, and the inhabitants were so eager to see the entertainment, that some disturbances took place at the door of the coffee-house where they were amusing themselves. This so alarmed the lieutenant-governor, council, and house of representatives, that, "For preventing and avoiding the many and great mischiefs which arise from public stage-plays, &c. which not only occasion great and unnecessary expenses, and discourage industry and frugality, but likewise tend generally to increase immorality, impiety, and a contempt of religion," they enacted as follows: "that from and after the publication of this act, no person or persons whatsoever may, for his or their gain, or for any price or valuable consideration, let, or suffer to be used or improved, any house, room, or place whatsoever, for acting or carrying on any stage-plays, interludes, or other theatrical entertainments, on pain of forfeiting and paying for each and every day, or time, such house, room, or place, shall be let, used, or improved, contrary to this act, twenty pounds. And if, at any time or times whatsoever, from and after the publication of this act, any person or persons shall be present as an actor in or spectator of any stage-play, &c. in any house, &c. where a greater number of persons than twenty shall be assembled together, every such person shall forfeit for each time five pounds. One-half to his majesty, and one-half to the informer."

Such were the feelings and opinions of the representatives of the people of Massachusetts in 1750; "but," says the author of Dramatic Reminiscences in the New England Magazine, "as the Puritanic sentiments of the older inhabitants gave place to more liberal and extended views in religion and morals, much of the prejudice against theatrical amusements subsided."

After Wignell had separated from Hallam and Henry, they, foreseeing that he would occupy the south, petitioned the legislature of Massachusetts, on the 5th of June, 1790, "for leave to open a theatre in Boston, under proper regulations." The petition was not granted.

In 1791, a petition was presented to the select men of Boston, drawn up by Perez Morton, Esq., and signed by him and thirty-eight other gentlemen of the town, setting forth "the advantages of well regulated public amusements in large towns," and stating that, "being desirous of encouraging the interests of genius and literature, by encouraging such theatrical exhibitions as are calculated to promote the cause of morality and virtue, and conduce to polish the manners and habits of society," and for other reasons assigned, they respectfully solicit the board of select men to take the opinion of the inhabitants "on the subject of admitting a theatre in the town of Boston," and of instructing their representatives "to obtain a repeal" of the prohibitory act of 1750, which law had been revived in 1784, to be in force fifteen years.

On the 26th of October, this subject was debated in town-meeting, and a committee appointed to prepare instructions to the representatives of the town in the legislature, and on the 9th of November following, the committee presented their report to the adjourned town-meeting, which was accepted.

The instructions state, that the inhabitants of Boston consider the prohibitory law of 1750 as an infringement of their privileges; and that a "theatre, where the actions of great and virtuous men are represented, will advance the interests of private and political virtue." They, for these and similar reasons, instruct the representatives to endeavour to effect the "repeal of the law alluded to, so far, at least, as respects the town of Boston." They farther instruct, that "the law of repeal may be so constructed that no dramatic composition shall be the subject of theatrical representation," till sanctioned "by some authority appointed for the purpose;" that no "immoral expressions may ever disgrace the American stage;" but, on the contrary, all "subserve the great and beneficial purposes of public and private virtue."

In January, 1792, Mr. Tudor brought the subject before the house of representatives, and moved for a committee to "consider the expediency of bringing in a bill to repeal the prohibitory law of 1750." After opposition, a committee was appointed, and "a remonstrance against the repeal" was referred to the same committee.

The committee reported on the 20th that it was inexpedient to repeal the law. Notwithstanding the efforts of Mr. Gardiner and Dr. Jarvis against this report, it was accepted on the 25th. The names of Samuel Adams and Benjamin Austin are enrolled as opponents to a theatre. The latter wrote "a series of essays," says the author of Reminiscences, "to prove that Shakspeare had no genius." The principal advocates for stage exhibitions were William Tudor and Dr. Charles Jarvis.

We see from the above instructions, given by Boston to her representatives, that the opinions of the people of the capital of Massachusetts had undergone a change. We shall soon see, that, notwithstanding present opposition to these opinions, they were triumphant, and the drama established in the cradle of the liberties of America.

The secession of Wignell from the old American Company, and his crossing the Atlantic in search of performers, caused the immediate voyage of John Henry, also for the same purpose. It has been stated that Mr. and Mrs. Morris and Stephen Wools were sharers in the *scheme* of the old company. Harper was not. Mr. and Mrs. Morris took their part with Wignell, and were, during his absence, to seek employment. Harper was not engaged with either party. Wools adhered to the property in which he was a sharer, but was left for the present unemployed.

Under these circumstances, the above-named four individuals united for the purpose of trying their fortunes in Boston, invited by the efforts for the establishment of a theatre which a portion of the inhabitants were making. Notwithstanding the refusal of the legislature to repeal the law of 1750, a number of gentlemen formed an association for the purpose of introducing the drama. A committee was formed to carry their purpose into effect, and ground purchased on which to erect a building in Broad-alley, near Hawley-street. The committee were, according to Mr. Buckingham, "Joseph Russell, Esq., who also acted as treasurer to the association, Dr. Jarvis, Gen. Henry Jackson, Joseph Barrell, and Joseph Russell, Jun." "A theatre in every thing but the name" was erected. A pit, one row of boxes, and a gallery, could contain about five hundred persons, and it was called the "New Exhibition Room." "The boxes formed three sides of a regular square, the stage making the fourth. The scenery was tolerably well executed." But before its completion, Charles Powell arrived from England, and advertised an entertainment, which he called "The Evening Brush for rubbing off the Rust of Care," to consist of songs and farcical recitations. This was on Monday, August 13th, 1792, and on the 16th, the New Exhibition Room was opened by Harper as manager, with feats on the tight rope by Mons. Placide, songs by Mr. Wools, feats on the slack rope and tumbling by Mons. Martine, hornpipes and minuets by Mons. and Madame Placide, and the gallery of portraits by Mr. Harper, the manager. "These entertainments," says the New England Magazine, "continued, with slight variations, for several weeks."

Thus we see a theatre was put in operation in open defiance of the law of the state, and, as the good people of Boston were denied rational amusement, they accepted the efforts of the tumbler and rope-dancer, and eagerly seized on the entertainments of Sadler's Wells, when prohibited by law from listening to the lines of the wit or the poet, as recited at Old Drury or Covent Garden.

But this could not last long; the company of performers increased in numbers: Mr. and Mrs. Morris, and Harper, were really actors; to these were added the names of Mr. and Mrs. Solomon, Messrs. Roberts, Adams, Watts, Jones, Redfield, Tucker, Murry, Mrs. Gray, Miss Smith, and Miss Chapman— names only mentioned as being the first professional actors who performed plays in Boston. Roberts was deformed, and almost an idiot; Watts a vulgar fellow, with a wry neck; Miss Smith became soon after Mrs. Harper: the rest are only names. Charles Powell joined Harper.

Plays were now performed; but, as the theatre was called an exhibition room, *Douglas* was represented as a Moral Lecture in five parts, "delivered by Messrs." so and so; and all the songs of *The Poor Soldier* were to be "delivered by Messrs. Watts, Murry, Redfield, Solomon, Jones, Mrs. Solomon, and Miss Chapman." The play-bill for this entertainment, *Douglas* and *The Poor Soldier*, thus disguised, was dated September 26th, 1792. Wools, who was attached to Hallam and Henry's company, had before this joined his leaders, they having opened the old theatre in Philadelphia.

Thus were the laws defied, and the people and their magistrates insulted for several weeks. The municipal authorities criminally suffered this nuisance to exist until "about the end of October or beginning of November, when," as Mr. Buckingham says, "during the representation of *The School for Scandal,* while Morris and his wife were on the stage in the characters of Sir Peter and Lady Teazle, the sheriff of the county suddenly and very unexpectedly *made his first appearance on that stage,* and arrested them by virtue of a peace-warrant." Some of the audience leaped on the stage from the pit, "tore down the arms of the state, which decorated a tablet between one of the stage-boxes and the door, and trampled it under their feet. Several gentlemen immediately came forward and became bound for the appearance of the persons arrested;" and shortly after, an association was formed for erecting a permanent theatre.

"It does not appear," says Mr. Buckingham, who writes on the spot, and has every source of information at command, "that those whose duty it was to see the laws executed, pursued the offenders with much rigour."

The legislature of Massachusetts at this time sat at Concord, and Governor Hancock, in his speech, thus alludes to what he justly considered "an open insult upon the laws and government of the Commonwealth."

"Whether the apprehensions of the evils which might flow from theatrical exhibitions, so fully expressed in the preamble of that act" (the act of 1750, to be continued in force till 1799), "are well founded or not, may be a proper subject of legislative disquisition, on a motion for the continuance or the repeal of the law; but the act is now a law of the commonwealth; the principles on which it is predicated have been recognised by and derive support from several legislatures, and surely it ought to claim the respect and obedience of all persons who live, or happen to be, within the commonwealth. Yet a number of aliens or foreigners have lately entered the state, and, in the metropolis of the government, under advertisements insulting to the habits and education of the citizens, have been pleased to invite them to, and to exhibit before such as have attended, stage-plays, interludes, and theatrical entertainments, under the style and appellation of moral lectures." He proceeds to say, "no measures have been taken to punish a most open breach of the laws, and a most contemptuous insult upon the powers of government." He then calls upon the legislature to take measures to rectify the abuse, and punish the offenders.

The legislature in reply concur with the governor, and promise to endeavour to remedy any defect that may be found in the statute. The consequence was, that, in December, a warrant, was issued for the apprehension of the offenders, and the sheriff, in obedience to his precept, took the body of Mr. Harper, and as to the rest returned *non inventus*. The justices (Barrett and Greenleaf), with a view to accommodate the numerous spectators, who waited with anxious expectation the result of this important inquiry, held their sitting at Faneuil Hall. Upon Mr. Harper's appearance before them, the attorney-general read a special order from the governor and council, directing him to prosecute and bring to condign punishment these contemners of the law; and then read his complaint filed with the aforesaid justices, upon which they had issued their warrant as above.

Messrs. Tudor and Otis, for the defendant, suggested the illegality of the complaint, it not being grounded upon an oath, as required by the 14th article of the declaration of rights. The objection prevailed, and Mr. Harper was released from his arrest, amid the loud applauses of a "numerous and respectable audience."

On the 5th of December, a few evenings subsequent to the preceding measures, just after the first act of the play had been performed, the sheriff executed a second warrant on Mr. Harper, and put a stop to the performance. The audience, finding themselves thus disappointed, became riotous, and it was at this time (according to this statement) that the painting of the state arms was pulled down and torn to pieces. Judge Tudor addressed the audience, and begged the company to withdraw, which had its effect, and great order was observed in retiring from the house.

The existence of a legislative enactment, which has become obsolete, or is contrary to the sense or will of the community, is at all times the source of evil. It is broken with impunity, or, if the offender is punished, he is considered as a martyr, and praised and supported, while the laws, the only safeguard of society, are rendered of less effect in the eyes of the people, both of those they are intended to restrain, and those for whose protection they are enacted.

In 1793, the legislature of Massachusetts repealed the law against theatrical amusements, and the Federal-street theatre was opened February 4th, 1794, with a prologue written by Thomas Paine, the son of the Honourable Robert Treat Paine, one of the signers of the Declaration of Independence.

1833

FRANCES TROLLOPE

In their accounts of their travels, English visitors to the young Republic, among them Captain Basil Hall (1829), the actress Fanny Kemble (1835), Captain Marryat (1839), and Charles Dickens (1842), displayed an anti-Jeffersonian bias and disapproved of much of what they saw. Most censorious of the lot was Frances Trollope (1780–1863), who wrote of the Americans: "I do not like them. I do not like their principles, I do not like their manners, I do not like their opinions." Mother of the future novelists Anthony and his lesser-known elder brother, Thomas, Trollope had come to frontier Cincinnati to make money with an ambitious "Bazaar"; when her emporium failed badly, she moved around the United States for the next two and a half years. Her *Domestic Manners of the Americans* (1832), a pot-boiler written to repair her ruined fortunes, almost created an "international incident." Bawdy puns on her name proliferated, and she was caricatured as the pretentious Amelia Wollope in Kirke Paulding's comedy *The Lion of the West* (1831). For all that, Mark Twain considered "Dame Trollope" the most accurate and the most readable of the English travelers.

FROM

Domestic Manners of the Americans

THE theatre at Cincinnati is small, and not very brilliant in decoration; but in the absence of every other amusement, our young men frequently attended it, and in the bright clear nights of autumn and winter, the mile and a half of distance was not enough to prevent the less enterprising members of the family from sometimes accompanying them. The great inducement to this was the excellent acting of Mr. and Mrs. Alexander Drake,* the managers. Nothing could be more distinct than their line of acting, but the great versatility of their powers enabled them often to appear together. Her cast was the highest walk of tragedy, and his the broadest comedy; but

---

*Mr. Drake was an Englishman.

yet, as Goldsmith says of his sister heroines, I have known them change characters for a whole evening together, and have wept with him and laughed with her, as it was their will and pleasure to ordain. I think in his comedy he was superior to any actor I ever saw in the same parts, except Emery. Alexander Drake's comedy was like that of the French, who never appear to be acting at all; he was himself the comic being the author aimed at depicting. Let him speak whose words he would, from Shakspeare to Colman, it was impossible not to feel that half the fun was his own; he had, too, in a very high degree, the power that Fawcett possessed, of drawing tears by a sudden touch of natural feeling. His comic songs might have set the gravity of the judges and bishops together at defiance. Liston is great, but Alexander Drake was greater.

Mrs. Drake, formerly Miss Denny, greatly resembles Miss O'Neil; a proof of this is, that Mr. Kean, who had heard of the resemblance, arrived at New-York late in the evening, and having repaired to the theatre, saw her for the first time across the stage, and immediately exclaimed, "That's Miss Denny." Her voice, too, has the same rich and touching tones, and is superior in power. Her talent is decidedly first-rate. Deep and genuine feeling, correct judgment, and the most perfect good taste, distinguish her play in every character. Her last act of Belvidera is superior in tragic effect to any thing I ever saw on the stage, the one great exception to all comparison, Mrs. Siddons, being set aside.

It was painful to see these excellent performers playing to a miserable house, not a third full, and the audience probably not including half a dozen persons who would prefer their playing to that of the vilest strollers. In proof of this, I saw them, as managers, give place to paltry third-rate actors from London, who would immediately draw crowded houses, and be overwhelmed with applause.

Poor Drake died just before we left Ohio, and his wife, who, besides her merit as an actress, is a most estimable and amiable woman, is left with a large family. I have little, or rather no doubt, of her being able to obtain an excellent engagement in London, but her having property in several of the Western theatres will, I fear, detain her in a neighbourhood where she is neither understood nor appreciated. She told me many very excellent professional anecdotes collected during her residence in the West; one of these particularly amused me as a specimen of Western idiom. A lady who professed a great admiration for Mrs. Drake had obtained her permission to be present upon one occasion at her theatrical toilet. She was dressing for some character in which she was to stab herself, and her dagger was lying on the table. The visitor took it up, and examining it with much emotion, exclaimed, "What! do you really jab this into yourself sevagarous?"

We also saw the great American star, Mr. Forrest. What he may become I will not pretend to prophesy; but when I saw him play Hamlet at Cincinnati, not even Mrs. Drake's sweet Ophelia could keep me beyond the third act. It is true that I have seen Kemble, Macready, Kean, Young, C. Kemble, Cook, and Talma play Hamlet, and I might not, perhaps, be a very fair judge of this young actor's merits; but I was greatly amused when a gentleman, who asked my opinion of him, told me upon hearing it, that he would not advise me to state it freely in America, "for they would not bear it."

The theatre was really not a bad one, though the very poor receipts rendered it impossible to keep it in high order; but an annoyance infinitely greater than decorations indifferently clean, was the style and manner of the audience. Men came into the lower tier of boxes without their coats; and I have seen shirt-sleeves tucked up to the shoulder; the spitting was incessant, and the mixed smell of onions and whiskey was enough to make one feel even the Drakes' acting dearly bought by the obligation of enduring its accompaniments. The bearing and attitudes of the men are perfectly indescribable; the heels thrown higher than the head, the entire rear of the person presented to the audience, the whole length supported on the benches, are among the varieties that these exquisite posture-masters exhibit. The noises, too, were perpetual, and of the most unpleasant kind; the applause is expressed by cries and thumping with the feet, instead of clapping; and when a patriotic fit seized them, and "Yankee Doodle" was called for, every man seemed to think his reputation as a citizen depended on the noise he made.

Two very indifferent figurantes, probably from the Ambigu Comique, or la Gaieté, made their appearance at Cincinnati while we were there; and had Mercury stepped down, and danced a *pas seul* upon earth, his godship could not have produced a more violent sensation. But wonder and admiration were by no means the only feelings excited; horror and dismay were produced in at least an equal degree. No one, I believe, doubted their being admirable dancers, but every one agreed that the morals of the Western world would never recover the shock. When I was asked if I had ever seen any thing so dreadful before, I was embarrassed how to answer; for the young women had been exceedingly careful, both in their dress and in their dancing, to meet the taste of the people; but had it been Virginie in her most transparent attire, or Taglioni in her most remarkable pirouette, they could not have been more reprobated. The ladies altogether forsook the theatre; the gentlemen muttered under their breath, and turned their heads aside when the subject was mentioned; the clergy denounced them from the pulpit; and if they were named at the meetings of the saints, it was to show how deep the horror such a theme could produce. I could not but ask myself if virtue were a plant, thriving under one form in one country, and flourishing under a different one in another? If these Western Americans are right, then how dreadfully wrong are we! It is really a very puzzling subject.

1832

ALEXIS DE TOCQUEVILLE

In James Barker's Philadelphia comedy *Tears and Smiles* (1807), the Frenchman Monsieur Gaillard rhapsodizes over America: "C'est un bon pays; ver good fine countree; tous les hommes, all de people happy; all de vomen belle, beautiful! By gar, I am ravish'd!" The first French visitors, such as Crèvecoeur and Chateaubriand, had projected just such a rosy view of North America as a cradle of liberty, rocked by noble savages. The aristocrat Alexis de Tocqueville (1805–1859), arriving as Jacksonian democracy was supplanting Revolutionary ideals, was more guarded in his praise. Although most art and music left him cold, Tocqueville valued the theatre as an asset in creating "association," the bond that nurtures civic engagement and common action. In this chapter from *Democracy in America* (1835–40), he shrewdly recognized the difference between drama as literature, appreciated by the elite, and theatre as a shared collective experience available to the masses. His own favorite playwright, Racine, was, he granted, an acquired taste, yet he was delighted to find that "there is hardly a pioneer's hut which does not contain a few odd volumes of Shakespeare. I remember that I read the feudal drama of Henry V for the first time in a log cabin." So did the young Abraham Lincoln.

Some Observations on the Theater of Democratic Peoples

WHEN a revolution that has changed the social and political state of an aristocratic people begins to affect literature, it generally manifests itself first in drama and remains conspicuous there long afterward.

The theatergoer is in a sense taken unawares by the impressions he receives. He has no time to quiz his memory or consult the experts. It does not occur to him to resist the new literary instincts he has begun to feel. He yields to them, not knowing what he is yielding to.

Authors are quick to divine which way the taste of the audience is secretly leaning, and they shape their work accordingly. Drama, having given the first signs of a literary revolution in the making, soon brings that revolution to completion. For a foretaste of what the literature of a people making the transition to democracy will be like, study its theater.

Even in aristocratic nations, plays constitute the most democratic part of literature. No literary pleasures are more accessible to the crowd than those that come from seeing a play. To experience them requires neither study nor preparation. They grip you in the midst of your preoccupations and your ignorance. When a class of citizens first begins to feel for the pleasures of the mind a love still half-uncivilized, it immediately takes to drama. The theaters of aristocratic nations have always been filled with non-aristocrats. Only in the theater did the upper classes mingle with the middle and lower classes and agree, if not to accept their opinion, then at least to suffer them to express one. It is in the theater that scholars and men of letters have always had the greatest difficulty establishing the supremacy of their taste over that of the people and resisting the influence of the people's taste on their own. The pit has often imposed its law on the boxes.

If it is difficult for an aristocracy to keep the people from invading the theater, it is easy to see that the people will reign over the theater as masters when, democratic principles having seeped into laws and mores, ranks blend and intellects as well as fortunes become comparable, and the upper class loses not only its hereditary wealth but also its power, traditions, and leisure.

The natural literary tastes and instincts of democratic peoples will therefore manifest themselves first in theater, and we may anticipate that they will do so in a violent manner. In written works, aristocratic literary canons will be amended little by little, by gradual and so to speak legal means. In the theater, they will be overturned by riot.

The theater brings out most of the qualities and nearly all the vices inherent in democratic literatures.

Democratic peoples hold erudition in very low esteem and care little about what happened in Rome and Athens. What they want to hear about is themselves, and what they ask to be shown is a picture of the present.

So when ancient heroes and mores are frequently reproduced on stage, and great care is taken to remain faithful to the traditions of Antiquity, it is safe to conclude that the democratic classes do not yet rule the theater.

Racine, in his preface to *Britannicus*, very humbly excuses himself for making Junia a vestal virgin, because according to Aulus-Gellius "no one under the age of six or above the age of ten was accepted." Were he writing today, he surely would never dream of accusing himself of such a crime or of defending himself against such an allegation.

An action of this kind sheds light not only on the state of literature at the time it occurred but also on the state of society itself. A democratic theater does not prove that a nation is a democracy, because, as we have just seen, democratic tastes can influence the drama even in aristocracies. But when the spirit of aristocracy reigns alone in the theater, that is incontrovertible proof that the entire society is aristocratic, and one can make so bold as to conclude that the same erudite and literate class that guides authors also commands citizens and takes the lead in public affairs.

When the aristocracy rules the theater, its refined tastes and arrogant penchants seldom fail to result in a rather selective view of human nature. The aristocracy is primarily interested in certain social conditions, and it likes to see these portrayed on stage. Certain virtues and even certain vices seem, in its eyes, particularly worthy of being reproduced. It applauds representations of these qualities while averting its eyes from all others. In the theater, as elsewhere, it does not wish to encounter any but great lords and is stirred only by kings. So, too, with styles. An aristocracy deliberately imposes on dramatic authors certain ways of saying things. It wants to set the tone for how everything is said.

Thus drama often portrays only one side of man and at times even depicts traits not found in human nature. It rises above human nature and goes beyond it.

In democratic societies, audiences have no such preferences and rarely display antipathies of this kind. What they like to see on stage is the same confused mixture of conditions, sentiments, and ideas that they find in life. Theater becomes more striking, more vulgar, and more true.

Sometimes, though, the people who write for the theater in democracies also go beyond human nature but in a different way from their predecessors. Aiming to reproduce the little singularities of the present moment in minute detail and to describe the peculiar physiognomies of certain individuals, they forget to delineate the general features of the species.

When the democratic classes rule the theater, they introduce freedom not only in the choice of subjects but equally in the manner in which those subjects are treated.

Since love of the theater is, of all literary tastes, the most natural in democratic peoples, the number of dramatic authors, the size of the audience, and the number of theatrical productions all increase steadily in democracies. Such a multitude, composed of such diverse elements and spread about so many different locations, cannot be subject to one set of rules or one body of laws. No agreement is possible among such a large number of judges, who, because they have no way of meeting, render their verdicts independently. If the effect of democracy is in general to cast doubt on literary rules and conventions, in the theater it abolishes them entirely only to replace them with nothing more than the whim of each author and each audience.

The theater also offers an excellent example of what I said earlier about style and art in democratic literature in general. In reading criticism inspired by the dramatic works of the age of Louis XIV, one is surprised to discover that audiences set great store by plausibility and attached considerable importance to consistency of characterization, so that no character in a play ever does anything that cannot be easily explained and understood. It is also surprising to see how much value was attached in those days to forms of language and what nitpicking criticisms were made of dramatic authors for their choice of words.

Apparently, people in the age of Louis XIV greatly exaggerated the value of such details, which can be perceived in private but go unnoticed on the stage. After all, the chief purpose of a play is to be performed, and its chief merit is to move its audience. If the theatergoers of that time exaggerated the value of details, it was because they were also readers. After leaving the performance, they expected to renew their acquaintance with the writer at home in order to round off their judgment of him.

In democracies, people listen to plays, but they do not read them. Most people who attend plays go in search of intense emotions of the heart rather than pleasures of the intellect. They expect to find not a work of literature but a show, and provided that the author speaks the language of the country correctly enough to make himself understood and his characters arouse curiosity and awaken sympathy, they are happy. Immediately thereafter, they return to the real world, without asking anything more of the fiction. Hence style is less necessary on the democratic stage, where the breaking of rules is more likely to pass unnoticed.

As for the rules of plausibility, it is impossible to respect them while at the same time rapidly turning out novel and unexpected work. So authors neglect them, and audiences are forgiving. If you touch the audience, you can be sure that it will not worry about the route you took to get it there. It will never reproach you for breaking the rules in order to move it.

When Americans go to the theater, they clearly exhibit all the instincts I have been discussing. Note, however, that to date only a small number of them do in fact go. Although both the size of the audience and the number of plays have increased prodigiously in the United States over the past forty years, most of the population is still extremely reluctant to participate in this kind of amusement.

There are specific reasons for this with which the reader is already familiar, so that a brief reminder will suffice.

The Puritans, who founded the American republics, were not only enemies of pleasure but professed a special abhorrence of the theater. They looked upon it as an abominable diversion, and as long as their spirit reigned uncontested, dramatic performances remained wholly unknown. The views of the founding fathers of the colonies on this subject left a deep imprint on the minds of their descendants.

Furthermore, the extreme regularity of habit and the great rigidity of mores that one finds in the United States have thus far done little to encourage the development of dramatic art.

Drama wants for subjects in a country that has never witnessed a great political catastrophe and in which love always leads directly and easily to marriage. People who spend every weekday making their fortunes and every Sunday in prayer do not lend themselves to the comic muse.

One fact by itself is enough to show how unpopular the theater is in the United States.

Americans, whose laws authorize freedom and even license of speech in all matters, have nevertheless imposed a kind of censorship on dramatic authors. Plays can be performed only when town officials allow. This shows clearly that peoples are like individuals. They indulge their principal passions to the hilt and then take care lest they yield more than they should to tastes they do not possess.

No part of literature is more closely or more abundantly linked to the present state of society than the theater.

The theater of one period will never suit the next if a major revolution has changed mores and laws in between.

People still study the greater writers of previous centuries, but they do not go to plays written for another audience. The dramatic authors of the past live only in books.

Traditional tastes in certain individuals, vanity, fashion, an actor's genius—each of these things may sustain or revive aristocratic theater in a democracy for a while, but before long it will collapse of its own weight, not overthrown but abandoned.

1840

EDGAR ALLAN POE

Edgar Allan Poe (1809–1849) was proud that his parents had been actors, and a few months after his birth, they presciently appeared together in the Gothic melodrama *The Castle Spectre*. Poe himself did not gravitate to playwriting; his only attempt is a fragment, *Politian* (1835), based on a contemporary murder case but reset in 17th-century Rome. Typically, it includes a drunken orgy in a wine cellar filled with the corpses of plague victims. Established as a book reviewer, Poe enlarged his coverage to the theatre when he lived in New York City, with its six playhouses, circus, and dramatic museum. His critiques were so savage that one manager withdrew his free pass. The essay "Does the Drama of the Day Deserve Support?" condemned it as artificial, "essentially imitative," mired in soliloquies, asides, and "absurd conventionalities." What Poe hoped to see on stage was, as he wrote of the comedy *Tortesa the Usurer* by his former employer Nathaniel Parker Willis (1839), "naturalness, truthfulness and appropriateness . . . of sentiment and language, a manly vigor and breadth in the conception of character; and a few ideal elevations or exaggerations throughout. . . ."

In March 1845, when Poe heard that the gentlewoman Anna Cora Mowatt was to have a comedy produced at the Park Theatre, he asked to read the manuscript, which she sent him. He attended the opening night of *Fashion*, and his initial review was unsympathetic. However, he continued to visit the next seven performances and, uncharacteristically, offered a revised opinion, praising the original concept of satirizing fashion *as* fashion. He became a steadfast supporter of Mrs. Mowatt when she went on the stage, and included a character sketch of her in a *Godey's Lady's Book* series in 1846.

On Anna Cora Mowatt's Fashion

THE NEW COMEDY BY MRS. MOWATT

The plot of "Fashion" runs thus: Adam Trueman, a blunt, warm-hearted, shrewd, irascible, wealthy, and generous old farmer of Cattaraugus county, N.Y., had a daughter, (Ruth) who eloped with an adventurer. The father forgave the daughter, but resolving to disappoint the hopes of the fortune hunter, gave the couple a bare subsistence. In consequence of this, the husband maltreated, and finally abandoned the wife, who returned, broken-hearted, to her father's house and there died, after giving birth to a daughter, Gertrude. That *she* might escape the ills of fortune-hunting by which her mother was destroyed, Trueman sent the child, at an early age, to be brought up by relatives in Geneva; giving his own neighbours to understand that she was dead. The Geneva friends were instructed to educate her in habits of self-dependence, and to withhold from her the secret of her parentage, and heirship;—the grandfather's design being to secure for her a husband who will love her solely for herself. The friends by advice of the grandfather, procured for her when grown up to womanhood, a situation as music teacher in the house of Mr. Tiffany, a quondam footpedlar, and now by dint of industry a dry-goods merchant doing a flashy if not flourishing business; much of his success having arisen from the assistance of Trueman, who knew him and admired his honest industry as a travelling pedlar.

The efforts of the dry goods merchant, however, are insufficient to keep pace with the extravagance of his wife, who has become infected with a desire to shine as a lady of *fashion*, in which desire she is seconded by her daughter, Seraphina, the musical pupil of Gertrude. The follies of the mother and daughter so far involve Tiffany as to lead him into a forgery of a friend's endorsement. This crime is suspected by his confidential clerk, Snobson, an intemperate blackguard, who at length extorts from his employer a confession, under a promise of secrecy provided that Seraphina shall become Mrs. Snobson. Mrs. Tiffany, however, is by no means privy to this arrangement: she is anxious to secure a title for Seraphina, and advocates the pretensions of Count Jolimaitre, a quondam English cook, barber, and valet, whose real name was Gustave Treadmill, and who, having spent much time at Paris, suddenly took leave of that city, for that city's good, and his own; abandoning to despair a little laundress (Millinette) to whom he was betrothed, but who had rashly entrusted him with the whole of her hard earnings during life.

Gertrude is beloved (for her own sake) by Colonel Howard "of the regular army," and returns his affection. The Colonel, however, makes no proposal, because he considers that his salary of "fifteen hundred a year" is no property of his own, but belongs to his creditors. He has endorsed for a friend to the amount of seven thousand dollars, and is left to settle the debt as he can. He talks, therefore, of resigning, going west, making a fortune, returning, and then offering his hand with his fortune, to Gertrude.

At this juncture, Trueman pays a visit to his old friend Tiffany, and is put at fault in respect to the true state of Gertrude's heart (and indeed of every thing else) by the tattle of Prudence, Mrs. Tiffany's old-maiden sister. She gives the old man to understand that Gertrude is in love with T. Tennyson Twinkle, a poet who is in the sad habit of reading aloud his own verses, but who has really very respectable pretensions, as times go. T. T. T. nevertheless, has no thought of Gertrude, but is making desperate love to the imaginary money-bags of Seraphina. He is rivalled, however, not only by the Count, but by Augustus Fogg, a gentleman of excessive *haut ton*, who wears black and has a general indifference to every thing but hot suppers.

Millinette, in the mean time, has followed her deceiver to America, and happens to make an engagement as *femme de chambre* and general instructor in Parisian modes, at the very house (of all houses in the world) where her Gustave, as Count Jolimaitre, is paying his addresses to Miss Tiffany. The laundress recognizes the cook, who, at first overwhelmed with dismay, finally recovers his self-possession, and whispers to his betrothed a place of appointment at which he promises to "explain all." This appointment is overheard by Gertrude, who for some time has had her suspicions of the Count. She resolves to personate Millinette in the interview, and thus obtain means of exposing the impostor. Contriving therefore to detain the *femme de chambre* from the assignation, she herself (Gertrude) blowing out the candles and disguising her voice, meets the Count at the appointed room in Tiffany's house, while the rest of the company (invited to a ball) are at supper. In order to accomplish the detention of Millinette, she has been forced to give some instructions to Zeke (re-baptized Adolph by Mrs. Tiffany) a negro footman in the Tiffany livery. These instructions are overheard by Prudence, who mars everything by bringing the whole household into the room of appointment before any secret has been extracted from the Count. Matters are made worse for Gertrude by a futile attempt on the Count's part to conceal himself in a closet. No explanations are listened to. Mrs. Tiffany and Seraphina are in a great rage—Howard is in despair—and Trueman entertains so bad an opinion of his grandaughter that he has an idea of suffering her still to remain in ignorance of his relationship. The company disperse in much admired disorder, and everything is at odds and ends.

Finding that she can get no one to hear her explanations, Gertrude writes an account of all to her friends at Geneva. She is interrupted by Trueman—shows him the letter—he comprehends all—and hurries the lovers into the presence of Mr. and Mrs. Tiffany, the former of whom is in despair, and the latter in high glee at information just received that Seraphina has eloped with Count Jolimaitre.

While Trueman is here avowing his relationship, bestowing Gertrude upon Howard, and relieving Tiffany from the fangs of Snobson by showing that person that he is an accessary to his employer's forgery, Millinette enters, enraged at the Count's perfidy to herself, and exposes him in full. Scarcely has she made an end when Seraphina appears in search of her jewels, which the Count, before committing himself by the overt act of matrimony, has insisted upon her securing. As she does not return from this errand, however, sufficiently soon, her lover approaches on tip-toe to see what has become of her; is seen and caught by Millinette; and finding the game up, confesses every thing with exceeding nonchalance. Trueman extricates Tiffany from his embarrassments on condition of his sending his wife and daughter to the country to get rid of their fashionable notions; and even carries his generosity so far as to establish the Count in a *restaurant* with the *proviso* that he, the Count, shall in the character and proper habiliments of cook Treadmill, carry around his own advertisement to all the fashionable acquaintances who had solicited his intimacy while performing the *rôle* of Count Jolimaitre.

We presume that not even the author of a plot such as this, would be disposed to claim for it any thing on the score of originality or invention. Had it, indeed, been designed as a burlesque upon the arrant conventionality of stage incidents in general, we should have regarded it as a palpable hit. And, indeed, while on the point of absolute unoriginality, we may as well include in one category both the events and the characters. The testy yet generous old grandfather, who talks in a domineering tone, contradicts every body, slaps all mankind on the back, thumps his cane on the floor, listens to nothing, chastises all the fops, comes to the assistance of all the insulted women, and relieves all the *dramatis personae* from all imaginable dilemmas:—the hen-pecked husband of low origin, led into difficulties by his vulgar and extravagant wife:—the die-away daughter aspiring to be a Countess:—the villain of a clerk who aims at the daughter's hand through the fears of his master, some of whose business secrets he possesses:—the French grisette metamorphosed into the dispenser of the highest Parisian modes and graces:—the intermeddling old maid making bare-faced love to every unmarried man she meets:—the stiff and stupid man of high fashion who utters only a single set phrase:—the mad poet reciting his own verses:—the negro footman in livery impressed with a profound sense of his own consequence, and obeying with military promptness all orders from every body:—the patient, accomplished, and beautiful governess, who proves in the end to be the heiress of the testy old gentleman:—the high-spirited officer, in love with the governess, and refusing to marry her in the first place because *he* is too poor, and in the second place because *she* is too rich: and, lastly, the foreign impostor with a title, a drawl, an eye-glass, and a *moustache*, who makes love to the supposititious heiress of the play in strutting about the stage with his coat-tails thrown open after the fashion of Robert Macaire, and who, in the end, is exposed and disgraced through the instrumentality of some wife or mistress whom he has robbed and abandoned:—these things we say, together with such incidents as one person supplying another's place at an assignation, and such *equivoques* as arise from a surprisal in such cases—the concealment and discovery of one of the parties in a closet—and the obstinate refusal of all the world to listen to an explanation, are the common and well-understood property of the play-wright, and have been so, unluckily, time out of mind.

But, for this very reason, they should be abandoned at once.

Their hackneyism is no longer to be endured. The day has at length arrived when men demand rationalities in place of conventionalities. It will no longer do to copy, even with absolute accuracy, the whole tone of even so ingenious and really spirited a thing as the "School for Scandal." It was comparatively good in its day, but it would be positively bad at the present day, and imitations of it are inadmissible at any day.

Bearing in mind the spirit of these observations, we may say that "Fashion" is theatrical but not dramatic. It is a pretty well-arranged selection from the usual *routine* of stage characters, and stage manœuvres—but there is not one particle of any nature beyond greenroom nature, about it. No such events ever happened in fact, or ever could happen, as happen in "Fashion." Nor are we quarrelling, now, with the mere *exaggeration* of character or incident;—were this all, the play, although bad as comedy might be good as farce, of which the exaggeration of possible incongruities is the chief element. Our fault-finding is on the score of deficiency in verisimilitude —in natural art—that is to say, in art based in the natural laws of man's heart and understanding.

When, for example, Mr. Augustus Fogg (whose name by the bye has little application to his character) says, in reply to Mrs. Tiffany's invitation to the conservatory, that he is "indifferent to flowers," and replies in similar terms to every observation addressed to him, neither are we affected by any sentiment of the farcical, nor can we feel any sympathy in the answer on the ground of its being such as any human being would naturally make at all times to all queries—making no other answer to any. Were the thing absurd in itself, we should laugh, and a legitimate effect would be produced; but unhappily the only absurdity we perceive is the absurdity of the author in keeping so pointless a phrase in any character's mouth. The shameless importunities of Prudence to Trueman are in the same category—that of a total deficiency in verisimilitude, without any compensating incongruousness—that is to say, farcicalness, or humor. Also in the same category we must include the rectangular crossings and recrossings of the *dramatis personae* on the stage; the coming forward to the foot-lights when any thing of interest is to be told; the reading of private letters in a loud rhetorical tone; the preposterous soliloquising; and the even more preposterous "asides." Will our play-wrights never learn, through the dictates of common sense, that an audience under no circumstances can or will be brought to conceive that what is sonorous in their own ears at a distance of fifty feet from the speaker cannot be heard by an actor at the distance of one or two?

No person of common ingenuity will be willing to admit that even the most intricate dramatic narrative could not be rendered intelligible without these monstrous inartisticalities. They are the relics of a day when men were content with but little of that true Art whose nature they imperfectly understood, and are now retained solely through that supine spirit of imitation which grows out of the drama itself as the chief of the imitative arts, and which has had so much to do in degrading it, in effect, by keeping it stationary while all of its sisters have been making rapid progress. The drama has not declined as many suppose: it has only been left out of sight by every thing else. We must discard all models. The Elizabethan theatre should be abandoned. We need thought of our own—principles of dramatic action drawn not from the "old dramatists" but from the fountain of a Nature that can never grow old.

It must be understood that we are not condemning Mrs. Mowatt's comedy in particular, but the modern drama in general. Comparatively, there is much merit in "Fashion," and in many respects (and those of a *telling* character) it is superior to any American play. It has, in especial, the very high merit of simplicity in plot. What the Spanish play-wrights mean by dramas of *intrigue* are the worst acting dramas in the world:—the intellect of an audience can never safely be fatigued by complexity. The necessity for verbose explanation on the part of Trueman at the close of "Fashion" is, however, a serious defect. The *dénouement* should in all cases be full of *action* and nothing else. Whatever cannot be explained by such action should be communicated at the opening of the play.

The colloquy in Mrs. Mowatt's comedy is spirited, generally terse, and well seasoned at points with sarcasm of much power. The *management* throughout shows the fair authoress to be thoroughly conversant with our ordinary stage effects, and we might say a good deal in commendation of some of the "sentiments" interspersed:—we are really ashamed, nevertheless, to record our deliberate opinion that if "Fashion" succeed at all (and we think upon the whole that it will) it will owe the greater portion of its success to the very carpets, the very ottomans, the very chandeliers, and the very conservatories that gained so decided a popularity for that most inane and utterly despicable of all modern comedies—the "London Assurance" of Boucicault.

The above remarks were written before the comedy's representation at the Park, and were based on the author's original MS., in which some modifications have been made—and not at all times, we really think, for the better. A good point, for example, has been omitted, at the *dénouement*. In the original, Trueman (as will be seen in our digest) pardons the Count, and even establishes him in a *restaurant*, on condition of his carrying around to all his fashionable acquaintances his own advertisement as *restaurateur*. There is a *piquant*, and dashing deviation, here, from the ordinary *routine* of stage "poetic justice," which could not have failed to tell, and which was, perhaps, the one original point of the play. We can conceive no good reason for its omission. A scene, also, has been introduced, to very little purpose. We watched its effect narrowly, and found it null. It narrated nothing; it illustrated nothing; and was absolutely nothing in itself. Nevertheless it *might* have been introduced for the purpose of giving time for some other scenic arrangements going on out of sight.

The comedy was thus cast:

Adam Trueman . . . . Mr. Chippendale.
Count de Jolimaitre . . . . W. H. Crisp.
Colonel Howard . . . . Dyott.
Mr. Tiffany . . . . Barry.
Mr. T. Tennyson Twinkle . . . . . . De Walden.
Mr. Augustus Fogg . . . . Bridges.
Mr. Snobson . . . . Fisher.
Zeke, a colored servant . . . . Skerrett.
Master of the ceremonies . . . . Gallot.
Mrs. Tiffany . . . . Mrs. Barry.
Gertrude . . . . Miss Clara Ellis.
Seraphina Tiffany . . . . Miss Kate Horn.
Prudence . . . . Mrs. Knight.
Millinette . . . . Dyott.

A well written prologue was well delivered by Mr. Crisp, whose action is far better than his reading—although the latter, with one exception, is good. It is pure irrationality to recite verse, as if it were prose, without distinguishing the lines: —we shall touch this subject again. As the Count, Mr. Crisp did every thing that could be done:—his grace of gesture is prëeminent. Miss Horne looked charmingly as Seraphina. Trueman and Tiffany were represented with all possible effect by Chippendale and Barry:—and Mrs. Barry as Mrs. Tiffany was the life of the play. Zeke was caricatured. Dyott makes a bad colonel—his figure is too diminutive. Prudence was well exaggerated by Mrs. Knight—and the character in her hands, elicited more applause than any one other of the *dramatis personae.*

Some of the author's intended points were lost through the inevitable inadvertences of a first representation—but upon the whole, every thing went off exceedingly well. To Mrs. Barry we would suggest that the author's intention was, perhaps, to have *élite* pronounced *ee-light*, and *bouquet*, bokett:—the effect would be more certain. To Zeke we would say, bring up the table bodily by all means (as originally designed) when the *fow tool* is called for. The scenery was very good indeed—and the carpet, ottomans, chandelier, etc. were also excellent of their kind. The entire "getting up" was admirable. "Fashion," upon the whole, was well received by a large, fashionable, and critical audience; and will succeed to the extent we have suggested above. Compared with the generality of modern dramas it is a good play—compared with most American dramas, it is a *very* good one—estimated by the natural principles of dramatic art, it is altogether unworthy of notice.

———

PROSPECTS OF THE DRAMA. —
MRS. MOWATT'S COMEDY.

So deeply have we felt interested in the question of Fashion's success or failure, that we have been to see it every night since its first production; making careful note of its merits and defects as they were more and more distinctly developed in the gradually perfected representation of the play.

We are enabled, however, to say but little either in contradiction or in amplification of our last week's remarks—which
were based it will be remembered, upon the original MS. of
the fair authoress, and upon the slightly modified performance
of the first night. In what we then said we made all reasonable
allowances for inadvertences at the outset—lapses of memory
in the actors—embarrassments in scene-shifting—in a word
for general hesitation and want of *finish*. The comedy now,
however, must be understood as having all its capabilities fairly
brought out, and the result of the perfect work is before us.

In one respect, perhaps, we have done Mrs. Mowatt unin-
tentional injustice. We are not quite sure, upon reflection, that
her entire thesis is not an original one. We can call to mind no
drama, just now, in which the design can be properly stated as
the satirizing of fashion *as* fashion. Fashionable follies, indeed,
as a class of folly in general, have been frequently made the
subject of dramatic ridicule—but the distinction is obvious—
although certainly too nice a one to be of any practical avail to
the authoress of the new comedy. Abstractly we may admit
some pretension to originality of plan—but, in the representation, this shadow of originality vanishes. We cannot, if we
would, separate the *dramatis personae* from the moral they illustrate; and the characters overpower the moral. We see before
us only personages with whom we have been familiar time out
of mind:—when we look at Mrs. Tiffany, for example, and hear
her speak, we think of Mrs. Malaprop in spite of ourselves, and
in vain endeavour to think of anything else. The whole conduct and language of the comedy, too, have about them the
unmistakeable flavor of the green-room. We doubt if a single
point either in the one or the other, is not a household thing
with every play-goer. Not a joke is any less old than the hills—
but this conventionality is more markedly noticeable in the
sentiments, so called. When, for instance, Gertrude in quitting
the stage, is made to say, "if she fail in a certain scheme she will
be the first woman who was ever at a loss for a stratagem," we
are affected with a really painful sense of the antique. Such
things are only to be ranked with the stage "properties," and
are inexpressibly wearisome and distasteful to every one who
hears them. And that they are sure to elicit what appears to be
applause, demonstrates exactly nothing at all. People at these

points put their hands together, and strike their canes against the floor for the reason that they feel these actions to be required of them as a matter of course, and that it would be ill-breeding not to comply with the requisition. All the talk put into the mouth of Mr. Truman, too, about "when honesty shall be found among lawyers, patriotism among statesmen," etc. etc. must be included in the same category. The error of the dramatist lies in not estimating at its true value the absolutely certain "*approbation*" of the audience in such cases—an approbation which is as pure a conventionality as are the "sentiments" themselves. In general it may be boldly asserted that the clapping of hands and the rattling of canes are no tokens of the *success* of any play—such success as the dramatist should desire:—let him watch the *countenances* of his audience, and remodel his points by these. Better still—let him "look into his own heart and write"—again better still (if he have the capacity) let him work out his purposes *à priori* from the infallible principles of a Natural Art.

We are delighted to find, in the reception of Mrs. Mowatt's comedy, the clearest indications of a revival of the American drama—that is to say of an earnest disposition to see it revived. That the drama, in general, can go down, is the most untenable of all untenable ideas. Dramatic art is, or should be, a concentralization of all that which is entitled to the appellation of Art. When sculpture shall fail, and painting shall fail, and poetry, and music;—when men shall no longer take pleasure in eloquence, and in grace of motion, and in the beauty of woman, and in truthful representations of character, and in the consciousness of sympathy in their enjoyment of each and all, then and not till then, may we look for *that* to sink into insignificance, which, and which alone, affords opportunity for the conglomeration of these infinite and imperishable sources of delight.

There is not the least danger, then, that the drama shall fail. By the spirit of imitation evolved from its own nature and to a certain extent an inevitable consequence of it, it has been kept absolutely stationary for a hundred years, while its sister arts have rapidly flitted by and left it out of sight. Each progressive step of every other art *seems* to drive back the drama to the exact extent of that step—just as, physically, the objects by the way-side seem to be receding from the traveller in a coach. And the practical effect, in both cases, is equivalent:—but yet, in fact, the drama has not receded: on the contrary it has very slightly advanced in one or two of the plays of Sir Edward Lytton Bulwer. The apparent recession or degradation, however, will, in the end work out its own glorious recompense. The extent—the excess of the seeming declension will put the right intellect upon the serious analysis of its causes. The first noticeable result of this analysis will be a sudden indisposition on the part of all thinking men to commit themselves any farther in the attempt to keep up the present mad—mad because false —enthusiasm about "Shakspeare and the musical glasses." Quite willing, of course, to give this indisputably great man the fullest credit for what he has done—we shall begin to ask our own understandings why it is that there is so very—very much which he has utterly failed to accomplish.

When we arrive at this epoch, we are safe. The next step may be the electrification of all mankind by the representation of *a play* that may be neither tragedy, comedy, farce, opera, pantomime, melodrama, or spectacle, as we now comprehend these terms, but which may retain some portion of the idiosyncratic excellences of each, while it introduces a new class of excellence as yet unnamed because as yet undreamed-of in the world. As an absolutely necessary condition of its existence this play may usher in a thorough remodification of the theatrical *physique*.

This step being fairly taken, the drama will be at once side by side with the more definitive and less comprehensive arts which have outstripped it by a century:—and now not merely will it outstrip them in turn, but devour them altogether. The drama will be all in all.

We cannot conclude these random observations without again recurring to the effective manner in which "Fashion" has been brought forward at the Park. Whatever the management and an excellent company could do for the comedy, has been done. Many obvious improvements have been adopted since the first representation, and a very becoming deference has been manifested, on the part of the fair authoress and of Mr. Simpson, to every thing wearing the aspect of public opinion—in especial to every reasonable hint from the press. We are proud, indeed, to find that many even of our own ill-considered suggestions, have received an attention which was scarcely their due.

In "Fashion" nearly all the Park company have won new laurels. Mr. Chippendale did wonders. Mr. Crisp was, perhaps, a little too gentlemanly in the Count—he has *subdued* the part, we think, a trifle too much:—there is a *true* grace of manner of which he finds it difficult to divest himself, and which occasionally interferes with his conceptions. Miss Ellis did for Gertrude all that any mortal had a right to expect. Millinette could scarcely have been better represented. Mrs. Knight as Prudence is exceedingly comic. Mr. and Mrs. Barry do invariably well—and of Mr. Fisher we forgot to say in our last paper that he was one of the strongest points of the play. As for Miss Horne—it is but rank heresy to imagine that there could be any difference of opinion respecting *her*. She sets at naught all criticism in winning all hearts. There is about her lovely countenance a radiant *earnestness* of expression which is sure to play a Circean trick with the judgment of every person who beholds it.

1845

WALT WHITMAN

That the poet who boasted of his "barbaric yawp" should be a fan of *bel canto* ought to come as no surprise. After all, Walt Whitman (1819–1892) insisted that he contained multitudes. He first attended plays between 1832 and 1836 when he worked as a teenaged journeyman compositor in Brooklyn and took the ferry to Manhattan in the evening. "I spent much of my time in the theatres then, seeing everything, high, low, middling—absorbing theatres at every pore"—and spouting Shakespeare from the tops of buses. New York City had five playhouses by then, but Whitman most often frequented the cheap seats of the Bowery Theatre, luxuriating in its full-blooded melodramas. His favorite actor was the temperamental (some said insane) English tragedian Junius Brutus Booth. A populist who hobnobbed with actors, Whitman preferred a vociferous and demonstrative exchange between the stage and the audience. In the 1840s, when he was editing the *Brooklyn Eagle*, he felt guilty about sitting in the parquet on a press pass. With typical self-contradiction, however, he projected his own growing class consciousness on the spectators and deplored Edwin Forrest's "loud mouthed ranting style." Complaining that the critics were mere "slaves of the paid puff system," he pleaded for American plays informed by American ideas, particularly abolition. Eventually, he turned his attention from the theatre to opera and the visual arts and, after a few more years of journalism, published *Leaves of Grass* in 1855. Very late in life, he recalled with pleasure his time in the Bowery, even softening his appraisal of Forrest amid the haze of nostalgia.

The Gladiator—Mr. Forrest—Acting

FROM footlights to lobby doors—from floor to dome—were packed crowds of people last night (25th) at the Park Theatre, N. Y., to see Mr. Forrest in the Gladiator. . . . This play is as full of 'Abolitionism' as an egg is of meat. It is founded on that passage of Roman history where the slaves—Gallic, Spanish, Thracian and African—rose against their masters, and formed themselves into a military organization, and for a time successfully resisted the forces sent to quell them. Running

o'er with sentiments of liberty—with eloquent disclaimers of
the right of the Romans to hold human beings in bondage—it
is a play, this Gladiator, calculated to make the hearts of the
masses swell responsively to all those nobler manlier aspirations in behalf of mortal freedom!—The speech of Spartacus,
in which he attributes the grandeur and wealth of Rome, to
her devastation of other countries, is fine; and Mr. Forrest delivered it passing well. Indeed, in the first part of the play, this
favorite actor, with his herculean proportions, was evidently i'
the vein—but the later parts were not so well gone through
with. . . .

We do not intend the following reflections—which started
during the view of Mr. Forrest's performances—to bear directly
on that actor. Mr. F. is a deserved favorite with the public—
and has high talent in his profession. But the danger is, that as
he has to a measure become identified with a sort of American
style of acting, the crowd of vapid imitators may spread quite
all the faults of that style, with none of its excellencies. Indeed,
too, in candor, all persons of thought will confess to no great
fondness for acting which particularly seeks to "tickle the ears
of the groundlings." We allude to the loud mouthed ranting
style—the tearing of every thing to shivers—which is so much
the ambition of some of our players, particularly the young
ones. It does in such cases truly seem as if some of Nature's
journeymen had made men, and not made them well—they
imitate humanity so abominably. They take every occasion, in
season and out of season, to try the extremest strength of their
lungs. They never let a part of their dialogue which falls in the
imperative mood—the mood for exhorting, commanding, or
permitting—pass by without the loudest exhibition of sound,
and the most distorted gesture. If they have to enact passion,
they do so by all kinds of unnatural and violent jerks, swings,
screwing of the nerves of the face, rolling of the eyes, and so
on. To men of taste, all this is exceedingly ridiculous. And even
among the inferior portion of the audience, it does not always
pass safely. We have frequently seen rough boys in the pit, with
an expression of sovereign contempt at performances of this
sort.—For there is something in real nature which comes home
to the "business and bosoms" of all men.—Who ever saw love
made as it is generally made upon the stage? How often have

we heard spontaneous bursts of approbation from inferior audiences, toward acting of the most unpretending kind, merely because it was simple, truthful, and natural!

If we thought these remarks would meet the eye of any young theatrical artist, we would like through him to beg all—for we cannot call to mind any who are not more or less tainted with this vice—to take such hints as the foregoing, to their hearts—aye, to their heart of hearts. It is a common fallacy to think that an exaggerated, noisy, and inflated style of acting—and no other—will produce the desired effect upon a promiscuous audience. But those who have observed things, Theatres, and human nature, know better. Where is there a good, truthful player that is not appreciated? Who, during the past season, has dared compare the quiet polish of Mrs. Kean with the lofty pretensions of the general run of tragedy queens?

In all the intervals between the appearance of these much trumpetted people, the theatre is quite deserted, though the plays and playing are often far better than during some star engagement. We have seen a fine old English drama, with Miss *Cushman* and her sister—Mrs. *Vernon*, *Placide*, *Fisher*, and several others whose betters in their departments could hardly be found—we have seen such a beautiful piece, well put upon the stage, and played to a forlorn looking audience, thinly scattered here and there through pit and box—while the very next week, crowds would crush each other to get a sight of some flippant well-puffed star, of no real merit, and playing a character written (for the play consists of nothing but *one*, in such cases) by nobody knows whom—probably an ephemeral manufacturer of literature, with as little talent as his employer.

If some bold man would take the theatre in hand in this country, and resolutely set his face against the starring system, as a system,—some *American* it must be, and not moulded in the opinions and long established ways of the English stage,—if he should take high ground, revolutionize the drama, and discard much that is not fitted to present tastes and to modern ideas,—engage and encourage American talent, (a term made somewhat nauseous by the use it has served for charlatans, but still a good term,) look above merely the gratification of the vulgar and of those who love glittering scenery—give us

American plays too, matter fitted to American opinions and institutions—our belief is he would do the republic service, and himself too, in the long round.

1846

Miserable State of the Stage
Why Can't We Have Something Worth the Name of American Drama?

OF all '*low*' places where vulgarity (not only on the stage, but in front of it) is in the ascendant, and bad-taste carries the day with hardly a pleasant point to mitigate its coarseness, the New York theatres—except the Park—may be put down (as an Emeralder might say,) at the top of the heap! We don't like to make these sweeping assertions in general—but the habit of such places as the Bowery, the Chatham, and the Olympic theatres, is really beyond all toleration; and if the N.Y. prints who give dramatic notices, were not the slaves of the paid puff system, they surely would sooner or later be 'down' on those miserable burlesques of the histrionic art. Yet not one single independent dramatic critic seems to be among many talented writers for the N.Y. press. Or rather, we should say, not one single upright critic is permitted to utter candidly his opinions of the theatricals of the metropolis; for we would not insult the good taste of the intelligent literary men connected with the press over the river, so much as to suppose that their eyes and ears do not make the same complaint to them as ours make to us in the matter alluded to.

We have excepted the Park theatre in the charge of vulgarity, because the audiences there are always intelligent, and there is a dash of superiority thrown over the performances. But commendation can go not much further. Indeed it is not a little strange that in a great place like New York, acknowledged as the leading city of the western hemisphere, there should be no absolutely *good* theatre. The Park, once in a great while, gives a fine play, performed by meritorious actors and actresses. The Park is still very far, however, from being what we might reasonably expect in the principal dramatic establishment of the metropolis. It is but a third-rate imitation of the best London theatres. It gives us the cast off dramas, and the unengaged players of Great Britain; and of these dramas and players, like garments which come second hand from gentleman to valet, every thing fits awkwardly. Though now and then there is ground for satisfaction, the average is such as men of refinement cannot applaud at all. A play arranged to suit an English audience, and to jibe with English localities, feelings, and domestic customs, can rarely be represented in America, without considerable alteration. This destroys its uniformity, and generally deprives it of all life and spirit. One of the curses of the Park, and indeed of nearly all theatres now, is the *star* system. Some actor or actress flits about the country, playing a week here and a week there, bringing as his or her greatest recommendation, that of *novelty*—and very often indeed having no other.—

1847

The Old Bowery
A Reminiscence of New York Plays and Acting Fifty Years Ago.

In an article not long since, "Mrs. Siddons as Lady Macbeth," in "The Nineteenth Century," after describing the bitter regretfulness to mankind from the loss of those first-class poems, temples, pictures, gone and vanish'd from any record of men, the writer (Fleeming Jenkin) continues:

If this be our feeling as to the more durable works of art, what shall we say of those triumphs which, by their very nature, last no longer than the action which creates them—the triumphs of the orator, the singer or the actor? There is an anodyne in the words, "must be so," "inevitable," and there is even some absurdity in longing for the impossible. This anodyne and our sense of humor temper the unhappiness we feel when, after hearing some great performance, we leave the theatre and think, "Well, this great thing has been, and all that is now left of it is the feeble print upon my brain, the little thrill which memory will send along my nerves, mine and my neighbors, as we live longer the print and thrill must be feebler, and when we pass away the impress of the great artist will vanish from the world." The regret that a great art should in its nature be transitory, explains the lively interest which many feel in reading anecdotes or descriptions of a great actor.

All this is emphatically my own feeling and reminiscence about the best dramatic and lyric artists I have seen in bygone days—for instance, Marietta Alboni, the elder Booth, Forrest, the tenor Bettini, the baritone Badiali, "old man Clarke"—(I could write a whole paper on the latter's peerless rendering of the Ghost in "Hamlet" at the Park, when I was a young fellow) —an actor named Ranger, who appear'd in America forty years ago in *genre* characters; Henry Placide, and many others. But I will make a few memoranda at least of the best one I knew.

For the elderly New Yorker of to-day, perhaps, nothing were more likely to start up memories of his early manhood than the mention of the Bowery and the elder Booth. At the date given, the more stylish and select theatre (prices, 50 cents pit, $1 boxes) was "The Park," a large and well-appointed house on Park Row, opposite the present Post-office. English opera and the old comedies were often given in capital style; the principal foreign stars appear'd here, with Italian opera at wide intervals. The Park held a large part in my boyhood's and young manhood's life. Here I heard the English actor, Anderson, in "Charles de Moor," and in the fine part of "Gisippus." Here I heard Fanny Kemble, Charlotte Cushman, the Seguins, Daddy Rice, Hackett as Falstaff, Nimrod Wildfire, Rip Van Winkle, and in his Yankee characters. (See pages 19, 20, *Speciman Days.*) It was here (some years later than the date in the headline) I also heard Mario many times, and at his best. In such parts as Gennaro, in "Lucrezia Borgia," he was inimitable—the sweetest of voices, a pure tenor, of considerable compass and respectable power. His wife, Grisi, was with him, no longer first-class or young—a fine Norma, though, to the last.

Perhaps my dearest amusement reminiscences are those musical ones. I doubt if ever the senses and emotions of the future will be thrill'd as were the auditors of a generation ago by the deep passion of Alboni's contralto (at the Broadway Theatre, south side, near Pearl street)—or by the trumpet notes of

Badiali's baritone, or Bettini's pensive and incomparable tenor in Fernando in "Favorita," or Marini's bass in "Faliero," among the Havana troupe, Castle Garden.

But getting back more specifically to the date and theme I started from—the heavy tragedy business prevail'd more decidedly at the Bowery Theatre, where Booth and Forrest were frequently to be heard. Though Booth *père*, then in his prime, ranging in age from 40 to 44 years (he was born in 1796,) was the loyal child and continuer of the traditions of orthodox English play-acting, he stood out "himself alone" in many respects beyond any of his kind on record, and with effects and ways that broke through all rules and all traditions. He has been well describ'd as an actor "whose instant and tremendous concentration of passion in his delineations overwhelm'd his audience, and wrought into it such enthusiasm that it partook of the fever of inspiration surging through his own veins." He seems to have been of beautiful private character, very honorable, affectionate, good-natured, no arrogance, glad to give the other actors the best chances. He knew all stage points thoroughly, and curiously ignored the mere dignities. I once talk'd with a man who had seen him do the Second Actor in the mock play to Charles Kean's Hamlet in Baltimore. He was a marvellous linguist. He play'd Shylock once in London, giving the dialogue in Hebrew, and in New Orleans Oreste (Racine's "Andromaque") in French. One trait of his habits, I have heard, was strict vegetarianism. He was exceptionally kind to the brute creation. Every once in a while he would make a break for solitude or wild freedom, sometimes for a few hours, sometimes for days. (He illustrated Plato's rule that to the forming an artist of the very highest rank a dash of insanity or what the world calls insanity is indispensable.) He was a small-sized man—yet sharp observers noticed that however crowded the stage might be in certain scenes, Booth never seem'd overtopt or hidden. He was singularly spontaneous and fluctuating; in the same part each rendering differ'd from any and all others. He had no stereotyped positions and made no arbitrary requirements on his fellow-performers.

As is well known to old play-goers, Booth's most effective part was Richard III. Either that, or Iago, or Shylock, or Pescara in "The Apostate," was sure to draw a crowded house.

(Remember heavy pieces were much more in demand those days than now.) He was also unapproachably grand in Sir Giles Overreach, in "A New Way to Pay Old Debts," and the principal character in "The Iron Chest."

In any portraiture of Booth, those years, the Bowery Theatre, with its leading lights, and the lessee and manager, Thomas Hamblin, cannot be left out. It was at the Bowery I first saw Edwin Forrest (the play was John Howard Payne's "Brutus, or the Fall of Tarquin," and it affected me for weeks; or rather I might say permanently filter'd into my whole nature,) then in the zenith of his fame and ability. Sometimes (perhaps a veteran's benefit night,) the Bowery would group together five or six of the first-class actors of those days—Booth, Forrest, Cooper, Hamblin, and John R. Scott, for instance. At that time and here George Jones ("Count Joannes") was a young, handsome actor, and quite a favorite. I remember seeing him in the title role in "Julius Cæsar," and a capital performance it was.

To return specially to the manager. Thomas Hamblin made a first-rate foil to Booth, and was frequently cast with him. He had a large, shapely, imposing presence, and dark and flashing eyes. I remember well his rendering of the main role in Maturin's "Bertram, or the Castle of St. Aldobrand." But I thought Tom Hamblin's best acting was in the comparatively minor part of Faulconbridge in "King John"—he himself evidently revell'd in the part, and took away the house's applause from young Kean (the King) and Ellen Tree (Constance,) and everybody else on the stage—some time afterward at the Park. Some of the Bowery actresses were remarkably good. I remember Mrs. Pritchard in "Tour de Nesle," and Mrs. McClure in "Fatal Curiosity," and as Millwood in "George Barnwell." (I wonder what old fellow reading these lines will recall the fine comedietta of "The Youth That Never Saw a Woman," and the jolly acting in it of Mrs. Herring and old Gates.)

The Bowery, now and then, was the place, too, for spectacular pieces, such as "The Last Days of Pompeii," "The Lion-Doom'd" and the yet undying "Mazeppa." At one time "Jonathan Bradford, or the Murder at the Roadside Inn," had a long and crowded run; John Sefton and his brother William acted in it. I remember well the Frenchwoman Celeste, a splendid pantomimist, and her emotional "Wept of the Wish-ton-Wish." But certainly the main "reason for being" of the Bowery Theatre those years was to furnish the public with For-rest's and Booth's performances—the latter having a popular-ity and circles of enthusiastic admirers and critics fully equal to the former—though people were divided as always. For some reason or other, neither Forrest nor Booth would accept en-gagements at the more fashionable theatre, the Park. And it is a curious reminiscence, but a true one, that both these great actors and their performances were taboo'd by "polite society" in New York and Boston at the time—probably as being too robustuous. But no such scruples affected the Bowery.

Recalling from that period the occasion of either Forrest or Booth, any good night at the old Bowery, pack'd from ceiling to pit with its audience mainly of alert, well dress'd, full-blooded young and middle-aged men, the best average of American-born mechanics—the emotional nature of the whole mass arous'd by the power and magnetism of as mighty mimes as ever trod the stage—the whole crowded auditorium, and what seeth'd in it, and flush'd from its faces and eyes, to me as much a part of the show as any—bursting forth in one of those long-kept-up tempests of hand-clapping peculiar to the Bowery —no dainty kid-glove business, but electric force and muscle from perhaps 2000 full-sinew'd men—(the inimitable and chromatic tempest of one of those ovations to Edwin Forrest, welcoming him back after an absence, comes up to me this moment)—Such sounds and scenes as here resumed will surely afford to many old New Yorkers some fruitful recollections.

I can yet remember (for I always scann'd an audience as rigidly as a play) the faces of the leading authors, poets, edi-tors, of those times—Fenimore Cooper, Bryant, Paulding, Irving, Charles King, Watson Webb, N. P. Willis, Hoffman, Halleck, Mumford, Morris, Leggett, L. G. Clarke, R. A. Locke and others, occasionally peering from the first tier boxes; and even the great National Eminences, Presidents Adams, Jack-son, Van Buren and Tyler, all made short visits there on their Eastern tours.

Awhile after 1840 the character of the Bowery as hitherto described completely changed. Cheap prices and vulgar pro-grammes came in. People who of after years saw the pandemonium of the pit and the doings on the boards must not gauge by them the times and characters I am describing. Not but what there was more or less rankness in the crowd even then. For types of sectional New York those days—the streets East of the Bowery, that intersect Division, Grand, and up to Third Avenue—types that never found their Dickens, or Hogarth, or Balzac, and have pass'd away unportraitured—the young ship-builders, cartmen, butchers, firemen (the old-time "soap-lock" or exaggerated "Mose" or "Sikesey," of Chanfrau's plays,) they, too, were always to be seen in these audiences, racy of the East River and the Dry Dock. Slang, wit, occasional shirt sleeves, and a picturesque freedom of looks and manners, with a rude good-nature and restless movement, were generally notice-able. Yet there never were audiences that paid a good actor or an interesting play the compliment of more sustain'd attention or quicker rapport. Then at times came the exceptionally deco-rous and intellectual congregations I have hinted at; for the Bowery really furnish'd plays and players you could get no-where else. Notably, Booth always drew the best hearers; and to a specimen of his acting I will now attend in some detail.

I happen'd to see what has been reckon'd by experts one of the most marvelous pieces of histrionism ever known. It must have been about 1834 or '35. A favorite comedian and actress at the Bowery, Thomas Flynn and his wife, were to have a joint benefit, and, securing Booth for Richard, advertised the fact many days before-hand. The house fill'd early from top to bot-tom. There was some uneasiness behind the scenes, for the afternoon arrived, and Booth had not come from down in Maryland, where he lived. However, a few minutes before ringing-up time he made his appearance in lively condition.

After a one-act farce over, as contrast and prelude, the cur-tain rising for the tragedy, I can, from my good seat in the pit, pretty well front, see again Booth's quiet entrance from the side, as, with head bent, he slowly and in silence, (amid the tempest of boisterous hand-clapping,) walks down the stage to the footlights with that peculiar and abstracted gesture, musingly kicking his sword, which he holds off from him by its sash. Though fifty years have pass'd since then, I can hear the clank, and feel the perfect following hush of perhaps three thousand people waiting. (I never saw an actor who could make more of the said hush or wait, and hold the audience in an indescribable, half-delicious, half-irritating suspense.) And so throughout the entire play, all parts, voice, atmosphere, magnetism, from

"Now is the winter of our discontent,"

to the closing death fight with Richmond, were of the finest and grandest. The latter character was play'd by a stalwart young fellow named Ingersoll. Indeed, all the renderings were wonderfully good. But the great spell cast upon the mass of hearers came from Booth. Especially was the dream scene very impressive. A shudder went through every nervous system in the audience; it certainly did through mine.

Without question Booth was royal heir and legitimate representative of the Garrick-Kemble-Siddons dramatic traditions; but he vitalized and gave an unnamable *race* to those traditions with his own electric personal idiosyncrasy. (As in all art-utterance it was the subtle and powerful something *special to the individual* that really conquer'd.)

To me, too, Booth stands for much else besides theatricals. I consider that my seeing the man those years glimps'd for me, beyond all else, that inner spirit and form—the unquestionable charm and vivacity, but intrinsic sophistication and artificiality —crystallizing rapidly upon the English stage and literature at and after Shakspere's time, and coming on accumulatively through the seventeenth and eighteenth centuries to the beginning, fifty or forty years ago, of those disintegrating, decomposing processes now authoritatively going on. Yes; although Booth must be class'd in that antique, almost extinct school, inflated, stagy, rendering Shakspere (perhaps inevitably, appropriately) from the growth of arbitrary and often cockney conventions, his genius was to me one of the grandest revelations of my life, a lesson of artistic expression. The words fire, energy, *abandon*, found in him unprecedented meanings. I never heard a speaker or actor who could give such a sting to hauteur or the taunt. I never heard from any other the charm of unswervingly perfect vocalization without trenching at all on mere melody, the province of music.

So much for a Thespian temple of New York fifty years since, where "sceptred tragedy went trailing by" under the gaze of the Dry Dock youth, and both players and auditors were of a character and like we shall never see again. And so much for the grandest histrion of modern times, as near as I can deliberately judge (and the phrenologists put my "caution" at 7)— grander, I believe, than Kean in the expression of electric passion, the prime eligibility of the tragic artist. For though those brilliant years had many fine and even magnificent actors, undoubtedly at Booth's death (in 1852) went the last and by far the noblest Roman of them all.

1885

PHILIP HONE

Walt Whitman's distaste for Edwin Forrest's robustious style of performance was a minority report. By the mid-1840s, Forrest was lauded as the very model of the native American tragedian, not just in Shakespeare but in plays he had commissioned or inspired: as the Indian chief Metamora and the mutinous slave Spartacus, his stentorian voice and muscular physique roused the groundlings. A tour of England sparked a rivalry with the restrained and intellectual actor-manager William Charles Macready, and what began as a histrionic competition became a full-fledged grudge match. When Macready visited New York in 1849, Forrest fanned the flames of anti-British feeling among the Irish working class and helped foment a riot in which 31 people were killed and a large number were wounded.

Among those who spoke out against Forrest's demagoguery and its results were Washington Irving, Herman Melville, and Philip Hone (1780–1851). Hone, the son of an immigrant German joiner, made a fortune as an auctioneer and became a local celebrity who preferred the company of other celebrities. He was briefly mayor of New York. The Whig Party relied on him as a sagacious counselor and Manhattan society's old families valued his exquisite manners and impeccable taste. The diary Hone kept from 1826 until his death is richly detailed and observant, but regularly displays a backward-looking regret that things are going to hell in a handbasket.

The Astor Place Riot

MAY 8.—Mr. McCready commenced an engagement last evening at the Opera-House, Astor place, and was to have performed the part of "Macbeth," whilst his rival, Mr. Forrest, appeared in the same part at the Broadway theatre. A violent animosity has existed on the part of the latter theatrical hero against his rival, growing out of some differences in England; but with no cause, that I can discover, except that one is a gentleman, and the other is a vulgar, arrogant loafer, with a pack of kindred rowdies at his heels. Of these retainers a regularly organized force was employed to raise a riot at the Opera-House and drive Mr. McCready off the stage, in which, to the disgrace of the city, the ruffians succeeded. On the appearance of the "Thane of Cawdor," he was saluted with a shower of missiles, rotten eggs, and other unsavoury objects, with shouts and yells of the most abusive epithets. In the midst of this disgraceful riot the performance was suspended, the respectable part of the audience dispersed, and the vile band of *Forresters* were left in possession of the house. This cannot end here; the respectable part of our citizens will never consent to be put down by a mob raised to serve the purpose of such a fellow as Forrest. Recriminations will be resorted to, and a series of riots will have possession of the theatres of the opposing parties.

MAY 10.—The riot at the Opera-House on Monday night was children's play compared with the disgraceful scenes which were enacted in our part of this devoted city this evening, and the melancholy loss of life to which the outrageous proceedings of the mob naturally led.

An appeal to Mr. McCready had been made by many highly respectable citizens, and published in the papers, inviting him to finish his engagement at the Opera-House, with an implied pledge that they would stand by him against the ferocious mob of Mr. Forrest's friends, who had determined that McCready should not be allowed to play, whilst at the same time their oracle was strutting, unmolested, his "hour upon the stage" of the Broadway theatre. This announcement served as a firebrand in the mass of combustibles left smouldering from the riot of the former occasion. The *Forresters* perceived that their previous triumph was incomplete, and a new conspiracy was formed to accomplish effectually their nefarious designs. Inflammatory notices were posted in the upper ward, meetings were regularly organized, and bands of ruffians, gratuitously supplied with tickets by richer rascals, were sent to take possession of the theatre. The police, however, were beforehand with them, and a large body of their force was posted in different parts of the house.

When Mr. McCready appeared he was assailed in the same manner as on the former occasion; but he continued on the stage and performed his part with firmness, amidst the yells and hisses of the mob. The strength of the police, and their good conduct, as well as that of the Mayor, Recorder, and other public functionaries, succeeded in preventing any serious injury to the property within doors, and many arrests were made; but the war raged with frightful violence in the adjacent streets. The mob—a dreadful one in numbers and ferocity— assailed the extension of the building, broke in the windows, and demolished some of the doors. I walked up to the corner of Astor place, but was glad to make my escape. On my way down, opposite the New York Hotel, I met a detachment of troops, consisting of about sixty cavalry and three hundred in- fantry, fine-looking fellows, well armed, who marched steadily to the field of action. Another detachment went by the way of Lafayette place. On their arrival they were assailed by the mob, pelted with stones and brickbats, and several were carried off severely wounded.

Under this provocation, with the sanction of the civil au- thorities, orders were given to fire. Three or four volleys were discharged; about twenty persons were killed and a large num- ber wounded. It is to be lamented that in the number were several innocent persons, as is always the case in such affairs. A large proportion of the mob being lookers-on, who, putting no faith in the declaration of the magistrates that the fatal order was about to be given, refused to retire, and shared the fate of the rioters. What is to be the issue of this unhappy affair cannot be surmised; the end is not yet.

MAY 11.—I walked up this morning to the field of battle, in As- tor place. The Opera-House presents a shocking spectacle, and the adjacent buildings are smashed with bullet-holes. Mrs. Langdon's house looks as if it had withstood a siege. Groups of people were standing around, some justifying the interfer- ence of the military, but a large proportion were savage as tigers with the smell of blood.

MAY 12.—Last night passed off tolerably quietly, owing to the measures taken by the magistrates and police. But it is consola- tory to know that law and order have thus far prevailed. The city authorities have acted nobly. The whole military force was under arms all night, and a detachment of United States troops was also held in reserve. All the approaches to the

Opera-House were strictly guarded, and no transit permitted. The police force, with the addition of a thousand special constables, were employed in every post of danger; and although the lesson has been dearly bought, it is of great value, inasmuch as the fact has been established that law and order can be maintained under a Republican form of government.

1849

ANNA CORA MOWATT

Anna Cora Ogden (1819–1870) enjoyed a pampered girlhood, writing poems and starring in amateur theatricals, activities she continued after she secretly married the New York lawyer James Mowatt in 1834. When he lost his money, she found herself constrained to give public readings, with some success. Illness cut off this avenue of financial recovery, and so she wrote a comedy, *Fashion*, to be acted at the Park Theatre in 1845. It became the first American play to enjoy a long run, and her prejudices against the professional stage began to evaporate. To the horror of her friends and relatives, who shared the common view of actresses as little better than prostitutes, she made a debut at the Park and performed throughout America and England until 1854. Poe, who became a friend, praised "her own grace of manner—her own sense of art—her own rich and natural elocution." Her refinement and hard work helped to qualify the stage as a viable profession for respectable women. Mowatt's autobiography (1854) and her reality-based fiction *Mimic Life; or Before and Behind the Curtain* (1856) promoted this purpose. In these theatrical equivalents of *Uncle Tom's Cabin*, a class of exploited laborers is portrayed as virtuous, moral, and worthy of society's consideration.

FROM

Mimic Life;
or, Before and Behind the Curtain

It was the morning of Stella's début. As she drew back the curtains of her window, the sight of her own name, in huge characters, on a placard opposite, sent an electric shock through her frame. The novel sensation could hardly be designated as pain, yet it would be mistermed pleasure. There was too much incertitude, too much thrilling expectancy, too many turbulent thoughts contending in her mind, for the sense of enjoyment to predominate. She had broken the thrall of tyrannous custom, she had triumphed over all opposition; and yet the canker-worm of discontent entered her breast, and blasted the spring blossoms of her youth. The unrelaxed tension of her nerves, her mental unrest, had quenched the sparkle of her effervescing spirits. Her state constantly alternated between high excitement and an oppressive weariness.

As soon as her determination to become an actress was bruited in the public ear, she was, of course, besieged by the remonstrances of friends. But their opinions she set at naught. Her independent tone and resolute manner silenced exhortation. To her mother's presence no one gained admission.

Mr. Oakland declined to accompany his pupil to her second rehearsal. His tenderness towards the unprotected girl had induced him to violate a principle, at her strong entreaty, but he saw no cause to subject himself to further slight without being of essential service to her.

The clock had struck its tenth warning on that eventful day, and the ten minutes' theatrical grace had expired, before Stella, with Mattie at her side, once more entered the theatre. They found the company already assembled, but rehearsal had not commenced. Everybody awaited the appearance of the great tragedian. Punctuality would have been derogatory to the dignity of Mr. Tennent. To cause his co-laborers as much annoyance as possible was to impress them with a due sense of his own importance.

Mr. Belton saluted Stella more cordially than on a previous occasion. He was gratified to find that Mr. Oakland's presence was not considered indispensable. Fisk bestowed on her a familiar nod. The stage-manager and actors curtailed their civilities to the utmost brevity. The profession never pay homage in anticipation. Miss Rosenvelt's assumed position in the theatre as yet lacked the stamp of public recognition. All novices are looked upon as pretenders until success proclaims their legitimacy.

Mr. Belton chanced to be called away. Stella was left standing in the centre of the stage, beside Mattie, looking wretchedly uncomfortable and out of place.

Mrs. Fairfax, who had just entered, joined her at once, and ordered Fisk to bring a chair.

"You will learn the ways of a theatre, little by little, my dear. Every one feels strange at first." She placed the chair beside the manager's table. "You can sit here or in the green-room, just as you please. It is the privilege of stars to take their seat on the stage and watch the rehearsal. The rest of the company are not allowed this liberty. How flushed you look! Will you not be more comfortable if you lay aside your bonnet? You will rehearse better."

Stella willingly removed her hat, for even its light weight seemed to press painfully on her throbbing brain.

Mrs. Fairfax hinted that Mattie had better keep a little more in the background. She might subject herself to reproof from the austere stage-manager. Mattie, at a word, retreated behind the scenes. But her honest, anxious face was constantly visible, peeping round one of the wings, and watching Stella.

After half an hour's delay, Mr. Tennent made a pompous entrance. The stage echoed with his heavy tread. His deep, sonorous voice, as he issued some despotic orders, his imperious bearing, his athletic frame, cast in one of nature's rudest moulds, inspired Stella with a feeling akin to awe.

Mr. Belton presented him.

"Sorry you've got me a novice! Detest acting with *amateurs!*" was his audible observation, as he eyed the young girl with supercilious scrutiny. "Poor Lydia! we shan't soon see her match again." He turned on his heel without addressing a single syllable to the discomfited novice.

"And *he* is to enact Virginius!" thought Stella to herself. "How will I ever imagine myself his daughter? If he had only spoken one word to me, it would make such a difference!"

Rehearsal commenced. To Stella's great surprise, Mr. Tennent rattled over the language of his rôle in the same senseless manner as the other actors, pausing now and then to explain his particular "business," and ejaculating "Brute!" in an undertone, every time some unfortunate individual failed to comprehend him.

Stella summoned all her energy, and successfully assumed a bearing which might have been mistaken for composure. She went through her allotted duties without hesitation, and apparently undismayed. Mrs. Fairfax congratulated her on her newly-acquired self-possession. Mr. Tennent occasionally instructed her in "business," but without unbending from his stately demeanor.

As Virginia is seen no more after the fourth act, Stella was at liberty to absent herself before rehearsal concluded. She re-

turned to the chair upon which she had placed her bonnet.
Mr. Finch was unconsciously sitting upon both. He laughed
unconcernedly, and made a clumsy attempt to pull the hat into
shape, but uttered no apology. Then, thrusting it into her extended hand, he said:

"No use of crying over spilled milk! If you don't put your
foot in it to-night, and make a failure, you can afford to buy
yourself twice as fine a kickshaw as this."

Stella's mind was too much engrossed to dwell upon trifles,
but she recoiled from contact with coarse natures. It was less
mortification to be forced to wear the damaged hat through
the streets than to be treated with such rude indifference.

She was passing out behind the scenes, when Mrs. Fairfax
once more joined her.

"Call upon me for any assistance you may need this evening.
You will, of course, have the 'star dressing-room.' The luxury
of an apartment to one's self is reserved for stars only. The
room in which I dress, with four other ladies, adjoins yours.
You had better come early,—at least an hour and a half before
the curtain rises,—so that you can walk about, after you are
dressed, and collect your thoughts. Don't forget that I will assist you with pleasure."

Mrs. Fairfax's partiality for her profession, as well as her native kindness of heart, interested her in a novice who apparently possessed histrionic qualifications of a rare order. The
compassionate actress stretched out a loving hand to this young
girl, whose uncertain feet were forcing their way within the
briery circle which bounded that miniature world, a theatre.

Stella was thanking her new friend with much warmth,
when a ballet-girl timidly approached. Her face was grief-worn
and sickly, but of touching loveliness. Oppression looked out
from her meek eyes. Her coarse and insufficient garb betokened penury. Her attenuated fingers were rapidly knitting
lace, and her needles never ceased their motion as she spoke.

"May Floy carry your basket, miss?"

"My basket?"

"The basket with your dresses. Floy carries all the baskets."

Stella looked inquiringly at Mrs. Fairfax.

"You should have a basket for your costumes. A basket is
lighter and more convenient than a trunk. This is Floy's sister.

He takes charge of all our baskets. Poor fellow! we ought to help him as much as we can." She added, in an under-tone, "The unfortunate boy is half-witted, but very honest."

"Mattie shall purchase me a basket. Let your brother call for it, by all means," said Stella.

"And tell him to be sure to call early, Perdita," added Mrs. Fairfax.

"O, never fear! Thank you, kindly, Miss Rosenvelt." Still knitting as she walked away, Perdita returned to the green-room.

*   *   *

The afternoon was one of long expectancy to Stella. The thoughtful Mattie had persuaded her to lie down; but she tossed uneasily on her pillow, finding no repose. Every few minutes she turned to the clock; there was surely some clog upon its hands, they moved so slowly. O, that the night had come and had passed! Then, as the longed-for time drew near, suddenly she grew sick at heart, and was seized with faintness. The thought flashed through her mind that she would fail at the last moment; that she lacked strength to carry the burden which she had lifted upon her own shoulders with such head-strong will.

Half-past seven was the hour at which the curtain must rise. She had been apprised that Mr. Belton enforced the strictest punctuality at night. Even when stars of first magnitude solicited a few moments' delay, it was denied. Mrs. Fairfax had cautioned her to be at the theatre in ample time. It wanted but a quarter of six.

A knock at the door. The pale-faced Perdita stood without. She was accompanied by a tall, ungainly stripling. The extreme sharpness of his countenance reminded Stella of the "profile" shows she had that morning seen scattered about the stage. His large projecting eyes, of faintest blue, seemed starting from their sockets. His nether limbs bore a strong resemblance to a pair of compasses, and his long, lank arms reached below his knees. His mouth remained open with an expression of silly wonder. When he caught Stella's eye, he shook his head, agitating a profusion of straight, tow-colored locks, and chuckled and laughed, as child does with child when they are bent upon some forbidden frolic.

"I have brought my brother," said Perdita, advancing into the room. "He has come for the basket. I show him the way the first time he goes to a strange place. He always remembers it after that."

The serene, sweet face of that humble girl, who had passed calmly through such soul-harrowing trials, who faithfully performed so many difficult duties, had more effect in composing Stella's excited nerves than all the hartshorn and sal-volatile which Mattie solicitously administered.

The basket was already packed. Mattie strapped the cover with leathern girths, and Floy delightedly received his new burden.

Stella's adieu to her mother was very brief. She only trusted herself to say, "I hope I shall bring you good news, mother; and the promise of laurels hereafter, even if I win none to-night."

She was equally surprised and gratified when her mother asked for a copy of Virginius to peruse in her daughter's absence.

Mattie, who was now and then a little tyrannical, had persisted in ordering a carriage, though Stella declared herself quite able to walk. Soon after six, they were driving to the theatre. They presented themselves at the stage-door just as Perdita and Floy arrived with the basket. The door-keeper brusquely questioned Stella as to her identity before he admitted them.

The dreary gloominess of a theatre behind the scenes, when twilight is chasing the out-spent day, must be seen and felt to be fully comprehended. The desolate cheerlessness of the place has struck a chill to the heart of many a novice. The crowded scenery looks rougher and dingier; the painted tenements, groves, gardens, streets, more grotesque; the numberless stage anomalies more glaringly absurd.

The sea-weed floating on the waves in feathery sprays of brilliant red and vivid green, that, seized for closer scanning, turns to an unsightly, shapeless mass, fitly typifies the stage in its resplendent wizard-robe of night enchantment, and its unideal, lugubrious daytime garb.

"Where am I to go?" Stella inquired of Perdita.

"The dresser, Mrs. Bunce, has not come yet, and the gas will not be turned on until half-past six. Mr. Belton only allows it to be lighted for one hour before the curtain rises; but, if you please, I can show you the star dressing-room."

Perdita led the way up a long flight of stairs, then through a narrow entry, or, rather, gallery. On one side appeared a row of small doors, very like those of a bathing-machine. They opened into the rooms of the ladies of the company. A wooden railing extended on the other side. To any one who leaned over this rude balcony the larger portion of the stage became visible. Five or six persons were often crowded into one dressing-room. The apartments were portioned off into set spaces, and every cramped division labelled with a name. The room at the end of the gallery was appropriated solely to the lady "star." The dressing-rooms devoted to the use of gentlemen were located beneath the stage.

Perdita opened the door of this modern "star-chamber." The apartment was very small, the atmosphere suffocatingly close. Mattie at once threw up the tiny, cobweb-draped window. A shelf ran along one side of the wall, after the manner of a kitchen dresser. In front lay a narrow strip of baize; the rest of the floor was bare. On the centre of the shelf stood a cracked mirror. A gas-branch jutted out on either side. Two very rickety chairs, a crazy washstand, a diminutive stove, constituted the furniture of the apartment. In this unseemly chrysalis-shell the butterflies of the stage received their wings. Little did the audience, who greeted some queen-like favorite, sumptuously attired in broidered velvet and glittering with jewels, imagine that such was the palace-bower from which she issued!

The year had just ushered in its most wayward child, smiling, frowning April. Frowns thus far predominated; the unsunned air had all the searching bleakness of March. Mattie threw her own shawl over her shivering charge, and examined the unlighted stove.

"Set down the basket, Floy, and run for a match," said Perdita.

The boy, as he removed the basket from his shoulder, looked at Stella with evident admiration, winked at her, chuckled again, and ran down the stair. He was strongly attracted by this new face. He comprehended that something was going on which principally concerned its possessor; but what it was he could not have defined.

Floy returned with the match, and Mattie was lighting the fire which she found prepared for kindling, when Perdita whispered, "Here comes Mrs. Bunce!" and hurried away with her brother, apparently awed by the approach of some august personage.

Mrs. Bunce, a portly, middle-aged woman, now bustled in. What a voice that Mrs. Bunce had! It was so shrill that, when she spoke, Stella almost fancied her ears were suddenly pierced by a sharp instrument. All Mrs. Bunce's words were darted out with amazing rapidity.

"Here in time, eh? That's a good sign for a novice. This is the young lady, I suppose," examining Stella. "Quite a stage face. How do you do, my dear? This is your maid, I presume?"

"Her maid, or her nurse, or her costumer, or anything she is pleased to want," replied Mattie, with dignity.

"Ah! that's well. No doubt a very serviceable person. So you've set the fire going? That's a pity! You may be smoked out soon; all the stoves here smoke when the wind's contrary. Out with the dresses! Hang them up on those nails. Her toilet things go here. Never been on the stage before, miss? It's a trying thing for beginners. I've seen hundreds of débuts in my day. Most of the young ones think a deal of themselves until they get before the lights; then they find out what they're made of. Not one in fifty succeeds. Hope you're not scared? Don't show it to the audience, or they'll think it good fun. They always laugh at the fright of novices; you know it makes the poor, simple things look so ridiculously awkward! Here, Jerry," calling over the gallery to the gas-lighter, "if you can't light up that gas yet, give us a candle, will you? The young person is a novice, and I may have trouble dressing her."

"Thank you, Mrs. Bunce," Stella ventured to say; "but Mattie has been accustomed to dress me."

"Yes, that I have, ever since she was that high!" added Mattie, affectionately, and designating with her hand a stature of some few inches.

"Ah! I dare say, but not for the stage. Mr. Belton depends upon me to look after the novices on their first night, and see that they don't disfigure themselves."

Mattie, when her legitimate office was thus peremptorily snatched from her hands, looked like a suppressed thunder-gust;

but, considerate even in her wrath, she feared to distress Stella by remonstrating. Not without difficulty, she controlled a strong temptation to forcibly eject Mrs. Bunce from the apartment.

As Mattie opened the basket, Mrs. Bunce seized upon the contents, and dragged them to light without ceremony.

"White merino: that's right. Has it got a sweep? Not too long, I hope; if she's awkward, she'll trip. Those folds are too small for a Roman dress. She has such a wisp of a figure, she could wear loose folds, which are more correct. Where's your key border?"

"*Key border?*" asked Stella.

"Yes, round the bottom of the dress; it's Roman. We always dress our Virginias with key-border trimming."

"I like the dress better without. Virginia's character is marked by so much girlish simplicity that her attire should be unadorned."

"O, very well! It's no great matter; you are not expected to know much about it as yet."

Mrs. Bunce chattered on without pause, while Stella commenced her toilet. The busy fingers of the dresser made several desperate attempts to assist in the arrangement of the novice's hair; but this Stella would not allow. She folded back the waving, golden-tinted tresses from her pure brow, gathered them in a classic knot, and encircled her head with a white fillet. A stray lock here and there escaped its bonds, and was permitted to curl down her finely-curved throat.

The gas was by this time lighted. Stella was just receiving her dress from the hands of Mattie. Mrs. Bunce snatched it away.

"Wait, wait a bit!" said she. "Where's your paint and your powder?—but you're white enough without powdering— where's your *rouge*?"

"I have none. There is nothing in the poet's description of Virginia to make one suppose that she was particularly ruddy; besides, excitement has given me too much color already."

"Does very well now, but it can't be depended upon like *rouge*. It won't last when you're frightened out of your wits, that's the mischief. Better let me borrow some *rouge* from the ladies."

"No, I would rather not. I don't see the necessity."

Mrs. Bunce persisted; Stella refused.

"O, of course you can do just as you please," said the officious dresser, in an irate tone.

"I always do," replied Stella, quietly.

Stella's Roman toilet was completed. Even the critical Mrs. Bunce was forced to confess herself satisfied with the young débutante's appearance; it was so chastely classic, so befitting the patrician maiden, so indicative of vestal purity.

It wanted more than half an hour of the rising of the curtain. The small stove had been gradually sending out thin wreaths of smoke. The atmosphere was becoming unendurable, as Stella's smarting eyes and irritated lungs began to testify.

"I shall have neither sight nor voice, if I am shut up here any longer," thought she, "and this chattering woman will drive my part quite out of my head."

Then she remembered the kind offer of Mrs. Fairfax, and requested Mrs. Bunce to see if she were dressed. In the Roman matron who returned with the messenger Stella hardly recognized her friend; the *make up* of the practised actress was so elaborate, so striking, so full of character.

Mrs. Fairfax shook hands, and held the novice at arm's length with a look of unmistakable pleasure; then retouched Stella's dress, disposed a fold here and there with more statuesque grace, and said, affectionately,

"I have seen at last my *beau ideal* of Virginia! I hope you feel quite collected?"

"Tolerably; but this room is so close, the smoke chokes me. Might we not go down?"

"Certainly. Come, and I will show you the green-room, and teach you your way behind the scenes; that will help wear off the newness."

Mattie followed, carefully protecting from contact with the ground Virginia's spotless vesture. To Stella's great relief, Mrs. Bunce remained behind.

"This is the green-room," said Mrs. Fairfax.

Stella looked in curiously. It was a long, narrow apartment. At one end sofas, throne-chairs, and other stately seats for stage use, stood crowded together. On either side of the wall a cushioned bench was secured, the only article of stationary furniture, except the full-length mirror. On this bench lay an actor in Roman apparel. Stella's uninitiated eye failed to detect that he was indebted to art for his white locks and venerable aspect. He appeared to be studying, but every now and then gave vent to an uneasy groan.

"That is Dentatus—Mr. Martin. Don't you recognize him?" inquired Mrs. Fairfax. "He is a martyr to inflammatory rheumatism, and can scarcely stand. He has suffered for years, and finds no relief."

Stella called to mind the gentleman on crutches whom she had seen at rehearsal.

"But how can he act?" she asked.

"That is one of the stage mysteries which it requires some wisdom to solve. You will see him, when he is called, hobble with his crutches to the wing, groaning at every step, and really suffering, there is no doubt about that; but, the instant his cue is spoken, his crutches will very likely be flung at Fisk's head, and, lo! Dentatus walks on the stage, erect and firm as though he had never known an ache. He is a great favorite with the audience, and generally manages to keep them convulsed with laughter, though he never ceases complaining and groaning himself, when he is out of their presence."

Two other Romans were walking up and down the green-room, repeating their parts in a low tone. At the further end, where the sofas and chairs were huddled together, sat a group of girls in Roman costume. Stella recognized Perdita among them. She was knitting lace with a rapidity positively wonderful.

Mrs. Fairfax next conducted Stella to the prompter's nook on the right of the stage. There Mr. Finch sat, arranging his prompt-book, and Fisk was going through a series of ludicrous antics at his side.

The latter nodded to Stella, and inquired, patronizingly, "How d' ye do? How do you feel *now*?"

Mrs. Fairfax checked him by a light box on the ear, and led Stella to the stage. It was covered with green baize; the scene was set for a street in Rome.

"Come and take your first look at the audience," said her cicerone, pointing out a small aperture that had been surreptitiously made in the green curtain. They looked through, and saw the boxes, pit, and gallery, rapidly filling.

At this moment, Floy glided up to Stella, rubbing his bony hands. "Such a house! such a house!" he exclaimed, and then darted away again.

Stella's heart began to leap as though it would bound into her throat, as she caught sight of the thronged audience.

"You won't mind them, when you are once engrossed in your part," said Mrs. Fairfax, noticing her sudden trepidation. "Never think of an audience, if you can help it."

They walked up and down behind the scenes. Stella remarked the broken windows, the open doors through which rushed strong currents of cold air, the dilapidated condition of the walls, and wondered at the comfortlessness of the place.

"It's the same in all theatres, my dear. I never knew a manager yet who thought it necessary to render the members of his company comfortable behind the scenes. Those windows have been broken all winter. Nobody ever dreams of having them mended. A good many of us have nearly perished in our light clothing. But I dare say we get accustomed to it; and, on the stage, in the excitement of acting, one is not conscious of heat or cold."

The door-keeper came up to them. "There is a gentleman asking to see you, miss. He says you desired him to call. It's against the rules to admit strangers, and I had to take his name to Mr. Belton to get consent. Mr. Belton said he didn't mind your seeing any one to-night, as you were a novice; but he wants you to learn the rules, and the sooner the better."

"It's Mr. Oakland! I begged him to come for one moment. How kind he is!"

Mr. Oakland was standing at the stage-door, somewhat discomposed by the door-keeper's rebuff. Fastidious and sensitive as he was, that he subjected himself to these annoyances, was an eloquent proof of his attachment to the fatherless girl.

"How good you are! The sight of you revives me, and gives me courage!"

"Fair Virginia! Yes—you *are* Virginia in looks—be nothing but Virginia to-night! I must say adieu, for I could not stay here" (and he looked around with an expression of slight disgust) "amongst these dramatic savages. Be natural; do not aim at too much; don't try to act, but to feel; don't *declaim*, but *talk*; remember the good rule: colloquial, but not prosaic;

forcible, but not declamatory. Good-by, and Heaven help you!"

Just then, Fisk darted by her, twisting his body into ludicrous contortions as he ran up the stairs, crying, at the top of his piping voice, "First musi-ic—ic—ic! First musi—ic—ic—ic!"

Along the gallery, past all the dressing-room doors, he sped, repeating, "First musi—ic—ic!" Down the staircase, beneath the stage, making the circuit of the gentlemen's dressing-rooms, he pursued his rapid flight, still shouting, "First musi—ic—ic!"

"What *is* that strange boy about?" asked Stella of Mrs. Fairfax.

"He is making the *first music call*. It is given a quarter of an hour before the curtain rises."

The musicians could now be heard tuning their instruments. Stella continued promenading up and down with Mrs. Fairfax. After the lapse of five minutes, Fisk was seen rolling himself from side to side, in sailor-like fashion, as he climbed the stairs again, screaming, "Second musi—ic—ic—*ic*! Second musi—ic—ic—*ic*!" He made the same tour, and then rolled back to the prompter's seat.

"Now it wants ten minutes of the time," said Mrs. Fairfax.

Stella was seized with an uncontrollable fit of gasping and trembling. Her head grew giddy; the same sickening faintness which she had experienced at home now nearly overpowered her. Mattie ran for a glass of water. The members of the company, who were on their way to the green-room, stopped to stare at the novice, to nudge each other, and jest at an alarm which most of them had suffered themselves.

"Last musi—ic—ic—*ic*! Last musi—ic—ic—*ic*!" screeched Fisk, with a new variation of his fantasticalities.

The orchestra was playing vociferously.

"Now, my dear, you had better forget everything else, and think over your part. It wants but five minutes of the rising of the curtain."

"O, don't leave me! don't leave me! What would I do without you?" supplicated Stella, for she saw her friend about to mount the stair.

"I will return directly. You don't appear until the second scene. I go on a moment before you, and from the same entrance. I shall be by your side. Now walk about quietly with Mattie, and try to think only of the play."

"I shall fail! I shall fail!" murmured Stella, in an agony of fear. "I shall never be able to articulate a word! O! if Mr. Oakland were here, or my brother, or any one who loved me!"

She was wringing her hands in absolute despair, when Perdita passed her and went up to a man in the garb of a Roman citizen, who was extended on the ground, in one corner. He appeared to be asleep; his head rested on a pile of shields, breastplates, and other warlike accoutrements. Perdita laid her hand gently on his shoulder.

"Father! father, dear! the last music is called; you will be wanted in a moment."

"Get out! get out! don't disturb me; get out, I say!" was the rough reply, accompanied by a motion that somewhat resembled a kick.

"Father, you *must* wake up! The curtain is going to rise! You are on in the first scene!—*do* wake!"

"What is it? Who is it?" asked the man, with a vacant stare. "Perdy, it's you, is it? Always bothering me! no quiet to be found anywhere; no rest!"

"I was forced to wake you, father; for you are called for the stage."

She smoothed his disordered hair, and arranged the tumbled folds of his toga.

He rose unwillingly, shaking himself after the fashion of a huge mastiff. His form was tall and finely proportioned. His countenance must once have been handsome; but the defacing fingers of passion and sensuality had ploughed furrows that destroyed its comeliness. He was not precisely intoxicated, but in that semi-stupid state which habitual intemperance renders second nature.

Stella forgot herself and her approaching trial as she watched the noble girl patiently waiting upon and soothing her brutal father.

"Everybody called for First Act of Virginius!" bellowed Fisk, gambolling up to the green-room door. "Servius, Cneius, Virginius, Titus, and all the Roman citizens!"

"O, where is Mrs. Fairfax?" cried Stella, as she seized Mattie's arm to support herself, "Why don't she come? Do try and find her room, and beg her to come, Mattie! No! no! don't leave me here alone! If she would only come! I go on at that entrance, over there. I must get there quickly."

She was walking across the stage, with Mattie's arm encircling her waist, when the orchestra ceased.

"Clear the stage, ladies and gentlemen," called out Mr. Finch.

The prompter's tinkling bell sounded. Stella's white dress and sandalled feet were visible for a second, as the curtain slowly rose.

The first scene commenced. Where Stella stood, she commanded a full view of the stage. But she saw nothing, heard nothing,—not even the stately Virginius, not the shouts of applause with which his entrance was greeted.

"Courage! courage!" said a kind voice at her side. It was Mrs. Fairfax.

"O, madam, I feel as if I were under water—stifling—drowning!"

"It's only *stage fright*, my dear; it will pass off by and by. All actors suffer more or less from its paralyzing influence. Even our veterans are not proof against occasional attacks of the monster. Try and collect yourself, and think of what you have to do."

"Virginius—Servia—Virginia," cried Fisk, in a more subdued tone; for, now that the curtain had risen, his former key would have been heard by the audience. Fisk looked saucily in Stella's face, his head on one side, and a sagacious expression upon his countenance, which seemed to ask, "How d' ye like it? Pleasant feeling, isn't it?" And then he repeated almost in her ear, "Vir-gin-ia-a-a call-*alled*!"

"Go away, you young pest!" said Mrs. Fairfax, giving him a shove.

A shrill whistle sounded; it penetrated Stella's very brain. The scene changed to an apartment in the house of Virginius.

"There's Virginia's broidery," said Fisk, giving Mrs. Fairfax a frame with worsted-work of by no means classic appearance. "There's your Virginia painting," he added, handing Stella a colored engraving. "That's the picture of Achilles, which looks so wonderful like your belov*ed* Icilius. An't it fine?"

At the sound of the changing scene all the company poured

from the green-room and gathered around the wings, to witness Stella's débût. Actors invariably entertain a sovereign contempt for novices. The stage tremors of youthful aspirants are a fruitful source of mirth. They delight in confusing and tormenting a débûtante.

Virginius enters with Servia. She points out the tell-tale letters L and I twined with a V, in Virginia's embroidery. After a brief dialogue, Servia is despatched for the maiden.

Mrs. Fairfax returned to the place where she had left the panic-stricken Stella, and found her lying in Mattie's arms, breathless with the intensity of her emotion, her face and lips colorless, her eyes half closed.

The actress grasped her by the shoulder with pretended roughness, and shook her, saying, "Rouse yourself, child! rouse yourself! You've only a second now. You're not going to make a failure? Think of what a disgrace it would be! Think of the one whom you wish most to please—who is dearest to you —and rouse yourself. Virginius' soliloquy is just over. 'Soft she comes'—that is your cue; go on bravely."

She clasped Stella's icy hand, and with gentle force pressed her forward. Stella was scarcely conscious of what she was doing, as she tottered on the stage and approached Virginius, saying, in a tremulous tone, "Well, father, what's your will?"

Those foot-lights sent forth a dazzling glare, but Stella was in total darkness. The air grew so thick she could not breathe; her "soul of lead" "staked her to the ground;" she could not move. There was a sound of noisy hands, a prolonged acclamation, but Stella paid no heed to these, as she stood spellbound before Virginius.

He attempted to speak, but the applause drowned his voice. As it was bestowed upon another, he would gladly have hushed it down, by proceeding with his part (a favorite trick of actors); but the audience was resolute in obtaining some recognition from the stupefied novice.

Mr. Tennent now churlishly whispered, "Curtsey, curtsey— can't you?" Muttering to himself, "Defend me from novices!"

Stella, thus prompted, turned mechanically to the audience and bended slightly, for her quivering limbs rendered the genuflexion somewhat difficult of accomplishment. The darkness was partially dispelled, but the still misty atmosphere seemed full of floating atoms; her Roman father was enveloped by them. The air was less stifling, but were they not flakes of ice which she inhaled at every breath? Silence was restored, and the dialogue proceeded.

The graceful simplicity of Stella's attire, the changing beauty of her countenance, the refinement of her mien, her rich, well-cadenced voice, made an instantaneous impression on the audience.

Virginius despatches her for her "last task." Mrs. Fairfax had thoughtfully taken the painting from Stella's hand, and was now holding it in readiness. Stella drew one long breath of relief as she passed out of sight of the audience. Only three lines are spoken by Virginius before Virginia reënters. Stella would certainly have forgotten herself but for Mrs. Fairfax. Virginia returns with the painting. Dentatus enters a moment afterwards. There was no trace of the crippled rheumatic in his gait or mien. Dentatus and Virginius retire together.

It was passing strange, but Stella, now that she was left alone upon the stage, felt as though the freezing influences that begirt her had suddenly melted away. The spell was broken; her lost faculties were restored. Her form dilated, the truant blood rushed back to her cheeks, the lustre to her dimmed eyes, her thoughts concentrated themselves on her part; with an involuntary self-surrender, she became Virginia. Nothing could surpass the girlish naturalness, the earnest sweetness, with which she uttered:

> "How is it with my heart? I feel as one
>   That has lost everything, and just before
>   Had nothing left to wish for. He will cast
>   Icilius off! I never told it yet;
>   But take of me, thou gentle air, the secret—
>   And ever after breathe more balmy sweet—
>   I love Icilius!
>   He'll cast Icilius off! Not if Icilius
>   Approve his honor. That he'll ever do;
>   He speaks, and looks, and moves, a thing of honor,
>   Or honor never yet spoke, looked, or moved,
>   Or was a thing of earth!"

The audience testified their approval. She had taken her first step on the steep, flinty mount. That over, at every tread she gained a securer foothold.

Icilius enters. Virginia has but a few lines to speak in this scene, but the maidenly modesty with which she confessed her love,—

> "My secret's yours;
> Keep it, and *honor it*, Icilius,—"

her drooping head, the unconscious picturesqueness of her *pose*, drew down a second round of plaudits.

When the act closed, Mrs. Fairfax embraced her warmly. "You will be an actress. I thought so; now I know it!"

"But what I have suffered, and how much I owe to your sympathy and encouragement!" replied Stella.

By the time that the call-boy's summons for the second act was given, she had entirely regained her self-possession. Every time she appeared, she grew in favor with the audience. There is no field for a striking display of dramatic abilities in the simple character of Virginia, as portrayed by Knowles; but Stella's unaffected, artless delineation left a deep impression.

In the fourth act, as Virginius raises his knife to stab his daughter, Stella gave utterance to an irrepressible shriek, which imparted unusual reality to the scene. Virginius, the instant he had struck the blow, dropped the young girl from his arms upon the ground, and, with upraised knife, rushed towards Claudius, exclaiming:

> "Lo! Appius, with this innocent blood
> I do devote thee to the infernal Gods!"

Stella felt the trampling of the citizens' and soldiers' feet over her dress and on her loosened hair, as they gathered round to form the closing *tableau*; but she lay motionless, inwardly sending up thanks to Heaven that her trial was over. The curtain rapidly descended. Mr. Belton assisted her to rise.

"You have done well, you give promise," were his chary words of commendation.

There was, of course, a "call" for the débûtante. The manager requested Mr. Tennent to be kind enough to lead on Miss

Rosenvelt. The pompous tragedian complied somewhat sulkily. As Stella made her obeisance before the foot-lights, every chord of her heart vibrated with a strange, wild delight. It was the first sensation of unalloyed pleasure she had experienced that night.

While she resumed her every-day attire, the tearful congratulations of Mattie drew from her eyes responding tokens of joy.

Floy came for the basket. That he noticed her streaming eyes was obvious. "O! O! O!" he murmured, pityingly; then, when she smiled, he shook his head, rubbed his hands gleefully, and repeated his favorite ejaculation, "Such a house! such a house!"

Half an hour later, the débûtante was sobbing in her mother's arms. "Mother, I have succeeded! Forgive my waywardness!"

1856

MARK TWAIN

Theatre went West for the same reason most pioneers did, to make its fortune. Eager to profit from the Gold Rush of 1848, performers played mining camps and frontier settlements; some, like the child Lotta Crabtree, got rich in the process. By 1849 Sacramento had a permanent playhouse and San Francisco followed suit soon after. Samuel Langhorne Clemens (1835–1910), a former Mississippi riverboat pilot, also drifted westward, becoming a reporter in Virginia City in 1862. Under the name Mark Twain, he proceeded to chronicle such attractions as "the naked lady" Adah Isaacs Menken in a facetiously ironic vein. (The extravagant career of Menken—sometimes billed as "The World's Delight"—encompassed marriage to a champion prizefighter, alleged affairs with Swinburne and Alexandre Dumas, and authorship of a book of cloying prose poems.) For Twain, fame came in 1865 with his short story "The Jumping Frog of Calaveras County" and he moved to New York, where he made a triumphant debut as a lecturer at Cooper Union in 1867. He also reported for the *Alta California* on Manhattan amusements, among them the scandalous new genre, the burlesque. He knew his readers in the West would be excited to hear of moral peril on the stages of the civilized East.

The eroticism of the "leg show" stood in sharp contrast to the respectability of the minstrel show, which Twain recalled not long before his death. The first public display of minstrelsy had taken place at the Bowery Amphitheatre in New York in 1843, when a quartet of fiddle, tambourine, banjo, and bones was played by white men in blackface. Minstrelsy became the most popular form of indigenous American entertainment, its traditions surviving well into the 20th century.

Twain hoped that the theatre might serve as his own private gold strike, but his collaborations and adaptations—*Colonel Sellers* (1874), *Ah Sin* (1877) and *The American Claimant* (1887)—failed to pan out. Aware of his weakness as a playwright, he assumed an insouciant pose: addressing the opening night audience at *Ah Sin*, Twain said, "I never saw a play that was so much improved by being cut down, and I believe it would have been one of the very best plays in the world if [the manager's] strength had held out so that he could cut out the whole of it."

The Menken
Written Especially for Gentlemen

WHEN I arrived in San Francisco, I found there was no one in town—at least there was no body in town but "the Menken" —or rather, that no one was being talked about except that manly young female. I went to see her play "Mazeppa," of course. They said she was dressed from head to foot in flesh-colored "tights," but I had no opera-glass, and I couldn't see it, to use the language of the inelegant rabble. She appeared to me to have but one garment on—a thin tight white linen one, of unimportant dimensions; I forget the name of the article, but it is indispensable to infants of tender age—I suppose any young mother can tell you what it is, if you have the moral courage to ask the question. With the exception of this super-fluous rag, the Menken dresses like the Greek Slave; but some of her postures are not so modest as the suggestive attitude of the latter. She is a finely formed woman down to her knees; if she could be herself that far, and Mrs. H. A. Perry the rest of the way, she would pass for an unexceptionable Venus. Here every tongue sings the praises of her matchless grace, her sup-ple gestures, her charming attitudes. Well, possibly, these tongues are right. In the first act, she rushes on the stage, and goes cavorting around after "Olinska"; she bends herself back like a bow; she pitches headforemost at the atmosphere like a battering-ram; she works her arms, and her legs, and her whole body like a dancing-jack: her every movement is as quick as thought; in a word, without any apparent reason for it, she car-ries on like a lunatic from the beginning of the act to the end of it. At other times she "whallops" herself down on the stage, and rolls over as does the sportive pack-mule after his burden is removed. If this be grace then the Menken is eminently graceful. After a while they proceed to strip her, and the high chief Pole calls for the "fiery untamed steed"; a subordinate Pole brings in the fierce brute, stirring him up occasionally to make him run away, and then hanging to him like death to keep him from doing it; the monster looks round pensively upon the brilliant audience in the theatre, and seems very willing to stand still—but a lot of those Poles grab him and hold on to him, so as to be prepared for him in case he changes his mind. They are posted as to his fiery untamed nature, you know, and they give him no chance to get loose and eat up the orchestra. They strap Mazeppa on his back, fore and aft, and face uppermost, and the horse goes cantering up-stairs over the painted mountains, through tinted clouds of theatrical mist, in a brisk exciting way, with the wretched victim he bears unconsciously digging her heels into his hams, in the agony of her sufferings, to make him go faster. Then a tempest of applause bursts forth, and the curtain falls. The fierce old circus horse carries his prisoner around through the back part of the theatre, behind the scenery, and although assailed at every step by the savage wolves of the desert, he makes his way at last to his dear old home in Tartary down by the footlights, and beholds once more, O, gods! the familiar faces of the fiddlers in the orchestra. The noble old steed is happy, then, but poor Mazeppa is insensible—"ginned out" by his trip, as it were. Before the act closes, however, he is restored to consciousness and his doting old father, the king of Tartary; and the next day, without taking time to dress—without even borrowing a shirt, or stealing a fresh horse—he starts off on the fiery untamed, at the head of the Tartar nation, to exterminate the Poles, and carry off his own sweet Olinska from the Polish court. He succeeds, and the curtain falls upon a bloody combat, in which the Tartars are victorious. "Mazeppa" proved a great card for Maguire here; he put it on the boards in first-class style, and crowded houses went crazy over it every night it was played. But Virginians will soon have an opportunity of seeing it themselves, as "the Menken" will go direct from our town there without stopping on the way. The "French Spy" was played last night and the night before, and as this spy is a frisky Frenchman, and as dumb as an oyster, Miss Menken's extravagant gesticulations do not seem so overdone in it as they do in "Mazeppa." She don't talk well, and as she goes on her shape and her acting, the character of a fidgety "dummy" is peculiarly suited to her line of business. She plays the Spy, without words, with more feeling than she does Mazeppa with them.

I am tired writing, now, so you will get no news in this letter. I have got a note-book full of interesting hieroglyphics, but I am afraid that by the time I am ready to write them out, I shall have forgotten what they mean. The lady who asked me to furnish her with the Lick House fashions, shall have them shortly—or if I ever get time, I will dish up those displayed at the great Pioneer ball, at Union Hall, last Wednesday night.

1863

The Model Artists

WHEN I was here in '53, a model artist show had an ephemeral existence in Chatham street, and then everybody growled about it, and the police broke it up; at the same period "Uncle Tom's Cabin" was in full blast in the same street, and had already run one hundred and fifty nights. Everybody went there in elegant toilettes and cried over Tom's griefs. But now, things are changed. The model artists play nightly to admiring multitudes at famous Niblo's Garden, in great Broadway—have played one hundred and fifty nights and will play one hundred and fifty nights more, no doubt—and Uncle Tom draws critical, self-possessed groups of negroes and children at Barnum's Museum. I fear me I shall have to start a moral missionary society here. Don't you suppose those friends of mine in San Francisco were jesting, when they warned me to be very choice in my language, if I ever lectured here, lest I might offend?

In '53 they called that horrid, immoral show I was speaking of, the "Model Artists," and people wouldn't go to see it. But now they call that sort of thing a "Grand Spectacular Drama," and everybody goes. It is all in a name. And it is about as spectacular as anything I ever saw without sinking right into the earth with outraged modesty. It is the wickedest show you can think of. You see there is small harm in exhibiting a pack of painted old harlots, swathed in gauze, like the original model artistes, for no man careth a cent for them but to laugh and jeer at them. Nakedness itself, in such a case, would be nothing worse than disgusting. But I warn you that when they put beautiful clipper-built girls on the stage in this new fashion, with only just barely clothes enough on to be tantalizing, it is a shrewd invention of the devil. It lays a heavier siege to public morals than all the legitimate model artist shows you can bring into action.

The name of this new exhibition that so touches my missionary sensibilities, is the "Black Crook." The scenic effects—the waterfalls, cascades, fountains, oceans, fairies, devils, hells, heavens, angels—are gorgeous beyond anything ever witnessed in America, perhaps, and these things attract the women and the girls. Then the endless ballets and splendid tableaux, with seventy beauties arrayed in dazzling half costumes; and displaying all possible compromises between nakedness and decency, capture the men and boys—and so Niblo's has taken in twenty-four hundred dollars a night, (seven nights and a matinee a week,) for five months, and sometimes twenty-seven hundred dollars. It is claimed that a multitude equal to the entire population of the State of California, Chinamen included, have visited this play. The great *Herald* newspaper pitched into it, and a sensation parson preached a sermon against it; this was sufficient to advertise it all over the continent, and so the proprietor's fortune was made.

The scenery and the legs are everything; the actors who do the talking are the wretchedest sticks on the boards. But the fairy scenes—they fascinate the boys! Beautiful bare legged girls hanging in flower baskets; others stretched in groups on great sea shells; others clustered around fluted columns; others in all possible attitudes; girls—nothing but a wilderness of girls—stacked up, pile on pile, away aloft to the dome of the theatre, diminishing in size and clothing, till the last row, mere children, dangle high up from invisible ropes, arrayed only in a camisa. The whole tableau resplendent with columns, scrolls, and a vast ornamental work, wrought in gold, silver and brilliant colors—all lit up with gorgeous theatrical fires, and witnessed through a great gauzy curtain that counterfeits a soft silver mist! It is the wonders of the Arabian Nights realized.

Those girls dance in ballet, dressed with a meagreness that would make a parasol blush. And they prance around and expose themselves in a way that is scandalous to me. Moreover, they come trooping on the stage in platoons and battalions, in most princely attire I grant you, but always with more tights in view than anything else. They change their clothes every fifteen

minutes for four hours, and their dresses become more beautiful and more rascally all the time.

1867

The Minstrel Show

WHERE now is Billy Rice? He was a joy to me, and so were
the other stars of the nigger show—Billy Birch, David Wambold, Backus, and a delightful dozen of their brethren who
made life a pleasure to me forty years ago and later. Birch,
Wambold, and Backus are gone years ago; and with them departed to return no more forever, I suppose, the real nigger
show—the genuine nigger show, the extravagant nigger show
—the show which to me had no peer and whose peer has not
yet arrived, in my experience. We have the grand opera; and I
have witnessed and greatly enjoyed the first act of everything
which Wagner created, but the effect on me has always been so
powerful that one act was quite sufficient; whenever I have
witnessed two acts I have gone away physically exhausted; and
whenever I have ventured an entire opera the result has been
the next thing to suicide. But if I could have the nigger show
back again in its pristine purity and perfection, I should have
but little further use for opera. It seems to me that to the elevated mind and the sensitive spirit, the hand organ and the
nigger show are a standard and a summit to whose rarefied altitude the other forms of musical art may not hope to reach.

I remember the first negro musical show I ever saw. It must
have been in the early forties. It was a new institution. In our
village of Hannibal we had not heard of it before, and it burst
upon us as a glad and stunning surprise.

The show remained a week and gave a performance every
night. Church members did not attend these performances,
but all the worldlings flocked to them and were enchanted.
Church members did not attend shows out there in those
days. The minstrels appeared with coal-black hands and faces
and their clothing was a loud and extravagant burlesque of the
clothing worn by the plantation slave of the time; not that the

rags of the poor slave were burlesqued, for that would not
have been possible; burlesque could have added nothing in the
way of extravagance to the sorrowful accumulation of rags and
patches which constituted his costume; it was the form and
color of his dress that was burlesqued. Standing collars were in
fashion in that day, and the minstrel appeared in a collar which
engulfed and hid the half of his head and projected so far forward that he could hardly see sideways over its points. His coat
was sometimes made of curtain calico with a swallowtail that
hung nearly to his heels and had buttons as big as a blacking
box. His shoes were rusty and clumsy and cumbersome, and
five or six sizes too large for him. There were many variations
upon this costume and they were all extravagant, and were by
many believed to be funny.

The minstrel used a very broad negro dialect; he used it
competently and with easy facility, and it was funny—delight-
fully and satisfyingly funny. However, there was one member
of the minstrel troupe of those early days who was not extrav-
agantly dressed and did not use the negro dialect. He was
clothed in the faultless evening costume of the white society
gentleman and used a stilted, courtly, artificial, and painfully
grammatical form of speech, which the innocent villagers took
for the real thing as exhibited in high and citified society, and
they vastly admired it and envied the man who could frame it
on the spot without reflection and deliver it in this easy and
fluent and artistic fashion. "Bones" sat at one end of the row of
minstrels, "Banjo" sat at the other end, and the dainty gentleman just described sat in the middle. This middleman was the
spokesman of the show. The neatness and elegance of his dress,
the studied courtliness of his manners and speech, and the
shapeliness of his undoctored features made him a contrast to
the rest of the troupe and particularly to "Bones" and "Banjo."
"Bones" and "Banjo" were the prime jokers and whatever fun-
niness was to be gotten out of paint and exaggerated clothing
they utilized to the limit. Their lips were thickened and
lengthened with bright red paint to such a degree that their
mouths resembled slices cut in a ripe watermelon.

The original ground plan of the minstrel show was maintained without change for a good many years. There was no
curtain to the stage in the beginning; while the audience

waited they had nothing to look at except the row of empty chairs back of the footlights; presently the minstrels filed in and were received with a wholehearted welcome; they took their seats, each with his musical instrument in his hand; then the aristocrat in the middle began with a remark like this:

"I hope, gentlemen, I have the pleasure of seeing you in your accustomed excellent health, and that everything has proceeded prosperously with you since last we had the good fortune to meet."

"Bones" would reply for himself and go on and tell about something in the nature of peculiarly good fortune that had lately fallen to his share; but in the midst of it he would be interrupted by "Banjo," who would throw doubt upon his statement of the matter; then a delightful jangle of assertion and contradiction would break out between the two; the quarrel would gather emphasis, the voices would grow louder and louder and more and more energetic and vindictive, and the two would rise and approach each other, shaking fists and instruments and threatening bloodshed, the courtly middleman meantime imploring them to preserve the peace and observe the proprieties—but all in vain, of course. Sometimes the quarrel would last five minutes, the two contestants shouting deadly threats in each other's faces with their noses not six inches apart, the house shrieking with laughter all the while at this happy and accurate imitation of the usual and familiar negro quarrel, then finally the pair of malignants would gradually back away from each other, each making impressive threats as to what was going to happen the "next time" each should have the misfortune to cross the other's path; then they would sink into their chairs and growl back and forth at each other across the front of the line until the house had had time to recover from its convulsions and hysterics and quiet down.

The aristocrat in the middle of the row would now make a remark which was surreptitiously intended to remind one of the end men of an experience of his of a humorous nature and fetch it out of him—which it always did. It was usually an experience of a stale and moldy sort and as old as America. One of these things, which always delighted the audience of those days until the minstrels wore it threadbare, was "Bones's" account of the perils which he had once endured during a storm at sea. The storm lasted so long that in the course of time all the provisions were consumed. Then the middleman would inquire anxiously how the people managed to survive.

"Bones" would reply, "We lived on eggs."

"You lived on eggs! Where did you get eggs?"

"Every day, when the storm was so bad, the Captain laid *to*."

During the first five years that joke convulsed the house, but after that the population of the United States had heard it so many times that they respected it no longer and always received it in a deep and reproachful and indignant silence, along with others of its caliber which had achieved disfavor by long service.

The minstrel troupes had good voices and both their solos and their choruses were a delight to me as long as the negro show continued in existence. In the beginning the songs were rudely comic, such as "Buffalo Gals," "Camptown Races," "Old Dan Tucker," and so on; but a little later sentimental songs were introduced, such as "The Blue Juniata," "Sweet Ellen Bayne," "Nelly Bly," "A Life on the Ocean Wave," "The Larboard Watch," etc.

The minstrel show was born in the early forties and it had a prosperous career for about thirty-five years; then it degenerated into a variety show and was nearly all variety show with a negro act or two thrown in incidentally. The real negro show has been stone dead for thirty years. To my mind it was a thoroughly delightful thing, and a most competent laughter-compeller and I am sorry it is gone.

As I have said, it was the worldlings that attended that first minstrel show in Hannibal. Ten or twelve years later the minstrel show was as common in America as the Fourth of July but my mother had never seen one. She was about sixty years old by this time and she came down to St. Louis with a dear and lovely lady of her own age, an old citizen of Hannibal, Aunt Betsey Smith. She wasn't anybody's aunt in particular, she was aunt to the whole town of Hannibal; this was because of her sweet and generous and benevolent nature and the winning simplicity of her character.

Like my mother, Aunt Betsey Smith had never seen a negro show. She and my mother were very much alive; their age counted for nothing; they were fond of excitement, fond of novelties, fond of anything going that was of a sort proper for members of the church to indulge in. They were always up early to see the circus procession enter the town and to grieve because their principles did not allow them to follow it into the tent; they were always ready for Fourth of July processions, Sunday-school processions, lectures, conventions, camp meetings, revivals in the church—in fact, for any and every kind of dissipation that could not be proven to have anything irreligious about it—and they never missed a funeral.

In St. Louis they were eager for novelties and they applied to me for help. They wanted something exciting and proper. I told them I knew of nothing in their line except a Convention which was to meet in the great hall of the Mercantile Library and listen to an exhibition and illustration of native African music by fourteen missionaries who had just returned from that dark continent. I said that if they actually and earnestly desired something instructive and elevating, I would recommend the Convention, but that if at bottom they really wanted something frivolous, I would look further. But no, they were charmed with the idea of the Convention and were eager to go. I was not telling them the strict truth and I knew it at the time, but it was no great matter; it is not worth while to strain one's self to tell the truth to people who habitually discount everything you tell them, whether it is true or isn't.

The alleged missionaries were the Christy minstrel troupe, in that day one of the most celebrated of such troupes and also one of the best. We went early and got seats in the front bench. By and by when all the seats on that spacious floor were occupied, there were sixteen hundred persons present. When the grotesque negroes came filing out on the stage in their extravagant costumes, the old ladies were almost speechless with astonishment. I explained to them that the missionaries always dressed like that in Africa.

But Aunt Betsey said, reproachfully, "But they're niggers."

I said, "That is no matter; they are Americans in a sense, for they are employed by the American Missionary Society."

Then both the ladies began to question the propriety of their countenancing the industries of a company of negroes, no matter what their trade might be, but I said that they could see by looking around that the best people in St. Louis were present and that certainly they would not be present if the show were not of a proper sort.

They were comforted and also quite shamelessly glad to be there. They were happy now and enchanted with the novelty of the situation; all that they had needed was a pretext of some kind or other to quiet their consciences, and their consciences were quiet now, quiet enough to be dead. They gazed on that long curved line of artistic mountebanks with devouring eyes. The middleman began. Presently he led up to that old joke which I was telling about a while ago. Everybody in the house except my novices had heard it a hundred times; a frozen and solemn and indignant silence settled down upon the sixteen hundred, and poor "Bones" sat there in that depressing atmosphere and went through with his joke. It was brand new to my venerable novices and when he got to the end and said, "We lived on eggs," and followed it by explaining that every day during the storm the Captain "laid *to*," they threw their heads back and went off into heart-whole cackles and convulsions of laughter that so astonished and delighted that great audience that it rose in a solid body to look, and see who it might be that had not heard that joke before. The laughter of my novices went on and on till their hilarity became contagious, and the whole sixteen hundred joined in and shook the place with the thunders of their joy.

Aunt Betsey and my mother achieved a brilliant success for the Christy minstrels that night, for all the jokes were as new to them as they were old to the rest of the house. They received them with screams of laughter and passed the hilarity on, and the audience left the place sore and weary with laughter and full of gratitude to the innocent pair that had furnished to their jaded souls that rare and precious pleasure.

1906

CHARLES KING NEWCOMB

The New England Transcendentalists had no time for the theatre, their minds set on higher things. An exception was one of their fellow-travelers, Charles King Newcomb (1820–1894), who boarded at Brook Farm between 1841 and 1845, courted Margaret Fuller, but never formally joined the commune. Newcomb seemed incapable of committing to any doctrine: his poetry, exuding a romantic Catholicism, a nebulous Swedenborgianism, and a fleshly sensuousness, combines Bunthorne and Grosvenor—the rival poets of Gilbert and Sullivan's *Patience*—in one. In similar fashion, his room was decorated with crucifixes, saints' images, and a portrait of the dancer Fanny Elssler. When he published a threnody on the death of Emerson's son Waldo in 1842, the sage of Concord praised Newcomb as "a true genius," but six years later downgraded him to "the spoiled child of culture" and by 1857 declared that his potential amounted to "zero." Newcomb's sensibilities show most to advantage in his journals, especially after he moved to Philadelphia. They illustrate the aesthetic tastes of a dilettante bachelor. Like most inveterate playgoers of the 19th century, he saw enough performances of the standard repertoire to be able to compare actors' interpretations with critical acumen and committed large chunks of Shakespeare to memory. Still, with typical eclecticism, Newcomb welcomed both the underclad "leg show" and the new game of baseball.

FROM
The Journals

OCTOBER 16, 1866

The exquisite art, in its kind, of Shakspear makes his plays as interesting, instructive, & suggestive on the stage as in the book. Last evening, at the theater, where I went to see Edwin Booth as Iago, the moral of the play & Shakspear's qualities were the prominent & main interests of the performance. At first, the imperfection of the acting was annoying, & the evening promised tediousness; but the theme & the dramatist redeemed the time.—Booth is little like his father. When he came on the stage, I could not think it was he, now so famous, though the part was Iago's; his person, excepting his large head, was ordinary; his voice husky; & his acting second rate, though distinguished by earnestness, sentiment, & genius of a kind. I noted in picking him out amongst a group of other actors, that the mien of genius is marked boldly: this man could hardly be the son of his father & not have some genius. . . . One could easily see why girls were wild about him; he was too pensive & isolated for Iago; too much like Hamlet, in reflectiveness; & too much like Mephistopheles, in abstruseness & idiosyncracy of relation & posture; he was not accurate in his memory, like Charles Kean; he seems to have an organisation affected by his father's eccentricities. Othello was dressed, & acted somewhat, like an Indian; but the text was almost if not quite as well, pronounced by the actor of this part as by Booth.

November 1, 1866

To advertise the play of Richard 3^d, as produced last night at the Walnut, as Shakspear's Play, was an act of forgery & fraud. No high toned actor could lend himself to such a snare & perversion. It was probably the usual stage-version: a blended medley of Shakspear & of Colman. Henry 6th is the hero of the 1st act; an allotment of which Shakspear was incapable.

November 10, 1866

The naturalness of theatrical representations is attested by the propensity of children to play at dramas of dolls, horses, & society; & invites the normal adaptation & uses of the theater for practical purposes in the training of all ages of life in experience.—Was reminded of this, at the Chestnut Street last evening, where I sat beside two little boys, absurdly misplaced indeed, at their age; but there they were. At first, I thought they would see no more in the stage-scenes than scenes, similar in kind to those they saw everyday & that they would wonder at the reproduction of life in what would seem to them unreality, & something like mimicry: but I remembered the fondness of children for playing social parts, & so was in their secret & also thought better of the theater than before.

November 15, 1866

Conjoint artlessness, energy & sensibility are principle in-gredients in the effective & pervasive power of what is called genius. Men who feel warmly & act determinately tend to make impressions on other people in favor of both themselves & their cause. Edwin Booth's performance of Hamlet, which I went to see at the Walnut last eve'g, was an illustration of this fact. Although not a first rate actor, he threw himself so dili-gently, sympathetically, & artlessly into the part, that he was something, in kind, positive, whatever it was, & drew the rapt attention of a miscellaneous house. He gave to Hamlet too mobile & demonstrative an impatience & restlessness, but his exaggeration served as an emphasis on the reading of the char-acter. His husky voice, which was suited to Richard 3^d, gave to Hamlet the effect of a cold in the lungs, but did not prevent what impression he produced. I doubt if any delineation of Hamlet ever before so much interested an audience: & the cause was the greater zeal & simplicity of the actor.—As I looked around once at the audience, understanding the attrac-tive nature of Booth's standpoint too well to be surprised at its effect, I was filled with admiration at the engagedness of the spectators in the performance. Here were people of all ranks drinking in with their eyes the type of men of all ranks. Shop-men, stockbrokers, lawyers, apprentices, news-boys, sailors, loafers, scholars, & hod-carriers were listening to a problem which all the ingenuity & mythology of Greece & Egypt had not presented to their schoolmen & kings.

December 20, 1866

The contrast of an Italian to an American or English actor, in the part of Macbeth, reminds one of the greater predomi-nance of consideration & composure in the Anglo-Saxon race. The Italian made a good & interesting Macbeth, of its kind; but it was, on the one hand, too arbitrary, as before the Witches, &, on the other hand, too ecstatic, as in his remorse. Scotch witches would have never answered so domineering a man; & a Scotch Lady Macbeth would have been disgusted with such maniacal morbidness.

April 3, 1867

Noticed that Murdoch, who played Hamlet last evening, very well,—being a better elocutionist . . . but less of a man of genius, than Edwin Booth—prudishly substituted "trull" for "whore" in Hamlet's soliloquy, "ay, so"; that, amongst a few other mistakes, he left out, probably in a momentary embarrassment of memory, the word "What" in the address to the ghost, "say, why is this? wherefore? what should we do?" . . . that he put "the" before "fardels" in Hamlet's "To be"; & that—I think, like Booth—he repeated the word "play" in the line, "the play's the thing." . . .

May 20, 1867

It would be a good point for an actor, as I felt at reciting the passage on Saturday, to burst into tears at Hamlet's adjuration of his father, "Do you not come your tardy son to chide." . . . The pathetic currents of extraordinary & harassing relation to two parents meet at that point & overwhelms him with, at least, emotion & tenderness.

April 27, 1868

The beauty in the gorgeous spectacle of men & women—in part derived through flesh-colored tights, made such an impressive scene at the theater, night before last, that the incessant & inconsiderate abuse which, on account of attire, the piece, The Black Crook,—has occurred for the year past, recurred to my thought as an act of impiety on the part of silly prudes, & of mongering conventionalists. The correlation of prudity with profanity is an inevitable conclusion from the correlation of every principle of divine, & of human, art with the mere person of god-erected & god-like man.—The entire indecency of the play consisted not in the dress, but in some double-entendre, unnecessary & untimely, in the speech of the fellow who played Steward: &, perhaps, in the gestures of one of the dancers, in one particular, Egyptian-like, dance.—Not only the morale, but the Maker, of man is maligned & insulted when the mere form of men & women is stigmatised as indecent. . . .

December 31, 1868

Noted in the mien of an English company of Actors at the Academy of Music, last night, that the English especially in contrast with the Americans, have marked aplomb, but, also, marked unripeness. . . . I noticed also, that Mrs Scott-Siddons carried an English nature to the part of Lady Macbeth, which served toward the reproduction of a Lady Macbeth, in her own account, whether or no on Shakspear's account. In some points, she was remarkable as, in herself, such as she then was, a powerful & influential woman. In the first act, she was splendidly suggestive; & I could at once comprehend that Mrs Siddons, her namesake & kinswoman, merited contemporary & national fame in the part. In the other acts she was not much anyways: excepting once or twice, when she threw herself especially upon herself—like a person who takes deep breaths—in such a way as to revive the semblance which she wore in the first act, & as to explain why she had appeared so differently at first than afterwards. The dress assisted her abnormal prestige of power. It, together with her mien, gave her the aspect of a Scotch Medea. As an exceptional, rather than ordinary & somewhat feminine Lady Macbeth she was more impressive & picturesque than Ristori; but she did not hold out. She did not keep to the same key . . . throughout the play, that she pitched herself by at first. Little Mary McVickars was, in American style, more intense & interesting, as a whole, but Mrs Siddons was, in English style, more mechanical & substantial.

January 28, 1869

Malvolio, well impersonated, is, on the stage, one of the most marked & graphic personages in Shakspear's plays. He is a diluted & damaged first class sort of Shakspearian personage. He is a cross of Hamlet & of Romeo, of Polonius & of Jaques. Barton Hill did it well, excepting in the cross-gartered scene which was superficial & flat. Mrs Drew, the enterprising manageress, took the part of Viola, instead of assigning it to a young actress: but though she was corporally too old for full verisimilitude she played it with a character which, in part, justified her ambition & persistency; soul, after all, is the life of sense . . . Sir Andrew, who is a sly-witted, flat-headed, knight, was shown up as a wholly soft nimcompoop & coward. Caricature spoils an actor, as farcicality spoils comedy.

September 24, 1869

Booth made a tolerable point, the other night, by sitting down after pronouncing Hamlet's invective against Claudius, "lecherous, treacherous, kindless villain,"—& then, after a pause,—as if, either . . . stopping to regret his impulsive indulgences in mere words, or remembering & renewing himself —continuing, "Why, what an ass am I,"—But, Hamlet is so swift in thought & emotion that he needs little self-recollection so far as mere thought & emotion in his kind & degree, is concerned. This invective against Claudius, & his invective against himself, were part & parcel of the same surcharged & general mind & mood. His wits are ahead of his words, always. I make no break & no pause in reciting that, or any, soliloquy of Hamlet's, & so do not think Booth's point a strong one.

Booth said, "bawd," for "whore," in the words, "& like a whore." He put "heel" before "sequel," in the line, "But is there no sequel at the heels of this monster's admiration," but soon corrected himself. . . .

November 16, 1869

The comparative flatness of Forrest's Lear, at the Walnut last night, suggested, at first thought, whether literal & mere verisimilitude to a part, in either actor or author, were sufficient to procure large & telling interest for it; but I soon saw that the cause of the deficiency in the tone of the whole piece, as then played, was a lack of a sort of leading consciousness & generalisation,—such as almost every active-minded & active-willed man has during the enactment of daily experience on the part of the actor. Forrest threw himself, as it were, point blank,—when he was at all remarkable & effective in the personation of Lear—into his part, without maintaining a free range & conduct of general relation to it. He was, as it were, an abjected Lear . . . he neither maintained his mere assumption of the part, throughout, nor gave it at any time the buoyant rampancy of its intellectually moral motive. Part of it was very tedious; & I doubted if it was not the tediousness of the

morbid old Lear himself; but Forrest's self-recovery of dramat-
ical standpoint, & flashes of strength, revived the interest of
Lear himself & showed that the fault was mostly the
actor's. . . .

March 8, 1870
    Fechter is an extraordinary actor without being, on the
whole, a great one. I do not wonder that he was made much of
by those to whom, before he was famous, he was a surprise, as
perhaps he was to Dickens, who advertised & recommended
him to the Americans. . . . He has a feverish energy, which
would have made the part of Hamlet in actual life an impossibility to him. Such determination & vigor as he showed, was
inconsistent with the feeble conclusions to which the part constrained him to come. He did not suborn his energy to his
role, & was thus inconsistent & untrue as an actor. His acting
was, in some respects, a cross between fine & coarse . . . it
was questionable whether he was very effective, or extremely
ridiculous. He was too external to identify himself with Hamlet. . . . There is a pathos & plaintiveness in his voice which
would become the part of Hamlet, if he knew the part better,
or if he cared for it more. The soliloquies of Hamlet were
never recited on the stage with such aplomb as he gave
them. . . . I never before saw Hamlet so effectively played in
respect of distinctness . . . positiveness, & pronouncement.
. . . His yellow wig was becoming to the play & to himself.
He reminded me of a man of sentiment of the times of Sir Horace Walpole. He omitted the soliloquy on Claudius at prayer,
& the lines on his killing of Polonius, "but heaven hath
pleased it so," which are two important key notes of the
play. . . .

June 6, 1870
    The air of the theater, the other night, smelt, as I entered it,
as if a concocted mass of tobacco-juice, peanut-shells, old
clothes, blacked shoes, & stale perspirations & respirations had
been simmered & stewed down by the heat of the room into
steaming dregs. All of our public and private edifices are badly
ventillated; but theaters are scarcely ventillated at all. . . .

September 24, 1870

The length of the play, the lateness of the hour,—it was after twelve when I got home from the Walnut St. last night,—& the blasted, & literally blasting, atmosphere of unventilated theaters, commonly make Hamlet, after the third act, a tedious performance; & to these causes of fatigue must be added the lack,—especially as the motive of the play is commonly taken & played,—of positive & heroical action in the piece itself. In the first parts, last night, I thought that Forrest, because of his prestige, & the reserves of his stronger physique, made, or would make, the acting less tedious than Booth made it; it suggested, at least, the rough, but solid, scaffolding & under-flowing of the histrionic edifice; & even near the last I thought the performance more tedious in itself than Forrest was in himself; but his voice was not up to the promise of such a big chest & frame, not only having the huskiness, or what not,—something as Booth has it,—which seems peculiar to actors, but, becoming lower than was agreable, & even the burley & ambitious Forrest fell flat toward the end. The brisk & clear voice of Chapman, as first grave-digger, relieved the whole house, &, which is uncommon, made the principal actor, under the circumstances, insignificant in comparison. Still, Hamlet is a play to be performed,—not only for sake of the unlettered, who would otherwise never see it, but of the lettered who are served by the palpableness of the action, by the suggestion of the performance, by their scenic readings of the text, & by the impressions of, even, the fatigue of the last act. . . .

December 13, 1870

The Play of Hamlet was never before such a sustained & rich treat to me as it was last night at the Walnut St. Sometimes I thought I was getting tired of such a profuse feast of meats & wines,—& if I had tired, it were not to the discredit of the play, for one cannot, at one sitting, eat up the whole of a feast; but, as a whole, my interest lasted to the end. Edwin Booth was at his best, & won the attention of the audience by his earnestness. He took the part to himself, instead of on himself: yet the text, not the actor, was almost the only & not merely the chief, cynosure of the evening. His unaffectedness & zeal were admirable, but he lacks particular power as a person, being neither stately, vigorous, or loud-voiced. He was too scholar-likely rapt, moreover, in his part, for Hamlet himself. His expostulation with his mother was sweetly done, & his rudeness to Ophelia was tactive & self-explained. . . . Shakspear is a standing repast of human & intellectual significance to one who, as I have learned to do, takes in every word as it is uttered or read.

OLIVE LOGAN

Although she was born into a theatrical family, her father a Yankee comic and her two sisters actresses, Olive Logan (1839–1909) was deeply conflicted about being on stage. Her need for respectability warred with her livelihood, and she was even embarrassed by newsboys hawking her photograph with the cry "Have Olive Logan. Only 10¢." In 1868, she retired from the profession. Encouraged by Artemus Ward and touted by her journalist second husband, she toured the lecture circuit with some brief success, a success that Mark Twain for one considered to be an undeserved fluke. Logan's favorite topics were equal rights for women and condemnation of what she called "the leg business." The musical extravaganza *The Black Crook*, which opened in New York in 1866, had enjoyed such success with its scantily clad chorines that at one time 14 out of 16 theatres in New York were housing burlesque or comic operas. Logan believed that this trend set back the acceptance of acting as a legitimate profession, especially for women. She harped on this in three books: *Apropos of Women and Theatres* (1869), *Before the Footlights and Behind the Scenes* (1870) and *Get Thee Behind Me, Satan!* (1872). Despite the strident tone, they are valuable repositories of information about the workings of the stage in the Gilded Age. Three times married, Logan died destitute and demented.

About Nudity in Theatres

"NUDE. Bare."—*Webster.*
"BARE. Wanting clothes, or ill-supplied with garments."—*Johnson.*

THERE were always great evils attaching to the theatrical profession. I have always deplored them deeply. Some of them I have touched upon in the preceding chapters. No one who has read my articles, or listened to my lectures, will say that I have not earnestly defended the theatrical profession,—as such. I have also said, honestly, how I loathe the evils which attach to it. In this feeling of loathing, I have expressed the sentiments of a large class of people who were, like myself, bred to the stage, but who could not shut their eyes to the evils referred to.

Within a few years, these evils had grown to appalling dimensions. Decency and virtue had been crowded from the ranks by indecency and licentiousness. A coarse rage for nudity had spread in our theatres, until it had come to be the ruling force in them.

Seeing this truth, I shuddered at it. Seeing its effects, I mourned over them. In every place where I spoke of the stage, I denounced this encroaching shame; but I always coupled with denunciation of it defence of THE DRAMA.

At the Woman's Suffrage Convention in New York, in May, 1869, I denounced this thing again; but, as I was not speaking at length upon this subject, but only touched upon it in passing, and by way of illustration, I did not, as usual, defend THE DRAMA.

At once, there rose so wild a yell, as all the fiends from heaven that fell were furious at my course.

Certain portions of the press attacked me, and accused me of slandering the profession to which I once belonged. Anonymous letters poured in upon me at the office of the Authors' Union in a sort of flood, villifying me, upbraiding me, covering me with coarse and gross revilings.

I was asked to explain such base conduct. It was demanded that I should take back my rash and reckless statements. I was requested to remember that I had once been very glad to think well of the theatrical profession. How *dared* I say I could advise no honorable woman to turn to the stage for support?

In a word, I was put upon my defence.

Turning the matter over in my mind carefully, I came to the conclusion that I had in my hands an opportunity for doing a great deal of good by the simple course of making my defence.

And I concluded, also, that my testimony in this matter had peculiar weight, as coming from one who is of a dramatic family, and may be presumed to speak from close and immediate observation, if not from experience.

I, therefore, wrote the words which follow; and, in reproducing them here, I shall only express the sincere hope that when this book is read, the evil here treated of will be so much a thing of the past, that this chapter shall possess no other value than as a record of a dark page in the history of the theatre.

Though for some years I have not played a part in a theatre, I have not been altogether separated from association with its people. The ties which bind me to these people are strong and close. I never expect to sever them wholly; but they shall never prevent me from giving my allegiance to the cause of morality, virtue, honor, and integrity, though, as a consequence of this, the theatrical heavens fall.

That curse of the dramatic profession, for which editors, critics, authors, and managers struggle to find a fitting name, is my general theme in this article; which is, at the same time, my defence against the charge of slandering the dramatic profession.

What the *Tribune* calls the Dirty Drama, the *World* the Nude Drama, the *Times* the Leg Drama, and other journals various other expressive adjective styles of *drama*, I call the Leg *Business*, simply.

Does any one call the caperings of a tight-rope performer the Ærial Drama?—the tricks of an educated hog the Porcine Drama?

There is a term in use among "professionals" which embraces all sorts of performances in its comprehensiveness, to wit: The Show Business.

In this term is included every possible thing which is of the nature of an entertainment, with these three requirements: 1. A place of gathering. 2. An admission fee. 3. An audience.

This remarkably comprehensive term covers with the same mantle the tragic Forrest, when he plays; the comic Jefferson, when *he* plays; the eloquent Beecher, when he lectures; and the sweet-voiced Parepa, when she sings. It also covers with the same mantle the wandering juggler, who balances feathers on his nose; the gymnast, who whirls on a trapeze; the danseuse, who interprets the poetry of motion; the clown, who cracks stale jokes in the ring; the performer on the tight-rope, the negro minstrel, the giant and the dwarf, the learned pig, and the educated monkey. Therefore, it includes the clog-dancing creature, with yellow hair and indecent costume.

All these things being included in the show business, you

see it is almost as wide a world as the outer world. It must be a
very wide world which should include Mr. Beecher with the
learned pig.

It must be a very wide world which should include Rachel,
Ristori, Janauschek, and Lander with the clog-dancing creature of indecent action and attire.

But, by as good a right as you would call Mr. Beecher and
the learned pig performers in the intellectual sphere, you would
call Janauschek and the clog-dancing creature interpreters of
THE DRAMA.

How, then, does it happen that in attacking these yellow-
haired nudities, I am compelled to say that they disgrace the
dramatic profession?

In this wise: These creatures occupy the temples of the
drama; they perform in conjunction with actors and actresses,
on the same stage, before the same audience, in the same hour.
They are made legitimate members of our theatrical companies, and take part in those nondescript performances which
are called burlesques, spectacles, what you will. They carry off
the chief honors of the hour; their names occupy the chief
places on the bills; and, as I said in my speech at the Equal
Rights Meeting at Steinway Hall, they win the chief prizes in
the theatrical world.

A woman, who has not ability enough to rank as a passable
"walking lady" in a good theatre, on a salary of twenty-five
dollars a week, can strip herself almost naked, and be thus
qualified to go upon the stage of two-thirds of our theatres at
a salary of one hundred dollars and upwards.

Clothed in the dress of an honest woman, she is worth
nothing to a manager. Stripped as naked as she dare—and it
seems there is little left when so much is done—she becomes a
prize to her manager, who knows that crowds will rush to see
her, and who pays her a salary accordingly.

These are simple facts, which permit of no denial. I doubt if
there is a manager in the land who would dream of denying
them.

There are certain accomplishments which render the Nude
Woman "more valuable to managers in the degree that she
possesses them." I will tell you what these accomplishments

are, and you shall judge how far they go toward making her, in any true sense, an actress.

They are: 1. The ability to sing. 2. The ability to jig. 3. The ability to play on certain musical instruments.

Now that I have put them down, I perceive that they need explanation, after all; so complete is the perversion of everything pertaining to this theme, that the very language is beggared of its power of succinct expression.

To sing. Yes, but not to sing as Parepa sings; nor such songs as she sings. The songs in demand in this sphere are vulgar, senseless—and, to be most triumphantly successful, should be capable of indecent constructions, and accompanied by the wink, the wriggle, the grimace, which are not peculiar to virtuous women, whatever else they are. The more senseless the song, the more utterly it is idiotic drivel, the better it will answer in the absence of the baser requisites. Here is a specimen:

> "Little Bo-peep, she lost her sheep,
>   And don't know where to fi-*ind* her;
> Leave her alone and she'll come home,
>   And fetch her tail behi-*ind* her."

A simple nursery song; and, if men were babies, innocent and harmless in itself; but men are not babies, and the song is not sung in a simple or harmless manner, but with the wink or the idiotic stare that means a world, and sets the audience into an extatic roaring.

To jig. Let no one confound jig-dancing with the poetry of motion which is illustrated by a thoroughly organized and thorough-bred body of ballet-dancers.

Ballet-dancing is a profession by itself, just as distinctly as is singing in opera. A danseuse, like Fanny Elssler or Taglioni, or, to come to the present moment, like Morlacchi, is no more to be ranked with these nude jiggers than an actress like Mrs. Lander is.

The ability to jig is an accomplishment which any of these nude creatures can pick up in a few weeks. A danseuse, who has any claim whatever to the title of *artiste*, must be bred to her profession through years of toil and study.

In this country, the ballet proper has had little illustration.

Yet it is a branch of art,—not the noblest art, it is true; but, by the side of the jigging woman, almost rising to dignity.

To play on certain musical instruments. These instruments should be such as to look queer in a woman's hands,—such instruments as the banjo and the bugle.

Now, I am not saying that the ability to sing silly songs, to jig, or to play the banjo, in itself disgraces a woman, however little it may entitle her to my esteem. I am only calling attention to them as valuable aids to the nude woman in her business, and letting you judge whether they give her any right to the name of *actress.*

You, no doubt, will at once remark that these accomplishments have hitherto been peculiar to that branch of the show business occupied by the negro minstrel. But in the hands of the negro minstrel, these accomplishments amuse us without disgusting us. They are not wedded to bare legs, indecent wriggles, nor suggestive feminine leers and winks; nor is there a respectable minstrel band in the United States to-day which would tolerate in its members the *double entendres* which fly about the stages of some of the largest temples of the drama in this city. The minstrels would not dare utter them. Their halls would be vacated, and their business ruined. It requires that a half-naked woman should utter these ribaldrous innuendoes, before our fastidious public will receive them unrebukingly.

To what branch of the show business, then, do these creatures belong?

I answer, to that branch which is known by the names of variety-show, concert-saloon, music-hall, and various other titles, which mean nothing unless you already know what they mean.

No one in the show business needs to be told what a variety-show is. It certainly is not a theatre.

Until the reign of the nude woman set in, variety-halls were the resort of only the lowest and vilest, and women were not seen in the audience.

The nude woman was sometimes seen upon the stage, but she was only one of a large variety of attractions,—she was a tid-bit, hugely relished by the low and vile who went to see her; but only permitted to exhibit herself economically, for fear of cloying the public appetite.

Delicate caution! but how useless, her later career in our theatres has shown.

There, she is exhibited ceaselessly for three hours, in every variety which an indecent imagination can devise.

When the *Black Crook* first presented its nude woman to the gaze of a crowded auditory, she was met with a gasp of astonishment at the effrontery which dared so much. Men actually grew pale at the boldness of the thing; a death-like silence fell over the house, broken only by the clapping of a band of *claqueurs* around the outer aisles; but it passed; and, in view of the fact that these women were French ballet-dancers after all, they were tolerated.

By slow and almost imperceptible degrees, this shame has grown, until to-day the indecency of that exhibition is far surpassed. Those women were ballet-dancers from France and Italy, and they represented in their nudity imps and demons. In silence they whirled about the stage; in silence trooped off. Some faint odor of ideality and poetry rested over them.

The nude woman of to-day represents nothing but herself. She runs upon the stage giggling; trots down to the foot-lights, winks at the audience, rattles off from her tongue some stupid attempts at wit, some twaddling allusions to Sorosis, or General Grant, or other subject prominent in the public eye, and is always peculiarly and emphatically herself,—the woman, that is, whose name is on the bills in large letters, and who considers herself an object of admiration to the spectators.

The sort of ballet-dancer who figured in the *Black Crook* is paralleled on the stage of every theatre in this city, except one, at this time.

She no longer excites attention.

To create a proper and profitable sensation in the breast of man, she no longer suffices. Something bolder must be devised, —something that shall utterly eclipse and outstrip her.

Hence, the nude woman of to-day,—who outstrips her in the broadest sense. And, as if it were not enough that she should be allowed to go unhissed and unrotten-egged, she must be baptized with the honors of a profession for which Shakespeare wrote!

Managers recognize her as an actress, and pay her sums

ranging from fifty to a thousand dollars a week, according to her value in their eyes. Actresses, who love virtue better than money, are driven into the streets by her; and it becomes a grave and solemn question with hundreds of honorable women what they shall do to earn a livelihood.

I say it is nothing less than an insult to the members of the dramatic profession, that these nude women should be classed among actresses and hold possession of the majority of our theatres. Their place is in the concert-saloons or the circus tents. Theatres are for artists.

A friend said to me the other day that it was inconsistent in me to find indecency in women exposing their persons, when men constantly do the same; that, as an honest exponent of Woman's Rights, I ought to see no more immodesty in a woman dancing a jig in flesh-colored leggings than in a man performing a circus feat in the same costume.

I reply, that I think such shows are indecent in both sexes. Yet, nevertheless, in woman a thousand times more indecent than in man; for the simple reason, that the costume of the sexes in every-day life is different.

To ignore this fact is to just wilfully shut one's eyes to a reasonable argument.

Women in society conceal all the lower part of their bodies with drapery,—and for good and sufficient reasons, which no man, who has a wife or mother, should stop to question.

But set this aside. Circus men, who strip to the waist in this fashion, don't claim to be actors.

Now, I come back to the words I said at the Woman Suffrage Convention. They have been variously reported by the newspapers. They were exactly as follows,—

> "I can advise no honorable, self-respecting woman to turn to the stage for support, with its demoralizing influences, which seem to be growing stronger and stronger day by day; where the greatest rewards are won by a set of brazen-faced, clog-dancing creatures, with dyed yellow hair and padded limbs, who have come here in droves from across the ocean."

I have been astonished and pained at the extent to which the meaning of these words has been distorted. The press and my anonymous letter critics seem to be agreed in taking the view, that I attack, in these words, the profession in which I was reared, and all my family.

Some of the letters sent me are from religious people, encouraging me to go on; others are from actors and actresses, seeking to dissuade me,—not always in gentle language.

The first letter on which I lay my hands, so gross in its language that I suspect it to be from one of the nude women themselves, says,—

"You were, no doubt, satisfied with the stage so long as it paid. Now, don't swear at the bridge that carried you over."

Perhaps this person, being new to the country, thinks it is true, as a newspaper once said, that I was formerly a ballet-girl.

Hitherto, I have only laughed at this story, as on a par with that of the person who thought me a daughter of the negro preacher, Loguen; or that of the "dress reform" scarecrow, who believed me "formerly a ballad songstress."

I laugh at it no longer. I answer, in all gravity, that I never was a ballet-girl, nor even a jig-dancer.

It is true that I was once a member of the theatrical profession; so were my father and my mother; so were my five sisters; but I say with pride that never was there a Logan who sought any connection with the stage save in the capacity of a legitimate player.

There were no nude women on the stage in my father's day. Such exhibitions as are now made on the stage of many leading theatres were, in his day, confined to that branch of the show business known as the *Model Artists*,—another perversion of words; but most people know their meaning in their present acceptation.

Across this infamous bridge no Logan ever walked.

And, one by one, every member of our family has left the stage behind, until, at this writing, not one remains upon it; though of their number, there are seven still living who have trod the boards.

Here it is proper that I should say why I left the stage. The *Commercial Advertiser* and the *Philadelphia Dispatch* are the only journals I have seen which have intimated that my hatred of indecency is born of jealousy; thus implying that I ceased to be an actress because these nude women had encroached upon my territory so far that I was forced to leave, or do what they do.

This is not true. As for the nude women, their reign had not yet set in at the time I left the stage. But I was not forced from the stage at all. My success as an actress was always fully equal to my deserts; and, up to the very day I retired from the stage, I was in receipt of large sums for my services as an actress. As a star (in which capacity I played in the leading theatres of this country, from Wallack's, in New York, to McVicker's, in Chicago) my earnings were very large,—sometimes reaching one thousand dollars per week. When I played for a salary, the lowest sum I ever received—save when I was a mere child—was one hundred dollars per week.

I left the stage respecting it and many of its people; but my resolve was to live, henceforth, by my pen. I preferred literature to acting, simply on the score of congeniality; and I have never regretted the day when I turned to it. I love it with all my soul, and have several times refused most tempting offers to leave it and return to the stage.

How, then, can I be *jealous* of these women? I am no longer a rival for their place in the theatres. No, it is no such ignoble feeling as this which animates me; it is a feeling of shame that the stage should be so degraded, the drama so disgraced, by the place the nude woman has taken, united to a feeling of sympathy with the numerous modest and virtuous actresses who are crowded from a sphere which they could adorn and honor,—crowded from it *not* by superior talent, nor even by greater beauty, but by sheer brazen immodesty, and by un-blushing vice.

I take up next an anonymous letter, dated at Boston, and signed, "A Sister Member of the Profession."

The writer says she is a respectable actress, and professes to be ignorant that gross evils prevail in the theatrical world.

She refers to my letter in the New York *Times*, and asks at what theatre such questions were ever put to an applicant for employment.

In my letter to the *Times*, I said,—

"I referred the other night to decent young women who are

not celebrities,—merely honest, modest girls, whose parents have left them the not very desirable heritage of the stage, and who find it difficult to obtain any other employment, being uneducated for any other. When these girls go into a theatre to apply for a situation now, they find that the requirements of managers are expressed in the following questions,—

"1. Is your hair dyed yellow?

"2. Are your legs, arms, and bosom symmetrically formed, and are you willing to expose them?

"3. Can you sing brassy songs, and dance the can-can, and wink at men, and give utterance to disgusting half words, which mean whole actions?

"4. Are you acquainted with any rich men who will throw you flowers, and send you presents, and keep afloat dubious rumors concerning your chastity?

"5. Are you willing to appear to-night, and every night, amid the glare of gas-lights, and before the gaze of thousands of men, in this pair of satin breeches, ten inches long, without a vestige of drapery upon your person?

"If you can answer these questions affirmatively, we will give you a situation; if not, there's the door."

At nothing have I been more astonished than at the manner in which this letter has been received by certain "professionals."

When one of our daily newspapers says that the streets of this city are in a filthy condition, does a resident of Fifth Avenue rush down to the editor's sanctum to call him a liar, and point him to the cleanliness of Fifth Avenue?

It seems incredible that any one could be so stupid as to imagine me making reference to such managers, for instance, as Edwin Booth, Mr. Field, of the Boston Museum, or Mrs. John Drew, of Philadelphia!

These managers, and a few like them, form the exception to the rule. To such, all honor! But it is a sufficient indication of the enormity of this shame to say that the rage for nudity has intruded in some shape upon the stage of every theatre in this city, *except one.*

Here is a list of the places in this city where the English drama claims, or has claimed, a place, at one time or another, in its highest or its lowest manifestations,—

Academy of Music,	Booth's,
Fisk's Grand Theatre,	Wood's Museum,
Fifth Avenue Theatre,	Theatre Comique,
Wallack's,	The Tammany,
New York Theatre,	The Waverly,
Olympic,	Niblo's Garden,
Broadway Theatre,	Bowery Theatre,
Theatre Français,	Pastor's Opera House.

Two of the above-named places are now closed; but, at this writing, it is rumored that one of them is to be opened for the use of a newly organized troupe of nude women.

Of this whole list, there is but one (Booth's, which is only a few months old) which can claim that it has always been free from any symptom of this licentious fever.

"Four weeks from this time," says the *New York Review* of May 15, "there will be only two theatres in New York that will offer dramatic works. The rest will be show-shops, having as little to do with dramatic art as so many corner groceries."

As to the questions themselves, as printed above, they are, of course, suppositious. It is not said that managers put these exact questions to applicants. It is said that "*the requirements of managers are expressed in these questions.*"

This is strictly true.

It is not necessary, I suppose, to give with the accuracy of a criminal trial report the exact questions which pass between managers and actresses who seek for employment. Their purport is unmistakable. Take this one which was asked a beautiful and modest young woman whom I have known for years, an actress by profession, who was quietly edged out of her last situation because she carried decency and womanly reserve too far in the presence of an audience which cheered to the echo the nude creatures who trod the same stage with her,—

"*Are you up in this style of business?*"

This question needed no interpreter,—for the manager pointed, as he spoke, to one of the members of his company, photographed in an immodest attitude, with her legs clad in flesh-colored silk and her body in a tight-fitting breech-cloth, richly embroidered.

She was not "up in" this sort of business; she sought em-

ployment as *an actress*; there was none for her, and she went
away, to apply with like results at other theatres.

She sought employment, as a respectable actress, at fifteen
or twenty dollars a week. She would have refused five hundred
dollars a week salary to do what the nude woman does.

If the above instance does not indicate managerial requirements sufficiently, take these statements from managerial lips,—

"Devil take your legitimate drama! I tell you if I can't draw
the crowd otherwise, I'll put a woman on my stage without a
rag on her."

So said a manager of this city in the hearing of a dozen
people; and the disgusting remark was bandied about from
mouth to mouth as if it had been wit.

A proprietor of one of the theatres above-named, where a
legitimate play was running without paying expenses, rubbed
his dry old hands together, and said,—

"Aha! we must have some of those *fat young women* in this
piece to make it draw."

I go down to Boston for a moment, where lives this anonymous letter-writing actress who is so singularly ignorant of
what is passing about her, to mention the rumor which was set
afloat *by a manager* of a certain one of the blonde nudities, to
the effect that she was once the mistress of the Prince of Wales.

This manager deemed it to his interest to keep this vile story
afloat. It gave an added piquancy to the creature who nightly
wriggled about his stage in a dress of silk which fitted her form
all over as tightly as a glove.

I stay in Boston long enough to note that, in the late Working-
woman's Convention there, a lady related the trials of a young
friend of hers, who went upon the stage and endured insult
and wickedness from managers. The same lady corroborated
my own observations, with the statement, that managers look
upon the girls they employ as women of the town.

My anonymous "sister member of the profession" has been
fortunate beyond most actresses of this period, in coming in
contact with nothing of this sort.

I return to New York, to direct attention to that manager of
blonde nudities who has won, probably, the most money for

his speculations in yellow hair and padded legs of any one in the business.

This person is an Englishman,—said to be, by birth, a gentleman (in the English or aristocratic sense of the word), and who, on entering the theatrical world, concealed his real name.

It is known that this man is a most licentious and shameless *roué*, who publicly boasts of the number of blonde women who have been his mistresses at different times; who actually perpetrated the monstrous indecency of making these infamous boasts in a speech at a dinner where women were present!

Among other things this disgraceful creature said was this: that a certain woman who had broken her professional engagement with him ought to have remembered the fact that she had once been his mistress, and had borne him children!

This infamous boast was coupled with the jeering remark that, in spite of the fact that he had no legal claim upon her services, he had *a moral one* in the fact just stated.

Shame! that such a monster as this should be permitted to remain in this country, the master of a drove of nude women, who are exhibiting themselves nightly to crowded houses, at the largest theatre on Broadway, and fill his already gorged pockets at the expense of disgrace to the dramatic profession, and distress to many of its members!

Were he to be hooted and stoned through the streets of this city, and packed off to England, covered with obloquy, it would be well. But packing him off would hardly rid the stage of this curse, since there are plenty of men besides him who are as vile as he, in all save the infamy of boasting.

With a sigh of relief, I turn to another anonymous letter, dated at New Haven, and signed "One who loves Jesus."

The writer of this letter is evidently a woman. It is tender and sweet in its tone. "I assure you," says the good lady, "your noble stand will be esteemed by all good, moral people." I have abundant proof of that; and if I, in my turn, can lead all such people to think more gently of good and true actors and actresses, I shall thank heaven with a full heart.

"As a child of God," this letter says, "I must esteem the theatre as the devil's play-house."

There was a time, not very long ago, when I should have

taken great offence at this. That time is past. I recognize the devil's play-house in the theatre where the nude woman jigs and wriggles.

If there be any such actual entity as that same old theological devil, I can easily imagine him kicking up his hoofs in Mephistophilean joy at the harvests that are falling into his lap from the temples of the nude.

But, dear lady,—you who write me from New Haven,—on the middle ground where I stand, I see what you can not see, and know what you can not know. All theatres do not deserve the stigma of this term. It is true that the theatres which still remain devoted to the drama proper are very, very few; but there are such; and they are no more the "devil's play-house" than is the concert-room where Parepa sings. They are not consecrated to the service of God, it is true; but, at least, they are not given over to the devil's work.

I respect the theatre in its purity. I respect the actor who is an artist,—even the harmless clown of the pantomime, who makes us laugh without offending decency. That I love so many good and lovely women who are actresses, is my chief reason for deploring the reign of a class of women who are neither good nor lovely,—but coarse, indecent, painted, padded, and dyed.

If it were possible to treat the Nude Woman Question, and leave the nude woman herself out of it, I should be glad to do so. I am the last to wish to give pain to any person; but, in the path of clear duty, there is no choice. When it becomes a question between suffering, struggling virtue, and vice which rolls in luxury, and gathers unto itself wealth by the sheer practice of its wickedness, no woman who loves honor in her sex can hesitate as to the course to be taken.

The spirit of most of the anonymous letters I have received is one which might well cause me to hesitate in the path I have chosen, if fear were stronger in me than principle. But neither the sneers of low-class newspapers, nor the threats of anonymous correspondents, shall have weight with me. I see no other way to effect a cure of this nude woman evil but to make it odious. To that end, I shall do what in me lies. This article is but a beginning. I shall not cease to combat the encroachments of the nude woman upon the domain which should be occupied by true artists, and by virtuous men and women.

Firm in the belief that this indecent army *can* be routed, I call on all honorable souls, both in and out of the profession, to stand by my side and strike hard blows. We shall get hard blows in return, no doubt; but poor indeed must be the panoply of that warrior who can not hold his own against the cohorts of the nude woman. Whatever falls on my head in consequence of my words, I promise to give thrust for thrust. I do not fear the issue.

"Thrice is he armed that hath his quarrel JUST."

1869

EDWARD P. HINGSTON

The great popularity in the mid-19th-century English-speaking world of the humor of the Ohio reporter Charles Farrar Browne is difficult to explain. His comic letters, attributed to itinerant showman Artemus Ward, depend on an appreciation of illiteracy: they are misspelled, ungrammatical, and packed with groan-worthy puns. Ward's show is said to consist of "three moral Bares, a Kangaroo . . . besides several miscellanyus moral statoots of celebrated piruts & murderers &c." Even so, Abraham Lincoln quoted him frequently and Mark Twain was inspired to imitate Ward's poker-faced lectures, delivered tongue-in-cheek. Edward Hingston (c. 1823–1876) was an English theatrical agent who came to the United States in 1856 as advance man for the magician John Henry Anderson, "the Wizard of the North." After working for Anderson until 1863, he managed Ward's tour to the Western territories. His reminiscences of that tour, *The Genial Showman* (1870), provide a picturesque account of an adolescent America. Hingston's record of a trip to San Francisco's Chinatown to see a Peking opera is off-putting in its blatant racism, but he took seriously the Mormon respect for theatre, a rare commodity among religious communities. Artemus Ward's explication of Mormonism became his most demanded lecture, and, after it was delivered at Egyptian Hall in London in 1868, accompanied by a panorama, Hingston edited it for publication.

FROM

The Genial Showman

The Church in the Theatre and the Theatre in the Church

"THE theatre will be open to-night. The play will be *The Stranger*. Brigham Young will be there with most of his family. You must go."

So said one of the cavalry officers to Artemus Ward a few hours after our arrival in Salt Lake City.

Unfortunately poor Artemus was too jaded, travel-worn, and exhausted to avail himself of the opportunity. To me the attraction was powerful enough to overcome my fatigue, and draw me away from a bright fire and an easy-chair.

A theatre in the midst of the wilderness! A theatre in a valley shut in by mountains and surrounded by a thousand square miles of desert! A theatre with Indian savages almost within hail! A theatre near the shores of the great Dead Sea of America! A theatre belonging to a Church—erected, managed, and frequented by "Saints!" Could a showman abstain from going?

The City of the Saints is the favourite name for the metropolis of Utah among the Mormons. Its inhabitants manifest no diffidence in arrogating to themselves peculiar holiness. They consider the saintly character to be exclusively their own, and all who are not Mormons are "Gentiles."

Brigham Young, arch-priest and saintliest of the "Saints," built the theatre; to maintain it the Church lends its authority, and to go to the play is a duty in the code of Mormon ethics.

I left Artemus slumbering before the fire; and in the midst of a heavy snow-storm sought my way to the theatre. I found it on the corner of an adjacent street. People were wending their way to it along the middle of the road, for the snow-drift was too deep for them to use the footpath. There were a few small houses with wooden pales in front of them, and beyond them a large rectangular building, so large as to dwarf every other structure in the neighbourhood. The long black side wall visible through the snow-storm, recalled to my recollection the Waterloo Road side of the Victoria Theatre in London as seen from the New Cut. On a nearer inspection I found the building to present few claims to architectural merit externally, though it is but fair to acknowledge that its exterior was then incomplete. The style of architecture was the Doric, with Mormon modifications.

In a small office to the left of the entrance was the money-taker, handing out tickets at a window. I found that admission to the dress circle was only a dollar. As I paid the amount in a gold coin bright and fresh from the Californian mint, I noticed that the money-taker took stock of me. I returned the compliment and listened to him whistling the air of "The Groves of Blarney." I was not aware at the time that I was gazing at a bishop!

Internally the theatre presented as incomplete an appearance as the exterior. There was very little attempt at decoration, other than that obtainable by the use of white paint and gilding. There was a large pit or "parquette" as the Americans call it, having a high rake from the orchestra towards the back, thus allowing occupants of seats in the rear to have as good view of the stage as those in front. I counted the pit, and found that there were about eight hundred people in it. The price of admission was seventy-five cents. Over the dress-circle was an upper box tier the admission to which was fifty cents, and over that again a gallery to which the charge was twenty-five cents, or about one English shilling.

Some of my cavalry friends undertook to point out the arrangements of the house. They told me that the dress-circle was the part which Gentiles frequented, and that the pit was specially reserved for Mormons, with their families. I noticed that nearly every man in it was accompanied by two, three, or more ladies, and that in some instances an entire family occupied a row, there being only one adult male among the number.

On each side of the proscenium was a private box on the same plane as the dress-circle. These boxes were fitted up with green curtains. No other drapery was used for decoration elsewhere in the house.

Under the dress-circle to my right, and a little more elevated than the floor of the pit, were a series of seats like pews, running parallel with the side wall of the theatre. Occupying them were fifty-nine women and children, all very plainly dressed, and none of them remarkable for good looks.

"That is the Prophet's Pen," said my Gentile informant, "and those are his wives and daughters. There are more of them in those seats of the parquette where you see the large rocking-chair."

"Whose is that, and why is it there?" I asked.

"That's where the Prophet sits when he is in the bosom of his family. It's a pretty large bosom," remarked the officer, dryly.

"But where is the Prophet himself?"

"That's he. Over in yon proscenium box with the green curtains to it. The lady beside him is his favourite wife—Sister Amelia. Brigham likes to sit up there because he can keep an eye upon his family down below, and see the Gentiles in the dress-circle. He's having a look through his opera-glass at the General just now."

The General referred to was General Connor, the commander of the troops in Camp Douglas. As I was subsequently informed, the General had been stationed in Utah for nearly two years, and during the whole of that time had resolutely refused to have any intercourse with Brigham Young, regarding him in the light of an enemy to the United States, with whom one day he might have to come in conflict. General Connor was a frequent visitor to the theatre, where he was in full view of the Mormon President, but no sign of recognition passed between them.

The *Mrs. Haller* of the evening was Mrs. Irwin, a lady who under her maiden name of Miss Rainforth I had seen a few years before on the stage of the Museum in Boston. Mr. Irwin, her husband, enacted the part of *The Stranger.* Both were Gentile "stars" who had come on a professional trip to Utah. Some days after my visit to the theatre I had an opportunity of spending an evening with them at their private residence, and found them to be loud in their praises of the kindly treatment they had received among the saints. Their eulogies were many, not only of the hospitality they had experienced, but also of the general management of the theatre, and of the courtesy shown to them by all behind the curtain. They were almost the first "stars" who had found their way across the wilderness to play in Brigham Young's theatre. Since then many actors and actresses of note have appeared on those boards. With the Pacific Railway in full operation there will be few histrionic artistes in the United States who will not take a trip to the Mormons, don the sock and buskin, and use the hare's foot on the shores of the Great Salt Lake.

I asked who were the other ladies and gentlemen of the company, and received my reply in nearly the following words:—

"They are all Mormons—every one of them. The part of *The Baron* is being played by Mr. Caine, the stage-manager. *Countess Wintersen* is Mrs. Clawson, wife of Hiram Clawson, the manager. He has three wives. This lady is No. 2. The part of *Peter* is being played by Mr. Margetts, he is one of their low comedians, a very good fellow. He has three wives also. All their wives learn to play; so that if one gets ill they can easily send on another for the part."

After the play of *The Stranger* came the farcical piece known as *Paddy Miles's Boy*. The part of *Henry*, according to the bills, was played by Mr. Sloan. So soon as that gentleman came on the stage I recognised him as being the money-taker to whom I had paid my dollar on entering.

The Mormon President left his box, came down to the pit, and took his seat in the rocking-chair. During the performance of the farce he laughed heartily, and entered into conversation with two or three of his wives. I had been led to expect that in Brigham Young I should find a man of severe aspect, stately presence, and solemn demeanour. My misconceptions were dissipated when, looking at him through an opera-glass, I saw a robust, jolly, pleasant-faced gentleman, with a ruddy complexion, hair of the colour of sand, light eyes, the lines of the face curving upwards instead of downward, his chest broad, his hands large, his age apparently about sixty; his appearance that of a well-to-do farmer, and his manner cheerful and agreeable as became a man who had forty of his children around him, and I know not how many of his wives. In the early morning I had crossed the Jordan, the waters of the Dead Sea of the West were not far from me.—Could time have gone backwards with me to patriarchal days, and was it Solomon in modern clothes who sat before me?

So cold was the evening and so chilly the interior of the theatre that the Prophet, like everybody else, was well wrapped up. Nothing in his attire denoted his rank, nor was there any attempt at dress among the members of his household. There was no display of silks and satins. Every one was plainly clad. Most of the ladies wore on the head what in the States is called a "Nubia"—a sort of knitted woollen scarf, with long ends to it. The men were mostly clad in homespun. As I afterwards learned, the policy of the Mormon leader is to discourage the wearing of any articles of attire not manufactured in the territory. His aim is to make his people independent of the outer world, and with that end in view he has established and owns cotton mills and woollen factories. The Gentile traders at Salt Lake take care to import novelties and fineries from New York; but Brigham Young has a keen eye and a denunciatory voice for those who indulge in the pomps and vanities of fashion. He once preached a sermon against the use of crinoline. The language he used on that occasion, and the plain, strong, coarse phrases and allusions in which he indulged, have become historical. He characterized the wearing of hoops as a nasty practice, and in denouncing it he used the nastiest language.

No audience could have behaved better than did the one I saw at Salt Lake. There was no whistling in the gallery; no cries of "Now then, catgut!" no stamping of feet, nor vacating seats before the downfall of the curtain. The performers on the stage met with much applause and very deservedly so, for the amateurs were not far behind the professional stars in their knowledge of stage business. Every performer was well dressed for his part. The scenery was good, and there were no mishaps on the part of the stage carpenters. Evidently the rehearsals had been well attended to; there was no laxity of management behind the curtain, and the voice of the prompter was not heard in the land.

"*Panem et circenses!*" cried the old Romans. "Corn and comedies!" cries Brigham Young. He desires that his people shall have food alike for their hunger and their laughter. Hence he disapproves of tragedies, and prefers that comedy and farce should constitute the chief performances at his play-house. Mr. Irwin told me that there were two or three tragic parts he wished to play, but that Brigham Young opposed the pieces being put in rehearsal. Said Mr. Irwin: "Brigham is of opinion that there is grief enough in this world without having it in imitation on the stage." I subsequently learned that the "Lady of Lyons" and the "Marble Heart" were two very favorite dramas among the Mormons, and that the Prophet had no objection to plays in which the crime of adultery is represented as being severely punished, but that he preferred dramas wherein the passion of love is depicted, and the comic and sentimental elements well blended. Considering that Brigham Young "loves not wisely but two hundred well"—to use a joke belonging to poor Artemus—it is not incomprehensible that he should uphold the claims of love to public appreciation. Perish the man who in Utah would decry the tender passion! "*Chi dice mal d'amore, dice la falsità!*"

Digressing from my narrative of what I saw at the theatre on

the evening of my first visit, it may not be out of place to refer
to the position of the play-house among the institutions of Salt
Lake. The theatre is essentially a national concern. It enters
into the general system of government—social, moral, and religious. Socially, because all classes visit it; morally, because
Brigham Young considers it the best substitute for amusements of a less harmless character; and religiously, because its
profits go to the support of what is called "The Church." The
performances are advertised from the pulpit, and attendance at
the play-house is preached to the people as a portion of their
duty. The actresses are for the most part the wives and daughters of church dignitaries. Even the daughters of the Prophet
himself occasionally assist in the representations; and Mr. Hiram Clawson, on whom the management devolves, is a son-in-
law of Brigham Young.

Mr. Clawson was kind enough to take me over the theatre a
few days after my arrival in the city. Well acquainted with some
hundreds of theatres, I do not remember one in which the
comfort of the actors is more studied than in the theatre at Salt
Lake, nor one where the arrangements for the business of the
stage have been more thoughtfully attended to. The ward-
robes are extensive, clean, and commodious. There is a capital
workshop for the tailors, and equally as good apartments for
the dressmakers. The library is nicely arranged, free from dust,
and well stocked with plays. The property-man has excellent
accommodation and a large stock of well-made properties. No
dressing-rooms could be more convenient, nor any green-
room better fitted for its purpose.

Brigham Young is as careful of the comfort of his audiences
as he is of that of his actors. The theatre was built under his inspection, and he has taken care that visitors shall not be in-
commoded. In all his arrangements the fact is apparent that
he understands what so many managers in London and elsewhere do not comprehend—that the auditorium of a theatre
should be attractive simply for its qualifications as a place in
which to sit at ease without being cramped, crushed, or annoyed,
—that it should be the drawing-room to retire to after dinner.
He understands also—and herein he is ahead of many other
managers, and anticipates the theatre of the future—that the
play-house should be a place for Paterfamilias, to which

without apology he could fearlessly take all his kith and kin, not an institution depending for its success upon ministering to the tastes of fast young men, nor for its patronage on its advantages as an exhibition-room for marketable beauty. But a place to which human beings with head and brains can go, and feel that they are not degrading themselves by witnessing senseless trash, nor having their patience tested by listening to uneducated and unqualified performers.

The Salt Lake City Theatre is open in winter and closed in summer. If the season of the year admits of agricultural labours being attended to, Brigham Young requires his flock to work. If the weather be ungenial, the shepherd allows his lambs to play. Better he thinks that they should laugh than moan; better be histrionic than hypochondriac. If they have no money with which to pay at the doors, they can take their flour or their dried peaches to the "tithing office" during the day, and barter them for tickets of admission to the theatre. At the tithing office, anything of any value will be accepted—eggs, apples, wool, cabbages, or feathers. During my stay in Salt Lake I remember a man obtaining entrance to the theatre for half a dozen glass bottles. Let it be borne in mind how many mountain tops those glass bottles had to be brought over before they arrived in the city, and it will be understood how they grew in value with every mile traversed. Should it be that a newly-arrived immigrant wishes to visit the playhouse, that he be poor and have no resources, he may go to the tithing office and obtain a dozen *coupons* of admission by pledging a portion of his labour during the ensuing summer to assist in building the great temple, or by otherwise devoting himself to the service of the Church.

Just as the people can visit the theatre when they have no labour to occupy their time, so the actors can learn new parts and study for the stage when they cannot carry on their ordinary occupations. I met an amateur tragedian who owned a saw-mill, and the best low comedian in the city was a blacksmith. The saw-mill tragedian—Mr. Bernard Snow—played *Matthew Elmore* in the drama of *Love's Sacrifice*, one evening during my stay. I have seen the part played much worse on the boards of a large theatre in London. In Great Salt Lake City it is not thought to be derogatory to the highest and holiest lady in the land to play even a subsidiary part on the stage. Three of Brigham Young's daughters posed for the statues of the three Graces in the *Marble Heart*; and I looked in at the theatre one morning when the daughter of an "apostle" was practising for the *rôle* of Columbine.

My first experiences of the Mormon theatre were on a Saturday night. On the morning of Sunday Artemus and I determined on paying a visit to the great Tabernacle in the hope of hearing Brigham Young preach. As we strolled towards it, we met many Mormon families on their way to the same place. Every one was clad in garments of warm but coarse texture, and there was no display of finery. Half a dozen wives of the same husband walked along lovingly together; their children following after them, hand-in-hand.

On the Mississippi River, far away up, just where the stream leaves the fields of Iowa to fertilize those of Missouri, stands a ruin on a bluff, the only ruin, worthy of being so called, I saw anywhere in the United States. It is that of the first temple of the Mormons, destroyed by fire in 1848. Driven from Nauvoo, on the Mississippi, and their lands taken possession of by a party of French socialists, led by M. Cabet, the Mormons planned the erection of a larger and far more magnificent temple in their new home at Salt Lake. Whether it will ever be completed is doubtful. In the state in which I saw it, it appeared as much of a ruin as its prototype at Nauvoo. Pending its erection the services of the church are carried on in what is termed the Tabernacle—a long building with a semi-cylindrical roof, situated within a walled enclosure. Beside it is a singular structure called the Bowery, consisting of a number of poles stuck in the ground, supporting a roof formed of branches of trees, and sheltering a vast space covered with settles and forms. Under the green leaves of the Bowery, with the sunbeams swooping down through their interstices, and the cool breezes from the Sea of Salt blowing in at the sides, the Mormons worship in the summer; during winter they assemble in the Tabernacle.

Snow underfoot and a bright blue sky overhead, Artemus and I found our way to the doors of the sacred edifice. On entering I noticed an organ to our left, and looking down the long tunnel-like interior, perceived the pulpit backed by a rostrum, on which were raised seats for the elders. The congregation came in slowly; as they took their seats we had an opportunity of observing their faces and scanning their outward developments. There were very few who arrested attention by attractiveness of feature or intelligence of expression,—a single glance was enough to ascertain that none of them could boast of "blue blood," noble birth, gentle nurture, or high intellectual culture. A similar assemblage might be seen at a Methodist meeting-house in a Lancashire manufacturing town, or attending an open-air discourse in the neighbourhood of Whitechapel, with the exception that cleanliness reigned supreme, and that no one had ragged attire.

The service commenced by the choir singing a hymn, accompanied by the organ and a small instrumental band. The congregation preserved silence. After the hymn an elder came forward from among the group on the rostrum, advanced to the pulpit, or tribune, and prayed an extempore prayer. Then came more singing, more organ, and more band; following on which the presiding elder rose and called on "Brother Sloan" to preach to the people.

Brother Sloan advanced to the pulpit.

"What are you excited about?" whispered Artemus. "Who is that preacher?"

"He?—he's the very man who took my dollar at the door of the theatre last night, and who played in *Paddy Miles's Boy*!"

1870

HENRY JAMES

The Complete Plays of Henry James, published in 1949, is a stout volume of nearly 850 double-column pages. Its contents range from a two-person farce written in 1869 to a monologue for Ruth Draper contrived in 1913. Henry James (1843–1916), subtlest of American novelists, never gave up the idea that somewhere in him lurked a popular playwright, despite all evidence to the contrary. He was stage-struck from boyhood and in his 70s lovingly recollected the New York entertainments his parents treated him to in the 1850s. Trips to London and Paris deepened his understanding of acting, and from 1874 to 1887 he reviewed plays for *The Atlantic, The Century, The Galaxy* and *The Nation*. James was bothered by the compromises drama as literature had to make with theatre as performance. "The drama at large in America, just now, is certainly neither artistic nor fine," he opined in 1874; it offered a field for improvement. At the age of 46, when his novels were not selling very well, he set to writing plays.

Taking as his mentor the French critic Francisque Sarcey, who prescribed workmanlike rules for a well-made play, James decided that "the fine thing in a real drama, generally speaking, is that, more than in any other work of literary art, it needs a masterly structure." But the Master was not a master builder. As Leon Edel puts it, "His plays became the prisoners of his theories"; and when *Guy Domville* was produced in London in 1895, it was hooted down. James took rejection hard. "I may have been meant for the Drama—God knows!—but I certainly wasn't meant for the theatre." In the 1890s, guided by the American actress Elizabeth Robins, he became an enthusiast for Ibsen; the influence shows in one of his last plays, *The Other House*. In the end, James' interest in theatre is best expressed in his novel *The Tragic Muse*, whose heroine was based on the great French tragedienne Rachel.

Notes on the Theatres

If one held the belief that there is any very intimate relation between the stage, as it stands in this country, and the general cause of American civilization, it would be more than our privilege, it would be our duty, as vigilant observers, to keep an attentive eye upon the theatres. For in New York, at least, these establishments have rarely been more active than during the past few weeks, and the moment would be highly opportune for drawing from the national diversions a critic's moral as to the national state of mind. In fact, however, we suspect that moralizing too rigidly here is a waste of ingenuity, inasmuch as the diversions in question are not especially national. New York possesses half-a-dozen theatres of the so-called first class, in addition to a host of play-houses of the baser sort, whose performances are dramatic only by that extension of the term under which the romances in the Sunday papers may be spoken of as literary. These theatres are all, for the time, working at high pressure. Each has brought forward its *pièce de résistance*. The trumpets are blown and the public is convoked. The public assembles in varying numbers—on the whole, it seems to us, in very goodly ones. The public evidently likes play-going, and is willing to pay for it—to pay a good deal, and to pay often. But except at the Fifth Avenue Theatre, it does not go with the expectation of seeing the mirror held up to nature as it knows nature—of seeing a reflection of its actual, local, immediate physiognomy. The mirror, as the theatres show it, has the image already stamped upon it—an Irish image, a French image, an English image. The French and English images indeed are multiplied, and an Italian image, we perceive, looms above the horizon. The images may be true to an original or not; the public doesn't care. It has gone to look and listen, to laugh and cry—not to think. This is so true that we fancy it must have resented even the very slight intellectual effort necessary for finding "Women of the Day" at the Fifth Avenue as preposterous an attempt to portray as it was a dreary attempt to entertain. Nevertheless, if the theatre with us *is* a superficial institution, it shares the peculiarity with other social phenomena, and the observer may commit as great a fault in taking it too easily as in taking it too hard.

Our drama seems fated, when it repairs to foreign parts for its types, to seek them first of all in the land of brogue and "bulls." A cynic might say that it is our privilege to see Irish types enough in the sacred glow of our domestic hearths, and that it is therefore rather cruel to condemn us to find them so inveterately in that consoling glamour of the footlights. But it is true that an Irish drama is always agreeably exciting; whether on account of an inherent property in the material, or because it is generally written by Mr. Boucicault, we are unable to say. "The Shaughraun" will, we suppose, have been the theatrical event of the season; and if a play was to run for four or five months there might have been a much worse one for the purpose that this. There is no particular writing in it, but there is an infinite amount of acting, of scene-shifting, and of liveliness generally; and all this goes on to the tune of the finest feelings possible. Love, devotion, self-sacrifice, humble but heroic bravery, and brimming Irish *bonhomie* and irony, are the chords that are touched, and all for five liberal acts, with a great deal of very clever landscape painting in the background, and with Mr. Boucicault, Mr. Montagu, Mr. Becket, and Miss Dyas in the foreground. For Mr. Boucicault, both as author and actor, it is a great triumph—especially as actor. His skill and shrewdness in knocking together effective situations and spinning lively dialogue are certainly commendable: but his acting is simply exquisite. One is hard cleverness, polished and flexible with use; the other is very like genius. The character of the Shaughraun is very happily fancied, but the best of the entertainment is to see the fancy that produced it still nightly playing with it. One hears it said sometimes that an actor acts with "authority"; certainly there is rarely a higher degree of authority than this. Mr. Boucicault smiles too much, we think; he rather overdoes the softness, the amiability, the innocence of his hero; but these exaggerations perhaps only deepen the charm of his rendering; for it was his happy thought to devise a figure which should absolutely, consummately, and irresistibly please. It has pleased mightily.

"The Two Orphans" at the Union Square Theatre, a piece which has been running a race with the "Shaughraun" in popularity, is an American rendering of an elaborate French *drame* of the old "boulevard" school. The original play ran all last winter in Paris, and fairly rejuvenated the rather defunct type to which it belonged. It is prodigiously clever, and we doubt whether for the time and the money one spends it would be possible to give one fuller measure, pressed down and running over, of surprises, sensations, and bewilderments. What is

offered at the Union Square is the mere gaunt, angular skeleton of the original. The whole thing, both as to adaptation and
rendering, is very brutally done. It hangs together as it can.
There is no really delicate acting in the piece, with the exception, in a sense, of Miss Kate Claxton's representation of the
blind maiden. She goes through the part with the pretty dis-
malness required, and with the enunciation of a young lady
reciting a "piece" at a boarding-school. But "The Two Orphans" is worth seeing simply for the sake of sitting in one's
place and feeling the quality of a couple of good old-fashioned
coups de théâtre as your French playwright who really knows
his business manages them. The first is when one of the Orphans, hearing in her garret the voice of the other, who is wandering in the street, sightless and helpless, and singing a song
addressed, through the mercy of chance, to her sister's ear, and
being about to fly to her rescue, is arrested on her threshold by
a *lettre de cachet.* The other is the cry of that sadly unwholesome cripple, Pierre (badly played, we should say, if the part
were not in its nature an impossible one), when, after being
trampled upon through the whole play, he turns upon his
hulking, blackguard brother: "As you say yourself, we come of
a race that kills!" These are very telling strokes, but if you wait
for them at the Union Square you pay for them well. You are
kept in patience, it is true, by some very pretty scenery.

The Fifth Avenue Theatre, we believe, makes a specialty of
"American comedy," eschews for the time at least Parisian orphans and heroic bog-trotters, and gives us our fellow-citizens
in their habits as they live. Some one ought to be held morally
accountable for such an unqualifiable mess of vulgarity as
"Women of the Day." It is a pity to talk about this thing, even
explicitly to pass it by; but we believe it is one of a series, and
under these circumstances one strikes out instinctively in self-
defence. It was ghastly, monstrous, a positive nightmare. It ran
for several weeks, and one wonders whether the public was an
active or a merely passive accomplice. Did it like it, or did it
simply endure it? The public at large is very ignorant and very
good-natured, and anything is possible.

One is bound to regret, in the presence of such a phenomenon as "Women of the Day," that the wholesome old fashion
of hissing has in the English theatre fallen into disuse. It was of

course liable to abuse; but what is one to say, on the other hand, of the spectator's patience? It would seem at least that, short of the privilege of absolute hissing (which ceases to be brutal only when it is directed at the play, and not at the performers), the disappointed, the deceived spectator ought to hold in his hand some instrument of respectful but uncompromising disapproval. We made this reflection as we watched the celebrated Mrs. Rousby, who has been interpreting historic blank-verse for a month at the Lyceum. It is hard to speak rigidly of so handsome a woman, but Mrs. Rousby's histrionic powers are about equivalent to those of some pretty trained animal—a pet lamb, say, or a white rabbit, or a snowy-breasted dove. Her acting is absolutely flat and weak—uninspired, untrained, unfinished. It was singular to see so extremely pretty a person take so little the critical chill off the atmosphere. Mrs. Rousby is distinctly incompetent. She has been followed at the same theatre by another English artist, a real artist this time— Mr. Toole. Mr. Toole has solved the problem of making low comedy charming. It must be admitted that in one of his parts —the "Artful Dodger"—the lowness is more apparent than the charm.

A more important dramatic enterprise than any we have mentioned has been the revival at Booth's Theatre, as a great spectacle, of "Henry V." We can spare but a word to it. The play could be presented only as a kind of animated panorama, for it offers but the slenderest opportunities for acting. These all fall to the lot of Mr. George Rignold, a young English actor, who, as the victor of Agincourt, has made a very charming impression. He plays the part in the most natural fashion, looks it and wears it to perfection, and declaims its swelling harangues with admirable vigor and taste. He is worth looking at and listening to. The scenic splendors of the play have received many compliments, though, as such things go, they seem to us to have a number of weak spots. But even if they had fewer, they would still, to our sense, be founded on a fallacy. Illusion, as such an enterprise proposes to produce it, is absolutely beyond the compass of the stage. The compromise with verisimilitude is not materially slighter than in the simple days before "revivals" had come into fashion. To assent to this you have only to look at the grotesqueness of the hobby-horses on the field of Agincourt and at the uncovered rear of King Harry's troops, when they have occasion to retire under range of your opera-glass. We approve by all means of scenic splendors, but we would draw the line at invading armies. Mr. Rignold, as we say, however, really produces a very grateful illusion.

1875

FROM

A Small Boy and Others

I TURN round again to where I last left myself gaping at the old ricketty bill-board in Fifth Avenue; and am almost as sharply aware as ever of the main source of its spell, the fact that it most often blazed with the rich appeal of Mr. Barnum, whose "lecture-room," attached to the Great American Museum, overflowed into posters of all the theatrical bravery disavowed by its title. It was my rueful theory of those days—though tasteful I may call it too as well as rueful—that on all the holidays on which we weren't dragged to the dentist's we attended as a matter of course at Barnum's, that is when we were so happy as to be able to; which, to my own particular consciousness, wasn't every time the case. The case was too often, to my melancholy view, that W. J., quite regularly, on the non-dental Saturdays, repaired to this seat of joy with the easy Albert—*he* at home there and master of the scene to a degree at which, somehow, neither of us could at the best arrive; he quite moulded, truly, in those years of plasticity, as to the æsthetic bent and the determination of curiosity, I seem to make out, by the general Barnum association and revelation. It was not, I hasten to add, that I too didn't, to the extent of my minor chance, drink at the spring; for how else should I have come by the whole undimmed sense of the connection?—the weary waiting, in the dusty halls of humbug, amid bottled mermaids, "bearded ladies" and chill dioramas, for the lecture-room, the true centre of the seat of joy, to open: vivid in especial to me is my almost sick wondering of whether I mightn't

be rapt away before it did open. The impression appears to
have been mixed; the drinking deep and the holding out,
holding out in particular against failure of food and of stage-
fares, provision for transport to and fro, being questions
equally intense: the appeal of the lecture-room, in its essence a
heavy extra, so exhausted our resources that even the sustaining
doughnut of the refreshment-counter would mock our desire
and the long homeward crawl, the length of Broadway and
further, seem to defy repetition. Those desperate days, none
the less, affect me now as having flushed with the very complexion of romance; their aches and inanitions were part of
the adventure; the homeward straggle, interminable as it appeared, flowered at moments into rapt contemplations—that
for instance of the painted portrait, large as life, of the celebrity
of the hour, then "dancing" at the Broadway Theatre, Lola
Montes, Countess of Lansfeldt, of a dazzling and unreal
beauty and in a riding-habit lavishly open at the throat.

It was thus quite in order that I should pore longest, there
at my fondest corner, over the Barnum announcements—my
present inability to be superficial about which has given in fact
the measure of my contemporary care. These announcements
must have been in their way marvels of attractive composition,
the placard bristling from top to toe with its analytic "synopsis
of scenery and incidents"; the synoptical view cast its net of
fine meshes and the very word savoured of incantation. It is
odd at the same time that when I question memory as to the
living hours themselves, those of the stuffed and dim little hall
of audience, smelling of peppermint and orange-peel, where
the curtain rose on our gasping but rewarded patience, two
performances only stand out for me, though these in the highest relief. Love, or the Countess and the Serf, by J. Sheridan
Knowles—I see that still as the blazonry of one of them, just as
I see Miss Emily Mestayer, large, red in the face, coifed in a
tangle of small, fine, damp-looking short curls and clad in a
light-blue garment edged with swansdown, shout at the top of
her lungs that a "pur-r-r-se of gold" would be the fair guerdon
of the minion who should start on the spot to do her bidding at
some desperate crisis that I forget. I forget Huon the serf, whom
I yet recall immensely admiring for his nobleness; I forget
everyone but Miss Mestayer, who gave form to my conception

of the tragic actress at her highest. She had a hooked nose, a great play of nostril, a vast protuberance of bosom and always the "crop" of close moist ringlets; I say always, for I was to see her often again, during a much later phase, the midmost years of that Boston Museum which aimed at so vastly higher a distinction than the exploded lecture-room had really done, though in an age that snickered even abnormally low it still lacked the courage to call itself a theatre. She must have been in comedy, which I believe she also usefully and fearlessly practised, rather unimaginable; but there was no one like her in the Boston time for cursing queens and eagle-beaked mothers; the Shakespeare of the Booths and other such would have been unproducible without her; she had a rusty, rasping, heaving and tossing "authority" of which the bitterness is still in my ears. I am revisited by an outer glimpse of her in that after age when she had come, comparatively speaking, into her own— the sight of her, accidentally incurred, one tremendously hot summer night, as she slowly moved from her lodgings or wherever, in the high Bowdoin Street region, down to the not distant theatre from which even the temperature had given her no reprieve; and well remember how, the queer light of my young impression playing up again in her path, she struck me as the very image of mere sore histrionic habit and use, a worn and weary, a battered even though almost sordidly smoothed, *thing* of the theatre, very much as an old infinitely-handled and greasy violoncello of the orchestra might have been. It was but an effect doubtless of the heat that she scarcely seemed clad at all; slippered, shuffling and, though somehow hatted and vaguely veiled or streamered, wrapt in a gauzy sketch of a dressing-gown, she pointed to my extravagant attention the moral of thankless personal service, of the reverse of the picture, of the cost of "amusing the public" in a case of amusing it, as who should say, every hour. And I had thrilled before her as the Countess in "Love"—such contrasted combinations! But she carried her head very high, as with the habit of crowns and trains and tirades—had in fact much the air of some deposed and reduced sovereign living on a scant allowance; so that, all invisibly and compassionately, I took off my hat to her.

To which I must add the other of my two Barnumite scenic

memories, my having anciently admired her as the Eliza of
Uncle Tom's Cabin, her swelling bust encased in a neat cotton
gown and her flight across the ice-blocks of the Ohio, if I
rightly remember the perilous stream, intrepidly and gracefully
performed. We lived and moved at that time, with great intensity, in Mrs. Stowe's novel—which, recalling my prompt and
charmed acquaintance with it, I should perhaps substitute for
The Initials, earlier mentioned here, as my first experiment in
grown-up fiction. There was, however, I think, for that triumphant work no classified condition; it was for no sort of
reader as distinct from any other sort, save indeed for Northern as differing from Southern: it knew the large felicity of
gathering in alike the small and the simple and the big and the
wise, and had above all the extraordinary fortune of finding itself, for an immense number of people, much less a book than
a state of vision, of feeling and of consciousness, in which they
didn't sit and read and appraise and pass the time, but walked
and talked and laughed and cried and, in a manner of which
Mrs. Stowe was the irresistible cause, generally conducted themselves. Appreciation and judgment, the whole impression,
were thus an effect for which there had been no process—any
process so related having in other cases *had* to be at some
point or other critical; nothing in the guise of a written book,
therefore, a book printed, published, sold, bought and "noticed," probably ever reached its mark, the mark of exciting interest, without having at least groped for that goal *as* a book or
by the exposure of some literary side. Letters, here, languished
unconscious, and Uncle Tom, instead of making even one of
the cheap short cuts through the medium in which books
breathe, even as fishes in water, went gaily roundabout it altogether, as if a fish, a wonderful "leaping" fish, had simply
flown through the air. This feat accomplished, the surprising
creature could naturally fly anywhere, and one of the first
things it did was thus to flutter down on every stage, literally
without exception, in America and Europe. If the amount of
life represented in such a work is measurable by the ease with
which representation is taken up and carried further, carried
even violently furthest, the fate of Mrs. Stowe's picture was
conclusive: it simply sat down wherever it lighted and made itself, so to speak, at home; thither multitudes flocked afresh and

there, in each case, it rose to its height again and went, with all its vivacity and good faith, through all its motions.

These latter were to leave me, however, with a fonder vision still than that of the comparatively jejune "lecture-room" version; for the first exhibition of them to spring to the front was the fine free rendering achieved at a playhouse till then ignored by fashion and culture, the National Theatre, deep down on the East side, whence echoes had come faintest to ears polite, but where a sincerity vivid though rude was now supposed to reward the curious. Our numerous attendance there under this spell was my first experience of the "theatre party" as we have enjoyed it in our time—each emotion and impression of which is as fresh to me as the most recent of the same family. Precious through all indeed perhaps is the sense, strange only to later sophistication, of my small encouraged state as a free playgoer—a state doubly wondrous while I thus evoke the full contingent from Union Square; where, for that matter, I think, the wild evening must have been planned. I am lost again in all the goodnature from which small boys, on wild evenings, could dangle so unchidden—since the state of unchiddenness is what comes back to me well-nigh clearest. How without that complacency of conscience could every felt impression so live again? It is true that for my present sense of the matter snubs and raps would still tingle, would count double; just wherefore it is exactly, however, that I mirror myself in these depths of propriety. The social scheme, as we knew it, was, in its careless charity, worthy of the golden age—though I can't sufficiently repeat that we knew it both at its easiest and its safest: the fruits dropped right upon the board to which we flocked together, the least of us and the greatest, with differences of appetite and of reach, doubtless, but not with differences of place and of proportionate share. My appetite and my reach in respect to the more full-bodied Uncle Tom might have brooked certainly any comparison; I must have partaken thoroughly of the feast to have left the various aftertastes so separate and so strong. It was a great thing to have a canon to judge by—it helped conscious criticism, which was to fit on wings (for use ever after) to the shoulders of appreciation. In the light of that advantage I could be *sure* my second Eliza was less dramatic than my first, and that my first "Cassy," that of the great and blood-curdling Mrs. Bellamy of the lecture-room, touched depths which made the lady at the National prosaic and placid (I could already be "down" on a placid Cassy;) just as on the other hand the rocking of the ice-floes of the Ohio, with the desperate Eliza, infant in arms, balancing for a leap from one to the other, had here less of the audible creak of carpentry, emulated a trifle more, to my perception, the real water of Mr. Crummles's pump. They can't, even at that, have emulated it much, and one almost envies (quite making up one's mind not to denounce) the simple faith of an age beguiled by arts so rude.

However, the point exactly was that we attended this spectacle just in order *not* to be beguiled, just in order to enjoy with ironic detachment and, at the very most, to be amused ourselves at our sensibility should it prove to have been trapped and caught. To have become thus aware of our collective attitude constituted for one small spectator at least a great initiation; he got his first glimpse of that possibility of a "free play of mind" over a subject which was to throw him with force at a later stage of culture, when subjects had considerably multiplied, into the critical arms of Matthew Arnold. So he is himself at least interested in seeing the matter—as a progress in which the first step was taken, before that crude scenic appeal, by his wondering, among his companions, where the absurd, the absurd for *them*, ended and the fun, the real fun, which was the gravity, the tragedy, the drollery, the beauty, the thing itself, briefly, might be legitimately and tastefully held to begin. Uncanny though the remark perhaps, I am not sure I wasn't thus more interested in the pulse of our party, under my tiny recording thumb, than in the beat of the drama and the shock of its opposed forces—vivid and touching as the contrast was then found for instance between the tragi-comical Topsy, the slave-girl clad in a pinafore of sackcloth and destined to become for Anglo-Saxon millions the type of the absolute in the artless, and her little mistress the blonde Eva, a figure rather in the Kenwigs tradition of pantalettes and pigtails, whom I recall as perching quite suicidally, with her elbows out and a preliminary shriek, on that bulwark of the Mississippi steamboat which was to facilitate her all but fatal immersion in the flood. Why should I have duly noted that no little game on her part could well less have resembled or simulated an accident, and yet have been no less moved by her reappearance, rescued from the river but perfectly dry, in the arms of faithful Tom, who had plunged in to save her, without either so much as wetting his shoes, than if I had been engaged with her in a reckless romp? I could count the white stitches in the loose patchwork, and yet could take it for a story rich and harmonious; I could know we had all intellectually condescended and that we had yet had the thrill of an æsthetic adventure; and this was a brave beginning for a consciousness that was to be nothing if not mixed and a curiosity that was to be nothing if not restless.

The principle of this prolonged arrest, which I insist on prolonging a little further, is doubtless in my instinct to grope for our earliest æsthetic seeds. Careless at once and generous the hands by which they were sown, but practically appointed none the less to cause that peculiarly flurried hare to run—flurried because over ground so little native to it—when so many others held back. Is it *that* air of romance that gilds for me then the Barnum background—taking it as a symbol; that makes me resist, to this effect of a passionate adverse loyalty, any impulse to translate into harsh terms any old sordidities and poverties? The Great American Museum, the downtown scenery and aspects at large, and even the up-town improvements on them, as then flourishing?—why, they must have been for the most part of the last meanness: the Barnum picture above all ignoble and awful, its blatant face or frame stuck about with innumerable flags that waved, poor vulgar-sized ensigns, over spurious relics and catchpenny monsters in effigy, to say nothing of the promise within of the still more monstrous and abnormal living—from the total impression of which things we plucked somehow the flower of the ideal. It grew, I must in justice proceed, much more sweetly and naturally at Niblo's, which represented in our scheme the ideal evening, while Barnum figured the ideal day; so that I ask myself, with that sense of our resorting there under the rich cover of night (which was the supreme charm,) how it comes that this larger memory hasn't swallowed up all others. For here, absolutely, *was* the flower at its finest and grown as nowhere else—grown in the great garden of the Ravel Family and offered again and again to our deep inhalation. I see the Ravels, French acrobats, dancers and pantomimists, as representing, for our culture, pure grace and charm and civility; so that one doubts whether any candid community was ever so much in debt to a race of entertainers or had so happy and prolonged, so personal and grateful a relation with them. They must have been, with their offshoots of Martinettis and others, of three or four generations, besides being of a rich theatrical stock generally, and we had our particular friends and favourites among them; we seemed to follow them through every phase of their career, to assist at their tottering steps along the tight-rope as very small children kept in equilibrium by very big balancing-poles (caretakers here walking under in case of falls;) to greet them as Madame Axel, of robust maturity and in a Spanish costume, bounding on the same tense cord more heavily but more assuredly; and finally to know the climax of the art with them in Raoul or the Night-Owl and Jocko or the Brazilian Ape—and all this in the course of our own brief infancy. My impression of them bristles so with memories that we seem to have rallied to their different productions with much the same regularity with which we formed fresh educational connections; and they were so much our property and our pride that they supported us handsomely through all fluttered entertainment of the occasional Albany cousins. I remember how when one of these visitors, wound up, in honour of New York, to the very fever of perception, broke out one evening while we waited for the curtain to rise, "Oh don't you hear the cries? They're *beating* them, I'm sure they are; can't it be stopped?" we resented the charge as a slur on our very honour; for what our romantic relative had heatedly imagined to reach us, in a hushed-up manner from behind, was the sounds attendant on the application of blows to some acrobatic infant who had "funked" his little job. Impossible such horrors in the world of pure poetry opened out to us at Niblo's, a temple of illusion, of tragedy and comedy and pathos that, though its *abords* of stony brown Metropolitan Hotel, on the "wrong side," must have been bleak and vulgar, flung its glamour forth into Broadway. What more pathetic for instance, so that we publicly wept, than the fate of wondrous Martinetti Jocko, who, after befriending a hapless French family wrecked on the coast of Brazil and bringing back to life a small boy rescued from the waves (I see even now, with every detail, this inanimate victim supine on the strand) met his death by some cruel bullet of which I have forgotten the determinant cause, only remembering the final agony as something we could scarce bear and a strain of our sensibility to which our parents repeatedly questioned the wisdom of exposing us.

These performers and these things were in all probability but of a middling skill and splendour—it was the pre-trapèze age, and we were caught by mild marvels, even if a friendly good faith in them, something sweet and sympathetic, was after all a value, whether of their own humanity, their own special quality, or only of our innocence, never to be renewed; but I light this taper to the initiators, so to call them, whom I remembered, when we had left them behind, as if they had given us a silver key to carry off and so to refit, after long years, to sweet names never thought of from then till now. Signor Léon Javelli, in whom the French and the Italian charm appear to have met, who was he, and what did he brilliantly do, and why of a sudden do I thus recall and admire him? I am afraid he but danced the tight-rope, the most domestic of our friends' resources, as it brought them out, by the far stretch of the rope, into the bosom of the house and against our very hearts, where they leapt and bounded and wavered and recovered closely face to face with us; but I dare say he bounded, brave Signor Léon, to the greatest height of all: let this vague agility, in any case, connect him with that revelation of the ballet, the sentimental-pastoral, of other years, which, in The Four Lovers for example, a pantomimic lesson as in words of one syllable, but all quick and gay and droll, would have affected us as classic, I am sure, had we then had at our disposal that term of appreciation. When we read in English storybooks about the pantomimes in London, which somehow cropped up in them so often, those were the only things that didn't make us yearn; so much we felt we were masters of the type, and so almost sufficiently was that a stop-gap for London constantly deferred. We hadn't the transformation-scene, it was true, though what this really seemed to come to was clown and harlequin taking liberties with policemen—these last evidently a sharp note in a picturesqueness that we lacked, our own slouchy "officers" saying nothing to us of that sort; but we had at Niblo's harlequin and columbine, albeit of less pure a tradition, and we knew moreover all about clowns, for we went to circuses too, and so repeatedly that when I add them to our list of recreations, the good old orthodox circuses under tents set up in vacant lots, with which New York appears at that time to have bristled, time and place would seem to have shrunken for most other pursuits, and not least for that of serious learning. And the case is aggravated as I remember Franconi's, which we more or less haunted and which, aiming at the grander style and the monumental effect, blazed with fresh paint and rang with Roman chariot-races up there among the deserts of Twenty-ninth Street or wherever; considerably south, perhaps, but only a little east, of the vaster desolations that gave scope to the Crystal Palace, second of its name since, following—not *passibus æquis*, alas—the London structure of 1851, this enterprise forestalled by a year or two the Paris Palais de l'Industrie of 1855. Such as it was I feel again its majesty on those occasions on which I dragged—if I must here once more speak for myself only—after Albany cousins through its courts of edification: I remember being very tired and cold and hungry there, in a little light drab and very glossy or shiny "talma" breasted with rather troublesome buttonhole-embroideries; though concomitantly conscious that I was somehow in Europe, since everything about me had been "brought over," which ought to have been consoling, and seems in fact to have been so in some degree, inasmuch as both my own pain and the sense of the cousinly, the Albany, headaches quite fade in that recovered presence of big European Art embodied in Thorwaldsen's enormous Christ and the Disciples, a shining marble company ranged in a semicircle of dark maroon walls. If this was Europe then Europe was beautiful indeed, and we rose to it on the wings of wonder; never were we afterwards to see great showy sculpture, in whatever profuse exhibition or of whatever period or school, without some renewal of that charmed Thorwaldsen hour, some taste again of the almost sugary or confectionery sweetness with which the great white images had affected us under their supper-table gaslight. The Crystal Palace was vast and various and dense, which was what Europe was going to be; it was a deep-down jungle of impressions that were somehow challenges, even as we might, helplessly defied, find foreign words and practices; over which formidably towered Kiss's mounted Amazon attacked by a leopard or whatever, a work judged at that day sublime and the glory of the place; so that I felt the journey back in the autumn dusk and the Sixth Avenue cars (established just in time) a relapse into soothing flatness, a return to the Fourteenth Street horizon from a far journey and a hundred looming questions that would still, tremendous thought, come up for all the personal answers of which one cultivated the seed.

1913

ALAN DALE

In 1869, the London *Daily News* warned that the New York daily newspapers were bringing the profession of journalism into contempt by a "kind of toadyism or flunkeyism, which they call 'interviewing.'" One of the most proficient practitioners of this new form was English-born, Oxford-educated Alfred J. Cohen, who wrote under the name Alan Dale (1861–1928). As a novelist, Dale is noteworthy for *A Marriage Below Zero* (1889), which introduced the first homosexual villain in American fiction, a sinister force undermining middle-class marriage. Many in the theatre world regarded Dale himself as a sinister force. He signed on as dramatic critic for Joseph Pulitzer's New York *Evening World* (1887–95), but abandoned it for the New York *Journal*, where his independent, bright, acerbic style better suited William Randolph Hearst's brash editorial policies. Dale became the most feared reviewer on "the Great White Way," a term he popularized; his vitriolic opinions were considered so influential that producers tried to ban him. In 1914 when one such complaint managed to get him demoted to a stringer at $25 per review, Dale quit the *Journal*, only to turn up at the New York *American*. There his notices were marginally more temperate and he was an early booster of Jerome Kern. At his death he had served longer than any other New York theatre reviewer.

By the time she granted Dale an audience, Clara Morris was past her prime as America's answer to Sarah Bernhardt. In her heyday, she had been heralded as an actress of such intense emotional power that audiences underwent paroxysms of sympathetic feeling during her climactic scenes. Dale, who dubbed her "Queen of Spasms," maintained a typically ironic attitude to the star in her decline. In his references to her happy home life, he may have been aware that she was a morphine addict, saddled with a free-spending husband. In its balance of respect and sarcasm, his interview is a classic of the genre.

Clara Morris

THERE have been few actresses who have been more discussed and analyzed in their day than Miss Clara Morris, the "queen of emotion;" few actresses have enjoyed a more brilliant and more successful day. If Miss Morris were to retire at the present time, she would do so in comparatively unrivalled glory. The indications, however, are that she will play herself into old age, struggle with those odious comparisons, which, miasma-like, are beginning to arise, and end in the sorrowful way made known by the great Ristori, who returned to America for a last tour, to ruin a perfect fortification of illusion.

Of one thing I am deeply regretful. It is that I never saw Clara Morris at her greatest; when the American people raved about the sublimity of her emotional work and listened eagerly to countless stories of her studies in mad-houses, of her nocturnal visits to hospitals and dissecting rooms, and to various other little tales as profitable as they were interesting. I saw Clara Morris within the last five years, and set her down as the "queen of spasms." The electrical effect of her work is undoubtedly as forcible as it ever was; she can still thrill an audience with the absolute reality of her emotion; the women can yet weep, as they look at Miss Morris' eyes, into which the real wet tears well so genuinely, but save for these spasms, I must confess that Miss Morris was to me a grievous disappointment. In her quieter moments, she appeared crude and unrefined, and there were times when I could quite understand the feelings of those who portrayed her as "wildly western."

But in spite of all her faults, Clara Morris is a case of genius, and her name in the annals of the American stage is luminous for all time.

Miss Morris has won her fame amid obstacles that in the present state of the drama, when pretty faces and handsome forms are looked upon as unquestioned passports to success, would seem unconquerable. She has a face that is far from beautiful, and a figure that is gaunt and unlovely. I always think of Gilbert and that "left shoulder blade, which is a miracle of loveliness," when I see Clara Morris. I do hope that she possesses this boon, even if we are never to know the truth for ourselves. She looks like a thoroughly healthy, robust woman, and it requires the most vivid imagination to give credence to the stories of her ineffably exhausted state, her broken nerves, her need of drugs, and other requirements.

It would be awful to believe that so great an artist would have recourse to feeble fiction. When, however, one sits for

half an hour in utter impatience between every act of a performance, to be told that Miss Morris' nerves need attending to,
the inner self talks unkindly.

Actresses, strange to say, love to give the impression that
they feel the griefs they portray so intensely, that it affects their
domestic life. Sarah Bernhardt would have a fit if you dared to
suggest health to her. Only the other day I read of her intense
suffering, during which she sat up in bed, in a white satin
night-gown, her hair in picturesque confusion, and her room
filled with artists, who took turns sitting by her bedside. Think
of the intense suffering that will permit such obtrusive idiocy;
picture the tortured frame in the white satin frills, or the
throbbing head with the Psyche knot!

Miss Clara Morris is very much in this style. When a newspaper man asks her if she is well, this is a specimen reply:

"Well, did you say? Yes, for me; but not perfectly well. I
never expect to be that in this world. Perhaps when I get to a
better, with a good many other people, I may enjoy perfect
health for the first time."

Now, Miss Morris is one of those women who thoroughly
enjoy this wicked world. Why it should make her ill, I can't
make out. She has a devoted husband, F. C. Harriott, and a
lovely home at Riverdale-on-the-Hudson. When she is not
acting, she is placidly enjoying herself. She is an accomplished
equestrienne, and is a well-known figure, on horseback, in the
leafy lanes of Riverdale. Supreme health seems to hover
around her. Isn't it funny that these stage people can't be absolutely natural off the stage? Is it not equally ludicrous that
perfect health, God's most lovely gift, should be looked upon
as unromantic, prosaic, detrimental to success? Our consumptive Sarah, and our nerve-racked Clara are peculiar instances of
those idols the people love to worship. Sarah's tuberculosis is a
dainty little recognition of the requirements of her supporters;
Clara's nerves have made a fortune all by themselves.

Miss Morris was born at Morristown, Canada, in 1848, and
began her stage career in Cleveland, in 1862.

"I was living in Cleveland," said Miss Morris, "and there
boarded in the same house with my mother, a Mrs. Bradshaw,
an actress, and her daughter Blanche. John Ellsler produced
'The Seven Ravens,' and Blanche had a place in the ballet. She

worried my mother to let me join her, and made my mother's life miserable until she gained her consent. Blanche took me down to the theatre, but Mr. Ellsler said I was too little, and that unless he could find somebody to march with me, he could not give me a place. I burst into tears. John Ellsler seemed to be sorry for me. He patted me on the head, and told me to come to the theatre. He secured an old-fashioned little woman to walk with me, and everything went well. I appeared as a fairy, and a very strange fairy I looked. After that I was a zouave, and went on the stage in boy's clothes. Blanche and I used to chew gum, and it didn't seem to interfere with our acting. 'The Seven Ravens' ran for two weeks, and my salary was $3 per week. Mr. Ellsler asked me if I would remain with him the following season. My mother refused his request at first, but finally gave her consent, saying that I might as well do this as anything else. That is how I came to go upon the stage."

Miss Morris lived in Cleveland for a number of years, and appeared in Buffalo in 1866. She also played in Cincinnati, where for one season she occupied the position of leading lady, at a salary of $35 per week. She supported her mother, and, as may be imagined, was not able to enjoy a very luxurious life. Her local reputation as an actress was excellent, but actresses don't care very much for local reputations, unless the locality be the metropolis. Miss Morris, however, received some very good offers, one from Augustin Daly, of New York City. She packed up her trunk, bade a temporary good-bye to her mother, and set out for the metropolis, at her own expense.

When Miss Morris first came to New York, she had in her pocket a contract with Mr. Maguire, of California. He pledged himself to give her $100 per week "in gold," two benefits, and the right to choose her own parts as leading lady. But Miss Morris sighed for New York; it was the Mecca of her hopes. She had but two dresses in the world, and a very meagre stage wardrobe. She possessed none of those sartorial "dreams" that actresses of the present day seem to consider as necessary as dramatic talent. Talking of dresses reminds me that on one occasion I had to criticise a feminine star who was playing the part of a governess. To my astonishment, she appeared in the most gorgeous gowns, Worth-made and exceedingly costly. I mentioned the incongruity of a governess donning such garbs. This was her reply:

"I know they are gorgeous, but if I appear out of town in cheap clothes, people will say that I am not a success, and am unable to wear startling dresses. I have got to make an 'appearance.'"

This, by-the-way, of course.

Miss Morris describes her own appearance when she presented herself before the austere Augustin Daly for the first time, as follows:

"Mr. Daly had been accustomed to the magnificence of Miss Morant, Fanny Davenport, Agnes Ethel, and others of his splendid stock company. He looked down upon my five feet three inches, clad in a rusty linen gown, and carrying a satchel. He shrugged his shoulders, and there was doubt expressed in every line of his face. He engaged me to play any part save that of soubrette and general utility. My salary was to be $40 per week, with the understanding that if I made a distinct hit, it was to be doubled. Upon this sum I was to live, support my mother, and buy my stage dresses."

Miss Morris declares that when she had brought her mother to New York, and settled down, she had not one dollar to her credit. Mother and daughter were so cramped for means, that meat once a day was a luxury. The young actress was often so weak at rehearsal, that she was unable to do herself justice. Her mother used to ask if she would have her chops to rehearse upon or to act upon. Miss Morris often used to think that in those days Daly was convinced that she would make a fearful *fiasco*. She suffered very acutely herself. Her stage wardrobe was no use at all for the modern society plays in which she was called to appear, while the tortures of shabbiness were felt when she mingled at rehearsal with the beautifully dressed women of the company.

Miss Morris met with her first metropolitan triumph through the usual accidents. In theatrical life, accidents are very frequently blessings. Mr. Daly was to present "Man and Wife," a dramatization of Wilkie Collins' famous novel. Miss Agnes Ethel was cast for the part of *Anne Sylvester*; Miss Morris was to appear as *Blanche*, a comparatively insignificant role. At the last moment Miss Ethel refused to act, with the charming caprice of the successful actress. Miss Morris received the part, and was told that she would be required to play *Anne Sylvester* that night. She did so unhesitatingly. It is in just this way that dramatic reputations are made. Her *Anne Sylvester* was a triumph. She was called five times before the curtain on the opening night. Her metropolitan reputation was established.

Miss Morris has made her principal successes as *Camille*, as *Mercy Merrick* in "The New Magdalen," as *Cora* in "Article 47," as *Alixe* and as *Renée de Moray*.

Her *Camille* has always attracted a great deal of attention. The death scene is a wonderful piece of work. Miss Morris has always disliked the part, and declares that she never really intended to play it. She first appeared as Dumas' consumptive heroine very unwillingly. She had just returned to New York after a long absence, to find that the theatres had decided upon giving an entertainment for the benefit of the poor. The winter had been a hard one, and the distress in New York, in the tenement districts, had been very great. Miss Morris consented to appear, and a list of parts was given to her to select from. It was headed by *Camille*, through which she immediately drew a pencil. Her wish was disregarded. A couple of days before the performance she found that she must appear as *Camille*, or remain out of the programme.

Miss Morris made the best of matters, and studied the objectionable role. There was but one rehearsal, and Frank Mayo, well known now in connection with "Nordeck" and "Davy Crockett," was the *Armand Duval*. The fateful night arrived, as fateful nights have a way of doing. Miss Morris selected her dresses with a great deal of care. Her manager was having scenery painted for a new French play that he was to produce. It was never produced. "Camille" was a gigantic success, and Miss Morris found the part foisted upon her.

She then made it a special study. "I learned from my physician," she said upon one occasion, "that there are two coughs peculiar to lingering consumption. One of them is a little hacking cough that interferes with the speech, and injures the throat; the other is a paroxysm brought on by extra exertion. I chose the paroxysm, and introduced it in the first scene, after I have been dancing. *Camille* says at one time that all pain is gone. My doctor told me that this was on account of entire loss of the lungs. He cautioned me against saying much after that, and told me that the tubes of the throat could be used for a few words. I studied *Camille* in this manner, and not in the coarse way that has been attributed to me."

A great deal of nonsense has been written on the subject of Miss Morris' ideas. Probably but very little of it emanated from the artist herself. The St. Louis *Post Despatch* printed a very interesting account of Miss Morris' views on emotion, and as her manager has had the talk printed for circulation, it is worth giving in part:

"You cannot affect other people except by feeling yourself," she said. "You must feel, or all the pretty and pathetic language in the world won't make people sympathize with you. You must cry yourself, and tears alone won't do it. There must be tears in your voice, in order to bring them forth from other people. Before I appear on the stage, I am in a nervous tremor, all because I am afraid that I shan't cry in the play. I spend an hour or two with my company, making just as much fun as I possibly can, so as to get all the laughter out of me. Then I shut myself up, and work up an artificial agony. To do this, I think of some sad incident, or read a sad story. One of Bret Harte's books supplied me with emotion for two years.

"I get the story fixed in my mind, and dwell upon the most pathetic incident in it until my feelings are completely aroused. Then I cry, and the whole thing is done. I have to look out for the other danger, and keep from being overcome. All the false sobs in the world will never take the place of real emotion. There must be real tears in eyes or voice. This is very hard on the eyes, of course. Mine are sometimes so inflamed that I can scarcely use them. We cannot play emotional scenes as they were formerly played. It used to be that there was only one way of dying on the stage. All that has been changed."

Clara Morris is an ardent admirer of Sarah Bernhardt. "Her *Camille* is perfect," she said on one occasion. "She has a wonderful voice, that thrills her audiences, but she does not make you cry. She is a supreme artist. I went to see her in 'Adrienne Lecouvreur,' and was beginning to be deeply moved. But the crisis came too quickly. The large audience was waiting in pained expectancy. I leaned forward and listened. Every word fell upon my ear. I was harrowing rapidly, when—she cleared her throat. The spell was broken. Nothing could move the audience. Too much nature is unpardonable; too much art is death."

Miss Morris is frequently asked whether she loses her own identity in the character she plays. Here is a story she tells:

"Once, in New York, when a number of us were at dinner, Mr. Stuart, one of the party, asked me the same thing. I told him to wait until after the play, and he would see if I lost myself in my role. We were very merry at dinner—you know I can be merry—and when it was over, Stuart, who had been laughing uproariously, said, 'You needn't think you can make me cry to-night, after seeing your mirth at this table!' Well, we went to the theatre. The play was 'Miss Multon.' It has a very strong climax. The scene is very forcible. It is brought to a close by *Miss Multon* casting herself, or rather falling upon the floor, very nearly in convulsions. I fell down as usual. I felt the part very acutely. My heart was beating violently, and I was red with excitement. As I lay there, I happened to look at the box overhead. There I saw Stuart. Even in my anguish, I recognized him.

"His nose was red from excessive weeping, and I could distinctly see the tears tracing themselves down his cheeks. I caught his eye, and—yes, I will say it—gave him a very decided wink. He was furious, and made some remark. The audience hissed him, and he went quietly to the back of the box. He has always declared that he would never forgive me for that wink."

Miss Morris says that it is dangerous to be too sympathetic. Nature must be tempered with art. "I must cry in my emotional roles, and feel enough to cry; but I must not cry enough to mumble my words, to redden my nose, or to become hysterical."

Although the actress relies very little upon the attractions of her person, she does not despise dress. She thinks that good clothes have a great deal to do with a part, and she is decidedly correct. Miss Morris, however, deals very artistically with this question. Her motto is not "Worth; *encore* Worth; *toujours* Worth." On one occasion, in the days to which I have before referred, when her stage wardrobe was decidedly meagre, her waiting-maid appeared in a pink silk dress, with lace and diamonds. Miss Morris has never forgotten that. The maid entirely eclipsed the mistress.

Many a maid nowadays would be willing to do the same thing. The question of dress is far too forcibly emphasized. Women who are known to dress well stand far better chances of engagement than those who are not. And it is the same with the men. Visit the dramatic agencies, and you will always hear the same thing: "He is a good dresser"; or "He has an excellent wardrobe." Very few stars appear in plays that give them no opportunity to "dress." Of course, I do not include the Shakespearian actresses. Even playwrights have become aware of the fact that plays without a drawing-room scene, or a reception incident where costumes can be as extravagant as possible, are unwelcome.

Miss Morris can discuss the question of dress as readily as she can those connected with the more important questions of theatrical interests. She has read a great deal, and has digested all that she has read. She studies intricacies very carefully, and does not cast them aside as unnecessary, as many less worthy actresses are inclined to do. The greater the artist, the more willing will he or she be to clutch at every possible hint that may be given.

Miss Morris is always extremely interesting. She understands her profession from its alpha to omega, and is always willing to talk. She has been frequently misrepresented, but it has done her little harm. As I said before, her name in the annals of the American stage is luminous for all time. She should, however, not abide with us until her greatness has become a memory.

1890

WILLIAM WINTER

When William Winter (1836–1917) began reviewing plays for the New York *Albion* in 1861, he signed his pieces "Mercutio," although "Polonius" might have been more apt. Deeply influenced by Long-fellow, Winter was a forerunner of Santayana's Genteel Tradition, a champion of the ideally beautiful and a determined preceptor of those less cultured. Secure in his post at the New York *Tribune* from 1865 to 1909, Winter came to be regarded as America's foremost dramatic critic, whose long experience enabled him to tease out the subtleties of the actor's art. He had a knack for a memorable phrase, character-izing Edwin Forrest's style "the school of limb and larynx" and the commercial appeal of *Camille* as "tears . . . crystallized into cur-rency." As these examples show, he preferred intellectual acting to the emotional; and he hailed Edwin Booth as its paragon. Booth made history by playing his saturnine Hamlet 100 times at the Winter Gar-den Theatre in 1864–65, and later he produced what was considered a definitive production at his own New York playhouse in 1870. Win-ter's evaluation matched the performance in its detail and judicious-ness. Some may see a conflict of interest here, since Booth was a good friend, but Winter cast himself as counselor to the prince.

By the 1890s, although still widely respected, Winter was regarded as a back number by the younger generation. Like his English counter-part Clement Scott, he voiced a ferocious animosity to Ibsen's plays and scolded Ibsen's American exponent Mrs. Fiske for "stooping" to drama that "banishes poetry and nobility." Still, shortly before his death, the theatrical profession presented him a testimonial signed by both Theodore Roosevelt and Woodrow Wilson.

The Art of Edwin Booth: Hamlet

BOOTH's impersonation of Hamlet was one of the best known works of the dramatic age. In many minds the actor and the character had become identical, and it is not to be doubted that Booth's performance of Hamlet will live, in commemora-tive dramatic history, with great representative embodiments of the stage—with Garrick's Lear, Kemble's Coriolanus,

Edmund Kean's Richard, Macready's Macbeth, Forrest's Othello, and Irving's Mathias, and Becket. That it deserved historic permanence is the conviction of a great body of thoughtful students of Shakespeare and of the art of acting, in Great Britain and Germany as well as in America. In the elements of intellect, imagination, sublimity, mystery, tenderness, incipient delirium, and morbid passion, it was exactly consonant with what the best analysis has determined as to the conception of Shakespeare; while in sustained vigour, picturesque variety, and beautiful grace of execution, it was a model of executive art,—of demeanour, as the atmosphere of the soul,—facial play, gesticulation, and fluent and spontaneous delivery of the text; a delivery that made the blank verse as natural in its effect as blank verse ought to be, or can be, without ever dropping it to the level of colloquialism and commonplace.

In each of Booth's performances a distinguishing attribute was simplicity of treatment, and that was significantly prominent in his portrayal of Hamlet. The rejection of all singularity and the avoidance of all meretricious ornament resulted in a sturdy artistic honesty, which could not be too much admired. The figure stood forth, distinct and stately, in a clear light. The attitudes, movements, gestures, and facial play combined in a fabric of symmetry and of always adequate expression. The text was spoken with ample vocal power and fine flexibility. The illustrative "business" was strictly accordant with the wonderful dignity and high intellectual worth of Shakespeare's creation. The illusion of the part was created with an almost magical sincerity, and was perfectly preserved. Booth's Hamlet was—as Hamlet on the stage should always be—an imaginative and poetic figure; and yet it was natural. To walk upon the stage with the blank verse stored in memory, with every particle of the business pre-arranged, with every emotion aroused yet controlled, and every effect considered, known, and pre-ordained, and yet to make the execution of a design seem involuntary and spontaneous,—that is the task set for the actor, and that task was accomplished by Booth.

Much is heard about "nature" in acting, and about the necessity of "feeling," on the part of an actor. The point has been too often obscured by ignorant or careless reasoning. An actor who abdicates intellectual supremacy ceases to be an actor, for he never can present a consistent and harmonious work. To yield to unchecked feeling is to go to pieces. The actor who makes his audience weep is not he who himself weeps, but he who seems to weep. He will have the feeling, but he will control it and use it, and he will not show it in the manner of actual life. Mrs. Siddons said of herself that she had got credit for the truth and feeling of her acting, when she was only relieving her own heart of its grief; but Mrs. Siddons knew how to act, whatever were her personal emotions,—for it was she who admonished a young actor, saying, "You feel too much." Besides, every artist has a characteristic, individual way. If the representative of Hamlet will express the feelings of Hamlet, will convey them to his audience, and will make the poetic ideal an actual person, it makes no difference whether he is excited or quiescent. Feeling did not usually run away with Dion Boucicault: yet he could act Daddy O'Dowd so as to convulse an audience with sympathy and grief. Jefferson, the quintessence of tenderness, has often accomplished the same result with Rip Van Winkle. In one case the feeling was assumed and controlled; in the other, it is experienced and controlled. Acting is an art, and not a spasm; and when you saw Booth as Hamlet you saw a noble exemplification of that art,—the ideal of a poet, supplied with a physical investiture and made actual and natural, yet not lowered to the level of common life.

The tenderness of Hamlet toward Ophelia—or, rather, toward his ideal of Ophelia—was always set in a strong light, in Booth's acting of the part. He likewise gave felicitous expression to a deeper view of that subject—to Hamlet's pathetic realisation that Ophelia is but a fragile nature, upon which his love has been wasted, and that, in such a world as this, love can find no anchor and no security. The forlorn desolation of the prince was thus made emphatic. One of the saddest things in Hamlet's experience is his baffled impulse to find rest in love— the crushing lesson, not only that Ophelia is incompetent to understand him, but that the stronger and finer a nature is, whether man or woman, the more inevitably it must stand alone. That hope by which so many fine spirits have been lured and baffled, of finding another heart upon which to repose when the burden of life becomes too heavy to be borne alone, is, of all hopes, the most delusive. Loneliness is the penalty of greatness. Booth was definite, also, as to the "madness" of Hamlet.* He was not absolutely mad, but substantially sane,— guarding himself, his secrets, and his purposes by assumed wildness; yet the awful loneliness of existence to which Hamlet has been sequestered by his vast, profound, all-embracing, contemplative intellect, and by the mental shock and wrench that he has sustained, was allowed to colour his temperament. That idea might, in its practical application, be advantageously carried much further than it ever was by any actor; for, after the ghost-scene, the spiritual disease of the Dane would augment its ravages, and his figure should then appear in blight, disorder, dishevelment, and hopeless misery. Poetic gain, however, may sometimes be dramatic loss. To Hamlet the dreamer, Booth usually gave more emphasis than to Hamlet the sufferer —wisely remembering therein the value of stage effect for an audience. His Hamlet was a man to whom thoughts are things and actions are shadows, and who is defeated and overwhelmed by spiritual perceptions too vast for his haunted spirit, by griefs and shocks too great for his endurance, by wicked and compelling environments too strong for his nerveless opposition, and by duties too practical and onerous for his diseased and irresolute will. That was as near to the truth of Shakespeare as acting can reach, and it made Hamlet as intelligible as Hamlet can ever be.

*In reply to a question on this subject, Booth wrote the following letter, which was printed by its recipient, in the *Nashville* (Tenn.) *Banner:*—

DEAR SIR: The subject to which you refer is, as you well know, one of endless controversy among the learned heads, and I dare say they will "war" over it "till time fades into eternity." I think I am asked the same question nearly three hundred and sixty-five times a year, and I usually find it safest to side with both parties in dispute, being one of those, perhaps, referred to in the last line of the following verse:—

"Genius, the Pythian of the beautiful,
   Leaves her large truths a riddle to the dull;
   From eyes profane a veil the Isis screens,
   And fools on fools still ask what Hamlet means."

Yet, I will confess that I do not consider Hamlet mad,—except in "craft." My opinion may be of little value, but 'tis the result of many weary walks with him, "for hours together, here in the lobby."

Truly yours,
EDWIN BOOTH.

To a man possessing the great intellect and the infinitely
tender sensibility of Hamlet, grief does not come in the form
of dejection, but in the form of a restless, turbulent, incessant
agonising fever of vital agitation. He is never at rest. The grip
that misery has fastened upon his soul is inexorable. Contemplation of the action and reaction of his spirit and his anguish
is, to a thoughtful observer, kindred with observance of the
hopeless suffering of a noble and beloved friend who is striving
in vain against the slow, insidious, fatal advance of wasting disease, which intends death, and which will certainly accomplish
what it intends. The spirit of Hamlet is indomitable. It may be
quenched, but it cannot be conquered. The freedom into
which it has entered is the awful freedom that misery alone can
give. Beautiful, desolate, harrowed with pain, but ever tremulous with the life of perception and feeling, it moves among
phantom shapes and ghastly and hideous images, through
wrecks of happiness and the glimmering waste of desolation. It
is a distracted and irresolute spirit, made so by innate gloom
and by the grandeur of its own vast perceptions. But it is never
supine.

That pathetic condition of agonised unrest, that vitality of
exquisite torture in the nature and experience of Hamlet, was
indicated by Booth. He moved with grace; he spoke the text
with ease, polish, spontaneous fluency, and rich and strong
significance. The noble ideal and the clear-cut execution were
obvious. But he crowned all by denoting, with incisive distinctness and with woful beauty, the pathetic vitality of the Hamlet
experience. His impersonation had wealth of emotion, exalted
poetry of treatment, and a dream-like quality that could not
fail to fascinate; but, above all, when at its best, it had the terrible reality of suffering. There was no "realism" in it, no fantastic stage business, no laboured strangeness of new readings: it
was a presentment of the spiritual state of a gifted man, whom
nature and circumstance have made so clear-sighted and yet so
wretchedly dubious that his surroundings overwhelm him,
and life becomes to him a burden and a curse. Hamlet is a
mystery. But, seeing that personation, the thinker saw what
Shakespeare meant. Many a human soul has had, or is now enduring, this experience, confronted with the duty of fulfilling
a rational life, yet heartbroken with personal affliction, and

bewildered with a sense of the awful mysteries of spiritual destiny and the supernal world. This is the great subject that Booth's performance of Hamlet presented—and presented in an entirely great manner. His scenes with the Ghost had a startling weirdness. His parting from Ophelia had the desolate and afflicting and therefore right effect of a parting from love, no less than from its object. His sudden delirium, in the killing of the concealed spy upon Hamlet's interview with the Queen, was wonderfully fine, and it always evoked a prodigious enthusiasm.

Booth's Hamlet did not love Ophelia. He had left behind not only that special love, but love itself—which was something that he remembered but could no longer feel. His Hamlet retained, under all the shocks of spiritual affliction, and through all the blight of physical suffering, a potent intellectual concentration and a princely investiture of decorous elegance: it was not a Hamlet of collapse and ruin: it was neither "fat" nor "scant of breath"—neither lethargic with the languor of misery, nor heavy with the fleshly grossness of supine sloth and abject prostration. The heart was corroded with sorrow, but the brain stood firm. Yet there were moments when the sanity of Booth's Hamlet lapsed into transient frenzy. A pathetic, involuntary tenderness played through his manner toward Ophelia, whom once he has loved and trusted, but whom he now knows to be a frail nature, however lovely and sweet. The pervasive tone of the embodiment was that of a sad isolation from humanity, a dream-like vagueness of condition, —as of one who wanders upon the dusky confines of another world,—and a drifting incertitude, very eloquent of the ravages of a terrible spiritual experience. The latter attribute was the poetic charm of Booth's Hamlet, and the poetic charm, the fine intellectuality, and the graceful execution of the work gave it at once extraordinary beauty and remarkable influence.

Acting, at its best, is the union of perfect expression with a true ideal. Booth's ideal of Hamlet satisfied the imagination more especially in this respect, that it left Hamlet substantially undefined. The character, or rather the temperament, was deeply felt, was imparted with flashes of great energy, and at moments was made exceedingly brilliant; but, for the most part, it was lived out in a dream, and was left to make its own way. There was no insistence on special views or on being specifically understood. And this mood mellowed the execution and gave it flexibility and warmth. Booth was an actor of uncertain impulses and conditions, and he was rightly understood only by those who saw him often, in any specified character. Like all persons of acute sensibility, he had his good moments and his bad ones—moments when the genial fire of the soul was liberated, and moments when the artistic faculties could only operate in the hard, cold mechanism of professional routine. Sometimes he seemed lethargic and indifferent. At other times he would put forth uncommon power, and in the ghost scenes and the great third act, would create a thrilling illusion and lift his audience into noble excitement. At its best his performance of Hamlet exalted the appreciative spectator by arousing a sense of the pathos of our mortal condition as contrasted with the grandeur of the human mind and the vast possibilities of spiritual destiny; and therein it was a performance of great public benefit and importance.

Booth's Hamlet was poetic. The person whom he represented was not an ancient Dane, fair, blue-eyed, yellow-haired, stout, and lymphatic, but was the dark, sad, dreamy, mysterious hero of a poem. The actor did not go behind the tragedy, in quest of historical realism, but, dealing with an ideal subject, treated it in an ideal manner, as far removed as possible from the plane of actual life. Readers of the play of Hamlet are aware that interest in the Prince of Denmark is not, to any considerable extent, inspired by the circumstances that surround him, but depends upon the quality of the man—his spirit and the fragrance of his character. There is an element in Hamlet no less elusive than beautiful, which lifts the mind to a sublime height, fills the heart with a nameless grief, and haunts the soul like the remembered music of a gentle voice that will speak no more. It might be called sorrowful grandeur, sad majesty, ineffable mournfulness, grief-stricken isolation, or patient spiritual anguish. Whatever called, the name would probably be inadequate; but the power of the attribute itself can never fail to be felt. Hamlet fascinates by his personality; and no man can succeed in presenting him who does not possess in himself that peculiar quality of fascination. It is something that cannot be drawn from the library, or poured from the flagon, or bought in the shops. Booth possessed it—and that was the first cause of his great success in the character.

Booth's Hamlet was likewise spiritual. Therein the actor manifested not alone the highest quality that can characterise acting, but a perfectly adequate intuitive knowledge of the Shakespearian conception. It is not enough, in the presentation of this part, that an actor should make known the fact that Hamlet's soul is haunted by supernatural powers: he must also make it felt that Hamlet possesses a soul such as it is possible for supernatural powers to haunt. In Shakespeare's pages it may be seen that—at the beginning, and before his mind has been shocked and unsettled by the awful apparition of his father's spirit in arms—Hamlet is a man darkly prone to sombre thought upon the nothingness of this world and the solemn mysteries of the world beyond the grave; and this mental drift does not flow from the student's fancy, but is the spontaneous, passionate tendency of his soul—for, in the very first self-communing passage that he utters, he is found to have been brooding on the expediency of suicide; and not long afterwards he is found avowing the belief that the powers of hell have great control over spirits as weak and melancholy as his own. A hint suffices. The soul of Hamlet must be felt to have been—in its original essence and condition, before grief, shame, and terror arrived, to burden and distract it—intensely sensitive to the miseries that are in this world; to the fact that it is an evanescent pageant, passing, on a thin tissue, over what Shakespeare himself has greatly called "the blind cave of eternal night;" and to all the vague, strange influences, sometimes beautiful, sometimes terrible, that are wafted out of the great unknown. Booth's embodiment of Hamlet was so thoroughly saturated with this feeling that often it seemed to be more a spirit than a man.

The statement of those felicities indicates Booth's natural adaptability and qualification for the character. Nature made it in him "a property of easiness" to be poetic and spiritual, according to the mood in which Hamlet is depicted. Hence the ideal of Shakespeare was the more easily within his grasp, and he stood abundantly justified—as few other actors have ever been—in undertaking to present it. The spiritualised intellect, the masculine strength, the feminine softness, the over-imaginative reason, the lassitude of thought, the autumnal gloom, the lovable temperament, the piteous, tear-freighted humour, the princely grace of condition, the brooding melancholy, the philosophic mind, and the deep heart, which are commingled in the poet's conception, found their roots and springs in the being of the man. Booth seemed to live Hamlet rather than to act it. His ideal presented a man whose nature is everything lovable; who is placed upon a pinnacle of earthly greatness; who is afflicted with a grief that breaks his heart and a shock that disorders his mind; who is charged with a solemn and dreadful duty, to the fulfilment of which his will is inadequate; who sees so widely and understands so little the nature of things in the universe that his sense of moral responsibility is overwhelmed, and his power of action arrested; who thinks greatly, but to no purpose; who wanders darkly in the borderland between reason and madness, haunted now with sweet strains and majestic images of heaven, and now with terrific, uncertain shapes of hell; and who drifts aimlessly, on a sea of misery, into the oblivion of death. This man is a type of beings upon the earth to whom life is a dream, all its surroundings too vast and awful for endurance, all its facts sad, action impossible or fitful and fruitless, and of whom it can never be said that they are happy till the grass is growing on their graves. That type Booth displayed, with symmetry and grace of method, in an artistic form which was harmony itself. If to be true to Shakespeare, in that vast, complex, and difficult creation, and to interpret the truth with beautiful action, is to attain to greatness in the dramatic art, then surely Booth was a great actor.

Booth's method in the scenes with the Ghost would endure the severest examination, and in those sublime situations he fully deserved the tribute that Cibber pays to the Hamlet of Betterton. Those are the test scenes, and Booth left his spectators entirely satisfied with the acting of them.

If I were to pause upon special points in the execution,—which, since they illumine the actor's ideal and vindicate his genius, are representative and deeply significant,—I should indicate the subtlety with which, almost from the first, the sense of being haunted was conveyed to the imagination; the perfection with which the weird and awful atmosphere of the ghost-scenes was preserved, by the actor's transfiguration into tremulous suspense and horror; the human tenderness and heartbreaking pathos of the scene with Ophelia; the shrill, terrific cry and fate-like swiftness and fury that electrified the moment of the killing of Polonius; and the desolate calm of despairing surrender to bleak and cruel fate, with which Hamlet, as he stood beside the grave of Ophelia, was made so pitiable an object that no man with a heart in his bosom could see him without tears. Those were peaks of majesty in Booth's impersonation.

Thought is not compelled, in remembering Booth's Hamlet, to stop short with the statement that the thing was well done. It may go further than that, and rejoice in the conviction that the thing itself was right. There are in the nature of Hamlet—which is grace, sweetness, and grandeur corroded by grief and warped by incipient insanity—depths below depths of misery and self-conflict; and doubtless it was a sense of this that made Kemble say that an actor of the part is always finding something new in it; but Booth's ideal of Hamlet possessed the indescribable poetic element which fascinates, and the spiritual quality which made it the ready instrument of "airs from heaven or blasts from hell." The heart had been broken by grief. The mind had been disordered by a terrible shock. The soul,—so predisposed to brooding upon the hollowness of this fragile life and the darkness of futurity that already it counsels suicide before the great blow has fallen and the prince confronts his father's wandering ghost,—was full of vast, fantastic shapes, and was swayed by strange forces of an unknown world. The condition was princely, the manner exalted, the humour full of tears, the thought weighed down with a wide and wandering sense of the mysteries of the universe; and the power of action was completely benumbed. That is Shakespeare's Hamlet, and that nature Booth revealed;—in aspect, as sombre as the midnight sky; in spirit, as lovely as the midnight stars. That nature, furthermore, he portrayed brilliantly, knowing that sorrow, however powerful in the element of oppression, cannot fascinate. The Hamlet that is merely sorrowful, though he might arouse pity, would not inspire affection. It is the personality beneath the anguish that makes the anguish so stately, so awful, so majestic. By itself the infinite grief of Hamlet would overwhelm with the monotony of gray despair; but, since the nature that shines through it is invested with the mysterious and fascinating glamour of beauty in ruin, the grief becomes an active pathos, and the sufferer is loved as well as pitied. Nor does it detract from the loveliness of the ideal, that it is cursed with incipient and fitful insanity. Thought is shocked by the word and not the thing, when it rejects this needful attribute of a character otherwise eternally obscure. No one means that Hamlet needs a strait-jacket. The insanity is a cloud only, and only now and then present—as with many sane men whom thought, passion, and suffering urge at times into the border-land between reason and madness. That lurid gleam was first conspicuously evident in Booth's Hamlet after the first apparition of the Ghost, and again after the climax of the play scene; but, flowing out of an art-instinct too spontaneous always to have direct intention, it played intermittently along the whole line of the personation, and added weight and weirdness and pathos to remediless misery.

Booth's embodiment of Hamlet was a pleasure to the eye, a delight to the sense of artistic form and moving, a thrilling presence to the imagination, and a sadly significant emblem to the spiritual consciousness. Booth was never at any time inclined, when impersonating Hamlet, to employ those theatrical expedients that startle an audience and diffuse nervous excitement. Except at the delirious moment when the prince rushes upon the arras, and stabs through it the hidden spy whom he wildly hopes is the king, his acting was never diverted from that mood of intellectual concentration which essentially is the condition of Hamlet. In that moment his burst of frensied eagerness—half horror, and half-exultant delight— liberated the passion that smoulders beneath Hamlet's calm, and it was irresistibly enthralling. There were indications of the same passion, in the delivery of the soliloquy upon the artificial grief of the player, at the climax of the play scene, and in the half-lunatic rant over Ophelia's grave. But those variations only served to deepen the darkness of misery with which his embodiment of Hamlet was saturated, and the gloomy grandeur of the haunted atmosphere in which it was swathed.

Booth's ideal of Hamlet was a noble person overwhelmed

with a fatal grief, which he endures, for the most part with a patient sweetness that is deeply pathetic, but which sometimes drives him into delirium and must inevitably cause his death. In the expression of that ideal, which is true to Shakespeare, he never went as far as Shakespeare's text would warrant. He never allowed his votaries to see Hamlet as Ophelia saw him, in that hour of eloquent revelation when,—without artifice and in the unpremeditated candour of involuntary sincerity,—his ravaged and blighted figure stood before her, in all the pitiable disorder of self-abandoned sorrow. To show Hamlet in that way would be to show him exactly as he is in Shakespeare; but in a theatrical representation that expedient, while it might gratify the few, would certainly repel the many. Real grief is not attractive, and the grief of Hamlet is real; it is not simply a filial sorrow for the death of his beloved father; a mournful shame at his mother's hasty marriage with his uncle; an affliction of the haunted soul because it knows that his father's spirit is condemned to fast in fires and to walk the night. It is deeper still. It is an elemental misery, coexistent with his being; coincident with his conviction of the utter fatuity of this world and with his mental paralysis of comprehension,—awe-stricken and half insane,—in presence of the unfathomable mystery that environs man's spiritual life. Entirely and literally to embody the man whose nature is convulsed in that way would be to oppress an audience with what few persons understand, and most persons deem intolerable, the reality of sorrow. Hamlet upon the stage must be interesting, and, in a certain sense, he must be brilliant; and Booth always made him so. But that noble actor—so fine in his intuitions, so just in his methods—could not be otherwise than true to his artistic conscience. He embodied Hamlet not simply as the picturesque and interesting central figure in a story of intrigue, half amatory and half political, in an ancient royal court, but as the representative type of man at his highest point of development, vainly confronting the darkness and doubt that enshroud him in this pain-stricken, transitory mortal state, and—because his vision is too comprehensive, his heart too tender, and his will too weak for the circumstances of human life—going to his death at last, broken, defeated, baffled, a mystery among mysteries, a disastrous failure, but glorious through it all, and infinitely more precious, to those who even vaguely comprehend his drift, than the most successful man that ever was created.

Treating Hamlet in that spirit Booth was not content merely to invest him with symmetry of form, poetry of motion, statuesque grace of pose, and the exquisite beauty of musical elocution, and to blend those gracious attributes with dignity of mind and spontaneous, unerring refinement of temperament and manner. He went further, because he illumined the whole figure with a tremulous light of agonised vitality. That was the true ideal of Hamlet—in whose bosom burns the fire that is not quenched. Students of Shakespeare,—who are, of course, students of human life and of themselves, and who think that perhaps they are in this world for some higher purpose than the consumption of food and the display of raiment,—could think upon it, and gather strength from it. Booth's art, in the acting of Hamlet, was art applied to its highest purpose, and invested with dignity, power, and truth.

1893

WILLA CATHER

While still a student at the University of Nebraska, Willa Cather (1876–1947) was named dramatic critic for the *Nebraska State Journal* and later for the *Lincoln Courier*. When the impresario Gustave Frohman said that "Lincoln newspapers are noted for their honesty," Cather was on his mind. Her standards were high, for she expected artists to give their all to their art. "Genius means relentless labor and passionate excitement from the hour one is born until the hour one dies." She soon became known to actors as "that meatax young girl"; subscribers opened their papers with excitement to enjoy her frank, often tactless criticism, delivered with the authority and verve of a veteran. "A critic's first instincts are the best," declared Cather, "because they are the truest . . . the great object [is] to have a notice live, to have the glare of the footlights and the echo of the orchestra in it," to recreate it for the imagination.

After the Civil War, the expanding network of railroads enabled performers to bring their talents to even the remotest villages. Almost every town boasted an "opera house" that might play host to Shakespeare one week, comic opera the next, and living statuary after that. The division between highbrow and lowbrow was porous; it all counted as theatre. Cather holds a traveling "Tom show" that boasted "20 ponies, donkeys and burros" and "a pack of man-eating Siberian bloodhounds" to the same high standards as a production of a Shakespearean history. Cather's theatre criticism continued for five years after she moved to Pittsburgh in 1896, and her views are vividly expressed in her novels *The Song of the Lark*, based on the career of the operatic soprano Olive Fremstad, and *My Mortal Enemy* with its "Dead Poets' Society."

Uncle Tom's Cabin

THE Rusco & Swift "Uncle Tom's Cabin" company played that classic drama at the Lansing last night. All "Uncle Tom's Cabin"companies are bad, this being one of the worst. The companies who play the immortal production are usually made up of mongrel nondescript actors, a very sleepy and sometimes very pretty little girl, and a few hungry-looking curs that have become stage-struck and have left the ordinary walks of life, cultivated a tragic howl and seek for glory on the histrionic boards. These stage-struck dogs are peculiar creatures and are very much like all other actors. They are generally of plebeian extraction, as their color, in spite of all their paint and "make-up," always shows. On the stage they are very fierce and coura-geous, but behind the flies they whine about the manager with their tail between their legs and patiently submit to the ca-resses of the soubrette. They are vain in the extreme and will go without their bone to wear a silver collar. They are pitiably fond of praise and pitiably sensitive to censure. If the transmi-gration theory is true, then surely in their previous incarnation these dramatic dogs wore checked trousers and a red tie and diamonds and walked the Rialto.

Uncle Tom's Cabin is old, older than almost any other play, because it never had enough vitality in it to keep it young. In point of construction it is about the poorest melodrama on the American stage, and that is saying a good deal. From a literary point of view the play is like the book, exaggerated, over-drawn, abounding in facts but lacking in truth. The work of a woman who sat up under cold skies of the north and tried to write of one of the warmest, richest and most highly-colored civilizations the world has ever known; a Puritan blue-stocking who tried to blend the savage blood of the jungle and the ro-mance of Creole civilization. The play is like the whooping cough or the measles, an experience that must be gone through with some time, and it is least painful in extreme youth.

The Rusco & Swift company is made up of an Uncle Tom who suffers from obesity, who also doubled for George Harris; an Eliza with a painful nasal twang, who also doubled for Miss Ophelia; a very wishy-washy St. Clair, a little Eva who was really very pretty and natural, and a very disgusting Topsy who wore her dresses above her knees and who must have been reading Trilby, as her feet and legs were very insufficiently clothed by a thin coat of black paint. I never realized until last night why Mr. Du Maurier's novel was immoral or what evil influence it could have, but that Topsy opened every eye. It is said that after the appearance of Rose in "Robert Elsmere" all the young ladies in society at once began to play the violin. Now, if all the young ladies in society should begin to imitate Trilby's noted peculiarity in the matter of footwear, it would make matters awkward indeed. No, the shoe dealers cry out against the immorality of Trilby.

With these talented actors the play went along in the usual manner. Eliza crossed the river on floating ice to slow music, George Harris shot off a blank cartridge at the slave trader, Eva read Uncle Tom words of hope and comfort about the new Jerusalem out of a city directory, and promptly at 9:45 little Eva expired, and not being interested in funerals I departed.

1894

Antony and Cleopatra (1)

THE serpent of old Nile uncoiled at the Funke last night before a large and amused audience. While the text was considerably mutilated in places, still the general outline of the play was recognizably Shakespearean. The fortune telling scene was put first and after that a barge drew up and from it descended a large, limp, lachrymose "Kleo-paw-tra," with an Iowa accent, a St. Louis air and the robust physique of a West England farmer's wife. This ponderous personage descended from the barge and perching upon the back of a stuffed tiger somewhat moth-eaten she began gleefully coquetting with Mark Antony, recently of Rome, whom she occasionally called "Me Anthony," which showed that she had been reading "The Prisoner of Zenda."

Mark Antony, impersonated by Edward Collier, was the only piece of legitimate acting in the whole production. In spite of a decided tendency to continually declaim and fling the Shakespearean lines about like banners, he has the conventional intelligent conception of his part and that is something, nay, in this company it was much.

The Enobarbus of George Wessell was certainly as remote as

possible from that of Shakespeare. The real Enobarbus was a gentleman somewhat more shrewd than frank, wise in wine and women and wiser still in war, low of voice and smooth of tongue. Mr. Wessell shouted like a free silver advocate and that beautiful description of Cleopatra on the Cydnus, that paragraph that is almost as full of delicate poetry as Mercutio's Queen Mab speech, he mouthed as though he was shouting "Spartacus the Gladiator."

The gorgeous stage settings were certainly all that could be asked of a one-dollar attraction, but the crops must have failed in Egypt that year. During the battle of Actium the audience was treated to stereopticon views. It only needed a lecture. It's not every production of "Cleopatra" that's embellished by magic lantern slides. The bare-footed ballet was there, with both feet, but even it did not bring relief to the weary souls who longed for it.

And how was it with the rural, robust queen, the royal Kleopawtra? Miss Lewis walks like a milkmaid and moves like a housemaid, not a movement or gesture was dignified, much less regal. She draped and heaped her ample form about over chairs and couches to imitate oriental luxury. She slapped her messenger upon the back, she tickled Mark Antony under the chin. She fainted slouchily upon every possible pretext and upon every part of the stage. And it was no ordinary faint either, it was a regular landslide. When the messenger brings the tidings of Antony's marriage she treats him exactly as an irate housewife might treat a servant who had broken her best pickle dish. When she lavishes her affection upon Antony, she is only large and soft and spoony. To call her amorous would be madness, she was spoony, and it was large, 200 pounds, matronly spooniness.

Her death scene was done in the modern emotional drama ten, twenty and thirty-cent carnival style. She took a few tears from "Camille," a few from "Article 47," a few from "Credit Lorraine," a few from "As in a Looking Glass" and made a death scene. She sat down upon a cane bottom dining room chair, took her crown from a little sixteenth century oak table, sighed and wept and heaved her breast and then died from an imaginary serpent hidden in a ditch of lettuce after having worn most atrocious gowns and having drawn and quartered and mangled some of the greatest lines in all the poetry of the world. *Requiescat in pace.* Was ever Shakespeare in this fashion played?

1895

Antony and Cleopatra (2)

When Homer wished for a tongue of iron and a throat of brass that he might tell the ships and the number of them that came from distant Argos, he should have saved time and eloquence and merely wished to be an advance man. Advance men can talk till the town clock stops, till the cows come home, till the grass on your grave grows green. And of all advance men I never met no one who could out-talk Mr. Lawrence Marston, the husband and playwright of Lillian Lewis. A good share of his conversation Mr. Marston devoted to Cleopatra, and to clearing Cleopatra's record, which latter was kind and considerate of him. Mr. Marston is very sure that Antony and Cleopatra were married. I think he even has theories as to who performed the ceremony and knows who were the bridesmaids and best men. "Of course she was married to Antony," quoth he. "Why, just think how that affair would have hurt her social standing in Egypt if she had not been!" Truly. Then Mr. Marston thinks that Cleopatra was married to Julius Cæsar also, despite the fact that Julius was no longer young and had a wife in Rome. When humbly asked as to whether this much married queen were Pompey's wife also, Mr. Marston hedged and said he thought that little story about Pompey and the languid lily of the Nile was all gossip. And the numerous slave stories he is sure were all slander. He thinks, too, that Cleopatra was very domestic, that she used to butter Antony's toast and patch his tunic and darn the stockings of the numerous little Antonys.

I feel that I am not at all able to do justice to Lillian Lewis as the Egyptian lotus bud. I shall see her in my dreams, that coy, kittenish matron, bunched up on a moth-eaten tiger stroking Mark Antony's double chin. I never saw a less regal figure and carriage. I have seen waiters in restaurants who were ten times more queenly. Her movements were exactly like those of the women who give you Turkish baths in Chicago. And ah! the giddy manner in which she buckled on his armor and the fulsome way in which she gurgled,

> but, since my lord
> Is Antony again, I will be Cleopatra.

I suppose that is what the learned Malaprop of the *Evening News* would call "cloyish abandon." And the queer little motions she made when she put that imaginary snake in her bosom, it was so suggestive of fleas. And her resounding faint when she saw a vision of Mark Antony in his cunning little pink wedding tunic being married to *Octavia*.

There was just one good thing about Lillian Lewis' *Cleopatra*, and that was that, as hunger makes one dream of banquets, it recalled the only Cleopatra on earth worth the seeing, the royal Egyptian of Sarah Bernhardt. I could see it all again, that royal creature with the face of flame, every inch a queen and always a woman. The bewildering reality of that first scene with *Mark Antony* in which her caresses are few, fitful, unexpected, light as air and hot as fire. The regal queenliness with which she sends him from her back to Rome, when she touches his sword with her lips and invokes the god of victory, and one feels that in her veins there flows the blood of a hundred centuries of kings. And the restlessness of her when he is gone. How she beats the heated pillows with feverish impatience and strains her eyes out across the glowing desert and the sleepy Nile. The madness of her fury when the messenger delivers his news, how her face became famished and hungry and her eyes burned like a tiger's and her very flesh seemed to cleave to her bones. How, but bah! it is not possible to describe it. It was like the lightning which flashes and terrifies and is gone. Through it all she keeps doing little things that you do not expect to see on the stage, things that make you feel within yourself how she loves and how she hates. She gives you those moments of absolute reality of experience, of positive knowledge that are the test of all great art. The thing itself is in her, the absolute quality that all books write of, all songs sing of, all men dream of, that only one in hundreds ever knows or realizes. It leaps up and strikes you between the eyes, makes you hold your breath and tremble. And this reminds me of what Plutarch says, that Cleopatra's chiefest charm was not in her beautiful face, nor her keen wit, nor her wealth of wisdom, but "in the immensity of what she had to give," in her versatility, her intensity, her sensitiveness to every emotion, her whole luxuriant personality.

I wish it had been Sardou's Cleopatra that Miss Lewis played, for, compared to Shakespeare's it is cheap and tawdry, it has less beauty to mar, less dignity to lose. There have been innumerable attempts to dramatize that greatest love story of the ages. They began with Virgil, who tried to do it in that dramatic fourth book of the Aeneid in the person of the *infelix Dido*. Since then poets and dramatists and novelists galore have struggled with it. But among them all the great William is the only man who has made a possible character of the Egyptian queen. Some wise men say, indeed, that he had a living model for it, and that his Cleopatra "with Phœbus' amorous pinches black and wrinkled deep in time" was none other than the Dark Lady of the sonnets. The more one reads the sonnets the more probable that seems, and yet I think he was great enough to have done it without a model. He had no model for Caesar or Brutus or Antony and certainly none for Juliet. His mind worked independently of any romances or tragedies in his own life. It, in itself, had loved all loves, suffered all sorrow, known all tragedies. I sometimes think that if there is anything in the theory of re-incarnation he must have been them all, Troilus, Antony, Romeo, Hamlet. No personal experience in fog-clouded England, no love in dusky Elizabethan London could have brought to him the sun and langor of the south, the beauty and luxury and abundant life of the lotus land. It was amusing even while it was painful to see the childish way in which they played with his great purposes and mangled his great art the other night. "Father, forgive them, for they knew not what they did." The gleeful, irresponsible way in which they went through that first scene where Antony is down in Egypt kissing away kingdoms and provinces. But Cleopatra was one woman of the ages, one unique product of the centuries, she had more than mortal resources and the love she inspired was almost more than mortal. No ordinary woman could be expected to enact it. As Antony said, if she would set a limit to the love she made men feel she "must needs find out new heaven, new earth." Well, she found them. She was more than a woman, she was a realization of things dreamed. As that shrewd philosopher, Enobarbus, said to Antony when a repentant mood was on him,

> "O, sir, you had then left unseen
> A wonderful piece of work,
> Which not to have been blest withal
> Would have discredited your travel"

To know Cleopatra was then a sort of finishing touch to a great man's education. If a man was to be traveled and experienced he must see her, as today, he must see the pyramids. All the greatest Romans took post graduate work in Egypt.

The finest drinking scene in literature was cut out the other night, while a dozen trivial scenes were left in. The talk about the serpents of Egypt which takes place between *Lepidus* and *Antony* Miss Lewis and her versatile husband saw fit to have spoken by Lepidus and Enobarbus. Now the only purpose of that scene is to recall to Antony Egypt and that one queen of serpents, recall them until he drinks and drinks again, till his foot steps are unsteady and he finally goes out flushed and reeling, leaning on the steady arm of Caesar, the beginning to the end. They failed utterly to bring out the meaning of that scene where the fight is declared by sea, where the gods have first made mad he whom they would destroy and Antony cries, "By sea, by sea!"

I wonder if any other poet could have given to Antony the dignity and majesty that Shakespeare gives him in defeat. After Actium, when Antony meets the queen he says,

> O, whither hast thou led me, Egypt?
> . . . .
> Thy full supremacy thou knewest,
> And that thy beck might from the bidding of the Gods
> Command me.

It is said with a simplicity and pathos that dignify even its weakness. And O, the greatness of him after the last defeat. Well does Enobarbus call him an old lion dying. When they tell him that the queen is dead, all the simple manliness in him comes out. "The long day's task is done, and we must sleep." When the ruse is confessed he is not angry, he is beyond all that now. The key note of the whole tragedy, the grand motif rounds once again. He does what he has always done. He has always gone back to her, after every wrong, after every treachery. He has left kingdoms and principalities to go to her, thrown away half the world to seek her, and now of his old captain, he asks one last favor, that they carry him to her now that he cannot go himself anymore, and he goes, for the last time.

That last meeting, that awful scene in which Antony, bleeding and dying, is dragged up to the sides of the monument, Miss Lewis omits. Possibly because it is almost impossible to represent it on the stage, possibly because the play is long and something must be cut to give time to the barefoot ballet. At any rate to cut it is to divest the play of half its greatness. For the "moral" of the play, if there be one, is in the last line that Antony speaks before the mists cloud over him and he begins to wander back to the old days of empire and delight.

> One word, sweet queen:
> Of Caesar seek your honor, with your safety.

That he should have lived for her and died for her, lost the world for her and yet should have had to say that at the end! There is a tragedy for you, in its darkest melancholy. The tragedy of all such love and such relations, of everything on earth that hides shame at its heart, that is without honor and absolute respect. All the hundreds of French novels that have been written upon the *union libre* have told us nothing new about it after that. That one line has in it all the doubt and dark tragedy of the whole thing. We Anglo-Saxons have no need of a "Sapho" or of the numerous and monotonous works of M. Paul Bourget. That story has all been written for us once as it never can be again, by a master whose like no one world can bear twice, whose ashes one planet can carry but once in its bosom.

1895

HUTCHINS HAPGOOD

In his lifetime, the radical Hutchins Hapgood (1869–1944) was over-shadowed by his more respectable brother, the dramatic critic and crusading editor Norman Hapgood and Norman's wife, Elizabeth Reynolds, the authorized translator of Stanislavsky's works. He dwelt as a bohemian on the fringes of the Greenwich Village and the Provincetown Players circles. An avowed follower of Nietzsche and the anarchist Max Stirner, Hapgood preached free love and practiced what he preached. Most of Hapgood's books championing the underdog—*Autobiography of a Thief, Story of a Lover, Anarchist Woman, The Spirit of Labor*—are what he called "assisted biography," modeled on Defoe's *Moll Flanders.* "I consider the general character of my work an interpretation of the developing labor, sociological, philosophical and aesthetic movements of the country." *The Spirit of the Ghetto,* which first appeared as a series of articles in *Atlantic Monthly* in 1901, illustrated by the sculptor Jacob Epstein, sought to demystify the East European Jewish immigrants of New York's Lower East Side for the rest of America. Hapgood's sympathetic treatment is that of an outsider, a sound position from which to interpret the arcana of proletarian Yiddish culture to readers who shared his own genteel WASP background. If his book lacks the reforming zeal of Jacob Riis or Jane Addams, it compensates with psychological acumen and a novelist's eye for colorful detail.

FROM

The Spirit of the Ghetto

THEATRES, ACTORS AND AUDIENCE

In the three Yiddish theatres on the Bowery is expressed the world of the Ghetto—that New York City of Russian Jews, large, complex, with a full life and civilization. In the midst of the frivolous Bowery, devoted to tinsel variety shows, "dive" music-halls, fake museums, trivial amusement booths of all sorts, cheap lodging-houses, ten-cent shops and Irish-American tough saloons, the theatres of the chosen people alone present the serious as well as the trivial interests of an entire community. Into these three buildings crowd the Jews of all the Ghetto classes—the sweat-shop woman with her baby, the day-laborer, the small Hester Street shopkeeper, the Russian-Jewish anarchist and socialist, the Ghetto rabbi and scholar, the poet, the journalist. The poor and ignorant are in the great majority, but the learned, the intellectual and the progressive are also represented, and here, as elsewhere, exert a more than numerically proportionate influence on the character of the theatrical productions, which, nevertheless, remain essentially popular. The socialists and the literati create the demand that forces into the mass of vaudeville, light opera, historical and melodramatic plays a more serious art element, a simple tran-script from life or the theatric presentation of a Ghetto prob-lem. But this more serious element is so saturated with the simple manners, humor and pathos of the life of the poor Jew, that it is seldom above the heartfelt understanding of the crowd.

The audiences vary in character from night to night rather more than in an up-town theatre. On the evenings of the first four week-days the theatre is let to a guild or club, many hun-dred of which exist among the working people of the east side. Many are labor organizations representing the different trades, many are purely social, and others are in the nature of secret societies. Some of these clubs are formed on the basis of a common home in Russia. The people, for instance, who came from Vilna, a city in the old country, have organized a Vilna Club in the Ghetto. Then, too, the anarchists have a society; there are many socialistic orders; the newspapers of the Ghetto have their constituency, which sometimes hires the theatre. Two or three hundred dollars is paid to the theatre by the guild, which then sells the tickets among the faithful for a good price. Every member of the society is forced to buy, whether he wants to see the play or not, and the money made over and above the expenses of hiring the theatre is for the benefit of the guild. These performances are therefore called "benefits." The widespread existence of such a custom is a striking indication of the growing sense of corporate interests among the laboring classes of the Jewish east side. It is an ex-pression of the socialistic spirit which is marked everywhere in the Ghetto.

On Friday, Saturday and Sunday nights the theatre is not let, for these are the Jewish holidays, and the house is always completely sold out, altho prices range from twenty-five cents to a dollar. Friday night is, properly speaking, the gala occasion of the week. That is the legitimate Jewish holiday, the night before the Sabbath. Orthodox Jews, as well as others, may then amuse themselves. Saturday, altho the day of worship, is also of holiday character in the Ghetto. This is due to the Christian influences, to which the Jews are more and more sensitive. Through economic necessity Jewish workingmen are compelled to work on Saturday, and, like other workingmen, look upon Saturday night as a holiday, in spite of the frown of the orthodox. Into Sunday, too, they extend their freedom, and so in the Ghetto there are now three popularly recognized nights on which to go with all the world to the theatre.

On those nights the theatre presents a peculiarly picturesque sight. Poor workingmen and women with their babies of all ages fill the theatre. Great enthusiasm is manifested, sincere laughter and tears accompany the sincere acting on the stage. Pedlars of soda-water, candy, of fantastic gewgaws of many kinds, mix freely with the audience between the acts. Conversation during the play is received with strenuous hisses, but the falling of the curtain is the signal for groups of friends to get together and gossip about the play or the affairs of the week. Introductions are not necessary, and the Yiddish community can then be seen and approached with great freedom. On the stage curtain are advertisements of the wares of Hester Street or portraits of the "star" actors. On the programmes and circulars distributed in the audience are sometimes amusing announcements of coming attractions or lyric praise of the "stars." Poetry is not infrequent, an example of which, literally translated, is:

> Labor, ye stars, as ye will,
> Ye cannot equal the artist;
> In the garden of art ye shall not flourish;
> Ye can never achieve his fame.
> Can you play *Hamlet* like him?
> The *Wild King*, or the *Huguenots?*
> Are you gifted with feeling

So much as to imitate him like a shadow?
Your fame rests on the pen;
On the show-cards your flight is high;
But on the stage every one can see
How your greatness turns to ashes,
Thomashevsky! Artist great!
No praise is good enough for you;
Every one remains your ardent friend.
Of all the stars you remain the king.
You seek no tricks, no false quibbles;
One sees Truth itself playing.
Your appearance is godly to us;
Every movement is full of grace;
Pleasing is your every gesture;
Sugar-sweet your every turn;
You remain the King of the Stage;
Everything falls to your feet.

On the playboards outside the theatre, containing usually
the portrait of a star, are also lyric and enthusiastic announcements. Thus, on the return of the great Adler, who had been
ill, it was announced on the boards that "the splendid eagle
has spread his wings again."

The Yiddish actors, as may be inferred from the verses
quoted, take themselves with peculiar seriousness, justified by
the enthusiasm, almost worship, with which they are regarded
by the people. Many a poor Jew, man or girl, who makes no
more than $10 a week in the sweat-shop, will spend $5 of it on
the theatre, which is practically the only amusement of the
Ghetto Jew. He has not the loafing and sporting instincts of
the poor Christian, and spends his money for the theatre
rather than for drink. It is not only to see the play that the
poor Jew goes to the theatre. It is to see his friends and the actors. With these latter he, and more frequently she, try in every
way to make acquaintance, but commonly are compelled to
adore at a distance. They love the songs that are heard on the
stage, and for these the demand is so great that a certain bookshop on the east side makes a specialty of publishing them.

The actor responds to this popular enthusiasm with sovereign contempt. He struts about in the cafés on Canal and

Grand Streets, conscious of his greatness. He refers to the crowd as "Moses" with superior condescension or humorous vituperation. Like thieves, the actors have a jargon of their own, which is esoteric and jealously guarded. Their pride gave rise a year or two ago to an amusing strike at the People's Theatre. The actors of the three Yiddish companies in New York are normally paid on the share rather than the salary system. In the case of the company now at the People's Theatre, this system proved very profitable. The star actors, Jacob Adler and Boris Thomashevsky, and their wives, who are actresses—Mrs. Adler being the heavy realistic tragedienne and Mrs. Thomashevsky the star soubrette—have probably received on an average during that time as much as $125 a week for each couple. But they, with Mr. Edelstein, the business man, are lessees of the theatre, run the risk and pay the expenses, which are not small. The rent of the theatre is $20,000 a year, and the weekly expenses, besides, amount to about $1,100. The subordinate actors, who risk nothing, since they do not share the expenses, have made amounts during this favorable period ranging from $14 a week on the average for the poorest actors to $75 for those just beneath the "stars." But, in spite of what is exceedingly good pay in the Bowery, the actors of this theatre formed a union, and struck for wages instead of shares. This however, was only an incidental feature. The real cause was that the management of the theatre, with the energetic Thomashevsky at the head, insisted that the actors should be prompt at rehearsals, and if they were not, indulged in unseemly epithets. The actors' pride was aroused, and the union was formed to insure their ease and dignity and to protect them from harsh words. The management imported actors from Chicago. Several of the actors here stood by their employers, notably Miss Weinblatt, a popular young ingénue, who, on account of her great memory is called the "Yiddish Encyclopedia," and Miss Gudinski, an actress of commanding presence. Miss Weinblatt forced her father, once an actor, now a farmer, into the service of the management. But the actors easily triumphed. Misses Gudinski and Weinblatt were forced to join the union, Mr. Weinblatt returned to his farm, the "scabs" were packed off to Philadelphia, and the wages system introduced. A delegation was sent to Philadelphia to throw cabbages at the new actors, who appeared in the Yiddish performances in that city. The triumphant actors now receive on the average probably $10 to $15 a week less than under the old system. Mr. Conrad, who began the disaffection, receives a salary of $29 a week, fully $10 less than he received for months before the strike. But the dignity of the Yiddish actor is now placed beyond assault. As one of them recently said: "We shall no longer be spat upon nor called 'dog.'"

The Yiddish actor is so supreme that until recently a regular system of hazing playwrights was in vogue. Joseph Latteiner and Professor M. Horowitz were long recognized as the only legitimate Ghetto playwrights. When a new writer came to the theatre with a manuscript, various were the pranks the actors would play. They would induce him to try, one after another, all the costumes in the house, in order to help him conceive the characters; or they would make him spout the play from the middle of the stage, they themselves retiring to the gallery to "see how it sounded." In the midst of his exertions they would slip away, and he would find himself shouting to the empty boards. Or, in the midst of a mock rehearsal, some actor would shout, "He is coming, the great Professor Horowitz, and he will eat you"; and they would rush from the theatre with the panic-stricken playwright following close at their heels.

The supremacy of the Yiddish actor has, however, its humorous limitations. The orthodox Jews who go to the theatre on Friday night, the beginning of Sabbath, are commonly somewhat ashamed of themselves and try to quiet their consciences by a vociferous condemnation of the actions on the stage. The actor, who through the exigencies of his rôle, is compelled to appear on Friday night with a cigar in his mouth, is frequently greeted with hisses and strenuous cries of "Shame, shame, smoke on the Sabbath!" from the proletarian hypocrites in the gallery.

The plays at these theatres vary in a general way with the varying audiences of which I have spoken above. The thinking socialists naturally select a less violent play than the comparatively illogical anarchists. Societies of relatively conservative Jews desire a historical play in which the religious Hebrew in relation to the persecuting Christian is put in pathetic and melodramatic situations. There are a very large number of "culture" pieces produced, which, roughly speaking, are plays in which the difference between the Jew of one generation and the next is dramatically portrayed. The pathos or tragedy involved in differences of faith and "point of view" between the old rabbi and his more enlightened children is expressed in many historical plays of the general character of *Uriel Acosta*, tho in less lasting form. Such plays, however, are called "historical plunder" by that very up-to-date element of the intellectual Ghetto which is dominated by the Russian spirit of realism. It is the demand of these fierce realists that of late years has produced a supply of theatrical productions attempting to present a faithful picture of the actual conditions of life. Permeating all these kinds of plays is the amusement instinct pure and simple. For the benefit of the crowd of ignorant people grotesque humor, popular songs, vaudeville tricks, are inserted everywhere.

Of these plays the realistic are of the most value, for they often give the actual Ghetto life with surprising strength and fidelity. The past three years have been their great seasons, and have developed a large crop of new playwrights, mainly journalists who write miscellaneous articles for the east side newspapers. Jacob Gordin, of whom we shall have frequent occasion to speak, has been writing plays for several years, and was the first realistic playwright; he remains the strongest and most prominent in this kind of play. Professor Horowitz, who is now the lessee of the Windsor Theatre, situated on the Bowery, between Grand and Canal Streets, represents, along with Joseph Latteiner, the conservative and traditional aspects of the stage. He is an interesting man, fifty-six years of age, and has been connected with the Yiddish stage practically since its origin. His father was a teacher in a Hebrew school, and he himself is a man of uncommon learning. He has made a great study of the stage, has written one hundred and sixty-seven plays, and claims to be an authority on *dramaturgie*. Latteiner is equally productive, but few of their plays are anything more than Yiddish adaptations of old operas and melodramas in other languages. Long runs are impossible on the Yiddish stage and consequently the playwrights produce many plays and are not very scrupulous in their methods. The absence of dramatic criticism and the ignorance of the audience enable them to "crib" with impunity. As one of the actors said, Latteiner and Horowitz and their class took their first plays from some foreign source and since then have been repeating themselves. The actor said that when he is cast in a Latteiner play he does not need to learn his part. He needs only to understand the general situation; the character and the words he already knows from having appeared in many other Latteiner plays.

The professor, nevertheless, naturally regards himself and Latteiner as the "real" Yiddish playwrights. For many years after the first bands of actors reached the New York Ghetto these two men held undisputed sway. Latteiner leaned to "romantic," Horowitz to "culture," plays, and both used material which was mainly historical. The professor regards that as the bright period of the Ghetto stage. Since then there has been, in his opinion, a decadence which began with the translation of the classics into Yiddish. *Hamlet*, *Othello*, *King Lear*, and plays of Schiller, were put upon the stage and are still being performed. Sometimes they are almost literally translated, sometimes adapted until they are realistic representations of Jewish life. Gordin's *Yiddish King Lear*, for instance, represents Shakespeare's idea only in the most general way, and weaves about it a sordid story of Jewish character and life. Of *Hamlet* there are two versions, one adapted, in which Shakespeare's idea is reduced to a ludicrous shadow, the interest lying entirely in the presentation of Jewish customs.

The first act of the Yiddish version represents the wedding feast of Hamlet's mother and uncle. In the Yiddish play the uncle is a rabbi in a small village in Russia. He did not poison Hamlet's father but broke the latter's heart by wooing and winning his queen. Hamlet is off somewhere getting educated as a rabbi. While he is gone his father dies. Six weeks afterwards the son returns in the midst of the wedding feast, and turns the feast into a funeral. Scenes of rant follow between mother and son, Ophelia and Hamlet, interspersed with jokes and sneers at the sect of rabbis who think they communicate with the angels. The wicked rabbi conspires against Hamlet, trying to make him out a nihilist. The plot is discovered and the wicked rabbi is sent to Siberia. The last act is the graveyard scene. It is snowing violently. The grave is near a huge windmill. Ophelia is brought in on the bier. Hamlet

Yiddish Playwrights Discussing the Drama

mourns by her side and is married, according to the Jewish custom, to the dead woman. Then he dies of a broken heart. The other version is almost a literal translation. To these translations of the classics, Professor Horowitz objects on the ground that the ignorant Yiddish public cannot understand them, because what learning they have is limited to distinctively Yiddish subjects and traditions.

Another important step in what the professor calls the degeneration of the stage was the introduction a few years ago of the American "pistol" play—meaning the fierce melodrama which has been for so long a characteristic of the English plays produced on the Bowery.

But what has contributed more than anything else to what the good man calls the present deplorable condition of the theatre was the advent of realism. "It was then," said the professor one day with calm indignation, "that the genuine Yiddish play was persecuted. Young writers came from Russia and swamped the Ghetto with scurrilous attacks on me and Latteiner. No number of the newspaper appeared that did not contain a scathing criticism. They did not object to the actors, who in reality were very bad, but it was the play they aimed at. These writers knew nothing about *dramaturgie*, but their heads were filled with senseless realism. Anything historical and distinctively Yiddish they thought bad. For a long time Latteiner and I were able to keep their realistic plays off the boards, but for the last few years there has been an open field for everybody. The result is that horrors under the mask of realism have been put upon the stage. This year is the worst of all —characters butchered on the stage, the coarsest language, the most revolting situations, without ideas, with no real material. It cannot last, however. Latteiner and I continue with our real Yiddish plays, and we shall yet regain entire possession of the field."

At least this much may fairly be conceded to Professor Horowitz—that the realistic writers in what is in reality an excellent attempt often go to excess, and are often unskilful as far as stage construction is concerned. In the reaction from plays with "pleasant" endings, they tend to prefer equally unreal "unpleasant" endings, "onion" plays, as the opponents of the realists call them. They, however, have written a number of plays which are distinctively of the New York Ghetto, and which attempt an unsentimental presentation of truth. A rather extended description of these plays is given in the next section. Professor Horowitz's plays, on the contrary, are largely based upon the sentimental representation of inexact Jewish history. They herald the glory and wrongs of the Hebrew people, and are badly constructed melodramas of conventional character. Another class of plays written by Professor Horowitz, and which have occasionally great but temporary prosperity, are what he calls *Zeitstucke*. Some American newspaper sensation is rapidly dramatized and put hot on the boards, such as *Marie Barberi*, *Dr. Buchanan* and *Dr. Harris*.

The three theatres—the People's, the Windsor and the Thalia, which is on the Bowery opposite the Windsor—are in a general way very similar in the character of the plays produced, in the standard of acting and in the character of the audience. There are, however, some minor differences. The People's is the "swellest" and probably the least characteristic of the three. It panders to the "uptown" element of the Ghetto, to the downtown tradesman who is beginning to climb a little. The baleful influence in art of the *nouveaux riches* has at this house its Ghetto expression. There is a tendency there to imitate the showy qualities of the Broadway theatres—melodrama, farce, scenery, etc. No babies are admitted, and the house is exceedingly clean in comparison with the theatres farther down the Bowery. Three years ago this company were at the Windsor Theatre, and made so much money that they hired the People's, that old home of Irish-American melodrama, and this atmosphere seems slightly to have affected the Yiddish productions. Magnificent performances quite out of the line of the best Ghetto drama have been attempted, notably Yiddish dramatizations of successful up-town productions. Hauptman's *Versunkene Glocke*, *Sapho*, *Quo Vadis*, and other popular Broadway plays in flimsy adaptations were tried with little success, as the Yiddish audiences hardly felt themselves at home in these unfamiliar scenes and settings.

The best trained of the three companies is at present that of the Thalia Theatre. Here many excellent realistic plays are given. Of late years, the great playwright of the colony, Jacob Gordin, has written mainly for this theatre. There, too, is the best of the younger actresses, Mrs. Bertha Kalisch. She is the prettiest woman on the Ghetto stage and was at one time the leading lady of the Imperial Theatre at Bucharest. She takes the leading woman parts in plays like *Fedora*, *Magda* and *The Jewish Zaza*. The principal actor at this theatre is David Kessler, who is one of the best of the Ghetto actors in realistic parts, and one of the worst when cast, as he often is, as the romantic lover. The actor of most prominence among the younger men is Mr. Moshkovitch, who hopes to be a "star" and one of the management. When the union was formed he was in a quandary. Should he join or should he not? He feared it might be a bad precedent, which the actors would use against him when he became a star. And yet he did not want to get them down on him. So before he joined he entered solemn protests at all the cafés on Canal Street. The strike, he maintained, was unnecessary. The actors were well paid and well treated. Discipline should be maintained. But he would join because of his universal sympathy with actors and with the poor—as a matter of sentiment merely, against his better judgment.

The company at the Windsor is the weakest, so far as acting is concerned, of the three. Very few "realistic" plays are given there, for Professor Horowitz is the lessee, and he prefers the historical Jewish opera and "culture" plays. Besides, the company is not strong enough to undertake successfully many new productions, altho it includes some good actors. Here Mrs. Prager vies as a prima-donna with Mrs. Karb of the People's and Mrs. Kalisch of the Thalia. Professor Horowitz thinks she is far better than the other two. As he puts it, there are two and a half prima-donnas in the Ghetto—at the Windsor Theatre there is a complete one, leaving one and a half between the People's and the Thalia. Jacob Adler of the People's, the professor thinks, is no actor, only a remarkable caricaturist. As Adler is the most noteworthy representative of the realistic actors of the Ghetto, the professor's opinion shows what the traditional Yiddish playwright thinks of realism. The strong realistic playwright, Jacob Gordin, the professor admits, has a "biting" dialogue, and "unconsciously writes good cultural plays which he calls realistic, but his realistic plays, properly speaking, are bad caricatures of life."

The managers and actors of the three theatres criticise one another indeed with charming directness, and they all have their followers in the Ghetto and their special cafés on Grand or Canal Streets, where their particular prejudices are sympathetically expressed. The actors and lessees of the People's are proud of their fine theatre, proud that no babies are brought there. There is a great dispute between the supporters of this theatre and those of the Thalia as to which is the stronger company and which produces the most realistic plays. The manager of the Thalia maintains that the People's is sensational, and that his theatre alone represents true realism; while the supporter of the People's points scornfully to the large number of operas produced at the Thalia. They both unite in condemning the Windsor, Professor Horowitz's theatre, as producing no new plays and as hopelessly behind the times, "full of historical plunder." An episode in *The Ragpicker of Paris*, played at the Windsor when the present People's company were there, amusingly illustrates the jealousy which exists between the companies. An old beggar is picking over a heap of moth-eaten, coverless books, some of which he keeps and some rejects. He comes across two versions of a play, *The Two Vagrants*, one of which was used at the Thalia and the other at the Windsor. The version used at the Windsor receives the beggar's commendation, and the other is thrown in a contemptuous manner into a dust-heap.

1902

ROLLIN LYNDE HARTT

A whole library could be made up of sermons, tracts, and similar clerical denunciations of the stage in America. By the turn of the century, some religious leaders were taking a different tack. In his anonymous *Confessions of a Clergyman* (1915), Rollin Lynde Hartt (1869–1946) says of Jesus, "He softened the rigors of Rabbinism, and I think He is not displeased when we soften the rigors of Puritanism." Hartt, son of a prominent zoologist, a graduate of Williams College and the Andover Theological Seminar, was influenced by the YMCA movement. His time as a Congregational minister made him a firm defender of Christian "modernism" against fundamentalism. As a contributor to *Atlantic Monthly* and a staff columnist for the Boston *Transcript*, he wrote with understanding about Mormons, mountain folk, "the new Negro," and the "Scopes Monkey Trial." His progressive defense of the Jews caused him to be attacked by Henry Ford in Ford's ferociously anti-Semitic paper *The Dearborn Independent*. *The People at Play* (1909), which *The New York Times* called "a valuable and entertaining work of sociology," was intended to survey the popular amusements of the working-class and justify them to the white-collar public that looked down its nose at them. Even novelists such as Frank Norris in *McTeague* and Stephen Crane in *Maggie: A Girl of the Street* had portrayed vaudeville as a degrading and sensually arousing diversion. Like an experienced safari leader, Hartt led his readers through the steamy undergrowth of burlesque houses, amusement parks, dime museums, nickelodeons, dance halls, baseball diamonds, and, in the chapter included here, popular melodrama, pointing out the occasional danger, but more often lingering over the benefits to the proletariat of its new-found leisure.

Melodrama

At the Grand—temple of Melodrama—"the villain still pursues her." From this you infer that he has been at it for a somewhat protracted period, as is only too true. Curse him!—he has hounded that angelic creature for more than two centuries. He began it in France, when *les mélodrames* introduced the "brigand chieftain, stained with all the vices" pursuing an "innocent heroine endowed with all the virtues"; while from the *poulailler* (which is French for "chicken-roost") there descended, I doubt not, the gallery-god's cries of "Cheese it!" and "Sick 'em!" And in those days, even as now, all ended sweetly. "Saved, mon Dieu!"

But why the term "melodrama"? Rinuccini, who invented it, applied it to the opera. Later, the Germans used it to denote plays in which instrumental accompaniment to spoken lines heightened the thrill. The French borrowed it from the Germans because the new *tragédie du peuple* had orchestral interludes and a ballet. We retain it, lax Grecians that we are, and may defend the practice by adducing the "chills-and-fever music" that rages *molto tremoloso* while Sam, the assistant villain, says boldly to Sir Lionel Crowninshield, "I'll lie for you, I'll steal for you, I'll fight for you, but I'll be damned if I'll kill that beautiful little girl for you!"

Now, I take it that, when any artistic genre has persisted for two hundred years, it deserves your contemplation. In this case, happily, you can't altogether escape. The monster besieges your very porch, flinging upon it a prospectus intended for the housemaids but appealing irresistibly to their employer's sense of fun. One such prospectus I have by me now. It affords a synopsis of that solemn and awful melodrama, "Red-Handed Bill, the Hair-Lifter of the Far South-West." Read here the synopsis, and tremble:—

ACT I. A Mountain Pass in the Rockies. In Pursuit. Kate saved by the Cattle King. The Assault of Red-Handed Bill and his Brazen Bandits. "Avaunt! This lady is under my protection."

ACT II. Golden Gulch and Exterior of the Bucket-of-Blood Saloon. The Rustic Lover. Bob accused of Horse-stealing. The Struggle and Capture of the Cattle King. "Coward, I'll do for you yet!"

ACT III. A Mountain Gorge. The Captives. Preparing for Death. The Equine Friend to the Rescue of his Master. "Saved!"

ACT IV, *Scene 1*. Don Pedro's Ranch. Red-Handed Bill's Visit. The Attack. *Scene 2*. Bob and the Irishman. "An eye for an eye." *Scene 3*. Interior of the Bucket-of-Blood Saloon. Playing for High Stakes. "Come and take them if you dare!"

ACT V, *Scene 1*. Interior of Don Pedro's Ranch. Red-Handed

Bill and Barney. *Scene 2*. Heart of the Rockies. The Marriage Ceremony. Terrific Knife-fight on Horseback between Red-Handed Bill and Nebraska Jim. "At last!"

ACT VI. Parlor in Don Pedro's Ranch. The Threat. Timely Arrival of the Cattle King. Carlotta's Dying Confession. Bob and Kate happy.

And, as if this were not enough, the promoter of melodramas declares that "the breakage of costly bric-a-brac during the fight in the Bucket-of-Blood Saloon makes a weekly expense equal to the entire salary list of some companies."

Charming, is it not? Equally charming, and not less insistent, are the gaudy lithographic "eight-sheets" that assail your eye from a hundred bill-boards, foretelling hair's-breadth 'scapes, miraculous rescues, and scenes that freeze the blood. Sometimes the producer designs the lithographs first and orders up "script" to match. For a docile crew are his dramatists. They have to be. Early in life they learn submissiveness. The very laws of their craft forbid originality, since blood-and-thunder, like architecture, adheres of necessity to established principles. Attempt variation, and you cease to please. In fact, the following clever jingle by Mr. Franklin P. Adams might almost have been written in French during the earliest days of melodrama:—

> "If you want a receipt for a melodramatical,
>   Thrillingly thundery popular show,
> Take an old father, unyielding, emphatical,
>   Driving his daughter out into the snow;
> The love of a hero, courageous and Hacketty;
>   Hate of a villain in evening clothes;
> Comic relief that is Irish and racketty;
>   Schemes of a villainess muttering oaths;
> The bank and the safe and the will and the forgery—
>   All of them built on traditional norms—
> Villainess dark and Lucrezia Borgery
>   Helping the villain until she reforms;
> The old mill at midnight, a rapid delivery;
> Violin music, all scary and shivery;
> Plot that is devilish, awful, nefarious;
> Heroine frightened, her plight is precarious;

> Bingo!—the rescue!—the movement goes snappily—
> Exit the villain and all endeth happily!
>> Take of these elements any you care about,
>> Put 'em in Texas, the Bowery, or thereabout;
>> Put in the powder and leave out the grammar,
>> And the certain result is a swell melodrammer."

Unhappily this prescription overlooks a most essential detail, the title. Authors of "hurrah stuff" (so they call their creations) comprehend that the Grand's patrons never choose the player first and the play afterward, as we do; with them it is not Mr. Sothern in what-you-will, it is "Red-Handed Bill" performed by whom-you-will; the title is everything. Alluring, compelling titles, it appears, array themselves in four categories:—

1. *The Blunderbuss Title.* Examples: "Red-Handed Bill," "Queen of the Outlaw Camp," "The Card King of the Coast."

2. *The Another-Girl-Like-You Title.* Examples: "Lottie, the Poor Saleslady," "Nellie, the Beautiful Cloak-Model," "Bell, the Typewriter Girl."

3. *The Heart-Throb Title.* Examples: "For His Sister's Honor," "For Her Children's Sake," "For His Brother's Crime."

4. *The Too-Dreadful-for-Anything Title.* Examples: "His Terrible Secret," "Why Girls Leave Home," "The Worst Woman in London."

But dear me, how we tarry in realms of theory, while yonder at the Grand concrete realities will so soon be thundering with unstinted fury. Come! what ho for the Grand!

Reduce the conventional theatre to a state of dog-eared shabbiness; write commercial advertisements on the curtain; borrow a whiff or so of the Dime Museum's aroma, and fill the house with office-boys, bell-boys, messengers, common laborers, factory-girls, shop-girls, waitresses, and "generals." There you have the Grand, wanting only the music, in which the drum predominates. To you, its incessant throbbing becomes oppressive. Not to those about you, though. One and all, they would indorse the sentiment if you quoted:—

> "Bang-whang-whang! goes the drum. Tootle-te-tootle, the fife!
>   No keeping one's haunches still; it's the greatest pleasure in
>   life!"

RED-HANDED BILL,
THE HAIR-LIFTER of the FAR SOUTH-WEST

And now the curtain goes up. It little matters what scene it discloses. Be it Chinatown or the Riverside Drive, New Orleans or the Bad Lands, the same thrilling deeds of derring-do will be enacted by the same conventional machine-made characters as in the famous "Boulevard du Crime" two hundred years ago. Milieu may vary, types never.

Consider those types, those presumably immortal types, so dear to the popular heart. First the heroine:—

She is "in-no-cent." With "quivering lips and moistened eye, her hands clasped meekly across her breast as though life was too heavy to bear," she tremulously reiterates the fact. Yet upon her, despite that aureole of angelic hair, those eyes so virtuously limpid, that rounded, maidenly figure, and the madonna-like sweetness of her ways, they have fastened accusations of arson, safe-cracking, forgery, and the murder of her husband. She is driven from home and kin. She is hounded by detectives. As the plot thickens, she grows eloquent. "Oh misery, misery!" she sobs. "I am alone forever! The thought will drive me frantic! I am wretched, mad! What is left to me now but the deepest, darkest despair? Oh, I cannot bear it! My heart will break! Why do I not die?—why do I not die?" She has life in her, though; lots of it. Wait till the villain sets about feeding her baby to the stone-crusher. It is with no little vigor, then, that she shrieks, "Me child! Me chi-i-i-ild!!!"

Or wait till he makes love to her. Zounds, what a counterblast! "Thou cur!" she snaps. "Unhand me, coward! The devilish cunning of your nature makes me shudder!" In moments like these she towers up in a physical grandeur well suiting her moral sublimity. And she needs a quite marvelous vitality, you discover, to go through the harrowing and terrific adventures this villain prepares for her. He loves her furiously and would be gentler if he understood. But villainy is not to be ranked among the learned professions. It is singularly without intellect. In "Nellie, the Beautiful Cloak-Model," the villain begins by causing the heroine to fall from the Brooklyn Bridge. Next, he pitches her overboard in mid-Atlantic. After that, he throws her under a freight elevator. Ultimately he says to her, "Why do you fear me, Nellie?"

What made him a villain, "no fellow can find out." He is a villain out of a clear sky, without motive or provocation, a "bold bad man" by nature, who has done all in his power to cultivate the gift. Hence a huge and horrid unpopularity, which he persistently augments till even the tiniest, tenderest gallery-god thirsts for his gore. The audience becomes so enraged that it hisses every time he comes on. Some cherish an abiding hatred; meeting him on the street next day, they openly insult him. In Texas, villains have been shot at. And as a final proof of villainy, the fiend glories in his shame, taking obloquy as a sort of laurel-crown, a tribute to his art.

Art it is, gadzooks! To be called "liar," "scoundrel," "puppy," "toad," yet never reply in more ferocious terms than "A time —will—come! Ha! Ha!"—this, methinks, argues that self-command which is the soul of virtuosity. Splendid, too, is the villain's talent for dropping flat when only half poked at by the hero; for never recognizing a detective disguised in a Piccadilly collar; for falling back foiled, although armed to the teeth, when the "comic relief" comes at him with bare knuckles, and for purloining wills and looting safes only at moments when witnesses swarm at his elbow. Moreover, if "genius is patience," this demon possesses a really dazzling brand of genius. "Foiled again"—and again and again—he pursues the evil tenor of his way.

And now the hero. Whereas the villain is completely and exhaustively villainous, the hero is completely and exhaustively heroic. You know it by his grand-opera stride, his righteously erect carriage, and the ring in his voice. Also by the creditable sentiments he exclaims while posing like any Olympian. "What! tell a falsehood? Let me die first!" "Fear a treacherous foe? Never, while a brave heart beats within me bosom!" "I swear that with the last drop of me blood I will defend yonder hunted but innocent girl!" To live up to this last proclamation requires a certain acrobatic nimbleness and a downright marvelous clairvoyance. Just when the heroine is about to be disintegrated by the sausage-machine, or reduced to longitudinal sections by the buzz-saw, or run over by the express-train as she lies bound across the rails, or blown to bits by the powder-barrel as the fuse sputters nearer and nearer, then—whoopla!—in jumps the hero, who has foreseen all and turned up not a second too late. Down chimneys he comes, up woodchuck-holes, over yawning chasms, across tottering bridges, and along the ridge-poles of flaming buildings, to thwart the villain and succor beauty in distress. A demigod, that hero! He will maul a villain twice his size; in "His Terrible Secret; or, Melmoth, the Man Monkey," the hero mauls two tremendous villains simultaneously.

But discerning melodramatists have discovered that our world is not wholly composed of the incurably good and the incurably bad. Ah, no! Witness the adventuress—the terrible, man-eating adventuress—who was once as "in-no-cent" as the heroine, yet who now sports a diabolical red gown, a nefarious

plumed hat, and exceedingly devilish high-heeled slippers.
Having depicted the facile Avernus-ward tendency of human
character, our author shows us how facile is return thence. The
ogress reforms. "It was you," she shrieks—"it was you, you,
Sir Lionel Crowninshield, who dragged me down into the
mire! Puppy! Snake! I was happy till I met you. And to-day
you would cast me off—ha! ha!—to marry Violet St. Claire!
Curse you! Leave me forever! I will return to the paths of
virtue. Ay—ha! ha!—I will have revenge! I will fly to Violet
St. Claire and say to her, 'Come, let me prove his perfidy to
you!' " A jolly enterprise, and one likely to succeed,—especially
when you recall the vigor with which Sir Lionel has pitched
poor, tearful Violet about.

And in real life, as the melodramaturge has noticed, one
finds here and there a character part good and part bad. So, if
Blaney's learned sock be on,—or Ried's, or Kremer's, or
Owen Davis's,—we shall expect from the assistant villain some
up-spoutings of ethical fervor. Sam will do Sir Lionel's will
until bidden, let us say, to strangle Violet St. Claire, or boil
the baby in oil. Then his conscience asserts itself. He rebels,
while storms of applause acclaim his extraordinary delicacy of
feeling. He would leave Sir Lionel's service altogether but for
past crimes that his employer might then make known to the
constable.

A few more characters will complete the cast. We shall encounter that hard-hearted father who so eagerly drove Violet
from home the moment suspicion fell upon her. We shall meet
a friend of the hero, who extricates him from the various blast-
furnaces, prison cells, and bottomless pits into which a man
of honor is so prone to fall. We shall track the lynx-eyed
detectives as they hound the quivering heroine by day and by
night. And, at fixed intervals, we shall welcome the "comic re-
liefs." Says Dickens, "It is the custom on the stage, in all good
murderous melodramas, to present the tragic and the comic
scenes in as regular alternation as the layers of white and red in
a side of well-streaked bacon." When the hero has come
ashore on the life-line, hanging by his teeth, with the heroine
under his arm, then, sure enough, out prance the comedy-
team—rustics, negroes, or merry Celts—to dance and sing

and crack jokes. But for this happy intervention, the audience would blow up.

At times—arbitrarily, quite—the curtain drops, and they call it the end of an act. A hundred lads and lasses bolt for the doors, to flirt among themselves, gaze forth upon the passing multitudes, and get a breath of fresh air, while inside the Grand the orchestra plays "Harrigan" and the gallery sings the chorus. There is much neighborly stepping to and fro, a hum of conversation, and no little munching of caramels. Or perhaps, instead of music, the Grandscope displays a flickering film or so in hope to discourage the all too serious tendency of the fickle to desert melodrama for the motion-picture show. Then up goes the curtain, and blood-and-thunder resumes.

Where it left off? It were rash to say so. The same characters, to be sure, go at the same frightful, blood-curdling business,— villain pursuing, hero thwarting, heroine escaping by the skin of her innocent teeth. But how, pray, came this about? Absolutely without connection with the preceding act. The more you watch the thing, the more it is borne in upon you that a melodrama, far from being a play, is merely a vaudeville,—a string of hair-lifting playettes, with comic specialties interspersed. They no more constitute a play than the detached adventures of Mr. Sherlock Holmes constitute a novel.

Still, as the riot of incidents had a beginning, it must have an ending. The detectives handcuff the fainting Violet St. Claire, when behold! the hero rushes on with a missive which the (reformed) adventuress has received from the Dead Letter Office. It was written by Violet's husband, shortly after his death, and declares that the combined charges of arson, forgery, safe-cracking, and murder should rest solely upon that black-hearted scoundrel, Sir Lionel Crowninshield. Violet comes to. The detectives loose the shackles. A policeman enters. The hero, with his left arm about the heroine and his right hand pointing at the villain, shouts majestically, "Mr. Officer, arrest that man!" Violet's father steps out from behind a boulder, and blesses the happy pair; the reformed adventuress falls upon the shoulder of the assistant villain, who has now no obstacle left between him and reform; the detectives slink off, cowering, R. and L.; and the villain is dragged away to the dungeon he so richly deserves. Tableau. Impassioned music. Slow curtain. Deafening and hilarious applause.

As the spectators rise up to go, you note in every face the gleam of triumph. Virtue victorious, vice vanquished,—such might be the perennial and suitably alliterative boast of melodrama. That, chiefly, is why the people love it. A crude motif? Say, rather, a primal,—the motif of old legends, of monkish morality plays, of fairy tales, of Sunday-school classics, of camp-meeting anecdotes. Vice, to be sure, gets frank statement, yet ever from virtue's point of view. Well may Blaney autograph his portrait, "Author of clean plays." Well may he exclaim, "I have never written a suggestive line, never allowed vice or wrong-doing to seem even temporarily to be in the ascendant!" How many dramatists in less lowly zones of art can say as much? Indeed, one recalls how a citizen once approached the box-office of a theatre and inquired, "Is this play a melodrama?" whereupon the official replied, "Mellow! It's rotten." No such fear at the Grand. The spectators, by long experience, know that invariably the wicked marionettes will be punished hideously, while the righteous marionettes will be sumptuously rewarded. What if, by reason of having baseless suspicions cast upon her, the heroine is compelled to wear black? In the last scene she will strut resplendent in a pink-and-blue evening gown (it is morning, there in the Klondike, but who cares?) and blaze with monstrous jewels. Then cries every flaming heart, "I told you so!"—which is on the whole the most joyous and soul-satisfying sentence the tongue can fashion.

Have we caught our balance sufficiently to attempt criticism? Then let us begin with the actors, who are the worst—and the best—in the world: the worst because their machine-made technique misinterprets reality; the best because it is their mission to misinterpret reality, and they fulfill that mission sublimely. They personify those theoretic types which the densely ignorant audience accepts as lifelike. The hero writes heroism in bill-board capitals, the heroine weaves lachrymose innocence into a motto to go on the wall, the villain does villainy into scare-heads. It is clean-cut, unequivocal acting, blatant and megaphonic. It takes the citadel of stupidity by a frontal attack, covered by artillery. As well might each player wear a label denoting his quality, and light the label with electricity.

Such players, methinks, would hardly shine in a drama like "Why They Felt as They Did Instead of Slightly Differently," though even there they might introduce a merit now rare and little prized,—the merit, I mean, of clear utterance. With them, no affected, incomprehensible chirpings or cooings; instead, a fine, bold vocalization, straight from the diaphragm and audible in the very garret. Sometimes, however, noise were better if muffled; in "His Terrible Secret," one regretted the bluster with which the actors kept addressing the adventuress in two syllables,—"Salome!"

And melodrama itself,—I find it perfect. Consider its problem. Wanted: By an incredibly dull audience, ten thousand thrills. To deliver those thrills takes something stronger, quicker, and simpler than the conventional play. Something stronger because the very dull require powerful stimulants to stave off torpor. These are they who love Salvationist rantings and whoopings, the yellow journal's tom-tom, and the dime novel's inspired hydrophobia; mild appeals leave them listless. Hence the merits of melodrama's wild and outrageous fury, a fury which no one but Mr. Franklin Adams, who is as skilled in mathematics as in song, has ever dared to compute. Writing of Mr. Owen Davis's thrillers, he declares, "If all the blood spilled in the one hundred and seventeen Davidramas were put into one caldron, it would equal the average rainfall for Asia, Rhode Island, and Tasmania. The blank cartridges shot off in those same plays would supply the Bulgarian army for 1342 years, 7 months, and 12 days. All the curse-yous and other oaths, placed end on end, would reach from Oneonta, New York, to Nashotah, Wisconsin, while the virtue triumphant on a field of vice scarlet would—" But here even an Adams gives over, and one doubts if any statistician, however valiant, would have the hardihood to continue.

Tepid, anæmic, and neutral-tinted by comparison, is our aristocratic drama, though the poor thing can't help it. We bring to the theatre a fastidiousness that precludes the grander flights of art. That "terrific knife-fight on horseback in the Bucket-of-Blood Saloon" is not for natures depleted by a false culture; neither is "the breakage of costly bric-a-brac" that "makes a weekly expense equal to the entire salary list of some companies." I question, too, whether Mr. Winter or Mr.

William Archer could appreciate the scene in "Chinatown Charley" where a troop of little girls ascend a telegraph pole, and form a sort of chain which swings across to the window and affords a human bridge for the heroine to escape by when tragically cornered by the villain. They have small compunction in melodrama; they go it strong.

Note, I beg you, the vigor displayed by the author of "The White Squadron." His hero, as I remember, has been enslaved by the heroine's cruel father, and made a brother to the ox,— quite literally, for he has his head through the yoke, side by side with the beast. Worse, he burns with thirst. He cries piteously for water. His master refuses, but at last, when the fiend has turned his back, the girl brings a cooling cup and presses it to the lips of the captive, who cries, "O, thou dove, sprung from the loins of a tiger!"

Now I call that genuinely remarkable. Barrie at his best has given us nothing at all resembling it. Or again, recall the avalanche scene in "The Card King of the Coast." A cabin containing hunted innocence and predatory stealth is buried in the snow. After a moment of harrowing suspense, in bursts the hero, who has easily won to the door and smashed it through. Forthwith he assists the heroine to ascend the red-hot stove, stands beside her on top of it, and little by little pokes a hole in the ceiling. Through this and the forty feet of snow overhead the pair make their escape.

But for the very thriller of thrillers, I point you to "His Terrible Secret; or, Melmoth, the Man Monkey." I consider it indubitably "the limit." Melmoth's father, it appears, was erroneously believed to have been strangled by a gorilla. Consequently, Melmoth resembles an ape. Mr. Charles E. Blaney, who made that shilling-shocker, is too honest to claim originality; he confesses that his plot is "based on Darwin's theory of evolution." Obviously, for Melmoth cherishes a desire to "return to the jungle and live among his forefathers." By allowing the mind to dwell upon this idea, one obtains a degree of æsthetic satisfaction equaled only by the exultancy with which one watches the many displays of ultra-simian ferocity afforded by fight after fight, as the ape nature periodically reasserts itself to the detriment of the villain. Besides, there's the pathos of it all. "A great mind, a great heart, and a monkey face." Think of it,—and it might have happened to any one of us! Never shall I forget that final scene, in which, just as the curtain is about to fall, the sweet heroine asks, "And Melmoth, Melmoth, what will *you* do?" He replies, "I will return to the jungle, where alone is peace and contentment for the Man Monkey!" So this was the "terrible secret,"—this circumstance of having had a father who wasn't strangled by a gorilla, and of having consequently the visage of a gorilla,— rather a difficult secret to keep, which was why Melmoth told it to everybody in the play at the outset.

Situations sufficiently appalling and incidents sufficiently cataclysmic are not wholly wanting upon our own stage. To Melmoth one may oppose that other unfortunate curio, the Sieur de Bergerac, whose nose was as astonishing in its way as Melmoth's ape-like visage. Yet in general our dramatists are but a timid race. For often they conduct their most awesome horrors behind the scenes. Not so here, where one gets the full effect, helped out not infrequently by those ministrants to realism, the live horse, the live dog, the bona fide waterfall, and such hurricanes and thunderings as cause one's head to duck. These crude phenomena "take the skin off," as the saying goes; as the saying ought to go, they take most of the flesh along too. And the crowd adores them. It especially adores the shower of "fire-proof theatrical snow" (I quote from the dealer's catalogue), and will enjoy deathly pangs of compassion as the heroine, hatless and without her shawl, exposes herself to the cold.

Let us do the square thing by that snow. Addison has said that it consists of dismembered manuscripts of unsuccessful playwrights,—which is misleading. Mr. Jerome K. Jerome remarks, "One thing that must irritate the stage heroine very much, on these occasions, is the way the snow seems to lie in wait for her, and follow her about. It is quite a fine night before she comes on the scene; the moment she appears, it begins to snow. The way the snow 'goes' for that poor woman is most unfair. It always snows much heavier in the particular spot where she is sitting than it does anywhere else in the whole street. We have even known a more than usually malignant snow-storm to follow a heroine three times round the stage, and then go off R. with her. A stage snow-storm is the

kind of snow-storm that would follow you upstairs and want
to come into bed with you." Clever, this, and once true. Now,
however, the snow-storm behaves much better. Though it still
times its precipitation so as to afford the lady a foregone pneu-
monia, and though it still contrives to let up as soon as she has
withdrawn, it yields a fine, even, undiscriminating shower of
highly realistic flakes, whose verisimilitude may rank among
the most praiseworthy shockers of melodrama.

Next to shock, in the technique of thrill-carpentry, comes
quickness. In "Ten Nights in a Bar-Room," two gentlemen sit
playing at cards. The ensuing tragedy runs thus, if I recall.

"You cheated!"

"You lie!"

"You die!"

Bang!!!

Such alacrity, one appreciates, is in principle only a response
to a natural requirement of stagecraft. Once, when Sarah
Bernhardt had been rehearsing a death-scene, her uncle expos-
tulated, "But don't you know, Sarah, that rigor mortis doesn't
set in till six hours after death?"—"Yes, yes," cried the divine
Sarah, "I know that,—*ah, parfaitement!* But do you expect an
audience to wait six hours to see me stiffen?" At the Grand,
the audience can scarce wait six minutes, so, however grave the
business in hand, there's not a moment to lose. You should
see them make love at the Grand. One proposes, there, with
the brevity and abruptness of a brakeman bawling the name of
the next station. Without preliminary hoverings or flutterings
or hesitant, lyrical circumlocutions, one hurls a declaration
straight from the shoulder. "Will you marry me?" The impact,
as it hits the lady, must be terrific, yet she replies firmly, "I
will!" Which closes the incident.

And think not that transitions from scene to scene demand
delicate shading. The more sudden and extreme, the better. In
a delicious melodrama I remember, the curtain falls upon the
pursuit of a murderer; immediately the murderer comes before
the curtain and disports himself in song and dance. The spectator's mood will change in a twinkling. A gifted melodrama-
tist of my acquaintance has accomplished the feat of turning a
hanging into a wedding. "Think of that!" he exclaims. "Never
was done before. Here I have the hero with the rope around

his neck and the black cap drawn down and the drop about to fall. You get ready for the dull, sickening thud. Then—wow!—in an instant, I have the bridal party rush on, breathless, and I marry that hero before he knows where he's at!"

Meanwhile, in the nine-and-twenty hair's-breadth-escape scenes of a melodrama, rapidity is everything. For three reasons. First, the audience knows what's coming; familiarity with "hurrah stuff" enables it to keep always at least a minute ahead of the action. In the next place, it absolutely forgets itself. "Save her!" it shrieks. "Save her!" Or even, "Look out, Bill, he's under the sofa!" They tell how Salvini once choked his Desdemona in good faith; here it is the audience that is run away with by the convincing potency of art. And that mood won't last; one must strike while the iron is hot. Finally, melodrama is not got up for psychologists. Its devotees care nothing for the portrayal of the inner life, save in its crudest, most ferocious manifestations; a few wild cries suffice. They want "sump'n doin'." Strip the action, therefore, of all those interpretative, significant, philosophic touches that make it human. Give it go. Give it noise and bluster as it goes. Let it career madly, in a cloud of dust and with sparks flying.

And make it simple. The reason, really, why blood-and-thunder has for two centuries adhered to the rules set by the French *mélodrames*, is that their simplicity was absolute and final. They reduced character, incident, structure, and ideas to their lowest terms, enabling the Neolithic mind (and such is the Grand's) to comprehend. A *reductio ad absurdum* for you, "hurrah stuff" becomes for the housemaid and the office-boy a vehicle of truth.

To that coterie of ridiculously simplified and outrageously overdrawn types—hero, heroine, villain, and the rest—you exclaim, as did Alice in Wonderland, "Who cares for you? You are nothing but a pack of cards!" Nevertheless, it is beyond the power of the Neolithic mind to distinguish between the visible representation and the thing it claims to represent. At a much higher stage of development, men were wont to adduce the clincher, "Is it not written?" At the Grand one encounters the clincher, "Is it not acted?" Why question the existence of characters as completely virtuous or as completely infamous as those of melodrama? Can't you see them, yonder on the stage, performing at this moment the so-called impossibilities, exemplifying the so-called impossible humanity? Trust your eyes! And, to a degree, even the educated fall prey to this pleasing fallacy. Cartoons, however irrational, have still their persuasiveness. If you scorn the Grand for accepting Red-Handed Bill, ask yourself if you can think of Senator Hanna as clad otherwise than in dollar signs.

The incidents, too,—despite their magnified, galvanized outlandishness, they are the simplest of all imaginable thrillers. Into a scrape and out of it. *Voilà tout!* Call them false and you err. False they may be, to life as it commonly runs and to life as you see it. Meanwhile they are true, to life as it occasionally runs and as the Neolithic see it; for only the glaringly sensational gets through their armor of stupidity to leave a vivid impression. And have I not with these eyes beheld melodrama turned loose in the public street? For instance, when the old-time firemen were marshaling their parade. Let me sketch it for you.

A city square, packed with people. Battalions of red-shirted braves waiting the order to march. Suddenly, a distant cry. Then more cries and louder. Then the throng split in twain, and through the gap dashed a runaway horse, foam-flecked and without a driver. At his heels swung a coupé, now tilted to left and now to right, with a woman and a baby girl inside. An instant later a red-shirted fellow sprang tigerlike from among the terror-stricken crowd. With one terrific bound he seized the bridle and clung. He was dragged—oh yes,—and hurt. But he had saved two lives; and I was there and saw it. It is the livest, cleanest-cut recollection of my boyhood. Never till I die shall I forget the red flash of that leap or the ring of applause that followed it. It was melodrama, real and perfect.

In the Grand's audience, pray notice, there are many who have had first-hand—or at least second-hand—acquaintance with the melodramatic. From among the Neolithic come firemen, policemen, seamen, and those who gain their bread in trades replete with danger and daring. Meanwhile the tenement street has its daily melodramas, such as they are,—melodramas of crime, drunkenness, and frightful vice, though generally lacking the completeness that would fit them for the stage. You know what happens when philanthropists transplant a family from the slum to the village. The family returns. It returns because its removal has involved an exchange of melodrama for "the legitimate."

While the life of the people gives a tremendous reality to the melodramatic, their reading superemphasizes that reality. In your evening newspaper, somewhere among the items under inconspicuous headlines, you are told that when Mrs. Ahearn, who dwells in a certain remote city, stood shrieking at the window of a blazing tenement, it was her own son, Terence (of Hook-and-Ladder Three), who carried her fainting to the ground. In the Neolithic newspaper, on the other hand, the story fills half a page, with colossal headlines and thrilling illustrations. A dozen despatches of international importance are "killed" to make room for it. So you need hardly marvel that, when the Grand presents incidents familiar through experience and reading, the people accept them. They are plausible, stirring, and readily comprehended.

But the way melodrama combines its incidents—is that so simple? For the Neolithic, yes, though not for you. Conceived as a play, "Red-Handed Bill" involves non sequiturs, discrepancies, contradictions; it makes your head swim. Conceived as a random series of playettes, it exactly suits the short-distance intellect, which would droop with exhaustion should it attempt to follow the plot of "The Hypocrites," for instance, or even of "Leah Kleschna." It wants not dramas but scenes, and the Grand's stage is peopled with characters who have little hesitation about making scenes. Nobody cares if there are too many scenes. Nobody cares if the scenes won't hang together; they should of right "hang separately." Mr. Owen Davis, author of "Nellie, the Beautiful Cloak-Model," says, "Frankly, I wrote it as a burlesque. Often, while working on it, I had to laugh at its incongruities and impossible situations,—Nellie faced certain death seventeen times from curtain to curtain,— but it was a big financial success and is now in its third season." Mr. Davis, being a Harvard graduate, might well deride Nellie's seventeen escapes; he could view the performance in its entirety, get all seventeen into his mind at once. His audience, on the contrary, took the performance one inning at a time, each new shocker obliterating its predecessor. And it is precisely this brevity of perspective that makes a series of unrelated

episodes more facile of interpretation than the sustained elab-
oration we demand of a play. Make scene depend upon scene
and you cruelly overtask the Neolithic mentality.

That mentality demands likewise an extreme simplicity and
perspicuity of idea, a stripping of truth to the bone. I say truth
advisedly. However wild and unrepresentative the incident, and
however crude (even to grotesquerie) the depiction of character, the underlying notions must consist solely of platitudes,—
or, to put it more genially, of fundamental verities. Mr.
Chesterton remarks with absolute justice, "Melodrama is popular because it is profound truth; because it goes on repeating
the things which humanity has found to be central facts. This
endless repetition profoundly annoys the sensitive artist inside
you and me. But it ought to profoundly please the realist. The
melodrama is perpetually telling us that mothers are devoted
to their children, because mothers are devoted to their children. Humanity may in time grow tired of hearing this truth;
but humanity will never grow tired of fulfilling it. The melodramas say that men are chiefly sensitive upon honor and upon
their personal claim to courage. Men are. It bores one to hear
one's honor reiterated; but it would startle one to hear it denied. In so far as the melodrama is really bad, it is not bad
because it expresses old ideas; it is bad because it so expresses
them as to make them seem like dead ideas."

Dead ideas? So they may seem to Mr. Chesterton while
"hurrah stuff" rages before his eyes and chills-and-fever music
rings in his ears. So they most emphatically do not seem to the
Neolithic. In "A Wife's Secret," the heroine flees to a belfry at
dead of night. The villain, still pursuing, climbs the roof of the
church and enters the belfry. "Ha!" he cries, "at last I have got
you alone!" The heroine answers, "Ah, no! Not—not alone!
For God is ev-er-y-where!" A dead idea? Then why the exul-
tant tempest of applause, which swells, and bursts, and, were it
only a little louder, would lift the very roof?

Mr. Charles E. Blaney, author of many terrific melodramas,
has now and then a half-repentant mood. He confesses that
perchance he may have "over-stimulated young minds." I
would bid him and all his guild be of good comfort. Young
minds, of the grade they address, will seek overstimulation,
Grand or no Grand, and it is the glory of melodrama that it

preaches nightly a gospel that gives the mere platitudes of morals a glaring, thrilling intensity that finds the heart and sets it leaping.

And what, after all, is melodrama? The Ten Commandments in red fire.

1909

LOTTIE BLAIR PARKER

The melodramatic device of turning an erring daughter out into a blinding snowstorm with her love-child in her arms has a long history. It appears on the London stage in Prince Hoare's *Indiscretion* (1800) and subsequently—minus the blizzard but with the injunction, "Quit this house and never darken the theshold of its door again"—in Dion Boucicault's *Flying Scud* (1866). The American playwright Steele Mackaye put back the snowstorm in *Hazel Kirke*; by 1883 his play had been performed more than 2,000 times, thanks to the innovative concept of multiple companies. One of the many players of Hazel was Lottie Blair Parker (1868–1937); when she took up playwriting, she consciously or unconsciously lifted Mackaye's plot for *Way Down East*. What novelty it had came, paradoxically, from familiarity. Parker set her play on a farm in rural Maine, the kind of bucolic background already popular from the folksy comedies of Denman Thompson, James Herne, and a score of others. *Way Down East* became a perennial hit all over the States, and as late as 1920 D. W. Griffith paid $175,000 for the screen rights. Sensationalizing it with the ice-floes of *Uncle Tom's Cabin*, he perpetuated its phenomenal success for a new generation.

My Most Successful Play

THE consensus of opinion seems to be that "Way Down East" is my best play. For this reason if for no other I must so consider it myself. The only play yet produced from my pen which can contest the supremacy of "Way Down East" is my romance of the South, "Under Southern Skies." A careful comparison of these rival plays shows that the New England one scores its point of advantage over the Southern in the greater simplicity, concentration and power of its sympathetic appeal.

"Way Down East" was written almost at the beginning of my career as a writer of plays. I had already gained recognition through the production, by Mr. Daniel Frohman, of a one-act play, "White Roses." Never, I believe, was a one-act play put upon the stage with so perfect a cast, such artistic setting and careful attention to every detail of production. It was correspondingly successful and I was thus encouraged to keep on writing other plays—offering them where I thought they might be found available.

One of these manuscripts I sent to Miss Effie Ellsler. Mr Weston, her manager, returned it as not suitable for her use, but he was much pleased with the quality and workmanship of the play and asked me to send anything else I had or might write that I thought would fit Miss Ellsler. Here was an opening for a production, but I had nothing that I thought would do; I began casting about for some idea upon which a play might be built for this charming actress.

In this process of mental rummaging, the outlines of a story —long forgotten—read years before—emerged from some mysterious store-house of memory. From this outline the form of the young woman, now known to the stage as "Anna Moore," seemed to step forth as the very character for Miss Ellsler— whose exquisite rendition of "Hazel Kirke" was still fresh in my mind.

I had no copy of the story and, after one or two ineffectual attempts to get one, decided that the play would possess more originality if written from a hazy recollection than if all the details were fresh in my mind from a rereading.

After several weeks of steady application the play was finished. I had retained such characters as I thought necessary, added others, and located the play in New England for the purpose of gaining "atmosphere" through characterization and stage setting. My several years' experience on the stage had given me a knowledge of the practical requirements of playbuilding, and when my manuscript was dispatched to Miss Ellsler it was in thorough good form for production. So sure was I that Miss Ellsler would see herself as clearly in the part of "Anna" as I did that not a shadow of doubt as to her acceptance of the play entered my calculations.

The measure of my disappointment may be judged when the script came back. It was not just what she was looking for. But one other attempt was made at placing the play—with one of our leading managers—before it was sent to Mr. Wm. A. Brady.

That gentleman received it, figuratively speaking, with open arms and, in so short a time that it made my head swim, the play was read, accepted and contracts for its production signed. It is scarcely necessary to say I had told Mr. Brady that I had used the plot of a story for its basis.

Having written and disposed of "Way Down East" it might seem that the caption of this article had been fully complied with. But it is seldom indeed that an author parts company with his manuscript at this point. He usually finds more or less work to do at rehearsals and even after production changes are often found desirable.

"Way Down East" did not prove singular in this respect, although the nature and scope of the changes have at times been misrepresented and greatly exaggerated.

One thing which seemed to please Mr. Brady very much was the shortness of the cast—there were but nine characters. He objected, however, to the title (which was then "Annie Laurie") and he thought the last act would have to be changed. I thought it was a pretty good last act—and as Mr. Brady could not just place the trouble, beyond the fact that he thought the set too cold (it was a winter landscape)—too much snow following the snowstorm in the third act—he said the last act might wait until rehearsal, when something would probably develop towards its improvement.

A new title, however, he wanted as speedily as possible. In a day or two I sent him a list of names from which he chose "Way Down East."

It was in August 1896 that these arrangements were concluded, and a production was confidently expected to be made during the season. With characteristic energy Mr. Brady began making efforts to get time for an extended engagement, considering suitable actors for the different parts and arranging for the scenery. It may serve as an interesting item that one of the first women mentioned by Mr. Brady as being a representative type of the part was—Miss Ellsler!

Mr. Brady also sent the manuscript about that he might get the opinions of the various readers. From the late Mr. W. J. Le Moyne came a verdict that was very gratifying to me. Mr. Le Moyne wrote:

"The movement throughout the play is quite remarkable. The characters are strongly individualized, the comedy is good and natural throughout." Here followed some exceptions taken to incidents in the last act (that last act was assuming dubious proportions). Mr. Le Moyne's letter concluded: "These few remarks are submitted for what they are worth. They embody the few trifling defects that appear to me in a very interesting play."

That so able and experienced a man as Mr. Le Moyne should be so favorably impressed gave me added hope that the play would prove a success. But unforeseen events interposed and all work toward production was put off indefinitely.

Not until April 1897 was any move made. Then the play was put in rehearsal with Mr. Brady's "Under the Polar Star" company, for one performance to be given in a New England town. This performance, owing to the unexpected closing of the company, was not given and the incident would call for no mention but for one thing. The rehearsals had given a better "line" upon the manuscript than even careful reading could give.

These rehearsals were under the direction of Mr. George F. Marion. I felt that his report would have much weight with Mr. Brady and naturally I was anxious to know what it might be. I think it is pertinent to quote here a few lines of a letter from Mr. Marion to Mr. Brady:

"I have tried to avoid anything stagey, keeping as close to the homely atmosphere as possible. The play improves on acquaintance, even the last act rehearsing better than it reads."

This was encouraging to me and I believe it was to Mr. Brady; at all events I think it determined him on giving the last act a trial without any changes being made in it.

Arrangements were made to open the following September for a trial tour of four weeks through New England. A fine company, including Miss Phoebe Davies, was engaged. Mr. Joseph R. Grismer directed the rehearsals. The text and general business of the manuscript were followed almost without change for this production. But one alteration was made which would come under the category "worth mentioning"—and this proved very much worth mentioning. I refer to "Pickin's from Puck." I had provided "Hi" with different matter to read which I had thought he could give humorously, but at rehearsal Mr. Grismer told me that Mr. Clay Greene had suggested that "Hi" read instead some old jokes. This appealed to

me at once and then and thereafter "Pickin's from Puck" became one of the features of the performance. Mr. Grismer,
past-master of this art, further enhanced the effectiveness of
the performance by adding much irresistibly funny "business"
—as well as many touches which helped the sentimental or serious situations. Lack of space, not lack of appreciation, keeps
me from enumerating all of these, but I may recall here the
blowing of the dinner-horn; the tying of Kate's shoe into the
"bow-knot;" "driving tandem" business; the Professor pouring
hot water into the flower vase.

The play opened in Newport R. I., September 3d, 1897, and
met with instant favor.

After two or three performances, however, Mr. Grismer,
saying that the actors felt a paucity of words in the two last
scenes of the first act, suggested some lines for "padding"
them. The added lines rounded out the scenes advantageously,
although in no way changing their meaning or the general
structure and the climax remained the same.

No other changes were made during the four weeks' tour,
barring the expected and inevitable smoothing and polishing
of a new work, and the invention of stage business under Mr.
Grismer's skilled supervision, except an alteration of one scene
in the last act which I shall refer to later.

I had gone up into New Hampshire for a few days after the
opening of the play. While on my return trip to New York I decided to stop over and see the performance again. Although
the press notices had been very good—throughout the four
weeks' tour they compared favorably with those the play has
since received—the receipts were very light. Many causes might
have been urged to account for slim attendance, but nevertheless I felt a bit anxious.

I watched the play carefully, trying to criticise it, to see if it
were lacking, and where. It was at this point a feeling came to
me, that if two or three more people were introduced—
characters such as might naturally be found about a farm—the
play would be benefitted.

I did not think Mr. Brady would view such a proposition
with much favor—he had seemed so pleased in the beginning
with the small cast—but I told Mr. Grismer my idea before

leaving the company, and at once upon my return to New York sought Mr. Brady for the same purpose.

He received my suggestion as Mr. Grismer had done, without comment; but he wanted to know about "that last act." I confessed that I was still unable to find anything especially wrong with it; I thought that with sympathetic treatment and a complete setting as planned in the manuscript it would be all right.

From this time no information came to me from Mr Brady relative to the play until the receipt of two telegrams sent to me by him from Chicago on October 25th and 27th. As a result of these telegrams I hastened to Chicago.

Arrived there I learned from Mr. Grismer that "Way Down East" was to be produced in Chicago on November 14th for two weeks; also I was now told for the first time that my suggestion of adding some characteristic minor parts was to be adopted, and that other changes had been decided upon.

Mr. Grismer was prepared with the idea of "Seth Holcomb," a character who was to be a persistent admirer of "Martha Perkins," a sort of "I'll go where Tildy goes" part, who was also to be devoted to a bottle—supposedly a patent-medicine but in reality whiskey—for the benefit of his health. A "country doctor" was also suggested as a character to be brought in with advantage. It was quickly agreed that these characters should be used—they were satisfactory to Mr. Grismer and they seemed very good to me—as good as—perhaps better than—any others I might think of, and time was saved by adopting them. Also a quartet (the Village Choir) was to be introduced.

A scene in the original last act had been cut out and one written in its place, during the fall tour of the play, without consulting me. This change was now explained. As it seemed immaterial to me—although I really preferred the original idea—I allowed the change to be continued.

It was now, and for the first time, that a serious point of difference arose. "Mr. Brady and I have decided," said Mr. Grismer, "that the last act must be played in three scenes, so that the last one may end the play in the sitting-room at the Squire's. It is merely a rearrangement of the material and will be no trouble to you as I have it all laid out as I want it rehearsed."

I was decidedly opposed to cutting the last act into different scenes.

"I cannot consent to that," I said.

"Then the production cannot be made," Mr. Grismer replied.

"Very well then; it cannot."

I wonder now at my temerity in setting my judgment against that of men so much more experienced and resourceful than myself. But my reasons seemed to me so clear—and the effect of such a change so vital—that I felt I could not yield the point. My reasons for objecting were several. Changes of scene had gone out of favor. Authors were avoiding them whenever possible, except in sensational melodrama. The interest in the story would be broken instead of cumulative, and any complete, effective stage setting would be impossible.

After giving Mr. Grismer these reasons I proposed, as a compromise, the set as now used—the interior of a maple-sugar shed, with a part exterior winter landscape, to which idea Mr. Grismer finally assented.

I should like to note here that, with my permission, the three-scene arrangement was tried during the Chicago engagement. All the objections I had urged against it were apparent and it was not again used.

Having reached an agreement as to what was to be done, the work of putting in the new parts began. Mr. Grismer and I first went over the manuscript together, marking the points where the new scenes might best come in. With pencil, paste-pot and shears I then set to work writing in the dialogue for "Seth," the "doctor" and the other characters brought into conjunction with them in their scenes, cutting the dialogue which could best be spared to make room for the new material, and going back and forth over the manuscript to make sure that no "loose ends" should be left.

Daily I submitted these changes to Mr. Grismer for his approval, acting upon such suggestions as he made for their betterment, until the work was finished.

With the passing of this manuscript into Mr. Grismer's hands for rehearsal the "How" of my writing "Way Down East" has been told.

Yet two points should be touched upon before this article

can be properly brought to a conclusion. "Anna," "The Squire," "Mrs. Bartlett," "David," "Kate," "The Professor," "Hi Holler," "Sanderson" and "Martha Perkins" are the original parts.

I have told of the introduction of "Seth Holcomb" and "Doc Wiggin." There remains one other part—"Rube Whipple," the constable, who made his first appearance in the cast at the Manhattan Theatre when the play received its New York première. As I knew nothing of the preparations for a New York opening, was not present at rehearsals and did not see a performance for some time, I can not say where credit belongs for this diverting character.

These changes, which I have enumerated as carefully as allotted space will permit, are perhaps what have given rise to the statement that "Way Down East" was "re-written."

To this I must take exception. To say that a play has been "re-written" or "revised" implies the existence originally of defects in its theme or the manner of its development which it has been found necessary to correct.

Such changes as were made in "Way Down East" were in the nature of additions or embellishments—not correctives. They in no way disturbed or changed the general structure of the play and however much they increased the effectiveness of the performance or added to the commercial value of the play they must be classed under another head than that of "re-writing," or "revision."

A careful comparison of the original manuscript with the copy printed for copyright purposes shows that the great body of the play is to-day just what it was when first written. It is the same in every essential detail of its story, in its principal people, in their characteristics, in their relation to each other and their relation to the plot, and in its situations.

Save for the scene in the last act referred to early in this article, the principal scenes are unaltered in their meaning. The bulk of the dialogue and general stage business remains the same. The climax of every act is the same and is led up to by the same series of events.

1911

CHANNING POLLOCK

Channing Pollock (1880–1946) was the all-purpose Broadway facto-
tum. He served his apprenticeship as dramatic critic of *The Washington Post* in 1898, before becoming a press agent for the managers
William A. Brady and the Shuberts. Without any sense of conflict of
interest, he regularly reviewed plays for several publications, including
The Smart Set and *The Green Book*, often biting the hands that had fed
him. He also promoted his own works for the stage, including a
dramatization of Frank Norris's *The Pit*. Pollock contributed sketches
to three versions of the *Ziegfeld Follies* (1911, 1915, and 1921), composing the English lyrics for "My Man," Fanny Brice's rendition of the
French torch song "Mon Homme." His sanctimonious anti-war play
The Fool was a popular if not a critical success in 1924, but his dramatic
career was dealt a lethal blow in 1931 when Dorothy Parker wrote of
his latest effort: "*The House Beautiful* is the play lousy." Pollock's ample store of stage lore is illustrated in his essay "Stage Struck," from
his collection *The Footlights Fore and Aft* (1911), which indicates just
how popular the theatre as a profession and how widespread the concept of "stardom" had become since the days of Anna Cora Mowatt.

Stage Struck

*Being a diagnosis of the disease, and a description of its
symptoms, which has the rare medical merit of
attempting a cure at the same time.*

"From the stern life of an officer in Uncle Sam's Navy to a
merry job carrying a spear in the chorus of a musical comedy
may be a far cry", but that is the step which a metropolitan
newspaper recently recorded as having been taken by a young
man named in the story whose beginning is quoted above. On
another page of this same newspaper was an article which announced that "because pink teas, bridge whist, and dances no
longer amused her", a certain "society woman" had joined the
chorus of a company appearing at the Casino. These two cases
composed a single day's list of casualties from the malignant
disease known as stage-fever.

"The malignant disease"

When my eye had finished its journey over the accounts of the "society woman" and the naval officer, I paused to wonder whether either of these aspirants would be checked by seeing spread-headed over the first page of the journal in question the horrid details of a theatrical suicide. The night before, an actress of reputation—a woman who had won everything that these new-comers had but a faint chance of winning—had killed herself in an hotel in Baltimore. Of course, it had not been shown that this "star" was influenced by any circumstance connected with her work, and, of course, it is true that people of various professions are self-slain, and yet—I wondered.

If the naval officer was restrained in his resolve it was not for long. A week or so later I saw this impetuous youth, who couldn't stand "being bottled up on a battle-ship", on the stage of an up-town theater. He was standing near the middle of a row of young men, waving his hands at stated intervals, and singing "yes—yes" at the end of every second line rendered by the principal comedian. He had but to wave his hands a moment too soon or too late in order to incur a fine or a reprimand. Perhaps by this time he has discovered that there are worse misfortunes than being "bottled up on a battleship."

Whether he does or not, the stream of the stage-struck will continue to flow like the brook poeticized by Tennyson. There is no stopping it. Youth has a better chance of missing measles or scarlet-fever than of escaping that consuming passion to "go on the stage." Nearly everyone struggles with the mania for a time; the wise conquer it, the foolish make up the comic opera choruses, the unimportant road companies, and the stage-door-keeper's list of "extra ladies and gentlemen." From every class and walk of life, from every town and city troop the victims, abandoning their vocations and their homes, as though they had heard the witching notes of a siren song. They come with high hopes and bright dreams, most of them to the great, gay city of New York, where they besiege the agencies, and the managers, and the teachers of acting until their dreams fade, or their money gives out, or they are smitten with realization. There is hardly a community in the country so small as to be without its "amateur dramatic club", and no one even distantly connected with the theatrical profession has lacked his or her experience with the inoculated unfortunate who knows that "I could succeed if I only had a chance."

Some time ago I happened to be in Syracuse, and used the long-distance telephone to communicate with New York. My conversation over, I sat down in the hotel lobby, and had just lit a cigar when a page announced: "Long distance wants you." I returned to the booth. "Yes?" I inquired. A woman's voice replied: "I overheard enough of your talk with New York to judge that you're in the theatrical business."

"I'm indirectly connected with it", I replied.

"Well", said the voice, "I'm the long-distance operator, and I want to go on the stage. Please get me an engagement."

I explained my misfortune in being acquainted with no manager who was likely to consider extensive training in enunciation of "hello" and "busy" sufficient education for the stage. The lady probably didn't believe me, for it is the popular impression that anyone concerned in the business of the playhouse has only to ask in order to receive a contract for whomever he wishes to assist. That song-heroine, who declared herself "an intimate friend of an intimate friend of Frohman", has her prototype in real life. Moreover, no aspirant to footlight honors ever can be convinced that actors must be made as well as born, and that there may be a few people in the world, who, given the opportunity, would not become Modjeskas and Mansfields.

William A. Brady once was served at dinner by a waitress whose surliness astonished him. He made no remark, however, and at last the waitress addressed him. "You're William A. Brady", she said; "ain't you?"

Mr. Brady confessed.

"Well", exclaimed the duchess of dishes, "my name's Minnie Clark. I've been a waitress since I was fourteen years old, and I think I can stand it until about next Wednesday. Give me a job, will you?"

David Belasco had a less amusing experience with a chambermaid in Attleboro, Mass., where he spent a night with the organization supporting David Warfield in "The Auctioneer." This girl, whose tap at the door interrupted the wizard producer while he was blue-penciling a scene, had just heard of his

" 'You're William A. Brady, ain't you?' "

presence in town, and lost no time approaching him. She had been stage-struck since childhood. Hearing of Mr. Belasco's success in teaching dramatic art, she had determined to visit him in New York. "I saved my money for three years", she said, "and then I went up to you. I called at your office every day, but they wouldn't let me in. When all my money was spent I came back home, and began saving again. I had about half enough when I found that you were coming to Attleboro." Mr. Belasco was unable to give the girl the least encouragement. She was wholly illiterate, and, moreover, her death warrant was writ on her face. She was suffering from an incurable disease of the lungs.

Collin Kemper, one of the managers of the Astor Theater, recently had a letter from an elderly priest, who, after twenty years in the pulpit, felt that he wanted "a larger field of expression", and yearned to play Shakespeare. A wrinkled old woman of sixty sought the late Edward Marble, when he was conducting a school of acting in Baltimore, and confided in him her desire to be seen as Juliet. This desire she had cherished nearly half a century when the death of a relative gave her the means of gratifying her ambition. Daniel Frohman once received a young man, who laid on his desk a letter of introduction from an acquaintance in the West. "Ah!" said Mr. Frohman. "So you wish to become an actor?"

"Yes", replied the young man. "I'm puh-puh-puh-perfectly wa-wa-willing to ba-ba-ba-be-gin at the ba-bottom—"

He stuttered hopelessly.

The most astonishing feature of stage fever, however, is that its ravages are not confined to the ranks of people who would be bettered by success in their chosen profession. My wealthiest friend, a silk importer, who owns a charming home in Central Park West, dines alone while his wife stands in the wings of a dirty little theater in Paris, where their only daughter earns a hundred francs a week by dancing. A successful literary man of my acquaintance, who would cheerfully devote his entire income, something more than fifteen thousand a year, to making his young wife happy in his cozy apartment yields per force to her wish to appear in vaudeville. The most valuable member of the staff of an out-of-town newspaper, recipient of a big salary, suddenly threw up his position two years ago, since when he

"A wrinkled old woman confided her desire to be seen as Juliet"

has been employed seven weeks, and that seven weeks in an organization presenting "The Chinatown Trunk Mystery."

A. L. Wilbur, at the time when he conducted the well-known Wilbur Opera Company, printed in the program of his performances an advertisement for chorus girls. Successful applicants were paid twelve dollars a week, yet recruits came by the dozens from the best families in the territory through which the aggregation was touring. Scores of the young women who play merry villagers on Broadway today are well born and bred victims of the virus. "Society" has contributed even to the ranks of the chorus men, whose caste is far below that of their betighted sisters. When Maybelle Gilman opened her metropolitan season in "The Mocking Bird" a male chorister, whose weekly stipend was eighteen dollars, electrified the management by purchasing nine boxes. This Croesus of the chorus proved to be "Deacon" Moore, a Cornell graduate and son of one of the biggest mine operators in the West.

The germ of stage fever frequently is as slow to get out of the system as it is quick to enter it. Douglas Fairbanks is a clever comedian, who, after a long apprenticeship, has been elevated to the stellar rank by William A. Brady. Mr. Fairbanks fell in love with the daughter of Daniel J. Sully, and, according to report, was given parental permission to marry her if he would abandon his profession. Mr. Fairbanks retired from the stage, and was out of the cast of "The Man of the Hour" for a trifle less than two months. Margaret Fuller came to town a few years ago with an ambition to star. She enlisted the help of a well-known manager, who told her that he would give her a chance to play Camille if she could get rid of twenty pounds of superfluous flesh. Miss Fuller presented "Camille" at a special matinee, and has not been heard of since. She is still in the theatrical profession, content with minor roles, but clinging tenaciously to the vocation. There are hundreds of men and women haunting the agencies in New York, promenading that graveyard of buried hopes, The Great White Way, who might be enjoying the comfort of luxurious homes and the affectionate care of doting relatives.

In nine cases out of ten the mania to go on the stage is prompted by pure desire for glorification. Love of excitement, and the fallacious notion that the profession is one of comparative ease and luxury, may be alloying factors, but the essence of the virus is vanity. No other field offers the same quick approval of successful effort, and no other climber is quite so much the center of his eventual triumph. In the other arts, approbation follows less promptly and is less direct. The fortunate player hears the intoxicating music of applause a dozen times every evening and two dozen times on matinee days. He struts about his mimic world, the observed of all observers, conscious of the strained attention of the thousands who have paid to see him, profiting not only by his own achievements but by those of the author, the director, the scene-painter and the orchestra. The newspapers are full of his praise and his photographs, recording his slightest doing and giving to the opinions expressed by him, or by his press agent, an importance scarcely less than might be accorded the President of the United States. In the course of time he even begins to arrogate to himself the heroic virtues of the characters he impersonates. It is sweet to see one's name on the cover of a novel, sweet to scrawl one's autograph in the lower left-hand corner of a painting, but O, how doubly and trebly sweet to meet one's own image lithographed under a laudatory line and posted between advertisements of the newest breakfast food and the latest five cent cigar!

The temptation is the stronger, as the rewards are more numerous, if the aspirant happens to be a woman. The gentler sex may not have greater vanity than the stronger, but it takes greater delight in commendation and it has keener appreciation of luxury. If the much-mentioned "society belle" longs for the glitter and gaud supposed to exist behind the footlights, how can one blame the daughters of poverty and squalor who make up the rank and file of the chorus? James Forbes has embodied the minds of these girls in his Patricia O'Brien in "The Chorus Lady." What wonder that they try to escape the sordid commonplaces of their poor lives for the glory of the theater, and delight to strut their "brief hour" in a palace, even if that palace be of canvas and scantling? The prospect of diamonds and automobiles cannot exert a stronger appeal to the men and women who dwell in dreary drudgery than does the hope of becoming *somebody*, of enjoying even a temporary illumination of their obscurity.

"How sweet to meet one's own image"

Charles Dickens vividly explained the psychology of this longing for prominence in his chapter on "Private Theaters" in "Sketches by Boz." In his day there were scores of these institutions in London, each "the center of a little stage-struck neighborhood." In the lobby of each was hung a placard quoting the price for which willing amateurs might play certain desirable parts. To be the Duke of Glo'ster, in "Richard III", cost £2, the part being well worth that amount because "the Duke must wear a real sword, and, what is better still, he must draw it several times in the course of the piece." We have no such private theaters on this side of the water, but there are nearly two hundred amateur dramatic clubs in Brooklyn, while other communities possess these organizations in proportion to their size.

There are three well-trod roads to the stage. One wanders through membership in a society like those mentioned, another and straighter is by way of the dramatic schools, while the third, and most frequented, goes direct from the home to the office of agent or manager. Of dramatic schools the number is legion, but only those conducted by dishonest adventurers promise employment to the enrolled student. "Be an actor for $1", is the alluring caption of an advertisement carried weekly by a number of periodicals, but the aspirants who make it profitable for that institution to go on advertising must be exceptionally gullible. New York has many "academies" in which useful technicalities of the art are carefully taught, and the managers of several of these "academies" keep in close touch with the producing interests of the country. While they guarantee nothing, they frequently are able to place their graduates in small parts. Grace George, Margaret Illington, and other well-known stars have come out of these schools.

The direct path to which reference has been made is full of difficulties and obstacles. Agencies are established with the purpose of helping communication between managers and the actors most in demand. They are busy places, with little time to devote to the novice, and the average impresario is not more nearly inaccessible than their executive heads. Every year the producing manager is less inclined to see applicants or to make opportunities for people of whom he knows nothing. It is all very well to be recommended by some acquaintance of the man who "presents", but friendship is only friendship, and nobody will risk the success of a production that has cost thousands of dollars merely to please an associate. The current method of selecting a company is quick and simple. A copy of the play's cast is sent to the manager, who writes opposite each character the name of the actor whom he thinks most likely to interpret that role to advantage. Then the manager's secretary sends for the fortunate Thespian. This system is undeniably hard, and perhaps unjust to the beginner, but such sentiment as gets into the theater comes in manuscripts, and, in these days of severe critical judgment, the investor in drama has the fullest right to minimize his risk.

Out of every hundred tyros who come to town in search of an engagement ten may secure the coveted prize, and not more than one person out of that ten makes a decent living from his or her adopted profession. It is too much to say that one aspirant in a thousand achieves real success. The average salary in the chorus is $18, and for speaking parts in dramatic performances it cannot be more than $40. No one is paid during the period devoted to rehearsal, and a long season lasts somewhere between thirty and thirty-five weeks. The sane way of computing wages in the theatrical business, therefore, is to multiply by thirty and divide the result by fifty-two. Following this system, it will be seen that the seeming $40 a week really is only $23. The most ardent and ambitious among the stage-struck will admit that this is not an income permitting the employment of a chauffeur or the purchase of a palatial residence on Riverside Drive.

Nor is the matter or remuneration the only disappointment connected with entrance into the theatrical profession. This is the one vocation in which the worker must begin again every year. If the fairly-successful actor "gets something" for the current season, he will find almost equal difficulty in getting something else for the season to follow. Unless he has made a prodigious hit—and prodigious hits are very rare—he finds himself no farther advanced next June than he was last September. Should he be lucky enough to remain in New York, he occupies a hall room in a boarding house, and, failing in this doubtful good fortune, he faces a long term on "the road."

Excepting only solitary confinement in prison, the world probably holds no terror surpassing that of touring the "one night
stands." Lost to his best friends and companions, travelling at
all hours of the day and night, grateful for board and lodging
that would not be tolerated by a domestic servant, the player
with a small road company has ample reason to repent his
choice of a career. To illustrate the universal dread of this fate,
I quote the lines printed under a comic picture in the Christmas issue of a prominent dramatic weekly:

DOCTOR—You're pretty badly run down, my friend. I
should advise change of scene.

PATIENT—(Just returned from thirty weeks of "one night
stands" with the Ripping Repertoire Company). Heaven have
mercy on me! (He dies).

Of course, it is quite futile to recite facts like these to the victim of stage fever. That unhappy individual is certain that he or
she will positively enjoy such discomforts as your feeble fancy
can paint, and doubly sure that the ugly present will fade into
a roseate future just as it does in the transformation scene at
the end of "Uncle Tom's Cabin." Tell this adventurer that one
histrion in a thousand succeeds and your reply is bound to be:
"I'll be that one." And, to speak truth, he or she *may* be that
one. Celebrated actors are made from queer material sometimes, and the roster of well-known people on our stage includes the names of men and women who were originally
plumbers, waitresses, floor-walkers and cloak-models. The
beginner may be positive, however, that these players did not
advance while they still had the intellects and the training required in the occupations mentioned. No person can possibly
succeed on the dramatic stage without the foundation of genuine talent and a superstructure of culture and education. A
woman whose pronunciation betrayed the baseness of her
early environment could not win enduring fame if she had the
temperament of a Bernhardt.

Generally, however, the woman who thinks she has the temperament of a Bernhardt really has only anaemia and a great
deal of vanity. If she has not mistaken her symptoms, and,
besides genuine ability, has a good education, some money, infinite patience, an iron constitution, and a mind made up to

the bitterness of long waiting and constant disappointment, she may eventually win a position half as important and a fourth as agreeable as that which she pictured in her imagination.

She is far luckier if her desire to go on the stage proves akin to and as fleeting as the average small boy's desire to be a burglar.

1911

STARK YOUNG

Stark Young (1881–1963) was arguably the most poetically idealistic drama critic America has produced. The Mississippi-born aesthete studied theatre at Yale under the eminent Brander Matthews and managed to see all the great stars of the day, native and foreign, in New Haven and New York. In 1921, on resigning from Amherst College where he had been a popular instructor of literature, he became the dramatic critic of *The New Republic*, where he stayed until he retired in 1947; a supporter of the New Stagecraft, he also served as associate editor of its flagship publication, *Theatre Arts Monthly* (1921–30). Young quit a one-year stint at *The New York Times* because he disliked the daily grind, having to come up with an immediate response, provide a plot summary, and insert puff pieces. His preferred method was to choose which play he would review, attend it several times, and weigh his impressions before composing a well-wrought essay. He was able to convey the quintessence of a performance to a reader who had not seen it, as well as enlighten those who had.

In Harold Clurman's words, Young "stood for something." With his sensitivity to color, line, form, and the spoken word, that "something" was often Beauty with a capital B. Although he could draw on his wide knowledge of art and literature to make his points, Young was a hands-on critic. He worked with Eugene O'Neill and Robert Edmond Jones at the Provincetown Playhouse, wrote plays of his own, taught at the New School for Social Research, and learned Russian to translate *The Seagull* for the Lunts. His early essay arguing that the American South was a rich but unexploited field for drama bore fruit soon after with the plays of Hatcher Hughes, Paul Green, and, eventually, Tennessee Williams, Carson McCullers, and Lillian Hellman. Young's analysis of John Barrymore as the Hamlet of his generation deserves comparison with William Winter on Edwin Booth's Prince of Denmark (see page 150). This was the highwater mark of Barrymore's stage career; having begun as a light comedian, he had graduated to tragedy with Richard III and the protagonists of Galsworthy and Tolstoy. It was also the beginning of a decline, as he moved to Hollywood and (despite delightful, often self-mocking turns in such films as *Twentieth Century* and *The Great Man*) eventually projected the public image of a ham basted in Scotch.

Some American Dramatic Material

IT is doubtless a pleasant thing to think one's country the best country in the world, one's state the best state in the country, one's town the best town in the state, one's family the best family in the town, and one's self the best member of the family. That is not the attitude of this paper, however. What I shall say is not meant to be comparative. No sectional inferences for better or for worse are to be drawn. When a point is made about the South, there is no intention of implying that such is not more or less true about other parts of the country. What I am trying to do is simply to point out elements in the South that might serve as useful material in the development of American drama.

Nor am I saying that there ought to be a Southern drama. I have, generally speaking, small faith in localized art. Certainly we have in this country no such difference as obtains between Ireland and England. And even if we could have a localized drama, it would be of doubtful advantage.

The gain to drama that I am to point out would be rather a broadening than a provincializing. The American drama at present is almost as provincialized as it might be under the Merrie Monarch of Yvetot; for New York is the American drama. To hear that said, New York would smile. Nevertheless the fact remains that the verdict of New York is absurdly respected. The rest of the nation is like the citizens in the old plays, who are allowed to huzzah and acclaim, but enjoy little share in the action. To please New York is the ultimate desideratum; New York is the *arbiter elegantiarum* of all things dramatic; we have a Knickerbocker Petronius. This is to be regretted, for the East has much to contribute, and so have the West and the South.

What I shall say, then, is no plea for Southern drama, as if there could be such a thing nowadays, but rather an attempt to indicate the possibilities in the South of material that may be available for dramatic uses, and that might by supplying thus new matter, give to our drama a deeper and more widely national content and significance, and by reason of that fact a content and truth more universal and eternal.

At the mention of the dramatic material of a country, one thinks ordinarily of the history or legend of the country as material for incident and plot. That would be the popular impression certainly, since plot and situation are to the popular mind the most immediate substance for drama. Surely, Southern history does not fall below that of the rest of the country, to put the case mildly—since it comprises a gamut of effects, from the genteel and stately colonial, and those heroic Marathons of Vicksburg and the Alamo, to the later endurance and suffering, and actions more convincing and pathetic than those of war. The states are full of stories, of bravery, of a kind of Roman stateliness, of grief, of sacrifice, of deeds sometimes that show a strangely savage intensity, and sometimes are splendidly elemental and heroic. The history of events, however, affords but superficial material for drama—since incidents are easy to invent; it is the result of the past and present, as shown in the people, that really counts.

Now, it is the temperament of a people that must always be the matrix of drama. The struggle of the old and the new goes on over the entire South, and is rendered vivid by the particularly vivid nature of the old. Everywhere the new progress and energy goes side by side with the old memories, and is finding its own harmony and place. The old elegance and retirement and courtesy and manliness must shape itself to the hurry and the competitive progress and the heartiness of the new. The interurban wants a right of way through the colonel's garden!

Thus the new South finds itself with many new formative influences bearing upon its development. The field is full of grave matters: there is the race problem, the industrial problem, child labor, and so on; the South in the West, immigration, the inter-oceanic canal, the changing politics, with its severing of old ties, the decline of cultural interest before materialism, and other problems of the optimists and pessimists, socialists, atheists, Republicans, Democrats, Prohibitionists, Populists, what not?—people whom our grandfathers classed as Whigs and Democrats, as churchgoers and non-churchgoers.

Behind the life of latter years is a background—all the more glorious by contrast—of ante-bellum memories. What youth ever had his golden age so near as the young Southerner has! Behind, and near behind, lies a life that he has been taught to think of as beautiful and gallant and full and heroic. And yet he has not that sighing after dead days, that cry of the *avi famosi*, that Leopardi sang. He does not feel that he is born too late; but looks on his own time and on his future as full of promise, however different it may be in kind from the old. Thus—and it is an interesting situation, I think—what would otherwise be decadence is buoyed up with a new energy.

Your young Southerner of the best type remains true to the past, and at the same time stands by the future. Behind him he sees the past lovely and tender, before him the struggle; he loves them both. His convictions and instincts belong most often to the old régime; his exigencies and practical conclusions belong to the new; and he cares very little as a rule whether he be strictly consistent or not.

So far as that goes, the Southerner has no desire to establish his life and convictions on a basis of rigid logic. He likes sentiment and romance and a touch of heart. He goes not always in customary suits of solemn black. He has, as Rostand's old Patou would say, the courage of color on his wing. He has, too, to some extent, that good old Irish trait of not being afraid of making himself ridiculous. There is a wisdom of the heart, he knows, as well as of the head; and he knows that, as Molière says, reasoning is fatal to reason. Which is another way of saying that he is still a human being; not yet, at least, a machine in the service of society and progress. There is dramatic material enough in this struggle to live in the heart, to be human, irrational, individual, before the demands of that great, rational, impersonal thing called "progress." And the human and individual is the drama's first necessity.

The standard American temperament, as found in the newspapers, and banking-houses, and such plays as "Paid in Full," is somewhat lean; and, whatever else its excellencies may be, it is meagre in self-expression. To the Anglo-Saxon repression it adds nervous energy and haste. This standard—mind, I do not say ideal—American abhors any exhibition of emotion, and is apt to regard the display of feeling in general, and often the feelings themselves, as forms of weakness. Your Italian, your Frenchman, your German or Russian, delight in their sensations, in the play of their emotional selves, their enthusiasms, their admirations, their humors good and bad. The American often feels that the foreigner carries this to the point of excess; but is himself likely to err at the other extreme. Psychologically we know that unemployed faculties are apt to dwindle. At any rate, the point here is, that this standard temperament—though it may be excellent for banks and counting-houses—shows, so far as art is concerned, a lack of adaptability. When it does wish to run the scale of its complete self, it finds the action stiff and half the keys stuck. This reserve makes a temperamental miser, and, like Plautus' Euclio, shuts all the doors of the house and lets no stranger in. And what—as the servant asks—what if anyone should ask for fire? Alas, the fire on this hearth is fanned and fed so little that it is apt to be cold or out.

To return to the illustration taken, Mr. Walter's play "Paid in Full." The play was a shrewd and energetic American adaptation of "The Doll's House." It was entertaining; but, I think, not in the end satisfactory, because of the thinness of the characters. They were ordinary subordinates in the business world, true to the surface of their originals; neither they nor the author showed one flash of vision and insight; shrewdness and energy remain the keynote of the play. The average Southern temperament avoids at least this quality of leanness. Its keynote is a sort of Irish warm-bloodedness. Whatever its faults may be, of impulsiveness, easy-goingness, prejudice and pride, it has surely the qualities of full-bloodedness and sympathy. Even its faults are positive, are expressive. The point is, that the Southern nature is apt to be positive rather than negative; its faults and virtues are expressive, often explosive; and expressibility is one of the first essentials of dramatic material. For that matter, drama does not care particularly whether its material is labeled fault or virtue; and strongly suspects perhaps that the two cannot always be distinguished. Like Mr. Shaw's Napoleon making his chart, what it wants is "blood." In drama, blood is the thing; to have veins full of blood and a heart to drive it back and forth. The Southern faults and virtues possess a certain something of the elemental that has about it the flavor of humanity.

The life of the South, like the Latin life that underlies Terence and Plautus and Goldoni and Molière, smacks of the community; it is marked by its sociability. There is much speaking over gates, and the tram cars and shops are as friendly as parlors. Southerners are great conversers and great visitors, both of which aptitudes are conducive to self-expression and responsiveness. This may be related to another point: there is something about the strictly Southern temperament that might serve to counterbalance the tendency in serious modern drama to morbidity and excessive innerness. The Southerner has sentiment, sentimentality, romance, heroism, and heroics —even sensationalism—rather than morbidity; and exhibits more of the tender and emotional than of innerness.

Every hall-marked Southerner's forefathers have *lived*; they have all struggled and loved and hated; they have died on battle-fields and of broken hearts—whatever else may be said, they were not colorless. I know a man whose grandmother rode horseback from Georgia to Mississippi, eloped later and married, and years after died of a broken heart a few months after her husband. This man's father was killed at Shiloh, and his sword stands in the big parlor still, with the blood stains on the scabbard. The man's mother, brought up like a doll, faced marauders during the war and famine afterward; lifted the mortgage; educated her children; and lives to-day with the memory of the old courtesy and romance and gallantry still clinging about her brave little body and her tired eyes. The man himself ran away to the war when he was old enough; he was in Johnson's Island Prison, and received there letters and socks from a Kentucky girl, whom he afterward met face to face and married. Surely, we have here a whole family theatre.

All of us sigh sometimes at the too frequent absence—if not of kings and queens—at least of ladies and gentlemen from our stage; the absence, all too frequent, of the grand manner, and often even of good manners. Nietzsche remarks somewhere that the value of a man's life may be measured by the extent to which his words and deeds take on a lasting significance. To say that another way: it is the man behind the deed that makes the deed count. Surely, in many of our plays the deeds lose significance for lacking people of value to do them. Surely, we weary sometimes of people whose selves diminish the significance and appeal of their deeds. We have too many people who suffer because of what they cannot do. We would welcome more of those finer types of people who suffer because of things from the doing of which they restrain themselves for noble reasons, or reasons at least that seem to them noble. We have had something too much of shady persons who take the bit of passion between their teeth. We should like more of those to whom a fine restraint and control give a strength and a capacity for experience that is larger and more significant. Granting that we have plenty of ladies and gentlemen in our plays, we should like the outside of them, their manners, the daily painting of themselves on our minds, to have more of the earmarks of their quality. At the least we should like an external expression that might suggest breeding and the intention of nobility. All this is not meant so much to imply that Southerners have more gentility than the rest of the nation, but rather that they have a strong *sense* of gentility. The true Southerner has a strong sense of the genteel; he has many scruples of *noblesse oblige*; the family sense is strong in him. Whether he has it or not, he is apt to see himself picturesquely, as a personage of blood. He must refrain from certain things out of respect to his lineage. To an outsider this may seem superficial, grandiose, absurd. As a matter of fact, it is sometimes noble and splendid, sometimes pathetic, sometimes ludicrous. I know a woman whose husband is nephew to one of the oldest earldoms in Scotland; she tries to assist him in a little truck farm they manage; and her hands are hard and her face very worn. If ever there was a fine lady, she is one. She never apologizes and would resent sympathy; but her gracious dignity and courtesy and quietness are pathetic almost to tears. I know another, who is without descent, but thinks of herself as a *grande dame*, and measures her words and shapes her manners after the royal fashion. Every word and every movement conveys the high intent of Cæsar's daughter. She is a quaint sort of burlesque on aristocracy. But her solemn affectation serves at least to save her from a loud vulgarity. What I wish to say, in brief, is this: the South has a marked sense of gentility, of *noblesse obliqe*, of manners, which may serve to give a better surface for the painting of the dramatic picture; that this—if we stop there—may help to give a certain scope and suggestiveness to the characters; may keep out too much of the *bourgeois* and meagre; and may lead to such a presentation of words, actions, and attitudes as may be gracious and ornate as well as noble.

It goes without saying that one of the most powerful resources of literature lies in the quality of the language employed. To hit the word closest to the matter, to find the word of all words that will seem to be inevitable and unavoidable, is one of the first means towards that effect of innerness and truth that is a mark of great writing. Not all great writers possess it, and sometimes a man who is not great may have this one gift.

I have heard, in the course of my travels, language that seems never to touch life, language in the face of which a word of the slightest emotional color seems either intense or affected. *Very good* does the duty of a dozen other words; *very good* may mean passable, wonderful, lovely, delightful, delicious, beautiful. "Yes, Othello is very good," a man said to me once. And, in addition to this cool propriety and decorum, a sense of economy is apparent: one calls the starry innocents "bluets" because they are blue; one says "bone butter" for marrow; walnut and black walnut for hickory nut and walnut; "my hair sticks up" for cowlick, and so on and so on. Sometimes, too, there is a strong sense of logic. They smile at us when we say "mighty" good—how could it be mighty? Alas, for the purposes of literature the worst thing that can happen to a language is for logic to get hold of it, and make it explicable and systematic. Well for logic, perhaps, but for the language—"Ah me!" it may cry with Metadorus in the play, "Sister, you are knocking the brains out of me. You are speaking stones." The more logical, the more explicable and systematic a language is, the farther it is removed from elemental life; because that life is never explicable or systematic.

Among modern dramatists, the man in English who, in my opinion, has shown most of this word gift—within his peculiar limitations, of course—is John Synge. In reading his plays over and over, I have often been struck with the similarity in freshness between many of his phrases and phrases to be heard in the South. *To get shut of, a sprinkling of them, to be huffy,* and many others; not to speak of the many vivid ways of putting things, and the general vivacity. An interesting experiment in this direction was made by Mr. Edward Sheldon in his play "The Nigger." The means employed are worthy of the theory that colleges can teach anything beyond mere technique of the "small fry" variety, and worthy also of the American conviction that demand can create supply, even of the arts. Their expositions are good, their conclusions are bad; these young men can be taught to mix the cake, but they cannot bake it. The author goes at it by simply omitting all the r's in the book, wherever Southerners are speaking. Word becomes wo'd, bird becomes bi'd. This is, of course, provincialism in the young author, and is equivalent to saying that unless one pronounces a word as he does, one should change its usual spelling; that Mr. Forbes Robertson, for example, should spell work *wo'k*, because he does not pronounce the *r* as Mr. Sheldon does. All that, apart from the loss in artistic effect by the distraction of the spelling. That is not the point, however, which is that the play is without language gift, and that the machine-made method does all the work; and that beyond such superficial bits as "you all," there is scarcely a tang, scarcely the faintest savor, of Southern talk.

Just what this savor is, of course, would be hard to say; but every Southerner has memories from his childhood of talking that lingers and glows with him yet; words full of impulse, of tenderness, of quaintness, sentiment, passion, bitter prejudice; and of old phrases full of life and experience. And out-of-the-way words and phrases: *jackleg, thingum-doochy, the last of peapicking, to get a larruping, to know B from bull's foot*. And names of things: *piggins* and *ash-hoppers* and *clapboards* and *barlows* and *coverlids*.

Something in them, too, has shot this language of theirs upward. Southerners have a strong turn for eloquence and oratory. Over and over the pages of history say that for us in remembered great names. Oratory, as such, is something out of date nowadays; but in all public meetings down South its heat is still to be felt. And if there is one thing that the realistic drama of to-day needs, it is that its people should be allowed to indulge sometimes a natural craving for eloquence. We should all feel better if some one in Ibsen would go off some day and blow the cap from the scientific cylinder in which he has been condensed.

Apart, however, from any manifest quaintness or any eloquence, it is not too much to say, I think, that the talk of Southerners is marked by impetuosity and vividness, and given to idioms and the flavor of old time; that it is fairly undisturbed as yet by the leveling tendency of immigration and commercial democracy.

All art must work side by side with life. And those ages in which art grows most easily into greatness are the ages when art can find in the life and speech of men the material most ready to its hand. It was in that richest of our English periods, the Elizabethan, that our dramatists wrote most easily and best; for the glow and press of the time, the vision and spaciousness of that great day, and its reflection in speech, stood ready at hand. The naturalistic, the realistic, and the poetic were easily fused into one, for the poetry of that age was its life, and so its life was poetry.

I do not, of course, say that we have any such conditions as the Elizabethan; but I do say that there is something well worth while which the South may contribute to drama; that there are still among us memories of a rich and touching past, to which a living present and future are seeking readjustment; that we have a speech not void of brawn and impulse and feeling; and that we have in the South—though not so much as once, however fondly we may hope—a people of heart, with something fiery and tender showing yet, in spite of the straitness and necessity of the new conditions; and that all this, scarcely as yet touched upon in American drama, constitutes material from which that drama may draw to round out and enrich itself; and that, in conclusion, were I asked to name the particular traits most notable in this material that the South might contribute to the drama of America, I should mention sentiment and romance, and a sense of the heroic and the eloquent.

1912

Hamlet

The Tragedy of Hamlet.
Sam H. Harris Theatre. November 20, 1922.

MR. JOHN BARRYMORE seemed to gather together in himself
all the Hamlets of his generation, to simplify and direct everyone's theory of the part. To me his Hamlet was the most satisfying that I have seen, not yet as a finished creation, but a
foundation, a continuous outline. Mounet-Sully's Hamlet was
richer and more sonorous; Forbes-Robertson's at times more
sublimated; Irving's more sharply devised and Sothern's, so far
as we are concerned strictly with the verse pattern, was more
securely read. But there is nothing in Mr. Barrymore's Hamlet
to get in the way of these accomplishments also, with time and
study. And in what he has done there is no inherent quality
that need prevent his achieving the thing most needed to perfect, in its own kind, his Hamlet; I mean a certain dilation and
abundance in all his reactions. This Hamlet of Mr. Barrymore's must give us—and already promises—the sense of a
larger inner tumult and indeed of a certain cerebral and passionate ecstasy, pressing against the external restraint of him.
He needs the suggestion of more vitality, ungovernable and
deep, of more complex suffering, of not only intellectual subtlety but intellectual power as well, all this added to the continuity of distinction that he already has, the shy and humorous
mystery, the proud irony, the terrible storms of pain. Mr.
Barrymore brings to the part what is ultimately as necessary to
a fine actor as to a fine singer, the physical gifts that enable him
to express his idea. He has a beautiful presence, a profound
magnetism. His English, much of which is but recently acquired through the teaching of the remarkable Mrs. Margaret
Carrington, is almost wholly reborn from what it once was,
and is now almost pure, even and exact, though not yet wholly
flexible. His voice, also to a considerable extent Mrs. Carrington's production, is not supreme. It is not a rich and sonorous volume such as Mansfield had, but is capable of high,
intelligent training, and is already in the middle tones highly
admirable.

With such an artist as Mr. Barrymore has risen to be, one cannot escape the matter of the technical means by which he fills out and develops the kind of truth that he sees in his rôle, or confuses and prevents its realization. His chief technical triumph, I think, lies in the absence from his work of all essentially theatrical faults. There are no idle tricks of the voice, no empty display of actor vanity and professional virtuosity, no foolish strutting, none of the actor idol's way of feeling his oats. There is no egotistical intrusion on the play, no capricious distortion of the truth in the service of histrionic exhibitionism. Throughout the performance the technical method is invariably derived from the conception of the part and never allowed to run ahead of it.

Mr. Barrymore's important technical limitations at this stage of his achievement seem to me to be two. The first concerns the verse. The "resistant flexibility," to use an old phrase, that is the soul of fine reading, he has not yet completely acquired. Much of his reading is excellent; but now and again in his effort to keep the verse true to its inner meaning and to the spiritual naturalness that underlies it—and because, too, of a lack of concentration on his projection at times—Mr. Barrymore seems to be afraid to admit the line for what it is, verse. Sometimes he allows the phrases to fall apart in such a way that the essential musical pattern of the verse—which is a portion of the idea itself—is lost. In the line—to take an example—

> Why, she would hang on him,

he put a heavy stress on the word "hang" and almost let the "him" disappear; a useless naturalism, for the same effect of sense emphasis can be secured and yet the verse pattern of the lines preserved, by sustaining the nasals in "on" and "him" with no more actual stress on them than Mr. Barrymore used.

For one more instance out of a good many, take the line

> Must, like a whore, unpack my heart with words.

Mr. Barrymore let the phrase "like a whore" fall out solid from the verse, which then began anew with "unpack." But there is a certain sustained unity to the line; "must" and "unpack" have a resistant connection together—to be secured by the tone—which the intervening phrase does not break off. And, as a matter of fact, everywhere in Shakespeare the long, difficult, elaborate and complex passages depend above everything on their musical unity to recreate out of their many details that first profound unity of emotion from which they sprang. Without this unity these details appear to be—as in fact they often are, in the earlier plays especially—mere images and ornaments thrown in, whose artificiality is only embarrassing.

The other technical limitation that I feel in Mr. Barrymore is in his rendering of decreasing emotion. To be able to rise successfully to emotional heights is one measure of an actor's art; but this declining gradation is a no less sure test of it. For an illustration of what I mean, take the passage in the closet scene where the Ghost vanishes.

HAMLET: Why, look you there! look how it steals away!
My father in his habit as he lived!
Look, where he goes, even now, out at the portal!
QUEEN: This is the very coinage of your brain;
This bodiless creation ecstasy
Is very cunning in.
HAMLET: Ecstasy!
My pulse as yours doth temperately keep time,—

Mr. Barrymore repeats the word and goes on with the speech in a reasonable and almost even tone. But in such places a part of the effect of preceding emotion appears in the gradual lessening of it in the actor's manner and voice. This speech of Hamlet's is reasonable, yes, but the calm in the thought precedes the calm in the state of emotion; the will and the idea are to rule but only after conflict with the emotion.

I cannot admire too much Mr. Barrymore's tact in the scenes with Polonius. Most actors for the applause they get play up for all it is worth Hamlet's seemingly rude wit at the old man's expense. But Mr. Barrymore gave you only Hamlet's sense of the world grown empty and life turned to rubbish in this old counselor. And, without seeming to do so he made you feel that Polonius stood for the kind of thing in life that had taken Ophelia from him. How finely—even in that last entreaty to Laertes for fair usage—Mr. Barrymore maintained an absence of self-pity in Hamlet, and thus enlarged the tragic pity of the play! What a fine vocal economy he exercised in the scene where Horatio tells him of his father's ghost! And what a stroke of genius it was, when by Ophelia's grave Hamlet had rushed through those mad lines, piling one wild image on another, and comes to the

> Nay, and thou'lt mouth,
> I'll rant as well as thou

to drop on that last, on the "I'll rant as well as thou," into an aspirate tone, hoarse, broken with grief and with the consciousness of his words' excess and the excess of irony in all things!

And I must admire the economy of business—not all Mr. Barrymore's, of course, but partly due to Mr. Hopkins, Mrs. Carrington and Mr. Jones—all through the part. The nunnery scene with Ophelia was done with a reaching out of the hands almost; the relation of Hamlet to his mother and through her to the ghost was achieved by his moving toward the ghost on his knees and being caught in his mother's arms, weaving together the bodies of those two, who, whatever their sins might be, must belong to each other at such terrible cost. There were no portraits on the wall with a ghost stepping out, as Hackett used to do it in the sixties. There was no crawling forward on the floor to watch the King during the play, as so many actors have done; and none of Ophelia's peacock fan for Hamlet to tap his breast with and fling into the air, as Irving used to do. About all this production there were none of those accessories in invented business; there was for the most part, and always in intention, only that action proceeding from the inner necessity of the moment and leaning on life, not on stage expedients. The inner limitations of Mr. John Barrymore's Hamlet are both less tangible and less amendable perhaps. They are in the direction of the poetic and human. With time, meditation and repetition it will gain in these respects no doubt; but it needs now more warmth, more abundance in all the reactions, more dilation of spirit. It takes too much for granted, makes Hamlet too easy to understand, and so lacks mystery and scope. It needs a larger inner tumult, more of a cerebral and passionate ecstasy pressing against the outward restraint of the whole pattern. It needs more of the sense of an ungovernable vitality, more complex subtlety and power. It needs more tenderness and, above all, more, if you like, generosity.

Miss Fuller's Ophelia could not dominate the longer speeches in her first scenes. But in the mad scenes she sang her ballads with unheard-of poignancy; and the mere slip of her white, flitting body was itself the image of pathos. Miss Fuller sharpened the effect of madness by putting into it a hint of that last betrayal that insanity brings to Ophelia: indecency. Miss Yurka, though she subsided at times out of the part when she had nothing to do, read her lines admirably; and contrived to suggest without overstating it the loose quality in this woman that subjected her to the King. Mr. O'Brien's Polonius was good, simplified rather far, perhaps, but with a certain force of truth that rendered what Polonius, despite his fatuity, has: a kind of grotesque distinction. Mr. Reginald Pole brought to the Ghost's lines a fine ear and an exact method of reading the verse that you gratefully detect before he is three lines under way. The Laertes of Mr. Sidney Mather is the only very bad performance in the company. The role is extra difficult because of its Renaissance approach, through character and reality, to the flowery gallantry and lyric expedition required; though the bases of Laertes' feelings and actions seem to me fresh, accessible and human. The fact remains, nevertheless, that unless the actor gets the manner and flourish of Laertes, the expression of his vivid, poignant and decorative meaning cannot find its due outlet. Mr. Tyrone Power's King—superb in voice and metre—was admirable. He suggested not mere villainy but rather a tragic figure of force and heavy will. Mr. Power's King gave us also the sense of great charm exerted upon those around him that is attributed to the character in the play.

It is in the scene where Hamlet catches the King praying and does not kill him—the climax of the play—that the method of production employed by Mr. Hopkins and Mr. Jones is reduced, it seemed to me, to its most characteristic terms. The King enters through the curtain, already used a number of times, with the saints on it. He kneels, facing the audience. He lifts his hands and speaks to heaven. Hamlet enters through the same curtain. He debates the fitness of the

time for the King's murder, decides against it, withdraws. The
King says

> My words fly up, my thoughts remain below;
> Words without thoughts never to heaven go.

and rises and goes out. One man is here, one is there. Here are
the uplifted hands, there the sword drawn. Here, sick conscience, power, and tormented ambition; there, the torture of
conflicting thoughts, the irony, the resolution. Two bodies
and their relation to each other, the words, the essential
drama, the eternal content of the scene. No tricks, no plausible
business, no palace chapel. And no tradition.

Tradition of conception there is now and again, of course;
but throughout the entire production there is very little concern about external tradition. And what of it? If we had some
kind of Théâtre Français, a conservatory where a classic like
Hamlet would be seen from time to time as a star returns on
its course; or if in our theatre we had a succession of rival
Hamlets, as was once the case, the question of tradition would
be more important. Under such conditions a certain symbolism of stage business might develop, full of deep significance,
familiar and accepted, and not to be abandoned too readily.
But in the American theatre today the disregard of Shakespearean tradition is easy and commendable. To pursue it
doggedly is to block the way with dead husks of forms once
full of meaning. It only thwarts the audience and Shakespeare's living matter with a kind of academic archaism and,
even, with a certain fanaticism; which consists, as Santayana
says, in redoubling your effort when you have forgotten your
aim. Messrs. Hopkins and Jones and Barrymore have, for the
most part, let sleeping dogs lie. Nothing could be easier than
not to do so; hence their eminence.

Mr. Robert Edmond Jones has created a permanent setting
of architectural forms and spaces, bounded across the stage,
and down two-thirds to the front line of it, with a play of steps.
Within this, easy variations are possible to indicate the changes
of scene. The design of the setting cannot be conveyed in words,
of course, but it is princely, austere and monumental. It has no
clutter of costumes or elaborate variations in apartments, but
instead a central rhythm of images, of light and shade innate to

the dramatic moment. The shortcoming of this bold and eloquent setting is that it either goes too far or does not go far
enough. In this respect the limit was reached when the time
came for the scene of Ophelia's burial, where the setting was at
least enough like a palace to make the grave toward the front
of the stage—and therefore the whole scene —appear to be incongruous if not absurd. A greater vastness of imagination was
thus required of the designer. In his defense it should be said,
however, that our theatre does not easily allow for repeated experiment, with the discarding and choosing and the expense
involved.

This production of *Hamlet* is important and is out of class
with Shakespeare production from other sources. This is not
through any perfection in the field of the Shakespearean so
called; but because it works toward the discovery of the essential and dramatic elements that from the day it was written
have underlain this play. The usual Shakespeare production,
however eminent, goes in precisely the opposite direction. It
does not reveal the essential so much as it dresses up the scene
at every conceivable angle, with trappings, research, scenery,
business.

Such a production as this of *Hamlet* could not hope to be
uniformly successful. But in its best passages, without any
affectation of the primitive or archaic, it achieved what primitive art can achieve: a fundamental pattern so simple and so revealing that it appeared to be mystical; and so direct and
strong that it restored to the dramatic scene its primary truth
and magnificence. For a long time to come this *Hamlet* will be
remembered as one of the glories of our theatre.

1922

WILLIAM GILLETTE

The Edwardian English actor Gerald Du Maurier was said to underplay his partners off the stage. In fact, an understated, more natural style of acting had already taken root in America, exemplified by many Yankee comedians and in particular Joseph Jefferson. The trend culminated in William Hooker Gillette (1853–1937). Gillette was also a new breed of actor in being college-educated at Harvard and MIT. After his first stage appearance in 1875, he made a minor name in farce, light comedy, and Shakespeare. But his ambition led him to realize that actors became great "because of their successful use of their own strong and compelling personalities in the rôles which they made famous." The nine parts he enacted out of the 20 plays he wrote showcased him as a cool, polished, charming gentleman, always in control. These included the urbane sugar-plantation owner in *Too Much Johnson* (1894), the Union spy sending coded messages by telegraph in *Secret Service* (1895), and especially the lead in *Sherlock Holmes* (1899), which he played over 1,300 times before retiring in 1932. He became so identified with the legendary detective that Frederic Dorr Steele used his image in his illustrations for Conan Doyle's stories.

" 'The Illusion of the First Time' in Drama" was delivered as a lecture in November 1913 at the fifth joint session of the American Academy of Arts and Letters and the National Institute of Arts and Letters in Chicago. This bespeaks the hard-won prestige of the actor-manager in Progressive-Era America. Gillette mediated the age-old debate on whether an actor should be a creature of artifice or genuine emotion; his compromise was that the actor should not be absolutely true to nature, but must be situated in the character's mental and emotional position. At many points this matches Stanislavsky's contemporaneous ideas that would eventually dominate the American stage.

"The Illusion of the First Time" in Drama

I AM to talk a brief paper this morning on a phase of what is called Drama, by which is meant a certain well-known variety of stage performance usually but not necessarily taking place in a theatre or some such public building, or even transplanted out into the grass, as it occasionally is in these degenerate days.

If you care at all to know how I feel about having to talk on this subject—which I do not suppose you do—but I'll tell you anyway—I am not as highly elated at the prospect as you might imagine. Were I about to deliver a Monograph on Medicine or Valuable Observations on Settlement Work and that sort of thing—or even if I had been so particularly fortunate as to discover the Bacillus of Poetry and could now report progress toward the concoction of a serum that would exterminate the disease without killing the poet—that is, without quite killing him, I could feel that I was doing some good. But I can't do any good to Drama. Nobody can. Nothing that is said or written or otherwise promulgated on the subject will affect it in the slightest degree. And the reason for this rather discouraging view of the matter is, I am sorry to say, the very simplest in the world as well as the most unassailable, and that is, the Record.

And what is meant by a "Record" is, roughly speaking, a History of Behavior along a certain line—a history of what has been done—of what has taken place, happened, occurred—of what effect has been produced, in the particular direction under consideration. We might say that Records are past performances or conditions along a specified line.

And upon these Records or Histories of Behavior, Occurrences, or Conditions, depend all that we know or may ever hope to know; for even Experiment and Research are but endeavors to produce or discover Records that have been hidden from our eyes. To know anything—to have any opinion or estimate or knowledge or wisdom worth having, we must take account of Past Performances, or be aware of the results of their consideration by others—perhaps more expert than we. Yet, notwithstanding this perfectly elementary fact of existence, there is a group or class of these Records, many of them relating to matters of the utmost interest and importance, the consideration of which would at least keep people from being so shamelessly duped and fooled as they frequently are, to which no one appears to pay the slightest attention.

This class or group of forgotten or ignored Items of Behavior I have ventured, for my own amusement, to call the

Dead Records,—meaning thereby that they are *dead to us*— dead so far as having the slightest effect upon human judgment or knowledge or wisdom is concerned, buried out of sight by our carelessness and neglect. And in this interesting but unfortunate group, and evidently gone to its last long rest, reposes the Record of the Effect upon Drama of what has been said and written about it by scholars and thinkers and critics. And if this Record could be roused to life—that is, to consideration but for a moment, it would demonstrate beyond the shadow of a doubt that Drama is perfectly immune from the manœuvres of any germ that may lurk in what people who are supposed to be "Intellectual" may say or write or otherwise put forth regarding it.

The unending torrent of variegated criticism, condemnation, advice, contempt,—the floods of space-writing, prophesying, high-brow and low-brow dinner-table and midnight-supper anathematizing that has cascaded down upon Drama for centuries has never failed to roll lightly off like water from the celebrated back of a duck—not even moistening a feather.

From all of which you will be able to infer without difficulty that it is perfectly hopeless for me to try to do any good to Drama. And I can't do it any harm either. Even that would be something. In fact nothing at all can be done to it. And as I am cut off in that direction there seems to be nothing left but to try if, by describing a rather extraordinary and harassing phase of the subject involving certain conditions and requirements from a Workshop point of view, it is possible so to irritate or annoy those who sit helpless before me, that I can feel something has been accomplished, even if not precisely what one might wish.

It must be a splendid thing to be able to begin right—to take hold of and wrestle with one's work in life from a firm and reliable standing-ground, and to obtain a comprehensive view of the various recognized divisions, forms, and limitations of that work, so that one may choose with intelligence the most advantageous direction in which to apply his efforts. The followers of other occupations, arts, and professions appear to have these advantages to a greater or less degree, while we who struggle to bring forth attractive material for the theatre are

without them altogether; and not only without them, but the
jumble and confusion in which we find ourselves is infinitely
increased by the inane, contradictory, and ridiculous things
that are written and printed on the subject. Even ordinary
names which might be supposed to define the common varieties of stage work are in a perfectly hopeless muddle. No one
that I have ever met or heard of has appeared to know what
Melodrama really is; we know very well that it is *not* Drama-
with-Music as the word implies. I have asked people who were
supposed to have quite powerful intellects (of course the cheap
ones can tell you all about it—just as the silliest and most
feebleminded are those who instantly inform you regarding
the vast mysteries of the universe)—I say I have made inquiries
regarding Melodrama of really intellectual people, and none of
them have appeared to be certain. Then there's plain Drama—
without the Melo, a very loose word applied to any sort of performance your fancy dictates. And Comedy—some people tell
you it's a funny, amusing, laughable affair, and the Dictionar-
ies bear them out in this; while others insist that it is any sort
of a play, serious or otherwise, which is not Tragedy or Farce.
And there's Farce, which derives itself from force—to stuff,—
because it was originally an affair stuffed full of grotesque antics and absurdities;—yet we who have occasion to appear in
Farce at the present day very well know that unless it is not
only written but performed with the utmost fidelity to life it is
a dead and useless thing. In fact it must not by any chance *be*
Farce! And there is the good old word Play that covers any and
every kind of Theatrical Exhibition and a great many other
things besides. Therefore, in what appears—at least to us—to
be this hopeless confusion, we in the workshops find it necessary to make a classification of Stage Work for our own use. I
am not advising anyone else to make it, but am confessing, and
with considerable trepidation—for these things are supposed
to be sacred from human touch—that *we* do it. Merely to hint to
a real Student of the Drama that such a liberty has been taken
would be like shaking a red bull before a rag. Sacrilege is the
name of this crime.

More or less unconsciously, they end without giving any
names or definitions (I am doing that for you this morning),
we who labor in the shops divide Stage Performances in which

people endeavor to represent others than themselves for the amusement and edification of spectators, into two sections:

1. Drama.
2. Other Things.

That's all. It's so simple that I suppose you'll be annoyed with me for talking about it. Drama—in the dictionary which we make for ourselves, is that form of Play or Stage Representation which expresses what it has to express in Terms of Human Life. Other Things are those which do not. Without doubt those Other Things may be classified in all sorts of interesting and amusing ways, but that is not our department. What we must do is to extricate Drama from among them;— and not only that, but we must carefully clear off and brush away any shreds or patches of them that may cling to it. We do not do this because we want to, but because we have to.

For us, then, Drama is composed of—or its object is attained by—simulated life episodes and complications, serious, tragic, humorous, as the case may be; by the interplay of simulated human passion and human character.

Other Things aim to edify, interest, amuse, thrill, delight, or whatever else they may aim to do, by the employment of language, of voice, of motion, of behavior, etc., as they would not be employed in the natural course of human existence. These unlife-like things, though they may be and frequently are, stretched upon a framework of Drama, are not Drama; for that framework so decorated and encumbered can never be brought to a semblance or a simulation of life.

Although I have stated, in order to shock no one's sensibilities, that this is our own private and personal classification of Stage Work, I want to whisper to you very confidentially that it doesn't happen to be original with us; for the development and specialization of this great Life-Class, *Drama*—or whatever you may please to call it, has been slowly but surely brought about by that section of the Public which has long patronized the better class of theatres. It has had no theories— no philosophy—not even a realization of what it does, but has very well known what it *wants*—yet by its average and united choosing has the character of Stage Work been changed and shaped and moulded, ever developing and progressing by the survival of that which was fittest to survive in the curious world of Human Preference.

Be so good as to understand that I am not advocating this classification in the slightest degree, or recommending the use of any name for it. I am merely calling attention to the fact that this Grand Division of Stage Work is here—with us—at the present day; and not only here, but as a *class* of work—as a method or medium for the expressing of what we have to express—is in exceedingly good condition. After years and centuries of development, always in the direction of the humanities, it closely approximates a perfect instrument, capable of producing an unlimited range of effects, from the utterly trivial and inconsequent to the absolutely stupendous. These may be poetical with the deep and vital poetry of Life itself, rather than the pleasing arrangement of words, thoughts, and phrases; tragical with the quivering tragedy of humanity— not the mock tragedy of vocal heroics; comical with the absolute comedy of human nature and human character—not the forced antics of clowns or the supernatural witticisms of professional humorists.

The possibilities of the instrument as we have it to-day are infinite. But those who attempt to use it—the writers and makers and constructors of Drama, are, of course, very finite indeed. They must, as always, range from the multitudes of poor workers—of the cheap and shallow-minded, to the few who are truly admirable. I have an impression that the conditions prevailing in other arts and professions are not entirely dissimilar. Some one has whispered that there are quite a few Paintings in existence which could hardly be said to have the highest character; a considerable quantity of third, fourth, and fifth rate Music—and some of no rate at all; and at least six hundred billion trashy, worthless, or even criminally objectionable, Novels. It would not greatly surprise me if we of the theatre—even in these days of splendid decadence—had a shade the best of it. But whether we have or have not, the explanation of whatever decline there may be in Dramatic Work is so perfectly simple that it should put to shame the vast army of writers who make their living by formulating indignant inquiries regarding it. For the highest authority in existence has stated in plain language that the true purpose of the Play is to

hold the mirror up to Nature—meaning, of course, human nature; and this being done at the present day a child in a kinder-
garten could see why the reflections in that mirror are of the
cheapest, meanest, most vulgar and revolting description.
Imagine for one moment what would appear in a mirror that
could truthfully reflect, upon being held up to the average
Newspaper of to-day in the United States! But I admit that
this is an extreme case.

And now I am going to ask you—(but it is one of those
questions that orators use with no expectation of an answer)—
I am going to inquire if anyone here or any where else goes so
far as to imagine for an instant that a Drama—a Comedy—a
Farce—a Melodrama—or, in one word, a Play, is the manuscript or printed book which is ordinarily handed about as
such? And now I will answer myself—as I knew I should all the
time. One probably does so imagine unless he has thought
about it. Doubtless you all suppose that when a person hands
you a play to read he hands you that Play—to read. And I am
here with the unpleasant task before me of trying to dislodge
this perfectly innocent impression from your minds. The person does nothing of that description. In a fairly similar case he
might say, "Here is the Music," putting into your hands some
sheets of paper covered with different kinds of dots and things
strung along what appears to be a barbed-wire fence. It is
hardly necessary to remind you that that is not the Music. If
you are in very bad luck it may be a "Song" that is passed to
you, and as you roll it up and put it in your hand-bag or your
inside overcoat-pocket, do you really think that is the *Song* you
have stuffed in there? If so, how cruel! But no! You are perfectly well aware that it is not the Song which you have in your
hand-bag or music-roll, but merely the Directions for a Song.
And that Song cannot, does not, and never will exist until the
specific vibrations of the atmosphere indicated by those Directions actually take place, and only during the time in which
they *are* taking place.

And quite similarly the Music which we imagined in your
possession a moment ago was not Music at all, but merely a
few sheets of paper on which were written or printed certain
Directions for Music; and it will not be Music until those Directions are properly complied with.

And again quite similarly the Play which you were supposed to be holding in your hand is not a Play at all, but simply the written or printed Directions for bringing one into being; and that Play will exist only when these Directions for it are being followed out—and not then unless the producers are very careful about it.

Incredible as it may seem there are people in existence who imagine that they can *read* a Play. It would not surprise me a great deal to hear that there are some present with us this very morning who are in this pitiable condition. Let me relieve it without delay. The feat is impossible. No one on earth can read a Play. You may read the *Directions* for a Play and from these Directions imagine as best you can what the Play would be like; but you could no more read the *Play* than you could read a Fire or an Automobile Accident or a Base-Ball Game. The Play—if it is Drama—does not even *exist* until it appeals in the form of Simulated Life. Reading a list of the things to be said and done in order to make this appeal is not reading the appeal itself.

And now that all these matters have been amicably adjusted, and you have so quietly and peaceably given up whatever delusion you may have entertained as to being able to read a Play, I would like to have you proceed a step further in the direction indicated and suppose that a Fortunate Dramatic Author has entered into a contract with a Fortunate Producing Manager for the staging of his work. I refer to the Manager as fortunate because we will assume that the Dramatist's Work appears promising; and I use the same expression in regard to the Author, as it is taken for granted that the Manager with whom he has contracted is of the most desirable description—one of the essentials being that he is what is known as a Commercial Manager.

If you wish me to classify Managers for you,—or, indeed, whether you wish it or not,—I will cheerfully do so. There are precisely two kinds, Commercial Managers and Crazy Managers. The Commercial Managers have from fifty to one hundred and fifty thousand dollars a year rent to pay for their theatres, and, strange as it may seem, their desire is to have the productions they make draw money enough to pay it, together with other large expenses necessary to the operation of a modern playhouse. If you read what is written you will find un-ending abuse and insult for these men. The followers of any other calling on the face of the earth may be and are com-mercial with impunity. Artists, Musicians, Opera Singers, Art Dealers, Publishers, Novelists, Dentists, Professors, Doctors, Lawyers, Newspaper and Magazine Men and all the rest— even Secretaries of State—are madly hunting for money. But *Managers*—Scandalous, Monstrous, and Infamous! And because of a sneaking desire which most of them nourish to produce plays that people will go to see, they are the lowest and most contemptible of all the brutes that live. I am making no reference to the managerial abilities of these men; in that they must vary as do those engaged in any other pursuit, from the multitudinous poor to the very few good. My allusion is solely to this everlasting din about their commercialism; and I pause long enough to propound the inquiry whether other things that proceed from intellects so painfully puerile should receive the slightest attention from sensible people.

Well, then, our Book of Directions is in the hands of one of these Wretches, and, thinking well of it, he is about to assem-ble the various elements necessary to bring the Drama for which it calls into existence. Being a Commercial Person of the basest description he greatly desires it to attract the paying public, *and for this reason* he must give it every possible advan-tage. In consultation with the Author, with his Stage-Manager and the heads of his Scenic, Electric, and Property Depart-ments he proceeds to the work of complying with the require-ments of the Book.

So far as painted, manufactured, and mechanical elements are concerned, there is comparatively little trouble. To keep these things precisely as much in the background as they would appear were a similar episode in actual life under observation— *and no more*—is the most pronounced difficulty. But when it comes to the Human Beings required to assume the Charac-ters which the Directions indicate, and not only to assume them but to breathe into them the Breath of Life—and not the *Breath* of Life alone but all other elements and details and items of Life so far as they can be simulated, many and serious discouragements arise.

For in these latter days Life-Elements are required. Not long ago they were not. In these latter days the merest slip from true Life-Simulation is the death or crippling of the Character involved, and it has thereafter to be dragged through the course of the play as a disabled or lifeless thing. Not all plays are sufficiently strong in themselves to carry on this sort of morgue or hospital service for any of their important rôles.

The perfectly obvious methods of Character Assassination such as the sing-song or "reading" intonation, the exaggerated and grotesque use of gesture and facial expression, the stilted and unnatural stride and strut, cause little difficulty. These, with many other inherited blessings from the "Palmy Days" when there was acting that really amounted to something, may easily be recognized and thrown out.

But the closeness to Life which now prevails has made audiences sensitive to thousands of minor things that would not formerly have affected them. To illustrate my meaning, I am going to speak of two classes of these defects. I always seem to have two classes of everything—but in this case it isn't so. There are plenty more where these came from. I select these two because they are good full ones, bubbling over with Dramatic Death and Destruction. One I shall call—to distinguish it, "The Neglect of the Illusion of the First Time"; the other, "The Disillusion of Doing it Correctly." There is an interesting lot of them which might be assembled under the heading "The Illusion of Unconsciousness of What Could Not Be Known"—but there will not be time to talk about it. All these groups, however, are closely related, and the "First Time" one is fairly representative. And of course I need not tell you that we have no names for these things—no groups—no classification; we merely fight them as a whole—as an army or mob of enemies that strives for the downfall of our Life-Simulation, with poisoned javelins. I have separated a couple of these poisons so that you may see how they work, and incidentally how great little things now are.

Unfortunately for an actor (to save time I mean all known sexes by that), unfortunately for an actor he knows or is supposed to know his part. He is fully aware—especially after several performances—of what he is going to say. The Character he is representing, however, does *not* know what he is going to say, but, if he is a human being, various thoughts occur to him one by one, and he puts such of those thoughts as he decides to, into such speech as he happens to be able to command at the time. Now it is a very difficult thing—and even now rather an uncommon thing—for an actor who knows exactly what he is going to say to behave exactly as though he didn't; to let his thoughts (apparently) occur to him as he goes along, even though they are there in his mind already; and (apparently) to search for and find the words by which to express those thoughts, even though these words are at his tongue's very end. That's the terrible thing—at his tongue's very end! Living and breathing creatures do not carry their words in that part of their systems; they have to find them and send them there—with more or less rapidity according to their facility in that respect—as occasion arises. And audiences of today, without knowing the nature of the fatal malady are fully conscious of the untimely demise of the Character when the actor portraying it apparently fails to do this.

In matters of speech, of pauses, of giving a Character who would think time to think; in behavior of eyes, nose, mouth, teeth, ears, hands, feet, etc., while he does think and while he selects his words to express the thought—this ramifies into a thousand things to be considered in relation to the language or dialogue alone.

This menace of Death from "Neglect of the Illusion of the First Time" is not confined to matters and methods of speech and mentality, but extends to every part of the presentation, from the most climacteric and important action or emotion to the most insignificant item of behavior—a glance of the eye at some unexpected occurrence—the careless picking up of some small object which (supposedly) has not been seen or handled before. Take the simple matter of entering a room to which, according to the plot or story, the Character coming in is supposed to be a stranger: unless there is vigilance the actor will waft himself blithely across the threshold, conveying the impression that he has at least been born in the house—finding it quite unnecessary to look where he is going and not in the least worth while to watch out for thoughtless pieces of furniture that may, in their ignorance of his approach, have established themselves in his path. And the different scenes with the different people; and the behavior resulting from *their* behavior; and the love-scenes as they are called—these have a little tragedy all their own for the performers involved; for, if an actor plays his part in one of these with the gentle awkwardness and natural embarrassment of one in love for the first time—as the plot supposes him to be—he will have the delight of reading the most withering and caustic ridicule of himself in the next day's papers, indicating in no polite terms that he is an awkward amateur who does not know his business, and that the country will be greatly relieved if he can see his way clear to quitting the stage at once; whereas if he behaves with the careless ease and grace and fluency of the Palmy Day Actor, softly breathing airy and poetic love-messages down the back of the lady's neck as he feelingly stands behind her so that they can both face to the front at the same time, the audience will be perfectly certain that the young man has had at least fifty-seven varieties of love-affairs before and that the plot has been shamelessly lying about him.

The foregoing are a few only of the numberless parts or items in Drama-Presentation which must conform to the "Illusion of the First Time." But this is one of the rather unusual cases in which the sum of all the parts does *not* equal the whole. For although every single item from the most important to the least important be successfully safeguarded, there yet remains the Spirit of the Presentation as a whole. Each successive audience before which it is given must feel—not think or reason about it, but *feel*—that it is witnessing, not one of a thousand weary repetitions, but a Life Episode that is being lived just across the magic barrier of the footlights. That is to say, the Whole must have that indescribable Life-Spirit or Effect which produces the Illusion of Happening for the First Time. Worth his weight in something extremely valuable is the Stage-Director who can conjure up this rare and precious spirit!

The dangers to dramatic life and limb from "The Disillusion of Doing it Correctly" are scarcely less than those in the "First Time" class, but not so difficult to detect and eliminate. Speaking, breathing, walking, sitting, rising, standing, gesturing—in short behaving correctly, when the character under representation would not naturally or customarily do so, will either kill that character outright or make it very sick indeed. Drama can make its appeal only in the form of Simulated Life as it is Lived—not as various authorities on Grammar, Pronunciation, Etiquette, and Elocution happen to announce at that particular time that it ought to be lived.

But we find it well to go much further than the keeping of studied and unusual correctness *out*, and to put common and to-be-expected errors *in*, when they may be employed appropriately and unobtrusively. To use every possible means and device for giving Drama that which makes it Drama—Life-Simulation—must be the aim of the modern Play-Constructor and Producer. And not alone ordinary errors but numberless individual habits, traits, peculiarities are of the utmost value for this purpose.

Among these elements of Life and Vitality but greatly surpassing all others in importance is the human characteristic or essential quality which passes under the execrated name of Personality. The very word must send an unpleasant shudder through this highly sensitive assembly; for it is supposed to be quite the proper and highly cultured thing to sneer at Personality as an altogether cheap affair and not worthy to be associated for a moment with what is highest in Dramatic Art. Nevertheless, cheap or otherwise, inartistic or otherwise, and whatever it really is or is not, it is the most singularly important factor for infusing the Life-Illusion into modern stage creations that is known to man. Indeed it is something a great deal more than important, for in these days of Drama's close approximation to Life, it is essential. As no human being exists without Personality of one sort or another, an actor who omits it in his impersonation of a human being omits one of the vital elements of existence.

In all the history of the stage no performer has yet been able to simulate or make use of a Personality not his own. Individual tricks, mannerisms, peculiarities of speech and action may be easily accomplished. They are the capital and stock in trade of the "Character Comedian" and the "Lightning-Change Artist," and have nothing whatever to do with Personality.

The actors of recent times who have been universally acknowledged to be great have invariably been so because of their successful use of their own strong and compelling Personalities in the rôles which they made famous. And when they undertook parts, as they occasionally did, unsuited to their Personalities, they were great no longer and frequently quite the reverse. The elder Salvini's "Othello" towered so far above all other renditions of the character known to modern times that they were lost to sight below it. His "Gladiator" was superb. His "Hamlet" was an unfortunate occurrence. His personality was marvelous for "Othello" and the "Gladiator," but unsuited to the Dane. Mr. Booth's personality brought him almost adoration in his "Hamlet"—selections from it served him well in "Iago," "Richelieu," and one or two other rôles, but for "Othello" it was not all that could be desired. And Henry Irving and Ellen Terry and Modjeska, Janauschek and Joseph Jefferson and Mary Anderson, each and every one of them with marvelous skill transferred their Personalities to the appropriate rôles. Even now—once in a while—one may see "Rip Van Winkle" excellently well played, but without Mr. Jefferson's Personality. There it is in simple arithmetic for you—a case of mere subtraction.

As indicated a moment ago I am only too well aware that the foregoing view of the matter is sadly at variance with what we are told is the Highest Form of the Actor's Art. According to the deep thinkers and writers on matters of the theatre, the really great actor is not one who represents with marvelous power and truth to life the characters within the limited scope of his Personality, but the performer who is able to assume an unlimited number of totally divergent rôles. It is not the thing at all to consider a single magnificent performance such as Salvini's "Othello," but to discover the Highest Art we must inquire how many kinds of things the man can do. This, you will observe, brings it down to a question of pure stage gymnastics. Watch the actor who can balance the largest number of rôles in the air without allowing any of them to spill over. Doubtless an interesting exhibition if you are looking for that form of sport. In another art it would be: "Do not consider this man's paintings, even though masterpieces, for he is only a Landscape Artist. Find the chap who can paint forty different kinds." I have an idea the Theatre-going Public is to be congratulated that none of the great Stage Performers, at any rate of modern times, has entered for any such competition.

1914

EZRA POUND

Ezra Pound's (1885–1972) earliest connection with the theatre was when he allowed a stranded actress to spend the night in his rooms, an act of charity that caused him to be dismissed from his teaching post at Wabash College. By 1908 he had moved definitively to Europe, preaching the gospel of Imagism, "the very essence of poetry" in its use of novel rhythms, precise words, common speech, and freedom in choice of subject. In London, he assumed the function of a literary talent scout, promoting Robert Frost and later T. S. Eliot. In 1913 Pound's friend and mentor, the Irish poet William Butler Yeats, introduced him to the work of James Joyce, who was having trouble getting *Dubliners* and *A Portrait of the Artist as a Young Man* published. The two men had much in common, both being widely read polymaths with a knack for parody. Pound managed to get portions of *Portrait* placed, slightly expurgated, in *The Egoist*, one of the little magazines he advised. Joyce then sent Pound his only play, *Exiles*, based on Ibsen's *When We Dead Awaken*, about which Joyce had written an admiring essay. Pound found *Exiles* "exciting" but "not nearly so intense as Portrait." After a manager he had approached turned it down, he composed an article valuable for its statement of Pound's ideas on drama and the stage of his time. It appeared in the Chicago magazine *The Drama*, which rejected the play itself a few months later.

This "three cat and mouse acts," as Joyce called *Exiles*, was considered too daring for most stages. The Abbey Theatre and the Stage Society both refused it. George Bernard Shaw damned it as "obscene," although he later defended it in a debate. Its first production was in German in Munich in 1919, accompanied by a notice that it was not appropriate for the general public. Not until the Neighborhood Playhouse in New York staged it in 1925 was *Exiles* offered to an audience in Joyce's own words.

Mr. James Joyce and the Modern Stage

A Play and Some Considerations

Two months ago I set out to write an essay about a seventeenth century dramatist. As I had nearly finished translating one of his plays into English, my interest in him must have been more than that of a transient moment. His own life was full of adventure. The play had a number of virtues that one could quite nicely mark out on a diagram. It was altogether a most estimable "subject"; yet, when I began to ask myself whether my phrases really corresponded to fact, whether it was worth while causing a few readers to spend their time on the matter, I was convinced that it was not. I believed that old play and the author had fallen into desuetude from perfectly justifiable causes. I agreed to let the dead bury their dead, and to let other people write about the drama, and I returned to some original work of my own.

Last week I received a play by Mr. James Joyce and that argumentative interest, which once led me to spend two years of my life reading almost nothing but plays, came back upon me, along with a set of questions "from the bottom up": Is drama worth while? Is the drama of today, or the stage of today, a form or medium by which the best contemporary authors can express themselves in any satisfactory manner?

Mr. Joyce is undoubtedly one of our best contemporary authors. He has written a novel, and I am quite ready to stake anything I have in this world that that novel is permanent. It is permanent as are the works of Stendhal and Flaubert. Two silly publishers have just refused it in favor of froth, another declines to look at it because "he will not deal through an agent"—yet Mr. Joyce lives on the continent and can scarcely be expected to look after his affairs in England save through a deputy. And Mr. Joyce is the best prose writer of my generation, in English. So far as I know, there is no one better in either Paris or Russia. In English we have Hardy and Henry James and, chronologically, we have Mr. James Joyce. The intervening novelists print books, it is true, but for me or for any man of my erudition, for any man living at my intensity, these books are things of no substance.

Therefore, when Mr. Joyce writes a play, I consider it a reasonable matter of interest. The English agent of the Oliver Morosco company has refused the play, and in so doing the agent has well served her employers, for the play would certainly be of no use to the syndicate that stars *Peg o' My Heart*; neither do I believe that any manager would stage it nor that it could succeed were it staged. Nevertheless, I read it through at a sitting, with intense interest. It is a long play, some one hundred and eighty pages.

It is not so good as a novel; nevertheless it is quite good enough to form a very solid basis for my arraignment of the contemporary theatre. It lays before me certain facts, certain questions; for instance, are the excellences of this play purely novelist's excellences? Perhaps most of them are; yet this play could not have been made as a novel. It is distinctly a play. It has the form of a play—I do not mean that it is written in dialogue with the names of the speakers put in front of their speeches. I mean that it has inner form; that the acts and speeches of one person work into the acts and speeches of another and make the play into an indivisible, integral whole. The action takes place in less than twenty-four hours, in two rooms, both near Dublin, so that even the classical unities are uninjured. The characters are drawn with that hardness of outline which we might compare to that of Dürer's painting if we are permitted a comparison with effects of an art so different. There are only four main characters, two subsidiary characters, and a fishwoman who passes a window, so that the whole mechanics of the play have required great closeness of skill. I see no way in which the play could be improved by redoing it as a novel. It could not, in fact, be anything but a play. And yet it is absolutely unfit for the stage as we know it. It is dramatic. Strong, well-wrought sentences flash from the speech and give it "dramatic-edge" such as we have in Ibsen, when some character comes out with, "There is no mediator between God and man"; I mean sentences dealing with fundamentals.

It is not unstageable because it deals with adultery; surely, we have plenty of plays, quite stageable plays, that deal with adultery. I have seen it in the nickel-plush theatre done with the last degree of sentimental bestiality. I admit that Mr. Joyce once mentions a garter, but it is done in such a way . . . it is done in the only way . . . it is the only possible means of presenting the exact social tone of at least two of the characters.

"Her place in life was rich and poor between," as Crabbe says of his Clelia; it might have been done in a skit of a night club and no harm thought; but it is precisely because it occurs neither in fast nor in patrician circles, but in a milieu of Dublin genteelness, that it causes a certain feeling of constraint. Mr. Joyce gives his Dublin as Ibsen gave provincial Norway.

Of course, oh, of course, if, *if* there were an Ibsen stage in full blast, Mr. Joyce's play would go on at once.

But we get only trivialized Ibsen; we get Mr. Shaw, the intellectual cheese-mite. That is to say, Ibsen was a true agonist, struggling with very real problems. "Life is a combat with the phantoms of the mind"—he was always in combat for himself and for the rest of mankind. More than any one man, it is he who has made us "our world," that is to say, "our modernity." Mr. Shaw is the intellectual cheese-mite, constantly enraptured at his own cleverness in being able to duck down through one hole in the cheese and come up through another.

But we cannot see "Ibsen." Those of us who were lucky saw Mansfield do the *Peer Gynt*. I have seen a half-private resurrection of *Hedda*. I think that those are the only two Ibsen plays that I have ever had an opportunity of seeing performed, and many others must be in like case. Professionals tell us: "Oh, they have quickened the tempo. Ibsen is too slow," and the like. So we have Shaw; that is to say, Ibsen with the sombre reality taken out, a little Nietzsche put in to enliven things, and a technique of dialogue superadded from Wilde.

I would point out that Shaw's comedy differs essentially from the French comedy of Marivaux or De Musset, for in their work you have a very considerable intensity of life and of passion veiling itself, restraining itself through a fine manner, through a very delicate form. There is in Shaw nothing to restrain, there is a bit of intensity in a farce about Androcles, but it is followed by a fabian sermon, and his "comedy" or whatever it is, is based solely on the fact that his mind moves a little bit faster than that of the average Englishman. You cannot conceive any intelligent person going to Mr. Shaw for advice in any matter that concerned his life vitally. He is not a man at prise with reality.

It is precisely this being at grips with reality that is the core of great art. It is Galdos, or Stendhal, or Flaubert, or Turgenev or Dostoevsky, or even a romanticist like De Musset, but it is not the cheese-mite state of mind. It is not a matter of being glum; it can be carried into the most tenuous art.

The trouble with Mr. Joyce's play is precisely that he *is* at prise with reality. It is a "dangerous" play precisely because the author is portraying an intellectual-emotional struggle, because he is dealing with actual thought, actual questioning, not with clichés of thought and emotion.

It is untheatrical, or unstageable, precisely because the closeness and cogency of the process is, as I think, too great for an audience to be able to follow . . . under present conditions.

And that is, in turn, precisely the ground of my arraignment.

All of this comes to saying: can the drama hold its own against the novel? Can contemporary drama be permanent? It is not to be doubted that the permanent art of any period is precisely that form of art into which the best artists of the period put their best and solidest work.

That is to say, the prose of the *trecento* was not so good as Dante's poetry, and, therefore, that age remains in its verse. The prose of the Elizabethan period was at least no better than Shakespeare's plays and we, therefore, remember that age, for the most part, by drama. The poetry of Voltaire's contemporaries was not so good as his prose and we, therefore, do not remember that period of France by its verses. For nearly a century now, when we have thought of great writers, we have been quite apt to think of the writers of novels. We perhaps think of Ibsen and Synge. We may even think of some poets. But that does not answer our problem.

The very existence of this quarterly and of the Drama League means, I take it, that an appreciable number of people believe that the drama is an important part of contemporary art . . . or that they want it to be an important or even great art of today.

It is a very complex art; therefore, let us try to think of its possibilities of greatness first hand.

ACTING

I suppose we have all seen flawless acting. Modern acting I don't know, I should say flawless *mimetic* acting is almost as cheap and plentiful as Mr. A. Bennett's novels. There is plenty of it in the market. A lot of clever, uninteresting people doing clever, tolerable plays. They are entertaining. There is no reason to see anyone in particular rather than any other one or any six others. It is a time of commercial efficiency, of dramatic and literary fine plumbing.

But great acting? Acting itself raised to the dignity of an art?

Yes, I saw it once. I saw Bernhardt; she was so wobbly in her knees that she leaned on either her lover or her confidant during nearly all of the play, *La Sorcière*, and it was not much of a play. Her gestures from the waist up were superb. At one point in the play, she takes off a dun-colored cloak and emerges in a close-fitting gown of cloth of gold. That is all—she takes off a cloak. That much might be stage direction. But that shaky, old woman, representing a woman in youth, took off her cloak with the power of sculpture.

That is to say, she created the image, an image, for me at least, as durable as that of any piece of sculpture that I have seen. I have forgotten most of the play; the play was of no importance.

Here was an art, an art that would have held Umewaka Minoru, great acting.

SPEECH

But it is impractical? Perhaps only a crazy, romantic play would give a situation of abnormal tragedy sufficient to warrant such gestures? And so on.

I noticed, however, one other thing in that Bernhardt performance, namely, that the emotional effect was greater half an hour after I had left the theatre than at any time during the performance. That, of course, is a "secret of Bernhardt's success."

Maybe, but it is due to a very definite cause, which the practical manager will probably ridicule. It is possible, by the constant reiteration of sound from a very small bell, to put a very large room in a roar, whose source you cannot easily locate. It is equally possible by the reiteration of a cadence . . . say the cadence of French alexandrines, to stir up an emotion in an audience, an emotion or an emotional excitement the source of which they will be unable to determine with any ease.

That is, I think, the only "practical" argument in favor of plays in verse. It is a very practical argument . . . but it may need the skill of Bernhardt to make it of any avail.

I might almost say that all arguments about the stage are of two sorts: the practical and the stupid. At any rate, the rare actor who aspires to art has at his disposal the two means; that is, speech and gesture. If he aspires to great art, he may try to substitute the significant for the merely mimetic.

THE CINEMA

The "movie" is perhaps the best friend of the few people who hope for a really serious stage. I do not mean to say that it is not the medium for the expression of more utter and abject forms of human asininity than are to be found anywhere else . . . save possibly on the contemporary stage.

Take, for example, the bathos, the *bassesse*, the consummate and unfathomable imbecility of some films. I saw one a few weeks ago. It began with a printed notice pleading for the freedom of the film; then there was flashed on the screen a testimonial from a weeping Christian, a "minister of a gospel," who declared that having had his emotions, his pity, stirred by a novel of Dickens in his early youth, had done more to ennoble his life, to make him what he was than any sermons he had ever heard. Then we had some stanzas from a poem by Poe (Omission: we had had some information about Poe somewhere before this). Then we had some scenes out of a Poe story in before-the-war costume; then the characters went off to a garden party in quite modern raiment and a number of modern characters were introduced, also a Salome dance in which the lady ended by lying on her back and squirming (as is so usual at an American garden party). Then the old before-the-war uncle reappeared. There were a few sub-plots, one taken from a magazine story that I happened to remember; later there came Moses and the burning bush, a modern detective doing the "third degree," Christ on Golgotha, some supernatural or supernormal creatures, quite nondescript, a wild chase over the hills, the tables of the law marked, "Thou shalt not kill," some more stanzas from a lyric of Poe's, and a lady fell off, no, leapt off, a cliff. There had been some really fine apparitions of the uncle's ghost somewhere before this, and finally the murderer awakened to find that he had been dreaming for the last third of the film. General reconciliation!

This film, you will note, observes the one requirement for popular stage success; there is plenty of action . . . and no one but a demi-god could possibly know what is going to come next.

Nevertheless, the "c'mat" is a friend to the lovers of good drama. I mean it is certainly inimical to the rubbishy stage. Because? Because people can get more rubbish per hour on the cinema than they can in the theatre, *and* it is cheaper. And it is on the whole a better art than the art of Frohman, Tree and Belasco. I mean to say it does leave something to the imagination.

Moreover, it is—whether the violet-tinted aesthete like it or not—it is developing an art sense. The minute the spectator begins to wonder why Charles Chaplin amuses him, the minute he comes to the conclusion that Chaplin is better than X——, Y—— and Z——, because he, Chaplin, gets the maximum effect with the minimum effort, minimum expenditure, etc., etc., the said spectator is infinitely nearer a conception of art and infinitely more fit to watch creditable drama than when he, or she, is entranced by Mrs. So-and-So's gown or by the color of Mr. So-and-So's eyes.

On the other, the sinister hand, we have the anecdote of the proud manager of "the Temple of Mammon" (as a certain London theatre is nicknamed). It was a magnificent scene, an oriental palace *de luxe*, which would have rivalled Belasco's, and the manager, taking a rather distinguished dramatist across the stage, tapped the lions supporting the throne with his gold-headed cane and proudly said, "Solid brass!"

Is it any wonder that the simple Teuton should have supposed this country ripe for invasion?

Well, benevolent reader, there you have it. The drama, the art of Aeschylus and of Shakespeare, the art that was to cast great passions and great images upon the mind of the auditor! There is the "drama" staged for the most part by men who should be "interior decorators" furnishing the boudoirs and reception rooms of upper-class prostitutes, there is the faint cry for art-scenery with as little drama as possible, and there is the trivialized Ibsen, for Shaw is the best we get, and all Shaw's satire on England was really done long since in a sentence quoted by Sterne:

"Gravity: A mysterious carriage of the body to cover the defects of the mind."

Even so, Shaw is only a stage in the decadence, for if we must call Shaw trivialized Ibsen, what shall we say of the next step lower, to-wit: prettified Shaw?

What welcome is this stage to give the real agonist if he tries to write "drama"? These problems are your problems, gracious reader, for you belong to that large group whose hope is better drama.

Also, in your problem plays you must remember that all the real problems of life are insoluble and that the real dramatist will be the man with a mind in search; he will grope for his answer and he will differ from the sincere auditor in that his groping will be the keener, the more far-reaching, the more conscious, or at least the more articulate; whereas, the man who tries to preach at you, the man who stops his play to deliver a sermon, will only be playing about the surface of things or trying to foist off some theory.

So Mr. Joyce's play is dangerous and unstageable because he is not *playing* with the subject of adultery, but because he is actually driving in the mind upon the age-long problem of the rights of personality and of the responsibility of the intelligent individual for the conduct of those about him, upon the age-long question of the relative rights of intellect, and emotion, and sensation, and sentiment.

And the question which I am trying to put and which I re-form and reiterate is just this: Must our most intelligent writers do this sort of work in the novel, *solely in the novel*, or is it going to be, in our time, possible for them to do it in drama?

On your answer to that question the claims of modern drama must rest.

1916

ALEXANDER WOOLLCOTT

With her red hair and blue eyes, Minnie Maddern was from childhood one of the most popular ingénues on the postbellum American stage, but she retired in 1890 when she married Harrison Grey Fiske, influential editor of the New York *Dramatic Mirror*. Three years later she returned as Mrs. Fiske, but in a loftier repertoire, playing Nora in *A Doll's House* and Tess in *Tess of the D'Urbervilles*. Her comic talent gave relief to tragic situations, and her personal magnetism, combined with her husband's managerial skills, help naturalize Ibsen on the American stage. She played Hedda, Rebecca West, and Mrs. Alving; even William Winter, who otherwise had little use for Ibsen, had to grant that her Hedda was "remarkably effective—being mordant with sarcasm, keen with irony, dreadful with suggestion of watchful wickedness, and bright with vicious eccentricity." Settled in her own playhouse in Manhattan, she successfully battled the theatrical trust and was the first to stage a product of the Harvard playwriting workshop, Edward Sheldon's *Salvation Nell*. The last phase of her career saw her in regular revivals of her star vehicle *Becky Sharp*.

Mrs. Fiske was a favorite of Alexander Woollcott (1887–1943), whose other pets included Harpo Marx, Katharine Cornell, and Charlie Chaplin; the bouquets he threw to them were matched by the brickbats he hurled at Eugene O'Neill and Marcel Proust. Obese, bespectacled, gossipy, Woollcott was one of New York's most widely read dramatic critics from 1914 to 1928, writing successively for the *Times*, the *Herald*, and the *World*, and warring with the Shuberts, who tried to bar him from their productions. He then achieved nationwide notoriety as a columnist at *The New Yorker* and as a radio personality in *The Town Crier* at $3,500 a program. Woollcott the critic was shamelessly subjective, with a sentimental streak at odds with his waspish invective (he was one of the habitués of the Algonquin Hotel's "vicious circle"). His occasional collaborator, George S. Kaufman, immortalized him as the insufferable Sheridan Whiteside in *The Man Who Came to Dinner* (1939). The part was created on Broadway by Monty Woolley; when Woollcott undertook it on the road, critics found him to be unconvincing.

Mrs. Fiske on Ibsen the Popular

WE talked of many things, Mrs. Fiske and I, as we sat at tea on a wide veranda one afternoon last Summer. It looked out lazily across a sunlit valley, the coziest valley in New Jersey. A huge dog that lay sprawled at her feet was unspeakably bored by the proceedings. He was a recruit from the Bide-a-wee Home, this fellow, a Great Dane with just enough of other strains in his blood to remind him that (like the Danes at Mr. Wopsle's Elsinore) he had but recently come up from the people. It kept him modest, anxious to please, polite. So Zak rarely interrupted, save when, at times, he would suggestively extract his rubber ball from the pocket of her knitted jacket and thus artfully invite her to a mad game on the lawn.

We talked of many things—of Duse and St. Teresa and Eva Booth and Ibsen. When we were speaking casually and quite idly of Ibsen, I chanced to voice the prevailing idea that, even with the least popular of his plays, she had always had, at all events, the satisfaction of a great *succès d'estime*. I could have told merely by the way her extraordinarily eloquent fan came into play at that moment that the conversation was no longer idle.

"*Succès d'estime!*" she exclaimed with fine scorn. "Stuff and nonsense! Stuff, my friend, and nonsense."

And we were off.

"I have always been *embarrassed* by the apparently general disposition to speak of our many seasons with Ibsen as an heroic adventure,—as a *series* of heroic adventures, just as though we had suffered all the woes of pioneers in carrying his plays to the uttermost reaches of the continent. This is a charming light to cast upon *us*, but it is quite unfair to a great genius who has given us money as well as inexhaustible inspiration. It is unfair to Ibsen. I was really quite taken aback not long ago when the editor of a Western paper wrote of the fortune we had lost in introducing the Norwegian to America. I wish I knew some way to shatter forever this monstrous idea. Save for the first season of 'A Doll's House,' many years ago, our Ibsen seasons have invariably been profitable. Now and then, it is true, the engagement of an Ibsen play in this city or that would be unprofitable, but never, since the first, have we known an unprofitable Ibsen year.

"When I listen, as I have so often had to listen, to the ill-considered comments of the unthinking and the uninformed, when I listen to airily expressed opinions based on no real knowledge of Ibsen's history in this country, no real understanding whatever, I am silent, but I like to recall a certain final matinée of 'Rosmersholm' at the huge Grand Opera House in Chicago, when the audience crowded the theater from pit to dome, when the stairways were literally packed with people standing, and when every space in the aisles was filled with chairs, for at that time chairs were allowed in the aisles. And I like to remember the quality of that great audience. It was the sort of audience one would find at a symphony concert, an audience silent and absorbed, an overwhelming rebuke to the flippant scoffers who are ignorant of the ever-increasing power of the great theater iconoclast."

And so, quite by accident, I discovered that, just as you have only to whisper Chatterton's old heresy, "Shakespeare spells ruin," to move William Winter to the immediate composition of three impassioned articles, so you have only to question the breadth of Ibsen's appeal to bring Mrs. Fiske rallying to his defense. Then she, who has a baffling way of forgetting the theater's very existence and would always far rather talk of saints or dogs or the breathless magic of Adirondack nights, will return to the stage. So it happened that that afternoon over the tea-cups we went back over many seasons—"A Doll's House," "Hedda Gabler," "Rosmersholm" and "The Pillars of Society."

"As I say," she explained, "'A Doll's House' in its first season was not profitable; but, then, that was my own first season as Mrs. Fiske, and it was but one of a number of plays in a financially unsuccessful repertory. And even that, I suppose, was, from the shrewdest business point of view, a sound investment in reputation. It was a *wise* thing to do. But the real disaster was predicted by every one for 'Rosmersholm.' There was the most somber and most complex tragedy of its period. No one would go to see *that*, they said, and I am still exasperated from time to time by finding evidences of a hazy notion that it did not prosper. 'Rosmersholm' was played, and not particularly well played, either, for one hundred and ninety-nine consecutive performances at a profit of $40,000. I am never greatly interested in figures, but I had the curiosity to make sure of these. Of course that is a total of many profitable weeks and some unprofitable ones and of course it is not an overpowering reward for a half-season in the theater. In telling you that Ibsen may be profitable in a money sense, I am not so mad as to say other things may not be far more profitable. But $40,000 profit scarcely spells ruin.

"And I tell you all this because it is so discouraging to the Ibsen enthusiasts to have the baseless, the *false* idea persist that he and the box-office are at odds. Sensibly projected in the theater—"

"Instead," I suggested, "of being played by strange people at still stranger matinées—"

"Of course. Rightly projected in the theater, Ibsen always has paid and always will. And that is worth shouting from the housetops, because sensibly and rightly projected in the theater, the fine thing always does pay. Oh, I have no patience with those who descend upon a great play, produce it without understanding, and then, because disaster overtakes it, throw up their hands and say there is no public for fine art. How absurd! In New York alone there are two universities, a college or two, and no end of schools. What more responsive public could our producers ask? But let us remember that the greater the play, the more carefully must it be directed and acted, and that for every production in the theater there is a psychologically *right* moment. Move wisely in these things, and the public will not fail."

For many false but wide-spread impressions of Ibsen we were inclined to blame somewhat the reams of nonsense that have been written and rewritten about him, the innumerable little essays on his gloom.

"And none at all on his warmth, his gaiety, his infinite humanity," said Mrs. Fiske, her eyes sparkling. "When will the real book of Ibsen criticism find its way to the shelf? How can we persuade people to turn back to the *plays* and re-read them for the color, the romance, the *life* there is in them? Where in all the world of modern drama, for instance, is there a comedy so buoyant, so dazzlingly joyous as 'An Enemy of the People'?"

"They say he is parochial," I ventured.

"Let them say. They said it of *Hedda*, but that poor, empty, little Norwegian neurotic has been recognized all over the world. The trouble with *Hedda* is not that she is parochial, but that she *is* poor and empty. She was fascinating to play, and I suppose that every actress goes through the phase of being especially attracted by such characters, a part of the phase when the eagerness to 'study life' takes the form of an interest in the eccentric, abnormal, distorted—the *perverted* aspects of life. As a rôle *Hedda* is a marvelous portrait; as a person she is empty. After all, the empty evil, selfish persons are not worth our time—either yours or mine—in the theater any more than in life. They do not matter. They do not count. They are enormously unimportant. On the highway of life the *Hedda Gablers* are just so much *impedimenta*."

"Do you recall," I inquired, "that that is the very word Cæsar used for 'baggage'?"

Whereat Mrs. Fiske smiled so approvingly that I knew poor *Hedda* would be "impedimenta" to the end of the chapter.

"But she is universal," said Mrs. Fiske, suddenly remembering that some one had dared to call Ibsen parochial. "She was recognized all over the world. London saw her at every dinner-table, and I have watched a great auditorium in the far West—a place as large as our Metropolitan—held enthralled by that brilliant comedy."

"Which I myself have seen played as tragedy."

"Of course you have," she answered in triumph. "And that is precisely the trouble. When you think how shockingly Ibsen has been misinterpreted and mangled, it is scarcely surprising that there are not a dozen of his plays occupying theaters in New York at this time. It is only surprising he has lived to tell the tale. Small wonder he has been roundly abused."

And I mentioned one performance of "John Gabriel Borkmann" in which only the central figure was adequately played and which moved one of the newspaper scribes to an outburst against, not the players, but against Ibsen as the "sick man of the theater."

"Exactly," said Mrs. Fiske. "And so it has always gone. Ibsen's plays are too majestic and too complex to be so maltreated. To read 'Borkmann' in the light of some knowledge of life is to marvel at the blending of human insight and poetic feeling. How beautiful, how wonderful is that last walk with *Ella* through the mists! But played without understanding, this and the others are less than nothing at all. Yet with the published texts in every bookstore, there is no excuse for any of us blaming the outrage on Ibsen. We would attend a high-school orchestra's performance of a Wagnerian score and blame the result on Wagner. Or would we? We would have once."

And we paused to recall how curiously alike had been the advent and development of these two giants as irresistible forces.

"It was not so very long ago," said Mrs. Fiske with great satisfaction, "that a goodly number of well-meaning people dismissed Wagner with tolerant smiles. There is a goodly number of the same sort of people who still wave Ibsen away. Extraordinary questions are still asked with regard to him. The same sort of dazing questions, I suppose, were once asked about Wagner. I myself have been asked, 'Why do you like Ibsen?' And to such a question, after the first staggering moment, one perhaps finds voice to ask in return, 'Why do you like the ocean?' Or, 'Why do you like a sunrise above the mountain peak?' Or, possibly, 'What do you find interesting in Niagara?'

"But, then, the key is given in those delightful letters after 'An Enemy of the People.' You remember Ibsen admitted there that his abhorred 'compact majority' eventually gathered and stood behind each of his drama messages; but the trouble was that by the time it did arrive he himself was away on ahead—somewhere else."

And we went back with considerable enjoyment to the days when Ibsen was a new thing outside Germany and his own Scandinavia, when his influence had not yet transformed the entire theater of the Western world, remodeling its very architecture, and reaching so far that never a pot-boiling playwright in America today but writes differently than he would have written if Ibsen—or *an* Ibsen—had not written first. Then we moved gaily on to the Manhattan Theater in the days when the Fiskes first assumed control. It seems that on that occasion, Mr. Fiske consulted one of the most distinguished writers on the American theater for suggestions as to the plays that might well be included in Mrs. Fiske's program. And the answer, after making several suggestions, wound up by expressing the hope that, at all events, they would having nothing to do with "the unspeakable Mr. Ibsen."

And so at the first night of "Hedda Gabler"—that brilliant première which Mrs. Fiske always recalls as literally an ovation for William B. Mack and Carlotta Nillson, eleventh-hour choices both—there was nothing for the aforesaid writer to do but to stand in the lobby and mutter unprintable nothings about the taste, personal appearance, and moral character of those who were misguidedly crowding to the doors. But what had he *wanted* her to play? The recollection was quite too much for Mrs. Fiske.

"You'll never believe me," she said, amid her laughter. "But he suggested *Adrienne Lecouvreur*, *Mrs. Haller*, and *Pauline* in 'The Lady of Lyons.'"

A good deal of water has passed under the bridge since then, but even when the Fiskes came to give "Rosmersholm" there was enough lingering heresy to make them want to give that most difficult of them all a production so perfect that none could miss its meaning or escape its spell.

"I had set my heart on it," she said sadly. "It was to have been our great work. I was bound that 'Rosmersholm' should be right if we had to go to the ends of the earth for our cast. Mr. Fiske agreed. I do not know what other manager there has been in our time from whom I could have had such wholehearted coöperation in the quest of the fine thing. Mr. Fiske has been my artistic backbone. His theater knowledge, taste, and culture, his steadiness, have balanced my own carelessness. Without him I should have been obliterated long ago.

"Well, Mr. Fiske and I selected Fuller Mellish for *Kroll* in 'Rosmersholm.' He was perfect. For *Brendel* we wanted Tyrone Power, who, because *Brendel* appears in only two scenes, could not recognize the great importance of the rôle. That is a way actors have. So Mr. Arliss was *Brendel*. But we had wanted Mr. Arliss for *Mortensgård*, and of course as *Mortensgård* he would have been superb. And then there was *Rosmer*.

Spiritual, noble, the great idealist, for *Rosmer* of 'Rosmer-sholm' we had but one choice. It must be Forbes-Robertson. I sought Forbes-Robertson. But I suspect he thought I was quite mad. I suspect he had the British notion that Ibsen should be given only on Friday afternoons in January. I dare say he could not conceive of a successful production of 'Ros-mersholm' in the *commercial* theater."

"It flourished, though."

"Yes, and it was *fairly* good. But it was not perfect. It was not *right*. The company was composed of fine actors who were, however, not all properly cast. So it did not measure up to my ideal, and I was *not* satisfied. It drew, as Ibsen always draws, on the middle-class support. It packed the balconies—to a great extent, I imagine, with Germans and Scandinavians. It pleased the Ibsen enthusiasts; but, then I am *not* an Ibsen enthusiast."

This was a little startling.

"Or, rather, have not always been," she hastened to add. "For that, you must know him thoroughly, and such knowl-edge comes only after an acquaintance of many years. I have not always understood him. I might as well admit," she said guiltily, "that I once wrote a preposterous article on Ibsen the pessimist, Ibsen the killjoy, an impulsive, scatter-brained arti-cle which I would read now with a certain detached wonder, feeling as you feel when you are confronted with some incred-ible love-letter of long ago. And just when I think it has been forgotten, buried forever in the dust of some old magazine file, some one like Mr. Huneker, whom *nothing* escapes, is sure to resurrect it and twit me good-humoredly."

That acquaintance—when did it first begin?

"Years ago," said Mrs. Fiske. "It was when I was a young girl and given to playing all manner of things all over the coun-try. We were all imitating delightful Lotta in those days. You would never guess who sent it to me. Lawrence Barrett. Not, I think, with any idea that I should play it, for I was far too young then even for *Nora*. But here was the great, strange play every-one was talking about, and it was his kindly thought, I imag-ine, that I should be put in touch with the new ideas. Of course it seemed very curious to me, so different from every-thing I had known, so utterly lacking in all we had been taught to consider important in the theater. It was not until later that

I played *Nora*—emerged from my retirement to play it at a benefit at the Empire.

"No, there was no special ardor of enthusiasm then. I came to play the other parts because, really, there was nothing else. Shakspere was not for me, nor the standard repertory of the day. I *did* act *Frou Frou*, and I cannot *begin* to tell you how *dreadful* I was as *Frou Frou*. But I did *not* play *Camille*. As a matter of fact, I could not."

There had to be an explanation of this. Mrs. Fiske whispered it.

"I cannot play a love scene," she confessed. "I never could."

So it was from such alternatives that she turned to the great Ibsen rôles—rôles with such depths of feeling, such vistas of life as must inspire and exact the best from any player anywhere in the world.

"And now to play smaller pieces seems a little petty—like drawing toy trains along little tin tracks. No work for a grown-up. And if now I speak much of Ibsen, it is because he has been *my* inspiration, because I have found in his plays that *life-sized* work that other players tell us they have found in the plays of Shakspere."

Life-sized work. We thought of Irving fixing twenty years as a decent minimum of time in which a man of talent could be expected to "present to the public a series of characters acted almost to perfection." We spoke of Macready standing sadly in his dressing-room after his memorable last performance as the Prince of Denmark. "Good night, sweet Prince," he murmured as he laid aside the velvet mantle for good and all, and then, turning to his friend, exclaimed: "Ah, I am just beginning to realize the sweetness, the tenderness, the gentleness of this dear *Hamlet*." So we spoke of all the years of devotion Shakspere had inspired in the players of yesterday and the day before—"inexhaustible inspiration," such inspiration, Mrs. Fiske said, as awaits the thoughtful actor in the great rôles of Ibsen. She found it in *Nora* and *Lona* and *Hedda* and *Rebecca West*, and in other characters we have never seen her play and never *shall* see her play.

"There are," she said, "such limitless depths to be explored. Many a play is like a painted backdrop, something to be looked at from the front. An Ibsen play is like a black forest, something you can *enter*, something you can walk about in.

There you can lose yourself: you can lose *yourself.* And once inside," she added tenderly, "you find such wonderful glades, such beautiful, *sunlit* places. And what makes each one at once so difficult to play and so fascinating to study is that Ibsen for the most part gives us only the last hours."

Ibsen gives us only the last hours. It was putting in a sentence the distinguishing factor, the substance of chapters of Ibsen criticism. Here was set forth in a few words the Norwegian's subtle and vastly complex harmonies that weave together a drama of the present and a drama of the past. As in certain plays of the great Greeks, as in "Œdipus Tyrannus," for instance, so in the masterpieces of the great modern, you watch the race not in an observation train, but from the vantage-point of one posted near the goal. Your first glance into one of these forbidding households shows only a serene surface. It is the calm before the storm—what Mrs. Fiske likes to call "the *ominous* calm." Then rapidly as the play unfolds, the past overtakes these people. You meet the scheming *Hedda* on the day of her return from her wedding trip. In little more than twenty-four hours all she has ever been makes her kill herself. An ironic story of twenty years' accumulation comes to its climax in as many hours. You have arrived just in time to witness the end.

"Back of these Ibsen men and women," I put in tentatively, "there are dancing shadows on the wall that play an accompaniment to the unfolding of the play."

"A nightmare accompaniment," Mrs. Fiske assented. "Often he gives us only the last hours, and that, my friend, is why, in the study of Ibsen, I had to devise what was, for me, a new method. To learn what *Hedda was*, I had to imagine all that she had ever *been*. By the keys he provides you can unlock her past. He gives us the last hours: we must recreate all that have gone before.

"It soon dawned on me that studying *Hedda* would mean more than merely memorizing the lines. I had a whole summer for the work—a summer my cousin and I spent in all the odd corners of Europe. And so, at even odder moments, in out-of-the-way places, I set my imagination to the task of recreating the life of *Hedda Gabler*. In my imagination I lived the scenes of her girlhood with her father. I toyed with the shining pistols—"

"Those pistols that somehow symbolize so perfectly the dangers this little coward would merely play with," I interrupted. "How much he says in how little!"

Whereupon Mrs. Fiske shook hands with me. She *is* an enthusiast.

"I staged in my own ghost theater," she went on, "her first meeting with *Eilert Lövborg—Lövborg* whom *Hedda* loved, as so many women love, not with her heart, but with her nerves. I staged their first meeting and all other meetings that packed his mind and hers with imperishable memories all the rest of their days. I staged them as we sat in funny little German chapels or sailed down the Rhine. I spent the summer with *Hedda Gabler*, and when it came time to sail for home I knew her as well as I knew myself. There was nothing about her I did *not* know, nothing she could do that I could not guess, no genuine play about her—Ibsen's or another's—that would not play itself without invention. I had *lived Hedda Gabler*."

"It must have been pleasant for Miss Stevens," I hazarded.

Mrs. Fiske laughed gaily.

"Poor Cousin Emily!" she said. "I remember how biting she was one afternoon after she had been kept waiting an hour outside a little Swiss hotel while I was locked in the parlor, pacing up and down in the midst of a stormy scene with *Lövborg*.

"And so," she went on, "if *Hedda*, and better still, if both *Hedda* and *Lövborg*, have been studied in this way, the moment in the second act when these two come face to face after all their years of separation is for each player a tremendous moment. To *Hedda* the very sight of *Lövborg* standing there on the threshold of her drawing-room brings a flood of old memories crowding close. It must not show on the surface. That is not Ibsen's way. There are others—alien spirits— present, and *Hedda* is the personification of fastidious self-control. She has sacrificed everything for that. No, it may not show on the surface, but if the actress has lived through *Hedda's* past, and so realized her present, that moment is electrical. Her blood quickens, her voice deepens, her eyes shine. A curious magnetic something passes between her and

Lövborg. And the playgoer, though he has but dimly guessed all that *Hedda* and *Lövborg* have meant to each other, is touched by that current. For him, too, the moment is electrical."

"Taking," I suggested, "its significance, its beauty, its dramatic force from all that has gone before."

"From all the untold hours," said Mrs. Fiske. "And see how wonderfully it sharpens the brilliant comedy of that scene where *Hedda* and *Lövborg* are whispering cryptically across the photograph-album while the others chatter unconsciously about them. Think how significant every tone and glance and gesture become if these two have in their mental backgrounds those old afternoons when *General Gabler* would fall asleep over his newspaper and he and she would be left to talk together in the old parlor.

"And I must admit," she added, with a twinkle, "that in those recreations, *Lövborg* was sometimes quite unmanageable. He would behave very badly."

"Like *Colonel Newcome*," I exclaimed.

"Not at *all* like *Colonel Newcome*. What *do* you mean?"

"Exactly like," I went on enthusiastically. "Do you remember that time when, in the days Thackeray was deep in 'The Newcomes,' his hostess at breakfast asked him cheerily if he had had a good night? A good night! 'How could I?' he answered, 'with *Colonel Newcome* making such a fool of himself?' 'But why do you let him?' This, of course, from his bewildered hostess. 'Oh! It was in him to do it. He must.'"

"Thackeray understood," Mrs. Fiske agreed. "But I wonder if he really thought the death scene—the '*Ad-sum*' scene—intrinsically beautiful."

"I suspect so," I said. "It was the only part of the book he could not dictate. He had to write that alone. Anyway, Mr. Saintsbury thinks that *Lear's* is the only death scene that surpasses it in literature."

"Yet is it not so beautiful and so touching because of all that has gone before, because of all the affection for dear *Colonel Newcome* you have acquired in a thousand pages of sympathy? So it is, at least, with the great scenes in Ibsen, meaningless, valueless except in the light of what has gone before. He gives us the last hours. Behind each is a lifetime.

"And think how valuable is such a method of study in a play

like 'Rosmersholm,' how impossible for one to play *Rebecca* until one has lived through the years with the dead *Beata*. *Rosmer's* wife has already passed on before the first curtain rises, but from then on, nevertheless, she plays an intense rôle. She lives in the minds of those at Rosmersholm, in the very hearts of those who play the tragedy.

"And how crucially important it is that the *Rebecca* should have thought out all her past with *Dr. West*! It is the illumination of that past which she comes upon unexpectedly in a truth let fall by the unconscious *Kroll*—a truth so significant that it shatters her ambitions, sends her great house of cards toppling about her ears, touches the spring of her confession, and brings the tragedy to its swift, inevitable conclusion. Now, unless an actress be one of those rare artists who can put on and take off their emotions like so many bonnets, I do not see how she could make this scene *intelligible* unless she had perceived and felt its hidden meaning; nor how, having perceived and felt it, she could help playing it well. If her own response is right, the playgoer will be carried along without himself having quite understood the reason for her confession. This is curious, but it is true. I am sure of it. For, as a matter of fact, few *have* caught the half-revealed meaning of that scene between *Rebecca* and *Kroll*. It is one of the inexplicable stenches that *do* rise occasionally from Ibsen's play—like another in the otherwise beautiful 'Lady from the Sea.' It assailed me so directly that for a long time I hesitated to produce 'Rosmersholm' at all. Yet, of all the writers in America only two seemed to have been aware of it.

"But if the actress has not searched *Rebecca's* past, the key to the scene is missing. The actress must *know*, and, knowing, her performance will take care of itself. Go to the theater well versed in the *science* of acting, and knowing thoroughly the person Ibsen has created, and you need take no thought of how this is to be said or how that is to be indicated. You can *live* the play."

But with shallower pieces, with characters that come meaningless out of nowhere, could she follow this method of study?

"It would be a mountain bringing forth a mouse," she admitted; "and yet I suppose that now I always try it."

And it occurred to me that probably that delightful confession of *Erstwhile Susan's* in her present play—that harrowing return to the closed chapter back in the op'ry-house at Cedar Center when the faithless *Bert Budsaw* had deserted her at the altar—had probably crept into the comedy during Mrs. Fiske's own quest of a background for the lady elocutionist. I tried to find out, but she gave only an inscrutable smile, expended largely on Zak who was visibly depressed.

"If it is a real part in a real play," she said sternly. "That is the way to study it."

At this point Zak, who is always right in a matter of manners, rose and stared at me in such an expertly dismissive way that there was simply no escaping the suggestion. I started to go.

"And that," I concluded from the steps, "is the method of study you would recommend to all young players?"

"Indeed, indeed it is," said Mrs. Fiske, with great conviction. "I should urge, I should *inspire* my students to follow it if ever I had a dramatic school."

A dramatic school, Mrs. Fiske's dramatic school. But that is another story—the next, in fact.

1917

JAMES G. HUNEKER

Trained as a pianist in Philadelphia and Paris, James G. Huneker (1857–1921) was teaching piano at the New York National Conservatory when he began to contribute articles to New York and London musical journals. From 1891 to 1919, he served successively as either music or drama critic (or both) on several New York newspapers: the *Recorder*, the *Advertiser*, the *Sun*, the *Times*, and the *World*. A successor at the *Times*, Brooks Atkinson, lauded him as "the best critic Broadway ever had." Huneker, who in early youth had admired the acting of Salvini and Booth, grew up to be a missionary of European modernism. Painting, sculpture, and architecture joined music and drama in his synaesthetic approach, as he schooled his countrymen with wit and insight, beguiling them with anecdote and biographical detail. His cosmopolitan critiques were couched in a florid prose, often sensuously lush, in response to a given work. "I never preached aught but the beauty of art," he explained, but "I don't take criticism as seriously as I do manslaughter and prohibition." Although Huneker rarely lavished enthusiasm on an American artist in his essays, he helped sophisticate American taste and greatly influenced H. L. Mencken. One of his many books, *Iconoclasts*, deals exclusively with dramatists, among whom he preferred Ibsen and (with some reservations) Shaw. His essay on Wedekind, drawn from his 1917 miscellany *Ivory Apes and Peacocks*, demonstrates the audacity of his proselytizing. For an American theatre that was finding the Scandinavians and Russians tough pills to swallow, Frank Wedekind's "tragedies of sex" would have been regurgitative. Even now, his dramatic works have proved to be more acceptable as opera (Berg's *Lulu*) and musical (*Spring Awakening* by Duncan Sheik and Stephen Saiter) than as plays.

Frank Wedekind

A VERY deceptive mask is literature. Here is your Nietzsche with his warrior pen slashing away at the conventional lies of civilisation, a terrific figure of outraged manhood, though in private life he was the gentlest of men, self-sacrificing, lovable, modest, and moral to a painful degree. But see what his imitators have made of him. And in all the tons of rubbish that have been written about Tolstoy, the story told by Anna Seuron is the most significant. But a human being is better than a half-god.

Bearing this in mind I refused to be scared in advance by the notorious reputation of Frank Wedekind, whose chief claim to recognition in New York is his Spring's Awakening, produced at the Irving Place Theatre seasons ago. I had seen this moving drama of youth more than once in the Kammerspielhaus of the Deutsches Theater, Berlin, and earlier the same poet's drama Erdgeist (in the summer, 1903), and again refused to shudder at its melodramatic atrocities. Wedekind wore at that time the mask Mephistophelian, and his admirers, for he had many from the beginning, delighted in what they called his spiritual depravity—forgetting that the two qualities cannot be blended. Now, while I have termed Frank Wedekind the naughty boy of the modern German drama, I by no means place him among those spirits like Goethe's Mephisto, who perpetually deny. On the contrary, he is one of the most affirmative voices in the new German literature.

He is always asserting. If he bowls away at some rickety ninepin of a social lie, he does it with a gusto that is exhilarating. To be sure, whatever the government is, he is against it; which only means he is a rebel born, hating constraint and believing with Stendhal that one's first enemies are one's own parents. No doubt, after bitter experience, Wedekind discovered that his bitterest foe was himself. That he is a tricky, Puck-like nature is evident. He loves to shock, a trait common to all romanticists from Gautier down. He sometimes says things he doesn't mean. He contradicts himself as do most men of genius, and, despite his poetic temperament, there is in him much of the lay preacher. I have noticed this quality in men such as Ibsen and Strindberg, who cry aloud in the wilderness of Philistia for freedom, for the "free, unhampered life" and then devise a new system that is thrice as irksome as the old, that puts one's soul into a spiritual bondage. Wedekind is of this order; a moralist is concealed behind his shining ambuscade of verbal immorality. In Germany every one sports his Weltanschauung, his personal interpretation of life and its meanings. In a word, a working philosophy—and a fearsome thing it is to see young students with fresh sabre cuts on their honest countenances demolishing Kant, Schopenhauer, or Nietzsche only to set up some other system.

Always a system, always this compartmentising of the facts of existence. Scratch the sentimentalism and æstheticism of a German, and you come upon a pedant. Wedekind has not altogether escaped this national peculiarity. But he writes for tomorrow, not yesterday; for youth, and not to destroy the cherished prejudices of the old. His admirers speak of him as a unicum, a man so original as to be without forerunners, without followers. A monster? For no one can escape the common law of descent, whether physical or spiritual. Wedekind has had plenty of teachers, not excepting the most valuable of all, personal experience. The sinister shadow cast by Ibsen fell across the shoulders of the young poet, and he has read Max Stirner and Nietzsche not wisely, but too well. He is as frank as Walt Whitman (and as shameless) concerning the mysteries of life, and as healthy (and as coarse) as Rabelais. Furthermore, Strindberg played a marked rôle in his artistic development. Without the hopeless misogyny of the Swede, without his pessimism, Wedekind is quite as drastic. And the realism of the Antoine Theatre should not be omitted.

He exhibits in his menagerie of types—many of them new in the theatre—a striking collection of wild animals. In the prologue to one of his plays he tells his audience that to Wedekind must they come if they wish to see genuine wild and beautiful beasts. This sounds like Stirner. He lays much stress on the fact that literature, whether poetic or otherwise, has become too "literary"—hardly a novel idea; and boasts that none of his characters has read a book. The curse of modern life is the multiplication of books. Very true, and yet I find that Wedekind is "literary," that he could exclaim with Stéphane Mallarmé: "La chair est triste, hélas! et j'ai lu tous les livres."

Regarding the modern stage he is also positive. He believes that for the last twenty years dramatic literature is filled with half-humans, men who are not fit for fatherhood, women who would escape the burden of bearing children because of their superior culture. This is called "a problem play," the hero or heroine of which commits suicide at the end of the fifth act to the great delight of neurotic, dissatisfied ladies and hysterical men. Weak wills—in either sex—have been the trump card of the latter-day dramatist; not a sound man or woman who isn't at the same time stupid, can be found in the plays of Ibsen or Hauptmann or the rest. Wedekind mentions no names, but he tweaks several noses prominent in dramatic literature.

He is the younger generation kicking in the panels of the doors in the old houses. There is a hellish racket for a while, and then when the dust clears away you discern the revolutionist calmly ensconced in the seats of the bygone mighty and passionately preaching from the open window his version of New Life; he is become reformer himself and would save a perishing race—spiritually speaking—from damnation by the gospel of beauty, by shattering the shackles of love—especially the latter; love to be love must be free, preaches Wedekind; love is still in the swaddling clothes of Oriental prejudice. George Meredith once said the same in Diana of the Crossways, although he said it more epigrammatically. For Wedekind religion is a symbol of our love of ourselves; nevertheless, outside of his two engrossing themes, love and death, he is chiefly concerned with religion, not alone as material for artistic treatment, but as a serious problem of our existence. A Lucifer in pride, he tells us that he has never made of good evil, or vice versa; he, unlike Baudelaire, has never deliberately said: Evil, be thou my good! That he has emptied upon the boards from his Pandora-box imagination the greatest gang of scoundrels, shady ladies, master swindlers, social degenerates, circus people, servants, convicts, professional strong men, half-crazy idealists, irritable rainbow-eaters—the demi-monde of a subterranean world—that ever an astonished world saw perform their antics in front of the footlights is not to be denied, but it must be confessed that his criminal supermen and superwomen usually get their deserts. Like Octave Mirbeau, he faces the music of facts, and there are none too abhorrent that he doesn't transform into something significant.

On the technical side Strindberg has taught him much; he prefers the one-act form, or a series of loosely joined episodes. Formally he is not a master, nor despite his versatility is he objective. With Strindberg he has been called "Shakespearian"—fatal word—but he is not; that in the vast domain of Shakespeare there is room for them both I do not doubt; room in the vicinity of the morbid swamps and dark forests, or hard by the house of them that are melancholy mad.

The oftener I see or read Wedekind the more I admire his fund of humour. But I feel the tug of his theories. The dramatist in him is hampered by the theorist who would "reform" all life—he is neither a socialist nor an upholder of female suffrage —and when some of his admiring critics talk of his "ideals of beauty and power," then I know the game is up—the prophet, the dogmatist, the pedant, not the poet, artist, and witty observer of life, are thrust in the foreground.

There is Hermann Sudermann, for example, the precise antipodes of Wedekind—Sudermann, the inexhaustible bottle of the German theatre, the conjurer who imperturbably pours out any flavour, colour, or liquid you desire from his bottle; presto, here is Ibsen, or Dumas, or Hauptmann, or Sardou; comedy, satire, tragedy, farce, or the marionettes of the fashionable world! Frank Wedekind is less of the stage prestidigitator and more sincere. We must, perforce, listen to his creatures as they parade their agony before us, and we admire his clever rogues—the never-to-be-forgotten Marquis of Keith heads the list—and smile at their rough humour and wisdom. For me, the real Frank Wedekind is not the prophet, but the dramatist. As there is much of his stark personality in his plays, it would not be amiss to glance at his career.

He has "a long foreground," as Emerson said of Walt Whitman. He was born at Hanover, July 24, 1864, and consequently was only twenty-seven years old when, in 1891, he wrote his most original, if not most finished, drama, Spring's Awakening. He studied law four terms at Munich, two at Zurich: but for this lawless soul jurisprudence was not to be; it was to fulfil a wish of his father's that he consented to the drudgery. A little poem which has been reproduced in leaflet form, Felix and Galathea, is practically his earliest offering to the muse. Like most beginnings of fanatics and realists, it fairly swims and shimmers with idealism. His father dead, a roving existence and a precarious one began for the youthful Frank. He lived by his wits in Paris and London, learned two languages, met that underworld which later was to figure in his vital dramatic pictures, wrote advertisements for a canned soup—in Hauptmann's early play, Friedensfest, Wedekind is said to figure as Robert, who is a réclame agent—was attached to circuses, variety theatres, and fairs, was an actor in tingle-tangles, cabarets, and saw life on its seamiest side, whether in Germany, Austria, France, or England. Such experiences produced their inevitable reaction—disillusionment. Finally in 1905 Director Reinhardt engaged him as an actor and he married the actress Tilly Niemann-Newes, with whom he has since lived happily, the father of a son, his troubled spirit in safe harbour at last, but not in the least changed, to judge from his play, Franziska, a Modern Mystery.

Personally, Wedekind was never an extravagant, exaggerated man. A sorrowful face in repose is his, and when he appeared on Hans von Wolzogen's Ueberbrettl, or sang at the Munich cabaret called the Eleven Hangmen, his songs—he composes at times—Ilse, Goldstück, Brigitte B, Mein Liebchen, to the accompaniment of his guitar, there was a distinct individuality in his speech and gesture very attractive to the public.

But as an actor Wedekind is not distinguished, though versatile. I've only seen him in two rôles, as Karl Hetman in his play of Hidalla (now renamed after the leading rôle), and as Ernest Scholtz in The Marquis of Keith. As Jack the Ripper in The Box of Pandora I am glad to say that I have not viewed him, though he is said to be a gruesome figure during the few minutes that he is in the scene. His mimetic methods recalled to me the simplicity of Antoine—who is not a great actor, yet, somehow or other, an impressive one. Naturally, Wedekind is the poet speaking his own lines, acting his own creations, and there is, for that reason, an intimate note in his interpretations, an indescribable sympathy, and an underscoring of his meanings that even a much superior actor might miss. He is so absolutely unconventional in his bearing and speech as to seem amateurish, yet he secures with his naturalism some poignant effects. I shan't soon forget his Karl Hetman, the visionary reformer.

Wedekind, like Heine, has the faculty of a cynical, a consuming self-irony. He is said to be admirable in Der Kammersänger. It must not be forgotten that he has, because of a witty lampoon in the publication Simplicissimus, done his "little bit" as they say in penitentiary social circles. These few months in prison furnished him with scenic opportunities; there is more than one of his plays with a prison set. And how he does lay out the "system." He, like Baudelaire, Flaubert, and De Maupassant, was summoned before the bar of justice for outraging public morals by the publication of his play, The Box of Pandora, the sequel to Erdgeist. He had to withdraw the book and expunge certain offensive passages, but he escaped fine and imprisonment, as did his publisher, Bruno Cassirer. He rewrote the play, the second act of which had been originally printed in French, the third in English, and its republication was permitted by the sensitive authorities of Berlin.

If a critic can't become famous because of his wisdom he may nevertheless attain a sort of immortality, or what we call that elusive thing, by writing himself down an ass. The history of critical literature would reveal many such. Think of such an accomplished practitioner as the late M. Brunetière, writing as he did of Flaubert and Baudelaire. And that monument to critical ineptitude, Degeneration, by Max Nordau. A more modern instance is the judgment of Julius Hart in the publication, *Tag* (1901), concerning our dramatist. He wrote: "In German literature to-day there is nothing as vile as the art of Frank Wedekind." Fearing this sparkling gem of criticism might escape the notice of posterity, Wedekind printed it as a sort of motto to his beautiful poetic play (1902), Such Is Life. However, the truth is that our poet is often disconcerting. His swift transition from mood to mood disturbs the spectator, especially when one mood is lofty, the next shocking. He has also been called "the clown of the German stage," and not without reason, for his mental acrobatics, his grand and lofty tumblings from sheer transcendentalism to the raw realism, his elliptical style, are incomprehensible even to the best trained of audiences. As Alfred Kerr rightfully puts it, you must learn to see anew in the theatre of Wedekind. All of which is correct, yet we respectfully submit that the theatre, like a picture, has its optics: its foreground, middle distance, background, and foreshortening. Destroy the perspective and the stage is transformed into something that resembles staring post-Impressionist posters. The gentle arts of development, of characterisation, of the conduct of a play may not be flouted with impunity. The author more than the auditor is the loser. Wedekind works too often in bold, bright primary colours; only in some of his pieces is the modulation artistic, the character-drawing summary without being harsh. His climaxes usually go off like pistol-shots. Frühlings Erwachen (1891), the touching tale of Spring's Awakening in the heart of an innocent girl of fourteen, a child, Gretchen, doomed to a tragic ending, set all Germany by the ears when it was first put on in the Kammerspielhaus, Berlin, by Director Reinhardt at the end of 1906. During fifteen years two editions had been sold, and the work was virtually unknown till its stage presentation. Mr. Shaw is right in saying that if you wish to make swift propaganda seek the theatre, not the pulpit, nor the book. With the majority Wedekind's name was anathema. A certain minority called him the new Messiah, that was to lead youth into the promised land of freedom. For a dramatist all is grist that makes revolve the sails of his advertising mill, and as there is nothing as lucrative as notoriety, Wedekind must have been happy.

He is a hard hitter and dearly loves a fight—a Hibernian trait—and his pen was soon transformed into a club, with which he rained blows on the ribs of his adversaries. That he was a fanatical moralist was something not even the broadest-minded among them suspected; they only knew that he meddled with a subject that was hitherto considered tacenda, and with dire results. Nowadays the thesis of Spring's Awakening is not so novel. In England Mr. H. G. Wells was considerably exercised over the problem when he wrote in The New Machiavelli such a startling sentence as "Multitudes of us are trying to run this complex, modern community on a basis of 'hush,' without explaining to our children or discussing with them anything about love or marriage."

I find in Spring's Awakening a certain delicate poetic texture that the poet never succeeded in recapturing. His maiden is a dewy creature; she is also the saddest little wretch that was ever wept over in modern fiction. Her cry when she confesses the worst to her dazed mother is of a poignancy. As for the boys, they are interesting. Evidently, the piece is an authentic document, but early as it was composed it displayed the principal characteristics of its author: Freakishness, an abnormal sense of the grotesque—witness that unearthly last scene, which must be taken as an hallucination—and its swift movement; also a vivid sense of caricature—consider the trial scene in the school; but created by a young poet of potential gifts. The seduction scene is well managed at the Kammerspielhaus. We are not shown the room, but a curtain slightly divided allows the voices of the youthful lovers to be overheard. A truly moving effect is thereby produced. Since the performance of this play, the world all over has seen a great light. Aside from the prefaces of Mr. Shaw on the subject of children and their education, plays, pamphlets, even legislation have dealt with the theme. A reaction was bound to follow, and we do not hear so much now about "sex initiation" and coeducation. Suffice it to say that Frank Wedekind was the first man to put the question plumply before us in dramatic shape.

A favourite one-act piece is Der Kammersänger (1899), which might be translated as The Wagner Singer, for therein is laid bare the soul of the Wagnerian tenor, Gerardo, whose one week visit to a certain city results in both comedy and tragedy. He has concluded a brilliantly successful Gastspiel, singing several of the Wagnerian rôles, and when the curtain rises we see him getting his trunks in order, his room at the hotel filled with flowers and letters. He must sing Tristan the next night in Brussels, and has but an hour to spare before his train departs. If he misses it his contract will be void, and in Europe that means business, tenor or no tenor. He sends the servant to pack his costumes, snatches up the score of Tristan, and as he hums it, he is aware that some one is lurking behind one of the window-curtains. It is a young miss, presumably English— she says: "Oh, yes"—and she confesses her infatuation. Vain as is our handsome singer he has no time for idle flirtations. He preaches a tonic sermon, the girl weeps, promises to be good, promises to study the music of Wagner instead of his tenors, and leaves with a paternal kiss on her brow. The comedy is excellent, though you dimly recall a little play entitled: Fréderic Lemaître. It is a partial variation on that theme. But what follows is of darker hue. An old opera composer has sneaked by the guard at the door and begs with tears in his eyes that the singer will listen to his music. He is met with an angry refusal. Gradually, after he has explained his struggles of a half-century, he, the friend of Wagner, to secure a hearing of his work, the tenor, who is both brutal and generous, consents, though he is pressed for time. Then the tragedy of ill luck is unfolded. The poor musician doesn't know where to begin, fumbles in his score, while the tenor, who has just caught another woman behind a screen, a piano teacher—here we begin to graze the edge of burlesque—grows impatient, finally interrupts the composer, and in scathing terms tells him what "art" really means to the world at large and how useless has been his sacrifice to that idol "art" with a capital "A." I don't know when I ever enjoyed the exposition of the musical temperament. The Concert, by Bahr, is mere trifling in comparison, all sawdust and simian gestures. We are a luxury for the bourgeois, the tenor tells his listener, who do not care for the music or words we sing. If they realised the meanings of Walküre they would fly the opera-house. We singers, he continues, are slaves, not to our "art," but to the public; we have no private life.

He dismisses the old man.

Then a knock at the door, a fresh interruption. This time it is surely serious. A young, lovely society woman enters. She has been his love for the week, the understanding being that the affair is to terminate as it began, brusquely, without arrière-pensée. But she loves Gerardo. She clamours to be taken to Brussels. She will desert husband, children, social position, she will ruin her future to be with the man she adores. She is mad with the despair of parting. He is inexorable. He gently reminds her of their agreement. His contract does not permit him to travel in company with ladies, nor may he scandalise the community in which he resides. Tenors, too, must be circumspect.

She swears she will kill herself. He smiles and bids her remember her family. She does shoot herself, and he sends for a policeman, remembering that an arrest by superior force will but temporarily abrogate his contract. No policeman is found by the distracted hotel servants, and, exclaiming: "To-morrow evening I must sing Tristan in Brussels," the conscientious artist hurries away to his train, leaving the lifeless body of his admirer on the sofa. Played by a versatile actor, this piece ought to make a success in America, though the biting irony of the dialogue and the cold selfishness of the hero might not be "sympathetic" to our sentiment-loving audiences. The poet has protested in print against the alteration of the end of this little piece, *i.e.*, one acting version made the impassioned lady only a pretended suicide, which quite spoils the motivation.

Ibsen must have felt sick when such an artist as Duse asked him to let her make Nora in Doll's House return to her family. But he is said to have consented. Wedekind consented, because he was ill, but he made his protest, and justly so.

The Marquis of Keith is a larger canvas. It is a modern rogues' comedy. Barry Lyndon is hardly more entertaining. The marquis is the son of an humble tutor in the house of a count whose son later figures as Ernest Scholtz. The marquis is a swindler in the grand manner. He is a Get-Rich-Quick Wallingford, for he has lived in the United States, but instead of a lively sketch is a full length portrait painted by a master. You like him despite his scampishness. He is witty. He has a heart—for his own woes—and seems intensely interested in all the women he loves and swindles. He goes to Munich, where he invents a huge scheme for an exhibition palace and fools several worthy and wealthy brewers, but not the powerful Consul Casimir, the one man necessary to his comprehensive operation. When his unhappy wife tells him there is no bread in the house for the next day, he retorts: "Very well, then we shall dine at the Hotel Continental." Nothing depresses his mercurial spirits. He borrows from Peter to pay Paul, and an hour later borrows from Paul to pay himself. His boyhood friend he simply plunders. This Ernest, in reality the Graf von Trautenau, is an idealist of the type that Wedekind is fond of delineating. He would save the world from itself, rescue it from the morass of materialism, but he relapses into a pathological mysticism which ends in a sanitarium for nervous troubles. The marquis is a Mephisto; he is not without a trace of idealism; altogether a baffling nature, Faust-like, and as chockfull of humour as an egg is full of meat. He goes to smash. His plans are checkmated. His beloved deserts him for the enemy. His wife commits suicide. His life threatened, and his liberty precarious, he takes ten thousand marks from Consul Casimir, whose name he has forged in a telegram, and with a grin starts for pastures new. Will he shoot himself? No! After all, life is very much like shooting the chutes. The curtain falls. This stirring and technically excellent comedy has never been a favourite in Germany. Perhaps its cynicism is too crass. It achieved only a few performances in Berlin to the accompaniment of catcalls, hisses, and derisive laughter. I wonder why? It is entertaining, with all its revelation of a rascally mean soul and its shady episodes.

Space, I am sorry to say, forbids me from further exposition of such strong little pieces as Musik, a heart-breaking drama of a betrayed girl studying singing who goes to jail while the real offender, the man, remains at liberty (1907), or of Die Zensur, with its discussion of art and religion—the poet intrudes—and its terrible cry at the close: "Oh, God! why art thou so unfathomable?" Or of the so-called Lulu tragedy (Erdgeist and The Box of Pandora) of which I like the first act of the former and the second act of the latter—you are reminded at this point of the gambling scene in Sardou's Fernande—but as I do not care to sup on such unmitigated horrors, I prefer to let my readers judge for themselves from the printed plays.

Karl Hetman is an absorbing play in which a man loses the world but remains captain of his soul; actually he ends his life rather than exhibit himself as motley to the multitude. As a foil for the idealist Hetman—who is a sort of inverted Nietzsche; also a self-portrait in part of the dramatist—there is the self-seeking scamp Launhart who succeeds with the very ideas which Hetman couldn't make viable, ideas in fact which brought about his disaster. They are two finely contrasted portraits, and what a grimace of disgust is aroused when Launhart tells the woman who loves Hetman: "O Fanny, Fanny, a living rascal is better for your welfare than the greatest of dead prophets." What Dead-Sea-fruit wisdom! The pathos of distance doesn't appeal to the contemporary soul of Wedekind. He writes for the young, that is, for to-morrow.

The caprice, the bizarre, the morbid in Wedekind are more than redeemed by his rich humanity. He loves his fellow man even when he castigates him. He is very emotional, also pragmatic. The second act of his Franziska, a Karnevalgroteske, was given at the Dresden Pressfestival, February 7, 1913, with the title of Matrimony in the Year 2000, the author and his wife appearing in the leading rôles with brilliant success. It contains in solution the leading motives from all his plays and his philosophy of life. It is fantastic, as fantastic as Strindberg's

Dream Play, but amusing. In 1914 his biblical drama, Simson (Samson), was produced with mixed success.

Translated Wedekind would lose his native wood-note wild, and doubtless much of his dynamic force—for on the English stage he would be emasculated. And I wonder who would have the courage to produce his works.

Musik, for example, if played in its entirety might create a profound impression. It is pathetically moving and the part of the unhappy girl, who is half crazy because of her passion for her singing-master, is a rôle for an accomplished actress. If the public can endure Brieux's Damaged Goods, why not Musik? The latter is a typical case and is excellent drama; the French play is neither. For me all the man is summed up in the cry of one of his characters in Erdgeist: "Who gives me back my faith in mankind, will give me back my life." An idealist, surely.

The last time I saw him was at the Richard Strauss festival in Stuttgart, October, 1912. He had changed but little and still reminded me of both David Belasco and an Irish Catholic priest. In his eyes there lurked the "dancing-madness" of which Robert Louis Stevenson writes. A latter-day pagan, with touches of the perverse, the grotesque, and the poetic; thus seems to me Frank Wedekind.

1917

LEE SIMONSON

Lee Simonson (1888–1967) took part in George Pierce Baker's experimental playwriting laboratory at Harvard, then studied art in Paris for three years. He returned an apostle of the New Stagecraft, a blanket term for the reforms advocated by European directors and theorists of the intimate theatre movement. Simonson particularly appreciated the Swiss Adolphe Appia, who argued that two-dimensional scenery was inappropriate for a three-dimensional actor and that electric lighting could achieve effects painting could not. Along with Robert Edmond Jones and Norman Bel-Geddes, Simonson proclaimed, "We want to make the stage a world where the characters not only seem to live, but can initiate a new life." Simonson began to put these precepts into practice, starting with the Washington Square Players. He then helped found the Theatre Guild and designed over half of its productions, including the expressionistic *R.U.R.* and *The Adding Machine*, the constructivist *Dynamo*, and the spare *Joan of Lorraine*. His colleague Theresa Helburn recalled: "He could create miracles with light [to produce] some of the most interesting experimental sets seen on the American stage." Simonson, who often shared ownership of the production concept with the director, was far from doctrinaire in his use of "isms." In his opinionated and influential book *The Stage Is Set* (1932), he railed against one of the divinities of the New Stagecraft, Gordon Craig, for being dogmatic and impractical. His own preference was for a stripped-down, atmospheric, and functional synthesis of imagination and realism to fit the needs of a given play. His essay "The Painter and the Stage," one of the earliest American statements about the need to reform scene design, appeared in *Theatre Arts*, a magazine founded to promote the New Stagecraft.

The Painter and the Stage

I

THE importance of scenery is the importance of a background. Without its appropriate background nothing can be wholly sensed or completely experienced. In the end Art beautifies life by deliberately decorating everything that in life is "up stage"—the daily background of walls, furniture, balconies, gardens, streets, bridges and house fronts. And we are impelled to decorate the shifting backgrounds of the stage itself, the moment the stage becomes vital to us.

Perhaps because I am a decorator by instinct, nothing exists for me independently of its setting. The beauty of gothic tracery lived for me once in a hillside chapel in Brittany. I have seen far more important "examples" wedged in museums, and forgotten them. I can see no painting independently of the wall, or the other pictures near by. The physical appearance of a book affects my ability to read it. In a concert hall I long for a singer standing against a gold or flowered screen in order that I may surrender myself wholly to Schumann or Schubert. Wagner's *Ring* has always been an opera to me, never a legend, because of the dingy settings, slimy and dirty in color, dingy even when new, which the opera house of New York (and of Munich, for that matter) perennially offers. As the gods pick their way over sallow mounds, papier mâché rocks, so strangely stratified, I seem always to see a dreary corner of suburbia, as yet "undeveloped." At any moment a sign "Choice Lots for Sale" will gleam through the tree trunks, and the clang of a distant trolley rise above the dirge of Rhinemaidens. I have listened to Wagner's score. I have heard Fremstadt, or Goritz. But I have not been at the beginning of the world watching gods and heroes shape the destiny of men.

Now, it is this illusion of not being at a play, but in the domain of the play itself, which is the aim of all drama which pretends to express anything whatsoever. And in the matter of settings that will maintain this essential illusion, and not destroy it, there are only two alternatives: either the spectator's imagination must supply the background—and the *Ring* could be fitly sung against a gigantic curtain of blue, just as *A Midsummer Night's Dream* could be played against one of green—or the play must be acted before a background that is a piece with its intention. It was to preserve the essential illusion in the playhouse that every cult of what we call the modern scenic movement has arisen.

Unfortunately there is so little intention in current productions, let alone poetry and imagination, that our best talents, such as Robert Jones', are too often wasted in creating spacious backgrounds for polite farces. Scenery, to be sure, should heighten the mood of a play and dramatize its intention. But what is there to heighten, or dramatize with line and composition, in the flimsy whimsicality and the tepid wit of *Good Gracious Annabelle* or *A Successful Calamity*? The last act of *The Devil's Garden* was another instance of the artistry of a setting dwarfing the feebler artistry of a play. In that act a murderer is to wrestle with his soul. The room rose above with couch and chairs, and a hearth in firelight loomed stately and mysterious. One waited for the play to fill the scene. But the play maundered, babbled sentimental platitudes, and stumbled to a mechanical end. And the room stood waiting, while the play literally expired in it, as a sick puppy might die whimpering in the aisle of a church. Give Jones richer material, such as *Til Eulenspiegel* or Ridgely Torrence's negro plays, and we have a hint of what Jones might do with *The Misanthrope*, *Electra* or *Rosmersholm*. The dilemma is unavoidable, and it will persist until we evoke an indigenous Reinhardt, a Barker or a Copeau, producing in his permanent theatre plays that demand an artist to create their backgrounds, and providing a technical staff capable of teaching the stage designer his craft, and a workshop where he can execute his ideas.

At present the only such centers are the little theatres, the art theatres and the community playhouses which have been endowed or built until they begin to dot the width of the country from one seaboard to the other. Some like Maurice Browne's theatre in Chicago have maintained a unique standard, others have lapsed into fads, been merely smart when they intended to be witty, or speculated in thrillers like any vaudeville broker. But they continue to produce *Deirdre*, *The Life of Man*, *The Sea Gull*, *The Trojan Women* or *Bushido* about as frequently as Broadway continues to produce trash. They have, on the whole, achieved organization in which intelligent coöperation between a producer and scene designer is possible. And for that reason they will continue to breed scene designers faster than our chaotic "commercial theatres" can use them.

In fact, up to now this has been the little theatres' most emphatic contribution to the American stage and their most certain success. In New York, at any rate, they have as yet developed no school of acting as the Abbey Players did, nor bred a producer whose instinct for theatrical values could for a moment challenge Arthur Hopkins' or Mrs. Hapgood's; nor inspired a school of native playwrights. But they have everywhere stimulated the art of scene designing until it has begun to display the continuity and the momentum of what we call a "school" or a movement.

During the first year of the Washington Square Players at the Bandbox Theatre, Goodman and Moeller were, I imagine, often incensed at the frequent remark of critics and audiences, that the stage settings were better than the acting and the plays. They had a right to be incensed, for it is far easier to produce new stage settings than it is to achieve a new method of stage direction or write modern drama. Producers and actors bred upon Shaw's later plays are as bewildered by *The Sea Gull* or *The Cherry Orchard*, as conductors capable of successfully bringing their orchestras through *Tristan* once a week were bewildered by the first scores of Richard Strauss. Every tradition of acting, every trick of stage dialogue, every method of getting emphasis and "building up climaxes" is so completely ignored that an entirely new technique must be invented.

But the art of stage scenery has no tradition. It is the one craft which has remained wholly untouched by any trace of æsthetic taste. While successive publics assimilated Beardsley, Whistler, Degas and Renoir, audiences, whether at Bowery melodrama or at the Metropolitan Opera House, witnessed scenery invariably painted like the panoramic landscapes of the English Academy in the year 1852. So to-day a designer has only to transfer to the stage an adaptation of Beardsley's massing of black and white, the tinted monochromes of a Whistler nocturne, the elements of a Japanese print, a poster, or even an architectural water-color, and he is greeted with ripples of applause by astonished audiences who view him as a daring innovator. Every innovation in stage-craft we have witnessed in America is based upon the æsthetic discoveries of twenty years ago. We continue to be amazed by the presence within the frame of a proscenium of the very things that even the trustees of art museums now take for granted within a picture frame. In fact, it is impossible for any man capable of designing a poster, a piece of furniture, a book-cover, or any picture that would be rejected by the Academy, to design a stage setting that will not seem revolutionary. Given an instinct for decoration, the rudiments of good taste, an understanding of architectural form, and the sense of color which to-day any painter of twenty-five has inherited, a painter cannot avoid designing settings which in one way or another are significant.

We hear a great deal of a special "sense of the theatre," as though it were a separate intuition, developed only after a somewhat devout novitiate. Nothing is further from the truth. Precisely, because stage setting is but another form of decoration, a decorator can adapt himself as readily to the conditions of the stage as he adapts himself to the space allotted to him by an architect or determined by his own frame. So rarely is an American theatre equipped with a diffused lighting system, a dome or a "kuppelhorizont," a sliding stage or one capable of being raised and lowered in sections, that half a stage designer's energy is spent, not in designing, but in sacrificing the scale and scope of his original vision to devise something which the electrician can light with a row of footlights and one or two "spots," and a stage manager "fly," with a system designed for the wings and back drops of a Grand Opera House of thirty years ago. Craig, to be sure, banishes the painter from the theatre, along with the actor. But despite the prestige of this particular augur (pending the day when plays shall have become symbolic pantomimes), nothing is more patent than the fact that painters everywhere, though they have not changed the theatre's destiny, have been valuable recruits in its regeneration.

Maxime Dethomas, a French illustrator, at his first try designed settings for the *Théâtre des Arts* which achieved the most difficult of all things in stage setting,—stylistic realism,— the shop of a laundress, which had beauty of line, spacing and color. Fritz Erler, the Munich painter, designed the sets for one of Reinhardt's productions of *Hamlet*—a simpler and more intense background for a tragedy than Urban's stippled battlements, or his grandiose banquet hall for Hackett's recent production of *Macbeth*. Robert Lawson and I were painting when the Washington Square Players called upon us for scenery. Both of us, I think, had never been nearer the stage than an orchestra chair; within a season we had designed settings for every type of play,—comedies, pantomimes, fantasies and farce. Rollo Peters abandoned painting for scene designing. Bakst is another instance of a similar conversion. And in almost every case the stage settings of these painters have qualities of design, a pitch of style, never evinced in their painting. Dethomas' vigorous illustrations are far less significant æsthetically than his first stage set. Erler's portraits are competent and commonplace. The same holds true of Bakst's as compared with his work for the Russian Ballet, and of Orlik's canvases contrasted with his setting of *A Winter's Tale* at Reinhardt's Theatre. Dulac's masks and costumes for a play by Yeats escape just that element of prettiness which vitiates his successful illustrations. Hugo Ballin has recently staged "movies," and by all accounts his settings there are far more fundamentally decorative than his mural panels for which he has been thrice crowned by the Academy.

The catalogue is incomplete, but it will augment, because the stage to-day supplies the only opportunities for decoration capable of awakening a decorator's imagination and stimulating his creative energy. Mural painting is moribund as a result of the neo-classicism of American architects, who continue to turn Corinthian temples into post-offices, Roman baths into railway stations, and Doges' council chambers into the reading rooms of public libraries. In consequence, decorative painting in America is usually confined to the pages of a magazine or a picture frame. When I was installing a few stage-models at the first Independent Exhibition of Painters and Sculptors last year, Rockwell Kent admitted his eagerness to attempt scenery. To-day, a critic remarks of one of his Newfoundland landscapes: "A work which reaches force of statement through an appreciation of theatrical values." Why should the stage not profit by them? Jules Guerin, Henry McCarter and Maxfield Parrish are others who would gain stature on the stage. I hear of models for a production of *Snow-White* in Parrish's Cornish studio. Meanwhile we must read, in the program of *A Kiss for Cinderella*, Mr. Hewlett's acknowledgement that his most effective background is adapted from one of Parrish's pictures. And in the last act of Sheldon's *The Garden of Paradise* Urban transferred to the stage one of Parrish's covers for the "Ladies Home Journal," with the result that what we call a new era in the staging of musical comedy began. But Parrish himself is still without the theatre. Given a stage, adequately equipped and with a flexible lighting system, and I would set Kent designing *The Tempest*, Guerin *Aida* or *Cæsar and Cleopatra*, Parrish *The Merchant of Venice*, Dulac *The Magic Flute*, McCarter *Rheingold*, and using half a dozen more who had never staged plays before, provide an amazingly beautiful series of productions. Such a season might not produce the synthesis for which the devotees of the new theatre are waiting, but its visions would provide the most fertile soil in which a "newer" art of the theatre might grow.

II

Once within the theatre the artist's first battle is with the great American god—Grey. The constant prejudice he will have to overcome is the antipathy of audiences and actors to color. For on the stage it is still a dogma that a background must be dark or grey in order to stay back—a theory which in painting is always discredited and is applied only in such art schools as Julian's, into which the ambient light of day never enters. Painting has after a century struggled free of the omnipotence of brown.

The scene designer will have to struggle with the omnipotence of grey. A generation ago the way to make a portrait head "live" was to pick out the high-lights, particularly on the forehead, in a taffy-like mixture of ochre and white—this was light—and place the whole against a syrupy mixture of brown. This was shadow. Cezanne, Van Gogh and Renoir have taught us otherwise. And just as light in painting is no longer a subtle or sentimental spotlight, the light of the stage must achieve the harmonious welding of color masses.

The outcry comes, "But you can't see the actor." I reply that the actor is always visible. Any moving body is more conspicuous than the body against which it moves. A monk in grey against the flaming walls of the Grand Cañon would present an excellent target for any artillery officer. The most deliberate attempt to disguise moving objects—camouflage—succeeds so long as a gun or a man stands still. But no system of color-spotting will render invisible a ship on the sea or a cannon moving across a hill. It is true that a spot of yellow the size of a button will be conspicuous on a sheet of grey cardboard. And it is on this principle that most designing for the modern stage is based—color in the actor's costumes, and subdued backgrounds. But it is also true that a spot of yellow is even more conspicuous on a purple cardboard—a psychological law proven by countless posters as well as by half a century of impressionism. The scene of *Overtones* was based on the costumes Mrs. Holley had chosen for the four women: vivid green for two, purple for the others. I made the walls of the room gold, emphasized only by black lines, the door spaces backed with black velvet, the windows hung with orange silk. Nothing could have been more brilliant than this background, but the four women detached themselves completely and dominated the scene. They were, if anything, too visible. If Moors and Arabs can greet or stab each other against the vivid housefronts of their Mediterranean towns, why cannot the actors of a Biblical farce such as *The Sisters of Susannah* be seen against the orange walls I set for them, in Locker's costumes of emerald, turquoise and amethyst? In *The Magical City* Miss Mower stood robed in jonquil yellow in a room hung with purple burlap; through the window showed a silhouette of skyscrapers in a peacock sky. Would she have dominated the scene more completely had the walls been grey, and the furniture not blue with yellow cushions, but a somber mahogany brown, upholstered in discreet lilac?

As a nation we are unaccustomed to use our eyes. A spot of color distracts most of us, as a glass of wine befuddles a teetotaller, and for the next half hour we are unable to concentrate upon anything. On every steamer there are a goodly number who cannot look at the Bay of Naples except through smoked glasses. And in every audience a majority expects the designer to provide smoked glasses for them.

In deference to them, and from a false sense of chivalry to the play itself, has arisen the doctrine of the playwright's necessary humility. Jones has expressed this most picturesquely in an interview attributed to him: "I give this present form of stagecraft one more year to live—for one more year we will have Art Nouveau with us, striding across our backgrounds—distracting our gaze from the actors, and murdering thought. . . . For one more year orange and green hoops of gold and wigs of crimson will stagger zigzagging to reportorial bliss. For one more year these over-accentuated and inanimate objects will scream across the footlights and then——." One might retort: "For a few more years blank walls and towering draperies on which trickle blue or amber light will seem the only fitting background for poetry; for a few more years spewing floods of yellow from search-lights on a thousand figures prancing by night in a stadium will seem the acme of a beautiful festival—and then." It is a damning commentary on our plays if so many of them seem to require the discreet twilight of an invalid's room with the blinds drawn. Our thought in the theatre is not very vital if it so easily takes to cover at the sight of ornament, like a white rabbit scenting a hound. I long for plays in which we shall hear the baying of the hounds of spring or the hounds of heaven, and which will vibrate in dramatic unity with red and crimson, orange and gold.

Above all I crave the advent of drama vigorous enough to demand all the splendor, the color and the sensuous joy of which the modern palette is capable. The day must come when the scene designer need be no more concerned about distracting us from the play than the partisans who painted the jubilant windows of Chartres were fearful of distracting worshippers from the mysteries of high mass. Any ritual that has ever fundamentally answered the cravings of a group, has always accepted sumptuous and brilliant adornment. The screens of the temples of Japan are brilliant with silver and gold, the mosques of India and Persia begemmed with tiles. The Greeks gilded their Olympian Zeus and painted the metopes of the Parthenon. If acting ever becomes the ritual which Craig dreams, it will evolve its background of pomp and pageantry even in its most tragic moments.

The two most intensely tragic performances of Greek plays I have ever witnessed were in the brilliant sunlight of the open air. At the Harvard Stadium, in the *Agamemnon* of Æschylus, spears and helmets flashed, and the red scarfs of the heralds flamed in the happy radiance of a June day. But the wail of Cassandra was, none the less, infinitely terrible. At the New

York Stadium, during Barker's presentation of *The Trojan Women*, the lament of Hecuba evoked pity and terror, although she did not stand in the gloom of drapery and a dark portal.

So I would welcome modern painters to the theatre, hoping that they will bring with them not only the dusk of Appia and the moon of Craig, but also the sun.

1917

CARL VAN VECHTEN

Like Huneker, Carl Van Vechten (1880–1964) felt it his duty to introduce his fellow Americans to culture; unlike Huneker, he usually promoted culture that was homegrown and from the other side of the tracks. He too served as a music critic at *The New York Times*, swiftly shifting focus to report on exciting developments in dance exemplified by Loie Fuller and Isadora Duncan. In the 1920s he became known as white society's advance man for the Harlem Renaissance, sponsoring Langston Hughes and Ethel Waters and urging concertgoers to appreciate the blues. In 1922, he abandoned criticism for fiction; of his frivolous novels, reminiscent of a corn-fed Ronald Firbank, *Nigger Heaven* (1926) best encapsulates that moment. Van Vechten began to devote more of his time to photography and is now remembered chiefly for a luminous gallery of celebrity portraits and male nudes.

Van Vechten's eclectic enthusiasms are on display in "In the Theatre of the Purlieus," a survey of New York's minority theatres written in 1918–19. In addition to the section reprinted here, it also reported on an Italian variety artist, the Yiddish theatre, and the Negro drama. Given the received idea of Van Vechten as a booster of African-American art, it is surprising to find him writing, "I am afraid there will never be a Negro Theatre, and if there is one I am sure it will appeal more to whites than to blacks. The Negro will always prefer Mary Pickford to Bert Williams."

Salome with its Dance of the Seven Veils was an unavoidable fad at the time, a hangover from Mauve Era decadence. In the wake of Oscar Wilde's play came Richard Strauss's opera, Diaghilev's ballet, dance acts by Maud Allen and Gertrude Hoffman, Nazimova's silent film, and even Fanny Brice's "Sadie Salome." Mimi Aguglia had been on the Sicilian stage from childhood and managed her own company, playing the Americas in the verismo of Verga and early Pirandello. She was reputedly the first actress to bob her hair and, after becoming an American citizen, played Assunta in the Hollywood film of *The Rose Tattoo*.

Mimi Aguglia as Salome

THE great New York public—the public that patronizes Broadway successes, to be exact—plays with the foreign theatre,
both its dramas and its acting. Each of its elements may be a
sensation for a week or a month, whereupon, like the proverbial doll, it is tossed into the proverbial corner, and, with some
of its gloss worn off, it is given to the poor neighbour's child
in New Jersey or Colorado. New York can be constant to a
play like *Within the Law*, or to an actress like Maude Adams,
but the Russian Ballet, which has thrilled and amused Europe
for nearly a decade, excited curiosity here for a few weeks and
now is completely forgotten. We pull such plums out of the
foreign cake as Alla Nazimova or Bert Williams or Bertha
Kalich, and, in order to satisfy Broadway stomachs, they are
forced to alter the very qualities which made them palatable in
their original environment. Bert Williams is no more the player
who once delighted and amazed Eleonora Duse than Alla Nazimova is the woman who, as Regina, almost outplayed the
greatest of Oswalds.

Nevertheless, Broadway seems to continue to call for more.
It is fortunate that some of the great foreign actors who have
played in New York's minor theatres have resisted its alleged
desires, refused the proffered admiration, which certainly is
not to be depended upon for any extended period. Why,
Broadway even consigned Sarah Bernhardt to the music halls!
Mimi Aguglia, who, I am almost convinced, has more genius
than any other actress on the stage today, if we except the lyric
stage, has fortunately eluded Broadway. There have been ru-
mours from time to time that she would appear in English, a
language with which, I believe, she is tolerably familiar, but up
to now (and I hope the time will never come) she has not forsaken the darling theatres of the Italian purlieus of New York.
She has occasionally, to be sure, invaded Broadway, but such
invasions have been accomplished surreptitiously and under
the very conditions of her downtown appearances, that is, with
an Italian company, Italian stage decorations, and a prompter.

When, therefore, you go to see Signora Aguglia, you go to

see her under pretty nearly ideal conditions, with an audience that understands Italian, that admires, nay venerates, her performances, but which does not regard her as a freak, and that primarily attends the theatre to see a play. She appears in pieces by d'Annunzio, Giacosa, Shakespeare, and other authors whose names are not overly popular on Broadway. A curious fact about a typical Bowery audience of Jews or Italians is that it would just as soon see a good play as a bad one. It is even reasonable to believe that these people prefer good plays.

Unless, however, you happen to live in the neighbourhood of one of the theatrical temples which the signora adorns with her art, you will find it difficult to follow her movements. She may, indeed, be playing under your very nose without your being aware of the fact, unless you read the Italian newspapers. As for myself, I have a habit of wandering down unfrequented streets, sometimes in search of a new eating-place, sometimes in search of books; and in these streets, in the windows of hairdressers or macaroni merchants, or displayed prominently on the walls of pastry-shops, which, as any one who has lived in Naples knows, are the Italian clubs, the gathering places for neighbourhood gossip, such as our saloons afforded to our working men until our kindly-disposed government decided that only rich men should have clubs in this country, you may see posters announcing the "tragica Italiana," and telling you where and when and in what you may see her if you have the desire.

Usually a tour of Spring and Sullivan streets would give you this information if Mimi Aguglia were in town, but recently I was startled by running into an announcement on One Hundred and Twenty-fifth Street. If you happen to be a book collector, you may not be unaware that there is a row of old bookshops on this Harlem thoroughfare, running from Eighth Avenue to the New York Central Railroad tracks. A strange place for bookshops this, mingled with the homely life of Harlem, fish and vegetable markets, flashy haberdashers' shops, old and new furniture stores, cheap lunch counters, the Hotel Theresa, Pabst Harlem, moving-picture houses, and drug stores, the windows piled high with scented soaps. The external impression one gets is that Harlem never reads.

Nevertheless, several of these bookshops are large, and all seem to flourish.

Walking, then, from a tour of these shops to the Third Avenue Elevated, I passed the Gotham Theatre, a playhouse with which I had hitherto been unacquainted, and discovered that on the following Saturday night Mimi Aguglia would begin her Harlem season with a performance of Oscar Wilde's *Salome*, to be followed by a Sicilian comedy called *Mamma Rosa*. The doors of the theatre were nailed fast, and there seemed to be no way of purchasing tickets in advance, and so on the following Saturday, with those who accompanied me, I was on hand at a little after six to book places, which I secured in the tenth row.

Then we sought dinner in a near-by restaurant, a dinner which I can still recall with disgust; there was a lukewarm, thin, clam chowder which would have passed for dirty dishwater anywhere, a leathery finnan haddie, an inedible chunk of apple pie, weak beer, and unmentionable coffee. I cannot say that I was in the best of humours after this repast. Better dinners have spoiled an evening for me. We had been told that the play would begin at eight-thirty and, as in the theatres of the purlieus there are often discussions about tickets even if you possess checks for your seats, we were in our places by eight-fifteen. The theatre was large and painted a brilliant green, with a great deal of gold decoration. The seats were upholstered in red plush. The chandelier was a gorgeous monstrosity of brass branches bearing, in lieu of fruit or flowers, an infinitude of electric globes of many hues. There was no heat in this pretty playhouse on this cold November night, no heat at all. The place was icy cold, a cold which the green walls seemed to emphasize. Indeed, I had the impression of being imprisoned in a great green iceberg. We wrapped ourselves tightly in our coats and suffered. . . . The play did not begin at eight-thirty, nor yet at nine; it was indeed nearly nine-thirty before the curtain rose. Meanwhile, a young woman and a young man tortured, respectively, a piano and a violin: an hour of Rossini, of *Hearts and Flowers*, of *Faust*, of *Traviata*: an hour of scraping and pounding and thumping and groping and conscientious din. The audience became impatient, and whistled

and stamped and applauded; all to no end, and each separate
and good-natured person in this audience knew it would be to
no end, for Italians never do anything on time.

Nevertheless, may I state that two minutes after the curtain
had risen I had forgotten my bad dinner, forgotten the cold,
forgotten the long wait, forgotten the horrible music? Need I
say more for the compelling power of Mimi Aguglia?

The audience, as always in the Italian theatre, was delightful.
As I have intimated, these people came to see a play, not a
shocking drama by a social outcast named Oscar Wilde, who
went to jail for his sins and died a miserable death in Paris. I
venture to say that not ten individuals in that crowded theatre,
which, by the way, is bigger than most of the downtown
theatres, were in possession of any background whatever in regard to this piece. Probably not ten out of fifteen hundred had
ever heard of Oscar Wilde or knew anything about the play itself, except that it was a "biblica tragedia" (the program and
the posters said so much) and that Mimi Aguglia would appear
in it. No hysteria of shuddering repugnance informed this
mob, as we have been told informed that other mob which
watched and listened to Olive Fremstad in Richard Strauss's
music drama one Sunday morning at the Metropolitan Opera
House, and which filed out to register a solemn protest against
the exhibition in this sacred temple of art of a "toad upon
lilies." . . . Young mothers were there with their babes; they
suckled them, if nature so demanded. Young girls were there,
with lovely black hair and gold earrings; children were there, and
grandmothers. They had come to see a play. They applauded
Aguglia when she entered; they applauded vehemently at the
close of the drama, and recalled the protagonist several times,
but they did not rush into the lobby to consort in strange
groups to whisper about its indelicacies. No, to this audience
Salome was nothing "curious and sensual"; it was just a play.

Of all the conventions of the Italian theatre the prompter,
perhaps, is the most conspicuously esoteric to American eyes
and ears. He sits in a huge box, like an inverted chariot, in the
centre of the row of footlights, which is supposed to conceal
him, but often, in his excitement, his head protrudes, like that
of a turtle from its shell, or his arms, for sometimes he gesticu-
lates, the book in his hand! In any performance his voice is au-

dible, extremely audible; so that there is a likelihood that you will hear every line of the piece twice, for his office is not to prompt failing memories, but, rather, to give a line to an actor who may not have memorized it before. Therefore the Italian prompter reads every line of the play. I have known instances (the big scene in the fourth act of *Zaza* comes to mind) when the actors in their fury outstripped him by several speeches. But no self-respecting prompter is daunted by such a situation. Conscientiously he continues to read every line, and in time catches up with and even passes by the actors themselves. The effect is curious, and to some people it renders performances in the Italian theatre intolerable. For myself, I may say that either I ignore the presence of the prompter entirely, as when the acting is good enough to make me forget it, or else I find myself reflecting on the philosophy of the institution. It is almost, indeed, as if the poet himself were reading his play to the actors, who immediately grasp his lines and transmute them into emotional speech accompanied by gesture. With some such explanation you may easily persuade yourself that the spontaneity and adaptability and real power of the Italian actor far transcend that of the player of any other nation.

In some plays, notably in Sicilian pieces, or in such modern dramas as *Zaza* or *Madame X*, the unnamed (for the program does not list them) thespians that Signora Aguglia gathers around her give a great deal more than adequate performances. They are often atmospheric, suggestive, and emotionally sincere. *Salome*, however, was somewhat beyond the group I saw on this occasion. The page of Herodias, played by a woman in a sort of Viola costume with high gaiters, was a ridiculous figure; Narraboth, a stolid pink body; Herod, an incredible monstrosity in a Roman toga; and Herodias, in a mid-Victorian Greek gown cut low over the shoulders, with a diadem on her head, for all the world like an old print of Mrs. Somebody or Other as Lady Macbeth. There was, to be sure, a real Negro as the headsman, but he not only had to receive the command given by the playwright, but also whispered instructions as to where to descend, and what to do when he got to the bottom of the cistern. There were no signs of stage direction; I doubt if there had been a rehearsal. The scenery, evidently, had been borrowed from an Italian opera company which had been giving *Aida*, pieced out with stock wood scenes, thrones, etc. Herodias, finding herself without a throne, bade one of the attendants bring her a kitchen chair. . . . The play was considerably and advantageously cut. The Jews did not appear, and the Romans had little to do. Herod's speeches were chopped and hacked to pieces. And yet, bad dinner, cold theatre, long wait, prompter, bad stage direction, bad scenery, bad costumes, bad actors and all, I may say without qualification that this was the most effective performance of *Salome* I have ever seen, and one of the great evenings I have spent in the theatre. And for this satisfaction I must thank Mimi Aguglia.

Of such a performance a mere description of costume, gesture, and voice means very little. By such a process, how could I hope to recapture the electricity of Aguglia? . . . I doubt if Aguglia herself knows why or how she does certain things. This is one of the most curious phenomena of the art of acting. Given a suspicion of genius, a plan of attack, precision, authority, foresight, and sympathy, and the accidental gestures, or expedient gestures, fall into place and become essential parts of the interpretation. . . . The successor of Faure was not successful in the part of Hamlet at the Paris Opéra. He appealed to his great predecessor: "I have carefully studied you in the part; what have I forgotten to do?" Faure explained: on the opening night, finding his throat clogged at an important moment, he had turned aside and spat into his handkerchief, but to the audience the gesture suggested deep emotion, and it was greeted with a wave of applause. Thereafter Faure continued to do intentionally what he had first done accidentally. . . . So in Salome's long silent scene, between the entrance of the king and the dance, Aguglia's action provoked the most excited comment from us. It was open to many interpretations, but of one thing all of us were agreed, it was absolutely *right*. Salome Aguglia, repulsed by Jochanaan, in the depths of despair, suddenly started and threw back her head when the tetrarch entered. Did this signify merely the breaking of her mood, or did she then and there decide that it would be through Herod she would be enabled to fulfil her desire? Later, long before she promised to dance, she began to denude herself of her golden chains and her jewels. Had she made up her mind to accede to the king's request, or was she tossing her jewels off absent-mindedly while she thought of the prophet; or was she imagining herself as his jewelless companion in the wilderness? It is possible, indeed probable, that Aguglia thought none of these things. It is very likely that, with the practical carelessness incidental to the Italian theatre, while she was waiting she was preparing for the dance which was to follow. All that I mean to indicate is that these possibly careless gestures became almost great moments in the rhythm of the interpretation.

What a voice the woman has, now rich and full with the notes of the viola da gamba, now petulant and querulous like a clarinet, now rude and raucous like a bassoon! How well she plays on this superior instrument. In her scene with Narraboth he stood well up stage facing the audience. She played the scene with her back to the footlights; her whole effect was made with her voice and the sensuous curve of her spine. So, too, she played most of the following scene with Jochanaan, who by the way, never left the well. The cistern was built high, so that Salome might lean on it with her elbows while standing, an effect which might be imitated to advantage in more pretentious productions of this play. John lifted himself until his waist line was visible and then stood still, braced by his hands, his lower body concealed, while she played the scene about him. All this was marvellously mellow, marvellously plastic, extraordinarily intriguing, and there was no let-down in the crescendo of this performance.

Aguglia, as Salome, wore a wig of long, red hair and a trailing, transparent robe of tarnished silver, heavily embroidered in jewels. Her feet were incased in stilted sandals. For the dance she removed the outer garment and disclosed herself in the quaintest of gold tissue trousers decorated with the most fantastic bows of tied varicoloured ribbons. Above the bare abdomen she wore a short bolero jacket of gold and tassels. The dance was oriental, and centred in the stomach. . . . She made the first request for the head on a silver platter in a fittingly simple manner, but from then on she absolutely defied tradition. Instead of becoming angrier and more forceful, with each succeeding request she became more careless and childlike, running back and forth from the well, wrapping her veils about her, paying no heed whatever to the pleadings of the tetrarch, simply reiterating, "Give me the head of Jochanaan," not in a monotonous monotone, not with impatience, but with the ingenuous persistence of a spoiled child. Her antepenultimate repetition of the words was made with such legerity that the effect was almost too great to be borne in the theatre. I felt that the trumpets had blown and the walls of Jericho were falling, or that Samson was pulling the temple down around me. . . . Only the last time was she paramount, and Herod, startled by the sudden change of tone, yielded at once.

The scene with the head was conceived as something elementally sensuous, and was carried through unflinchingly. I suppose a chaste Broadway audience would have been shocked into getting thoroughly drunk in all available resorts before the night following such an interpretation was over. Aguglia had bound herself in a long, blue veil with thick meshes, wrapped it about her head, her face, her shoulders, her breast, and her thighs, but when the charger with its burden was given her the veil fell from her face, and on her knees before the head of Jochanaan she gradually unwound it from her body: the symbol of disrobing was obvious. Then she took the head from the charger and began pushing it about, following it on her knees from one side of the stage to the other, with little cries of delight, little exclamations of joy, little amorous coos, and finally came the embrace, in which everything was left to the imagination, because nothing was! The death was epileptic, a lesson learned probably from seeing Nijinsky die in *Scheherazade*.

We stayed for the beginning of *Mamma Rosa*, long enough to see a little of a very different Aguglia, with her own black hair, in a peasant dress, walking like a peasant, uttering comic lines in a Sicilian dialect, with an utterly different vocal apparatus, and for the audience this was just another play, and they enjoyed it almost as much as they had *Salome*.

November 28, 1918.

DOROTHY PARKER

Past mistress of the short form, Dorothy Parker (1893–1967) wrote dramatic criticism only for the smartest magazines, first *Vogue*, then *Vanity Fair*, as a replacement for P. G. Wodehouse, before taking over the department on her own in 1919. Unlike critics who sought to reproduce an experience or draw attention to "beauties," Parker used a production as the pretext for exercising her own acerbic wit. The point was to demonstrate that the writer was cleverer, more worldly-wise, and less gullible than the reader or even the artist. In the age of disillusionment that followed the Great War, the wisecrack best conveyed the fashion for cynicism. No wonder that the "Round Table" at the Algonquin Hotel, the journalists' luncheon club she frequented with Robert Benchley, Robert Sherwood, Franklin Pierce Adams, Alexander Woollcott, and George S. Kaufman, was commonly known as the Vicious Circle. The bon mots of these *mauvaises langues*—such as the barb that Katharine Hepburn "ran the gamut of emotions from A to B"—were made public in their columns the next day. Even Parker's praise, as in this review of a costume melodrama featuring those scions of an acting dynasty, the Barrymores, was tinged with acid. Complaints from producers led to Parker's dismissal from *Vanity Fair*, but, along with Benchley and Sherwood, she joined the newly founded *New Yorker* in 1925. There she was relegated to the safer realms of book reviewing and poetry. She did not lose her touch, however. Standing in for Benchley in 1931, she summed up her account of a popular drama about the Brownings: "In fact, now that you've got me right down to it, the only thing I didn't like about *The Barretts of Wimpole Street* was the play."

The Jest

WITHOUT wishing to infringe in any way on the Pollyanna copyright, there are times when one must say a few kind words for the general scheme of things. After all, the plan really has been worked out rather cleverly. When everything has gone completely bad and suicide seems the one way out, then something good happens, and life is again worth the cost of living. When things have sunk to their lowest depths, some really desirable event occurs, and business goes on again as usual. When clouds are thickest, the sun is due to come out strong in a little while. In fact, the darkest hour is just before the dawn. (No originality is claimed for that last one; it is just brought in for the heart interest and popular appeal.)

The Pollyanna system has recently been worked out with particularly brilliant effect, in the theatre. When the latest attractions at the local playhouses were so consistently poisonous that one had just about decided to give up the whole thing and stay at home in the evenings to see if there was anything in family life—then along came Mr. Arthur Hopkins and produced "The Jest." And, once again, all's well with the world.

It is difficult to write of "The Jest," for enough has been written about the thing to fill the Public Library comfortably, by this time. Everyone knows that it was written ten years ago by Sem Benelli—then in his late twenties—who was known in these parts heretofore only for his libretto of "L'Amore dei Tre Rei"; that in Italy, where its name is "La Cena Delle Beffe," it is practically a national institution; that Bernhardt played John Barrymore's part in French and another woman, Mimi Aguglia, played it in Italian; and that the present production at the Plymouth Theatre is the first English version of the play.

The name of the translator is no longer withheld; everyone knows that Edward Sheldon did the deed. Whether or not he has translated it into verse is still the subject of hot debates among the cultured. The ayes seem to have it, so far. If the English version is in what, in our youth, we used to speak of affectionately as dear old iambic pentameter, the actors mercifully abstain from reciting it that way; they speak their lines as good, hardy prose.

The Sunday supplements have printed long excerpts from the text, illustrated with scenes from the play and with weirdly blurred portraits of the author—portraits which look strangely like composite photographs of Harry Houdini and Josef Hofmann. The name Benelli has rapidly become a household word; little children in Greenwich Village chant it at their play, mothers hum it about the house; fathers whisper it through the smoke of their cigars. It is a good name for household pronunciation, too; you can't get into any arguments about it, the way you did about Ibanez.

It is even more difficult to write about the production and the acting of "The Jest"—superlatives are tiresome reading. The highest praise is the attitude of the audience, every evening. They say—they've been saying it for years—that it is impossible to hold an audience after eleven o'clock. The final curtain falls on "The Jest" at a quarter to twelve; until that time not a coat is struggled into, not a hat is groped for, not a sub-urbanite wedges himself out of his mid-row seat and rushes out into the night, to catch the 11:26. One wonders, by the way, how the commuters manage; they must just bring along a tube of toothpaste and a clean collar, and make a night of it. Anyway, there is not so much as a rustle before the curtain drops. Every member of the audience is still in his seat, clam-oring for more at the end of the last act.

There can be no greater tribute.

Once again the Barrymore brothers have shown what they can do when they try. They have easily outclassed all comers in this season's histrionic marathon—they have even broken their own records in "Redemption" and "The Copperhead." Their rôles—John plays Giannetto, the sensitive young artist, and Lionel, Neri, the great, swashbuckling mercenary—afford a brilliantly effective study in contrasts. The part of Giannetto, exquisitely portrayed no less by gesture and pose than by voice, is in its morbid ecstasies, its impotent strivings, its subtle shadings, undoubtedly far more difficult than the blustering rôle of Neri. Yet the physical strain of Lionel Barrymore's per-formance must in itself be enormous. How his voice can bear up all evening under Neri's hoarse roars of rage and reverber-ating bellows of geniality is one of the great wonders of the age. Not an extraordinarily big man in reality, he seems tremendous as he swaggers about the stage; in his fight scene, he goes through a mass formation of supernumeraries much as Elmer Oliphant used to go through the Navy line. And in some strange way, he manages to make the character almost likable.

Again, one must present it to the Barrymores; they are, in-dubitably, *quelque* family.

It is a bit rough on the other actors in "The Jest," for the Barrymores' acting makes one forget all about the other people concerned. It is all the more credit to Gilda Varesi that she can make her brief characterization stand out so vigorously. Maude Hanaford and E. J. Ballantine also contribute effective performances. But the Big Four of the occasion are unquestionably the Barrymore brothers, Arthur Hopkins, and Robert Edmond Jones.

Scenically, the production of "The Jest" reaches the high water mark of the season—which isn't putting it nearly strongly enough, unfortunately. Mr. Jones has devised a series of settings which are the most remarkable of his career; the year holds no more impressive picture than that of Giannetto's entrance, as he stands, cloaked in gleaming white, against a deep blue background, the dark figure of his hunchback servitor crouching at his side. The whole production is a succession of unforgettable pictures.

That, indeed, is just the quarrel that some people have with it. Those who have seen "La Cena Delle Beffe" on its home field say that the American production is a bit over-spectacular —that the production cuts in on the drama. The attention of the audience, they say, is diverted from the action by the amazing picturesqueness of the scenes. Well, their view is high over the heads of the untraveled. To one who has seen only this production, any better seems impossible. The simple, homely advice of one who has never been outside of these broadly advertised United States is only this: park the children somewhere, catch the first city-bound train, and go to the Plymouth Theatre, if you have to trade in the baby's Thrift Stamps to buy the tickets. The play will undoubtedly run from now on. You ought to be able to get nice, comfortable standing-rooms, any time after Labor Day.

1919

LUDWIG LEWISOHN

When eight-year-old Ludwig Lewisohn (1882–1955) was brought from
Berlin to Charleston, South Carolina, his Jewish parents converted to
Methodism in order to assimilate. However, as Lewisohn was finishing graduate school at Columbia in 1903, his advisers told him that no
college would hire a Jew to teach English literature. He left without
getting his doctorate, reaffirmed his Judaism, and concentrated on
teaching German literature at Midwestern universities. One of his
projects was to publish the complete plays of Gerhart Hauptmann in
English translation. In 1919 Lewisohn was appointed dramatic critic
of *The Nation,* and he served as its associate editor from 1920 to 1924.
Serious in intent, judicious in expression, his reviews sought to bring
the American theatre into the 20th century. The following two pieces
illustrate his values. He rejects the work of the superstar director and
playwright David Belasco, whose grandiose showmanship, which
Montrose Moses called "the Switchboard Theatre," was Broadway's
idea of "high art." He praises the Little Theatre Movement, in the
person of Susan Glaspell, who, with her husband George Cram Cook,
had been a prime mover behind the Provincetown Players. Lewisohn
moved to Paris, but in the face of Nazi incursions returned to New
York to translate Franz Werfel's pageant of Jewish travails, *The Eternal Road* (1937). It was directed by Max Reinhardt, then himself a
refugee from Hitler. An ardent Zionist, Lewisohn was one of the
founders of Brandeis University, where there was no bar to Jews in
the English Department.

Mr. Belasco Explains

FOR thirty-seven years Mr. David Belasco has devoted himself
to the art of the theatre. In remote cities where no other
American manager's name would be recognized, his is known.
If a girl is applauded in amateur theatricals in Peoria or Denver
she writes for counsel and help to David Belasco. There is a
Belasco legend composed of anecdotes that commercial travelers swap in smoking-cars; there is a Belasco biography in two
stout volumes by the late William Winter; there is, finally, issued

but the other day, the word of Mr. Belasco himself.* The critics may jeer mildly; the knowing ones among the public may show a correct disdain. They are all impressed. A Belasco opening—the first of any given season above all—still commands its very special little alertness and thrill.

And why should not these people be impressed? Mr. Belasco's dedication to his chosen art is as tireless as it is complete. He has spared no toil and no expense to produce what he considers beautiful things. He has never been cynical about his success, but has taken it to be the reward of his hard gained merits. He is satisfied with himself and with his public. He has made art pay. He still makes it pay. And who has the right to deny the unfailing qualities of every Belasco production—the silken delicacy of its surface, the unobtrusive perfection of its visible details, the gentle glow and harmony of its color schemes? Not those, assuredly, who daily applaud the less perfect productions of quite similar plays on another street. Nor those others who, in high places and humble ones, proclaim the theatrical theory of the drama—the theory, namely, that plays are "built" in the theatre, not written in solitude; that they are constructed to be gladly heard by any audience of the moment, not created to be overheard by the finer spirits of the age.

Of that theory Mr. Belasco's practice is the best of all possible illustrations. A manuscript to him is not something to be interpretatively bodied forth. It is a little raw material and a convenient starting-point. "Almost invariably," he tells us, "the exceptionally successful play is not written but re-written." During the crucial week of preliminary rehearsals, he continues, "I rewrite, transpose, change, and cut until the manuscript is so interlined that it is almost impossible to read it. . . . If it seems too heavy at a certain point, it must be lightened; if too tearful, laughter must be brought into it." It is no wonder that Mr. Belasco is the author or co-author of many of the plays he has produced, and that he has sedulously avoided the work of any master. What could he do with the method of production so truly attributed to another manager in another land, the method that strives to give to each play "its individual style, its

---

* *The Theatre through its Stage Door.* By David Belasco.

special atmosphere, its peculiar inner music."* "Who am I?" asked Oscar Wilde, only half in jest, when he was urged to make changes in *An Ideal Husband* for the production of the play, "Who am I to tamper with a masterpiece?" Mr. Belasco has not tampered with masterpieces. He has left them alone. And that is what every producing manager must do who desires —as our professors counsel and indeed command—to build successful plays in the theatre.

To Mr. Belasco, at all events, the play has been but one of many things. "The all-important factor in a dramatic production," he tells us, "is the lighting of the scenes." And again: "The greatest part of my success in the theatre I attribute to my feeling for colors translated into effects of light." He has ransacked the curio shops of ancient cities for furniture and the fabled East for silken draperies and has found in these "explorations in search of stage equipment really the most interesting part" of his work. And he has sought out charming and promising young persons and chosen and adjusted them as he would select and adjust folds of rich velvet or the glow of a new tint of light into the harmony of a production. He has "made" Frances Starr and Jeanne Eagels and Lenore Ulric and Ina Claire. He has fitted them like brilliant bits of glass into the shifting colors of his successive scenes. And yet this prestidigitator of light and shadows, this clever artificer, this glorified interior decorator, whose consciousness has never been touched by either life or art, holds himself to be a realist. "I am a realist," he proclaims proudly and sincerely. And he is a realist because on his stage he "will allow nothing to be built of canvas stretched on frames. Everything must be real." He is a realist because when he produced *The Music Master* he "searched for people in the theatres of the lower East Side"; because he employed real Japanese in *The Darling of the Gods* and caused the Uhlans in *Marie-Odile* to be represented by real Germans! In such preoccupations he has spent a lifetime of labor and has ended by impressing a nation. He has touched nothing that he has not, in his own inimitable sense, adorned.

What has he touched? He could never, as we have seen, produce the work of a great dramatist. No great dramatist would

---

* *Max Reinhardt.* By Siegfried Jacobsohn. Berlin. 1910.

have endured the process. He has given us one play by Pierre Wolff and one by Hermann Bahr. He saw the unfulfilled promise of Eugene Walter and staged *The Easiest Way*. The rest is sentiment and drapery—*The Music Master* and *Du Barry*, *The Auctioneer* and *The Darling of the Gods*. He ventured on *Tiger, Tiger*, but accompanied it by the ultrasaccharine *Daddies*; he re-wrote and re-built *Dark Rosaleen* until it was pretty and trivial enough; he engaged Mr. Albert Bruning only to load him with Chinese robes in a spectacle play by George Scarborough. He likes to have children on the stage as often as possible and hence avoids plays in which there are none. For such plays, in his opinion, "view life flippantly and cynically, like the comedies of Bernard Shaw"; he is blandly unconscious of the contemporary practice of his profession elsewhere, except to fling a querulous word at Max Reinhardt, a producing manager who, during the first eight years of his career, presented one play each by Aristophanes, Euripides, Calderon, Molière, Goldoni, Lessing, Henri Becque, Tolstoi, Hauptmann, Donnay, Chekhov, Gorki, and J. M. Synge, two by Hebbel, Kleist, Gogol, Strindberg and Schnitzler, three by Grillparzer, Wilde, and Maeterlinck; four by Schiller, Goethe, Wedekind, and Hofmannsthal; five by Ibsen; six by Shaw; and nine by Shakespeare!

The Gold Diggers by Avery Hopwood is a perfect example of Mr. Belasco's art. There is a foolish little story about a savage uncle who wishes to rescue his nephew from a chorus girl and himself falls a prey to the charms of another. There is a sunny little moral about chorus girls duly emphasized by a gray-haired mother. But neither the story nor the moral is very obtrusive. These, as well as Mr. Hopwood's little local jests, serve, after all, only to call attention to a burst of morning sunlight which Nature would do well to emulate more often, to Mr. Belasco's exquisite bits of color, to the influence of his training upon the talent and personality of his latest creation, Miss Ina Claire. The latter illustrates his most solid gift. He can train actresses. Miss Claire's rendering of her lines in the first act has the daintiest verisimilitude and the nicest precision in its miniature way; her crucial scene in the second act, in which she feigns intoxication so well and yet never lets us lose a sense of spiritual delicacy, is a little marvel of its kind. But the almost total waste of talent and hard work exemplified in these bits symbolizes once more and depressingly enough the character of Mr. Belasco's whole career. Miss Claire has intelligence and flexibility; Miss Jobyna Howland has her unfailing vein of natural and robust humor; Mr. Bruce McRae is a careful artist; quite minor members of the cast do credit to Mr. Belasco's persuasive methods. Thus a highly agreeable entertainment is offered, an entertainment that eludes criticism by never coming within its proper range. But we dare neglect neither the show nor the master of the show so long as any are left among us who believe that either one sustains the slightest relation to the drama or the drama's interpretation on the stage of our time.

1919

Susan Glaspell

I. *The Early Plays*

In the rude little auditorium of the Provincetown Players on MacDougall Street there is an iron ring in the wall, and a legend informs you that the ring was designed for the tethering of Pegasus. But the winged horse has never been seen. An occasional play might have allured him; the acting of it would invariably have driven him to indignant flight. For, contrary to what one would expect, the acting of the Players has been not only crude and unequal; it has been without energy, without freshness, without the natural stir and eloquence that come from within. This is the circumstance which has tended to obscure the notable talent of Susan Glaspell. The Washington Square Players produced *Trifles* and thus gave a wide repute to what is by no means her best work. *Bernice*, not only her masterpiece but one of the indisputably important dramas of the modern English or American theatre, was again played by the Provincetown Players with more than their accustomed feebleness and lack of artistic lucidity. The publication of Miss Glaspell's collected plays at last lifts them out of the tawdriness of their original production and lets them live by their own inherent life.

That life is strong, though it is never rich. In truth, it is thin. Only it is thin not like a wisp of straw, but like a tongue of flame. Miss Glaspell is morbidly frugal in expression, but nakedly candid in substance. There are no terrors for her in the world of thought; she thinks her way clearly and hardily through a problem and always thinks in strictly dramatic terms. But her form and, more specifically, her dialogue, have something of the helplessness and the numb pathos of the "twisted things that grow in unfavoring places" which employ her imagination. She is a dramatist, but a dramatist who is a little afraid of speech. Her dialogue is so spare that it often becomes arid; at times, as in *The Outside*, her attempt to lend a stunted utterance to her silenced creatures makes for a hopeless obscurity. The bleak farmsteads of Iowa, the stagnant villages of New England, have touched her work with penury and chill. She wants to speak out and to let her people speak out. But neither she nor they can conquer a sense that free and intimate and vigorous expression is a little shameless. To uncover one's soul seems almost like uncovering one's body. Behind Miss Glaspell's hardihood of thought hover the fear and self-torment of the Puritan. She is a modern radical and a New England school teacher; she is a woman of intrepid thought and also the cramped and aproned wife on some Iowa farm. She is a composite, and that composite is intensely American. She is never quite spontaneous and unconscious and free, never the unquestioning servant of her art. She broods and tortures herself and weighs the issues of expression.

If this view of Miss Glaspell's literary character is correct, it may seem strange upon superficial consideration that four of her seven one-act plays are comedies. But two of them, the rather trivial *Suppressed Desires* and the quite brilliant *Tickless Time*, were written in collaboration with George Cram Cook, a far less scrupulous and more ungirdled mind. Her comedy, furthermore, is never hearty. It is not the comedy of character but of ideas, or, rather, of the confusion or falseness or absurdity of ideas. *Woman's Honor* is the best example of her art in this mood. By a sound and strictly dramatic if somewhat too geometrical device, Miss Glaspell dramatizes a very searching ironic idea: a man who refuses to establish an alibi in order to save a woman's honor dies to prove her possessed of what he himself has taken and risks everything to demonstrate the existence of what has ceased to be. The one-act tragedies are more characteristic of her; they cleave deep, but they also illustrate what one might almost call her taciturnity. That is the fault of her best-known piece, *Trifles*. The theme is magnificent; it is inherently and intensely dramatic, since its very nature is culmination and crisis. But the actual speech of the play is neither sufficient nor sufficiently direct. Somewhere in every drama words must ring out. They need not ring like trumpets. The ring need not be loud, but it must be clear. Suppose in *Trifles* you do not, on the stage, catch the precise significance of the glances which the neighbor women exchange. There need have been no set speech, no false eloquence, no heightening of what these very women might easily have said in their own persons. But one aches for a word to release the dumbness, complete the crisis, and drive the tragic situation home.

The same criticism may be made, though in a lesser degree, of Miss Glaspell's single full-length play, *Bernice*. No production would be just to the very high merits of that piece which did not add several speeches to the first and third acts and give these the spiritual and dramatic clearness which the second already has. Crude people will call the play "talky." But indeed there is not quite talk enough. Nor does Miss Glaspell deal here with simple and stifled souls. That objection is the only one to be made. The modern American drama has nothing better to show than Miss Glaspell's portrait of the "glib and empty" writer whose skill was "a mask for his lack of power" and whose wife sought, even as she died, to lend him that power through the sudden impact of a supremely tragic reality. The surface of the play is delicate and hushed. But beneath the surface is the intense struggle of rending forces. Bernice is dead. The soft radiance of her spirit is still upon the house. It is still reflected in her father's ways and words. Her husband and her friend hasten to that house. And now the drama sets in, the drama that grows from Bernice's last words to her old servant. It is a dramatic action that moves and stirs and transforms. There is hardly the waving of a curtain in those quiet rooms. Yet the dying woman's words are seen to have been a creative and dramatic act. Through a bright, hard window one watches people in a house of mourning. They stand or sit and talk haltingly as people do at such times. Nothing is done. Yet everything happens—death and life and a new birth. What more can drama give?

II. *Inheritors*

While managers are returning from early spring trips to London and Paris with the manuscripts of plays ranging from Shaw to Bataille, our native drama is gathering an ever more vigorous life. The process has few observers. But all great things have had their origin in obscurity and have often become stained and stunted by contact with the world and its success. It need matter very little to Susan Glaspell whether her play *Inheritors*, which the Provincetown Players are producing, ever reaches Broadway. Nor need it affect her greatly whether the criticism of the hour approves it or not. If the history of literature, dramatic or non-dramatic, teaches us anything, it is that Broadway and its reviewers will some day be judged by their attitude to this work.

Inheritors is not, in all likelihood, a great play, as it is certainly not a perfect one. Neither was Hauptmann's *Before Dawn*. Like the latter it has too pointed an intention; unlike the latter its first act drifts rather than culminates and needs both tightening and abbreviation. But it is the first play of the American theatre in which a strong intellect and a ripe artistic nature have grasped and set forth in human terms the central tradition and most burning problem of our national life quite justly and scrupulously, equally without acrimony or compromise.

In 1879 two men occupied adjoining farms in Iowa: Silas Morton, son of the earliest pioneers from Ohio who fought Black Hawk and his red men for the land, and Felix Fejevary, a Hungarian gentleman, who has left his country and sought freedom in America after the abortive revolution of 1848. The two men were lifelong friends, and Morton, who had had but two months of schooling, absorbed from his Hungarian friend a profound sense of the liberation of culture and left the hill which the white man had wrung by force from the red to be the seat of a college that was to perpetuate the united spirits of liberty and learning. In the second act we are taken to the library of this college. The time is October, 1920. Felix Fejevary, 2nd, now chairman of the board of trustees, is in consultation with Senator Lewis of the finance committee of the State legislature. Fejevary wants an appropriation and recalls to the senator that the college has been one hundred per cent. American during the war and that the students, led by his son, have even acted as strike-breakers in a recent labor dispute. The son, Horace Fejevary, is introduced, a youth who thinks Morton College is getting socially shabby—too many foreigners!— and who is just now enraged at certain Hindu students who have plead the cause of the Indian revolutionists and quoted Lincoln in defense of their position. Senator Lewis thinks the lad a fine specimen. But, talking of appropriations, there is a certain Professor Holden who does not think that the Hindus ought to be deported, who has said that America is the traditional asylum of revolutionaries, and who seems to be a Bolshevik in other ways. Fejevary promises to take care of Holden, and the ensuing scene between these two with its searching revelation of spiritual processes, its bitter suppressions, its implication of an evil barter in values not made with hands touches a point of both dramatic truth and force which no other American playwright has yet rivaled. The ironic and tragic catastrophe is brought about by another member of the third generation, Madeline Fejevary Morton. To her mind, natural and girlish though it is, the monstrous inner contradictions of the situation are not wholly dark. It is two years after the armistice. Yet a boy chum of hers, a conscientious objector, is still in a narrow and noisome cell; the Hindu students who are to be sent to certain destruction are but following the precepts of Lincoln's second inaugural. She interferes in their behalf and proclaims in public, crudely but with the passionate emphasis of youth, the principles for which her two grandfathers founded Morton College. Her offense, under the Espionage Act, is no laughing matter. People with foreign names have got twenty years for less. Her uncle and her aunt plead with her; Holden asks her to let herself ripen for greater uses; her father's state pleads for itself. Miss Glaspell has been careful to make her neither priggish nor tempestuous. Some inner purity of soul alone prompts her to resist. Suddenly an outcast, she goes forth to face her judges and suffer her martyrdom.

No competent critic, whatever his attitude to the play's tendency, will be able to deny the power and brilliancy of Miss Glaspell's characterization. The delineation of the three Fejevarys—father, son and grandson—is masterly. Through the figures of these men she has recorded the tragic disintegration of American idealism. The second Felix remembers his father and his inheritance. But he has faced the seeming facts so long and compromised so much that he is drained dry of all conviction and sincerity. His son is an empty young snob and ruffian. With equal delicacy and penetration we are shown the three Morton generations—the slow, magnificent old pioneer, his broken son, his granddaughter Madeline whose sane yet fiery heart symbolizes the hope and the reliance of the future. Alone and pathetic among them all stands Holden, the academic wage slave who knows the truth but who has an ailing wife; who yearns to speak but who has no money laid by; a quiet man and a terrible judgment on the civilization that has shaped him.

In the second and third acts Miss Glaspell's dialogue expresses with unfailing fitness her sensitive knowledge of her characters. It has entire verisimilitude. But it has constant ironic and symbolic suppressions and correpondences and overtones. This power of creating human speech which shall be at once concrete and significant, convincing in detail and spiritually cumulative in progression, is, of course, the essential gift of the authentic dramatist. That gift Miss Glaspell always possessed in a measure; she has now brought it to a rich and effective maturity.

1919

ROBERT BENCHLEY

Although a charter member of the Algonquin Round Table, Harvard-educated Robert Benchley (1889–1945) employed a less aggressive form of mockery than his colleagues. As managing editor of *Vanity Fair*, columnist for the New York *World*, dramatic critic throughout the 1920s of the humor magazine *Life* and, from 1929, *The New Yorker*, he projected the persona of an easily befuddled, somewhat impatient, down-to-earth middlebrow. Everyday life was challenging enough, but the pretensions of art had to be withstood with exasperation and parody. Starting with "The Treasurer's Report," Benchley developed this alter ego into a number of monologues, and he appeared in *The Music Box Revue* and successful short films. There was "no better companion and no more ingratiating and intelligent humorist on stage or screen," attested the comic dramatist George Oppenheimer.

In 1922, Anne Nichols, author of half a dozen undistinguished plays, launched *Abie's Irish Rose*, a comedy about a mixed marriage between a Jew and an Irish Catholic. Benchley duly reviewed the play for *Life* in the three paragraphs which appear below. As Benchley's son Nathaniel Benchley tells the story in *Robert Benchley: A Biography* (1955): "It never occurred to Robert that the play would last, and he was therefore surprised the next week, when he came to make out the 'Confidential Guide' page, to see that it was still running. The 'Confidential Guide' was a listing of every show in town, with a one-sentence description, which he had to write for each issue. For *Abie's Irish Rose* he put down 'Something awful,' and let it go at that. The following week, with *Abie* incredibly still doing business, he was more specific; he wrote, 'Among the season's worst.' But this had no effect on *Abie*'s box office, and he found himself faced with the problem of saying the same thing, time and again. . . . The week after *Abie* closed, having run up a record of 2,327 performances, it was listed in the 'Confidential Guide' enclosed in a heavy black border and with 'In Memoriam' set in Gothic type." A selection of his comments between June of 1922 and November of 1927 follow the review.

Abie's Irish Rose *Review and Bulletins*

ON the night following the presentation of *The Rotters*, residents of Broadway, New York City, were startled by the sound of horse's hoofs clattering up the famous thoroughfare. Rushing to their windows they saw a man in Colonial costume riding a bay mare from whose eyes flashed fire. The man was shouting as he rode, and his message was: "*The Rotters* is no longer the worst play in town! *Abie's Irish Rose* has just opened!"

Abie's Irish Rose is the kind of play in which a Jewish boy, wanting to marry an Irish girl named Rosemary Murphy, tells his orthodox father that her name is Rosie Murphesky, and the wedding proceeds.

Any further information, if such could possibly be necessary, will be furnished at the old office of *Puck*, the comic weekly which flourished in the nineties. Although that paper is no longer in existence, there must be some old retainer still about the premises who could tell you everything that is in *Abie's Irish Rose*.

May 24, 1922

Eighty-ton fun.

Comic supplement stuff.

Made up of jokes from the files of *Puck* when McKinley was running for President the first time.

People laugh at this every night, which explains why a democracy can never be a success.

Just about as low as good, clean fun can get.

Contains everything of the period except a character who says, "Skiddoo."

It takes all kinds of people to make a world and a lot of them seem to like this.

For the people who like the "funnies."

Well, it seems there was a Jew and an Irishman walking down the street. . . .

Denounced continuously as cheap by this department since last May, but apparently unconscious of the fact.

The management sent us some pencils for Christmas; so maybe it isn't so bad after all.

We give up.

The success of this shows that the older a joke is, the better they like it.

Where do the people come from who keep this going? You don't see them out in the daytime.

A-ha-ha-ha-ha! Oh, well, all right.

All right if you never went beyond the fourth grade.

We were only fooling all the time. It's a great show.

The fact that there are enough people to keep this going explains why Hylan is Mayor of New York.

Showing that the Jews and the Irish crack equally old jokes.

The kind of comedy you eat peanuts at.

In its second year, God forbid.

The country's most popular comedy, constituting a reflection on either this department or the country.

America's favorite comedy, which accounts for the number of shaved necks on the street.

Probably the funniest and most stimulating play ever written by an American. (Now let's see what *that* will do.)

Judging from the thousands who see and like this play, Henry Ford has a good chance of being our next President.

In another two or three years we'll have this play driven out of town.

Answer to J.M.B.'s query: No, this was not written by Sir James Barrie.

Shall we join the ladies?

The one thing that will keep us from being President of the United States.

Heigh-ho!

An interesting revival of one of America's old favorites.

Fill this in for yourself. You know the idea.

The play which made Edwin Booth famous.

My, my, here it is November again!

Come on, now! A joke's a joke.

And a Merry Christmas to you, Miss Nichols!

For the best comment to go in this space, we will give two tickets to the play.

Contest line (in guide) closes at midnight, or at the latest, quarter past midnight, on Jan. 8. At present, Mr. Arthur Marx is leading with "No worse than a bad cold."

We've got those old pains in the back coming on us again. Every spring we have them.

The Phoenicians were among the early settlers of Britain.

Thirty days have September, April, June and November. All the rest have thirty-one, excepting February alone.

They put an end to the six-day bicycle races by tearing down Madison Square Garden. How about a nice, big office building on the present site of the Republic theatre?

The oldest profession in the world.

There is no letter "w" in the French language.

Four years old this week. Three ounces of drinking-iodine, please.

Viktusnak most már nines maradása otthon. Félti az 6 Jani urfijat, hogy valami Kart tesz magában.

There are 5,280 feet in a mile.

We will settle for $5,000.

The big Michael Arlen hit.

So's your old man.

See Hebrews 13:8.*

We might as well say it now as later. We don't like this play.

We see that earthquakes are predicted in these parts some time in the next seven years. Could it be that . . .

We understand that a performance of this play in modern dress is now under way.

Dun't esk.

Closing soon (Only fooling).

Flying fish are sometimes seen at as great a height as fifteen feet.

And that, my dears, is how I came to marry your grandfather.

---

*Jesus Christ the same yesterday, and today, and forever.

RING LARDNER

Ring Lardner (1885–1933) is best known for his sardonic stories skewering the stupidity and venality of baseball players, "a democracy of snobs, fools, and moral cowards," in Clifton Fadiman's words. These grew out of his experience as a sports reporter for several Chicago papers. His columns were often set up as dialogue, for even before his first newspaper job in 1905, Lardner had tried to write the lyrics and music for a minstrel show called *Zanzibar*. Throughout his short life, he was fascinated by the theatre, although it usually let him down. He contributed songs and sketches for Bert Williams and Will Rogers to the *Ziegfeld Follies*, but much of his material was rewritten. Collaborations with George M. Cohan and Robert Sherwood fell through, and his only successful play is a comedy of Tin Pan Alley, *June Moon*, written with George S. Kaufman. His eight nonsense plays best express his theatrical imagination when it is unfettered by pragmatism. *The Tridget of Greva* was performed in 1922 by members of the Algonquin Round Table in a revue, but the plays' surrealistic stage directions— "The curtain is lowered for seven days to denote the lapse of a week"—defeat normal stage practice. Lardner denied the charge that they were parodies of the Moscow Art Theatre, which had toured to New York; but they do seem inspired by the European modernist repertory adopted by the Washington Square Players and other progressive Greenwich Village troupes. Ernest Hemingway called them "native dada," and their closest equivalent is the Marx Brothers at their most physically and verbally exuberant.

I Gaspiri—"The Upholsterers"
A Drama in Three Acts
Adapted from the Bukovinan of Casper Redmonda

CHARACTERS
IAN OBRI, *a Blotter Salesman.*
JOHAN WASPER, *his wife.*
GRETA, *their daughter.*
HERBERT SWOPE, *a nonentity.*
FFENA, *their daughter, later their wife.*
EGSO, *a Pencil Guster.*
TONO, *a Typical Wastebasket.*

ACT I

(*A public street in a bathroom. A man named Tupper has evidently just taken a bath. A man named Brindle is now taking a bath. A man named Newburn comes out of the faucet which has been left running. He exits through the exhaust. Two strangers to each other meet on the bath mat.*)

FIRST STRANGER

Where was you born?

SECOND STRANGER

Out of wedlock.

FIRST STRANGER

That's a mighty pretty country around there.

SECOND STRANGER

Are you married?

FIRST STRANGER

I don't know. There's a woman living with me, but I can't place her.

(*Three outsiders named Klein go across the stage three times. They think they are in a public library. A woman's cough is heard off-stage left.*)

A NEW CHARACTER

Who is that cough?

TWO MOORS

That is my cousin. She died a little while ago in a haphazard way.

A GREEK

And what a woman she was!

(*The curtain is lowered for seven days to denote the lapse of a week.*)

ACT III

(*The Lincoln Highway. Two bearded glue lifters are seated at one side of the road.*)

(TRANSLATOR'S NOTE: *The principal industry in Phlace is hoarding hay. Peasants sit alongside of a road on which hay wagons are likely to pass. When a hay wagon does pass, the hay hoarders leap from their points of vantage and help themselves to a wisp of hay. On an average a hay hoarder accumulates a ton of hay every four years. This is called Mah Jong.*)

FIRST GLUE LIFTER
Well, my man, how goes it?
                    SECOND GLUE LIFTER
(*Sings "My Man," to show how it goes.*)
(*Eight realtors cross the stage in a friendly way. They are out of place.*)
                    CURTAIN

                                                            1924

GILBERT SELDES

The intellectual credentials of Gilbert Seldes (1893–1970) were impeccable. A Harvard graduate, Washington political correspondent of *L'Echo de Paris*, managing editor and dramatic critic of America's brainiest periodical, *The Dial*, New York correspondent to T. S. Eliot's *The Criterion*, adapter of Aristophanes' *Lysistrata* in a successful Broadway production, friendly with Picasso, Joyce, and Stravinsky, Seldes was in an unassailable position when he began to publish articles extolling what he called the popular arts. Collected in 1924 as *The Seven Lively Arts*, they took seriously what had hitherto been overlooked or slighted by serious criticism: vaudeville, musical comedy, comic strips, silent movies, and jazz. Later, Seldes characterized his book as "a record of crossing—crossing what were to me artificial lines of a map—between the fine and the popular arts, between Jews and non-Jews, between the academic or scholarly and the technological practical (as in the mass media)." His prose, shifting between the recondite and the colloquial, set the style for this sort of inquiry. Seldes never completely abandoned high ground; he continued to believe that "the greatest art is likely to be that in which an uncorrupted sensibility is worked by a creative intelligence," and so preferred the individual genius (Chaplin, Al Jolson, Irving Berlin, George Herriman of *Krazy Kat*) to the collective creativity to be found in jazz improvisations. His later experiences as the head of television programming for CBS and founding Dean of the Annenberg School of Communications at the University of Pennsylvania led him to recognize the dark side of mass culture as manipulated by big business. *The Great Audience* (1950) and *The Public Arts* (1956) were less exuberant inquiries into this "mass-produced mediocrity."

The Dæmonic in the American Theatre

ONE man on the American stage, and one woman, are possessed—Al Jolson and Fanny Brice. Their dæmons are not of the same order, but together they represent all we have of the Great God Pan, and we ought to be grateful for it. For in addition to being more or less a Christian country, America is a Protestant community and a business organization—and none of these units is peculiarly prolific in the creation of dæ-monic individuals. We can bring forth Roosevelts—dynamic creatures, to be sure; but the fury and the exultation of Jolson is a hundred times higher in voltage than that of Roosevelt; we can produce courageous and adventurous women who shoot lions or manage construction gangs and remain pale beside the extraordinary "cutting loose" of Fanny Brice.

To say that each of these two is possessed by a dæmon is a mediæval and perfectly sound way of expressing their intensity of action. It does not prove anything—not even that they are geniuses of a fairly high rank, which in my opinion they are. I use the word possessed because it connotes a quality lacking elsewhere on the stage, and to be found only at moments in other aspects of American life—in religious mania, in good jazz bands, in a rare outbreak of mob violence. The particular intensity I mean is exactly what you do not see at a baseball game, but may at a prize fight, nor in the productions of David Belasco, nor at a political convention; you may see it on the Stock Exchange and you can see it, canalized and disciplined, but still intense, in our skyscraper architecture. It was visible at moments in the old Russian Ballet.

In Jolson there is always one thing you can be sure of: that whatever he does he does at the highest possible pressure. I do not mean that one gets the sense of his effort, for his work is at times the easiest seeming, the most effortless in the world. Only he never saves up—for the next scene, or the next week, or the next show. His generosity is extravagant; he flings into a comic song or three-minute impersonation so much energy, violence, so much of the *totality* of one human being, that you feel it would suffice for a hundred others. In the days when the runway was planked down the centre of every good theatre in America, this galvanic little figure, leaping and shouting—yet always essentially dancing and singing—upon it was the con-centration of our national health and gaiety. In *Row, Row, Row* he would bounce up on the runway, propel himself by imagi-nary oars over the heads of the audience, draw equally imagi-nary slivers from the seat of his trousers, and infuse into the song something wild and roaring and insanely funny. The very phonograph record of his famous *Toreador* song is full of vital-ity. Even in later days when the programme announces simply

Fanny Brice

"Al Jolson" (about 10.15 P.M. in each of his reviews) he appears and sings and talks to the audience and dances off—and when he has done more than any other ten men, he returns and, blandly announcing that "You ain't heard nothing yet," proceeds to do twice as much again. He is the great master of the one-man show because he gives so much while he is on that the audience remains content while he is off—and his electrical energy almost always develops activity in those about him.

If it were necessary, a plea could be made for violence *per se* in the American theatre, because everything tends to prettify and restrain, and the energy of the theatre is dying out. But Jolson, who lacks discipline almost entirely, has other qualities besides violence. He has an excellent baritone voice, a good ear for dialect, a nimble presence, and a distinct sense of character. Of course it would be impossible not to recognize him the moment he appears on the stage; of course he is always Jolson—but he is also always Gus and always Inbad the Porter, and always Bombo. He has created a way of being for the characters he takes on; they live specifically in the mad world of the Jolson show; their wit and their bathos are singularly creditable characteristics of themselves—not of Jolson. You may recall a scene—I think the show was called *Dancing Around*—in which a lady knocks at the door of a house. From within comes the voice of Jolson singing, "You made me love you, I didn't wanna do it, I didn't wanna do it"—the voice approaches, dwindles away, resumes—it is a swift characterization of the lazy servant coming to open the door and ready to insult callers, since the master is out. Suddenly the black face leaps through the doorway and cries out, "We don' want no ice," and is gone. Or Jolson as the black slave of Columbus, reproached by his master for a long absence. His lips begin to quiver, his chin to tremble; the tears are approaching, when his human independence softly asserts itself and he wails, "We all have our *moments.*" It is quite true, for Jolson's technique is the exploitation of these moments; he has himself said that he is the greatest master of hokum in the business, and in the theatre the art of hokum is to make each second count for itself, to save any moment from dulness by the happy intervention of a slap on the back, or by jumping out of character and back again, or any other trick. For there is no question of legitimacy here—everything is right if it makes 'em laugh.

He does more than make 'em laugh; he gives them what I am convinced is a genuine emotional effect ranging from the thrill to the shock. I remember coming home after eighteen months in Europe, during the war, and stepping from the boat to one of the first nights of *Sinbad*. The spectacle of Jolson's vitality had the same quality as the impression I got from the New York sky line—one had forgotten that there still existed in the world a force so boundless, an exaltation so high, and that anyone could still storm Heaven with laughter and cheers. He sang on that occasion *'N Everything* and *Swanee*. I have suggested elsewhere that hearing him sing *Swanee* is what book reviewers and young girls loosely call an experience. I know what Jolson does with false sentiment; here he was dealing with something which by the grace of George Gershwin came true, and there was no necessity for putting anything over. In the absurd black-face which is so little negroid that it goes well with diversions in Yiddish accents, Jolson created image after image of longing, and his existence through the song was wholly in *its* rhythm. Five years later I heard Jolson in a second-rate show, before an audience listless or hostile, sing this outdated and forgotten song, and create again, for each of us seated before him, the same image—and saw also the tremendous leap in vitality and happiness which took possession of the audience as he sang it. It was marvelous. In the first weeks of *Sinbad* he sang the words of *'N Everything* as they are printed. Gradually (I saw the show in many phases) he interpolated, improvised, always with his absolute sense of rhythmic effect; until at the end it was a series of amorous cries and shouts of triumph to Eros. I have heard him sing also the absurd song about "It isn't raining rain, It's raining violets" and remarked him modulating that from sentimentality into a conscious bathos, with his gloved fingers flittering together and his voice rising to absurd *fortissimi* and the general air of kidding the piece.

He does not generally kid his Mammy songs—as why should he who sings them better than anyone else? He cannot underplay anything, he lacks restraint, and he leans on the second-rate sentiment of these songs until they are forced to render up the little that is real in them. I dislike them and dislike his doing them—as I dislike Belle Baker singing *Elie, Elie!* But it is quite possible that my discomfort at these exhibitions is proof of their quality. They and a few very cheap jokes and a few sly remarks about sexual perversions are Jolson's only faults. They are few. For a man who has, year after year, established an intimate relation with no less than a million people, every twelvemonth, he is singularly uncorrupted. That relation is the thing which sets him so far above all the other one-man-show stars. Eddie Cantor gives at times the effect of being as energetic; Wynn is always and Tinney sometimes funnier. But no one else, except Miss Brice, so holds an audience in the hollow of the hand. The hand is steady; the audience never moves. And on the great nights when everything is right, Jolson is driven by a power beyond himself. One sees that he knows what he is doing, but one sees that he doesn't half realize the power and intensity with which he is doing it. In those moments I cannot help thinking of him as a genius.

Quite to that point Fanny Brice hasn't reached. She hasn't, to begin with, the physical vitality of Jolson. But she has a more delicate mind and a richer humour—qualities which generally destroy vitality altogether, and which only enrich hers. She is first a great farceur; and in her songs she is exactly in the tradition of Yvette Guilbert, without the range, so far as we know, which enabled Mme Guilbert to create the whole of mediæval France for us in ten lines of a song. The quality, however, is the same, and Fanny's evocations are as vivid and as poignant as Yvette's—they require from us exactly the same tribute of admiration. She has grown in power since she sang and made immortal, *I Should Worry*. Hear her now creating the tragedy of *Second-Hand Rose* or of the one Florodora Baby who—"five little dumbells got married for money, And I got married for love. . . ." These things are done with two-thirds of Yvette Guilbert's material missing, for there are no accessories and, although the words (some of the best are by Blanche Merrill) are good, the music isn't always distinguished. And the effects are irreproachable. Give Fanny a song she can get her teeth into, *Mon Homme*, and the result is less certain, but not less interesting. This was one of a series of realistic songs for Mistinguett, who sang it very much as Yvonne

George did when she appeared in America. Miss Brice took it *lento affetuoso*, since the precise character of the song had changed a bit from its rather more outspoken French original. Miss Brice suppressed Fanny altogether in this song—she was being, I fear, "a serious artist"; but she is of such an extraordinary talent that she can do even this. Yvonne George sang it better simply because the figure she evoked as Mon Homme was exactly the fake apache about whom it was written, and not the "my feller" who lurked behind Miss Brice. It was amusing to learn that without a Yiddish accent and without those immense rushes of drollery, without the enormous gawkishness of her other impersonations, Miss Brice could put a song over. But I am for Fanny against Miss Brice and to Fanny I return.

Fanny is one of the few people who "make fun." She creates that peculiar quality of entertainment which is wholly light-hearted and everything else is added unto her. Of this special quality nothing can be said; one either sees it or doesn't, savours it or not. Fanny arrives on the scene with an indescribable gesture—after seeing it twenty times I believe that it consists of a feminine salute, touching the forehead and then flinging out her arm to the topmost gallery. There is magic in it, establishing her character at once—the magic must reside in her incredible elbow. She hasn't so much to give as Jolson, but she gives it with the same generosity, there are no reserves, and it is all for fun. Her Yiddish Squow (how else can I spell that amazing effect?) and her Heiland Lassie are examples—there isn't an *arrière-pensée* in them. "The Chiff is after me . . . he says I appil to him . . . he likes my type . . ." It is the complete give away of herself and she doesn't care.

And this carelessness goes through her other exceptional qualities of caricature and satire. For the first there is the famous Vamp, in which she plays the crucial scene of all the vampire stories, preluding it with the first four lines of the poem Mr Kipling failed to throw into the wastepaper basket, and fatuously adding, "I can't get over it"—after which point everything is flung into another plane—the hollow laughter, the haughty gesture, the pretended compassion, that famous defense of the vampire which here, however, ends with the magnificent line, "I may be a bad woman, but I'm awful good

AL JOLSON

company." In this brief episode she does three things at once: recites a parody, imitates the moving-picture vamp, and creates through these another, truly comic character. For satire it is Fanny's special quality that with the utmost economy of means she always creates the original in the very process of destroying it, as in two numbers which are exquisite, her present opening song in vaudeville with its reiterations of Victor Herbert's *Kiss Me Again*, and her Spring Dance. The first is pressed far into burlesque, but before she gets there it has fatally destroyed the whole tedious business of polite and sentimental concert-room vocalism; and the second (Fanny in ballet, with her amazingly angular parody of five-position dancing) puts an end forever to that great obsession of ours, classical interpretative dancing.

Fanny's refinement of technique is far beyond Jolson's; her effects are broad enough, but her methods are all delicate. The frenzy which takes hold of her is as real as his. With him she has the supreme pleasure of knowing that she can do no wrong —and her spirits mount and intensify with every moment on the stage. She creates rapidly and her characterizations have an exceptional roundness and fulness; when the dæmon attends she is superb.

It is noteworthy that these two stars bring something to America which America lacks and loves—they are, I suppose, two of our most popular entertainers—and that both are racially out of the dominant caste. Possibly this accounts for their fine carelessness about our superstitions of politeness and gentility. The medium in which they work requires more decency and less frankness than usually exist in our private lives; but within these bounds Jolson and Brice go farther, go with more contempt for artificial notions of propriety, than anyone else. Jolson has re-created an ancient type, the scalawag servant with his surface dulness and hidden cleverness, a creation as real as Sganarelle. And Fanny has torn through all the conventions and cried out that gaiety still exists. They are parallel lines surcharged with vital energy. I should like to see that fourth-dimensional show in which they will meet.

1924

EDMUND WILSON

The leg show, which had bemused Mark Twain and outraged Olive Logan, evolved into the burlesque show, with its strippers, baggy-pants comics, and runway. The monarchs of burlesque in New York were the four Minsky Brothers who reigned over an empire of 14 theatres. Beginning in 1912, they thrived despite raids and lockouts, eventually succumbing in 1937 to Mayor Fiorello La Guardia's morality campaigns. Many artists and writers looked to Minsky's for inspiration, as a Rabelaisian counterweight to establishment values.

Edmund Wilson (1895–1972) was among them. Like Henry James, he believed he had a theatrical vocation, composing a number of plays that went unproduced. One of his earliest statements on modern art concerns the dramatist; in 1922 he wrote, "The dramatic poet today has to take a naturalistic subject and try to knock poetry into it—just as the modern painter has to take a conventional still life and by main force hack it to pieces and shuffle the fragments into a novel pattern." His first wife, May Blair, was an actress with the Provincetown Players; there he became acquainted with Eugene O'Neill whom he liked "for drawing music from humble people." Wilson's first play, *The Crime in the Whistler Room*, elements of which, claimed his Princeton chum F. Scott Fitzgerald, were lifted from the yet unpublished *Great Gatsby*, received 25 performances in 1924; his next, *This Room and This Gin and These Sandwiches*, recounting the simultaneous breakup of the Provincetown Playhouse and his marriage, was unperformed. Not long before his death, when he enjoyed a reputation as a polyglot pundit, Wilson wrote to the cabaret-artist-turned-director Mike Nichols encouraging the foundation of a national theatre to revive such demotic pieces as *Uncle Tom's Cabin* and Mrs. Mowatt's *Fashion*.

Burlesque Shows

I. *The National Winter Garden*

THERE is a rumor that the National Winter Garden Burlesque has fallen a victim to the current purity wave and been obliged to abate the Aristophanic license for which it was formerly celebrated. The management of the National Winter Garden (not the Broadway Winter Garden, of course, but the one at Second Avenue and Houston Street) has been kind enough to supply the *New Republic* with a season pass, and, as the result of a recent visit, the writer of these notes is happy to announce that this report is entirely without foundation and to recommend the Minsky Brothers' Follies as still among the most satisfactory shows in town. The great thing about the National Winter Garden is that, though admittedly as vulgar as possible, it has nothing of the peculiar smartness and hardness one is accustomed to elsewhere in New York. It is refreshing because it lies quite outside the mechanical routine of Broadway. Though more ribald, it is more honest and less self-conscious than the ordinary risqué farce and, though crude, on the whole more attractive than most of the hideous comic-supplement humors of uptown revue and vaudeville. Nor is it to be confounded with the uptown burlesque show of the type of the Columbia, which is now as wholesome and as boring as any expensive musical comedy. The National Winter Garden has a tradition and a vein of its own.

For one thing, the Minsky Brothers go in for a kind of beauty which has long passed out of fashion elsewhere. The National Winter Garden has no use for the slim legs and shallow breasts the modern American taste for which has been so successfully exploited by Ziegfeld and the other uptown producers. Save for their bobbed hair and modern shoes, the chorus at the National Winter Garden might have come out of the pictures of Casino girls in old *Munsey's Magazines* of the nineties. And the humor of the National Winter Garden differs, also, from the humor of other shows. It mainly consists of gags, to be sure, but they are not the gags you are used to. For all their violence, the comic interludes have a certain freshness and wit. In the current version of *Anthony and Cleopatra*, a perennial Minsky classic, Julius Caesar, in a tin helmet and smoking a big cigar, catches Anthony (the Jewish comic) on a divan with Cleopatra (the principal strip-tease girl) and wallops him over the bottom with the flat of an enormous sword. "I'm dying! I'm dying!," groans Anthony, as he staggers around in a circle; and Caesar and Cleopatra, the Roman soldiers and the Egyptian slave-girls break into a rousing shimmy to the refrain of "He's dying! He's dying!" "I hear de voices of de angels!" says Anthony. "What do they say?" asks Caesar. "I don't know: I don't speak Polish." He is groggy; he totters; he faints. "I hear de cockroaches calling me!" he cries; and from the orchestra sounds, acrid and sinister, the cry of the expectant roaches. "Bring me the wassup," says Cleopatra, and her slave-girl, kneeling, presents a box, from which Cleopatra takes a huge property phallus. (At some point in the development of the ancient act, the word *asp* was evidently confused with *wasp*.) It is impossible to report in these pages all the incidents of the scenes that follow. Cleopatra falls prone on her lover's body, and Caesar, with pathetic reverence, places on her posterior a wreath, which he waters with a watering-pot. Charmian and Britannicus, after some play of their own with the wassup, finally fall lifeless, too, the girl as she flops on the soldier exploding a toy balloon which he has been wearing as a false chest. This curious piece of East Side folk-drama has been popular at Minsky's for years, and it is always a little different. Sometimes Caesar makes his entrance on a bicycle, blowing his own bugle; sometimes his entrance is heralded by a flourish of trumpets from the orchestra, as the company lines up and looks out the wings: Caesar enters from the other direction and gooses the last man, so that the whole row fall down like dominoes. There is also a remarkable gallows skit, which begins as an affecting piece of realism and ends as a low joke.

The orchestra at the National Winter Garden is energetic even in summer. The girls are not only robust but take a certain jolly interest in the show and sometimes betray their roles by laughing inappropriately at the jokes. The audience are keenly appreciative, and the house peals with easy thunder more infectious than the punctual crashes uptown. The theater, at the top of an office building, is very well ventilated; and just now you can see through an open exit the foothills of the downtown buildings against a pale lilac-gray sky. After the show, you can walk down the fire-escape.

The most celebrated performer of the National Winter Garden was a Yiddish comedian named Jack Shargel, who has now retired from the stage. To these raw buffooneries he is said to have brought a touch of the wistfulness of a Lew Fields or a

Charlie Chaplin. A connoisseur of the theater in its best days*
has described to me a scene in which Jack Shargel received a
rose from a beautiful lady just going off the stage. He kissed it,
he smelt it in ecstasy, then, with a graceful and infinitely tender
gesture, he stretched out his hand and tossed it away: it fell
with a crash of glass.

1925

II. *Peaches—A Humdinger*

The National Winter Garden Burlesque has been subjected
to a renovation since I wrote about it last summer. The poets,
the artists, and the smart magazines have been making it fashionable; and Mr. Minsky, the manager, feeling perhaps that the
shabbiness of the old productions was unworthy of his new
clientèle, has provided brighter and more elegant settings and
a slenderer bevy of girls, with a fresh repertoire of costumes.
At a recent performance I witnessed, one of the actors made a
speech in the intermission, in which he said that a critic had
written, apropos of some risqué Broadway musical comedy,
that if he wanted to hear "dubble entenders," he would rather
go to the National Winter Garden, "because here's where you
get burlesque as you like it, without any camouflage—sincere
dubble entenders." Nevertheless, a restraining taste has been
exercised, since I last was there, on the traditional Minsky humor. There is even a rumor that a gifted representative of the
non-commercial artistic theater is to write and design a sketch
for the National Winter Garden. At this rate, it will presently
be hardly distinguishable from the Music Box Revue.

To find burlesque in its primitive form, you must go to the
Olympic on Fourteenth Street. The Olympic, with more limited resources than the National Winter Garden, makes no attempt to give its patrons anything beyond the fundamentals—
that is, instalments of sidewalk conversation alternating with
instalments of girls. As for the former, it is mainly manufactured by three unvarying comedians, who reappear time after
time in front of the same prosaic backdrop advertising the

---

*This was E. E. Cummings, who loved burlesque and was able to make
some use of its methods. See the piece that follows on his play *Him*. He made
a drawing of Jack Shargel, which appeared in the *Dial*.

Monte Carlo Spaghetti House, the Cabin Dancing Academy, the White Rats Tonsorial Parlors and the D. and S. Pants Shop. (An act like the Anthony and Cleopatra of the National Winter Garden would be quite out of the range of the Olympic.) Of these merry-andrews and kings of fun, the leader is, of course, a spruce young man with a clean-shaven face and a straw hat. But, whereas, at Minsky's in its present phase, this conventional role has been given to a comparatively prepossessing fellow not unlike a musical-comedy hero, the "straight man," as he is called, at the Olympic follows the true burlesque tradition by making us feel that, though his neatly pressed clothes contrast with those of his disreputable companions, he is the greatest rogue of the three. The other two, the low comedians, have the appearance of unhappy monstrosities. One is dwarfish, with a very big head and the toil-toughened, staring and honest face of a German nibelung, and he embarks on his comic adventures invariably with the utmost solemnity; when these end in cruel disaster at the hands of his straw-hatted tormentor or of one of the disdainful cuties with bare legs and a brassière, he apostrophizes the audience in Yiddish on a note of bewildered complaint or rage. The other, more nondescript and stunted still, is dressed in clothes which produce a disconcerting effect, like those of a trained chimpanzee, from his inability to wear them in a human fashion, and his face presents no human expression but a heavy and cretinous mask, of which the closed-up slits of the eyes give the impression of some helpless abortion in which the faculty of sight has been scarcely developed. The dialogue of these three artists suffers sadly from a poverty of invention. Here are a couple of examples. One of the Girls: "I'm in love! I'm in love! I'm gonta jump off the Brooklyn Bridge!" The Man with the Straw Hat: "Don't do that: you'll get the water dirty!" The Man with the Straw Hat, who is trying to play a cornet, addressing the Nibelung: "Say, don't look at me! Don't look at me! I can't play when you look at me! Say, you've got the kind of face that only a mother could love! If I had a dog with a face like that, I'd shootum!"

The main thing, however, is the girls. The Olympic, like Earl Carroll's Vanities, is equipped with a double runway. This runway, though it is studded on the inside edge with a row of pink electric-light bulbs, has the aspect—to which, besides, the general appearance of the theater and the shirt-sleeved audience of men contribute—of some sort of bowling alley; but it figures, none the less, for the spectators, as the principal source of glamor. The leading women, with their sinewy thighs and their muscular abdomens, have learned the rhythmic contortions of the stomach-dance; and the chorus does its best to live up to them with such shaking of hips and breasts as it can clumsily manage. Some, evidently accepted for their beauty rather than for theatrical gifts, are too stolid or untrained to dance at all and, smiling at the audience below, merely parade back and forth on the runway. Some do not even smile. But all have their powerful effect on the clientèle of the house.

What strikes you at first, however, when you are new to this more primitive form of burlesque, is the outward indifference of the spectators. They sit in silence and quite without smiling and with no overt sign of admiration toward the glittering and thick-lashed seductresses who stand on a level with their shoulders and who address them with so personal a heartiness. The audience do not even applaud when the girls have gone back to the stage; and you think that the act has flopped. But as soon as the girls have disappeared behind the scenes and the comedians come on for the next skit, the men begin to clap, on an accent which represents less a tribute of enthusiasm than a diffident conventional summons for the girls to appear again. This is repeated from four to six times for every number in the show. The audience never betray their satisfaction so long as the girls are there; it is only when the performance is finished that they signify their desire to renew it. They have come to the theater, you realize, in order to have their dreams made objective, and they sit there each alone with his dream. They call the girls back again and again, and the number goes on forever. When the leading performer begins to strip, they watch the process in silence, recalling her with timid applause when she vanishes behind the wings. Finally, she shows them her breasts, but her smile is never returned; nor is there any vibration of excitement when she has finally got down to her G-string— merely the same automatic summons, to which this time she does not respond. In one of the numbers, the girls come out with fishing-rods and dangle pretzels under the noses of the spectators; the leading ladies have lemons. The men do not at first reach for them; they remain completely stolid. Then suddenly, when the lures have been played for some minutes, a few begin to grab at the pretzels, like frogs who have finally decided to strike at a piece of red flannel or like cats who, after simulating apathy while watching a cork on a string, at last find the moment to pounce on it. When they catch the pretzels, however, they do not take them off the strings or playfully refuse to release them; they let them go at the first jerk and relapse into their impassivity.

The truth is, I suppose, that this audience are struck by a kind of awe, as if before priestesses of Venus, in presence of these gorgeous creatures. Their decorum is not undermined by this brazenly sexual exhibition: on the contrary, it makes them solemn. They have come for the gratification that they hope to derive from these dances; but this vision of erotic ecstasy, when they see it unveiled before them—though they watch it with fascination—frightens them and renders them mute.

1926

ALAIN LOCKE

In 1916 the National Association for the Advancement of Colored People commissioned Angelina Weld Grimké to write a play to refute the vicious caricatures of blacks that had appeared in D. W. Griffith's film *The Birth of a Nation*. *Rachel*, whose heroine abjures mother-hood because her children will be subject to lynching and humilia-tion, was advertised as "the first attempt to use the stage for race propaganda in order to enlighten the people relative to the lamenta-ble condition of ten millions of colored citizens in this free republic." "It is not the business of plays to solve problems or to reform soci-ety," rejoined Alain Locke (1886–1934) as he resigned from the NAACP Drama Committee. A graduate of Harvard and the first African-American Rhodes scholar, Locke was counted one of the black urban intellectuals, along with W.E.B. Du Bois and James Wel-don Johnson. However, he disagreed with their methods and res-olutely refused to use art for social betterment. Inspired by the Abbey Theatre in Dublin and the Moscow Art Theatre, he subscribed to Brook Atkinson's belief that "in a country starved of folklore, the Southern negro with his natural eloquence and with the purity of his spirituals, is an inexhaustible source of materials." Locke's 1922 essay "Steps Towards the Negro Theatre" explained that the best way for an art theatre to avoid commercialism and propaganda was for it to be housed at a college. Once he became professor of philosophy at Howard University, he sponsored the Howard Players and an annual drama competition. Between 1925 and 1927, 30 prizes were awarded to 15 new African-American playwrights. Locke idealized rural South-ern blacks as unspoiled "peasants," but he extended his notion of folk theatre to the urban poor, writing in 1925: "Harlem has the same role to play for the New Negro as Dublin has had for the New Ireland."

The Negro and the American Stage

In the appraisal of the possible contribution of the Negro to the American theatre, there are those who find the greatest promise in the rising drama of Negro life. And there are others who see possibilities of a deeper, though subtler influence upon what is after all more vital, the technical aspects of the arts of the theatre. Certainly the Negro influence upon American drama has been negligible. Whereas even under the handicaps of second hand exploitation and restriction to the popular amusement stage, the Negro actor has considerably influenced our stage and its arts. One would do well to imagine what might happen if the art of the Negro actor should really become artistically lifted and liberated. Transpose the possible resources of Negro song and dance and pantomime to the serious stage, envisage an American drama under the galvanizing stimulus of a rich transfusion of essential folk-arts and you may anticipate what I mean. A race of actors can revolutionize the drama quite as definitely and perhaps more vitally than a coterie of dramatists. The roots of drama are after all action and emotion, and our modern drama, for all its frantic experimentation, is an essentially anemic drama, a something of gestures and symbols and ideas and not overflowing with the vital stuff of which drama was originally made and to which it returns for its rejuvenation cycle after cycle.

Primarily the Negro brings to the drama the gift of a temperament, not the gift of a tradition. Time out of mind he has been rated as a "natural born actor" without any appreciation of what that statement, if true, really means. Often it was intended as a disparaging estimate of the Negro's limitations, a recognition of his restriction to the interpretative as distinguished from the creative aspect of drama, a confinement, in terms of a second order of talent, to the status of the mimic and the clown. But a comprehending mind knows that the very life of drama is in dramatic instinct and emotion, that drama begins and ends in mimicry, and that its creative force is in the last analysis the interpretative passion. Welcome then as is the emergence of the Negro playwright and the drama of Negro life, the promise of the most vital contribution of our race to the theatre lies, in my opinion, in the deep and unemancipated resources of the Negro actor, and the folk arts of which he is as yet only a blind and hampered exponent. Dramatic spontaneity, the free use of the body and the voice as direct instruments of feeling, a control of body plastique that opens up the narrow diaphragm of fashionable acting and the conventional mannerisms of the stage—these are indisputably strong points of Negro acting. Many a Negro vaudevillian has greater store of them than finished masters of the polite theatre. And especially in the dawn of the "synthetic theatre" with the singing, dancing actor and the plastic stage, the versatile gifts of the Negro actor seem peculiarly promising and significant.

Unfortunately it is the richest vein of Negro dramatic talent which is under the heaviest artistic impediments and pressure. The art of the Negro actor has had to struggle up out of the shambles of minstrelsy and make slow headway against very fixed limitations of popular taste. Farce, buffoonery and pathos have until recently almost completely overlaid the folk comedy and folk tragedy of a dramatically endowed and circumstanced people. These gifts must be liberated. I do not narrowly think of this development merely as the extension of the freedom of the American stage to the Negro actor, although this must naturally come as a condition of it, but as a contribution to the technical idioms and resources of the entire theatre.

To see this rising influence one must of course look over the formal horizons. From the vantage of the advanced theatre, there is already a significant arc to be seen. In the sensational successes of *The Emperor Jones* and *All God's Chillun Got Wings* there have been two components, the fine craftsmanship and clairvoyant genius of O'Neill and the unique acting gifts of Charles Gilpin and Paul Robeson. From the revelation of the emotional power of the Negro actor by Opal Cooper and Inez Clough in the Ridgeley Torrence plays in 1916 to the recent half successful experiments of Raymond O'Neill's Ethiopian Art Theatre and the National Ethiopian Art Theatre of New York, with Evelyn Preer, Rose MacClendon, Sidney Kirkpatrick, Charles Olden, Francis Corbie and others, an advanced section of the American public has become acquainted with the possibilities of the Negro in serious dramatic interpretation. But the real mine of Negro dramatic art and talent is in the sub-soil of the vaudeville stage, gleaming through its slag and dross in the unmistakably great dramatic gifts of a Bert Williams, a Florence Mills or a Bill Robinson. Give Bojangles Robinson or George Stamper, pantomimic dancers of genius, a Bakst or an expressionist setting; give Josephine Baker, Eddie Rector, Abbie Mitchell or Ethel Waters a dignified medium, and they would be more than a sensation, they would be artistic revelations. Pantomime, that most essential and elemental of the dramatic arts, is a natural *forte* of the Negro actor, and the use of the body and voice and facile control of posture and rhythm are almost as noteworthy in the average as in the exceptional artist. When it comes to pure registration of the emotions, I question whether any body of actors, unless it be the Russians, can so completely be fear or joy or nonchalance or grief.

With his uncanny instinct for the theatre, Max Reinhardt saw these possibilities instantly under the tawdry trappings of such musical comedies as *Eliza, Shuffle Along* and *Runnin' Wild*, which were in vogue the season of his first visit to New York. "It is intriguing, very intriguing," he told me, "these Negro shows that I have seen. But remember, not as achievements, not as things in themselves artistic, but in their possibilities, their tremendous artistic possibilities. They are most modern, most American, most expressionistic. They are highly original in spite of obvious triteness, and artistic in spite of superficial crudeness. To me they reveal new possibilities of technique in drama, and if I should ever try to do anything American, I would build it on these things."

We didn't enthuse—my friend Charles Johnson of *Opportunity* and myself, who were interviewing Mr. Reinhardt. What Negro who stands for culture with the hectic stress of a social problem weighing on the minds of an over-serious minority could enthuse. *Eliza, Shuffle Along, Runnin' Wild!* We had come to discuss the possibilities of serious Negro drama, of the art-drama, if you please. Surely Director Reinhardt was a victim of that distortion of perspective to which one is so liable in a foreign land. But then, the stage is not a foreign land to Max Reinhardt; he has the instinct of the theatre, the genius that knows what is vital there. We didn't outwardly protest, but raised a brow already too elevated perhaps and shrugged the shoulder that carries the proverbial racial chip.

Herr Reinhardt read the gestures swiftly. "Ah, yes—I see. You view these plays for what they are, and you are right; I view them for what they will become, and I am more than right. I see their future. Why? Well, the drama must turn at every period of fresh creative development to an aspect which has been previously subordinated or neglected, and in this day of ours, we come back to the most primitive and the most basic aspect of drama for a new starting point, a fresh development and revival of the art—and that aspect is pantomime, the use of the body to portray story and emotion. And your people have that art—it is their special genius. At present it is prostituted to farce, to trite comedy—but the technique is there, and I have never seen more wonderful possibilities. Yes, I should like to do something with it."

With the New Russian Theatre experimenting with the "dynamic ballet" and Meierhold's improvising or creative actor, with Max Reinhardt's own recently founded International Pantomime Society inaugurated at the last Salzburg festival, with the entire new theatre agog over "mass drama," there is at least some serious significance to the statement that the Negro theatre has great artistic potentialities. What is of utmost importance to drama now is to control the primitive language of the art, and to retrieve some of the basic control which the sophisticated and conventionalized theatre has lost. It is more important to know how to cry, sob and laugh, stare and startle than to learn how to smile, grimace, arch and wink. And more important to know how to move vigorously and with rhythmic sweep than to pirouette and posture. An actor and a folk art controlling the symbolism of the primary emotions has the modern stage as a province ripe for an early and easy conquest. Commenting on the work of the players of the Ethiopian Art Theatre, discerning critics noticed "the freshness and vigor of their emotional responses, their spontaneity and intensity of mood, their freedom from intellectual and artistic obsessions." And almost every review of Paul Robeson's acting speaks of it as beyond the calculated niceties, a force of overwhelming emotional weight and mastery. It is this sense of something dramatic to the core that flows movingly in the blood rather than merely along the veins that we speak of as the racial endowment of the Negro actor. For however few there may be who possess it in high degree, it is racial, and is in a way unique.

Without invoking analogies, we can see in this technical and emotional endowment great resources for the theatre. In terms of the prevalent trend for the serious development of race drama, we may expect these resources to be concentrated and claimed as the working capital of the Negro Theatre. They are. But just as definitely, too, are they the general property and assets of the American Theatre at large, if once the barriers are broken through. These barriers are slowly breaking down both on the legitimate stage and in the popular drama, but the great handicap, as Carl van Vechten so keenly points out in his *Prescription for the Negro Theatre*, is blind imitation and stagnant conventionalism. Negro dramatic art must not only be liberated from the handicaps of external disparagement, but from its self imposed limitations. It must more and more have the courage to be original, to break with established dramatic convention of all sorts. It must have the courage to develop its own idiom, to pour itself into new moulds; in short, to be experimental. From what quarter this impetus will come we cannot quite predict; it may come from the Negro theatre or from some sudden adoption of the American stage, from the art-theatre or the commercial theatre, from some home source, or first, as so many things seem to have come, from the more liberal patronage and recognition of the European stage. But this much is certain—the material awaits a great exploiting genius.

One can scarcely think of a complete development of Negro dramatic art without some significant artistic reexpression of African life, and the tradition associated with it. It may seem a far cry from the conditions and moods of modern New York and Chicago and the Negro's rapid and feverish assimilation of all things American. But art establishes its contacts in strange ways. The emotional elements of Negro art are choked by the conventions of the contemporary stage; they call for freer, more plastic material. They have no mysterious affinity with African themes or scenes, but they have for any life that is more primitive and poetic in substance. So, if, as seems already apparent, the sophisticated race sense of the Negro should lead back over the trail of the group tradition to an interest in things African, the natural affinities of the material and the art will complete the circuit and they will most electrically combine. Especially with its inherent color and emotionalism, its freedom from body-hampering dress, its odd and tragic and mysterious overtones, African life and themes, apart from any sentimental attachment, offer a wonderfully new field and province for dramatic treatment. Here both the Negro actor and dramatist can move freely in a world of elemental beauty, with all the decorative elements that a poetic emotional temperament could wish. No recent playgoer with the spell of Brutus Jones in the forest underbrush still upon his imagination will need much persuasion about this.

More and more the art of the Negro actor will seek its materials in the rich native soil of Negro life, and not in the threadbare tradition of the Caucasian stage. In the discipline of art playing upon his own material, the Negro has much to gain. Art must serve Negro life as well as Negro talent serve art. And no art is more capable of this service than drama. Indeed the surest sign of a folk renascence seems to be a dramatic flowering. Somehow the release of such self-expression always accompanies or heralds cultural and social maturity. I feel that soon this aspect of the race genius may come to its classic age of expression. Obviously, though, it has not yet come. For our dramatic expression is still too restricted, self-conscious and imitative.

When our serious drama shall become as naïve and spontaneous as our drama of fun and laughter, and that in turn genuinely representative of the folk spirit which it is now forced to travesty, a point of classic development will have been reached. It is fascinating to speculate upon what riotously new and startling may come from this. Dramatic maturings are notably sudden. Usually from the popular sub-soil something shoots up to a rapid artistic flowering. Of course, this does not have to recur with the American Negro. But a peasant folk art pouring out from under a generation-long repression is the likeliest soil known for a dramatic renascence. And the supporters and exponents of Negro drama do not expect their folk temperament to prove the barren exception.

1926

DON MARQUIS

"In 1916 to hold a job on a daily paper, a columnist was expected to be something of a scholar and a poet—or if not a poet at least to harbor the transmigrated soul of a dead poet." So wrote E. B. White in his tribute to Don Marquis (1878–1937), who had lived up to that criterion. After a journalistic apprenticeship in Atlanta under Joel Chandler Harris, father of Br'er Rabbit, Marquis was taken on by the New York *Sun* and from 1913 to 1922 filled a 23-inch column six days a week. Over time he developed a cast of garrulous characters, including the genial victim of prohibition The Old Soak and, more memorably, Archy and Mehitabel. Archy was a press-room cockroach, who after hours composed free verse on a manual typewriter; incapable of using the shift, he wrote in lower-case, without punctuation. Mehitabel was an alley-cat of low morals and high spirits ("Toujours gai!") whose adventures often supplied copy for Archy.

Marquis was a popular member of The Players, a club founded by Edwin Booth, where he may have encountered the model for Archy's "old trouper." That poem predates T. S. Eliot's "Gus the Theatre Cat," written sometime in the 1930s, but they are both threnodies to a lost but more red-blooded stage. Marquis' own theatrical career was checkered; his dramatization of *The Old Soak* was a Broadway hit and he even played the lead in summer stock. It made him a fortune, which he then lost years later when he financed a play he had written about Christ's crucifixion, directed by his actress wife. Archy and Mehitabel turned up in Mel Brooks' first musical, *Shinbone Alley* (1957), with Eddie Bracken and Eartha Kitt in the leading roles.

the old trouper

i ran onto mehitabel again
last evening
she is inhabiting
a decayed trunk
which lies in an alley
in greenwich village
in company with the
most villainous tom cat

i have ever seen
but there is nothing
wrong about the association
archy she told me
it is merely a plutonic
attachment
and the thing can be
believed for the tom
looks like one of pluto s demons
it is a theatre trunk
archy mehitabel told me
and tom is an old theatre cat
he has given his life
to the theatre
he claims that richard
mansfield once
kicked him out of the way
and then cried because
he had done it and
petted him
and at another time
he says in a case
of emergency
he played a bloodhound
in a production of
uncle tom s cabin
the stage is not what it
used to be tom says
he puts his front paw
on his breast and says
they don t have it any more
they don t have it here
the old troupers are gone
there s nobody can troupe
any more
they are all amateurs nowadays
they haven t got it
here
there are only
five or six of us oldtime

troupers left
this generation does not know
what stage presence is
personality is what they lack
personality
where would they get
the training my old friends
got in the stock companies
i knew mr booth very well
says tom
and a law should be passed
preventing anybody else
from ever playing
in any play he ever
played in
there was a trouper for you
i used to sit on his knee
and purr when i was
a kitten he used to tell me
how much he valued my opinion
finish is what they lack
finish
and they haven t got it
here
and again he laid his paw
on his breast
i remember mr daly very
well too
i was with mr daly s company
for several years
there was art for you
there was team work
there was direction
they knew the theatre
and they all had it
here
for two years mr daly
would not ring up the curtain
unless I was in the
prompter s box

they are amateurs nowadays
rank amateurs all of them
for two seasons i played
the dog in joseph
jefferson s rip van winkle
it is true i never came
on the stage
but he knew i was just off
and it helped him
i would like to see
one of your modern
theatre cats
act a dog so well
that it would convince
a trouper like jo jefferson
but they haven t got it
nowadays
they haven t got it
here
jo jefferson had it he had it
here
i come of a long line
of theatre cats
my grandfather
was with forrest
he had it he was a real trouper
my grandfather said
he had a voice
that used to shake
the ferryboats
on the north river
once he lost his beard
and my grandfather
dropped from the
fly gallery and landed
under his chin
and played his beard
for the rest of the act
you don t see any theatre
cats that could do that

nowadays
they haven t got it they
haven t got it
here
once i played the owl
in modjeska s production
of macbeth
i sat above the castle gate
in the murder scene
and made my yellow
eyes shine through the dusk
like an owl s eyes
modjeska was a real
trouper she knew how to pick
her support i would like
to see any of these modern
theatre cats play the owl s eyes
to modjeska s lady macbeth
but they haven t got it nowadays
they haven t got it
here

mehitabel he says
both our professions
are being ruined
by amateurs

                              archy

                                      1927

GEORGE JEAN NATHAN

André Gide, asked to name the greatest French poet, famously replied, "Victor Hugo, hélas!" An American critic of the 1930s or '40s asked who was the greatest American playwright might have answered, "Eugene O'Neill, sorry!" From the one-acts put on by the Provincetown Players before World War I to the Broadway success of *The Iceman Cometh* after World War II, O'Neill was one of the few American writers to stake his all on the drama. Experimenting with Strindbergian angst, Expressionist masks, Freudian subtext, Greek choruses, African drums, he restlessly sought the theatrical incarnation of his personal demons and his misanthropic view of human striving. Critics followed his creative zigzags attentively if impatiently, in the hope that he would be delivered of the great American masterpiece. They found him at his best powerfully moving, at his worst gaseous and awkward.

Through thick and thin, O'Neill's staunchest supporter was George Jean Nathan (1882–1958). Nathan's career as a dramatic critic was long and distinguished; few magazines or newspapers of note were without a piece from his hand, though he was most closely associated with the iconoclastic and irreverent journals *The Smart Set, The American Mercury*, and *The American Spectator*. Like his editorial partner H. L. Mencken, Nathan launched shock attacks on American values and institutions in language that shuttled between the lecture hall and the beer garden. At first, he occupied an elevated position, deploring the American theatre's crudeness and promoting European modernism. As Nathan judged the national drama to be improving through the efforts of O'Neill and Saroyan, he began to extol popular entertainments at the expense of pretentious pseudo-sophistication. Nathan's tastes were unpredictable. He admired both the rabble-rousing Sean O'Casey and the effete Noël Coward; he despised both David Belasco as a whited sepulchre and Thornton Wilder as a plagiarist of Joyce. Nathan's bachelor ways, his taste for young women, his natty wardrobe, and his regular table at the Stork Club helped make him the model for the waspish Addison DeWitt in the film *All About Eve*. DeWitt is first shown at a banquet for the fictitious Sarah Siddons Award for acting. Dramatic criticism, which Nathan considered "the intelligent exercise of the emotions," was honored for real when his will established the George Jean Nathan Award.

The Audience Emotion

THE world may grow more civilized as the centuries pass, but I doubt whether the emotion of the theatre audience in any period or over any stretch of time, however great, shares in the proportionate increase of civilization. The nature of that emotion and of its reactions may alter in detail, usually negligible, but I have a feeling that it is, in sum, pretty much today what it was in the beginning, and that its fundamental innocence will remain inviolate until the world returns to dust. This, of course, is like saying in different words that human nature does not change and that, in the mass, it responds always in much the same way to the various phenomena of life with which it is brought into contact. But there is a difference, and this is it. A theatre audience enters a theatre with the deliberate intention either of forgetting itself for a couple of hours or of being reminded of half-remembered phases of itself, of its life, and of its dreams and despairs. In the matter of the former of these two psychological businesses it tacitly requests of the dramatist that he render it other than it actually is, that, as the phrase goes, he take it out of itself—in short, that he treat it not as it really is, whether in habitual thought or feeling, but as it would like to be. In the direction of thought, it urges the dramatist to rid it of its stereotyped mental processes and, in the direction of feeling, of its conventional emotions and substitute for them new and more soothingly desirable ones. It comes to the theatre ready, willing and eager to be made, for the nonce, other than it is. At home or in the street it is in its divers elements content to be conventional, average, normal. In its reaction to the various affairs of the world it is even insistent upon this conventionality and this normality. But in the theatre, on the occasions I allude to, it pays out its money with the deliberate motive of constituting itself other than in its heart and mind it is. It wants a momentary spree, a night off. And yet, try as a dramatist will to give it what it wants, try itself as it will to make itself other than it is, it cannot. The so-called crowd psychology has nothing to do with the matter. The truth of the contention would hold were the theatre to be occupied by only two or four such persons, for the fact is that what is true of a thousand boobs is true of two boobs, and that what is true of two is equally true of the thousand.

Matthew Arnold may have been right about the world, but he was wrong about that part of it that is the theatre. The theatre, in so far as the emotional quality of its audiences is concerned, does not move; it stands still. The audience emotion follows always an absolutely cut-and-dried routine, varied only superficially, and any fine attempt to change its course must, by the very nature of God's magnificent images, come to grief. Across the centuries, the signal fires in Aeschylus's *Agamemnon* evoke the same emotional response as those in Bronson Howard's *Shenandoah*; the audience's tears for Sophocles's Antigone when she seeks to follow her unfortunate sister are the same tears that are spilled over the girl in *The Two Orphans* who would do likewise; the laughter that was vouchsafed the drunk Dikaiopolis twenty-three hundred years ago is the same as that which is today vouchsafed the drunk Old Soak. We are asked by gentlemen who write books to believe that, where Sixteenth and early Seventeenth Century audiences viewed insanity as a comic affliction, modern audiences view it as a tragic one, but the gentlemen who write books have evidently never been members of the audiences who have roared over a score of shows beginning with *The Belle of New York* and ending with *The Misleading Lady* and *Chicago*. And they certainly are not vaudeville goers or they would know about the laughing success that has followed the Sam Mann sketch for many years. We are also asked to believe that physical deformity, once regarded as extremely jocose, is no longer so regarded, and that, as a consequence, Mr. Glass's One-Eye Feigenbaum and Miss Loos's Spoffard *père* are instruments of profound grief, and that it is all that a modern side-show audience can do to keep from crying out loud over the fat woman, the living skeleton and the bearded lady.

These general reflections occur to me in specific connection with the play called *Spread Eagle*, by the Messrs. Brooks and Lister. It was the intention of these novices in the business of playwriting to persuade their audiences to gag at jingoism and the wars it periodically leads the nation into by playing upon the emotions of those audiences with the various instruments of jingoism and then to make the audiences honorously self-critical, skeptical and ashamed of their own facile reaction. And what did the novices discover? They discovered that the aforesaid instruments for the furtherance of jingoism were so much more powerful in the audience's case than the latter's talent for self-criticism and skepticism that, far from making it catch on to its evergreen credulousness and susceptibility, they actually convinced it all over again. Though they suggested forcibly to the audience that they were playing "The Star Spangled Banner" with their tongues in their cheeks, and were showing it rousing movies of Our Boys going off to the front with their fingers crossed, and were making Liberty Loan speeches with a wink of the eye, the audience would have none of the derision and accepted the whole thing literally, and at one gulp. And what degree of success their play has had or may have, accordingly, was and will be due not to what they put into it but what they tried and hoped and yet failed to keep out of it. What they endeavored to do was to show a theatre audience, in terms of sardonic melodrama, the chicanery, mountebankery and nonsense of unthinking and blind patriotism; what they succeeded in doing was only to make their boob customers' hearts beat with the same old boob emotion when the drums got busy and the orators began orating and the flag was let loose. Their play, from any critical point of view, is a very bad play, but its badness has nothing to do with its failure to move an audience in the way they desired to move it. The same basic theme and the same central theatrical device are present in a good play by Galsworthy called *The Mob*, and *The Mob* fails with an audience quite as *Spread Eagle* fails. Genius and hack alike inevitably fall before a mere brass band.

The one thing that a dramatist, however gifted, apparently cannot monkey with is the fixed and changeless emotional credo of the masses of the people. It is for this reason that satire is so seldom financially prosperous at the popular box-office. Now and again, to be sure, a freak play that assails the popular heart-beat achieves a moderate, freak success, but as a rule the play that wins the public is the play that in some relatively novel manner merely restates the ancient and time-honored emotional principles of the public. From the time of Aristophanes and his *Knights* to that of *Spread Eagle*—there are points of similarity in the former's Cleon, promoter of war, and the latter's Martin Henderson, ditto—the public of the moment has been found to react left-handedly to the intention of dramatists who would whip its emotions in a direction that tradition opposes. A dramatist may play with superficially new ideas, new philosophies and new points of view, but down under them he must invariably cause to flow in a steady stream the old and tried emotions. Shaw is an excellent example of a dramatist who sagaciously appreciates the truth of this. Even a superficial glance at his plays from beginning to end reveals his wise timidity in offering his audiences any thing unsual or new in the way of emotional values. The Shaw dramatic canon is grounded upon a bedrock of grandma emotions tricked out, for the pleasurable deception of his customers, in the latest styles of philosophical and controversial millinery. Shaw simply asks his audience to feel the old feeling lightly instead of gravely; he never on a single occasion has asked it to alter the intrinsic nature of those feelings. There isn't an emotional note in any one of his plays that the lowliest doodle cannot respond to safely and very comfortably, however much the doodle may be horrified by the ironic counterpoint that Shaw synchronously plays.

1927

On Vaudeville

WHAT has killed vaudeville as much as anything else, I suppose, is the departure of what may be called the vaudeville mood from life itself. The leisurely nonchalance, the caprice, the happy irresolution that blessed living in the America of another day have long since been drowned out by the loud whirr of the machine that has got most of us in its grip. Even among the rich, there is no leisure; there is only loafing. And the difference is readily graspable. A gentleman has leisure; a barbarian loafs. Taste, culture, experience and charm are essential to an appreciation and execution of leisure; loafing is the refuge of the unimaginative bounder. Vaudeville, like the vanished hansom cab, the window tables at Delmonico's and Sherry's, the four-hour lunches at Luchow's and checkers at the Lafayette, has paid the price of modern speed, money-grubbing and excited boredom. No longer is there time for such things; no longer are ease and casualness part of our lives; no longer are evenings to be sampled haphazardly. "Dinner at 7:30 sharp; the theatre at 8:50 sharp; the motor at 11:05 sharp; supper at 11:20 sharp"—life has become sharp, too sharp. Punctuality, once the privilege of princes, has become the command of stockbrokers. A cocktail, once a drink, has become a drug; and a dinner, once an event, has become an eventuality. Conversation has been supplanted by nervous wisecracks fighting against time, and love is made in taxicabs. Vaudeville was a symptom of the earlier dispensation, of a time and a year when there was place for boyish fun and simple nonsense and engaging unconcern. It was a kid game for men in their kid moments. And men don't seem to have such moments any more.

It is not that the old-time vaudeville show was a good show; it often, certainly, was anything but that. It was rather that it had an innocence and artlessness that made it appealing to men who prefer to take their diversion in an easy-come-easy-go fashion instead of in the railroad-schedule manner imposed upon them by present-day theatrical managers and traffic cops. That is the trouble with amusement in America under existing conditions. It has become a business where once it was a pleasure—and that is true not only of the theatre but of drinking, under the strictures of Prohibition; of reading, under the strictures of book-of-the-month clubs; of dancing, under the boiled-shirt and boiled-collar strictures of gunmen-operated night clubs; of eating, under the protein and vitamin strictures of quack dietitians; and of almost everything else, including what the poets call love. Vaudeville, whatever its asininity, was at least to be taken casually and the worse it was the more jocular it seemed to fellows who didn't mind throwing away a dollar but who currently object to throwing away six to see the same *Schuhplättler* and acrobats performing in front of a diamond revue curtain instead of in front of the good old drop of Union Square peopled by Pepsin Gum, Moe the Tailor and Root Beer advertisements. No one complains about a drugstore sandwich, because a drugstore sandwich is taken for granted. But anyone has a right to complain if one gets a drugstore sandwich at Café de Paris prices.

1931

Eugene O'Neill

Wɪᴛʜ the appearance of *The Iceman Cometh*, our theatre has become dramatically alive again. It makes most of the plays of other American playwrights produced during the more than twelve-year period of O'Neill's absence look comparatively like so much damp tissue paper. In it there is an understanding of the deeper elements of human nature, a comprehension of the confused instincts that make up the life of mortals, and an evocation of pity for the tortured existence of dazed mankind that not merely most but all of those plays in combination have not faintly suggested. It is, in short, one of the best of its author's works and one that again firmly secures his position not only as the first of American dramatists but, with Shaw and O'-Casey, one of the three really distinguished among the world's living.

These, I appreciate, are big words and probably contributive to the suspicion that their inditer has forgone his old Phyrronism. They are also doubtless obnoxious and challenging to such persons as either resent what seems to be extravagant praise at the expense of other playwrights or are constitutionally averse to superlatives of any kind and ready to throw off their coats if anyone has the gall to say even that Bach was the greatest composer who ever lived or that horseradish sauce is the best of all things to go with boiled beef. But the words, I believe, are none the less in good order. If they are not and if the play is not what I think it is, I am prepared to atone for my ignorance by presenting gratis to anyone who can offer convincing contrary evidence the complete bound works of all our American playwrights from Bronson Howard through Charles Klein, David Belasco and Augustus Thomas down to the geniuses responsible for *Joan of Lorraine, Another Part of the Forest, Dream Girl,* and *Maid in the Ozarks.*

Laying hold of an assortment of social outcasts quartered in a disreputable saloon on the fringe of New York in the year 1912 and introducing into their drunken semblance of contentful hope an allergy in the shape of a Werlean traveling salesman, O'Neill distils from them, slowly but inexorably, the tragedy that is death in life. Superficially at times suggesting a cross between Gorki's *The Lower Depths* and Saroyan's *The Time of Your Life,* let alone Ibsen's *The Wild Duck,* the play with its author's uncommon dramaturgical skill gradually weaves its various vagrant threads into a solid thematic pattern and in the end achieves a purge and mood of compassion that mark it apart from the bulk of contemporary drama. There are repetitions in the middle sections which O'Neill has deemed necessary to the impact of the play but which in this opinion might be got rid of with no loss. There is also still an excess of profanity, for all the author's liberal cutting, that becomes disturbing to any ear that gags at such overemphasis. And since the uncut version of *Hamlet,* which is a good play too, can be played in its entirety in little more than three and a half hours, the longer running time of *The Iceman Cometh* may seem to some, and quite rightly, not only superfluous but a little pretentious. Yet small matter. In the whole history of drama there has been only one really perfect tragedy—incidentally, only one-third as long—and, while this of O'Neill's is scarcely to be compared with it, it still rises far above its possible errors.

With a few nimble strokes, O'Neill pictures vividly the innards of even the least of his variegated characters, from the one-time circus grifter to the one-time police lieutenant, from the quondam boss of a Negro gambling den to the erstwhile Boer War correspondent, and from the night and day bartenders and the wreck of a college graduate to the former editor of Anarchist magazines and the old captain once in the British armed services. Only in the characters of his three street-walkers does he work rather obviously; truthfully, perhaps, but in a theatrically routine manner. Yet in his major figures, Slade, the one-time Syndicalist-Anarchist, Hickey, the hardware salesman, Hope, the proprietor of the saloon, etc., the hand is as steady and sure as ever.

The long monologue, only now and then momentarily interrupted, wherein toward the drama's conclusion the salesman relates the relief from himself secured by the murder of
his wife, is one of the most impressive pieces of writing in contemporary dramatic literature: emotionally searching and definitely moving. The relations of Slade and the young man with
memory of his betrayed mother on his agonized conscience
are maneuvered with high suspensive dexterity, even if at one
or two points to the hypercritical slightly overplanted. The dialogue throughout is driving; there is robust humor to allevi-
ate the atmospheric sordidness; and out of the whole emerges
in no small degree the profound essences of authentic tragedy.

In the author's own analysis of his play as he has confided it
to me the dominant intention has been a study in the workings
of strange friendship. That intention, it is not to be gainsaid,
has been fully realized. But as I read the script and see it in stage
action it seems to me that, far above and beyond it, there rises
the theme of the tragedy which lies in bogus self-substantiation
and the transient, pitiable satisfaction which it bequeaths. That,
however, is the play's virtue: to different men it may convey
different things. But to all with any emotional understanding
and to all with any appreciation of the drama it must convey
the satisfaction of a theatre that, if only for a short while, has
again come into its rightful own.

In a setting by Robert Edmond Jones which catches perfectly the atmosphere of the play and with lighting that alternately gives the stage and groupings the effect of Daumier and
George Bellows, Eddie Dowling, with many acceptable critical
suggestions from the author, has accomplished an impressive
example of direction. In only two or three details has he
missed, and the fault in those cases was scarcely his. O'Neill's
men's toilet to the far left of the stage with the "This Is It"
sign is gratuitous, since it is strangely, even phenomenally,
never once used by any of the hard-drinking denizens of the
saloon and since it thus serves no purpose and is simply a gesture in juvenile waggery. Dowling's idea that it be given some
small justification by installing Hugo Kalmar, the drooling
Anarchist editor, in it at one point and having him declaim his
parrot lines from its interior—an excellent comedy touch that
would have suited the action with no slightest violation of the

text—was vetoed by O'Neill. The play's ending, which presently goes a little flat, might also, as Dowling wished, have been inspirited if, as counterpoint to Slade's final "Be God, I'm the only real convert to death Hickey made here; from the bottom of my coward's heart I mean that now!," the drunken singing and wild pounding on the table by the assembled, happily unredeemed bibuli had not been cut by the author and had been moved a bit forward from its place in the original script. And if the director had been allowed to lend a greater touch of his familiar "mood" staging to the play, which he was not, the spirit of the drama would have been materially aided.

O'Neill is the only dramatist in the history of the American theatre who has achieved real world status. His plays have been produced in most of the civilized countries of the globe; he has been awarded the Nobel prize for the body of his work; he has been the subject of critical discussion in South America, England, Germany, France, Italy, Greece, Russia, the Scandinavian lands, the Balkans, Australia, Japan and China. Almost as much has been written about him as about one-half all the living playwrights rolled together. Only Shaw has consumed more space.

In the United States, South America, France, Italy, Russia, the Scandinavian countries, Rumania, Greece, Australia, Japan and China, the critical attitude toward him in the main has been extremely favorable. In Germany, when criticism was operating freely, it was, with a few exceptions, highly appreciative. In England alone has there most often been either a lukewarm or chilly attitude toward him.

Here in America his preëminence as the first dramatist of his nation is taken by the great majority of the critics for granted. Now and again a small voice from the sidelines lifts itself in contradiction and puts in some peculiar nomination for the honor, but in the aggregate his position is unchallenged. In France, where his plays have had their chief hearing at the hands of Pitoëff, all save one or two of the recognized critics have been impressed. In Russia, praise of him has been pretty uniform, and understandably, since his dramatic philosophy and usual attitude toward his subject matter find a sympathetic echo in the Slav temperament. In Italy, those of his plays that have been shown have fared well at most critical hands; his

Days without End, which strikes a Catholic note, has received the Church's imprimatur and has been produced under the auspices of the Vatican. South America has paid him homage. Sweden has acclaimed him, and so has the theatre of Norway. Various of his plays have proved successes, both popular and critical, in Rumania, and Hungary, though to a lesser degree, has received him with hospitality. German critics, save in the few instances noted, have in the past treated him with respect, and in Japan and China the younger element, which alone is interested dramatically in the outside world, regards him, along with Shaw, as the most important of the Western playwrights.

On the other hand, though he has intermittently been accepted in England and even treated with considerable esteem by men of letters like Spender, *et al.*, the general run of drama criticism has frequently shown misgivings about him. In some cases, indeed, the misgivings have been accompanied by lofty derision.

For an example of the English attitude, we may turn to Eric Bentley and his recent observations in *The Playwright as Thinker*. I quote four typical samples:

a. "Among the untragic tragedians the most spectacular is Eugene O'Neill. At everything in the theatre except being tragic and being comic he is a success. . . . Tragedy is transported to the intense inane. . . . The tension that is missing in his work is inner tension."

b. "O'Neill has not as yet been able adequately to represent the bourgeois world as the nightmare which in the twentieth century it became, though his portraits of neurosis and decay are a labored and overconscious striving in that direction. O'Neill's more powerful, *unconsciously* symbolic tendency was to try to flee the bourgeois world, not like Wedekind by standing it on its head, but by trying to deny its existence, by proclaiming exclusive reality for the eternal. It was O'Neill himself who stood on his head."

c. "T. S. Eliot's 'conception' (in *The Family Reunion*) is clear, noble, and mature. . . . O'Neill's 'conception' (in *Mourning Becomes Electra*) is rude, simple-minded, gaga."

d. "Where Wedekind seems silly and turns out on further inspection to be profound, O'Neill seems profound and turns out on further inspection to be silly. . . . O'Neill has yet to show us he has a mind. So far he has only been earnest after the fashion of the popular pulpit or of professors who write on the romance of reality. Precisely because he pretends to be too much, he attains too little. He is false, and he is false in a particularly unpleasant way. His art is *faux-bon*. The 'good clean fun' of a Hitchcock movie is better."

Since every critic has a right to his opinion, and in view of the differences thereof which have been O'Neill's portion, I now that he has reappeared with *The Iceman Cometh* as a produced dramatist venture my own on the plays which he has contributed to the stage since first he began to function. In chronological compositional order, herewith the plays and the present commentator's views on them *in piccolo*:

1913–14. *Thirst* and four other one-act plays. Wholly negligible and plainly the work of a novice.

1914. *Bound East for Cardiff.* The first of his sea plays and the first indication of a significant new dramatic talent. A striking performance containing the seed of its author's future mental cast.

1916. *Before Breakfast.* A trifle. Little in it to encourage the critical hopes found in *Bound East for Cardiff.*

1917. *In the Zone, Ile, The Long Voyage Home, The Moon of the Caribbees.* The hopes were here reinforced in this rounding out of the cycle of short sea plays. *In the Zone* is the weakest of the four, melodramatically effective but built around an all too obvious theatrical device. *Ile* and *The Long Voyage Home*, however, show an advance in character portrayal, thematic feel, and dramaturgical expertness. *The Moon of the Caribbees*, the best of the four plays, is remarkable for the dramatic capturing of a mood and its projection. It remains one of the few genuinely important one-act plays in American dramatic literature.

1918. *The Rope, Beyond the Horizon, The Dreamy Kid, Where the Cross Is Made. The Rope* is an only fair excursion into psychopathic melodrama. *Beyond the Horizon*, his first full-length play (there were two or three written in his nonage which he destroyed and of which no traces remain), may be said to have influenced perceptibly the course of American drama. Its honest realism filtered through a poetic impulse came as a revelation to a stage chiefly given over, at its serious best, to rhinestone imagination and, at its worst, to vacuity illuminated by Broadway lamplight. While here and there suggesting a certain infirmity in dramaturgy, it betokened clearly the more finished work that was to come. *The Dreamy Kid* was and is a distinctly minor effort, and of no consequence. *Where the Cross Is Made*, the germ of the later full-length play, *Gold*, was and remains a fabricated one-acter partly redeemed by a potentially serviceable thematic idea.

1919. *Chris, The Straw*. Produced briefly in Philadelphia and withdrawn, *Chris* was a crude attempt at the play, *Anna Christie*, into which it was subsequently developed. *The Straw*, in its treatment of tuberculosis, is an unusual achievement of a difficult dramatic problem. Its emotional orchestration is one of O'Neill's best accomplishments.

1920. *Gold, Anna Christie, The Emperor Jones, Diff'rent*. *Gold*, though possessing several unmistakable virtues, fails in its entirety because of intermittent aberrant planning and uncertain playwrighting. *Anna Christie* is a new and forceful handling of a familiar theme, deep in its characterizations, driving in its firm composition, and etched with real observation and understanding. *The Emperor Jones* is a masterpiece of its kind. Its cumulative dramatic effect is irresistible. The tom-toms starting, in Richard Dana Skinner's apt phrase, at the rate of the human pulse beat and rising bit by bit as a fevered pulse would rise and which are of the warp and woof of the drama itself, sweep one along and up into a mighty climax and leave one without breath. Into this study of the Negro's dream of release from bondage to the whites and, upon the dream's coming true, his defeat by the very tricks of the whites which in practise have brought him release, or what he images is release, O'Neill has introduced a symbolic fancy uncommon to American dramatic writing. The succeeding *Diff'rent*, however, is of small moment, a feeble distillation of Strindberg further debilitated by its author's handling of its materials.

1921. *The First Man, The Hairy Ape*. The former, with the later *Welded*, is one of O'Neill's two worst full-length performances. Here again, in both cases, close imitation of Strindberg has brought its penalties. Aping the technic of Strindberg, as I observed at the time, O'Neill sets himself so to intensify and even hyperbolize a theme as to evoke the dramatic effect from its overtones rather than, as is the more general manner, from its undertones. His attempt is to duplicate the technic of such a drama as *The Father*, the power of which is derived not by suggestion and implication but from the sparks that fly upward from a prodigious and deafening pounding on the anvil. The attempt is a failure, for all that one gets in O'Neill's case is the prodigious and deafening pounding; the sparks simply will not come out. Now and again one discerns something that looks vaguely like a spark, but on closer inspection it turns out to be only an artificial theatrical firefly which has been cunningly concealed up the actors' sleeves. The author goes aground on the rocks of exaggeration and overemphasis. His philosophical melodrama is so full of psychological revolver shorts, jumps off the Brooklyn Bridge, incendiary Chinamen, galloping hose carts, forest fires, wild locomotives, sawmills, dynamite kegs, time fuses, infernal machines, battles under the sea, mine explosions, Italian blackhanders, sinking ocean liners, fights to the death on rafts, and last-minute pardons that the effect is akin to reading a treatise on the theme on a bump-the-bumps. He rolls up his sleeves and piles on the agony with the assiduity of a coalheaver. He here misjudges, it seems to me completely, the Strindberg method. O'Neill intensifies his theme from without. He piles psychological and physical situation on situation until the structure topples over with a burlesque clatter, Strindberg magnified the psychos of his characters. O'Neill here magnifies their actions.

The Hairy Ape is in a class apart. Partly expressionistic and written with greater restraint if with greatly increased and sounder dramatic intensity, the play dramatizes its theme of despairing humanity gazing blinded at the stars with a signal drive.

1922. *The Fountain.* A very uneven and not particularly successful fantasy dealing with the quest of Ponce de Leon. Some of the writing is eloquent, but more seems labored. The protagonist is described as "a romantic dreamer governed by the ambitious thinker in him." The protagonist's confusion is shared by the playwright.

1923. *Welded, All God's Chillun Got Wings.* As for the former, see the above comment on *The First Man.* *All God's Chillun Got Wings* is a study of miscegenation wrought with honesty, sympathetic comprehension, and proficient dramaturgy. Its basic idea, the tragic difficulty in man's acceptance of reality and truth, is boiled out of the theme with a steaming emotionalism and persuasion.

1924. *Desire under the Elms.* The Strindberg influence is here again clear, but in this instance O'Neill has exercised greater caution and selection and has not allowed himself so fully to be dominated. The result is a drama of passion and incest that does not get out of hand and that by and large amounts to a satisfactory realistic treatment of some of the elements in the classic Greek drama.

1925. *Marco Millions, The Great God Brown.* *Marco Millions* is a witty satire, crossed with the poetic mood, dealing with the exploits of that prototype of the American go-getter, Marco Polo. It is everything that *The Fountain* is not. Much of the writing is delightful and the sentiment in, for example, the little Princess Kukachin's eager search for the lost suggestion of her hero's soul has real body. *The Great God Brown*, with its employment of masks, is one of O'Neill's major efforts and in many respects comes off laudably despite the difficult problems it offers to stage presentation. The psychological essences of the drama are craftily distilled and, for all the complexities projected by the frequent mask-changing on the part of the characters, the play manages much of the impression designed by its author. What confusion there is is less inherent in the theme than in the mechanical adornments visited upon it.

1926. *Lazarus Laughed.* An unsuccessful attempt at what seems to be operatic Biblical fantasy. Less a theatre play than a libretto.

1927. *Strange Interlude.* A notable contribution to the drama. On an unusually broad canvas, O'Neill has plumbed the psyche of a woman in relation to her men with a handsome understanding. His knowledge of character has never been better displayed by him. There are one or two moments when matters seem to evade him, but he thereafter recaptures his purpose and pushes ahead with entire comprehension. On the whole, a psychological drama again touched by the Strindberg philosophy which leaves its immediate subject matter convincingly exhausted.

1928. *Dynamo*. A conflict between the depths and surfaces of man resolved into a drama that is overwritten, overstuffed, and that does not come off. Isolated scenes are dramatically stimulating, but the drama in its entirety becomes lost in its own tortuous philosophical alleys and leaves one with the impression that less symbolism and more simplicity would have served the playwright's purpose infinitely better.

1931. *Mourning Becomes Electra*. A fine paraphrase of the classic Greek drama. Bringing the incestuous theme of revenge into modern recognition, O'Neill has fashioned a tragedy that stands largely on independent feet and that presents his dramaturgical gifts in full flower.

1932. *Ah, Wilderness!* Turning from tragedy to comedy, the author has here achieved the tenderest and most amusing comedy of boyhood in the American drama. It is an answer to those who believe that he is without humor, a belief held by such as have engaged some of his antecedent work with a predetermined lack of humor.

1933. *Days without End*. Rewriting has spoiled a play that in its original conception was not without some merit. As it stands, it is an anachronistic treatment of its single-standard sex theme wedded to psychic release through religious faith. The many revisions made by the author in his several earlier drafts weakened the play's directness and have botched it. A poor performance.

1939. *The Iceman Cometh*. One of O'Neill's top achievements. A drama of the submerged tenth which, as previously noted, vaguely suggests Gorki's *The Lower Depths* but which is not only an immeasurably better play but one that explores the confused and agonized souls of mankind with rare understanding and with powerful dramatic result.

Two additional plays have been completed during the last four years and are awaiting metropolitan production: *A Moon for the Misbegotten*, already tried out in the Mid-West, and *A Touch of the Poet*. Pending a view of them, what is O'Neill's critical status to date?

That he is the foremost dramatist in the American theatre is, as has been recorded, generally granted. His eminence is predicated on the fact that no other has anything like his ability to delve into and appraise character, his depth of knowledge of his fellow man, his sweep and pulse and high resolve, his command of a theatre stage and all its manifold workings, and his mastery of the intricacies of dramaturgy. His plays at their best have in them a real universality. His characters are not specific, individual, and isolated types but active symbols of mankind in general, with mankind's virtues and faults, gropings and findings, momentary triumphs and doomed defeats. He writes not for a single theatre but for all theatres of the world.

It is argued by some against him that he is no poet, and that his drama hence misses true stature. Specifically and in the conventional sense, he may not be, but he is nevertheless, as must be evident to the close student of his work, driven ever by the poetic spirit. His weakness, where and when it exists, lies in his excesses—the excesses of overlength, overemphasis, overembroidery and overmelodramatization of the psychological aspects of his drama and of that drama itself. At his worst, these qualities edge him close to brooding travesty.

He has worked expertly in the field of tragedy, nimbly in the field of comedy, and less happily in that of fantasy. His brutality in tragedy is a handmaiden of the truth as he sees it. He cannot compromise with himself, right or wrong. Uncommonly gifted in a knowledge of the theatre, it may seem to some that he resorts occasionally to critically invalid devices to further his dramatic ends. If he does so, he does so unconsciously, never with calculation and deliberately. He would be content, I am assured, to publish his plays and forego the profits of production. He has written muddled and poor plays along with the valid, some very muddled and very poor. But the great body of his work has a size and significance not remotely approached by any other American. In a broader sense, he is certainly in no remotest degree the mind that Shaw is—his is an emotional rather than an intellectual; he is not by far the poet that O'Casey is, for in O'Casey there is the true music of great wonder and beauty. But he has plumbed depths deeper than either; he is greatly the superior of both in dramaturgy; and he remains his nation's one important contribution to the art of the drama.

Before the presentation of *The Iceman Cometh*, it was exactly twelve years and nine months since O'Neill's last previous play, *Days without End*, had seen production, and in the long intervening spell the theatre had had small news of him. Now and then came vague and contradictory reports that he was working on a cycle of eight or nine plays to be named by the general and somewhat turgid title, *A Tale of Possessors Self-Dispossessed*; that he was very ill and no longer able to do any work; and that he had successively retired from the theatre to Sea Island, Georgia, and the Valley of the Moon in California, there to devote the rest of his life to nursing his health, raising Dalmatian dogs, and laughing at most of current English dramatic criticism. But from the man himself there issued not so much as a whisper. What, really, was he up to?

It happens that we have been close friends for going on thirty years now, and that I am in a position to tell. That in the period of his absence he completed *The Iceman Cometh*, along with the subsequently to be produced *A Moon for the Misbegotten* and the still later to be produced *A Touch of the Poet*, the public had been apprised. These three plays, however, were by no means all. During the twelve-odd years, he not only outlined in minute detail not eight or nine but all of eleven plays of the cycle referred to—the eleven were to be played, however, as eight with three combined into duplex units and presented, like *Strange Interlude*, on the same afternoons, evenings and nights—but further definitely completed seven of them, including the three double-length ones, and got pretty well into the eighth. In addition, he finished a separate and independent play of full length called *Long Day's Journey into Night*, production of which he will not allow, for reasons which I may not specify, for many years. Nor, yet again, was that all. Besides *Long Day's Journey into Night*, he also completed the first play of a much shorter and entirely different cycle of which no word has reached anyone. Its title, like that of the contemplated briefer series in its entirety, is *By Way of Obit*. It runs for forty-five or so minutes and involves, very successfully I think, an imaginative technical departure from O'Neill's previous work. It contains but two characters and is laid in New York in approximately the same period as *The Iceman Cometh*.

All of which, one will agree, is not such bad going for a sick man.

The plays, *The Iceman Cometh* and *A Moon for the Misbegotten*, as well as the two last named, are distinct and wholly apart from the cycle of eleven plays. *A Touch of the Poet*, however, was to be first play of that cycle in revision. As to the cycle itself, he gradually convinced himself, after he had got as far as he had with it, that his dramaturgical plan was faulty. Without further ado, he destroyed two of the double-length, or four, of the plays he had written, preserving only *A Touch of the Poet*, the third double-header (*More Stately Mansions*), and one scene in another to be called *The Calms of Capricorn*. As for *A Touch of the Poet*, it seems to him to be a unit in itself and may well, he thinks, stand apart and alone. When and if he will return to work on the cycle as he has newly planned it, he does not know. In his head at the moment is an exciting idea for another play which bears no relation to the cycle. It will probably be his next effort after he has finished the production supervision of the other two plays noted.

The reason he withheld the three plays for so long is that he has made up his mind never again to permit a play of his to be produced unless he can be present. His health was such that it did not allow him to come to New York earlier. There was also another reason. He did not believe that, while the war was on, the theatre was right for the plays, though none is in any way related to it. It was simply his feeling that wartime audiences would not be in a mood for such serious dramas. His determination to be present at all future productions of his plays stems from his experience with his play *Dynamo*, which was shown in 1929. He was unable to come to New York for the casting and rehearsals of that one and learned all too late that the Theatre Guild had cast in the leading female role the fair young cute one, Claudette Colbert, famous for the symmetry of her legs, and not wholly unaware of the fact. Throughout the play, the young lady sought to extend her fame by placing the two reasons therefor on display whenever one of the other characters seemed to her to be diverting the attention of the audience, and the play as a consequence ran a bad second to her extremities.

"Henceforth," O'Neill averred, "I myself cast not only actresses but legs!"

In addition to the projected plays specified, the playwright has made copious notes on at least three or four others. Some of these notes were begun even before he went into retirement; others were made during that period. They include plans for, among the others, an heroic drama of ancient Chinese locale. This he has been mulling for fifteen years, though if he does it at all, which is doubtful, it would not be put into experimental preliminary writing until he finishes the one—with an American locale—alluded to as likely his next.

The long cycle, when and if he returns to it, will concern a single Irish-American family over a span of approximately one hundred and thirty years and will indicate broadly through its successive generations the changes in America and American life. Not the changes in the obvious theatrical sense, but the changes as they influence the members of the family. It will continue to be a study in character rather than a study in national progress. The latter will be held to a dramatic undertone. O'Neill's dissatisfaction with the work as far as it had gone proceeded from his conviction that it should deal with one family and not two, as it presently did. And also that, in the form he had written it, it began at the wrong point and overtold the story. Though he appreciated that he could rewrite what he had already done, he preferred to do away with much of it and to start afresh. The cycle, as he now envisages it, will begin with the French and Indian wars period and will present its first member of the family in the light of a deserter from the fighting forces.

O'Neill's attitude toward criticism of his work in particular and in general has not changed. However denunciatory and stinging it may be at times, he shows no indignation and maintains at least outwardly an appearance of smiling tolerance. Unlike a number of his playwrighting contemporaries, he never makes public reply to it, though now and again to a close friend he will privately express his amusement over certain of its more capricious aspects.

An English critic recently, for example, had at O'Neill with the old, familiar contention that, though he may think of himself as a poet, he is far from one. In proof whereof, the critic delightedly quoted this speech by Marsden in *Strange Interlude*:

"We'll be married in the afternoon, decidedly. I've already picked out the church, Nina—a gray ivied chapel, full of restful shadow, symbolical of the peace we have found. The crimsons and purples in the windows will stain our faces with faded passion. It must be in the hour before sunset when the earth dreams in afterthoughts and mystic premonitions of life's beauty," etc.

"Didn't he realize," chuckled O'Neill, "that the attempt there certainly wasn't poetry, but poetic travesty? Marsden, as anyone must easily see, is a sentimental throwback, a kind of *Yellow Book* period reversion, and I was deliberately using that 'crimsons and purples in the windows,' 'staining our faces with faded passion' and so on stuff to indicate it."

The notion that O'Neill entertains a profound satisfaction with everything he has written and resents any opposite opinion —a notion that pops up in various treatises on his work—is nonsensical. I give you several instances out of my own personal critical experience. When his *The First Man* was produced, I wrote acidly of it, even indulging in some ridicule. Reading the criticism, O'Neill grinned. "You let it down too easy," he observed. "It's no good." When subsequently I wrote in the same vein about *Welded*, which he seemed to have faith in when he gave me the script to read, he allowed, "I know now I was 'way off; the play is all wrong; it's no good." When, on the other hand, I found certain things to my liking in *Gold*, he took me to task. "You're wrong. It's a bad play. I'm telling you." He further believes that *The Fountain* is even more defective than I found it to be, and that *Dynamo*, though granting its lapses, is considerably less so. Only in the case of *Days without End*, which I could not critically stomach, has he vigorously opposed my opinion, and even in this case he allows that he now feels he must rewrite the play's ending for the definitive edition of his works. As originally conceived, this *Days without End* was, as I have said before, laid back in the year 1857 or thereabout. Bringing it up to the 1930's seemed to me, among others, to render its single-standard sex idea somewhat archaic and shopworn. O'Neill, however, was not to be persuaded. What he has persuaded himself, nevertheless, is that his hero's final gesture calls for alteration, though the alteration consists simply in reverting to the dramatic scheme as he first conceived it.

He is a stickler for casting and direction. As to the latter, his constant concern is any sentimentalization of his work. "Where sentiment exists," he says, "there is sufficient of it in the characters, and any directorial emphasis would throw it out of all proportion and make it objectionable." As to casting, he is generally opposed to so-called name actors. "They distract attention from the play to themselves," he argues. "My plays are not for stars but for simply good actors. Besides, you can never count on the idiosyncrasies of stars; they may not stick to a play and may so damage its chances on the road. I'm afraid of them, as I've had some experience with them. Also, they sometimes want you to change certain things in your play. Not for me!"

To return, finally, to *The Iceman Cometh*, I have already twice remarked that it may very roughly be described as a kind of American *The Lower Depths*. Like that play of Gorki's, though it in few other ways resembles it, it treats of a group of degenerate outcasts and the advent among them of a man with a philosophy of life new and disturbing to them. Its language is realistic, at times over-violently so; its cast of alcoholic down-and-outs includes gamblers, grafting cops, circus lot sharpers, whores, pimps, Anarchist riff-raff, military failures, college-educated wastrels, stool-pigeons, *et al.*; and it is written in four parts. It attests again to the fact, lost upon some of O'Neill's critics, that he is far from lacking a healthy sense of humor. Some of the comedy writing is irresistible. It also demonstrates again the most barbed appreciation of character known to any of his American playwriting contemporaries. And it embraces, among many other things, the most pitifully affecting picture of a woman—the unseen wife of the protagonist—that I, for one, have encountered in many years of playgoing.

Among the criticisms of the play is the argument that the characters "do not grow." That they do not grow is O'Neill's specific dramatic theme. Human beings sometimes change but change is not necessarily growth. Change is frequently imper-manent and retrogressive rather than advancing as O'Neill in-dicates. Another argument is that Hickey, the salesman of Death, in the end "explains himself with a textbook clarity that robs him of a truly dramatic role in the play, or a really human complexity." What of Nina in *The Sea Gull*? And a third con-descendingly observes, "As for O'Neill's 'thesis,' it would seem to be that men cannot live without illusions; hardly a new or very disputable idea." Hardly new, granted; but not very disputable? Come, come. What of the sufficient disputa-tions on occasion of Ibsen, Strindberg, Zola, Hauptmann, Tolstoi, Wedekind, Shaw . . . ?

1947

DJUNA BARNES

The Provincetown Players began in an abandoned fish-house on a Cape Cod wharf in the summer of 1915 as an amateur workshop for experiments in playwriting and stage lighting. Its elected head, George Cram "Jig" Cook, said its goal was "to give Americans a chance to work out their ideas in freedom." The group moved to a Greenwich Village stable and a membership subscription system, with new plays offered every three weeks. The fare was eclectic but fresh and ambitious: work by Eugene O'Neill, Cook's wife, Susan Glaspell, the Yiddish playwright David Pinski, Strindberg, even Gilbert and Sullivan. Growing dissension—some members wanted to continue experimenting, others to capitalize on success and go commercial—led to dissolution in 1924, but a second company took shape, formed by the disciples of New Stagecraft (O'Neill, Robert Edmond Jones, and Kenneth Macgowan), with an equally variegated repertory: Mrs. Mowatt's *Fashion*, *Desire Under the Elms*, plays by Stark Young and Paul Green. A third avatar was killed off by the Wall Street crash.

Among the 20-some hopefuls in at the birth of the Provincetown Players was the budding bohemian Djuna Barnes (1892–1982). She occasionally acted for them, in Tolstoy and Claudel, but chiefly contributed a number of one-act plays, some under the nom de plume Lydia Steptoe; "none of them," judges the critic Ruby Cohn, "can be taken seriously." Between 1929 and 1931, Barnes contributed a number of essays to *Theatre Guild Magazine*. Subjective to the point of idiosyncrasy, playing variations on the standard forms of the memoir and the celebrity profile, they were "op-eds" *avant la lettre*. Her tribute to the transplanted Russian actress Alla Nazimova, recognized as America's best interpreter of Ibsen and Chekhov, had piquancy for those who knew that both women were associates of the "Sewing Circle," a loose-knit coterie of lesbian artists.

The Days of Jig Cook

Recollections of Ancient Theatre History But Ten Years Old

THE world has grown a little older, the fat man even fatter, the local sponge has died, at a ripe old age at that, since the

Provincetown Players used to write and act their own plays in their Greenwich Village stable; the girls who used to fight to get into the Provincetown casts have withered, and others sit and cannot recall just what it was that used to make them get into such heated controversies. Only a few talk of the days when Jig Cook used to drink to inspire others, of the past when Eugene O'Neill was a boy who was too shy to speak.

Helen Westley tells me that youth alone is idealistic. But Helen is right only in regard to American youth. Those who were young when I was also very young have not, with the passing of time, become seasoned to the bone. The things that produced the Provincetown Players and made the group what it was, has not made them what they are. Therefore we hear much talk of "lost atmosphere." People speak of those early days as if they were a sort of collar stud which, by some diabolical mischance, had been mislaid by the injustice of God.

The French are otherwise. They too, to be sure, are idealistic in youth; but they are also idealistic in age. They do not speak of days "when." In their lives there is no mislaid stud of enthusiasm. They have, with the peculiarly economical spirit of their race, kept their stud where they can, at any moment, lay their hands on it. It is perhaps not quite the bright stud it used to be, it is indeed not a little dulled, but it will be found in their dress shirt when they are laid out for their grave.

Just what was the spirit that took us to the Brevoort in nineteen hundred and fifteen, sixteen, seventeen, with the eagerness of the devotee? America is the one country where the minority should die young. Jack Reed was right, and some, not all of us, are wrong; and we shall be wrong until we have the ability to keep that collar stud from start to finish.

It is perhaps this inability that has made those early days something we recall with sentiment and exasperation. We perhaps sensed that we would not live long, which is the essence of precocity. No, we would not live long, so we would live hard and reach high. Idah Rauh would not always want to be the Duse of Macdougal Street; Jig Cook was already fatal with his untimely end. The rhythm of his emotional life was that of one walk precariously on the hyphen of Jig versus Parnassus. Jig said "What is this thing called life? Where did it come

from? Where is it going? This past of life is just an accident . . . a moment."—And then it was a long while.

Our destiny made us speak before we understood, write
before we should and produce before we were able, the plays
of John Reed, of Eugene O'Neill, of Susan Glaspell and Floyd
Dell, of Maxwell Bodenheim, of George Cram Cook and Edna
St. Vincent Millay; of Wilson and Kreymborg, of Wellman, of
Steele and of Barnes. Before we were able we had mature grief
and fleeting immortality.

In those days Greenwich Village was to the Bronxite just another name for hell and the devil. Now it is no longer the Village that will get a girl by her back hair and sling her into
damnation, it is Paris. My own mother told me that I could
never expect to live down that city. And when she thinks I
am looking a little thin, or when she sees me watching a fly's
slow progress from wall to ceiling, or catches me being
introspective—"It's Paris! You needn't tell me. Don't I know
what that place can do? I accepted your father under the Arc
de Triomphe, and look at us now!"

Some said in those days that you could not get any nearer to
original sin than by renting a studio anywhere below Fourteenth Street. It was as good as suicide to write a one-act play,
have Norma Millay laugh at it, Charlie Ellis sit through it, or
hear Mary Blair connecting it with the Torah or Swedenborg,
which ability was one of her charms.

Poverty and paint, I was told, would bring about no good
end. We sat and cherished this possibility with a politic humor.
The Provincetown theatre was always just about to be given
back to the horses. It had been a stable, and a stable, said my
friends, it will be again. That this prophecy has never been fulfilled is due largely to M. Eleanor Fitzgerald, who by this organization has been turned into an eternal Eliza crossing the
ice, and by main strength, and gift of a pioneer right arm, has
so far kept the baby from drowning.

How can I recreate and analyse the spirit that was the early
Provincetown and its people? Did I once know? Did any of us
know? Do any of us know now since science has made the
analysing process a sort of social ping pong? I doubt it. I have
talked to Jimmy Light, and Jimmy does not seem to me to
know.

If it was just youth, are there not young people today? The answer is, there are. But not by so much as a single feature do they resemble this other youth. They have enthusiasm, but they are not the enthusiasms that we had. There are still Little Art Theatres, and one-act plays, actors and actresses clamoring for parts, but they are not related to us by so much as a wish-bone.

Why, in those days we used to sit on the most uncomfortable benches imaginable in that theatre, glad to suffer partial paralysis of the upper leg and an entire stoppage of the spinal juices, just to hear Ida Rauh come out of the wings and say: "Life, bring me a fresh rose!"

Our private lives were going all wrong in all directions; we did not eat for days that we might save up to dine at the Brevoort; we sat in the Hell Hole and became both foreign and philosophic under the "Hélas bébé!" of Hypolite Havel; and "Life teems with quiet fun" from Christine, who ran the Provincetown restaurant and who could be counted on to lose all her hairpins, thus loosing her lovely golden hair, by no later than twelve of the clock. We used to sit in groups and recall our earlier and divergent histories. One would say, "I was well smacked by my mother for chewing the paint off the gate post"; another maintained that he had learned the value of madness when his father jumped from a window in an effort to prove gravity, and was picked up convinced. So we talked, and so we went our separate ways home, there to write, out of that confusion which is biography when it is wedded to fact, confession and fancy in any assembly of friend versus friend and still friends.

Of such things were our plays made. Eugene O'Neill wrote out of a dark suspicion that there was injustice in fatherly love. Floyd Dell wrote archly out of a conviction that he was Anatole France. I wrote out of a certitude that I was my father's daughter, and Jig directed because he was the pessimistic Blue Bird of Greece.

Such things made atmosphere, as a chalk line on the floor of a magician's home makes terror and expectation,—atmosphere and a dead line over which the general public could not go.

Then where was the catch in the blood? When and on what day, or succession of days did we, unknowingly, walk over our own dead line and into the general life of a world which, until then, had been the audience?

For though some of us have "come through," we are less of that past than those who were never a part of it. This at least is true of me, and I think it is true of others.

Our legend was bought and paid for by those who did not live to walk over. That we are legend at all, that I have been asked to write of the days of Jig, that we are recalled by some with a sigh, by others with a shudder, is, I think, due to the lives we have lost and to the "ideals" that we cannot remember.

It was a kind of drunkenness that is beyond recall. Jig who could inspire divergent minds to work together for one idea, an ideal that was never quite clear to him, or if clear to him, one that he could not make clear to me nor to a number of others, sent his actors on the scent of no man's rabbit. It was, I think, Jig's rabbit, Jig's conjuring trick; he knew the passes, he spoke the formula, he had the hat, but—was he too proud, or was he too wise, or was he too limited to produce the hare? Who knows?—but it made good hunting.

1929

Alla Nazimova

Wнен was it that I first saw Alla Nazimova? In what was she playing? Certainly in none of the Ibsen plays which she made glorious, but in one of those emotional things that leave forethought to tomorrow. She wore ten good yards of that slinky material which, when molded about the hips, spells a woman bent on the destruction of the soul. She reclined upon a hundred cushions with but one idea, toying with a pistol with but one aim, the heart of the hero. Her managers had forbidden her to display any of her other myriad abilities, in order to set in relief her equally splendid physical ability to look "dangerous" and inexact, that look that is necessary to the popular conception of a thoroughly able adventurist. And all because this woman, born in Yalta, Crimea, Russia, and brought up in the Alps, had gorgeous eyes, winged nostrils and an upper lip to match, made doubly dangerous by a lower, which, for a brief inch in its middle, ran as straight as any Puritan praying for rain.

To Nazimova the memory of these plays is a neurosis, the radix of which is pain and calamity, because they obliged her to feed her great talents to a public which had appetite for nothing more than the conventional stage vampire. She took her beating without humor, because she is at heart a child pondering her adult childhood; otherwise she would be armoured with the very paradox of it, would be made inaccessible by a surmounted injustice, made a little witty at the hands of such a picturesque betrayal.

There has never been any reasonableness in her "fate"; a glance backward shows a meteoric condition that almost no one could cope with. Alla Nazimova was born in Russia and educated at Zurich. She studied the violin at Odessa and when she found that instrument "too difficult," entered Stanislavsky's dramatic school at Moscow. She played the provinces, she toured one night stands, she did the show boats on all the rivers; small parts, varied parts. She was noticed, forgotten, noticed again. She became the leading lady of a company in St. Petersburg, and presently joined Pavel Orlenev, visiting Berlin, London, and finally New York in some musty house on the east side. Sensation! Delirious enthusiasm! New York journeyed down through the smells to the Bowery to marvel at this miraculous pair—these two Russians whose language none could understand, but whose art pierced and dazzled all! And one of them anonymous. For Nazimova's name was not even on the program!

Then, almost as soon as it had appeared, this meteor was consumed in its own heat. Between Orlenev and Nazimova there arose a raging professional jealousy, made more bitter because of their mutual regard. The company dashed on the rocks. Orlenev escaped his creditors and fled back to Russia. Nazimova was stranded in an alien land.

Had it been the authentic fire of art, or only a flash of stage lightning? New York was soon to discover. The Messrs. Shubert, through an interpreter, offered this exotic actress a contract.

Within six months she had learned English and appeared on Broadway as Hedda, her newly acquired speech precise but slightly hatted with the gentle reluctance of a foreign tongue. She was no longer the extraordinary unknown. She was discussed and acclaimed. Her series of matinees gave way to regular evening performances, at the Princess. One after another Ibsen's women came to life before the eyes of astonished thousands. Hedda, Nora, and later Hilda Wangel and Rita Allmers —four utterly different persons, and each a universal, unforgettable type.

Then came the fall. Nazimova had a trace of that divine gullibility common to all who are greatly of the stage. She received, and took, bad advice. Her artistry was so extraordinarily flexible and persuasive that she could make a common vampire of melodrama seem, for the moment, as great a creation as Hedda. And the great public preferred vampires—or so it was commonly thought.

So, after toying through a dainty nothing called *Comtesse Coquette*, she began playing that series of lust-and-vengeance dramas which brought her nation-wide fame—and grief. *Comet*, *The Passion Flower*, *Bella Donna*, *The Marionettes*, *That Sort*—sorry plays that besmirched, rather than dimmed, her genius. She made huge sums of money, she was the darling of every tea, she was feted and cried over, complimented and kissed! One can see her longing in her every fiber to play parts that called for overtones and underacting. (She has the intelligence to know that quietly the world was made, and quietly it turns its sterner cheek.) One can see her valuing that sort of thing, the kind of thing she had once portrayed in Ibsen. And yet, like some one walking in the slow narcotic sleep of those banished to hell, for less than hell's requirements or reason, moved on in an ever narrower path of distaste, until with a grin of malice the devil took her by the heels and slung her into the Palace with *War Brides*; into *'Ception Shoals*. For a brief season she caught her breath and staggered back into Ibsen. And then, like the gentleman he is, the devil leaned out and gently pulled her into Hollywood and catastrophe.

B. A. Rolfe of the Metro pictures contracted her for an enormous sum, and what he wanted her to play she played. When she signed the contract she was fearful; for once before, under contract, she had been whistled for, to play Joan of Arc. Theresa Helburn had done the whistling, and Nazimova had been unable to come. What might happen now if she signed for the pictures? Was she, by trying to live, aiding and abetting that sinister faculty she had always been stalked by? She signed. There are stories of this Hollywood parenthesis that are too incredible to be false. Nazimova never could have played those amply elemental and passionate vampires if she had not been a very simple woman with a very guileless heart. Someone talked her money out of her—most of it. What was left she put into a production of Wilde's *Salome*, with settings designed by Natacha Rambova, and proved, though her friends said Hollywood had spoiled her, that she could get the head of her John with as authentic a conception of misdemeanor as has been seen since that act became common property.

And then there was silence.

What happened to Alla Nazimova as a woman, as an actress, as a thinking person who had felt too long and too little valued her own certitude, is matter for biography. If she is ever angry enough we shall hear of it. But in spite of her fame as a "tigress," as "passion's avenger," she is simple and quiet and small.

For a season she was with the Civic Repertory. Now she is again with her own people, with Turgenev, with the Theatre Guild.

Interviewing her after an evening with *A Month in the Country* I made my discovery. To me she had been entirely and rightly splendid, in one of splendor's many ways. To me my memory of her was the point where I had mounted romance; to her, where she had been thrown into the abyss.

"I wanted to do thoughtful things, things subtle and only hinted at. When anything is very great it is like that, is it not? When love is very great it is whispered perhaps; when one wants something terribly, there is only a motion of the hand. When one is horrified beyond words, one does not shout and scream; one says 'There,' and you can hardly hear it. So it is that I wanted to play. One fails when one is asked to give less than one has, though the public may think it is success. No, I do not want to do Ibsen now. I want to do some plays that America has little knowledge of, more Turgenev perhaps.

What do Americans really know of him? And there are others. Anyone can play a *Red Lantern*, a *Madame Peacock*, an *Eye for Eye*, because it means something to others. To me it means nothing. I feel like the woman in the *Makropoulos Secret* who had lived a thousand lives and was still young. Wise in youth!"

She broke off. She looked down at her dressing table and at all the things on it, then without raising her head repeated:

"Wise in youth! I have never been weighed down with knowledge of myself; I think it is a lack. It is called an inferiority complex, is it not?" she queried; and she laughed with her eyes, her mouth still mournful.

"Well, that is very wrong. But there is the solace, the pleasure of living by proxy. Other people's lives make me happy. I delight in their loves, I who have never known what it is to be in love." (What a gorgeous lie that was, what a brazen effort to say, "You do not see this face as you look at it!") "I have become a good mixer—ah yes, a very good mixer. I like other people's plans, I play the piano and I draw houses. I spend a lot of time drawing houses. I built some in California, you know—oh but they were ugly to look at and so comfortable!"

She smiled again. Suddenly I felt very tall and awkward. She is so little. I leaned down and said: "It's one of those quiet questions, Alla Nazimova. When was it you frightened yourself with what you are?"

She started, she turned halfway about.

"Oh," she said—and I swear she put her hands together like a child—"that night when I first saw my name in lights. I went up to my hotel room, way up under the roof and I opened the window and leaned on my arms, and I was afraid, terribly afraid. Then. It was then!"

1930

HAMLIN GARLAND

That James Herne came to be known as "the American Ibsen" demonstrates how desperately the American literati at the end of the 19th century felt the need to elevate the drama. Hamlin Garland (1860–1940), famous for his pessimistic stories of Midwestern farm life, jotted approvingly in his notebook in 1886, "the drama is following the lead of the novels and from the romantic is becoming realistic. The present is being studied." Garland befriended Herne, a San Francisco actor associated with David Belasco, who wrote plays to feature his wife Katharine Corcoran. Their success came from sure-fire effects, such as the two-act dream sequence in *Drifting Apart* (1888), along with a kind of surface realism that put on stage full-course meals or such specific locales as Gloucester, Massachusetts, Frenchman's Creek, Maine, and Sag Harbor, New York. Under the influence of Garland and William Dean Howells, Herne moved to a less superficial, more socially progressive realism. In "Art for Truth's Sake," published in 1897, Herne declared that the drama should "develop the commonplace aspects of life, dignify labor, and abhor injustice." It must "express some *large* truth" which is "not only beautiful, but in art for truth's sake it is indispensable." "Its mission is to interest and instruct."

His first attempt at this was *Margaret Fleming* (1890), a drama of a woman of moral strength and courage who takes in her husband's illegitimate baby and, blind by the last act, forgives her erring spouse. No commercial management would touch it, so Herne hired a Boston concert hall for its brief run; this is often cited at the first twitch of the Little Theatre Movement. Many found the play unwholesome, and the English critic William Archer dismissed the genre as "shirt-sleeve drama." Garland, however, in a review of *Margaret Fleming* in the October 1891 issue of *Arena*, applauded the play's "utter simplicity and absolute truth to life," superior to everything else on the American stage "in purpose, in execution, in power." His championing of the play established its reputation as an Ibsenite breakthrough, although *Margaret Fleming* was never published in Herne's lifetime. Herne and Garland also recognized that such plays, if they were to make their mark, needed to be seen in New York; this signaled the definitive end of Boston as a theatrical trend-setter.

James A. and Katharine Herne

I

As I think back into my busy Boston days, I am persuaded that my mental windows stood wide to every intellectual Old World breeze, no matter how unexpected. As in the past, though in somewhat lesser degree, New England was still a literary province whereon successive waves of European culture beat, and in Boston the high-thinking few prided themselves on being sensitive to each newest theory. French Impressionism and Russian Veritism were still in debate when the doctrine of dramatic realism swept upon us from the north, embodied in Henrik Ibsen's austere plays, and I, being already instructed in northland literature by Hurd of the *Transcript*, became its advocate.

I well remember the day when Edgar Chamberlin and I attended the first performance of "The Doll's House" (or The Doll Home, as Hurd declared it should have been translated) and saw Nora played by Beatrice Cameron, wife of Richard Mansfield. She had put the play on for a special matinée while engaged in another piece with her husband, but this afternoon was something more than a pleasing experiment to me. It was a revelation of the power, naturalness, and truth of the great Norwegian's methods.

Hitherto, in reading his plays, I had found the lines almost devoid of grace, dull and flat, but I now understood very clearly that they were only surface guides for the players. As in life, so his dramatic meanings lay below the lines, for these dull scenes when played by good actors gave the effect of life itself. Furthermore, the absence of all asides, soliloquies, and sensational climaxes made the conventions of the ordinary stage ridiculous. "This performance marks an epoch in American dramatic art," I said to Chamberlin. "It moves me more deeply than Shakespeare," he replied.

I left the theater that afternoon converted to the new drama, and like all recent converts I began to talk and write on Ibsenism as I had been talking and writing on Impressionism and Veritism. It became another "cause" for me.

There was method in my folly, however. In my poor, blundering fashion I was standing for all forms of art which expressed, more or less adequately, the America I knew. As I had welcomed the paintings which discarded the brown shadows of the German studios, so now I responded to the dialogue which aimed at representing life. That our artists in painting purple shadows were merely exchanging masters, I conceded, but Monet's canvases were more akin to the meadows and hills of New England than those of Corot. Similarly, Ibsen's method, alien as his material actually appeared, pointed the way to a new and more authentic American drama. "If we must imitate, let us imitate those who represent truth and not those who uphold conventions," was my argument.

Tea tables at once resounded with a new dramatic clamor. Those of us who scorned stage conventions, heard with eager attention descriptions of "The Independent Theater" in London and "The Free Stage" in Berlin, and deplored the absence of similar aspiring managers in New World cities, while earnest actresses announced their desire to uplift the stage.

All this has its amusing aspect now, but we were all very serious. None of us admitted that Ibsenism was just another wave of Old World influence sweeping over a bored provincial capital. America had been subject to such literary trade winds for two hundred years. Sometimes they came from Germany, sometimes from Italy, sometimes from France. Instructed by Howells, we had read the novels of Valdes, Tolstoy, and Flaubert. Now, through William Archer, we studied the dramas of Ibsen and Björnson. All these enthusiasms were natural phases of our development, but some of us said, "Ibsen will be a foolish fad if we do not advance the truth and power of our own writers. We are not to imitate Ibsen. We must accept his theory, but do our own work in our own color."

II

One afternoon in January, 1888, as Hurd and I were discussing plays, he handed me two theater tickets and asked if I had ever seen Jim Herne act. I told him I had not.

"Do so at once," he said, "for he is a local-color realist after your own heart. He's not an Ibsen, but he is trying to represent New England life."

I accepted the tickets with pleasure and that night witnessed the performance of "Drifting Apart" by James A. and Katharine Herne. They were playing at that time on a second-rate stage in the South End and their surroundings were cheap and tawdry, but I can still recall the profound impression which they made upon me by their action as well as by the play.

The plot of the piece was very simple. In the first act, Jack, the middle-aged husband of Mary Miller, was shaving himself in preparation for a trip to the village to purchase some Christmas presents, and all through the scene, which was charmingly set, Herne moved unaffectedly, joking, chuckling, making quaint gestures with a naturalism I had never before seen upon the stage; and Katharine was almost equally delightful as the wife, and when at the close of the joyous act her sailor husband returned from the village, his arms full of holiday presents, hopelessly drunk, her expression of grief, of shame, of despair formed a complete and piteous contrast to the homely comedy which preceded it.

The second and third acts, being a dream, were less moving, but the fourth act, which brought Jack back to tender sobriety in his own home, restored the reality of the opening scene, and was almost equally colloquial. The play closed on Christmas morning with a satisfying glow, with Jack repentant and Mary forgiving.

The quiet naturalism, the unaffected humor of the play so moved and interested me that I wrote immediately to Herne thanking him for the pleasure it had given me. I also expressed my admiration for the acting of "Miss Herne" and went on to say: "By such writings as that in the first and last acts of 'Drifting Apart' you have allied yourself with the best local-color fictionists of New England and deserve the encouragement and support of the same public."

A day or two later I received a modest and earnest letter in which he said:

"Your kindly conceived and earnestly written letter lies before me. I have read and reread it, and each perusal has added strength to the already firm conviction I had in the ultimate success of my play. By success, I mean that by which the managers measure—'financial,' for be the play or player never so fine, when there is no cash, there are no open doors. Your letter demonstrates the fact that as you saw my work, others will see it also, not so readily, nor so clearly—but they will see it. My task, and a difficult one at first, is to secure the attendance of the fine auditor—the others will follow. . . . It was, as you say, a daring thing to present such a subject in such a delicate form, but I have received many letters concerning it— none perhaps that I prize so much—for none bear such evidence of having given the subject deep thought. They are written from the heart, yours from the head *and* the heart. You say you would like to know more of me. I can only repeat that the desire is mutual. It will, however, be impossible for me to meet you during my present engagement. The past week has been devoted to *nine* performances of 'Drifting Apart' and six rehearsals of next week's production, 'The Minute Men' (please see that play), no small task you will admit, but when my season is ended and I return home, I will feel honored if you will spend a few hours and dine with Katharine C. (Mrs.) Herne, myself, and our three babies."

The wish was fulfilled some months later, when in answer to a cordial invitation I hastened to call upon him at his home. It was a small, plain, frame cottage such as a village carpenter might build, but Mrs. Herne, daintily gowned and looking quite like Mary Miller of the play, met me with charming grace and presented me to her sister and to her three little daughters, Julie, Chrystal, and Dorothy. They made me almost instantly a member of the family and listened to me with such respect that I hardly knew myself.

Our first evening, filled with cordial explanations and tumultuous debate, is still vivid in my memory. It was in effect a session of Congress, a Methodist revival, and an Irish comedy. Our clamor lasted far into the night, and when I went away at last, it was with a feeling that I had met people of my kind. I had never known such instant and warm-hearted understanding and sympathy. My head rang with their piquant phrases, their earnest and cheerful voices.

Still an active and, I fear, a pestiferous advocate of Henry George's land theories, I managed at our next meeting to switch our discussion to the single tax. Then having converted them to "Georgism," I fell upon the constitution of matter and outlined Spencer's theories of evolution. Mrs. Herne, a thinker of intuitive subtlety and a special lover of astronomy, took an active part in all our excited debates, wherein, beating the arms of our chairs, we warred over the nebular hypothesis with entire unconsciousness of the clock.

These extraordinary theatrical folk brought to me a wholly new world—a world of swift and pulsating emotion, a world of aspiration, and the story of brave battle for an art. It is difficult for me to express in a few lines how much they and their lovely children meant to me during the years that followed. They were at once a puzzle and a provocation.

Herne, I soon discovered, was only halfway on the road toward a finer form of dramatic art, and the tragic result of his aspiration seemed to be that just in proportion as his writing increased in truth and his acting gained in subtlety, he failed to interest the public, even the public he had already won in other plays. He confessed that he was deep in debt and sinking deeper day by day, and I dimly perceived that my influence was not helpful at this moment. My criticism rendered him discontented with the plays which had hitherto given him comfort, but did not materially aid him in his effort to achieve something better.

He had made a great deal of money with "Hearts of Oak," his first play, which was obviously only partly American, but he had lost heavily on his second play, "The Minute Men," a picturesque study of Colonial times, and was steadily dropping money on "Drifting Apart." Naturally he was discouraged, though never embittered.

"The managers all admit the good points of my play," he explained to me. "In fact they say it's too good. 'The public doesn't want a good play,' they say. 'It wants bad plays. Write a bad play, Jim. Not too bad but just bad enough.' Meanwhile I must play in theaters which are not suited to my way of doing things and am obliged to insert into my lines tricks and turns which I despise."

He related these experiences with a smile, but admitted that he was disheartened and with deepest sympathy I at once offered to assist him in finding an audience and a better theater. "There is a public for your plays if we can reach it," and I bluntly added, "You can do better work than any you have done and no play can be 'too good.' I want you to write a play in which there are no compromises at all."

Under the influence of my optimism, he took heart and began to revise "Drifting Apart" for the third time. It was stated at one time that I was working with him, but as a matter of fact I never suggested a line in any of his plays, though he read them to me scene by scene. In this case I followed his revisions day by day, encouraging him to cut out the very lines which his theatric advisers considered most vital. As he afterward wrote me, I upheld his elbow.

"I never was so much encouraged in the work I have laid out to accomplish as I have been by you," he wrote. "You have as it were endorsed my judgment, and showed me that it is possible to succeed and to force acknowledgment in spite of the opposition I have met with and the obstacles I have yet to overcome."

On August 5, 1889, he wrote me from Maine, "I will do no more with 'Drifting Apart' until I see you. I have done about all I can with it. After I have heard you fully and got closer to your idea, I will then scribble a little more on it, and try to get it nearly right by the time it gets to the stage again. I've finished 'The Hawthornes'—'rough finished'—and you'll like some of it."

This fixes the date of the first draft of the play which later became his enormously successful "Shore Acres."

III

My admiration for Mrs. Herne's art was almost unbounded. I felt that she could play other and much more important parts than Mary Miller, although there was in "Drifting Apart" a scene, in the dream, wherein the poor little mother sits holding her child in her lap while it dies of cold and hunger, which tested her art. The exquisite restraint, the marvelous fidelity to nature, and the grace with which she played this tragic episode convinced me that she was one of the subtlest actresses in America. The music which accompanied this scene, a wailing melody, came to embody, for me, all the pathos and defeat which lay in the failure of "Drifting Apart" and "The Minute Men."

My happiest days in Boston were associated with the Hernes. I loved the children, those vivid and dramatic little tow-haired girls, while their mother's lambent wit and their father's glowing humor enthralled me. I had never known such people. They were subject to all that is most typical in the Celt. Their extravagances of phrase and change of mood entranced me. They brought me to know many other figures in their strange world. They introduced me to William Gillette, Mary Shaw, and Robson and Crane, and before long I was not only thinking in terms of the theater but planning a general reform of the stage. I became one of the committee organized to promote the first Independent Theater Society in America. Herne, Flower, and Mary Shaw were among the promoters.

Having discovered the Hernes, I was eager to let all my friends know how fine, how important they were, and to that end I dragged Mr. Howells down to see the play and I insisted that Clement should comment upon it. I was a most indefatigable press agent and soon all my literary friends knew what the Hernes were trying to do, but my efforts proved of little financial value to them. They left the South End Theater, discouraged but not defeated. James A. had most marvelous resiliency. Just when I thought he was beaten to the earth, he rose with a chuckle and went at it again.

My brother Franklin joined the company in the autumn and during the next year we both shared the play's bewildering "ups and downs" on the road. I was present at the opening of the season in Troy, and when they reached Brooklyn I went on to New York to interest Gilder and Stedman in the Hernes. I suffered with them when the houses were small and exulted with them when the sales were large. I traveled with them to Buffalo, spending long hours on the train discussing why the play had no appeal in the East, and forecasting its chances of success in the West. I experienced the desolating effect which the sounds of slow-dropping seats in a half-filled auditorium has on a manager. The deep discouragement of watching streams of people pass the open door was another scarring experience.

In after years, when skies were fair, we were all able to laugh over these drab experiences, but they were not funny at the time, or at least if they were funny it was because Herne's irrepressible humor made them so. I suffered more than he— apparently, for I was wholly unaccustomed to the abrupt changes of mood which mark theatrical life and deceived by the readiness with which he turned a mood of defeat into laughter. I took his depressions (which always had in them a touch of exaggeration) to be despairs, and came slowly to a knowledge that his humorous sallies were meant to conceal from me the more poignant of his griefs. Altogether his friendship was a painful as well as a most beautiful experience. It gave me a deeper insight into that singular and passionate world in which the Hernes lived and had their being.

OTHER PLAYS AND PLAYERS

I

In the summer of 1890, Herne decided to give up "Drifting Apart" and produce a new play upon which he had been working called "Margaret Fleming." In this venture I was instantly and profoundly concerned. A volume of Ibsen's plays had just been translated and the discussion of "the Independent Theater" was in full swing. To every one I met I described Herne's new play, and I interviewed several managers, urging them to put it on—all to no purpose. The producers of Boston, like those of New York, would not consider it for a moment, although up to that time it was by all odds the most original of Herne's plays.

One day at a luncheon given to Herne by Howells, the dramatic situation was thoroughly gone into and James A. with boyish frankness confessed that he was at his wits' end. "All the theaters in New York and Boston have refused to consider my new play," he said, and to this I was able to bear corroborative testimony, for I had been personally rebuffed by five Boston managers.

Howells then spoke of a like situation in Berlin, and related the story of Sudermann and his associates, who secured a hall on a side street and made production of their plays there.

"They brought the public to them by the sheer force of their dramatic novelty," said Howells. "Why don't you do as they did—hire a sail loft or a stable and produce your play in the simplest fashion? The people will come to see it if it is new and vital."

Poor Herne did not instantly take fire at this suggestion, for he had reached almost the last ounce of his courage and pretty nearly the last dollar of his savings, but he went away with me, revolving the idea in his mind. "I'll do it," he said. "I'll hire Chickering Hall and remodel it into a little theater."

Of this music room which seated less than five hundred people (counting its small balcony) Herne made the first of the so-called "Little Theaters" in America, and all our dramatic reformers looked forward to the experiment with intense eagerness. In it Herne promised to produce effects hitherto unknown on our stage, and in all the rehearsals of the play he and Katharine had this in mind. They always and everywhere schooled their actors in a naturalism which, while not precisely the way in which the characters would speak in life, nevertheless produced that effect upon an audience.

To give up my own work and serve as press agent (without pay) was a joy, and while Herne carried on the rehearsals and supervised the construction of the stage, I bustled about the city, interesting the young men of the press and all my literary friends in the venture. Complimentary seats were sent to many of the most distinguished literary and artistic men and women of the region, and when, one night in the early autumn, the curtain rose on the first scene, the Hernes had one of the most notable audiences ever drawn together for a dramatic entertainment in Boston.

The performance was worthy of the audience. Not merely Herne but Mrs. Herne, and every one of the actors seemed to be actually presenting the unexaggerated gestures and accent of life. Katharine was especially moving in the title part, and the close of the play involved a touch of art which up to that time had never had its equal on our stage. After having refused reconciliation with her husband, *Philip Fleming, Margaret* was left standing in tragic isolation on the stage, and as the lights were turned out one by one, her figure gradually disappeared in deepening shadow, and when the heavy, soft curtains, dropping together noiselessly, shut in the poignant action of the drama, no one moved or spoke. The return to the actual world in which we lived was made silently.

There was a little pause, a considerable pause, before the applause came, and then the audience rose and slowly filed out. I saw Mr. and Mrs. Howells, Mr. and Mrs. Thomas Bailey Aldrich, Mr. and Mrs. Deland, Mrs. James T. Field, Sara Orne Jewett, William Lloyd Garrison, Mary E. Wilkins, John J. Enneking, and many others of the literary and artistic personalities of the day. Some of them spoke to me of the "wonderful play" and others of the "marvelous" acting, and, to my inexperienced mind, the Hernes had won. It seemed to me that the city must ring with applause of this courageous and distinguished performance.

Without question it was the most naturalistic, the most colloquial, and the most truthful presentation of a domestic drama ever seen on the American stage up to that time, and I am free to say that in some regards I do not think it has been surpassed since. But alas! while some of our most distinguished auditors came night by night, the general public could not be induced to flock in sufficient numbers to pay expenses, and after four weeks of losing business, poor Herne was obliged to leave the cast and go to New York under contract with a big commercial manager to produce a commercial success, "The Country Circus."

On October 7, 1891, he wrote me from New York:

"Klaw & Erlanger have no faith in the ability of 'Margaret Fleming' to pull out at Chickering Hall. They will probably close it there at the end of next week. Of course I have not the means to keep it on. They have not told me positively that they will close, but say 'It is madness to keep on,' etc. They talk of trying to get time in a theater for it, but you know if it fails in the hall the theaters will not have it at all. Our only hope lies in a success in Chickering Hall. Klaw got back this morning, and I presume, after they have conferred together, I'll get a decision. I feel what that decision will be. . . . If I had the means I would run it at the hall for another six weeks myself. It can be done for nine hundred or a thousand dollars, but I haven't got it and so there is an end. . . . Of course they only look at the money loss they've made. I look at the failure of my life. . . . The author of 'The Country Circus' read his play to the company to-day. *Oh, God!* But it'll go, I suppose. Oh; how I'd like to see such rot where it belongs!"

It was this letter which decided B. O. Flower to underwrite the extension of the play and I was glad to continue as "man in front" for another four weeks.

Naturally the play was widely discussed. Some could see no virtue in it, but others felt in it the beginning of a new and higher type of drama. Concerning Mrs. Herne's art there was no diversity of opinion. Praise was general. We could not then foresee the effect of our experiment, but we were satisfied. It had cost the Hernes several thousand dollars, but it had lifted them into the honorable position they deserved to fill.

II

Herne spent the winter in New York, working for a producing firm, and the following summer returned to Ashmont. For several seasons he had been in the habit of spending July and August at East Lemoyne on the coast of Maine, and being a close observer of life, had become keenly interested in his gnarly neighbors. He now began to think of putting them into a play. In a note to me I find this sentence: "I shall also try to do something more on 'The Hawthornes,'" and in all his letters, as well as those of Mrs. Herne, are humorous references to the curious and interesting characters they had met along the coast.

On his return in September he read to me the first act of "The Hawthornes." Later he spoke of it as "Uncle Nat" and finally as "Shore Acres." But the plot under all these names remained the same. The action involved two brothers, one, the elder, sweet, patient, self-sacrificing; the other discontented, sullen, and resentful, eager to make money without labor. The play was, in fact, the record of a bitter struggle over the question of "cuttin' the old farm up into buildin' lots," and as Herne read it to me scene by scene, the lines appealed to me as having something of the quality which made Mary E. Wilkins' stories so amusing and so vital.

It was by far the best play Herne had ever done, for it was written out of love for New England united to a thorough knowledge of coast characters. He tried all winter to get his new play produced, and it was not until the following spring that the manager of the Boston Museum, being in sore need of something to fill out the tag end of his season, yielded to Herne's plea, and put on "Shore Acres" for two weeks.

The opening night found me once more on hand as unofficial "man in front." Herne always declared that I stood in the door of a saloon opposite the entrance in order to gloat on the crowds filling the stairway and I guess I did. The piece was an instantaneous success. It drew great audiences from the first, and before the end of the first week half the managers in New York had written offering their theaters.

Among those who anxiously wired for the play was Harry Miner, a well-known New York theater owner, one of Herne's old acquaintances, and with him James A. signed a contract for the production of "Shore Acres" at the Broadway Theater the following autumn. Herne told me that in making out the contract he had insisted on the play being kept going for four weeks, no matter what the receipts were. "A most important proviso," he explained, "for 'Shore Acres' must have time for our kind of people to find out what sort of a play it is."

Naturally I was in New York to witness this opening, and my brother was in the cast. The play was greeted by a good house but fell off, as usual, on the second and third nights, and as I was behind the scenes a good deal of the time, I found Miner an interesting study. The first night he was jubilant. He posed in the lobby, glorious in evening dress, a shining figure. "We've got 'em coming, Jimmy, my boy," he said to Herne after the first act. But James A., whose face remained an impenetrable mask while Miner was looking at him, winked at me with full understanding of the situation.

"Watch him to-morrow night," he said after Miner left the dressing room.

Tuesday's house was light and Wednesday's still lighter, and on Thursday Miner fell into the dumps. "We've got to take it off, Jim," he mournfully announced.

"You'll do nothing of the kind," retorted Herne. "You'll keep it on four weeks according to contract, if it doesn't bring in a cent."

Miner was furious. He stormed about, declaring himself on the verge of ruin—all to no effect. Herne's face was stern as a New England granite boulder.

"You'll keep your contract," he calmly repeated.

Miner's attitude during the second week was comical. He became morose and was seen no more in the lobby. He brooded over the contract as though Herne had done him a grievous wrong, and all his employees came ultimately to share his resentful attitude. The house acquired a dank, depressing, tragic atmosphere and then, magically, came a change. The people began to come—our kind of people. At the end of the second week the house was filled. Miner ordered the lobby lighted up and reappeared in evening dress. He strutted once more in dazzling, confident splendor. He expanded. He appeared taller, larger. He clapped Herne on the back. "They're coming back, Jimmy, my boy!" he shouted, forgetting all his resentment, all his hard words, all his tragical gloom. "We'll be turning them into the street next week," he exultingly ended. "Your fortune is made."

This was almost literally true. The play ran the remainder of the season at the Broadway Theater and all the next year at Daly's, which was a phenomenal run in those days. It put Herne on his feet financially, as "Margaret Fleming" had established him artistically. He was now in the forefront of stage realists, quite independent of cheap theaters and cheaper managers and I was mightily relieved that he had succeeded in spite of my sinister influence.

III

Meanwhile Katharine had bought a handsome house on Convent Avenue in Harlem, and my brother and I were often there of a Sunday, and when we all came together in those days the walls resounded with our clamor. Herne was a great wag and story-teller and one of the most accomplished masters of dialect I have ever known. He could reproduce almost any accent and could dramatize at a moment's notice any scene or dialogue his wife demanded of him. Nevertheless, he took his art very seriously and was one of the best stage directors of his day, though his methods were so far in advance of his time that they puzzled or disgusted some of his subordinates. That he profoundly influenced the art of acting is admitted.

He was not only a good father in the ordinary sense, but an accepted comrade with his children. He played with them as if he were their own age, and was forever planning some new joke, some enterprise for their amusement. And yet with all his apparent simplicity and humor, he was a very complex and essentially a very sad character. In other words, he was a Celt. One of my friends upon seeing him for the first time in private life said, "His face is one of the saddest and sweetest I have ever seen." He was the Irish bard whose songs are compounded of laughter and a wailing keen.

Katharine Corcoran, his wife, was not merely of Irish temperament, she was Irish born and her laugh was one of the most infectious I have ever heard. Her speaking voice was very musical and expressive and her face could pass instantly from gay to grave like a sunny field over which the cloud shadows swiftly pass. Mr. Howells once said of her art, "I have never seen so many subtle expressions appearing in the lines of a woman's countenance."

"The both of them," as an Irishman would say, were capable of enthralling, spontaneous comedy on the stage and they were forever "guying" each other at home. Jim could not be trusted for one moment, but Katharine usually gave him as good as he sent. Indeed he was a little afraid of her keen wit, and often when she loosed her verbal arrows he quite frankly dodged.

He admired her profoundly, and generally remained silent during the call of a chance acquaintance or of a stranger. Only in the presence of intimate friends did he abandon his attitude of smiling and interested reticence. At the same time, his love and admiration for Katharine did not prevent him from observing every peculiarity which could be turned against her. One of his tricks was to rise gravely just as she had reached the middle of an eloquent period, and solemnly pretend to reverse a little switch at the top of her shoulder.

Sometimes she frowned for an instant at this outrage, but usually she acknowledged the justice of his action and broke into a ripple of laughter, with full appreciation of the fact that she had been "going it again."

They both held from the first an exaggerated notion of my importance in the world of letters and listened to me with a respect, a fellowship, and an appreciation which inspired me to better work. They called me "The Dean" on account of my supposed learning and often after dinner Herne would say, "Now, Dean, for the salt cellar."

In this way he always referred to an early discussion in which I had used a salt cellar to illustrate Spencer's theory of the constitution of matter. "We do not know what matter is. We cannot say this glass is solid, neither can we say it is made up of invisible molecules, etc."

We often harangued till long after midnight. Sometimes my brother was with me, sometimes not, but we were all flaming with hatred of land monopoly in those days, and when we were not advocating realism in fiction or impressionism in painting, we were quoting "Progress and Poverty."

Those were beautiful days to me and very successful days for the Hernes. Katharine in a recent letter refers to them as "the good old Convent Avenue days. But dearest of all we hold the little home in Ashmont."

In one of Herne's later letters I find the following reference to our first meetings:

"Yes, those Ashmont days were indeed glorious days. They laid the foundation of what success we have since achieved by strengthening and encouraging us in our work and making us steadfast to a purpose that we felt was the true one. And we believe that you, too, got something in your work and for your future out of them. They are gone but not forgotten. They change but cannot die."

IV

Inevitably I tried my hand at writing plays. Not to have done so would have been phenomenal stolidity, but I was never able to forget in those days that I was a reformer, so my first play dealt with land monopoly and was called "Under the Wheel," and my second was based on a celebrated investigation of the lobby by the legislature of Boston. I named it "A Member of the Third House." Whatever my plays possessed in the way of dramatic power, they were absolutely unsalable by reason of their austere content. Herne sympathized with them as documents, but was too wise to attempt to produce them.

In addition to these attempts I worked with him on a melodrama called "Fall River," he writing one act and I another, but they came to nothing. Then I worked with Katharine on an Irish comedy for her, which we named "Mrs. Crisp," but that also ran into the ditch. Then I induced Mr. Howells to work with me on a dramatization of "A Modern Instance." The net result of which is a manuscript, partly print and partly his own writing, nothing more.

Through Herne I met William Gillette, one of the handsomest and most talented of all the actor-dramatists of that day. I had seen him in "The Private Secretary," in which he appeared to be a forlorn, ganglionic individual about seven feet tall, and it was a pleasant shock to meet the man himself, so graceful and shapely, notwithstanding his height. I was greatly delighted by his alert and humorous mind and his clarity of expression.

Through Mrs. Herne I came to know Mary Shaw, whose voice had always delighted me. I had seen her several times in support of Julia Marlowe and considered her a better reader of Shakespeare than the star herself. She was in the fullness of her powers at this time, a noble actress and a cultivated woman. She had been a teacher in a Boston school and her taste and judgment made her impersonations among the best on the stage. She was of Irish parentage, blonde, gray-eyed, and humorous. She could tell a story with more effect than any of my acquaintances except Herne. She made fun of herself like a man and yet was essentially feminine.

One of the subjects of her monologues at our first meeting was an actor she called "Plim" and as I listened to her I was led into new regions. It did not seem possible that such amusing, carefree people could exist. They were characters in a novel. One of Herne's friends was a man he called "Putt," who was subject to illusions of grandeur. He had much to say of his "man Petah" and of his "paddock" and his "cobs." He went so far as to detail the way in which he shipped his horses to and from New York and how valuable "Petah" was. I met Putt one day and could not believe that he was the hero of Herne's stories, but he was! In truth he had no farm, no horses, and no paddock. They were all imaginary and "Petah" turned out to be a small boy of about fifteen. No character in fiction could surpass this braggart, who was a tall and graceful Englishman of fifty.

Up to this time the men and women of my world in Boston, as in the West, had been serious, restrained souls. Jesting of a quiet sort was common in my mother's family, but my father, although he told a story with dramatic power, was never comic, and most of the women I had known up to this time had been long-suffering and patient. Lambent spirits like Mary Shaw and Katharine Herne were new to me. I listened to their laughing comment with wonder and delight. That they did not openly make fun of me is proof of their kindly natures. No doubt they had their private opinion of me, but they never failed to treat me with highly flattering expressions of respect, even when I was most ponderous.

In order to be quite fair to myself, I must admit to being fairly well clothed at this time, and although a colossal bore when preaching the single tax or defining the local-color school in fiction, I had moments of being companionable. At times I laughed, especially when in the presence of Mary Shaw and Katharine Herne. In short, I was on my way to a mellow old age.

A relentless idealist in general and a Veritist in particular, I continued to uphold the fiction represented by Howells and to advocate similar drama. I commended Edward Harrigan for his attempts to put Harlem's shanty town on the stage and openly declared that Denman Thompson's "The Old Homestead" was also headed in the right direction.

Herne's use of my name in connection with that of Howells always made me wince. How little they knew of me! I tried to tell him that I was only a free-lance instructor and that no one would buy my stories, but he and Katharine continued to listen as though I were a philosopher and poet as well as a devoted friend. I repeatedly warned them against my cranky notions, but they persisted in seeking my judgment and while I did not suggest a line of "Shore Acres," Herne declared that I had profoundly influenced the structure of it.

We spent hours discussing plays like "Shenandoah," "My Partner," "Davy Crockett," and "The Henrietta," as well as farces like "The Hole in the Ground," "The Brass Monkey," and "Mulligan's Ball," assessing their value in terms of their truth to life. "I want to be truer than any of them," said Herne. "I want my 'Shore Acres' to be as true as Mr. Howells and Miss Wilkins." He included one or two of my short stories in this category, but as I had no book to my credit at this time, his judgment of me was based on faith in what I might do some time, rather than upon anything I had done.

As a writer, I included Augustus Thomas, Bronson Howard, and William Gillette among the forerunners of a new school of dramatists. They fitted into my lecture on "Local Color in Fiction and the Drama." It didn't harm them and it gave me and my pupils a great deal of satisfaction to have their plays arranged and classified. Moreover, Thomas and Herne both lived up to their label, Thomas with "In Missouri" and "The Hoosier Doctor" and Herne with "Shore Acres" and "Sag Harbor."

v

My interest in Herne, Gillette, and Thomas did not lessen my admiration for Edwin Booth. He was still the reigning king in my dramatic world, but each time I saw him play I sensed a decline in his vitality. He was growing old all too swiftly. He moved less alertly, and his voice, though beautiful as ever, was burdened with the tragedy of age, and when he uttered Macbeth's somber soliloquies he filled me with poignant regret that his day was falling "into the sere and yellow leaf."

Booth's founding of the Players and his retirement was soon followed by his death. Although I became a member of the club it was not till 1897, and so I never saw him there, but many of my friends have described to me how he came and went from his rooms on the second floor, a slight figure with a beautiful, sad face. He usually ate alone, not in austere mood but in gentle aloofness, and only his intimate friends ventured to join him. Occasionally when some question concerning the reading of a passage from Macbeth or Hamlet came up, his dark eyes flashed with remembered fire and his glorious voice was heard again for a moment. Mainly he was a shadowy figure, haunting the club he had created.

The rooms in which he died are preserved by the Players as a memorial, just as they were when he laid down his book and took to his final bed, and it is the custom of those who knew him to show visitors this chamber, together with the costumes and books which he bequeathed to the library. To those of us who remember him in these garments, the robe of Richelieu and the cloak of Hamlet bring glorious memories. They make the Players, small as it is, the most distinctive club in the New World, and in the square before the club, a beautiful bronze statue of him by Edmund Quinn stands as an evidence of the beauty of his face and the grace of his form as he appeared in Hamlet, a characterization which we all admired and in which we saw most of Edwin Booth the man.

1930

SIDNEY SKOLSKY

The theatrical gossip column made its bow in the 1880s, when Mary Hewins, posing as "The Giddy Gusher," introduced the novelty to the New York *Dramatic Mirror*. The sporting and theatrical journal the New York *Clipper* offered its own garner of inside information under the more manly pen name "Joe Hepp." By the 1920s, these columnists, writing in a snappy, up-to-date slang, were an important cog in the publicity machine of the professional theatre. There was often considerable slippage between their objectivity as reporters and their favor-seeking from producers. Sidney Skolsky (1905–1983) began as a Broadway press agent for Earl Carroll, impresario of the chorine-bedecked *Vanities*, before he took over Mark Hellinger's column in the New York *Daily News* in 1929. The youngest of that ilk, Skolsky was never as powerful as Walter Winchell, but his "Times Square Tin-types," character sketches of local personalities, was widely read until the column was terminated in 1981. With the westward drift of stage actors to appear in sound films, in 1934 Hearst's *New York Herald* sent Skolsky to Hollywood, where he made Schwab's Drugstore his headquarters. Quitting Hearst after a set-to with Louella Parsons, he supplied a syndicated column for the Los Angeles *Citizen News* which ran until the paper folded in 1970. "The little black mouse," as Skolsky was known, launched the (originally denigratory) term "Oscar" for the Academy Award and made the industry's "preview" and "take," "stand-in" and "stunt double" household words. Characteristically plying both sides of the street, he also became a producer of films about what he knew best, show business (*The Jolson Story*, *The Eddie Cantor Story*).

Cain's Warehouse

An author spends months writing a play. A producer stakes everything on it. Days and nights of weary rehearsals with stars sweating. The play opens. Evening dress and silk hats. Speculators selling tickets on the sidewalk. Everybody is so happy. A few months later a truck backs up at the stage door. The path of glory leads but to Cain's.

PATRICK CAIN is the owner of that theatrical storehouse. Everybody calls him Patsy.

He attended P.S. 32. Bows his head shamefully when admitting that he didn't have the honor of receiving a diploma.

His father, John J. Cain, a former policeman, started the trucking business forty-two years ago. He used to help his father just for the ride.

Seldom goes to an opening night. Producers, considering him a jinx, shoo him away. He has attended more closing nights than any other man in the world.

Has a broken nose. This he received in his youth during a block fight.

His warehouse is located at 530 West Forty-first Street. Directly opposite is an old brewery with a statue of a fallen man holding a schooner of beer. He seems to be saying to those shows entering their final resting place: "Here's to Better Days."

Is happily married and the proud possessor of four children. Has his own home in Flushing. It was built especially for him by a stage carpenter.

He doesn't drink, smoke or use profane language.

Rarely eats in restaurants. Has breakfast and dinner at home. Has lunch at his sister's, who lives two blocks from his place of business.

The storehouse consists of five stories and a basement.

The fifth floor is for the shows of Aarons and Freedley, Schwab and Mandel, Gene Buck and the personal belongings of W. C. Fields and Laurette Taylor. The fourth floor holds the last remains of Florenz Ziegfeld's *Follies* and George White's *Scandals*. Their mighty efforts for supremacy rest in peace. The third floor is for Sam H. Harris, Douglas Fairbanks, A. L. Erlanger and the Paramount Theatre. The second floor is occupied by Richard Herndon and others. The basement is for the canvas "drops." They are rolled neatly and lie row on row. Their tombstone is an identification tag on which is scrawled in pencil: "Garden Drop—Follies—1917."

He drinks two chocolate ice cream sodas every day. On Sunday evenings he takes the entire family to the neighborhood drug store and treats them to sodas.

Employs only four men—a night watchman, a day watchman, a bookkeeper and a superintendent. He hasn't a secretary. But the superintendent, attired in greasy overalls, takes great pride in referring to himself as "Patsy's typewriter."

He hires his help by the day. Employs exactly the number he needs for that day's work. While on a job if the men eat before three o'clock they must pay for the meal. If they eat after three he must. Every day he phones his men at exactly one o'clock and says: "Boys, I think you ought to knock off now and get yourselves a bite to eat."

He has eight gold teeth in his mouth. They make him look dignified.

Reads only two things. They are the dramatic reviews and the cartoons in the *New Yorker*.

Has the same amount of strength in his right hand as he has in his left. He can write just as unintelligibly with both.

His name often occurs in theatrical reviews. One critic referred to a show as "A typical Cain success." Another said: "The audience was so bored and quiet you could hear Cain's trucks carting the show away after each act was over." The prize of them all was the one by Rennold Wolf. For his review of Arthur Hopkins's first production, *Steve*, Mr. Wolf merely wrote: "A Voice From Cain's—I Gotcha, Steve."

Until three years ago he wore red flannel underwear. Now in the summer he wears balbriggan union suits and in the winter two-piece fleece-lined underwear.

He bought an automobile a year ago and is still learning how to drive it.

Nothing tickles his palate like a good plate of corn beef and cabbage—Irish style. Whenever the Cains have company for dinner they serve roast chicken. This he considers "living high."

Wallack's is his favorite theater. It is said that his horses stop there by force of habit.

His office is on the ground floor of the building. His desk is an old roll-top affair with hundreds of initials scratched on it. The drawers are filled with needles, sewing thread, penknives, old pen points, kodak photographs of his children and his house, screws, nails and holy pictures. The wall is decorated with a picture of his father, wooden cutouts of Dutch boys and girls and a large picture of an American flag with the caption

"Ours" under it. To the left of his desk a policeman's night-stick stands handy. To the right is a pail of milk for the office cat.

He attends the eleven o'clock mass at St. Andrew's Church, Flushing, every Sunday—hot or cold.

Always tucks the ends of his tie inside his shirt.

When his father died he willed Patsy his favorite horse. According to the terms of the will, he must take the horse for a vacation every summer.

He doesn't do any advertising. But if he did, his slogan would be: "Not a Show in a Carload."

1930

LANGSTON HUGHES

Langston Hughes (1902–1967) was the most politically engaged of the poetic dramatists of the Harlem Renaissance. Although the earliest of his one hundred plays were well-made melodramas about race relations and his last were folk musicals, in the 1930s his output was, in tune with the times, devoted to social change and political upheaval. Current events drove him to deal with union organizing, sharecroppers, and the Scottsboro Boys: *The Organizer. A Blues Opera in One Act* (1938) was a deliberate response to Odets' *Waiting for Lefty*. Hughes was instrumental in founding the New Negro Theatre in Los Angeles (1939) and the Skyloft Players in Chicago (1941–42), but as late as 1961 he was complaining that there was "no primarily serious colored theatre" in the United States.

One of the hits of the 1930–31 Broadway season had been *The Green Pastures* by Marc Connelly. It was based on Roark Bradford's sketches *Ol' Man Adam an' His Chillun* (1928), a white man's version of how the Bible might be retold by a backwoods Louisiana preacher. With an all-black cast and the Hall Johnson Choir intoning spirituals, this cartoon-version of the Old Testament ran for over a year on Broadway, toured widely, and was eventually filmed. Although James Weldon Johnson praised it, for Alain Locke it was insufficiently "apocalyptic." As for Langston Hughes, its stereotypes put his teeth on edge; he found it an inauthentic product of "paternalistic anti-Negro writers and folklorists of the South." In the socialist magazine *New Theatre* he published his account of discontent within the cast as it toured a segregated nation.

Trouble with the Angels

AT every performance lots of white people wept and almost every Sunday while they were on tour some white minister invited the Negro actor who played God to come and speak to his congregation of white Christians, and thus help improve race relations—because almost everywhere they needed improving. Although the play had been the hit of years in New York, the Negro actors and singers were paid much less than white actors and singers would have been paid for performing it. And although the dramatist and his backers made more than a half a million dollars, the colored troupers, now on tour, lived in cheap hotels and slept often in beds that were full of bugs. Only the actor who played God would sometimes, by the hardest effort, achieve accommodations in a white hotel, or be put up by some nice white family, or be invited to the home of the best Negro family in town. And thus God began to think that everything was lovely in the world. As an actor he really got awfully good write-ups.

Then they were booked to play Washington, and that's where the trouble began. Washington, the capital of the United States, is as every Negro knows, a town where no black man is allowed inside a theatre, not even in the gallery. Of course they have a few moving picture houses in their own African ghetto where they can go. But downtown in the legitimate playhouses, no accommodations are made for colored people. Washington is worse than the deep south in that respect.

But God wasn't at all worried about playing Washington. He thought sure his coming would improve race relations. He thought it would be fine for the good white people of the Capital to see him—a colored God—even if the Negroes couldn't. Not even those Negroes who worked for the government. Not even Congressman DePriest!

But several weeks before the Washington appearance of the famous "Negro" play about the charming darkies who drink eggnog and fry fish in heaven, and sing almost all the time, storm clouds began to rise. It seemed that the Negroes of Washington had decided, strangely enough, that they wanted to see this play. But when they approached the theatre management on the question, they got a cold shoulder in return. The theatre management said they didn't have any seats to sell to Negroes. They couldn't even allot a corner in the upper gallery—there was such a heavy demand from white folks.

Now this made the Negroes of Washington mad, especially those who worked for the government and constituted the best society. The colored singers got mad, too, and the teachers at Howard, and the ministers of the colored churches who wanted to see what a black heaven looked like on the stage.

But nothing doing, the theatre management was adamant.

They really couldn't sell seats to Negroes. Although they had
no scruples about making a large profit on the week's work of
the Negro actors, they just couldn't permit Negroes to sit in
their theatre.

So the Washington Negroes wrote to God, this colored God
who had been such a hit on Broadway. They thought sure he
would help them. (But Negroes have always been stupid about
God, even when he is white, let alone colored. They still keep
on expecting help.)

So the Ministerial Alliance wrote to him when he was playing in Philadelphia. What a shame, they said: white folks will
not allow us to come to see you perform in Washington! We
are getting up a protest. We want you to help us! Will you?

Now God knew that for many years white folks had not allowed Negroes in Washington to see any shows—not even in
the churches, let alone in the theatres! Of late even the
Catholic churches were barring them out of mass. So how
come they suddenly thought they ought to be allowed to see
Him in a white theatre?

Besides God was getting paid pretty well, and pretty well
known. So he answered their letters and said that his ink was
made of tears and his heart bled, but that he couldn't afford to
get into trouble with Equity. Also, it wasn't his place to go
around the country spreading dissension and hate, but love
and beauty. And it would surely do the white folks of the District of Columbia a lot of good to see Him, and it would
soften their hearts to hear the beautiful Negro spirituals, and
see the lovely black angels.

And maybe the company would try to give one special show
for the Race.

So the black drama lovers of Washington couldn't get any
satisfaction out of God by mail—their colored God. When the
company played Baltimore, a delegation of the "best" Washington Negroes went over to their neighboring city to interview God. In Baltimore, Negroes, at least, are allowed to sit in
the galleries of the theatres. After the play, God received the
delegation in his dressing room and wept about his inability
to do anything concerning the Washington situation. He had,
of course, spoken to his management about it and they
thought it might be possible to arrange a special Sunday night

performance for Negroes. God said it hurt him to his soul to think how his people were treated, but the play must go on.

The delegation left in a huff—but not before they had spread their indignation to other members of the cast of the big show. And among the angels there was a great discussion as to what they might do about the Washington situation. (Although God was the star, the angels, too, were a part of the play.)

Now, among the angels there was a young Negro named Johnny Logan, who had never really liked being an angel, but who, because of his baritone voice and his Negro features, had gotten the job during the first rehearsals of the play in New York. Now he was an old hand at being an angel, since the play had been running three years.

Logan was from the South—but he hadn't stayed there long after he grew up. The white folks wouldn't let him. He was the kind of a young Negro most Southern white people hate. He believed in fighting, in bucking against the traces of discrimination and Jim Crow, and in trying to knock down any white man who insulted him. So he was only about eighteen when the whites of Augusta ran him out of town.

He finally came to New York, married a waitress, got a job as a redcap and would have settled down forever in a little flat in Harlem, had not some of his friends discovered that he could sing, and persuaded him to join a Red Cap Quartette. And out of that had come this work as a black angel in what turned out to be a Broadway success.

Just before the show went on the road, his wife had their first kid, so he needed to hold his job as a singing angel, even if it meant going on tour. But the more he thought about their forthcoming appearance in a Washington theatre that wasn't even Jim Crow—but that barred Negroes altogether—the madder he got. And finally he got so mad that he caused the rest of the cast to get all worked up, too—except God. And the angels decided to organize a strike!

At that distance from Washington, the black angels—from tenors to basses, sopranos to blues singers—were up in arms, and practically everybody in the cast, except God, agreed to strike.

"The idea of a town where colored folks can't even sit in the gallery to see an all-colored show. I ain't gonna work there myself."

"We'll show them white folks we've got spunk for once. We'll pull off the biggest actor's strike you ever seen."

"We sho will."

That was in Philadelphia. In Baltimore, their ardor had cooled.

"Man, I got a wife to take care of. I can't lose no week's work!"

"I got a wife, too," said Logan, "and a kid besides, but I'm game."

"You ain't a trouper," said another.

"Naw, if you was you'd be used to playing all-white houses. In the old days . . . ," said the man who played Methusaleh, powdering his gray wig.

"I know all about the old days," said Logan, "when black minstrels blacked up even blacker and made fun of themselves for the benefit of white folks. But who wants to go back to the old days?"

"Anyhow, let's let well enough alone," said Methusaleh.

"You ain't got no guts," said Logan.

"You're just one of them radicals, son, that's all you is," put in the old tenor who played Saul. "We know when we wants to strike or don't."

"Listen, then," said Logan to the angels who were putting on their wings by now, as it was near curtain time, "if we can't make it a real strike, then let's make it a general walk-out on the opening night. Strike for one performance anyhow. At least show the white folks that we don't take it lying down. And show the Washington Negroes that we back them up— theoretically, at least."

"One day ain't so bad," said a skinny black angel. "I'm with you on that."

"Me, too," several others agreed as they crowded into the corridor at the curtain call, and went up on the stage. The actor who played God was standing in the wings in his frock coat.

"Shss-ss!" he said.

*

Monday in Washington. The opening of that famous white play of Negro life in heaven. Original New York cast. Songs as only darkies can sing them. Uncle Tom come back as God.

Negro Washington wanted to picket the theatre, but the police had an injunction against them. Cops were posted for blocks around the playhouse to prevent a riot. Nobody could see God. He was safely housed in the quiet home of a Negro professor, guarded by two detectives. The papers said black radicals had threatened to kidnap him, to kidnap God!

Logan spent the whole day rallying the flagging spirits of his fellow actors. They were solid for the strike when he was around, and weak when he wasn't. No telling what them Washington cops might do to them if they struck? They locked Negroes up for less than that in Washington. Besides they might get canned, they might lose their pay, they might never get no more jobs on the stage. It was all right to talk about being a man and standing up for your race, and all that—but hell, even an actor had to eat. Besides, God was right. It was a great play, a famous play! They ought to go on, and hold up its reputation. It did white folks good just to see Negroes in such a play. That nigger Logan was crazy!

"Listen here, you might as well get wise. Ain't nobody gonna strike tonight," one of the boys told him about six o'clock in the lobby of the colored Whitelaw Hotel. "You just as well give up. We ain't got no guts."

"I won't give up," said Logan.

When the actors reached the theatre, they found it surrounded by cops and the stage full of detectives. In the lobby there was a long line of people—white, of course—waiting to buy standing room. God arrived with motorcycle cops in front of his car. He had come a little early to address the cast. With him was the white stage manager and a representative of the New York producing office.

They called everybody together on the stage. The Lord wept as he spoke of all his race had borne to get where they were today. Of how they had struggled. Of how they sang. Of how they must keep on struggling and singing—until white folks saw the light. The strike would do no good. The strike would only hurt their cause. With sorrow in his heart—but more noble because of it—he would go on with the play. And he was sure his actors—his angels—his children—would, too.

The white men accompanying God were very solemn, also, as though hurt to their souls to think what their Negro employees were suffering—but far more hurt to think that they wanted to jeopardize a week's box office receipts by a strike! That would hurt everybody—*even white folks!*

Behind God and the white managers stood two big detectives.

All gave up but Logan. He went downstairs to fight, to drag them out by force, to make men of darkies just once, to carry through the strike. But he couldn't. Nobody really wanted to strike. Nobody really wanted to sacrifice anything for race pride, or decency, or elementary human rights. No, they only wanted to keep on appearing in a naive dialect play about a quaint funny heaven full of niggers.

The management sent two detectives downstairs to get Logan. They were taking no chances. Just as the curtain rose they dragged him off to jail—for disturbing the peace. All the other colored angels were massed in the wings for the opening spiritual when the police took the black boy out. They saw a line of tears running down his cheeks. Most of the actors thought he was crying because he was being arrested—and in their timid souls they were glad it wasn't them.

The Lord God Jesus in his frock coat did not even turn his head. He was getting "in the mood" for his triumphant first appearance before the Washington white folks.

1935

THOMAS WOLFE

Now remembered exclusively as a novelist, Thomas Wolfe (1900–1938) first aspired to be a playwright. While still an undergraduate at the University of North Carolina, he had several plays produced by the Carolina Playmakers. On graduating in 1920, he joined the famous 47 Workshop (English 47) initiated in 1913 under Professor George Pierce Baker at Harvard. This nursery of theatrical talent could boast such alumni as dramatists Eugene O'Neill, Sidney Howard, Edward Knoblock, Edward Sheldon, S. N. Behrman, and Philip Barry, critics Kenneth Macgowan and John Mason Brown, directors George Abbott and Hallie Flanagan, and designers Stanley McCandless and Donald Oenslager. Its benefits included group criticism and the staging of the students' efforts. Abandoning his local-color plays about Carolina mountain folk, Wolfe offered *Welcome to the City*, which enjoyed a Harvard production in 1923 but could not get a professional hearing. Despite moral and financial support from the stage designer Aline Bernstein, Wolfe was embittered when his Civil War drama *Mannerhouse* was also rejected; he turned definitively to the novel with his autobiographical *Look Homeward, Angel* (1929; ironically, its dramatization by Ketty Frings would win a Pulitzer Prize). Professor Baker also had reason to be bitter: Harvard adamantly refused to license a degree in playwriting. So he moved to New Haven in 1925 to found the Yale School of Drama. The 47 Workshop appears in Wolfe's novel *Of Time and the River* (1935) "not even thinly disguised" as "Professor Hatcher's Playwriting Course."

FROM

Of Time and the River

THE purposes of Professor Hatcher's celebrated school for dramatists seemed, as stated, to be plain and reasonable enough. Professor Hatcher himself prudently forebore from making extravagant claims concerning the benefits to be derived from his course. He did not say that he could make a dramatist out of any man who came to take his course. He did not predict a successful career in the professional theatre for every student who had been a member of his class. He did not even say he could teach a student how to write plays. No. He made, in fact, no claims at all. Whatever he said about his course was very reasonably, prudently, and temperately put: it was impossible to quarrel with it.

All Professor Hatcher said about his course was that, if a man had a genuine dramatic and theatric talent to begin with, he might be able to derive from the course a technical and critical guidance which it would be hard for him to get elsewhere, and which he might find for himself only after years of painful and even wasteful experiment.

Certainly this seemed reasonable enough. Moreover, Professor Hatcher felt that the artist would benefit by what was known as the "round table discussion"—that is by the comment and criticism of the various members of the class, after Professor Hatcher had read them a play written by one of their group. He felt that the spirit of working together, of seeing one's play produced and assisting in the production, of being familiar with all the various "arts" of the theatre—lighting, designing, directing, acting, and so on—was an experience which should be of immense value to the young dramatist of promise and of talent. In short, although he made no assertion that he could create a talent where none was, or give life by technical expertness to the substance of a work that had no real life of its own, Professor Hatcher did feel that by the beneficent influence of this tutelage he might trim the true lamp to make it burn more brightly.

And though it was possible to take issue with him on some of his beliefs—that, for example, the comment and criticism of "the group," and a community of creative spirits was good for the artist—it was impossible to deny that his argument was reasonable, temperate, and conservative in the statement of his purposes.

And he made this plain to every member of his class. Each one was made to understand that the course made no claims of magic alchemy—that he could not be turned into an interesting dramatist if the talent was not there.

But although each member of the class affirmed his understanding of this fundamental truth, and readily said that he accepted it, most of these people, at the bottom of their hearts, believed—pitiably and past belief—that a miracle would be wrought upon their sterile, unproductive spirits, that for them, for *them*, at least, a magic transformation would be brought about in their miserable small lives and feeble purposes—and all because they now were members of Professor Hatcher's celebrated class.

The members of Professor Hatcher's class belonged to the whole lost family of the earth, whose number is uncountable, and for this reason, they could never be forgotten.

And, first and foremost, they belonged to that great lost tribe of people who are more numerous in America than in any other country in the world. They belonged to that unnumbered horde who think that somehow, by some magic and miraculous scheme or rule or formula, "something can be done for them." They belonged to that huge colony of the damned who buy thousands of books that are printed for their kind, telling them how to run a tea shop, how to develop a pleasing personality, how to acquire "a liberal education," swiftly and easily and with no anguish of the soul, by fifteen minutes' reading every day, how to perform the act of sexual intercourse in such a way that your wife will love you for it, how to have children, or to keep from having children, how to write short-stories, novels, plays, and verses which are profitably salable, how to keep from having body odor, constipation, bad breath, or tartar on the teeth, how to have good manners, know the proper fork to use for every course, and always do the proper thing—how, in short, to be beautiful, "distinguished," "smart," "chic," "forceful," and "sophisticated"—finally, how to have "a brilliant personality" and "achieve success."

Yes, for the most part, the members of Professor Hatcher's class belonged to this great colony of the lost Americans. They belonged to that huge tribe of all the damned and lost who feel that everything is going to be all right with them if they can only take a trip, or learn a rule, or meet a person. They belonged to that futile, desolate, and forsaken horde who felt that all will be well with their lives, that all the power they lack themselves will be supplied, and all the anguish, fury, and unrest, the confusion and the dark damnation of man's soul can magically be healed if only they eat bran for breakfast, secure an introduction to a celebrated actress, get a reading for their manuscript by a friend of Sinclair Lewis, or win admission to Professor Hatcher's celebrated class of dramatists.

And, in a curious way, the plays written by the people in Professor Hatcher's class, illustrated, in one form or another, this desire. Few of the plays had any intrinsic reality, for most of these people were lacking in the first, the last, the foremost quality of the artist, without which he is lost: the ability to get out of his own life the power to live and work by, to derive from his own experience—as a fruit of all his seeing, feeling, living, joy and bitter anguish—the palpable and living substance of his art.

Few of the people in Professor Hatcher's class possessed this power. Few of them had anything of their own to say. Their lives seemed to have grown from a stony and a fruitless soil and, as a consequence, the plays they wrote did not reflect that life, save by a curious and yet illuminating indirection.

Thus, in an extraordinary way, their plays—unreal, sterile, imitative, and derivative as most of them indubitably were— often revealed more about the lives of the people who wrote them than better and more living work could do. For, although few of the plays showed any contact with reality— with that passionate integument of blood and sweat and pain and fear and grief and joy and laughter of which this world is made—most of them did show, in one way or another, what was perhaps the basic impulse in the lives of most of these people—the impulse which had brought them here to Professor Hatcher's class.

The impulse of the people in the class was not to embrace life and devour it, but rather to escape from it. And in one way or another most of the plays these people wrote were illustrative of this desire. For in these plays—unnatural, false, and imitative, as they were—one could discern, in however pale and feeble a design, a picture of the world not as its author had seen and lived and known it, but rather as he wished to find it, or believe in it. And, in all their several forms—whether sad, gay, comic, tragic, or fantastical—these plays gave evidence of the denial and the fear of life.

The wealthy young dawdler from Philadelphia, for example, wrote plays which had their setting in a charming little French Café. Here one was introduced to all the gay, quaint, charming

Frenchmen—to Papa Duval, the jolly proprietor, and Mama Duval, his rotund and no less jolly spouse, as well as to all the quaint and curious habitués that are so prolific in theatrical establishments of this order. One met, as well, that fixture of these places: old Monsieur Vernet, the crusty, crotchety, but kindly old gentleman who is the café's oldest customer and has had the same table in the corner by the window for more than thirty years. One saw again the familiar development of the comic situation—the day when Monsieur Vernet enters at his appointed time and finds at his table a total stranger, sacrilege! Imprecations! Tears, prayers, and entreaties on the part of Papa Duval and his wife, together with the stubborn refusal of the imperious stranger to move! Climax: old Monsieur Vernet storming out of the café, swearing that he will never return. Resolution of conflict: the efforts of Papa and Mamma Duval to bring their most prized customer back into the fold again, and their final success, the pacification and return of Monsieur Vernet amid great rejoicing, thanks to a cunning stratagem on the part of Henri, the young waiter, who wins a reward for all these efforts, the hand of Mimi, Papa Duval's charming daughter, from whom he has been separated by Papa Duval's stern decree.

Thus, custom is restored, and true love re-united by one brilliant comic stroke!

And all this pretty little world, the contribution of a rich young man who came from Philadelphia! How perfectly God-damn delightful it all was, to be sure!

The plays of old Seth Flint, the sour and withered ex-reporter, were, if of a different coloring, cut from the same gaudy cloth of theatric unreality. For forty years old Seth had pounded precincts as a newsman, and had known city-rooms across the nation. He had seen every crime, ruin, and incongruity of which man's life is capable. He was familiar with every trait of graft, with every accursed smell and smear of the old red murder which ineradicably fouled the ancient soul of man, and the stench of man's falseness, treachery, cruelty, hypocrisy, cowardice, and injustice, together with the look of brains and blood upon the pavements of the nation, was no new thing to old Seth Flint.

His skin had been withered, his eyes deadened, his heart and spirit burdened wearily, his faith made cynical, and his temper soured by the black picture of mankind which he had seen as a reporter—and because of this, in spite of this, he had remained or become—how, why, in what miraculous fashion no one knew—a curiously honest, sweet, and generous person, whose life had been the record of a self-less loyalty. He had known poverty, hardship, and self-sacrifice, and endured all willingly without complaint: he had taken the savings of a lifetime to send the two sons of his widowed sister to college, he had supported this woman and her family for years, and now, when his own life was coming to its close, he was yielding to the only self-indulgence he had ever known—a year away from the city-room of a Denver newspaper, a year away in the rare ether, among the precious and æsthetic intellects of Professor Hatcher's celebrated course, a year in which to realize the dream of a life-time, the vision of his youth—a year in which to write the plays he had always dreamed of writing. And what kind of plays did he write?

Alas! Old Seth did exactly what he set out to do, he succeeded perfectly in fulfilling his desire—and, by a tragic irony, his failure lay in just this fact. The plays which he produced with an astounding and prolific ease—("Three days is enough to write a play," the old man said in his sour voice. "You guys who take a year to write a play give me a pain. If you can't write a play a week, you can't write anything; the play's no good")—these plays were just the plays which he had dreamed of writing as a young man, and therein was evident their irremediable fault.

For Seth's plays—so neat, brisk, glib, and smartly done—would have been good plays in a commercial way, as well, if he had only done them twenty years before. He wrote, without effort and with unerring accuracy, a kind of play which had been immensely popular at the beginning of the twentieth century, but which people had grown tired of twenty years before. He wrote plays in which the babies got mixed up in the maternity ward of a great hospital, in which the rich man's child goes to the family of the little grocer, and the grocer's child grows up as the heir to an enormous fortune, with all the luxuries and securities of wealth around him. And he brought about the final resolution of this tangled scheme, the meeting of these scrambled children and their bewildered parents, with a skill of complication, a design of plot, a dexterity that was astonishing. His characters—all well-known types of the theatre, as of nurse tough-spoken, shop-girl slangy, reporter cynical, and so on—were well conceived to fret their purpose, their lives well-timed and apt and deftly made. He had mastered the formula of an older type of "well-made play" with astonishing success. Only, the type was dead, the interest of the public in such plays had vanished twenty years before.

So here he was, a live man, writing, with amazing skill, dead plays for a theatre that was dead, and for a public that did not exist.

"Chekhov! Ibsen!" old Seth would whine sourly with a dismissing gesture of his parched old hand, and a scornful contortion of his bitter mouth in his old mummy of a face. "You guys all make me tired the way you worship them!" he would whine out at some of the exquisite young temperaments in Professor Hatcher's class. "Those guys can't write a play! Take Chekhov, now!" whined Seth. "That guy never wrote a real play in his life! He never knew how to write a play! He couldn't have written a play if he tried! He never learned the rules for writing a play!—That *Cherry Orchard* now," whined old Seth with a sour sneering laugh, "—that *Cherry Orchard* that you guys are always raving about! That's not a play!" he cried indignantly. "What ever made you think it was a play? I was trying to read it just the other day," he rasped, "and there's nothing there to hold your interest! It's got no *plot*! There's no story in it! There's no suspense! Nothing happens in it. All you got is a lot of people who do nothing but talk all the time. You never get anywhere," said Seth scornfully. "And yet to hear you guys rave about it, you'd think it was a great play."

"Well, what do you call a great play, then, if *The Cherry Orchard* isn't one?" one of the young men said acidly. "Who wrote the great plays that you talk about?"

"Why George M. Cohan wrote some," whined Seth instantly. "That's who. Avery Hopwood wrote some great plays. We've had plenty of guys in this country who wrote great plays. If they'd come from Russia you'd get down and worship 'em," he said bitterly. "But just because they came out of this country they're no good!"

In the relation of the class towards old Seth Flint, it was possible to see the basic falseness of their relation towards life everywhere around them. For here was a man—whatever his defects as a playwright might have been—who had lived incomparably the richest, most varied and dangerous, and eventful life among them; as he was himself far more interesting than any of the plays they wrote, and as dramatists they should have recognized and understood his quality. But they saw none of this. For their relation towards life and people such as old Seth Flint was not one of understanding. It was not even one of burning indignation—of that indignation which is one of the dynamic forces in the artist's life. It was rather one of supercilious scorn and ridicule.

They felt that they were "above" old Seth, and most of the other people in the world, and for this reason they were in Professor Hatcher's class. Of Seth they said:

"He's really a misfit, terribly out of place here. I wonder why he came."

And they would listen to an account of one of Seth's latest errors in good taste with the expression of astounded disbelief, the tones of stunned incredulity which were coming into fashion about that time among elegant young men.

"Not really! . . . But he never really said *that*. . . . You *can't* mean it."

"Oh, but I assure you, he did!"

". . . It's simply past belief! . . . I can't believe he's as bad as *that*."

"Oh, but he *is*! It's incredible, I know, but you've no idea what he's capable of." And so on.

And yet old Seth Flint was badly needed in that class: his bitter and unvarnished tongue caused Professor Hatcher many painful moments, but it had its use—oh, it had its use, particularly when the play was of this nature:

Irene (*slowly with scorn and contempt in her voice*). So—it has come to this! This is all your love amounts to—a little petty selfish thing! I had thought you were bigger than that, John.

John (*desperately*). But—but, my God, Irene—what am I to think? I found you in bed with him—my best friend! (*with difficulty*). You know—that looks suspicious, to say the least!

Irene (*softly—with amused contempt in her voice*). You poor little man! And to think I thought your love was *so big*.

John (*wildly*). But I do love you, Irene. That's just the point.

Irene (*with passionate scorn*). Love! You don't know what love means! Love is bigger than that! Love is big enough for all things, all people. (*She extends her arms in an all-embracing gesture.*) My love takes in the world—it embraces all mankind! It is glamorous, wild, free as the wind, John.

John (*slowly*). Then you have had other lovers?

Irene: Lovers come, lovers go. (*She makes an impatient gesture.*) What is that? Nothing! Only love endures—my love which is greater than all.

Eugene would writhe in his seat, and clench his hands convulsively. Then he would turn almost prayerfully to the bitter, mummied face of old Seth Flint for that barbed but cleansing vulgarity that always followed such a scene:

"Well?" Professor Hatcher would say, putting down the manuscript he had been reading, taking off his eye-glasses (which were attached to a ribbon of black silk) and looking around with a quizzical smile, an impassive expression on his fine, distinguished face. "Well?" he would say again urbanely, as no one answered. "Is there any comment?"

"What is she?" Seth would break the nervous silence with his rasping snarl. "Another of these society whores? You know," he continued, "you can find plenty of her kind for three dollars a throw without any of that fancy palaver."

Some of the class smiled faintly, painfully, and glanced at each other with slight shrugs of horror; others were grateful, felt pleasure well in them and said underneath their breath exultantly:

"Good old Seth! Good old Seth!"

"Her love is big enough for all things, is it?" said Seth. "I know a truck driver out in Denver I'll match against her any day."

Eugene and Ed Horton, a large and robust aspirant from the Iowa cornlands, roared with happy laughter, poking each other sharply in the ribs.

"Do you think the play will act?" some one said. "It seems to me that it comes pretty close to closet drama."

"If you ask me," said Seth, "it comes pretty close to water-closet drama. . . . No," he said sourly. "What that boy needs is a little experience. He ought to go out and get him a woman and get all this stuff off his mind. After that, he might sit down and write a play."

For a moment there was a very awkward silence, and Professor Hatcher smiled a trifle palely. Then, taking his eyeglasses with a distinguished movement, he looked around and said:

"Is there any other comment?"

1935

S. J. PERELMAN

1935 was an *annus mirabilis* for Clifford Odets. A freshly minted member of the Communist Party, he became the house dramatist of the Group Theatre, a New York actors' collective influenced artistically by the Moscow Art Theatre and politically by the Moscow Presidium. After the success of his pro-union agitprop *Waiting for Lefty*, the Group staged in rapid succession *Till the Day I Die*, *Awake and Sing!*, and *Paradise Lost*, also to plaudits. His ear finely attuned to linguistic vagaries, both written and spoken, Sidney Joseph Perelman (1904–1971) was attracted to Odets' richly associative dialogue. A stint at *New Masses* had made Perelman immune to the leftist politics, but he reveled in Odets' blend of up-to-date slang, movie *marivaudage*, and Yiddishisms, which oddly resembled Perelman's own eclectic style. Whereas the humorist took metaphors literally, the playwright wrapped his rhetoric around bromidic slogans ("The world is supposed to be for us all!"). The following year Odets quit the Party, protesting, "I am a liberal, not a Communist," and signed a Hollywood studio contract; the screenwriter Frank Nugent, after seeing a melodramatic product of this sell-out, asked, "Odets, where is thy sting?" The *mot* was worthy of Perelman. An occasional screenwriter himself, most memorably for the Marx Brothers, he found a comfortable berth at *The New Yorker*, publishing short commentaries and parodies of lapidary brilliance. Of his infrequent theatrical ventures, the most successful were a collaboration with Ogden Nash on the book of the musical *One Touch of Venus* (1943) and a satirical comedy, *The Beauty Part* (1962), which furnished Bert Lahr with fodder for five outrageous caricatures.

Waiting for Santy

A Christmas Playlet
(With a Bow to Mr. Clifford Odets)

SCENE: *The sweatshop of S. Claus, a manufacturer of children's toys, on North Pole Street. Time: The night before Christmas.*
At rise, seven gnomes, Rankin, Panken, Rivkin, Riskin, Ruskin, Briskin, and Praskin, are discovered working furiously

to fill orders piling up at stage right. The whir of lathes, the hum of motors, and the hiss of drying lacquer are so deafening that at times the dialogue cannot be heard, which is very vexing if you vex easily. (Note: The parts of Rankin, Panken, Rivkin, Riskin, Ruskin, Briskin, and Praskin are interchangeable, and may be secured directly from your dealer or the factory.)

RISKIN (*filing a Meccano girder, bitterly*)—A parasite, a leech, a bloodsucker—altogether a five-star nogoodnick! Starvation wages we get so he can ride around in a red team with reindeers!

RUSKIN (*jeering*)—Hey, Karl Marx, whyn'tcha hire a hall?

RISKIN (*sneering*)—Scab! Stool pigeon! Company spy! (*They tangle and rain blows on each other. While waiting for these to dry, each returns to his respective task.*)

BRISKIN (*sadly, to Panken*)—All day long I'm painting "Snow Queen" on these Flexible Flyers and my little Irving lays in a cold tenement with the gout.

PANKEN—You said before it was the mumps.

BRISKIN (*with a fatalistic shrug*)—The mumps—the gout—go argue with City Hall.

PANKEN (*kindly, passing him a bowl*)—Here, take a piece fruit.

BRISKIN (*chewing*)—It ain't bad, for wax fruit.

PANKEN (*with pride*)—I painted it myself.

BRISKIN (*rejecting the fruit*)—Ptoo! Slave psychology!

RIVKIN (*suddenly, half to himself, half to the Party*)—I got a belly full of stars, baby. You make me feel like I swallowed a Roman candle.

PRASKIN (*curiously*)—What's wrong with the kid?

RISKIN—What's wrong with all of us? The system! Two years he and Claus's daughter's been making googoo eyes behind the old man's back.

PRASKIN—So what?

RISKIN (*scornfully*)—So what? Economic determinism! What do you think the kid's name is—J. Pierpont Rivkin? He ain't even got for a bottle Dr. Brown's Celery Tonic. I tell you, it's like gall in my mouth two young people shouldn't have a room where they could make great music.

RANKIN (*warningly*)—Shhh! Here she comes now! (*Stella*

Claus enters, carrying a portable phonograph. She and Rivkin embrace, place a record on the turntable, and begin a very slow waltz, unmindful that the phonograph is playing "Cohen on the Telephone.")

STELLA (*dreamily*)—Love me, sugar?

RIVKIN—I can't sleep, I can't eat, that's how I love you. You're a double malted with two scoops of whipped cream; you're the moon rising over Mosholu Parkway; you're a two weeks' vacation at Camp Nitgedaiget! I'd pull down the Chrysler Building to make a bobbie pin for your hair!

STELLA—I've got a stomach full of anguish. Oh, Rivvy, what'll we do?

PANKEN (*sympathetically*)—Here, try a piece fruit.

RIVKIN (*fiercely*)—Wax fruit—that's been my whole life! Imitations! Substitutes! Well, I'm through! Stella, tonight I'm telling your old man. He can't play mumblety-peg with two human beings! (*The tinkle of sleigh bells is heard offstage, followed by a voice shouting, "Whoa, Dasher! Whoa, Dancer!" A moment later S. Claus enters in a gust of mock snow. He is a pompous bourgeois of sixty-five who affects a white beard and a false air of benevolence. But tonight the ruddy color is missing from his cheeks, his step falters, and he moves heavily. The gnomes hastily replace the marzipan they have been filching.*)

STELLA (*anxiously*)—Papa! What did the specialist say to you?

CLAUS (*brokenly*)—The biggest professor in the country . . . the best cardiac man that money could buy. . . . I tell you I was like a wild man.

STELLA—Pull yourself together, Sam!

CLAUS—It's no use. Adhesions, diabetes, sleeping sickness, decalcomania—oh, my God! I got to cut out climbing in chimneys, he says—me, Sanford Claus, the biggest toy concern in the world!

STELLA (*soothingly*)—After all, it's only one man's opinion.

CLAUS—No, no, he cooked my goose. I'm like a broken uke after a Yosian picnic. Rivkin!

RIVKIN—Yes, Sam.

CLAUS—My boy, I had my eye on you for a long time. You and Stella thought you were too foxy for an old man, didn't you? Well, let bygones be bygones. Stella, do you love this gnome?

STELLA (*simply*)—He's the whole stage show at the Music Hall, Papa; he's Toscanini conducting Beethoven's Fifth; he's—

CLAUS (*curtly*)—Enough already. Take him. From now on he's a partner in the firm. (*As all exclaim, Claus holds up his hand for silence.*) And tonight he can take my route and make the deliveries. It's the least I could do for my own flesh and blood. (*As the happy couple kiss, Claus wipes away a suspicious moisture and turns to the other gnomes.*) Boys, do you know what day tomorrow is?

GNOMES (*crowding around expectantly*)—Christmas!

CLAUS—Correct. When you look in your envelopes tonight, you'll find a little present from me—a forty-percent pay cut. And the first one who opens his trap—gets this. (*As he holds up a tear-gas bomb and beams at them, the gnomes utter cries of joy, join hands, and dance around him shouting exultantly. All except Riskin and Briskin, that is, who exchange a quick glance and go underground.*)

CURTAIN

1936

BROOKS ATKINSON

"I tried to be on the level," was how Brooks Atkinson (1894–1984) summed up his career as theatre critic for *The New York Times* when he retired in 1960. To achieve this, from the time he took the job in 1926, he maintained as few personal relations with theatre people as possible. Unlike his predecessor Stark Young, he did not find the daily grind of reviewing uncongenial, but felt obliged to absent himself from it on occasion. During World War II, he spent two years as a correspondent in the Far East and won a Pulitzer Prize for his reporting from Moscow in 1945. Atkinson brought to his theatre writing a reporter's ability to sum up briskly and to maintain a show of objectivity. During a performance he would pencil notes on a yellow pad and in the hour following the final curtain send in his copy in one-paragraph increments that were rarely altered in proof. Given this rapidity, his judgments were surprisingly astute: he welcomed the first efforts of Wilder, Miller, Williams, and Beckett. Nor was he unwilling to revisit an opinion, reversing his initially unfavorable verdict on the cynical musical *Pal Joey*. Even so, it was during Atkinson's tenure that the legend began that a bad notice in the *Times* could sound the death knell of a show on Broadway.

Our Town

ALTHOUGH Thornton Wilder is celebrated chiefly for his fiction, it will be necessary now to reckon with him as a dramatist. His "Our Town," which opened at Henry Miller's last evening, is a beautifully evocative play. Taking as his material three periods in the history of a placid New Hampshire town, Mr. Wilder has transmuted the simple events of human life into universal reverie. He has given familiar facts a deeply moving, philosophical perspective. Staged without scenery and with the curtain always up, "Our Town" has escaped from the formal barrier of the modern theatre into the quintessence of acting, thought and speculation. In the staging, Jed Harris has appreciated the rare quality of Mr. Wilder's handiwork and illuminated it with a shining performance. "Our Town" is, in this column's opinion, one of the finest achievements of the current stage.

Since the form is strange, this review must attempt to explain the purpose of the play. It is as though Mr. Wilder were saying: "Now for evidence as to the way Americans were living in the early part of the century, take Grover Corners, N.H., as an average town. Mark it 'Exhibit A' in American folkways." His spokesman in New Hampshire cosmology is Frank Craven, the best pipe and pants-pocket actor in the business, who experimentally sets the stage with tables and chairs before the house lights go down and then prefaces the performance with a few general remarks about Grover Corners. Under his benign guidance we see three periods in career of one generation of Grover Corners folks—"Life," "Love" and "Death."

Literally, they are not important. On one side of an imaginary street Dr. Gibbs and his family are attending to their humdrum affairs with relish and probity. On the opposite side Mr. Webb, the local editor, and his family are fulfilling their quiet destiny. Dr. Gibbs's boy falls in love with Mr. Webb's girl —neighbors since birth. They marry after graduating from high school; she dies several years later in childbirth and she is buried on Cemetery Hill. Nothing happens in the play that is not normal and natural and ordinary.

But by stripping the play of everything that is not essential, Mr. Wilder has given it a profound, strange, unworldly significance. This is less the portrait of a town than the sublimation of the commonplace; and in contrast with the universe that silently swims around it, it is brimming over with compassion. Most of it is a tender idyll in the kindly economy of Mr. Wilder's literary style; some of it is heartbreaking in the mute simplicity of human tragedy. For in the last act, which is entitled "Death," Mr. Wilder shows the dead of Grover Corners sitting peacefully in their graves and receiving into their quiet company a neighbor's girl whom they love. So Mr. Wilder's pathetically humble evidence of human living passes into the wise beyond. Grover Corners is a green corner of the universe.

With about the best script of his career in his hands, Mr. Harris has risen nobly to the occasion. He has reduced theatre to its lowest common denominator without resort to perverse showmanship. As chorus, preacher, drug store proprietor and finally as shepherd of the flock, Frank Craven plays with great sincerity and understanding, keeping the sublime well inside his homespun style. As the boy and girl, John Craven, who is Frank Craven's son, and Martha Scott turn youth into tremulous idealization, some of their scenes are lovely past all enduring. Jay Fassett as Dr. Gibbs, Evelyn Varden as his wife, Thomas W. Ross and Helen Carew as the Webbs play with an honesty that is enriching. There are many other good bits of acting.

Out of respect for the detached tone of Mr. Wilder's script the performance as a whole is subdued and understated. The scale is so large that the voices are never lifted. But under the leisurely monotone of the production there is a fragment of the immortal truth. "Our Town" is a microcosm. It is also a hauntingly beautiful play.

1938

Standards in Drama Criticism

*Mrs. Roosevelt's Dissatisfaction With the Comments
on the Stage in This Newspaper and One Other*

As a dutiful New Dealer it is my custom to read Mrs. Roosevelt's column every evening. It sustains me; it gives me strength for the morrow. Particularly during the Winter months, when there is much work to do, it is refreshing to follow the mistress of the New Deal as she brightly scampers around the country—delivering a few words of encouragement here, nurturing a groping talent there or bravely discussing the illnesses of the grandchildren in the White House. Kindly and amiable, she listens to the growing pains of the country as though it were an adolescent boy to be cherished and guided to better things. Although he backslides occasionally, her patience is inexhaustible. During the daytime the politics and economics of the New Deal make the hair stand on end, but come evening, Mrs. Roosevelt is there in the paper to soothe the tired head. No country ever had a sweeter mother.

It was a shock, therefore, to find that Mrs. Roosevelt was cross the other day. More shocking than that: she was cross with me. After attending the opening night performance of Katharine (not Katherine) Dayton's "Save Me the Waltz" she was annoyed by the reviews in THE TIMES and The Herald Tribune, which, she says, "seem to infer that because this play does not teach a great lesson or pick any particular people to pieces it is worthless as a play." In spite of the churlish comments in THE TIMES and Herald Tribune, Mrs. Roosevelt was under the impression that she had had a pleasant evening before Miss Dayton's hackneyed hokum—which, incidentally, closed after one week of suicidal business. In fact, she had liked it more than "Our Town," which moved her and depressed her "beyond words." " 'Our Town,' " she says, "is more interesting and more original and I am glad I saw it, but I did not have a pleasant evening." Whereupon she outlines the New Deal program in drama criticism—

Sometimes we need a pleasant evening, so why must we have all our plays in the same vein? Why can't the critics have standards for different types of plays and give us an idea of the kind of evening we may have if we want to go to this play or that? Usually I want to be amused; then again I want to be stirred. But it is rather rare that you can find out what kind of play you are going to see by reading any of the criticisms.

Well, some people can. By sitting in one place long enough to get to the bottom of the column, they can find out a good many things about what is going on in the theatre. On the evenings when they do not want to be stirred they can find out that "Pins and Needles" is a gay, satirical revue, which is amusing, as Mrs. Roosevelt knows, for she has recently sealed it with the cachet of the White House; that Ed Wynn is the funniest man in New York, and by that sign amusing, and that "The Shoemakers' Holiday" is groaning with Elizabethan buffoonery, which is an amusing thing to encounter during a night on the town. For there are already viable standards of criticism, one of the chief ones being that it is not cricket to cry up the merits of a mediocre romance, like "Save Me the Waltz," by saying that a serious and notable work of imaginative art, like "Our Town," is depressing "beyond words."

And according to the standards of criticism that were written into the NRA code of the Critics Circle and are commonly accepted as equitable, even a second-rate work of art that throws some illumination on life ranks higher than a joint-piece that is produced solely for an evening's diversion. By the further use of logic, a second-rate joint-piece is scarcely worth anybody's while, since amusement is its only purpose and it is not amusing. Fortunately, the relations between the White House and Times Square are not hopelessly strained. In a second column, which concludes her current survey of Broadway, Mrs. Roosevelt says a word in appreciation of "Shadow and Substance," which is "whimsical and charming"; of "On Borrowed Time," which is "whimsical" and ends on a "happy note"; and she endorses ". . . one-third of a nation . . ." (not "A Third of the Nation") with the reservation that "private capital might carry its share of the housing burden," which is correct New Deal practice. Although "Shadow and Substance" is offered as rebellious thought, "On Borrowed Time" as guileless amusement and ". . . one-third of a nation . . ." as aggressive education, the editor of "My Day" responds impartially to their varying motives and gives credit impartially for individual merit, which is sound drama criticism in any administration.

What worries me, however, is the effect "Our Town" had on the busy wife of our leader. Although she was moved, she was depressed; although Mr. Wilder's play was original, it was unpleasant. According to Broadway's way of thinking, that is not giving a good notice to one of the finest dramas written in the last decade. I fear that Mrs. Roosevelt has done less than justice to a distinguished work of art, and precisely that is the sort of thing that gives critics the nightmare. If there is anything sacred in the theatre, it is an occasional statement of the truth amid the hubbub of the street. In the midst of Broadway's usual brummagem a genuine coin is discovered; that is time for rejoicing. "Our Town" is certainly moving; in fact, it is profoundly moving. By dispensing with all the realistic paraphernalia and bric-a-brac of the theatre, Mr. Wilder has looked

straight into the heart of an American village, and with the affection of a philosopher he offers evidence of living, loving
and dying, which are the imperishable truths of human existence. It is an idealized portrait. His characters are the salt of
the earth. His love for them is overflowing with compassion.
Far from being depressed, I came away from the theatre exalted by the bravery, kindliness and goodness of American
people. In the deepest sense of the word, "Our Town" is a religious play.

And that is the chief reason why the casual comments in
"My Day" disturbed me last week. As columnists we all work
under one grave disadvantage: we write too much and too rapidly. We do not reserve enough time for private thinking. But
a work of art, which helps to illuminate life, deserves the most
humble devotion we can bring to it. It is the richest source of
the more abundant life. As a dutiful New Dealer I like to see
the White House back of it to the last typewriter in the family.

1938

MORTON EUSTIS

In the 1920s, no one saw a conflict of interest in writing for the theatre while writing about it. George S. Kaufman worked on the drama desk of the New York *Tribune* and was dramatic editor of *The New York Times* at the same time that he was establishing himself as a comic dramatist with an uncanny skill at getting laughs. He invariably worked with a collaborator—Ring Lardner, Marc Connelly, Edna Ferber and, most successfully, Moss Hart—with Kaufman contributing the one-liners and surefire climaxes. Kaufman usually staged the plays himself, reshaping moments to deliver the greatest punch. Depression audiences welcomed the political satire of *Of Thee I Sing* (with Hart and George and Ira Gershwin, 1931), the first musical to win a Pulitzer Prize, and *You Can't Take It with You* (with Hart, 1936), a paean to taking life easy. *The Man Who Came to Dinner* (1939) was meant as topical fooling, with characters based on Alexander Woollcott, Noël Coward, and Harpo Marx; yet it has remained a perennial favorite. A valuable account of Kaufman molding the play was provided by Morton Eustis (1905–1944). A newspaperman from an old Virginia family, who grew up on a historic estate in Loudon County, Eustis joined the editorial staff of *Theatre Arts Monthly* in 1933. His series on the actor's work on his part, on the director, and on the business of theatre helped to promote it from a coterie journal to a widely read organ of opinion. In 1941, he left to serve in the army and was killed in August 1944 in Normandy where he was serving with the 2d Armored Division.

The Man Who Came to Dinner
With George Kaufman Directing

'ALL right, Mr. Kaufman?' the stage manager asks. . . . 'Yes, any time you're ready.' . . . George S. Kaufman has a whispered colloquy with Monty Woolley. He stands centre stage surveying the green living-room-hall in Mesalia, Ohio, which Donald Oenslager has designed for *The Man Who Came to Dinner*. He marks the spot where he wants Woolley's wheelchair to rest, opens and closes the big doors leading to the library on the left to see that they slide smoothly, and rubs the

445

edge of the stair bannisters in the centre to see that they are smooth enough for someone to slide down. Then he walks down the ramp which connects stage and auditorium during rehearsals and flops in an orchestra seat with his legs dangling over two of the chairs.

The scene is the Music Box Theatre. The time, 2 P.M., one Tuesday afternoon eight days after the Kaufman-Hart comedy has been in rehearsal. The first four days were passed sitting around a table, reading. Today a run-through of the entire play is to be attempted. Although the actors are still fumbling for their lines, none of them carry their 'sides', except Monty Woolley, who, in the Woollcottian role of Sheridan White-side—litterateur, lecturer, radio commentator, 'intimate friend of the great and near-great'—has a part which is almost as long as Hamlet's.

It is a little unusual in theatre practice to have the set in place so early. But Kaufman is such a stickler for assurance in detail that, when the play is not an elaborate, many-scened affair, he likes his actors to get the feel of the set as soon as they walk on in their parts. The stage manager sits at a prompt table on the right. A brilliant work-light hangs centre stage il-luminating the set and the dark and empty theatre in a garish manner.

'On stage for the end of the third act,' the stage manager calls out. Kaufman, a script in his hand, walks up the aisle to talk with his collaborator, Moss Hart. 'You may be right,' he says, 'but let's run through it this way and see how it plays.'

To see a play backwards—the final curtain first, then the last act, then the second and the first—is a curious and somewhat frightening experience to anyone who has ever tried to write a play. It shows—at any rate, this farce-comedy shows—that a play can be put together so that each scene is not only self-explanatory but a revelation of what has gone before. The last act of *The Man Who Came to Dinner* is just as funny, and just as clear, even if you have not seen the acts which preceded it and have but the haziest advance notion of what the play is about. Kaufman, in all the rehearsals of the show except the complete run-throughs, starts with the last act and works backward. Whether he does this deliberately because he thinks that it is one way to catch the dead spots—that each act, in other

words, should be able to stand on its own feet as an entity—
this writer cannot tell. But to see a backward run of a play that
is as expertly constructed as the present Kaufman-Hart script is
an object lesson in what William Archer calls 'playmaking'.

'All right, ready.' They start to run through the scene in
which Sheridan Whiteside takes his sarcastic leave of the Middle Western family on whom he has imposed himself for over a
month. Kaufman slumps in a seat next to Hart as the action
commences.

Whiteside, the bewhiskered 'Big Lord Fauntleroy', as his
secretary calls him in a moment of anger, bids farewell, in his
graciously ungracious style, to his long suffering host and
starts to make his exit.

'Merry Christmas, everybody,' he says as his parting thrust,
puts his hat on with a flourish and walks out of the house.

'Wait a minute,' Kaufman says. 'The gesture with the hat is
fine, Monty, but make it after the line. You'll hold the line that
way and sustain it.' The exit is repeated and Kaufman proves to
be right. The 'Merry Christmas' is funny in itself—after all that
has occurred—and the gesture holds and builds the laugh.

'Now let's get this sound right,' says Kaufman, as he ambles
up on stage and walks over to the stage manager's desk. Whiteside, in leaving the house, is supposed to slip on the icy stoop,
emitting a loud groan. 'I want to try dropping a sand bag for
the first sound. Then your groan, Monty, must be a long, agonized wail.' . . . 'How's this?' says Woolley, moaning eloquently. 'A little too sharp, I think,' Kaufman tells him. 'But
try it once.'

'Merry Christmas, everybody,' Woolley flourishes his hat
and goes out. A thud is heard, then Woolley's anguished
groan. 'No, Monty,' Kaufman calls out, 'I get the feeling that
you're standing right outside. Remember, the door is shut! All
right, now key it down a little—*there*, that's just right.'

They run through this exit several times as Kaufman stands
watching it, his long arms dangling loosely by his side, his
shock of black hair standing up in disarray.

Kaufman, the director, is the complete antithesis of Kaufman, the playwright. The pungent, volatile drive, the sheer
exuberance and vitality that illuminates almost every Kaufman

script, is completely lacking in Kaufman, the man. He is not, like Noel Coward, a whole show in himself at rehearsals. He is quiet, unobtrusive; he never raises his voice, even at the most exasperating moments; he is kindly, sympathetic, quizzical. There is nothing of the human dynamo hammering the beat of a speedy, perfectly timed charade. On the other hand, he gives almost immediately the impression that the jobs of playwriting and directing are two parts of the same thing; that gesture, and the movement of the actors, singly and together, are as much a part of the play as the words. This accounts for the way he rewrites as he goes along, shifting a phrase, a line, sometimes a whole speech to suit the tempo and the rhythm of movement he wants to secure. He is nothing if not thorough. And as you see him standing, his head tilted a little to one side, his forefinger cocked or in the corner of his mouth, listening to the sound of a play that will be as quickly paced as any in New York, you realize that his genius for direction lies as much in the infinite capacity for taking pains as in a natural theatre flair.

The new Kaufman-Hart opus is a kind of *You Can't Take It With You*, Algonquin style. Kaufman and Hart strand their Woollcottian prototype in Mesalia, Ohio, while on a lecture tour. The portly, quixotic 'road company Nero', as he describes himself in one bashful moment, breaks his hip (or is supposed to) when he slips on the ice on the doorstep of Mr. and Mrs. Ernest Stanley's home and he is obliged to spend a month in a wheel-chair in their house. He disrupts completely the life of every one in the establishment. He takes charge, arrogantly, of the living quarters; relegates the Stanleys to the service entrance; sends their children away from home and generally makes an alluring beast of himself. The thread of the play is hung on his thoroughly outrageous attempt to thwart his secretary's desire to marry a young reporter from the local gazette—an attempt which involves the kidnapping of an English actress he lures to Mesalia to entrap the young reporter. Like a good opus, it ends on the key in which it started—an exit and a fall on the ice.

'Hold it, Monty,' Kaufman calls out, 'I want to fill in here with a few little lines before you come in.' Whiteside's groan, on his final curtain fall, brings all the family and servants rushing into the room, down the stairs and from the doors to the left. After a moment's thought, as he scratches the edge of his steel-rimmed glasses, Kaufman gets the line he wants Whiteside's secretary to say: '"Bert, something's happened to Mr. Whiteside"—No, I beg your pardon. Bert's got to run out. I forgot. Turn to the doctor and say "Doctor—doctor". On that, you people run downstairs (the son and daughter and Mrs. Stanley). Not too highly keyed, please, you people on the stairs—*You* say (to the son) "What's the matter? What's wrong!"—You (to the girl) "Has something happened? What is it?"—You (to the mother) "What's the matter? What's the matter, Barbara!" . . . All right, try it.'

They run through it. 'Now a little faster,' Kaufman requests. 'You needn't wait for dead cues on this. You can overlap them. . . . "What's the matter? What's the matter?" sounds wrong. Let's see. Change that to "Oh dear! Oh dear!"'

Kaufman watches with Hart as they work out this scene. 'The group on the stairs a little stronger vocally, please,' he calls out. 'And Doctor, your entrance is too casual. You've got to come in with a good deal of eagerness.'

Back on stage he spends five minutes working out the cues with the stage manager so that each sound and movement is timed to create the right effect. The scene is played again and again. Whiteside is carried in for the final curtain, shouting for his nurse—whom he detested—and promising that he will sue the Stanley family for $350,000.

'We'll have to wait until we get this before an audience, Monty,' Kaufman says to Woolley, 'to see whether your line "I want Miss Preen, Miss Preen!" (the nurse) gets such a laugh that it will drown out the next one, or whether we can get the laugh and then build it again on "$350,000".'

'All right, let's try the third act from the beginning of the kidnap.' This is (or was) the scene in which a Harpo Marx character, named Banjo, and a crazy surrealist painter, named Miguel Santos, save the day for Whiteside by kidnapping the actress (played by Carol Goodner, the English actress). This is worked out very slowly, to get the mechanics of it exact. Binding the girl's legs and arms, and gagging her, require considerable routine work. Woolley also has a fast and continuous speech at this point and it is essential to have the kidnapping take no longer than Woolley's lines.

'All right, let's do this routine again,' Kaufman says, 'and time it.' It takes exactly twenty-seven seconds. 'We'll allow thirty seconds,' Kaufman says, 'in case of a slip.' They play it through again, first with the business alone, then with the lines. Kaufman calls: 'Put it together a few times, business and lines.' And he adds: 'Maybe in about two days, after this is better set, I'll fill it in a little more, but let's let it go as it is, now.'

Kaufman comes down into the house and has a long talk with Hart. Then he asks the stage manager to run through the third act.

Whiteside, looking intently at the picture of Mr. Stanley's sister, suddenly discovers that she is none other than Lizzie Borden, or as the dramatists choose to call her, Harriet Sedley. He looks at the picture, registers recognition, but that is all. Hart stands up. 'I think we've got to build this, George,' he tells Kaufman. 'I'd like to have him snap his fingers as he looks at the picture—and I'd even go so far as to have him say: "I knew I'd seen that face before." . . . You've got to let the audience realize the significance of what he's discovered and I don't think the facial expression is enough.'

Kaufman is a little uncertain. 'It may be too obvious,' he says, 'but O.K., let's try it.' Woolley does try it and it is much better. The slight confusion that was evident before is gone.

'I'd like you to run through the second act, Bernie,' Kaufman tells the stage manager. 'Then we'll try one little change.' And he and Hart retire to Sam Harris' office in the mezzanine to do some rewriting.

The second act runs fairly smoothly and without interruption, as its mentors are not present. There is a definite dead spot, however, in the middle where the Stanley son and daughter ask Whiteside to help them in their troubles. The son wants to become a professional photographer, 'but Dad won't hear of it'. The daughter has fallen in love with a young labor organizer and 'Dad won't hear of that' either. Each asks Whiteside's help, and of course he gives it, advising them to do exactly what their parents think they should not do. The two short scenes are nicely written. The son gives quite an eloquent speech, but somehow the interest lags the moment they start their pleas.

The run-through completed—to the tune of a typewriter pounding busily upstairs—Kaufman and Hart make their appearance with the new material. The sheets of paper are passed out to the company, Kaufman sits down on the sofa and asks them to read through the new scene, which is, needless to say, the dead spot of the second act. What Kaufman and Hart have done is quite simple. They have transposed, rearranged and cut the scene severely, giving to Whiteside the burden of the lines which the son and daughter formerly spoke. The net result is to keep Whiteside in the dominant position. He is now the one who suggests that the son should leave his family and follow his own bent; he is the one to tell the daughter that she must run away with her boyfriend. Even in a reading, the scene picks up. The sympathy of the audience is enlisted just as strongly on behalf of the children, but the fact that Whiteside, the supreme meddler, is the *deus ex machina* of the occasion, gives it a point and a breadth of humor lacking before.

'That's better, don't you think?' Kaufman says to the writer, as he strolls up the aisle. 'An audience always listens more to a lead than to a juvenile, and I think the shift has pulled up the scene. It's amazing, you know,' he says as he sits down. 'You think you have a script just as tight as possible. Then you get it on the stage and dead chunks appear all through it. When you get it in front of an audience, a whole new set of dead spots turn up. And three weeks after the New York opening you still find places you can cut.'

This, from a man of Kaufman's experience both as a playwright and a director, should be more than illuminating to young and earnest playwrights who feel that a script is an inviolable thing which cannot be desecrated by the change of even a word or a semi-colon. If anyone in our theatre should be able to write a 'tight' script, it is George Kaufman and Moss Hart. And yet you see these two glittering dramatic jitterbugs rewriting whole scenes, filling in others, and cutting, cutting, cutting all along the line.

You see them also writing almost as they go along, taking a

well-rounded script, not a skeleton by any means, and giving it a three-dimensional quality in terms of the complex medium in which it is expressed. Kaufman's method as a director is utterly different from that of Noel Coward or the Lunts, all three of whom are more dynamic in their approach than he is. Yet Kaufman, in his own way, produces a dynamic effect as well as anyone in our theatre. And he can mold a rollicking script like *The Man Who Came to Dinner* just as well as a sombre play like *Of Mice and Men*, and with equal variety.

'All right! Stand by for a complete run-through this time.'

'Four props came today, and one was right,' Kaufman tells Hart with a wry smile two days later, but he does not let this disturb his equanimity. He paces up and down, in front of the orchestra pit, as the company runs through the play—backwards again. Now he is concentrating upon cueing the action to the word, upon the thousand and one details that an audience is never aware of. Fully ten minutes is spent gauging the exact moment at which the slam of a door should be heard at a certain exit. All the spots where the props may hold up the action are studiously worked over. The opening of a package, for instance, is timed so that the actual work of undoing the string is at a minimum. One realizes as never before how important little details are; how the opening of a letter, say, can slow up the whole action of a play unless someone is given a line to fill in the pause.

'Keep perfectly serious,' Kaufman adjures the doctor, who enters disguised as Santa Claus. 'The moment you smile, the moment *you* think you're funny, it's gone!' . . . 'In the line "four telephones crying", don't lose the word "crying",' he tells the actor impersonating Banjo. 'You've got to heighten "crying", or you get the laugh on "telephones".'

He and Woolley work out little details of the characterization. Woolley will tell him, for example: 'I think I would be delighted, George, when she says that.' Kaufman agrees and suggests a way to register that delight. He rarely plays out a part for the actor, though sometimes he will illustrate a bit of business. He works mostly by a kind of suggestion; an encouragement of the actor's own feeling.

'That line is killed by having the radio men come in,' John

Hoysradt (the Beverly Carlton–Noel Coward of the play) tells Kaufman, which is quite true. So Kaufman has the men come in a beat later after the laugh is registered. But if an actor sees a line or a situation in a way that is out of key with the idea, Kaufman will tell him at once that that is not the way he wants the speech read, or the gesture made, and will explain his reasons.

One of the radio men has to enter a little later, to plug a cord into a light socket. 'Wait a minute,' Kaufman calls, after the actor has made his exit, 'I think we can get a laugh on that if you come in in a perfectly matter-of-fact manner, plug in, and then suddenly notice Miss Goodner standing there and retire in astonishment and confusion.' The actor tries it, looks up with a 'My-God-what's-this!' expression at the actress, turns quickly to run out and just before he exits casts another amazed glance over his shoulders at the siren. 'That's fine,' Kaufman says, 'particularly that last look.' And the point is proved emphatically at the first showing before an audience when the business gets a loud, spontaneous laugh—a perfect illustration of how a dull but essential bit of business can be transformed into a living part of the play by astute direction.

'Monty, I can't quite tell whether you're unsure of the lines or it's part of the characterization,' Kaufman says to Woolley after a run through of the first scene. 'That's bad.' Woolley *is* unsure of the lines, as is evidenced by his performance a few days later. His part is extremely difficult; he is on stage, seated in a wheel-chair, almost all the time, and he must dominate the scene even when he is not talking. Any actor knows how hard it is to get variety into a performance when he cannot move about the stage. And it is not until the lines and business are completely set that Woolley is able to incorporate the expressions and subtle gestures which enable him to dominate the show in eloquent fashion.

'If that's a laugh, take the door slam after the laugh,' Kaufman says to the stage manager, as he paces up and down, his right forefinger in the corner of his mouth.

He has an uncanny sense of rhythm—this playwright-director —even when he appears to be paying no attention to the goings-on. And he can tell instantly if, by accident, an actor inserts a word into his lines. His sense of timing is so acute that it may lead him, occasionally, to overlook details of characterization, providing only the time clock is clicking as he wants it to. People who have worked with him claim that sometimes he lets his ear control his mind. But there is only one scene in this play where there is evidence of that—a scene which, to these eyes, is badly overplayed by one of the actors, but which does not appear to bother Kaufman—perhaps because he knows that it is bad and that it can easily be remedied before the opening.

'Monty, when you say: "Two years ago I was in a diving suit with William Beebe, but she got me"' (*she* referring to Gertrude Stein who always calls up Whiteside on Christmas Eve to let him hear the bells of Notre Dame), 'Don't break the line on "Beebe". The laugh will come then, and kill it. The really funny part is not that you were in the diving suit, but that she got you by telephone there.'

Woolley has a line that he cannot remember. Every time he tries it, he loses it. It is simple enough, something to the effect: 'What kind of skullduggery have you been up to?' The line follows one in which he promises to give an iron toothpick as a wedding present to an English Lord whose teeth, he says, always remind him of Roquefort cheese. 'Think from the teeth to the skull and you'll get it,' Kaufman suggests—and Woolley does.

So it goes, day in, day out, for three weeks; heightening here, keying it down there, building it up, tearing it down, and cutting, cutting, cutting. Once the play opens before an audience it will have to be retimed, reset, because as Kaufman says, 'you can never be sure where the laugh will come,' and a long laugh requires re-spacing and lengthening of all the business that surrounds the words. For although the action of a comedy must never seem to stop to give the audience a chance to catch up, it must, in practice, take account of laughter or applause. The first dress rehearsal before an invited audience was almost wrecked by the prolonged laughter that greeted Monty Woolley's first speech and by the unexpected (though not unwarranted) applause that followed his 'Merry Christmas' exit. But Kaufman's imagination went to work at once to fill, with new business, the gaps which seemed to hold the play suspended.

'Dress parade at 8 P.M., please,' the stage manager calls out. 'Yes. Everyone except the choir boys,' Kaufman says, strolling up on stage. 'Oh, and Bernie, ask the three men who carry in the totem pole to come half an hour earlier; I want them to get the movements exactly; when they're set, we'll see whether we need to fill in there with any extra dialogue.'

Note from Hartford, after the out-of-town opening: 'You may want to make some slight changes in the article to fit changes that we are making in the play. We are re-writing Act Three, eliminating the character of the surrealist, who turned out not to be funny. The kidnapping remains but will be managed differently. The lady will not be tied up. Instead of a totem pole, the final gift will be a mummy case, and Miss Goodner will be carried out in it. . . . That's all—to date.'

G. S. K.

1939

HALLIE FLANAGAN

Hallie Flanagan (née Ferguson, 1889–1969) began to teach at Vassar College in 1925 and infused the Experimental Theatre she founded with ideas imbibed in Professor Baker's 47 Workshop at Harvard and from a Guggenheim-subsidized trip to Europe. German expressionism, Russian constructivism, the movement theories of Dalcroze and Duncan, the doctrines of Stanislavsky and Gordon Craig were fearlessly tried out on Flanagan's students. When, at the height of the Depression, President Roosevelt's Works Progress Administration appropriated six million dollars for a Federal Theatre Project, Flanagan was appointed to head it. Besides providing relief for unemployed theatre workers, Flanagan proclaimed that the Theatre's one necessity would be "that it help reshape American life." She hoped to offer plays that would "depict the struggle of many different kinds of people to understand the natural, social and economic forces around them and to achieve through these forces a better life for the people." From the start she and the Theatre were attacked as communist, but their artistic success was uncontestable. No touring was allowed so theatre could be cultivated within local communities; living newspaper techniques, children's theatre, puppetry, plays in the languages of immigrants aided in bringing a high level of professionalism to segments of the American public for whom theatre had been a dead letter. These successes increased the virulence of the political attacks, leading to Flanagan's summons before the House Un-American Activities Committee (described in the following excerpt from her autobiography *Arena*) and the eventual liquidation of the Federal Theatre Project by Congress in June 1939. Flanagan spent the rest of her career as chair of the theatre department of Smith College.

FROM
Arena

BEFORE me stretched two long tables in the form of a huge T. At the foot was the witness chair, at the head the members of the Committee. At long tables on either side of the T were reporters, stenographers, cameramen. The room itself, a high-walled chamber with great chandeliers, was lined with exhibits of material from the Federal Theatre and the Writers' Project; but all I could see for a moment were the faces of thousands of Federal Theatre people; clowns in the circus . . . telephone girls at the switchboards . . . actors in grubby rehearsal rooms . . . acrobats limbering up their routines . . . costume women busy making cheap stuff look expensive . . . musicians composing scores to bring out the best in our often oddly assembled orchestras . . . playwrights working on scripts with the skills of our actors in mind . . . carpenters, prop men, ushers. These were the people on trial that morning.

I was sworn in as a witness by Chairman Dies, a rangy Texan with a cowboy drawl and a big black cigar. I wanted to talk about Federal Theatre, but the Committee apparently did not. Who had appointed me? Harry Hopkins. Was that his own idea or did somebody put him up to it? I said I had no knowledge of any recommendations made in my behalf; I said that while the Committee had recently been investigating un-American activity, I had been engaged for four years in combating un-American inactivity. The distinction was lost on the Committee. I sketched the project's concern for the human values, the return of over 2,000* of our people to jobs in private industry, but the Committee was not interested in any discussion of the project. Wasn't it true I taught at Vassar? Yes. Went to Russia? Yes. Wrote a book about it? Yes. Praised the Russian theatre? In 1926 I had been appointed as a fellow of the Guggenheim Foundation to study the theatre in twelve European countries over a period of fourteen months; Russia was one of the countries in which I carried on such observations. What was it I found so exciting in the Russian theatre? It was at that time an interesting theatre about which little was known. It was my job at that time to study it. That, I pointed out, was twelve years ago. It was part of the background of my profession—the American theatre. The Committee was giving more time to the discussion of the Russian theatre than Federal Theatre had in the four years of its existence.

Mr. Starnes was curious about my visits to Russia. Had I

---

*When I spoke before the Sirovich Committee the number returned to private industry totaled 1,500. At the time the project ended the figure was 2,660.

gone there in 1931 as well as in 1926? Yes, for three weeks. Was I a delegate to anything? No, I had gone, as had many American theatre producers, to see the Russian theatre festival. Did I meet at the festival there any of the people later employed in the Federal Theatre? Certainly not.

Hadn't I written plays in Russian and produced them in Russia? I had not (I remembered my struggles to learn to order a meal or buy galoshes in Russian).

Then back to the project. Had communistic propaganda been circulated on the project? Not to my knowledge. Were there orders on my part against such activity? Yes, stringent orders which appear in the brief. Mr. Starnes took a different tack: Did I consider the theatre a weapon? I said the theatre could be all things to all men. "Do you see this?" Congressman Starnes suddenly shouted, waving a yellow magazine aloft. "Ever see it before?" I said it seemed to be an old *Theatre Arts Monthly*. This described a meeting of workers' theatres in New York in 1931. Hadn't I been active in setting them up? No. I had never been connected in any way with workers' theatres. I wrote a report on such theatres for *Theatre Arts Monthly* under the title "A Theatre Is Born." This theatre, however, was not born through me; I was simply a reporter.

How about these plays that had been criticized by witnesses before the Committee? Were they propaganda? For communism? "To the best of my knowledge," I told the Committee, "we have never done a play which was propaganda for communism; but we have done plays which were propaganda for democracy, for better housing. . . ."

How many people had we played to so far? Twenty-five million people, a fifth of the population. Where did our audience come from? Was it true that we "couldn't get any audiences for anything except communist plays"? No. The list submitted would show our wide audience support. Back to the article, "A Theatre Is Born," and the phrase where I had described the enthusiasm of these theatres as having "a certain Marlowesque madness."

"You are quoting from this Marlowe," observed Mr. Starnes. "Is he a Communist?"

The room rocked with laughter, but I did not laugh. Eight thousand people might lose their jobs because a Congressional

Committee had so pre-judged us that even the classics were "communistic." I said, "I was quoting from Christopher Marlowe."

"Tell us who Marlowe is, so we can get the proper references, because that is all we want to do."

"Put in the record that he was the greatest dramatist in the period of Shakespeare, immediately preceding Shakespeare."

Mr. Starnes subsided; Mr. Thomas of New Jersey took over. How about this play, *The Revolt of the Beavers?* Didn't Brooks Atkinson of the *New York Times* disapprove of the play? Yes, he did. But Mr. Hearst's *New York American* thought it a "pleasing fantasy for children," and an audience survey by trained psychologists brought only favorable reactions from children such as "teaches us never to be selfish"—"it is better to be good than bad"—"how the children would want the whole world to be nine years old and happy."

Was it true that we had been rehearsing *Sing for Your Supper*, the musical in New York, for thirteen months? It was true and the delays were not of our choosing. We kept losing our best skits and our best actors to private industry. Was that, I asked, un-American? Mr. Mosier brought us back to the question of propaganda. Had we ever produced any anti-fascist plays? Some people claimed that Shaw's *On the Rocks* was anti-fascist and others thought it was anti-communist; Shakespeare's *Coriolanus* caused the same discussion.

"We never do a play because it holds any political bias," I declared. "We do a play because we believe it is a good play, a strong play, properly handled, with native material."

Was it true that Earl Browder appeared as a character in *Triple-A Plowed Under?* Yes. Did he expound his theory of communism? He did not; he appeared as a shadow on a screen along with Al Smith, Senator Hastings, and Thomas Jefferson. Had we ever produced plays that were anti-religious? On the contrary, we had produced more religious plays than any other theatre organization in the history of the country. Was I in sympathy with communistic doctrines? I said:

"I am an American and I believe in American democracy. I believe the Works Progress Administration is one great bulwark of that democracy. I believe the Federal Theatre, which is one small part of that large pattern, is honestly trying in every possible way to interpret the best interests of the people of this democracy. I am not in sympathy with any other form of government."

What percentage of the 4,000 employees on the New York project were members of the Workers' Alliance, Mr. Thomas wanted to know. We had no way of knowing. Was it a very large percentage? No, we knew it could not be large because the vast majority belonged to the standard theatrical organizations like Actors' Equity and the various stage unions, and these unions did not permit their members to join the Workers' Alliance.

Chairman Dies asked if we were out to entertain our audiences or to instruct them. I said that the primary purpose of a play is to entertain but that it can also teach.

"Do you think the theatre should be used for the purpose of conveying ideas along social and economic lines?"

"I think that is one justifiable reason for the existence of a theatre."

"Do you think that the Federal Theatre should be used for the purpose of conveying ideas along social, economic, or political lines?"

"I would hesitate on the political."

"Eliminate political, upon social and economic lines?"

"I think it is one logical, reasonable, and I might say imperative thing for our theatre to do."

Could I give the Committee one play, dealing with social questions, where "organized labor does not have the best of the other fellows"? Certainly. I mentioned *Spirochete*, the living newspaper on the history of syphilis, endorsed by the Surgeon General of the United States Public Health Service. I mentioned the living newspapers being prepared on flood control (*Bonneville Dam*); the history of vaudeville (*Clown's Progress*); the history of California real estate (*Spanish Grant*). The Chairman waved these examples aside. Didn't *Power* imply that public ownership of utilities is a good thing? Is it proper for a government theatre to champion one side of a controversy? We do not choose plays by picking sides in a controversy.

On this matter of the writing of plays it was apparent that the Committee confused the Theatre and the Federal Writers' Project. Chairman Dies insisted that he had received admissions from Federal Theatre workers who were Communists, Communists who had placed their signatures openly in a book. I said this had not happened on our project.

"Well," declared the Chairman triumphantly, "Mr. De Solo said he was a Communist."

"But he is not on the Federal Theatre Project."

"He is on the Writers' Project."

"Yes, but not our project."

Suddenly Mr. Starnes remarked that it was a quarter past one, the Chairman announced an adjournment for an hour and said that Mr. Alsberg would be heard when they resumed.

"Just a minute, gentlemen," I interrupted. "Do I understand that this concludes my testimony?"

"We will see about it after lunch," the Chairman promised.

"I would like to make a final statement, if I may."

"We will see about it after lunch," the Chairman repeated and the gavel fell. We never saw about it after lunch.

As the hearing broke up I thought suddenly of how much it all looked like a badly staged courtroom scene; it wasn't imposing enough for a congressional hearing on which the future of several thousand human beings depended. For any case on which the life and reputation of a single human being depended, even that of an accused murderer, we had an American system which demanded a judge trained in law, a defense lawyer, a carefully chosen jury, and above all the necessity of hearing all the evidence on both sides of the case.

Yet here was a Committee which for months had been actually trying a case against Federal Theatre, trying it behind closed doors, and giving one side only to the press. Out of a project employing thousands of people from coast to coast, the Committee had chosen arbitrarily to hear ten witnesses, all from New York City, and had refused arbitrarily to hear literally hundreds of others, on and off the project, who had asked to testify.

Representative Dempsey, who throughout the hearing had been just and courteous, came up and told me that he felt my testimony had been "completely satisfactory." Congressman Thomas was jovial.

"You don't look like a Communist," he declared. "You look like a Republican!"

"If your Committee isn't convinced that neither I nor the Federal Theatre Project is communistic I want to come back this afternoon," I told him.

"We don't want you back," he laughed. "You're a tough witness and we're all worn out."

Mrs. Woodward and I weren't satisfied. We told the secretary of the Committee that I had not finished my testimony. He said, "In any case your brief will be printed." He accepted the brief for inclusion in the transcript. It was not included.

1940

THORNTON WILDER

Throughout a literary career rich in honors, Thornton Wilder (1897–1975) maintained a reputation for intellectuality without losing a popular audience. His close circle of friends encompassed both the Algonquin Round Table and Gertrude Stein. Wilder's early fame was built on his novels, particularly the best-selling *The Bridge of San Luis Rey.* "The novel is pre-eminently the vehicle of the unique occasion, the theater of the generalized one," he wrote, and his experimental one-acts of 1931 tend toward the imagistic and metaphoric: *The Long Christmas Dinner* covers the span of several generations of family life; and *The Happy Journey to Trenton and Camden* and *Pullman Car Hiawatha* use a couple of straight chairs to portray an American dynasty and human fate. The latter introduces a Stage Manager, a framing device Wilder would use again in his 1938 triumph *Our Town.* After the first shock of seeing a stage denuded of scenery, spectators took to their hearts this parable of love and death in rural New England. Wilder's vision is in fact less sentimental than his public's, and *The Skin of Our Teeth* (1942) is more ambitious and more sardonic in its coverage of human progress through the ages. Both Edmund Wilson and George Jean Nathan spotted its debt to Joyce's *Finnegans Wake.* In 1938, when the great German director Max Reinhardt fled to New York to escape Hitler, Wilder adapted one of his successes, a Viennese farce by Johann Nestroy, to Victorian New York, to provide him a vehicle for practicing his craft. *The Merchant of Yonkers* failed on Broadway, but a revised version, *The Matchmaker* (1954), was well-received. More playgoers have unwittingly made Wilder's acquaintance through its wildly successful musical-comedy remake *Hello, Dolly!* than through any of his original works.

Some Thoughts on Playwriting

Four fundamental conditions of the drama separate it from the other arts. Each of these conditions has its advantages and disadvantages, each requires a particular aptitude from the dramatist, and from each there are a number of instructive consequences to be derived. These conditions are:

I. The theater is an art which reposes upon the work of many collaborators;

II. It is addressed to the group-mind;

III. It is based upon a pretense and its very nature calls out a multiplication of pretenses;

IV. Its action takes place in a perpetual present time.

I

THE THEATER IS AN ART WHICH REPOSES
UPON THE WORK OF MANY COLLABORATORS.

We have been accustomed to think that a work of art is by definition the product of one governing selecting will. A landscape by Cézanne consists of thousands of brushstrokes each commanded by one mind. *Paradise Lost* and *Pride and Prejudice*, even in cheap frayed copies, bear the immediate and exclusive message of one intelligence. It is true that in musical performance we meet with intervening executants, but the element of intervention is slight compared to that which takes place in drama. Illustrations:

1. One of the finest productions of *The Merchant of Venice* in our time showed Sir Henry Irving as Shylock, a noble, wronged, and indignant being, of such stature that the merchants of Venice dwindled before him into irresponsible schoolboys. He was confronted in court by a gracious, even queenly Portia, Miss Ellen Terry. At the Odéon in Paris, however, Gémier played Shylock as a vengeful and hysterical buffoon, confronted in court by a Portia who was a *gamine* from the Paris streets with a lawyer's quill three feet long over her ear; at the close of the trial scene Shylock was driven screaming about the auditorium, behind the spectators' backs and onto the stage again, in a wild Elizabethan revel. Yet for all their divergences both were admirable productions of the play.

2. If there was ever a play in which fidelity to the author's requirements was essential in the representation of the principal rôle, it would seem to be Ibsen's *Hedda Gabler*, for the play is primarily an exposition of her character. Ibsen's directions read:

Enter from the left Hedda Gabler. She is a woman of twenty-nine. Her face and figure show great refinement and distinction. Her complexion is pale and opaque. Her steel-gray eyes express an unruffled calm. Her hair is of an attractive medium brown, but is not particularly abundant; and she is dressed in a flowing loose-fitting morning gown.

I once saw Eleonora Duse in this rôle. She was a woman of sixty and made no effort to conceal it. Her complexion was pale and transparent. Her hair was white, and she was dressed in a gown that suggested some medieval empress in mourning. And the performance was very fine.

One may well ask: Why write for the theater at all? Why not work in the novel, where such deviations from one's intentions cannot take place?

There are two answers:

1. The theater presents certain vitalities of its own so inviting and stimulating that the writer is willing to receive them in compensation for this inevitable variation from an exact image.

2. The dramatist through working in the theater gradually learns not merely to take account of the presence of the collaborators, but to derive advantage from them; and he learns, above all, to organize the play in such a way that its strength lies not in appearances beyond his control, but in the succession of events and in the unfolding of an idea, in narration.

The gathered audience sits in a darkened room, one end of which is lighted. The nature of the transaction at which it is gazing is a succession of events illustrating a general idea—the stirring of the idea; the gradual feeding out of information; the shock and counter-shock of circumstances; the flow of action; the interruption of action; the moments of allusion to earlier events; the preparation of surprise, dread, or delight—all that is the author's and his alone.

For reasons to be discussed later—the expectancy of the group-mind, the problem of time on the stage, the absence of the narrator, the element of pretense—the theater carries the art of narration to a higher power than the novel or the epic poem. The theater is unfolding action and in the disposition of events the authors may exercise a governance so complete that the distortions effected by the physical appearance of actors, by the fancies of scene-painters, and the misunderstandings of directors, fall into relative insignificance. It is just because the theater is an art of many collaborators, with the constant danger of grave misinterpretation, that the dramatist learns to turn his attention to the laws of narration, its logic, and its deep necessity of presenting a unifying idea stronger than its mere collection of happenings. The dramatist must be by instinct a storyteller.

There is something mysterious about the endowment of the storyteller. Some very great writers possessed very little of it, and some others, lightly esteemed, possessed it in so large a measure that their books survive down the ages, to the confusion of severer critics. Alexandre Dumas had it to an extraordinary degree; while Melville, for all his splendid quality, had it barely sufficiently to raise his work from the realm of nonfiction. It springs, not, as some have said, from an aversion to general ideas, but from an instinctive coupling of idea and illustration; the idea, for a born storyteller, can only be expressed imbedded in its circumstantial illustration. The myth, the parable, the fable are the fountainhead of all fiction and in them is seen most clearly the didactic, moralizing employment of a story. Modern taste shrinks from emphasizing the central idea that hides behind the fiction, but it exists there nevertheless, supplying the unity to fantasizing, and offering a justification to what otherwise we would repudiate as mere arbitrary contrivance, pretentious lying, or individualistic emotional association-spinning. For all their magnificent intellectual endowment, George Meredith and George Eliot were not born storytellers; they chose fiction as the vehicle for their reflections, and the passing of time is revealing their error in that choice. Jane Austen was pure storyteller and her works are outlasting those of apparently more formidable rivals. The theater is more exacting than the novel in regard to this faculty and its presence constitutes a force which compensates the dramatist for the deviations which are introduced into his work by the presence of his collaborators.

The chief of these collaborators are the actors.

The actor's gift is a combination of three separate faculties or endowments. Their presence to a high degree in any one person is extremely rare, although the ambition to possess them is common. Those who rise to the height of the profession represent a selection and a struggle for survival in one of the most difficult and cruel of the artistic activities. The three endowments that compose the gift are observation, imagination, and physical coordination.

1. An observant and analyzing eye for all modes of behavior about us, for dress and manner, and for the signs of thought and emotion in oneself and in others.

2. The strength of imagination and memory whereby the actor may, at the indication in the author's text, explore his store of observations and represent the details of appearance and the intensity of the emotions—joy, fear, surprise, grief, love, and hatred—and through imagination extend them to intenser degrees and to differing characterizations.

3. A physical coordination whereby the force of these inner realizations may be communicated to voice, face, and body.

An actor must *know* the appearances and the mental states; he must *apply* his knowledge to the rôle; and he must physically *express* his knowledge. Moreover, his concentration must be so great that he can effect this representation under conditions of peculiar difficulty—in abrupt transition from the nonimaginative conditions behind the stage; and in the presence of fellow actors who may be momentarily destroying the reality of the action.

A dramatist prepares the characterization of his personages in such a way that it will take advantage of the actor's gift.

Characterization in a novel is presented by the author's dogmatic assertion that the personage was such, and by an analysis of the personage with generally an account of his or her past. Since in the drama this is replaced by the actual presence of the personage before us and since there is no occasion for the intervening all-knowing author to instruct us as to his or her inner nature, a far greater share is given in a play to (1) highly characteristic utterances and (2) concrete occasions in which the character defines itself under action and (3) a conscious preparation of the text whereby the actor may build upon the suggestions in the rôle according to his own abilities.

Characterization in a play is like a blank check which the dramatist accords to the actor for him to fill in—not entirely blank, for a number of indications of individuality are already there, but to a far less definite and absolute degree than in the novel.

The dramatist's principal interest being the movement of the story, he is willing to resign the more detailed aspects of characterization to the actor and is often rewarded beyond his expectation.

The sleepwalking scene from *Macbeth* is a highly compressed selection of words whereby despair and remorse rise to the surface of indirect confession. It is to be assumed that had Shakespeare lived to see what the genius of Sarah Siddons could pour into the scene from that combination of observation, self-knowledge, imagination, and representational skill, even he might have exclaimed, "I never knew I wrote so well!"

II

THE THEATER IS AN ART ADDRESSED
TO A GROUP-MIND.

Painting, sculpture, and the literature of the book are certainly solitary experiences; and it is likely that most people would agree that the audience seated shoulder to shoulder in a concert hall is not an essential element in musical enjoyment.

But a play presupposes a crowd. The reasons for this go deeper than (1) the economic necessity for the support of the play and (2) the fact that the temperament of actors is proverbially dependent on group attention.

It rests on the fact that (1) the pretense, the fiction, on the stage would fall to pieces and absurdity without the support accorded to it by the crowd, and (2) the excitement induced by pretending a fragment of life is such that it partakes of ritual and festival, and requires a throng.

Similarly, the fiction that royal personages are of a mysteriously different nature from other people requires audiences, levées, and processions for its maintenance. Since the beginnings of society, satirists have occupied themselves with the descriptions of kings and queens in their intimacy and delighted in showing how the prerogatives of royalty become absurd when the crowd is not present to extend to them the enhancement of an imaginative awe.

The theater partakes of the nature of festival. Life imitated is life raised to a higher power. In the case of comedy, the vitality of these pretended surprises, deceptions, and *contretemps* becomes so lively that before a spectator, solitary or regarding himself as solitary, the structure of so much event would inevitably expose the artificiality of the attempt and ring hollow and unjustified; and in the case of tragedy, the accumulation of woe and apprehension would soon fall short of conviction. All actors know the disturbing sensation of playing before a handful of spectators at a dress rehearsal or performance where only their interest in pure craftsmanship can barely sustain them. During the last rehearsals the phrase is often heard: "This play is hungry for an audience."

Since the theater is directed to a group-mind, a number of consequences follow:

1. A group-mind presupposes, if not a lowering of standards, a broadening of the fields of interest. The other arts may presuppose an audience of connoisseurs trained in leisure and capable of being interested in certain rarefied aspects of life. The dramatist may be prevented from exhibiting, for example, detailed representations of certain moments in history that require specialized knowledge in the audience, or psychological states in the personages which are of insufficient general interest to evoke self-identification in the majority. In the Second Part of Goethe's *Faust* there are long passages dealing with the theory of paper money. The exposition of the nature of misanthropy (so much more drastic than Molière's) in Shakespeare's *Timon of Athens* has never been a success. The dramatist accepts this limitation in subject matter and realizes that the group-mind imposes upon him the necessity of treating material understandable by the larger number.

2. It is the presence of the group-mind that brings another requirement to the theater—forward movement.

Maeterlinck said that there was more drama in the spectacle of an old man seated by a table than in the majority of plays offered to the public. He was juggling with the various meanings in the word "drama." In the sense whereby drama means the intensified concentration of life's diversity and significance he may well have been right; if he meant drama as a theatrical representation before an audience, he was wrong.

Drama on the stage is inseparable from forward movement, from action.

Many attempts have been made to present Plato's dialogues, Gobineau's fine series of dialogues, *La Renaissance*, and the *Imaginary Conversations* of Landor, but without success. Through some ingredient in the group-mind, and through the sheer weight of anticipation involved in the dressing-up and the assumption of fictional rôles, an action is required, and an action that is more than a mere progress in argumentation and debate.

III
THE THEATER IS A WORLD OF PRETENSE.

It lives by conventions: a convention is an agreed-upon falsehood, a permitted lie.

Illustrations: Consider at the first performance of the *Medea*, the passage where Medea meditates the murder of her children. An anecdote from antiquity tells us that the audience was so moved by this passage that considerable disturbance took place.

The following conventions were involved:

1. Medea was played by a man.

2. He wore a large mask on his face. In the lip of the mask was an acoustical device for projecting the voice. On his feet he wore shoes with soles and heels half a foot high.

3. His costume was so designed that it conveyed to the audience, by convention: woman of royal birth and Oriental origin.

4. The passage was in metric speech. All poetry is an "agreed-upon falsehood" in regard to speech.

5. The lines were sung in a kind of recitative. All opera involves this "permitted lie" in regard to speech.

Modern taste would say that the passage would convey much greater pathos if a woman "like Medea" had delivered it—with an uncovered face that exhibited all the emotions she was undergoing. For the Greeks, however, there was no pretense that Medea was on the stage. The mask, the costume, the mode of declamation were a series of signs which the spectator interpreted and reassembled in his own mind. Medea was being re-created within the imagination of each of the spectators.

The history of the theater shows us that in its greatest ages the stage employed the greatest number of conventions. The stage is fundamental pretense and it thrives on the acceptance of that fact and in the multiplication of additional pretenses. When it tries to assert that the personages in the action "really are," really inhabit such-and-such rooms, really suffer such-and-such emotions, it loses rather than gains credibility. The modern world is inclined to laugh condescendingly at the fact that in the plays of Racine and Corneille the gods and heroes of antiquity were dressed like the courtiers under Louis XIV; that in the Elizabethan Age scenery was replaced by placards notifying the audience of the location; and that a whip in the hand and a jogging motion of the body indicated that a man was on horseback in the Chinese theater; these devices did not spring from naïveté, however, but from the vitality of the public imagination in those days and from an instinctive feeling as to where the essential and where the inessential lay in drama.

The convention has two functions:

1. It provokes the collaborative activity of the spectator's imagination; and

2. It raises the action from the specific to the general.

This second aspect is of even greater importance than the first.

If Juliet is represented as a girl "very like Juliet"—it was not merely a deference to contemporary prejudices that assigned this rôle to a boy in the Elizabethan Age—moving about in a "real" house with marble staircases, rugs, lamps, and furniture, the impression is irresistibly conveyed that these events happened to this one girl, in one place, at one moment in time. When the play is staged as Shakespeare intended it, the bareness of the stage releases the events from the particular and the experience of Juliet partakes of that of all girls in love, in every time, place, and language.

The stage continually strains to tell this generalized truth and it is the element of pretense that reinforces it. Out of the lie, the pretense, of the theater proceeds a truth more compelling than the novel can attain, for the novel by its own laws is constrained to tell of an action that "once happened"—"once upon a time."

IV

THE ACTION ON THE STAGE TAKES PLACE
IN A PERPETUAL PRESENT TIME.

Novels are written in the past tense. The characters in them, it is true, are represented as living moment by moment their present time, but the constant running commentary of the novelist ("Tess slowly descended into the valley"; "Anna Karenina laughed") inevitably conveys to the reader the fact that these events are long since past and over.

The novel is a past reported in the present. On the stage it is always now. This confers upon the action an increased vitality which the novelist longs in vain to incorporate into his work.

This condition in the theater brings with it another important element:

In the theater we are not aware of the intervening storyteller. The speeches arise from the characters in an apparently pure spontaneity.

A play is what takes place.

A novel is what one person tells us took place.

A play visibly represents pure existing. A novel is what one mind, claiming to omniscience, asserts to have existed.

Many dramatists have regretted this absence of the narrator from the stage, with his point of view, his powers of analyzing the behavior of the characters, his ability to interfere and supply further facts about the past, about simultaneous actions not visible on the stage, and, above *all*, his function of pointing the moral and emphasizing the significance of the action. In some periods of the theater he has been present as chorus, or prologue and epilogue, or as *raisonneur*. But surely this absence constitutes an additional force to the form, as well as an additional tax upon the writer's skill. It is the task of the dramatist so to coordinate his play, through the selection of episodes and speeches, that, though he is himself not visible, his point of view and his governing intention will impose themselves on the spectator's attention, not as dogmatic assertion or motto, but as self-evident truth and inevitable deduction.

Imaginative narration—the invention of souls and destinies—is to a philosopher an all but indefensible activity.

Its justification lies in the fact that the communication of ideas from one mind to another inevitably reaches the point where exposition passes into illustration, into parable, metaphor, allegory, and myth.

It is no accident that when Plato arrived at the height of his argument and attempted to convey a theory of knowledge and a theory of the structure of man's nature, he passed over into storytelling, into the myths of the Cave and the Charioteer; and that the great religious teachers have constantly had recourse to the parable as a means of imparting their deepest intuitions.

The theater offers to imaginative narration its highest possibilities. It has many pitfalls and its very vitality betrays it into service as mere diversion and the enhancement of insignificant matter; but it is well to remember that it was the theater that rose to the highest place during those epochs that aftertime has chosen to call "great ages" and that the Athens of Pericles and the reigns of Elizabeth I, Philip II, and Louis XIV were also the ages that gave to the world the greatest dramas it has known.

1941

ELIA KAZAN

When Elia Kazan (1909–2003) wrote this wartime piece for *Theatre Arts*—speculating on the G.I. as the cornerstone of a new audience and, incidentally, praising the emergence of Tennessee Williams—he was barely known to the wider public. An Anatolian Greek named Elias Kazanjoglu, he was brought to New York at the age of four. An education at Williams College and the Yale School of Drama led him to acting professionally, and in 1932 he joined the Group Theatre. In a company that included Lee Strasberg, Robert Lewis, and Stella Adler, he was cast chiefly as embattled proles and tough-talking gangsters, most memorably the union organizer Agate Keller in *Waiting for Lefty* and the racketeer Eddie Fuseli in *Golden Boy*. He was also, briefly, a card-carrying Communist, and would later name names before the House Un-American Activities Committee. In 1942 Kazan established himself as a director on Broadway with *The Skin of Our Teeth*. Ahead lay his groundbreaking productions of Arthur Miller (*All My Sons*, 1947; *Death of a Salesman*, 1949) and Williams (*A Streetcar Named Desire*, 1947; *Cat on a Hot Tin Roof*, 1955) which set new benchmarks for emotional authenticity in acting; his co-founding in 1947 with Strasberg and Cheryl Crawford of the Actors Studio to foster this new style; his hugely successful career as a Hollywood director; his unhappy leadership of the new Lincoln Center repertory company (1963–65); a belated career as a novelist; and the controversial acceptance of an Honorary Academy Award in 1999.

Audience Tomorrow

Preview in New Guinea

EDDIE MORAN wasn't going with us. He had a bad headache, and his bones ached. Some one suggested Eddie might have a touch of dengue fever, a fantastic disease that gives you the sensation that all your bones are breaking. It developed that he had nothing more exotic than a slight touch of flu, but the talk about dengue furnished a striking contrast to our 'cocktails and dinner downtown' before going to the theatre back in

New York. We climbed into Captain Lanny Ross' jeep and were off. The sky, for a change, was clear.

The War Department had sent us here to promote the Soldier Show program. With one eye on the fact that a happy soldier is a fighting-working soldier and with the other eye on the post-war period when restless occupation troops will have nothing but time on their hands, the Department was ready to push Soldier Shows. We were here to help set up G.I. production units, to size up the problems of the field, to recommend a program for the other theatres of war. I had thought some about the job at home and on our way over, but I had never anticipated the degree of hunger with which the men craved entertainment, the eagerness with which they offered to participate in programs. If they couldn't act, they'd bring hammers and saws. The theatre can use everybody. All you have to do is scratch around a little in each and every detachment and you are sure to turn up with an eager young man for every function. One has only to light the match—the forest is tinder.

Of course the shows are almost all variety. The favorite G.I. skits and parodies come from their own experiences, and the laughter they generate is all-healthy. Gripes, headaches, complaints and resentments when projected on stage become common property and tend to shrink. You might indulge in self pity on your own behalf, but it is unlikely that you will favor thousands of your mates with the same intensity. In the laughter something potentially dangerous is passed off. It's a simple kind of catharsis, though not, I suppose, what Aristotle meant.

Tonight we were to attend a G.I. Show at the Fifty-first General Hospital. Headquarters was situated on top of a hill which commanded a broad and beautiful valley. As we rode down, jeeps and 'six by six' trucks passed us going up. They were full of soldiers and Wacs, soldiers and Red Cross nurses, soldiers and unidentifiable women. In one of the Headquarters buildings there was an enlisted men's dance. This was social life in New Guinea. It always came to an abrupt close at midnight, when the Wac enlisted personnel had to be in. But now it was seven, the evening was young, and the kids were out 'to have themselves a ball'.

It was growing dark but we were each carrying a little beer, so it was pleasant riding that jeep bare-back through the evening that was closing in. Someone began to sing, and we joined in. You find you sing easily and readily here. And you sing for yourself. You sing to remember something or because you miss something, or because you are reminded of something or because you feel just fine. It's a natural outlet. It helps. Lanny Ross has a good big voice, but even he was singing to himself.

Passing through the gate at the Fifty-first we rode up the side of a hill, cut through the installations of the Hospital, somehow found a rocky half trail, forded a stream and pulled up in the very lobby of the Fifty-first's Theatre: The Medicine Bowl.

In each area there are many recreation halls and 'clubs', but the actual theatres are all out of doors, and all built on the side of hills. The Medicine Bowl was no exception. It was like the Jungle Bowl, the Sugar Bowl and the Iodine Bowl. The men either brought their own seats, chairs or boxes, or there were improvised benches. The Medicine Bowl's stage is set against a background of great trees, which in turn are framed against the mountains of Northern New Guinea. Later the trees would be silhouetted against mountains in flashes of lightning, but now the sky was clear and the night still and empty.

Then came the first shock. In the quiet sat hundreds and hundreds of men, all in pajamas. There are three thousand beds at the Fifty-first General Hospital. Most of them were empty tonight. The men were waiting, spread out around the Bowl. Men wait for hours in New Guinea to see a show. Chow is usually at four-thirty. The shows usually commence at seven. Except for a small officer's section, first come first seats. But that isn't why the men come early, and wait. I can't explain it except by saying that they just want to see the show. They want to bad. They wait with a quiet intensity. There is very little cutting up, shouting back and forth or rowdyism. If you want to see the original hunger for entertainment, come to New Guinea.

They sat in little groups of three and four, clumps of the comradeship the wounded have. These were the men from Leyte and from Luzon. Some had been there for weeks, forty had come south by plane that very morning. Their pajamas were faded from constant rewashing. Over their shoulders were Australian blankets, tough and durable. The boys in them were the kids from around the block. You kept feeling that you recognized someone. They did not seem like soldiers. Their stance was easy and casual, their smiles shy and fresh, never arrogant or domineering. They were the citizen soldiers of a democracy: tow heads, red heads, Italians, Negroes, Greeks, Irish. The mood was congenial, the night soft, all about was harmony.

Suddenly the two floodlights that, at best, barely illuminated the scene, went out and the single spotlight hit the front curtain. Revealed was a slim dark boy, the Hospital's Special Services officer. I had talked with him a few days ago. Like the other Special Services officers in the Base, he was overburdened with work. In the Army, Special Services is under Service of Supply. Entertainment is supplied to the men as a commodity along with rations, toothbrushes and waterproofing for their shoes. Not really the ideal organization to spur the production of more shows.

It was to be a night of informal entertainment, Lieutenant Braunstein said; in fact he didn't know himself what was in store. Whereupon he introduced Captain Lanny Ross and ducked. You felt that he had done his duty and was only too happy to turn the proceedings over to one of those incomprehensible beings who enjoy standing up before their fellow men. Lanny Ross, let me hasten to assure his friends back home, still has an excellent voice. He has the one first asset: he sings as easily as he talks, eats, or walks. There are men like this—Bing Crosby is the chief—for whom singing is a natural function of the body. Include Lanny . . .

He sang and sang as the boys egged him on. Their applause was a constant command for more. You wondered how he would ever manage to get off stage. When he did, you asked yourself: 'Now what in the world will they do?'

Lanny was saying something about an impromptu show. Suddenly onto the stage dashed three boys in pajamas; one fell at the foot of the mike, the others over him like cards. On their feet they were a strange sight. Two of the three were frightened and embarrassed, but enjoying it. The third boy was in his element. He was what the boys call 'a character'. Grinning, jittering and bobbing, he finally managed to ask Ross if they could take over for a while. They took over.

What would you expect? What they did was four little skits, each of which kidded the hospital, its staff, their wounds. It was wild! Only if I were Joyce could I hope to communicate the wild glee, the uproar in their hearts, their joy at being alive still, and the insult they paid their wounds. There were many ambulatory cases out front. There were the shell-shocked out front. They roared at themselves. (I remembered with a start of joy that 97% of the wounded in our army recover. All thanks to the New Medicine.)

And now the evening was off. The rest of the show was commonplace as to material, but spirited, too, to the point of abandon. As for the audience, everything was grist to its mill. I'm sure that many of the performers, their heads still ringing with the concussion of that applause, decided then and there that they had found their life work. There was the local Frank Sinatra (his imitators, by the way, outnumbering Crosby's) who did the same trick of suspiration, the faintmaking insinuation of voice that stirs the innards of our national virginhood. . . . There was a shy boy, with glasses, who sang like himself and had barely finished before he had shrunk off stage. There was a magician who was really deft, but seemed even nimbler in the irregular light. I watched the audience.

They were so mercurial. As quick as they were to roar irreverent laughter, just so ready were they to give in to sentiment. The laughter said: 'We're not going to take our wounds seriously; hell no. We're not going to brood over them. Don't pity us. We don't want your sympathy. We don't want to be treated like heroes either. We're ourselves, the same kids; we're normal. Don't forget that!' Then would come a sentimental song and sudden rapt attention and the silence said: 'That's right, talk to me. Talk to me of home and the things I miss, the happy times I knew and will know again—IF I don't get it when I go up north again.' Now they were tender kids, listening, with that look in their eyes that you will remember if you have ever watched children sitting before a show. Wonder is the word, or rapture. There was more; there was rain; but the show went on.

There is hell in the bowels of the weather here, but I have heard of only one audience completely and quickly dispersed, and it wasn't because of the weather. The occasion was the entrance down the centre aisle of a sixteen-foot python. He disappeared under the stage house, and the audience reconvened.

It was really coming down now. Lanny was trying to close the show, asking the boys of the band to put a climax on the evening. I felt he was asking for help. Half of the audience just wouldn't go. As a matter of fact, once the band, a hot six-piece combo, was going you could see many a boy settle as if for the real business of the evening. After the first number they took to calling for their favorites. They just had to hear certain numbers before the rain did its work. There was some community of taste. Duke Ellington's 'Take the A Train' won. Then a piece that was even 'hotter'. The boys were 'teeing off' in dead earnest. The only words seemed to be: 'You take it.' The audience shouted back, 'I got it,' 'You take it,' 'We got it.' The band was improvising. The brass section was battered, so was the music they produced. But always in beat. Each solo was acclaimed. The rain, coming down in horizontal slices, began to cut into the stage opening. Suddenly the boys brought the number to an abrupt close, someone threw a switch and the main lights bumped on. The show was over. In the rain the wounded walked back to their beds.

But that was not all we saw of the audience, or of drama. At the Officers' Club later there was cold Genesee beer. I looked around the club room. Someone had a monkey; they were getting it lively on beer. In a dark corner, a double date: Wacs. In another, two boys were writing. Right next to me, three boys were involved in a serious conversation. I leaned over and listened in. They were discussing the features of the jet plane. The language was highly technical, the faces new to a razor. I had gone through calculus at college—with difficulty, it's true . . . I read *The New York Times*, *PM*, *Life*, *Time*, *The New Yorker*, and all the latest books, but these kids made me feel out of it. Something had passed me by. Folks, there's a new generation.

The one thing these boys want more than anything else is to win the war and to go home. They are citizens, not soldiers. Our army is beautifully organized, beautifully equipped, and functions with efficiency, power and direction. But the men who run it and the men in the ranks don't impress you as professional soldiers, even when they most certainly are. The officers on Headquarters hill play volley ball each afternoon at five. You have to watch them only five minutes to get the indelible impression that here too are kids from around the block grown up, and nicely too.

You begin to wonder whether America, in getting back to its pursuit of happiness, won't run the danger of cancelling out this entire experience as a 'Bad Deal'. Significantly the one thing the boys will take home with them is an idealization of the 'States'. The States can't hope to live up to the picture these boys have in their mind's eye. These twelve million men are potentially the greatest unified body of Public Opinion our country has ever known. They could, if brought together, insist that an organization be found and made to function that would never permit a repetition and intensification of this nightmare.

I was sitting by myself, thinking of these things as I scraped the mud off those monuments to indestructibility, the G.I. shoe. It was time to go home. At first the road was through the jungle. We sloshed along, lurching here and there, over tree roots, till we hit the main highway. The jeep seemed pleased, spun up the hill. We drove through a cloud and out. And in a moment we were out of the rain. But the threat was still there, and later that night the rain picked up and came down in sheets almost horizontal, accelerating and accelerating till you felt it must soon reach some kind of breaking point, then slowing down suddenly as if to gain momentum. I lay in my bed thinking of home for the first time since my arrival. Thus I became one with the thousands of men over here. And that night I dreamt of home.

*　　*　　*

Coming back, I feel that the audience is ahead of us. We, the makers of entertainment, are faced with the job. We must try, in our field, to be as honest and grown-up as these kids. It is not a matter of chance any longer. The fellows who come back will be demanding. We'll have to be good to survive. If we're not, we'll feel our failure where it really hurts: at the box-office.

Those boys just won't pay a dollar plus for some of the celluloid I've seen. They're a lot tougher, more honest, and a lot more progressive.

It is encouraging to return and find Tennessee Williams' fine play, *The Glass Menagerie*, the reigning dramatic hit on Broadway. It's the kind of thing that wise and experienced showmen have always said didn't have a chance. I have often felt that the more experienced the showman is, the further behind the audience he is liable to be. Let's stop worrying about how intelligent the audience is. Let's think a little, we who make the stuff, about how good we can be. Because it is we who are challenged. We're behind. We're on the spot. Everyone is worried in Hollywood about the coming recession at the box-office. There's one way to avoid it. That is to make what is in the theatres a live experience for the people, not merely a kill-time. All the people of this nation have grown some during the war. Twelve million men have grown a lot. Some of us may not know it, but we are being challenged!

1945

MARY McCARTHY

For Mary McCarthy (1912–1989), the profession of theatre critic was adventitious. A lapsed Catholic graduate of Vassar, married to the minor actor and playwright Harald Johnsrud, she hung out in New York circles of bohemians, Trotskyites, and fellow-travelers. When invited to write for *The Nation*, in spring 1937 she contributed "Our Actors and Critics," a scathing attack on the current scene. Katharine Cornell was characterized as "an ambitious, unimaginative mediocre young woman whose fortune it is to own a face that is an exotic mask"; Lynne Fontanne was damned as a clapped-out no-talent. When McCarthy then was made a staff member of *Partisan Review*, the editors, who considered the stage of little importance to the political struggle, assigned her to a monthly "Theatre Chronicle." Her iconoclastic and contrarian opinions became required reading. Although they led the poet Lionel Abel to declare, "About the theatre she was almost always wrong," her reviews have to be seen as a liberal intellectual's polemical poke in the eye of establishment values. At a time when American drama was being praised for its "realism," she drew up an indictment: "the heroes are petty or colorless; the settings are drab; the language is lame" ("The American Realist Playwrights," 1961). Edmund Wilson, whom she married in 1938, offered to improve her criticism; instead she devoted more energy to fiction. Her best-selling novel *The Group* (1962) won McCarthy a wider audience than any critic, no matter how provocative, could achieve.

A Streetcar Called Success

You are an ordinary guy and your wife's sister comes to stay with you. Whenever you want to go to the toilet, there she is in the bathroom, primping or having a bath or giving herself a shampoo and taking her time about it. You go and hammer on the door ("For Christ's sake, aren't you through yet?"), and your wife shushes you frowningly: Blanche is very sensitive and you must be careful of her feelings. You get sore at your wife; your kidneys are sensitive too. My God, you yell, loud enough so that Blanche can hear you, can't a man pee in his own house, when is she getting out of here? You are pretty sick too of feeling her criticize your table-manners, and does she have to turn on the radio when you have a poker game going, who does she think she is? Finally you and your wife have a fight (you knew all along that She was turning the little woman against you), you decide to put your foot down, Blanche will have to go. Your wife reluctantly gives in—anything for peace, don't think it's been a treat for *her* ("But let me handle it, Stanley; after all, she's my own *sister!*"). One way or another (God knows what your wife told her) Blanche gets the idea. You buy her a ticket home. But then right at the end, when you're carrying her bags downstairs for her, you feel sort of funny; maybe you were too hard; but that's the way the world is, and, Boy, isn't it great to be alone?

This variation on the mother-in-law theme is the one solid piece of theatrical furniture that *A Streetcar Named Desire* can show; the rest is antimacassars. Acrimony and umbrage, tears, door-slamming, broken dishes, jeers, cold silences, whispers, raised eyebrows, the determination to take no notice, the whole classic paraphernalia of insult and injury is Tennessee Williams' hope-chest. That the domestic dirty linen it contains is generally associated with the comic strip and the radio sketch should not invalidate it for him as subject matter; it has nobler antecedents. The cook, one may recall, is leaving on the opening page of *Anna Karenina*, and Hamlet at the court of Denmark is really playing the part of the wife's unwelcome relation. Dickens, Dostoevsky, Farrell rattle the skeleton of family life; there is no limit, apparently, to what people will do to each other in the family; nothing is too grotesque or shameful; all laws are suspended, including the law of probability. Mr. Williams, at his best, is an *outrageous* writer in this category; at his worst, he is outrageous in another.

Had he been content in *A Streetcar Named Desire* with the exasperating trivia of the in-law story, he might have produced a wonderful little comic epic, The Struggle for the Bathroom, an epic ribald and poignant, a *comédie larmoyante* which would not have been deficient either in those larger implications to which his talent presumes, for the bathroom might have figured as the last fortress of the individual, the poor man's club, the working girl's temple of beauty; and the bathtub and the toilet, symbol of illusion and symbol of fact, the prone and the upright, the female and the male, might have faced each other eternally in blank, porcelain contradiction as the area for self-expression contracted to the limits of this windowless cell. Mr. Williams, however, like the Southern women he writes about, appears to have been mortified by the literary poverty of such material, by the pettiness of the arena which is in fact its grandeur. Like Blanche Du Bois in *A Streetcar Named Desire* and the mother in *The Glass Menagerie*, he is addicted to the embroidering lie, and though his taste in fancywork differs from these ladies', inclining more to the modernistic, the stark contrast, the jagged scene, the jungle motifs ("Then they come together with low, animal moans"), the tourist Mexican (*"Flores para los muertos, corones para los muertos"*), to clarinet music, suicide, homosexuality, rape, and insanity, his work creates in the end that very effect of painful falsity which is imparted to the Kowalski household by Blanche's pink lamp-shades and couch-covers.

To illustrate with a single instance, take the character of Blanche. In her Mr. Williams has caught a flickering glimpse of the faded essence of the sister-in-law; thin, vapid, neurasthenic, romancing, genteel, pathetic, a collector of cheap finery and of the words of old popular songs, fearful and fluttery and awkward, fond of admiration and over-eager to obtain it, a refined pushover and perennial and frigid spinster, this is the woman who inevitably comes to stay and who evokes pity because of her very emptiness, because nothing can ever happen to her since her life is a shoddy magazine story she tells herself in a daydream. But the thin, sleazy stuff of this character must be embellished by Mr. Williams with all sorts of arty decorations. It is not enough that she should be a drunkard (this in itself is plausible); she must also be a notorious libertine who has been run out of a small town like a prostitute, a thing absolutely inconceivable for a woman to whom conventionality is the end of existence; she must have an "interesting" biography, a homosexual husband who has shot himself shortly after their marriage, a story so patently untrue that the audience thinks the character must have invented it; and finally she must be a symbol of art and beauty, this poor flimsy creature to whom truth is mortal, who hates the feel of experience with a pathologic aversion—she must not only be a symbol but she must be given a poetic moment of self-definition; she who has never spoken an honest word in her life is allowed, indeed encouraged, to present her life to the audience as a vocational decision, an artist's election of the beautiful, an act of supreme courage, the choice of the thorny way.

In the same manner, Stanley Kowalski, the husband, who has been all too enthusiastically characterized as the man who wants to pee, the realist of the bladder and the genitals, the monosyllabic cynic, is made to apostrophize sexual intercourse in a kind of Odetsian or tin-pan alley poetry. Dr. Kinsey would be interested in a semi-skilled male who spoke of the four-letter act as "getting those colored lights going."

If art, as Mr. Williams appears to believe, is a lie, then anything goes, but Mr. Williams' lies, like Blanche's, are so old and shopworn that the very truth upon which he rests them becomes garish and ugly, just as the Kowalskis' apartment becomes the more squalid for Blanche's attempts at decoration. His work reeks of literary ambition as the apartment reeks of cheap perfume; it is impossible to witness one of Mr. Williams' plays without being aware of the pervading smell of careerism. Over and above their subject-matter, the plays seem to emanate an ever-growing confidence in their author's success. It is this perhaps which is responsible for Mr. Williams' box-office draw: there is a curious elation in this work which its subject-matter could not engender. Whatever happens to the characters, Mr. Williams will come out rich and famous, and the play is merely an episode in Mr. Williams' career. And this career in itself has the tinny quality of a musical romance, from movie usher to Broadway lights, like *Alexander's Ragtime Band* or *The Jolson Story*. Pacing up and down a Murray Hill apartment, he tells of his early struggles to a sympathetic reporter. He remembers his "first break." He writes his life-story for a Sunday supplement. He takes his work seriously; he does not want success to spoil him; he recognizes the dangers; he would be glad to have advice. His definition of his literary approach is a triumph of boyish simplicity: "I have always had a deep feeling for the mystery in life." This "Hello Mom" note in Mr. Williams' personality is the real, indigenous thing. He is the Aldrich Family and Andy Hardy and possibly Gene Tunney

and bride's biscuits and the mother-in-law joke. The cant of
the intelligentsia (the jargon, that is, of failure) comes from his
lips like an ill-learned recitation: he became, at one point, so
he says, "that most common American phenomenon, the
rootless, wandering writer"—is this a wholly fitting description
of a talent which is as rooted in the American pay-dirt as a
stout and tenacious carrot?

1948

HAROLD CLURMAN

Given his capacities as producer, director, critic, memoirist, and translator, the best descriptive term for Harold Clurman (1901–1980) is
homme du théâtre. It is also appropriate because he was a lifelong
Francophile. In his early 20s he shared an apartment in Paris with the
composer Aaron Copland and was greatly influenced by the innovations of the actor-manager Jacques Copeau; later, he would introduce
American audiences to the plays of Jean Anouilh and Jean Giraudoux
and receive the Légion d'Honneur in recognition of his services to
French culture. Back in New York, he worked as a playreader for the
Theatre Guild (1929–31) and, influenced by the Moscow Art Theatre,
in 1930–31 he co-founded with Cheryl Crawford the Group Theatre.
Although less politically committed than many of his colleagues,
the voluble and highly energized Clurman was the group's guiding
light. He promulgated the latest Russian ideas on acting, persuaded
his wife, Stella Adler, to join the ensemble, and staged the Group's
greatest successes with the plays of Paul Green, Clifford Odets, and
William Saroyan. His style drew directly from the teachings of
Richard Boleslavsky, with close attention to unifying the production
through textual analysis and thematic clarity. When the Group broke
up in 1941, Clurman was sought after by Broadway producers, and
until 1966 he applied his sedulous technique to staging works by
Arthur Miller, Carson McCullers, Eugene O'Neill, William Inge, and
Tennessee Williams. After he distilled his pungent recollections of the
Group into *The Fervent Years* (1945), his pointed and perceptive
theatre criticism appeared in *The New Republic* (1949–52), *The Observer* (1955–63), and *The Nation* (1953–80). By the time of his death,
he was regarded as the sagacious Elder Statesman of the American
Theatre.

Tennessee Williams

THE newest writing talent in the American theatre is that of
Tennessee Williams. His *The Glass Menagerie* was a lyric fragment of limited scope but undeniable poignancy. Tennessee
Williams' latest play—*A Streetcar Named Desire*—stands very
high among the creative contributions of the American theatre

since 1920. If we had a national repertory theatre, this play would unquestionably be among the few worthy of a permanent place there. Its impact at this moment is especially strong, because it is virtually unique as a stage piece that is both personal and social and wholly a product of our life today. It is a beautiful play.

Its story is simple. Blanche Du Bois, a girl whose family once possessed property and title to position in the circle of refined Southern respectability, has been reduced to the lowest financial estate. She has taught English in a high school, but when we meet her she has apparently lost her job and has come to stay with her younger sister Stella in New Orleans. Blanche expects to find Stella living in an environment compatible with their former background, but finds instead that Stella is in the kind of neighborhood that playgoers call sordid, though it happens to be no worse than any of the places inhabited by the majority of American people. Blanche is shocked at these Elysian Fields (literally the name of this particular spot in New Orleans, just as the streetcar she took to reach it is actually called Desire). She is even more shocked by her sister's husband, an American of Polish origin, an ex-sergeant, a machine salesman, and a rather primitive, almost bestial person. Her brother-in-law resents and then suspects the girl's pretentious airs, particularly her obvious disdain of him. Slowly he (and we) discover the girl's "secret": after an unfortunate marriage at an early age to a boy who turned out to be a homosexual, the boy's suicide, her family's loss of all its property, and the death of the last member of the older generation, Blanche has become a notorious person, whose squalid affairs have made it impossible for her to remain in her home town. She meets a friend of her brother-in-law whom she wants to marry because he is a decent fellow, but her brother-in-law, by disclosing the facts of the girl's life to her suitor, wrecks her hopes. Drunk the night his wife is in labor, the brother-in-law settles his account with Blanche by raping her. She is ordered out of Stella's house, and, when Blanche tells the story of the rape she is thought to be mad and is finally conducted unprotesting to a public institution for the insane.

Some of the reviewers thought Blanche Du Bois a "boozy prostitute," and others believed her a nymphomaniac. Such designations are not only inaccurate but reveal a total failure to understand the author's intention and the theme of the play. Tennessee Williams is a poet of frustration, and what his play says is that aspiration, sensitivity, departure from the norm are battered, bruised and disgraced in our world today.

It would be far truer to think of Blanche Du Bois as the potential artist in all of us than as a deteriorated Southern belle. Her amatory adventures, which her brother-in-law (like some of the critics) regards as the mark of her inferiority, are the unwholesome means she uses to maintain her connection with life, to fight the sense of death which her whole background has created in her. The play's story shows us Blanche's seeking haven in a simple, healthy man and that in this, too, she is defeated because everything in her environment conspires to degrade the meaning of her tragic situation. . . . Her lies are part of her will-to-beauty; her wretched romanticism is a futile reaching toward a fullness of life. She is not a drunkard, and she is not insane when she is committed to the asylum. She is an almost willing victim of a world that has trapped her and in which she can find "peace" only by accepting the verdict of her unfitness for "normal" life.

The play is not specifically written as a symbolic drama or as a tract. What I have said is implicit in all of the play's details. The reason for the play's success even with audiences who fail to understand it is that the characters and the scenes are written with a firm grasp on their naturalistic truth. Yet we shall waste the play and the author's talent if we praise the play's effects and disregard its core. Like most works of art the play's significance cannot be isolated in a single passage. It is clear to the attentive and will elude the hasty.

Still, the audience is not entirely to blame if the play and its central character are not understood. There are elements in the production—chiefly in the acting—that make for a certain ambiguity and confusion. This is not to say that the acting and production are poor. On the contrary, they are both distinctly superior. The director, Elia Kazan, is a man of high theatrical intelligence, a craftsman of genuine sensibility. . . . But there is a lack of balance and perspective in the production of *A Streetcar Named Desire* due to the fact that the acting of the parts is of unequal force, quality and stress. To clarify this I must digress here and dwell a bit on the nature of acting in general. What is acting? What is its function in the theatre? How does it serve the goal of art, which is at all times to give flesh to essential human meanings? The digression, we shall see, may lead to a greater insight into the outstanding theatrical event under discussion.

A pedant might characterize the actor as a person endowed with the capacity to behave publicly and for purposes of play as though fictional circumstances were real. The actor knows that the lines he speaks and the action he performs are merely invention, just as he knows the objects he deals with on the stage—scenery, properties, lights—are parts of an artificial world. His acting consists of his ability to make all these things take on a new reality for himself and for his audience. Just as the first step in painting is the "imitation" of an object, so the actor "imitates" a series of human events that in terms of real life are no more true than the apple or flower or horse that we see in a painting.

The actor is himself an instrument, and, if he is able to look right in terms of what he is "imitating," his very presence on the stage is already an accomplishment. Yet we know that an actor of a convincing presence who merely reads his lines intelligibly offers us little more than information, which is the small change of the theatre. The actor who adds visual illustration to what he is saying (beating his breast to indicate anguish!) provides a sort of lamp whereby we read the play more comfortably, although at times the illustration if well chosen may give special illumination. The actor becomes creative only when he reveals the life from which the play's lines may have emerged, a life richer perhaps than the lines' literal significance. The creative actor is the author of the new meaning that a play acquires on the stage, the author of a personal sub-text into which the play's lines are absorbed so that a special aesthetic body with an identity of its own is born. . . . Just as the painter who merely sets down the image of an apple that looks like one is not an artist, so the actor who merely "imitates" the surface impression that we might gather from a perusal of the play's text—an actor who does not create a life beyond what was there before he assumed his role—belies the art of the theatre.

The new meaning that the actor gives to the play emerges from what is popularly known as the actor's personality—not alone his physical "type," but the whole quality of his skill, emotion, insight, sensibility, character, imagination, spirit. These have an existence of their own, which the actor with the aid of the director must shape to the form of their interpretation or understanding of the problem they have set themselves for the play.

There are two things to be considered in any judgment of acting: the material of the actor himself and the use that the material has been put to in relation to the play as a whole. A very fine actor may utterly distort the intention of a play—that is, transform it with as much possibility of happy as of disastrous results. Bernard Shaw tells us that Duse was superior to Sudermann; it was her acting of that dramatist's play *Home* that made it a work of art. In Paris I saw the Laurette Taylor part in *The Glass Menagerie* very ably played in a way that robbed the character of all poetry. In my opinion, most of our highly regarded Hamlets are simply *readings* of the part but rather inferior acting or not acting at all. Katharine Cornell's Cleopatra may be said to have certain attractive aspects (no one need debate Miss Cornell's natural endowments), but, even aside from the question of physical qualifications, she creates nothing with the part, not only in the Shakespearean sense but within her own orbit. On the other hand, I have read that Michael Chekhov's Hamlet was not Hamlet (in the sense that there might be an "ideal" Hamlet) but that it was a true creation, albeit a very special one.

In *A Streetcar Named Desire* all the actors are good, but their performances do not truly convey Tennessee Williams' play. By virtue of its power and completeness the play pretty nearly succeeds in acting the actors, but the nature of the play's reception indicates a prevailing sentiment of excitement and glowing enthusiasm disassociated from any specific meaning.

Jessica Tandy's Blanche suffers from the actress' narrow emotional range. One of the greatest parts ever written for a woman in the American theatre, it demands the fullness and variety of an orchestra. Miss Tandy's register is that of a violin's A string. The part represents the essence of womanly feeling and wounded human sensibility. Blanche lies and pretends, but through it all the actress must make us perceive her truth. She is an aristocrat (regardless of the threadbare myth of Southern gentility); she is an aristocrat in the subtlety and depth of her feeling. She is a poet, even if we are dubious about her understanding of the writers she names; she is superior by the sheer intensity and realization of her experience, even if much of what she does is abject.

If she is not these things, she is too much of a fraud to be worthy of the author's concern with her. If the latter is true, then the play would be saying something rather surprising—namely, that frank brutality and naked power are more admirable than the yearning for tenderness and the desire to reach beyond one's personal appetites. When Blanche appeals to her sister in the name of these values, Miss Tandy is unable to make it clear whether she means what she says and whether we are supposed to attach any importance to her speech or whether she is merely spinning another fantasy. It is essential to the play that we believe and are touched by what she says, that her emotion convinces us of the soundness of her values. All through the play, indeed, we must be captured by the music of the girl's martyred soul. Without this there is either a play whose viewpoint we reject or no play at all—only a series of "good scenes," a highly seasoned theatrical dish.

Marlon Brando, who plays Stanley Kowalski (Blanche's brother-in-law), is an actor of genuine power. He has what someone once called "high visibility" on the stage. His silences, even more than his speech, are completely arresting. Through his own intense concentration on what he is thinking or doing at each moment he is on the stage all our attention focuses on him. Brando's quality is one of acute sensitivity. None of the brutishness of his part is native to him: it is a characteristic he has to "invent." The combination of an intense, introspective, and almost lyric personality under the mask of a bully endows the character with something almost touchingly painful. Because the elements of characterization are put on a face to which they are not altogether becoming, a certain crudeness mars our impression, while something in the nature of the actor's very considerable talent makes us wonder whether he is not actually suffering deeply in a way that relates him to what is represented by Blanche rather than to what his own character represents in the play. When he beats his wife or throws the radio out the window, there is, aside from the ugliness of these acts, an element of agony that falsifies their color in relation to their meaning in the play: they take on an almost Dostoevskian aspect.

For what is Stanley Kowalski? He is the embodiment of animal force, of brute life unconcerned and even consciously scornful of every value that does not come within the scope of such life. He resents being called a Polack, and he quotes Huey Long, who assured him that "every man is a king." He screams that he is a hundred percent American, and breaks dishes and mistreats his women to prove it. He is all muscle, lumpish sensuality and crude energy, given support by a society that hardly demands more of him. He is the unwitting antichrist of our time, the little man who will break the back of every effort to create a more comprehensive world in which thought and conscience, a broader humanity are expected to evolve from the old Adam. His mentality provides the soil for fascism, viewed not as a political movement but as a state of being.

Because the author does not preach about him but draws him without hate or ideological animus, the audience takes him at his face value. His face value on the stage is the face of Marlon Brando as contrasted to that of Jessica Tandy. For almost more than two-thirds of the play, therefore, the audience identifies itself with Stanley Kowalski. His low jeering is seconded by the audience's laughter, which seems to mock the feeble and hysterical decorativeness of the girl's behavior. The play becomes the triumph of Stanley Kowalski with the collusion of the audience, which is no longer on the side of the angels. This is natural because Miss Tandy is fragile without being touching (except when the author is beyond being overpowered by an actress), and Mr. Brando is tough without being irredeemably coarse.

When Kowalski tells his wife to get rid of Blanche so that things can be as they were (the author is suggesting that the untoward presence of a new consciousness in Kowalski's life—the appeal to forbearance and fineness—is a cruel disturbance and that he longs for a life without any spiritual qualms), the audience is all on Kowalski's side. Miss Tandy's speeches—which are lovely in themselves—sound phony, and her long words and noble appeals are as empty as a dilettante's discourse because they do not flow from that spring of warm feeling which is the justification and essence of Blanche's character.

One of the happiest pieces of staging and acting in the play is the moment when Kowalski, having beaten his wife, calls for her to return from the neighbor's apartment where she has taken momentary refuge. He whines like a hurt animal, shouts like a savage, and finally his wife descends the staircase to return to his loving arms. Brando has been directed to fall on his knees before his wife and thrust his head against her body in a gesture that connotes humility and passion. His wife with maternal and amorous touch caresses his head. He lifts her off her feet and takes her to bed. . . .

This, as I have noted, is done beautifully. Yet Brando's innate quality and something unresolved in the director's conception make the scene moving in a manner that is thematically disruptive. The pathos is too universally human (Kowalski at that moment is any man); it is not integrated with that attribute of the play which requires that Kowalski at all times be somewhat vile.

If Karl Malden as Blanche's suitor—a person without sufficient force to transcend the level of his environment—and Kim Hunter as Blanche's sister—who has made her peace with Kowalski's "normal life"—give performances that are easier to place than those of the two leading characters, it is not because of any intrinsic superiority to the other players. It is simply due to the fact that their parts are less complex. Miss Hunter is fairly good, Mr. Malden capital, but both appear in a sense to stand outside the play's interpretive problem. They are not struggling with a consciousness of the dilemma that exists in the choice between Kowalski's world and that of Blanche Du Bois.

As creative spectators, we cannot satisfy ourselves at a play like *A Streetcar Named Desire* with the knowledge that it is a wonderful show, a smash hit, a prize winner (it is and will be all of these). It is a play that ought to arouse in us as much feeling, thought and even controversy as plays on semipolitical themes; for it is a play that speaks of a poet's reaction to life in our country (not just the South), and what he has to say about it is much more far-reaching than what might be enunciated through any slogan.

I have heard it said, for example, that Tennessee Williams portrays "ordinary" people without much sense of their promise, and reserves most of his affection for more special people—that minority which Thomas Mann once described as life's delicate children. I find this view false and misleading, but I would rather hear it expressed than to let the play go by as the best play of the season, something you must see, "great theatre."

If the play is great theatre—as I believe—it is precisely because it is instinct with life, a life we share in not only on the stage, but in our very homes by night and day. If I have chosen to examine the production with what might seem undue minuteness, it is because I believe that questions of the theatre (and of art) are not simply questions of taste or professional quibbles, but life questions. I can think of no higher compliment to the director and actors of such a production than to take their work with utmost seriousness—even to the point of neglecting to make allowance for the difficulties attendant on the realization of so original a play on Broadway.

1948

The Famous "Method"

"ARE you in favor of grammar? Yes or no? God darn it!"

Can you conceive of people engaging in such a dispute? Do you suppose anyone could become fanatic about the subjunctive mood? In theatre circles something almost as absurd as this appears to be going on. The bone of contention is the famous Method—the grammar of acting.

Ordinarily it would hardly seem to me to be worth while to write about a matter of stagecraft for the general reader. It is not at all useful or particularly interesting for the playgoer to know how a performance he enjoys was prepared, any more than a knowledge of how pigments are mixed is helpful in the appreciation of painting. But the case of the Method has become a subject of inquiry for many theatregoers for reasons which I intend to explain.

The Method, an abbreviation of the term "Stanislavsky Method," is as its name indicates a means of training actors as well as a technique for the use of actors in their work on parts. This technique, formulated in 1909 by the Russian actor-director Konstantin Stanislavsky of the Moscow Art Theatre, and subsequently employed in the productions of that company, was introduced into this country by three of its actors: Leo Bulgakov, Richard Boleslavsky and Maria Ouspenskaya. After the Moscow Art Theatre had terminated its first Broadway engagement in 1923, these three actors decided to remain in the United States. They became the first teachers of the Method, which they and most other Russians referred to as the "System."

Among the young Americans who studied with Boleslavsky and Ouspenskaya between 1923–26 were Lee Strasberg, who today dominates the Actors Studio; Stella Adler, who now conducts a studio of her own; and, a little later, the present writer.

The Method had its first real trial and success on Broadway through the work of the Group Theatre (1931–41) of which Cheryl Crawford, Lee Strasberg and I were the leaders. In such productions as those of Kingsley's *Men in White* (directed by Strasberg), Odets' *Golden Boy* (directed by Clurman), Saroyan's *My Heart's in the Highlands* (directed by Robert Lewis), the Method—rarely touted beyond the confines of the Group's rehearsal hall—proved its value as a practical instrument in production.

I go into this now familiar history to stress the fact that by the year 1937 the "battle" of the Method had been won. By that time many theatre schools had been set up (among them the Neighborhood Playhouse whose main instructor, Sanford Meisner, had been an actor in the Group Theatre's permanent company) and an increasing number of well-known players— for example, Franchot Tone, who in 1933 left the Group for Hollywood—had made the Method part of their normal equipment. The Method was no longer a peculiarity of a few offbeat or off-Broadway actors.

It is true that a few critics still spoke of the Method and the schools or studios in which it was taught as a foreign excrescence unsuited to the American temperament, forgetting that in Stanislavsky's own company many of the actors had been just as skeptical as people anywhere else might be. But critics are notoriously behind the times.

How does it happen, then, that only in the past three or four years there has been such a rush and rash of publicity about the Method? What at this late date causes the endless palaver about Method and non-Method acting in and outside the theatrical profession?

Marilyn Monroe has a lot to do with it! That sumptuous lady in her eagerness to learn had begun to attend classes at the Actors Studio. Since all Miss Monroe's movements are carefully watched, the Studio began to attract attention far and wide. Everybody wanted to know what the Actors Studio was that the phosphorescent Marilyn should be concerned with it. What went on there? Who else participated? Then it was discovered that among other people who had been more or less attached to the Studio were Marlon Brando, Julie Harris, Kim Stanley, Maureen Stapleton, James Dean, Shelley Winters, Patricia Neal—with press emphasis, of course, on the Hollywood names.

If all these people had been adherents of the Studio, then the instruction there—mysteriously called the Method—had a gimmick fascination; there must certainly be something to it. Lee Strasberg might protest all he wanted that the Studio is not a school—nearly all its members had received their basic theatre instruction at schools or classes for beginners elsewhere —that many of its members were already well-known actors before they were invited into the Studio, that the Studio was simply a place where already trained actors thought particularly promising could pursue what might be called "postgraduate" work. None of this matters to the general public or to guileless aspirants to the stage; all they knew or cared about was the glamour and mystery that surrounded this nest of genius.

Of course, there was a more substantial reason for the Studio's hold on the acting profession. The practical eminence of the Studio's directorate—Crawford, Kazan, Strasberg—led aspirants to believe mistakenly that enrollment in the Studio was a gateway to employment.

None of this would be of much consequence if it did not result in certain misconceptions and confusion both outside the ranks of the acting profession and inside. Most members of the Studio—there is always a tendency in such organizations toward clannishness and cultism—are quite sane about their activities. The damage that is done is in the vastly larger body of "onlookers"—actors and those who have a general curiosity about the theatre. This damage ultimately injures the vital elements involved.

The Method, I have said, is the grammar of acting. There have been great writers who never studied grammar—though they usually possess it—but no one on that account proclaims grammar a fake and instruction in the subject futile. A mastery of grammar does not guarantee either a fine style or valuable literary content. Once in command of it, the writer is unconscious of method. It is never an end in itself. The same is true of the Stanislavsky Method.

There was grammar before there were grammarians. Great acting existed before the Method and great acting still exists unaware of it. A theatregoer who pays to see Michael Redgrave or Laurence Olivier cannot tell by watching them in performance which of the two was influenced by the Method.

The purpose of the Stanislavsky Method is to teach the actor to put the whole gamut of his physical and emotional being into the service of the dramatist's meaning. What Stanislavsky did was to observe great actors and study his own problems as an actor. In the process he began to isolate the various factors that composed fine acting. He systematized the way actors could prepare themselves for their task—the interpretation of plays. He detailed the means whereby actors might give shape and substance to the roles they were assigned.

There were acting methods before Stanislavsky, but none so thoroughgoing for the uses of all sorts of plays—from opera and farce to high tragedy—both classic and modern. Since the Method is a technique, not a style, there is no necessary connection between realism and the Method. In Russia, more nonrealistic plays than realistic plays were done with the aid of the Method.

Why was it necessary for Stanislavsky to evolve his Method? First, because the organization of knowledge about acting which the Method represents facilitates the first steps, diminishes the fumbling, wear and tear, waste of the apprentice years; and, second, because a conscious technique aids the actor, who has to repeat a part many times at specific hours, in gaining a greater mastery over his interpretation which without some form of conscious control tends to vanish through the capriciousness and fluidity of what is called inspiration.

All this is clearly set forth in Stanislavsky's three books—*My Life in Art, An Actor Prepares, Building a Character*—which have been available to the public for years. It is true that since the first of these volumes is an autobiography and the latter two technical handbooks, no one can learn to act merely by reading them. But the information they contain is neither mystic nor mysterious.

None of the American teachers of the Method (except Stella Adler, who worked with Stanislavsky in private sessions in Paris for six weeks in the summer of 1934) has ever known Stanislavsky personally and only two or three have ever seen any of his productions. I note this because it is always important to remember that just as every actor has his own individual personality which supersedes whatever technique he may employ or aesthetic doctrine he may profess, so every teacher of the Method lends it the quality of his own mind and disposition. There is no longer an "orthodox" Method, only a group of teachers (most of them trained in America) whose lessons derive from but are not limited to the Stanislavsky sources. As so often happens, on some points most of these teachers contradict one another violently. Which of them is in the right? For the laymen, it matters very little. Only results on the stage count.

Before abandoning the purely professional aspect of the subject and advancing to what I consider from the viewpoint of the general reader to be the more significant side, I should like to dispel some false notions which have arisen apropos the Method in the past five years or so. Those who are dubious or hostile to it (usually through misinformation) often mock it by saying that "Method actors"—a noxious term by the way—have slovenly diction, undistinguished voices, and conduct themselves on the stage with a singular lack of grace.

Needless to say, neither Stanislavsky nor any of the teachers who claim him as their guiding spirit are responsible for the professional or personal aberrations—real or imagined—of individual actors who study the Method. I have never heard anyone speak as long and as dogmatically on the importance of the voice and diction as did Stanislavsky to me on the several occasions of our meeting in Paris and Moscow. As for posture, physical deportment, correctness of carriage, discipline of manner: on these subjects Stanislavsky was almost fanatic. The actors of the Comédie Française (famous for fine voices and speech) had an inadequate vocal range of hardly more than three notes, he complained. The actress I most admired in his company was guilty of rather common speech and therefore could not gain his wholehearted approbation. Most actors walk badly, he pointed out. He was not satisfied that *anybody* anywhere had developed a voice to match the inherent demands of Shakespeare's verse.

American directors who were among the first followers of the Method and who have never renounced or denounced it have done shows such as *Brigadoon* (Robert Lewis) and *Tiger at the Gates* (Harold Clurman) which betrayed none of the traits of shabbiness in speech or behavior which many people associate with the Method. Indeed, it should be pointed out that a "classic" Method production, *Men in White*, was notable for a dignity which one critic declared attained a "concert beauty."

How then had this calumny about the drabness, not to say the grubbiness, of "Method acting" arisen? And is it only calumny? Marlon Brando's performance as Stanley Kowalski in Tennessee Williams' *A Streetcar Named Desire* was indirectly a major factor in the development of what might be dubbed a dreadful Method tradition or superstition. Brando's was a brilliant characterization and made a deep impression—unexpected as well as undesirable in its consequences.

It is worth mentioning that when I first heard that Brando was to do the part I thought he had been miscast. For I had known Brando, whom I had previously directed in a play by Maxwell Anderson, as an innately delicate, thoughtful and intellectually eager young man. No matter! For an alarming number of young people in the theatre Kowalski was Brando and Brando was great! The fact that Kowalski was largely a mug who frightened rather more than he fascinated the author himself—the play was intended to say that if we weren't careful such mugs might come to dominate our society—this fact escaped the host of Brando imitators. They equated the tough guy, delinquent aspect of the characterization with a heedlessness, a rebelliousness, a "freedom" and a kind of pristine strength which the performance seemed to them to symbolize. In it, they found combined their unconscious ideal: creative power in acting with a blind revolt against all sorts of conformity both in life and on the stage.

In France this is sometimes called *l'école Kazan*, although neither the muscularly energetic Kazan any more than the more intricately wrought Strasberg has ever made brutality a tenet of theatrical art. The fact that certain Method novitiates have confused realism with uncouthness in speech, manner and dress is an accident significant of the New York scene, not of the Method.

Too many of our younger actors have come to think of the refinement or decorum of the larger part of dramatic literature as somehow remote, old-fashioned, hypocritical—and alien. Their ideal is honesty, truth, down-to-earth simplicity, *guts.* "Down to earth" eventually becomes down to the gutter, and the only truth which is recognized as authentic is coarseness and ugliness.

This distortion is socially conditioned in the actors I refer to by an impulse to destroy the discipline of a gentility in their general environment, an environment usually without true roots in a meaningful and comprehensive culture. The distortion is also an unwitting protest against the streamlined efficiency of a too strictly business civilization or, so to speak, "Madison Avenue." These young actors fear nothing so much as any identification with the stuffed shirt.

The Method has influenced no theatre as much as the American. I have suggested one reason for this. Another has to do with one particular element of the Method—"affective memory" or the memory of emotions. I need not dwell here on the artistic validity, the use and abuse of this device. Suffice it to say that in the exercise of affective memory the actor is required to recall some personal event of his past in order to generate real feeling in relation to a scene in his part of the play.

This introspective action which—to an unusual degree—rivets the actor's attention on his inner life frequently strikes the novice as a revolutionary discovery. This is particularly true of the American, who, being part of an extroverted society which makes the world of *things* outside himself the focus of his hourly concern, seems to find in the technique of affective memory a revelation so momentous that it extends beyond the realm of its stage employment.

Most young actors who come upon it eat it up. Some it tends to make a little self-conscious, melancholy, "nervous," tense, producing a kind of constipation of the soul! Those with whom it agrees not only use it but often become consumed by it. With the immature and more credulous actor it may even develop into an emotional self-indulgence, or in other cases into a sort of private therapy. The actor being the ordinary neurotic man suffering all sorts of repressions and anxieties seizes upon the revelation of himself—supplied by the recollection of his past—as a purifying agent. Through it, he often imagines he will not only become a better actor, but a better person. It makes him feel that because of it he is no longer a mere performer but something like a redeemed human being and an artist. In this manner, the Method is converted into something akin not only to psychoanalysis but to "religion."

This was not Stanislavsky's aim nor does it represent the purpose of the Method teachers in America. It is, I repeat, an accident of our local scene to be explained by the psychological pressures and hunger of our youth. Where cultural activities are a normal part of daily life—as in most European countries—where self-expression is natural and habitual, the Method is taken as any other form of technical training—something to be learned and then "forgotten"—as grammar is forgotten when we have learned to use language properly.

Culture with us is still considered something apart from the main current of our lives. This is especially true of the stage. Since we have no national theatre, no repertory companies, no widespread stock companies, no consistent employment for the actor and since, too, channels for serious discussion, examination and practice of acting as an art are rare, the American actor clings to the Method and its ever-expanding centers of instruction as to a spiritual as well as a professional boon. It becomes manna from heaven.

I am glad the Method has "caught on." It has been of enormous benefit to our theatre and acting profession. Now that it has been established I hope to see it more or less taken as a matter of course. There is very little that is intrinsically controversial about it.

What the American actor really needs is more plays and productions in which to practice what has been preached. What actors of every kind need is a broader understanding of the Theatre as a whole: a general education in its relation to the world and to art in general. Young actors imbued with the Method have become so engrossed by what the Method can do for them that they forget that the Method exists for the Theatre and not the Theatre for the Method. What they must finally understand is that the Theatre is here for the pleasure, enlightenment and health of the audience—that is to say for all of us.

1958

FROM

The Theatre of the Thirties

THERE is a tendency nowadays to downgrade the thirties. The reason for this is that the prevailing mood of the thirties was what used to be called "left of center." Beginning with the late forties—from the time the phrase about the "iron curtain" became part of the common vocabulary—our "intelligentsia" sounded the retreat. The Roosevelt administration, subjected to sharp criticism not infrequently close to slander, seemed to be in bad odor. "Left of center" might be construed as something worse than liberalism. To be "radical" implied that one might be tainted with some degree of "pink."

A good many of the writers, artists and theatre folk in the thirties were inclined to radicalism. (Had not the Roosevelt administration sponsored the Projects for writers, artists and theatre?) In the early forties the fervor of the thirties was gradually absorbed by the pressures of the war. Since Russia was one of our allies there was less strictly political feeling: everyone was chiefly concerned with victory and the return to peaceful prosperity.

Shortly after the peace conference suspicion of the Soviet Union increased. Radicalism of any sort might be interpreted as "softness" toward the potential enemy. Our artists and writers, including theatre people, had not only shown too much sympathy for social experiment but had also been too emphatic about the real or supposed shortcomings of their own country. At best the enthusiasm of the thirties was now considered a sign of juvenile simple-mindedness, at worst something close to treason.

Around the year 1953 this reaction to the thirties had come close to hysteria. Today there is certainly more calm but the notion that the thirties was a foolish period persists. Presumably we are now far sounder in our thinking and work than we were then.

There is another aspect to the rather low esteem in which much of the dramatic work of the thirties is now held. The immediate past in the theatre always makes a poor impression. Writing about the twenties, which every student of our theatre history regards as a high point of the American theatre both in volume of activity and in achievement, Joseph Wood Krutch in the early thirties said that the record no longer seemed as bright as it once appeared. Very few of the best plays of that time would endure.

What most of us fail to note in this connection is that very few plays measured in the light of decades or generations have ever "endured." Shakespeare as we know Shakespeare is a nineteenth-century discovery! (He was neglected or disgracefully altered during the seventeenth and eighteenth centuries.) The number of plays which have come down to us from the

Greeks of the fifth century B.C. and from the Elizabethan era are a paltry few compared to the number produced. How cavalier was the attitude of our drama critics toward Marlowe's *Tamburlaine* because he was not equal to Shakespeare!

We may explain this paradox through our own theatregoing experience. A play may be both enjoyable and important to us at the moment we see it, but when the circumstances of our lives have changed, it may well have lost its appeal. One of the most popular plays the American theatre has ever produced is the dramatization of *Uncle Tom's Cabin*. No one can deny its importance for its day even if we no longer have much regard for it as literature.

It is downright stupid to sneer at our erstwhile excitement over *Waiting for Lefty* because today a good many people (in Europe at any rate) are waiting for Godot. As theatre-goers we are very rarely able to estimate a play in the present as we shall view it twenty-five years hence. What appeared a very inconsiderable play to England's finest dramatic critic, Bernard Shaw, Oscar Wilde's *The Importance of Being Earnest*, has proved durable beyond anyone's belief when it was first presented.

I recall having seen Robert Sherwood's *The Petrified Forest* (1935) in the company of one of our country's most astute men of letters. He enjoyed it thoroughly. A few days later we spoke on the phone. He remarked that the theatre was a hoax: he had been "taken in" by the play as he watched it, he said, but on further reflection he realized the play's flaws in thought and plot. Most readers who are also playgoers are like that.

We enjoy the "show," but we *think* about the play. There is often a disparity of judgment between the two activities. For though we are intellectually aware that literature and theatre are not identical, we are prone to assume that the text of a play is equivalent to the texture of its production. But a play in the theatre communicates qualities beyond—sometimes, in a bad performance, less than—what we find on the printed page. Thus to evaluate the theatre of any period only with regard to its texts is a falsification.

The plays of the thirties sharpen certain tendencies that were already evident, and comparatively new, in the plays of the twenties. For the twenties, which may be said to represent America's second coming of age in literature (the first might be dated around 1850) and its true coming of age in the theatre, were marked by a rather harsh critical realism. What such men as Frank Norris and Theodore Dreiser had been saying about us in their novels began to be said somewhat more lyrically (though no less vehemently) in the plays of Eugene O'Neill. The theatre is ideologically almost always behind the times because it is a mass medium. It takes a while for people to acknowledge publicly what a few individuals may think and say privately.

It was the artistic pleasure of the twenties to deride, curse, bemoan the havoc, spiritual blindness and absurdity of America's materialistic functionalism with its concomitant acquisitiveness and worship of success.

Another marked feature of the theatrical twenties was the fact that plays which had previously satisfied audiences with the mere tracing of types (or stereotypes) began to strike them as increasingly hollow. Characters began to show their faces on the stage. Psychology was "introduced." Men and women were no longer heroes or villains but "human," a mixture of contradictory traits. The standardized Puritanism typified by the old anti-vice societies became an object of scorn and ridicule.

The sentiment against war in *What Price Glory?* of the twenties was converted into the poignant and pointed satire of Paul Green's *Johnny Johnson* in the thirties. The sense of loneliness which informs O'Neill's pieces is rendered more acute and more general in Steinbeck's *Of Mice and Men* some ten years later. The plight of the colored people in the Heywards' *Porgy* or in Green's *In Abraham's Bosom* is intensified in John Wexley's *They Shall Not Die* in the thirties. The playful probing of Behrman's *The Second Man* in 1927 is given a social connotation in the same author's *Biography* and other of his later plays in the thirties. The laborer as a symbol of inner disharmony within the apparent health of the American commonwealth which we observe in O'Neill's *The Hairy Ape* (1922) becomes a leading theme on a more concrete basis in the thirties.

The most significant difference between the theatre of the twenties and that of the thirties is the emphasis in the later period on the social, economic and political background of the individual psychological case. The Wall Street crash of 1929, the Great Depression of the early thirties with its attendant scar of widespread unemployment, the hopeful attempt to remedy this bitter condition which ensued are the effective causes for the abrupt and drastic change.

The plays included in this volume are not all necessarily the "best" of the thirties, but all are representative. Space and other factors of publication permitting, I should certainly have included O'Neill's *Mourning Becomes Electra* (1931), an Irish play of Denis Johnston's, *The Moon in the Yellow River* (1932), Maxwell Anderson's *Winterset* (1935), Sidney Kingsley's *Dead End* (1935), Thornton Wilder's *Our Town* (1938), Robert Sherwood's *Abe Lincoln in Illinois* (1938), Lillian Hellman's *The Little Foxes* (1939).

Of the plays included one had to be the work of Clifford Odets. Historically speaking he is the dramatist of the thirties *par excellence*. His immediate sources of inspiration, his point of view, his language, his import and perhaps some of his weaknesses are typical of the thirties.

I am not at all sure that *Awake and Sing!*, first presented by the Group Theatre on February 19, 1935, is the best of Odets' plays. The 1937 *Golden Boy* has a more striking story line and is more varied and personal in its meaning. But *Awake and Sing!* contains the "seed" themes of the Odets plays and indicates most unaffectedly the milieu and the quality of feeling in which his work is rooted. One might even go so far as to say that there is hardly another play of the thirties—except perhaps John Howard Lawson's *Success Story* (1932)—which so directly communicates the very "smell" of New York in the first years of the depression.

The keynotes of the period are struck in *Awake and Sing!* as never again with such warm intimacy. There is first of all the bafflement and all-pervading worry of lower middle-class poverty. This is conveyed in language based on common speech and local New York (including Jewish) idiom, but it is not precisely naturalistic speech, for Odets' writing is a personal creation, essentially lyric, in which vulgarity, tenderness, energy, humor and a headlong idealism are commingled.

What is Odets' basic impulse; what is his "program"? They are contained in Jacob's exhortation to his grandson, "Go out and fight so life shouldn't be printed on dollar bills," and in another reflection, "Life should have some dignity." It seems to me that not only is most of Odets expressed in these bare words but the greater part of the whole cry of the American "progressive" movement—its radicalism if you will—as the artists of the thirties sensed it, is summed up in these innocent mottoes.

The "biblical" fervor in *Awake and Sing!* impels a "revolutionary" conviction expressed in Jacob's comment, "It needs a new world," which leads his grandson to take heart and proclaim, "Fresh blood, arms. We've got 'em. We're glad we're living." This was the "wave" of the thirties. If that wave did not carry us on to the millennium, it is surely the height of folly to believe that it had no vital force and accomplished nothing of value in the arts as well as in our community life.

S. N. Behrman's *End of Summer*, produced by the Theatre Guild on February 17, 1936, gives us the depression period seen from another angle: that of the "privileged" classes. It is a comedy of manners which besides its merits in the way of urbane dialogue, etc., presents a central character who (apart from having a decided semblance to the play's author) is kin to most of the folk who buy the best seats in our metropolitan theatres. Leonie, says Behrman, "is repelled by the gross and the voluptuary: this is not hypocrisy. . . . In the world in which she moves hypocrisy is merely a social lubricant, but this very often springs from a congenital and temperamental inability to face anything but the pleasantest and most immediately appealing and the most flattering aspect of things, in life and in her own nature."

What *End of Summer* presents is the spectacle of such a person confronted by the unhappy phenomenon of mass unemployment, nascent radicalism, spectres of fascism and the ambiguities of the psychoanalysts. The treatment is characteristic of Behrman—joshing, debonair, slightly more lighthearted than the author actually feels.

The lady of the play for the first time meets "the young radicals our colleges are said to be full of nowadays." One such radical, a somewhat fictitious Irish Catholic young fellow, tells the lady, "The world is middle-aged and tired," at which the lady queries, "Can you refresh us?" The young man rejoins, "Refresh you! Leonie, we can rejuvenate you." That was another hope of the youth which during the thirties had reached the ages of twenty-five to thirty-five. It was not altogether a vain hope for, as I have already indicated and shall continue to indicate, there was a young and invigorating spirit that relieved the thirties of its blues and led to concrete benefits.

One of the faults easily spotted in *End of Summer* is also evident in Robert Sherwood's *Idiot's Delight*, produced by the Theatre Guild in the spring of 1936. Just as the young radicals of Behrman's play seem to be known by hearsay rather than by intimate acquaintance, so in *Idiot's Delight* Sherwood's grasp of the European political situation is informed as it were by headlines rather than truly experienced. Thus he makes his French pacifist a Radical-Socialist who speaks of the workers' uprising and alludes to Lenin with reverence, whereas any knowledgeable foreign correspondent could have told Sherwood that the Radical-Socialists of France are the party of small business, abhor Lenin's doctrines and are neither radical nor socialist.

This slight error is worth mentioning because it is symptomatic of a not uncommon failing in American playwrights when they generalize or "intellectualize" on social or ethical themes. It is a species of dilettantism which consists of dealing with subjects in which one is certainly interested but not truly familiar.

More cogent than this flaw is the sentiment which inspired Sherwood to write *Idiot's Delight*. It echoes the American fear of and profound estrangement from the facts of European intrigue which led to war. One merit of Sherwood's play is that it gives us an inkling of the moral climate in our country shortly after the Italian-Ethiopian conflagration and at the outset of the Spanish civil conflict—two omens of the future scarcely understood by an average citizen. Sherwood's "solution" to the problem in his play is the idealistic injunction "You can refuse to fight."

This is significant because it shows that the attitude of our dramatists, generally speaking, was fundamentally moral rather than, as some are now inclined to believe, political. This explains why Sherwood, whose *Idiot's Delight* might indicate the opposition to war of the "conscientious objector," took a very different stand when Nazism threatened to engulf Europe and the world. The play also marks the transition from skepticism and pessimism in regard to modern life, suggested by several of Sherwood's earlier plays, to the willingness to be engaged in political struggle and an acceptance of war, exemplified by his *Abe Lincoln in Illinois.*

Sherwood was a shrewd showman: *Idiot's Delight* gives striking evidence of this. He himself is supposed to have said, "The trouble with me is that I start off with a big message and end with nothing but good entertainment." *Idiot's Delight* was good entertainment, particularly in the acting opportunities it afforded Alfred Lunt and Lynn Fontanne, just as Leonie in *End of Summer*, in itself a charming characterization, was given special fragrance by Ina Claire's delightful talent.

John Steinbeck's *Of Mice and Men*, produced by Sam H. Harris on November 23, 1937, is a parable of American loneliness and of our hunger for "brotherhood"—two feelings the depression greatly enhanced. This play, unlike most of the others we have cited, concentrates on the unemployed of the farm lands, the itinerants and ranch workers, while it alludes to the bus and truck drivers whose travels through the country permitted them to observe the state of the nation in its broad horizon.

The American theatre, centered in New York, is on the whole cut off from the rest of the country. The thirties was the time when the theatre, along with the other arts, rediscovered America. *Green Grow the Lilacs* (1931) is one of the several Lynn Riggs Oklahoma plays, Erskine Caldwell's *Tobacco Road* (1933), Osborn's *Morning's at Seven* (1939)—to mention only a few— are among the many which in one way or another perform a similar function. One of the reasons why Steinbeck's parable carries conviction on naturalistic grounds is that the author shares the background and the earthiness of his characters.

Steinbeck knows our longing for a home, not a mere feeding place. He has the same true sympathy for the lonesome devil whose sole companion is a mangy old dog as for the Negro cut off by his fellow workers because of his color. He suggests with something like an austere sorrow that America's "underprivileged" will never reach the home they crave till they arrive at greater consciousness.

Speaking of "austerity" I should point out that one of the

ground tones of American art and theatre (particularly the latter) is sentimentality. This is also true of Steinbeck's play, though he tries to control his sentimentality. Now sentimentality is usually accounted a vice, because it bespeaks a propensity to express a greater degree of feeling than a specific situation warrants. But sentimentality need not be a vital flaw; it isn't in *Of Mice and Men*. It is often the characteristic of a young and vigorous people whose experience of life is, so to speak, still new and uncontaminated by too frequent disillusionment. In this sense our history makes us a sentimental people and it is only natural that our arts, particularly our folk arts, should reveal this quality.

This brings us to the last play of this volume: William Saroyan's *The Time of Your Life*, presented by the Theatre Guild in association with Eddie Dowling on October 25, 1939. This sentimental comedy is by way of being a little classic. It marks the deliquescence of the aggressive mood of the thirties. For though the moralistic and critical rationale of the thirties is still present in *The Time of Your Life*, it is there in a lyrically anarchistic manner, a sort of sweet (here and there mawkish) dream.

Another way, distinctly 1959, of describing this play is to call is pre-beatnik! "I believe dreams more than statistics," one character says. "Everybody is behind the eight ball," says another. Money appears as the root of most evil—anyway it is the filthiest thing that goes and "there's no foundation all the way down the line," as the old man from the Orient mutters throughout the play.

In a way *The Time of Your Life* is a social fable: it turns its head away from and thumbs its nose at our monstrously efficient society which produces arrogance, cruelty, fear, headaches, constipation and the yammering of millions of humble folk, only to conclude that "all people are wonderful." Though this evinces more bewilderment than insight, it is nevertheless honestly American in its fundamental benevolence.

What saves this play, or rather what "makes" it, is its infectious humor, its anti-heroism (an oblique form of rebelliousness), its San Francisco colorfulness, its succulent dialogue, its wry hoboism and nonconformity. Though it is of another time, one still reads it with a sense of relief.

No account of the theatre of the thirties can convey any sense of its true nature and its contribution to our culture without emphasizing certain purely theatrical factors which played as decisive a role as the plays themselves.

The importance of the Group Theatre (1931–1941), whose origins may be traced back to the late twenties, can hardly be overestimated. (The first unofficial "group" meetings were held in 1928.) The Group Theatre was important not alone because it developed Odets from among its acting members, or even because it presented Sidney Kingsley's first play, *Men in White* (1933), Saroyan's first play, *My Heart's in the Highlands* (1939) as well as various plays by Paul Green, John Howard Lawson, Irwin Shaw and Robert Ardrey, but also because it organized its actors as a permanent company and trained them in a common craftsmanship which not only became emblematic for the era but which in many ways influenced the course of our theatre practice in the ensuing years.

Among the actors, directors, producers, designers, teachers trained or brought into prominence by the Group Theatre were: Stella Adler, Luther Adler, Boris Aronson, Harold Clurman, Lee Cobb, Cheryl Crawford, Morris Carnovsky, John Garfield, Elia Kazan, Mordecai Gorelik, Robert Lewis, Lee Strasberg, Franchot Tone.

The Group Theatre in certain respects continued a tradition established by such pioneer organizations as the Provincetown Players, the Theatre Guild, the Neighborhood Playhouse. In another way the Group served as a model for such organizations as the Theatre Union, the Theatre Collective, the Theatre of Action, which were "workers' theatres" with a more specifically political orientation. These were valuable organizations, particularly the Theatre Union, offering vivid productions of social plays. Our theatre needs more such organizations (there are none at present) which commit themselves to definite ideals or policies rather than wallowing in hit-or-miss show-shop opportunism.

Far more important than these special organizations was the Federal Theatre Project (1935–1939). Its rudest critics will not deny the interest of such productions as the "Living Newspaper," *One Third of a Nation*, the Negro *Macbeth*, Marlowe's *Dr. Faustus*, T. S. Eliot's *Murder in the Cathedral*, and the attempted production of Marc Blitzstein's momentous musical play, *The Cradle Will Rock*—ultimately presented under different auspices.

The Federal Theatre Project brought much excellent theatre fare to a national public at nominal prices, a public the greater part of which was barely acquainted with any form of "live" theatre. This was the first government-sponsored theatre in our history and it indicated how beneficial such an effort could be, even when circumstances were far from favorable.

Orson Welles was given his first opportunity as a director under the Federal Theatre Project. Because of his success there he was enabled to establish (with John Houseman) the short-lived but animated Mercury Theatre which produced a remarkably provocative *Julius Caesar* in the spirit of the times (1937).

Looking back from the vantage point of 1959 we may say that although admirable work still continues to be done on our constantly harassed and considerably shrunken stage, there are two virtues which may be claimed for the theatre of the thirties conspicuously lacking today. The theatre of the thirties attempted to make the stage an instrument of public enlightenment through a passionate involvement with the national scene. It made valiant and, to a remarkable degree, effective efforts to bring order and discipline into the helter-skelter of our theatre's artistic and financial organization.

An intelligent and successful Broadway producer of today recently said to me, "The theatre at present is twenty times more 'commercial' than it was in the thirties. For one thing, you could reach the hearts and souls of actors, playwrights, designers, etc., with good sense and considerations of sound craftsmanship. Today these people, whatever their personal dispositions, appear encircled by an iron ring forged by agents who protect their clients from all thought beyond income, percentages and publicity."

The lean days and hungry nights of the thirties were a brave time. Aren't we a little torpid now?

1959

JOHN MASON BROWN

John Mason Brown (1900–1969) was a classmate of Thomas Wolfe in Professor Baker's 47 Workshop at Harvard (1921–23), remembering him as the most earnest of the lot. Like many theatrical journalists, Brown pursued upward mobility from paper to paper, writing for the *Louisville Courier-Journal* and the *Boston Transcript* (1923–24), serving as dramatic critic for *Theatre Arts Monthly* (1925–28) and the *New York Evening Post*, writing the column "Two on the Aisle" from 1929 throughout the 1930s. He took up a similar position at the *New York World-Telegram* in 1941, but left it the next year to join the Navy as a lieutenant, seeing action in North Africa, Sicily, and Normandy. In 1944 he became associate editor and dramatic critic of the *Saturday Review* with the column "Seeing Things," which he continued to write until his death. John Simon's characterization of his style as "chatty urbanity" is too dismissive. Brown was an aphorist of considerable wit ("He played the king as if afraid someone else would play the ace"); his strong cultural background enabled him to compare plays in detail with the works on which they were based. And Brown's integrity was unassailable: in 1963 he resigned from the Pulitzer Prize Committee when the advisory board turned down his recommendation of Albee's *Who's Afraid of Virginia Woolf?*

Even as You and I

GEORGE JEAN NATHAN once described a certain actress's Camille as being the first Camille he had ever seen who had died of catarrh. This reduction in scale of a major disease to an unpleasant annoyance is symptomatic of more than the acting practice of the contemporary stage. Even our dramatists, at least most of them, tend in their writing, so to speak, to turn t.b. into a sniffle. They seem ashamed of the big things; embarrassed by the raw emotions; afraid of the naked passions; and unaware of life's brutalities and tolls.

Of understatement they make a fetish. They have all the reticences and timidities of the overcivilized and undemonstrative. They pride themselves upon writing around a scene rather than from or to it; upon what they hold back instead of upon what they release. They paint with pastels, not oils, and dodge the primary anguishes as they would the primary colors.

Their characters belong to an anaemic brood. Lacking blood, they lack not only violence but humanity. They are the puppets of contrivance, not the victims of circumstance or themselves. They are apt to be shadows without substance, surfaces without depths. They can be found in the *dramatis personae* but not in the telephone book. If they have hearts, their murmurings are seldom audible. They neither hear nor allow us to hear those inner whisperings of hope, fear, despair, or joy, which are the true accompaniment to spoken words. Life may hurt them, but they do not suffer from the wounds it gives them so that we, watching them, are wounded ourselves and suffer with them.

This willingness, this ability, to strike unflinchingly upon the anvil of human sorrow is one of the reasons for O'Neill's pre-eminence and for the respect in which we hold the best work of Clifford Odets and Tennessee Williams. It is also the source of Arthur Miller's unique strength and explains why his fine new play, *Death of a Salesman*, is an experience at once pulverizing and welcome.

Mr. Miller is, of course, remembered as the author of *Focus*, a vigorous and terrifying novel about anti-Semitism, and best known for *All My Sons*, which won the New York Critics Award two seasons back. Although that earlier play lacked the simplicity, hence the muscularity, of Mr. Miller's novel, it was notable for its force. Overelaborate as it may have been, it introduced a new and unmistakable talent. If as a young man's script it took advantage of its right to betray influences, these at least were of the best. They were Ibsen and Chekhov. The doctor who wandered in from next door might have been extradited from *The Three Sisters*. The symbolical use to which the apple tree was put was pure Ibsen. So, too, was the manner in which the action was maneuvered from the present back into the past in order to rush forward. Even so, Mr. Miller's own voice could be heard in *All My Sons*, rising strong and clear above those other voices. It was a voice that deserved the attention and admiration it won. It was not afraid of being raised. It spoke with heat, fervor, and compassion. Moreover, it had something to say.

In *Death of a Salesman* this same voice can be heard again. It has deepened in tone; developed wonderfully in modulation, and gained in carrying power. Its authority has become full-grown. Relying on no borrowed accents, it now speaks in terms of complete accomplishment rather than exciting promise. Indeed, it is released in a play which provides one of the modern theatre's most overpowering evenings.

How good the writing of this or that of Mr. Miller's individual scenes may be, I do not know. Nor do I really care. When hit in the face, you do not bother to count the knuckles which strike you. All that matters, all you remember, is the staggering impact of the blow. Mr. Miller's is a terrific wallop, as furious in its onslaught on the heart as on the head. His play is the most poignant statement of man as he must face himself to have come out of our theatre. It finds the stuffs of life so mixed with the stuffs of the stage that they become one and indivisible.

If the proper study of mankind is man, man's inescapable problem is himself—what he would like to be, what he is, what he is not, and yet what he must live and die with. These are the moving, everyday, all-inclusive subjects with which Mr. Miller deals in *Death of a Salesman*. He handles them unflinchingly, with enormous sympathy, with genuine imagination, and in a mood which neither the prose of his dialogue nor the reality of his probing can rob of its poetry. Moreover, he has the wisdom and the insight not to blame the "System," in Mr. Odets's fashion, for what are the inner frailties and shortcomings of the individual. His rightful concern is with the dilemmas which are timeless in the drama because they are timeless in life.

Mr. Miller's play is a tragedy modern and personal, not classic and heroic. Its central figure is a little man sentenced to discover his smallness rather than a big man undone by his greatness. Although he happens to be a salesman tested and found wanting by his own very special crises, all of us sitting out front are bound to be shaken, long before the evening is over, by finding something of ourselves in him.

Mr. Miller's Willy Loman is a family man, father of two sons.

He is sixty-three and has grubbed hard all his life. He has never possessed either the daring or the gold-winning luck of his prospector brother, who wanders through the play as a somewhat shadowy symbol of success but a necessary contrast. Stupid, limited, and confused as Willy Loman may have been, however, no one could have questioned his industry or his loyalty to his family and his firm. He has loved his sons and, when they were growing up, been rewarded by the warmth of their returned love. He loves his wife, too, and has been unfaithful to her only because of his acute, aching loneliness when on the road.

He has lived on his smile and on his hopes; survived from sale to sale; been sustained by the illusion that he has countless friends in his territory, that everything will be all right, that he is a success, and that his boys will be successes also. His misfortune is that he has gone through life as an eternal adolescent, as someone who has not dared to take stock, as someone who never knew who he was. His personality has been his profession; his energy, his protection. His major ambition has been not only to be liked, but well liked. His ideal for himself and for his sons has stopped with an easy, backslapping, sports-loving, locker-room popularity. More than ruining his sons so that one has become a woman chaser and the other a thief, his standards have turned both boys against their father.

When Mr. Miller's play begins, Willy Loman has reached the ebb-tide years. He is too old and worn out to continue traveling. His back aches when he stoops to lift the heavy sample cases that were once his pride. His tired, wandering mind makes it unsafe for him to drive the car which has carried him from one town and sale to the next. His sons see through him and despise him. His wife sees through him and defends him, knowing him to be better than most and, at any rate, well intentioned. What is far worse, when he is fired from his job he begins to see through himself. He realizes he is, and has been, a failure. Hence his deliberate smashup in his car in order to bring in some money for his family and make the final payment on his home when there is almost no one left who wants to live in it.

Although *Death of a Salesman* is set in the present, it also finds time and space to include the past. It plays the agonies of the moment of collapse against the pleasures and sorrows of recollected episodes. Mr. Miller is interested in more than the life and fate of his central character. His scene seems to be Willy Loman's mind and heart no less than his home. What we see might just as well be what Willy Loman thinks, feels, fears, or remembers as what we see him doing. This gives the play a double and successful exposure in time. It makes possible the constant fusion of what has been and what is. It also enables it to achieve a greater reality by having been freed from the fetters of realism.

Once again Mr. Miller shows how fearless and perceptive an emotionalist he is. He writes boldly and brilliantly about the way in which we disappoint those we love by having disappointed ourselves. He knows the torment of family tensions, the compensations of friendship, and the heartbreak that goes with broken pride and lost confidence. He is aware of the loyalties, not blind but open-eyed, which are needed to support mortals in their loneliness. The anatomy of failure, the pathos of age, and the tragedy of those years when a life begins to slip down the hill it has labored to climb are subjects at which he excels.

The quality and intensity of his writing can perhaps best be suggested by letting Mr. Miller speak for himself, or rather by allowing his characters to speak for him, in a single scene, in fact, in the concluding one. It is then that Willy's wife, his two sons, and his old friend move away from Jo Mielziner's brilliantly simple and imaginative multiple setting, and advance to the footlights. It is then that Mr. Miller's words supply a scenery of their own. Willy Loman, the failure and suicide, has supposedly just been buried, and all of us are at his grave, including his wife who wants to cry but cannot and who keeps thinking that it is just as if he were off on another trip.

"You don't understand," says Willy's friend, defending Willy from one of his sons, "Willy was a salesman. And for a salesman, there is no rock bottom to the life. He don't put a bolt to a nut, he don't tell you the law or give you medicine. He's a man way out there in the blue, ridin' on a smile and a shoeshine. And when they start not smilin' back—that's an earthquake. And then you get yourself a couple spots on your hat, and you're finished. Nobody dast blame this man. A salesman is got to dream, boy. It comes with the territory."

The production of *Death of a Salesman* is as sensitive, human, and powerful as the writing. Elia Kazan has solved, and solved superbly, what must have been a difficult and challenging problem. He captures to the full the mood and heartbreak of the script. He does this without ever surrendering to sentimentality. He manages to mingle the present and the past, the moment and the memory, so that their intertwining raises no questions and causes no confusions. His direction, so glorious in its vigor, is no less considerate of those small details which can be both mountainous and momentous in daily living.

It would be hard to name a play more fortunate in its casting than *Death of a Salesman*. All of its actors—especially Arthur Kennedy and Cameron Mitchell as the two sons, and Howard Smith as the friend—act with such skill and conviction that the line of demarcation between being and pretending seems abolished. The script's humanity has taken possession of their playing and is an integral part of their performances.

Special mention must be made of Lee J. Cobb and Mildred Dunnock as the salesman, Willy Loman, and his wife, Linda. Miss Dunnock is all heart, devotion, simplicity. She is unfooled but unfailing. She is the smiling, mothering, hard-worked, good wife, the victim of her husband's budget. She is the nourisher of his dreams, even when she knows they are only dreams; the feeder of his self-esteem. If she is beyond whining or nagging, she is above self-pity. She is the marriage vow— "for better for worse, for richer for poorer, in sickness and in health"—made flesh; slight of body but strong of faith.

Mr. Cobb's Willy Loman is irresistibly touching and wonderfully unsparing. He is a great shaggy bison of a man seen at that moment of defeat when he is deserted by the herd and can no longer run with it. Mr. Cobb makes clear the pathetic extent to which the herd has been Willy's life. He also communicates the fatigue of Willy's mind and body and that boyish hope and buoyancy which his heart still retains. Age, however, is his enemy. He is condemned by it. He can no more escape from it than he can from himself. The confusions, the weakness, the goodness, the stupidity, and the self-sustaining illusions which are Willy—all of these are established by Mr. Cobb. Seldom has an average man at the moment of his breaking been characterized with such exceptional skill.

Did Willy Loman, so happy with a batch of cement when puttering around the house, or when acquaintances on the road smiled back at him, fail to find out who he was? Did this man, who worked so hard and meant so well, dream the wrong dream? At least he was willing to die by that dream, even when it had collapsed for him. He was a breadwinner almost to the end, and a breadwinner even in his death. Did the world walk out on him, and his sons see through him? At any rate he could boast one friend who believed in him and thought his had been a good dream, "the only dream you can have." Who knows? Who can say? One thing is certain. No one could have raised the question more movingly or compassionately than Arthur Miller.

1949

FRANCES PARKINSON KEYES

One of the remarkable features of the American theatre in the 1920s and '30s was the number of women in charge: Eva Le Gallienne and Katharine Cornell heading their own companies, Alla Nazimova in Hollywood and Jessie Bonstelle in Detroit, Cheryl Crawford at the Group Theatre, Hallie Flanagan at the Federal Theatre Project. In advance of them all was Theresa Helburn, another product of George Pierce Baker's Harvard class. After serving a brief stint as a reviewer for *The Nation*, she became the iron-willed administrator of the Theatre Guild, an offshoot of the Washington Square Players, which championed Shaw and the New Stagecraft. To keep it on a financially even keel, she provided glamour by inviting Alfred Lunt and Lynn Fontanne into the company and produced both the groundbreaking musical comedy *Oklahoma!* and Paul Robeson's *Othello*. There is something piquant in the fact that, by a fluke of childhood friendship, the career of this no-nonsense lesbian should be chronicled by Frances Parkinson Keyes (1885–1970). Keyes, a convert to Roman Catholicism, a firm believer in virginity before marriage, married to a stodgy Republican senator, was a popular purveyor of "women's fiction." Her first writing had been a series of articles about life in Washington for *Good Housekeeping*. In the 1950s, she became a fixture of New Orleans society, which loosened her up. Her thoroughly researched novels now took the past of Southern Louisiana for their theme; the most entertaining is *Crescent Carnival*, about Mardi Gras in the 1890s.

Terry Helburn

I

I HAVE never lost my sense of sustained excitement, mingled with keen enjoyment, at a theatrical opening. The lights blazing above the entrance. The mounted police dashing back and forth. The long lines of shining limousines. The sidewalk crowds surging around nonchalant celebrities. The pompous critics taking their aisle seats. The exchange of greetings between established first-nighters. The condescending glances toward those who do not belong to the charmed circle. The suddenly subdued chatter, the slow rise of the curtain, the acclaim of the star. The stampede into the aisles at the end of the first act. The guarded expressions of those who await the critics' opinion. The candid praise or condemnation of those less timid. The final curtain, the frantic clapping. And then that kaleidoscopic street again. . . .

Perhaps the fact that I am essentially a country-woman accounts for the pleasure all this gives me. But only in part. In the last analysis, the fact that my presence at such functions is almost invariably due to a very remarkable woman, who is likewise a very old friend, is also largely accountable for my feeling about them. This woman is Theresa Helburn, Lawrence Langner's co-director in the Theatre Guild, who in such large measure, as he himself testifies, has contributed to the outstanding success they have shared through the development of a great theatrical idea. It is she who, on the occasion of an opening, often draws me into the charmed circle, which immediately becomes permeated with her friendliness and her vitality. Nothing in her speech or her manner betrays the struggle which has preceded success, the obstacles which have been overcome and the disasters which have threatened. And this is indubitably because of her lifelong, singlehearted, and unshakable conviction that "the play's the thing."

Except in our extreme youth, her approach to the drama and mine have always been from opposite directions: to me, it represents the most welcome and the most powerful means of relaxation that an overcrowded life affords; merely to sink into a seat at the theatre brings a sense of release that nothing else, short of an ocean voyage, provides. To Theresa Helburn, the drama represents not only supreme success in a chosen career, but the strenuous lifework to which all other pleasures and all other interests have been subordinated. (I do not say all other affections, because she has also been a devoted daughter, sister, aunt, wife, and friend.) Nevertheless, despite the difference in our approach to it, I believe, as she does, that without our common love for the theatre and the recurrent occasions on which it has served to reunite us after long periods of separation, our friendship might not have endured and flourished as it has ever since our school days.

My first impressions of Terry are not, however, centered on

her domination of a drama, but on a large, cold classroom at the rear of 94 Beacon Street, Boston, which, at the time, was the location of Miss Winsor's School. I had already been going to this school two or three years, but I still felt like an outsider: I had been away from Boston between the ages of ten and fourteen, part of the time in Vermont and part of the time in Europe, and I had ceased to belong exclusively to the Back Bay. I was troubled by this sense of strangeness. Terry was a newcomer who had never belonged and who was not in the least troubled by this circumstance. Business had brought her father to Boston and logically, but unenthusiastically, his wife and children had accompanied him. In consequence, Terry had been wrested from the Horace Mann School and thrust into Miss Winsor's.

It was a common saying among us that our teachers did not assign history and English lessons by the page, but by the number of inches that multitudinous pages would cover when pressed closely together. This was really not much of an exaggeration. Our algebra lessons did not cover quite so many pages, but our teacher of mathematics considered ten intricate problems a very reasonable number for daily solution. Some higher power decreed that not all of these should be classified as homework, but that we might spend the final period at school in solving, or attempting to solve, the first one or two. We were all extremely grateful for this concession.

The period lasted forty minutes, from ten minutes before one to one-thirty. On her first day at school, Terry raised her hand at ten minutes past one and, having attracted the room teacher's impersonal attention, inquired whether she might go home. Patiently the teacher explained that Theresa would be much freer that afternoon if she had made a good start on her problems.

"I've finished them," Terry announced tersely.

Involuntarily, the teacher glanced at the clock. There was a moment of electrified silence. It did not seem probable that this small cheerful child, who was actually the youngest girl in the class and who looked even younger than she was, could solve ten difficult problems at the rate of two minutes apiece. "Bring me your notebook, please," the teacher requested.

With complete self-possession, Terry rose, slid from her

seat, and approached the teacher's desk. The silence was now not only electric but breathless. It was broken by the crisp sound that the pages of the notebook made as the teacher turned them. Then she closed the book with a snap.

"The answers are all correct," she said levelly. "You may be excused. The rest of the class will please proceed with the problems."

Terry nodded and departed, her pleasant rosy face wreathed in smiles. She left no smiles in her wake. But she left ungrudging admiration. From that moment everyone knew that if she did not belong, it was because none of the rest of us was in her class, figuratively speaking, though, literally speaking, she was in ours.

2

None of us was ever to match wits with her successfully or to establish superiority on any other plane; her resourcefulness and her inventive powers were already greatly in evidence. But, after that, she made friends, happily for me, myself among them. When we left school, our feeling for each other continued to be friendly, but it did not find very frequent expression. Terry went on to college and her family moved back to New York, which became her logical center; I married at eighteen and went to live on a farm in New Hampshire, from which I did not often stray very far. Terry came to visit me two or three times and, in the course of these visits, coached our local Dramatic Club, of which I was then president. Then came several years in which I saw very little of her. I was more preoccupied with babies than I was with dramatics, and Terry was equally preoccupied, in very different ways. From Bryn Mawr, where she carried off both the Mary Helen Ritchie Prize and the George W. Childs Essay Prize, she went on to Radcliffe, where, as a graduate student, she joined Professor Baker's famous 47 Workshop, which was the prelude to all dramatic studies in universities. Later she matriculated at the Sorbonne; but she abandoned her courses, as she says semi-seriously, because no one would permit her to fling open the classroom windows, hitherto hermetically sealed, and admit currents of air to the venerable Paris buildings. (She has always been something of a fresh air fiend and to this day has to be closely watched lest she quickly reduce the comfortable temperature of a house to arctic chilliness.) Finally she settled down again, more or less, living with her parents on West End Avenue, and invited me to visit her there, so that we might "go the rounds of the theatres together."

I received the invitation with rapture, took the children to my mother-in-law's house in Boston, and prepared for flight. On the eve of my expected departure for New York, I came down with the flu or, as we still called it then, *la grippe.*

I was bitterly disappointed, but Terry's telegram, in response to mine voicing this disappointment, was reassuring: she either had changed or would change all our theatre tickets, and she had also managed to change the dates of all social engagements. Philosophically, I faced the postponement of two weeks. But when convalescence seemed assured, I had a relapse. This happened three times.

I cannot truthfully say that warmth was lacking in Terry's manner when she finally met me at the Grand Central Station, but still I thought I felt a certain constraint in it. Within twenty-four hours I was so sure of this that I questioned Terry about it. I realized all too well, I said, how inopportune my illness had been. If she would rather I cut my visit short. . . .

"Of course not," she said promptly. "But—well, I may as well confess. As you know, parties had been planned for you, and your prospective hostesses took one postponement in their stride. The second one was a little harder to face, but they were good sports about that, too. However, when it came to a third, I knew they *couldn't* face it. So I produced another Frances Parkinson Keyes."

"What do you mean, you produced another Frances Parkinson Keyes?"

"Well, of course that wasn't really her name, but everyone thought so then and everyone still thinks so. She'd just landed from England and she didn't know anyone when she got here. I met her as a result of a letter of introduction from mutual friends and I pressed her right into service—coached her about Pine Grove Farm and Harry's politics and the babies and all. She didn't slip up once and everyone thought she was charming. Incidentally, I explained her accent, too—it might have passed for Bostonian, but I wasn't taking any chances, so

I said you'd been to school in England for years. She went to all the parties that were given in your honor and now she's gone south and isn't coming back to New York before she returns to Europe. But I'm afraid you may have a rather dull time, because my aunt is bound to be the only person who'll give another party. I confessed to her this morning, too, and she thought it was a huge joke. I don't know how many other people would."

Neither do I. But from that time on, I never doubted that Terry Helburn was destined to be an impresario.

3

The stage had always attracted her very greatly, and I believe that if she had persisted in her desire to become an actress, she would have had an immense success. Though actually short of stature, she has always carried herself with such dignity and assurance, and moved with such easy grace, that her lack of height is not noticeable. And though she has never been beautiful, she has the type of personality which brings with it the illusion of beauty and qualities even better and brighter—vitality, mobility of expression, quick understanding, and wit unbarbed by venom, wisdom unburdened by pedantry. Above all, she has charm, which, as Barrie so rightly said, is that sort of bloom upon a woman that makes every other attribute secondary. When Terry was a girl, her abundant hair was very dark and rather shaggy-looking. It turned gray prematurely and she tried the somewhat startling experiment of wearing it dark blue. But her instinct for the appropriate had not led her astray; now, carefully coiffed and azure-tinted, it makes a becoming contrast to her fresh skin and gray eyes. She has equally happy results in her experiments with clothes. She appeared at one of my parties in Louisiana wearing a creation of stiff gray satin, made for her by the famous Valentina, from a dress length that had belonged to Terry's grandmother; afterward, one of her fellow guests, who met her then for the first time, pronounced her by far the loveliest and most striking woman present. On another occasion, when she was considering "something conservative in black," Valentina easily prevailed upon her to substitute sky-blue silk, caught up with pink roses, and admonished her that she must also put pink roses in her hair. "You will look like a French marquise," Valentina told her. And she did.

She could have acted such a part to perfection and any number of other parts as well; but to her conservative parents, the very word "actress" was anathema. I do not remember her father very clearly, but her mother was one of those lovely-looking women who create an impression of languor and deference which is as charming as it is misleading; as a matter of fact, she had unlimited energy and an iron will. Terry adored her. Feeling as she did about her, it is not surprising that Terry eventually yielded to her wishes, even though she had not only accepted a part in Lawrence Langner's *Licensed*, but actually started to rehearse. However, Langner says in his book *The Magic Curtain*, she later "sent in her regrets, stating that her family regarded the play as immoral and did not wish her to take up acting." Having renounced one form of dramatic expression, she speedily sought another; and this is not surprising, either, for as she herself puts it, she has been "in love with the theatre all her life." At first, she thought of this new expression almost wholly in terms of writing; besides numerous short stories and poems, all of which were eagerly accepted by the editors to whom they were submitted, she achieved a one-act play, entitled *Enter the Hero*, which to this day brings her substantial royalties; and later she became dramatic critic for *The Nation*. But, in spite of her success, such media were not the ones for which she was predestined; and opportunely, or perhaps we should say providentially, Lawrence Langner, with whom she had been so briefly associated in *Licensed* and the Washington Square Players, asked her if she would join a group that hoped to form an organization which would produce full-length plays on a strictly professional basis. (The Washington Square Players had produced one-act plays on a semi-professional basis.) She consented to attend a meeting and it was at this and at the gatherings held soon thereafter in a bare little office on the top floor of the Garrick Theatre that "a group of young enthusiasts, inspired by their faith that America wanted and needed a theatre devoted to ideas and ideals of maturity and integrity," laid the foundations of the great institution of the Theatre Guild.

Inevitably, the prevailing atmosphere at these meetings was

chaotic as well as zealous, and resignations occurred almost as frequently as discussions. When the first executive director announced that he was through, Terry Helburn reluctantly consented to "fill in" for a few weeks. Almost immediately, she proved to have a calming influence. This, she says with becoming modesty, was due less to her personally than to the fact that the previous director—a man—could not be expected to have such feminine traits as thriftiness and tact, and that it was because she—a woman—happened to have both qualities that she was successful. Certainly her salary—$30 a week and a promise of percentage on profits—could not have predisposed her to extravagance; and tact, like charm, was one of her fairy godmother's gifts.

The few weeks during which she was supposed to be filling in lengthened into months and then into years; and still nothing was said about another incumbent for the position. She married, and her marriage, like everything else in which she has been concerned, has been singularly successful. (Her husband is the well-known lexicographer, John Baker Opdycke— "Oliver Opdyke"—and they have so correlated their careers as to make these mutually agreeable and not mutually annoying, as might so easily have been the case. Of course, part of the credit for this belongs to Oliver, whom I like immensely; but, after all, this is not his story!) She bought a country place in Connecticut and converted it into a pleasurable rural center for herself, her husband, and her friends. She perfected her tennis, which she has only recently given up, at sixty, "because her doctor advised her to do so at forty"; also her swimming, which she has not the slightest intention of giving up. She began driving a car in 1905; she handles an automobile with the accomplished ease that comes partly from essential adaptability to such a function and partly from long familiarity; and long solitary drives among the hills satisfy both her need for quietude and her love of scenic beauty. Seascapes are not included in this affection; indeed, she rather dislikes the ocean in all its phases; nevertheless, Europe became a habit to her; she spent two or three months there every year, indulging her tastes for mountain climbing, for orchestral music, and for architecture. But none of these interests and none of these activities affected her association with the Guild. Instead, it became closer and closer all the time.

4

Terry says that for seven years she did her casting "from the pit of her stomach." Perhaps. But meanwhile she had revealed for such work a flair that was as unquestionable as it was outstanding. It was she who cast Laura Hope Crews for the leading part in *Mr. Pim Passes By*; it was she who took "the little round comedienne" June Walker out of bedroom farces and gave her an emotional role in *Processional*; it was she who insisted that Alfred Lunt and Lynn Fontanne should be acting together and cast them as the co-stars of *The Guardsman*—to give only a few examples of many which might be mentioned. And then there was that underlying fact, most important of all, that she was in love with the theatre. It is certainly not a feminine trait to abandon anything genuinely beloved; so she has gone on and on.

The crises which nearly always precede first nights may trouble her transiently; but before a play is a week old, she is telling funny stories about it. For instance, there were the pigeons, allegedly "trained by an expert," which were supposed "to add a rural touch" to a scene where she had declined to introduce pigs and cows. These pigeons were scheduled to soar across the stage at the Boston opening of *Oklahoma!* and then promptly wing their way back to their baskets. They were transported from New York at great expense, were duly released, and duly soared—completely out of sight. They have never been seen since, at least by Terry; presumably they are still raising families among the rafters of the Colonial Theatre. . . . Then there was the case of the snow-white steed on which George Washington was to make an impressive entrance in *Arms and the Girl*. It did not occur to anyone responsible for the production that such a noble animal would be unobtainable in Boston. But alas! the erstwhile reliable livery stables had all disappeared, and it was almost curtain time before "a horse of sorts" was found on a farm situated beyond the more remote suburbs. This animal proved to be a dingy gray and there were grave doubts as to its probable behavior under excitement; but it had to do.

An even greater cause for anxiety was Katharine Hepburn's inopportune attack of laryngitis; at noon on the day *The Millionairess* opened in New York last fall, it was still uncertain whether she could go on the stage at eight, or if she did, whether she could make herself heard beyond the first row. But Terry, telephoning me at five that afternoon, mentioned the matter with at least the effect of doing so more or less in passing: "Everything seems to be all right now. But perhaps we'd better not try to have dinner before the show. It might be pretty hurried. However, of course we're expecting you at the supper party for the cast that the Langners and I are giving at their house afterward."

It might be argued that the problems connected with openings, though vexatious, are inevitably short-lived and, therefore, do not constitute a real test of buoyant fidelity under difficulties. But no one could argue that it does not require stamina to take seven successive failures in one's stride as Terry did when *And Stars Remain, Prelude to Exile, But for the Grace of God, The Mask of Kings, Storm over Patsy, To Quito and Back,* and *Madame Bovary* followed one another without a break for the better. It also takes stamina—though of a different kind—to come through triumphantly when there is a long series of successes, which is what happened in the seasons that *Pygmalion, The Silver Cord, Porgy, The Doctor's Dilemma,* and *Strange Interlude* were among the dozen hits. Terry proved that she had both kinds.

Eventually, all the original board members, except herself and Mr. Langner, withdrew from the management of the Guild, and since 1939 they have been its sole directors. Either as playwright, producer, or director, Theresa Helburn has had a hand in almost all the plays—now nearly 200 in number—that it has presented in the thirty years of its existence. She has "been involved in the supervision of more Broadway plays than any other woman in the entire history of the American theatre"; and no theatrical organization in the history of the stage, with the exception of the state-supervised theatres in Europe, has lasted so long.

5

Inevitably, Terry succumbed to the temptation of accepting an invitation to Hollywood—extended, characteristically, by telephone and in the dead of night. "A lovely little pine-paneled office" in a leading studio had been prepared for her and a suite reserved at the Garden of Allah. But though she dutifully remained the eight months for which she was under contract, she realized almost immediately that she and Hollywood did not speak the same language. She was hardly settled in her new surroundings when she was handed a script for Grace Moore and told to go through it at once, as eight high executives were waiting for her opinion on a certain scene. Then she was catapulted into their presence before she had finished reading the script. "But it's impossible for me to give an opinion without knowing about the final scenes," she objected. "Does the heroine commit suicide or does she marry her admirer and live happily ever after?" . . . "Oh, we're shooting it both ways!" she was airily informed.

This was not her way of working; so as soon as she was free to do so, she went back to her beloved Broadway, to the supervision of the plays which she herself had discovered or chosen and to the companionship of the actors and authors who spoke her language and who had become her personal friends as well as her professional associates.

Visiting once more at Pine Grove Farm after the lapse of many—far too many—years, she tells endless enthralling stories. She recalls, for instance, that *John Ferguson*, "a rather heavy play" by St. John Ervine, which started late in the Guild's first season (1919), ran all summer and provided a nest egg which permitted the infant organization to start off in the fall with some badly needed capital, and that this was less because of the play's popular appeal than because of an actors' strike which had closed almost every other theatre in New York—"tourists had to see *John Ferguson* or nothing!" She recalls that Bernard Shaw—using a postcard—forbade the production of *Heartbreak House* until after the 1920 election, and that when she tried to persuade him that, in the United States, the election would not affect such a production, he declined to be convinced and said so—on another postcard. She remembers that Eugene O'Neill dined with her the night that Lindbergh flew the Atlantic in 1927 and that, of course, they completely forgot to discuss the current play; also that after the five-hour opening of *Mourning Becomes Electra* in 1931, one subscriber was overheard remarking to another, as they left the theatre, "Gosh, isn't it good to get out into the Depression again!" She recalls that John Golden called her up one day and said, "Little woman, I got a play for you up here. It's the kind you folks like—trampy, but true." Her recollections—all warm, all vivid, all kindly—of the Lunts, of Helen Hayes, of Maurice Evans, of Rodgers and Hammerstein, of Ferenc Molnar and Elmer Rice and Maxwell Anderson and countless others, go on and on.

When I reminded Terry that the first Guild production I had seen was a very gloomy Russian play (so gloomy that I went to a night club afterward to get cheered up) for which she had given me tickets, saying she had plenty to spare, I found I had started a train of thought—and of conversation— which, briefly and vividly, summarized the three principal periods in the Guild's progress.

"Don't you make fun of that gloomy Russian play, as you call it—probably you mean Tolstoy's *Power of Darkness* and probably you did have to go to a night club afterward to get cheered up. Very likely I was glad enough to give you the tickets, too. Just the same, when that play finished its run, we had a nice little profit although we had started with only $200 in the bank. We produced mostly foreign plays then, for the simple reason that our management was unknown and that we couldn't afford the road tryouts necessary to ensure success for American plays. In those days, of course, we didn't have the talkies, or the radio, or television with which to compete and, one by one, they've become formidable rivals of the theatre—we may as well face it. But two out of five plays would carry us—in fact, we could get by with one success in a season, if it was a *real* success. All costs were on a much smaller scale then. And from the beginning, we worked on the theory that the play's the thing rather than the star. We chose plays that had real literary value. We believed there was a public for them and we were right. For instance, *He Who Gets Slapped*, *Back to Methuselah*, *Peer Gynt*, and *Saint Joan*. Then I had a new idea—the idea that something which we had already produced, as a play, like *Porgy*, which inspired Gershwin's *Porgy and Bess*, might prove the basis for another musical comedy, with a different theme, but still one that was typically American. Well, you know what came of that idea."

I do—indeed we all do. When *Green Grow the Lilacs*, by Lynn Riggs, which was based on an American pioneer theme, was produced as a play in the '30–'31 season, it was pleasantly but temperately received. When *Oklahoma!*, which was based on that play, was produced as a musical in the '42–'43 season, "its color and spirit blew wholesome winds through what was fast becoming a hot-house form, its use of the ballet popularized the dance and set it as a fashion for other Broadway musical productions to copy." And, as Lawrence Langner says, "to Terry goes the full credit for having conceived the idea of producing *Oklahoma!*"

That idea was conceived more than ten years ago. Meanwhile, the Guild has produced *Carousel*, based on Molnar's *Liliom*, *Arms and the Girl*, based on *The Pursuit of Happiness*, and several other musicals, "each adding a new note to the development of the American musical theatre," but none detracting from the perennial success of *Oklahoma!*, which still seems as fresh, as vital, and as buoyant as when the curtain went up on it for the first time.

Governor Kerr, now Senator Kerr, came on to the opening of the National Company in Washington, as did large numbers of other prominent Oklahomans. But they felt that not enough of their fellow Oklahomans were seeing it; nothing would do but that Mohammed should go to the mountain, so to speak. A private car was put at the disposal of the directors and in this Mr. and Mrs. Langner, Mr. and Mrs. Mamoulian, Miss de Mille, Miss Helburn, Mr. and Mrs. Rodgers, and Mr. and Mrs. Hammerstein traveled in state. The president of the road and a party of other invited guests traveled in equal state in an adjoining private car. Upon arrival in Oklahoma City, the train was met by the governor and his suite, and the honor guests were escorted to their hotel to the music of a brass band. Cowboys had foregathered, tribes assembled, schools closed, and a holiday atmosphere prevailed. Unfortunately, a storm of unprecedented proportions necessitated the cancellation of the mammoth parade which had been planned. But at the dinner which took place after the opening performance, prodigality was the order of the day. Gifts took the form of tea sets made from local pottery, Indian costumes fashioned in soft white leather, miniature covered wagons. Ceremonial dances were presented with the participants in full regalia, and afterward Miss Helburn danced a *pas de deux* with the chief. Then she was inducted into the nation and given a tribal name which means "The little woman who sees far."

I can think of no designation which could be more appropriate. Even before Terry began to talk to me about the future plans, hopes, and projects of the Guild, I realized that the third stage of its progress was linked to its first, just as surely as its second had been, though in a different way. The Guild had already produced two of Shakespeare's plays—*The Taming of the Shrew* with the Lunts and *Twelfth Night* with Helen Hayes and Maurice Evans—before the revolutionary experiment which culminated in *Oklahoma!* And even the electrifying success of this did not divert its producers from their predilection for the classical. *Othello* with Paul Robeson, *The Winter's Tale* with Henry Daniell and Florence Reed, *The Merry Wives of Windsor* with Charles Coburn, and *As You Like It* with Katharine Hepburn followed each other in orderly and majestic progression; and out of this superb sequence came the conviction that there should be a nationally endowed Shakespearian Festival Theatre and Academy in America similar to the one in England.

This conviction has already resulted in tentative plans and preliminary arrangements. The project calls for a modern adaptation of Shakespeare's own Globe Theatre, in which such a Festival could be held, and the chosen locale is Connecticut, where the Langners and Miss Helburn both have homes; its accessibility to New York and other large centers, and its natural and climatic attractions also, make it a logical choice for such a venture, as the state authorities have been swift to recognize—indeed, Governor Lodge has already signed a bill incorporating this foundation under the laws of Connecticut. But the Festival would not function only there and only in the summer; during the winter the acting company would tour in all the larger cities of the United States. In other words, if hopes are fulfilled, Shakespearian drama, no less than musical comedy, and presented with equal skill and beauty, would be available for theatre lovers from Oregon to Florida and from Louisiana to Maine.

"And you'd produce some of the less-known plays, too, wouldn't you?" I asked Terry after she had told me this. I had put another log on the fire and adjusted the screen, and was still standing pensively between the hearthstone and the sofa where she sat.

"Yes, of course. . . . Which one did you have in mind, especially?"

"Well, perhaps *The Two Gentlemen of Verona* and—"

"*Measure for Measure?*"

"Yes, that's it."

"They've never been popular successes yet, you know, like—well, like *Twelfth Night*, for instance. But then, you liked *The Winter's Tale* best of all our Shakespearian productions, didn't you? Come to think of it, so did some other people, and that's not generally regarded as popular material, either. *The Two Gentlemen of Verona* and *Measure for Measure* . . . well, I don't see why not! Sometime. . . ."

For a few moments after that, Terry said nothing as she sat gazing into the fire. At least, she seemed to be gazing into the fire. But presently I knew she was not. I knew that "The little woman who sees far" was already watching the two gentlemen as they prepared to serenade Silvia, and Isabella pleading for her brother's life before a corrupt magistrate.

I am as sure as I can be of anything in this uncertain world that all America will be seeing them, too.

1953

ERIC BENTLEY

An Oxonian who studied under C. S. Lewis, Eric Bentley (b. 1916) met the refugee poet and playwright Bertolt Brecht while at UCLA and devoted much of his career to promoting him and his works, as critic, translator, and performer. He also admitted to following the advice of his hero Bernard Shaw by promoting himself. After Stark Young criticized Bentley's analytic study of modern drama *The Playwright as Thinker* (1946) as displaying no hands-on knowledge of the working theatre, Bentley served a four-year stint at *The New Republic* reviewing Broadway shows, sometimes so brutally that both Tennessee Williams and Arthur Miller threatened lawsuits. He later estimated those pieces—collected in *The Dramatic Event* and *What Is Theatre?*—as more insightful than his academic books, which he characterized as intellectually "arrogant." In 1950 he increased his theatrical savvy by directing Brecht in Munich, O'Neill in Zurich, and García Lorca in Dublin, and was then appointed Brander Matthews Professor of Dramatic Literature at Columbia University. In 1969 Bentley simultaneously resigned his chair and announced his homosexuality. (Consequently, his piece on *Tea and Sympathy* is of interest in showing a closeted man reviewing a closeted drama.) He began to write his own plays about injustice and political persecution, among them *Are You Now Or Have You Ever Been* (1972) and *Lord Alfred's Lover* (1979). Besides making Brecht a byword in American classrooms and rehearsal rooms, his work as a propagandist for "the modern repertoire" has been credited with inspiring the American regional theatre movement.

Folklore on Forty-Seventh Street

I HAVE seen two plays within a week about shy boy virgins finding their manhood in the arms of alluring widows. I need not mention the other soulful and problem-full adolescents of recent stage history, or the heartwarming spinsters and benign bachelors; for it is well-enough known by now that the bonnets of the grandmas and the blue-jeans of the bobby-soxers are but tokens of our playwrights' sad and startling incapacity to deal with the love of men and women.

While it took Freud to find "offence" in fairy tales, we should scarcely have needed his genius to spot neurotic fantasy in the folklore of the asphalt jungle around Times Square. Not that the American theatre is guiltier than others. The traditional function of entertainment everywhere has been to feed the appetite for consoling fantasy—exactly as the restaurant in the lucky European theatre addresses itself to the stomach. Dreams, drives, and yearnings dance before the theatre audience's eyes in disguises which may be pleasant or unpleasant in themselves but which at all events console and compensate. The image of an idealized mother caters to our lack of self-reliance. The image of a stage villain provides us with a scapegoat. The image of tenderness appeases our sense of isolation, the image of innocence our sense of guilt.

The great pioneers of modern drama presented these images only to smash them in the name of reality; other masters of the drama have begun by accepting the images and ended by transmuting them into something else. It would be folly to expect anything of either sort from the theatre as such. Great plays are miracles conferred with becoming infrequency, services rendered above and beyond the call of duty. The everyday theatre is nothing more than a day-dream factory. Tenderness, innocence, and the rest have to be mere commodities or they couldn't be produced quickly enough. While the artist transforms neurotic fantasies into a higher reality, the journeyman playwright is doomed simply, like the neurotic himself, to live with them. He does nothing to his fantasies except hand them over to the public. The public is excited by the contact. And the degree of excitement is the criterion of the dramatic critics.

Theatre is an escape, and "realist" theatre is no longer an exception to the rule: it differs from non-realistic theatre only in pretending to be so. For the escape here is into pretended realities like ideologies and psychological notions and scientific fetishes. Or reality, being relative, turns unreal when placed before the Broadway public: *Tobacco Road* was not reality, the play was a very titillating bit of slumming, and one didn't know why those silly people weren't eating cake. In the thirties, realist escapism signalized the flight of the intellectual middle class into the fun-world of proletarian legend. Today it signalizes the flight of that same public into a variety of notions, chiefly psychological. In the thirties you felt the reassuring presence of the "real" at the mention of a Worker. Today you feel it at the mention of a Homosexual.

Tea and Sympathy by Robert Anderson is about a private-school boy who is to lose the feeling that he is a homosexual by proving his potency with the housemaster's wife. The subject matter suggests a whole roster of other plays. (*The Green Bay Tree, The Children's Hour* . . .) but most of all *Tea and Sympathy* strikes me as the 1953 version of *Young Woodley*, not so much for its plot, or even its setting, as for its relation to the public's current view of what is scandalous. The formula for such a work is Daring as Calculated Caution. Or: Audacity, Audacity, But Not Too Much Audacity. Such a play must be "bannable" on grounds of what used to be considered immoral but also defensible on grounds of what is now considered moral. Sweet are the uses of perversity.

Tea and Sympathy is a highly superior specimen of the theatre of "realist" escape. Superior in craftsmanship, superior in its isolation, combination, and manipulation of the relevant impulses and motifs, its organization of the folklore of current fashion is so skilful, it brings us to the frontier where this sort of theatre ends. But not beyond it. One doesn't ask the questions one would ask of a really serious play. Here, in the cuckoo land of folklore, one doesn't ask how the heroine knows the hero is innocent, one doesn't permit oneself the thought that he may not be innocent, for he has an innocence of a kind the real world never supplies: an innocence complete and certified. One doesn't ask how her husband could be so unloving and yet have got her to love him: one accepts her neat, fairy-tale explanation that, one night in Italy, he needed her. One doesn't ask just how the heroine's motives are mixed—to what extent her favors are kindness, to what extent self-indulgence—for, in this realm, the author enjoys the privilege of dreamer, neurotic, and politician to appeal to whatever motive is most attractive at the moment.

Instead, one drinks the tea of sentiment and eats the opium of sympathy, realizing more and more, as the evening at the Ethel Barrymore Theatre races on, that these memoirs of an opium eater are not so much a play by Mr. Anderson as another essay of Elia, the latest phantasmagoria of Mr. Kazan, the

incarnate spirit of the age; I would call him a human seismograph if there were a seismograph which would not only
record tremors but transmit them. At every moment in the
evening, one can say: this *has* to be a hit, or men are not feck-
less dreamers, the theatre is not a fantasy factory, and this is
not the age of anxiety.

Technically, the production is perfection: the stage at all
times presents a dramatic picture, progression from moment
to moment is precisely gauged, every instant has its special
value, simultaneous action in three playing areas is beautifully
counterpointed. If the craftsmanship is expert, the casting is
inspired, for Mr. Kazan goes by what the actors will do under
his tutelage, not by what they have done when misled by
others. What Deborah Kerr has done in films I have forgotten;
what she does in this play I know I shall not forget; if the role
scarcely invites greatness, it certainly lets Miss Kerr display a
supple naturalness and delicate ardor we did not know were
hers. John Kerr, who last year in *Bernardine* was merely brilliant, has been guided into a timing and a subtlety of stance
and movement worthy of a veteran. And each minor role is
what a minor role should be and rarely is: a type, but alive and
concrete enough to come at you with the shock of recognition. Perhaps the greatest single pleasure of this evening of
many pleasures was to enjoy so much observation of American
life in such minor roles as our hero's roommate at school and
our hero's father (both of them confronted with the charge
that our hero is a "queer"). Here Mr. Anderson and Mr.
Kazan trespass in the realm of the really real.

Day-dreams are of course full of real objects, yet the effect
of the realities in *Tea and Sympathy* is strangely dual. At times
it lifts the show out of the commodity theatre altogether—and
into the theatre of the masters. At other times, Mr. Kazan seems
to say, No, day-dream it is, and day-dream it shall remain; and
he stylizes the action and has Miss Kerr stand like impatience
on a monument with one hand between her breasts and the
other outstretched, waiting for our hero to embrace her. The
total impression is of double exposure: two scenes, two realms,
blurred, not blended. The confusion is the greater in that, presumably, no one on Forty-seventh Street admitted the material
was folklore in the first place, and attempts are made in the

course of the evening to tell us it is not so, but that this is a demonstration of real evils and their real cure, heterosexuals shouldn't be accused of homosexuality, no one should be falsely accused of anything, manliness is not just bullying but also tenderness, we are all very lonely, especially at the age of seventeen, and so on.

Anyway, in the calculated caution of its audacity, it is a play for everyone in the family; the script is far better than most; folklore and day-dream are scarcely less interesting than drama; and the work of Elia Kazan means more to the American theatre than that of any current writer whatsoever.

1953

FROM

Bentley on Brecht

The Coronet Theatre, Los Angeles, California; July 31, 1947

LET me drop some names: I was seated beside Peter Lorre, behind Ingrid Bergman, and in front of Charlie Chaplin. Lorre alone would have been enough: he is probably the most intelligent actor I have ever met, even making allowances for the fact that, in front of the young Professor Bentley, he too much enjoyed showing off his erudition. ("Was sagt Heidegger dazu?"—"What does Heidegger say to that?") It is the first night of *Galileo*, and Lorre is telling me how *he* would do the play, how he would do other Brecht plays, and, yes, he would do *all* of them, he has known since the 1920s that BB is *the* dramatist, *the* poet, of our day . . . Brecht is nervous just before curtain time. He runs out of the theater to the nearest drugstore, exclaiming: "Ich muss ein Seven Up haben"—"I must have a Seven Up."

I had been staying at Jay Laughlin's ski lodge in Utah and drove down to Los Angeles with Maja, my wife and collaborator. The Brechts put us up in their garden house. I recall that the walls of the bathroom had been papered by Brecht's wife Helene Weigel with Chinese newspapers. She was an excellent

cook and a hospitable hostess: bourgeois regularity? No.
Brecht led a double life that made him hard to keep tabs on.
He might be at his family place for supper, but he had installed
Ruth Berlau in a house a mile or two off, and he would characteristically repair to her place during the evening, very likely
returning "home" in the morning to work in his study. Maja
and I would be driven between one house and the other at
need, occasionally taking in a call at the Peter Lorre residence,
which was on a grand scale. Horses! For Lorre, to be a star was
to have one's own stable. He also had his own Frau Hauptmann on the premises. No, not as mistress, but as counselor
and friend: she called the position "private secretary." (What is
a public secretary?)

Slightly unnerving, chez Brecht, the comings and goings.
Only Helene Weigel seemed to have settled in, to really reside
there. How she managed to cook for people who showed up
at different and unpredictable times one never knew. The son
and daughter—Stefan and Barbara—were already showing the
symptoms of whatever that malady should be called from
which the children of the conspicuous so often suffer. Signs of
strain, of wear and tear, and, yes, of rebelliousness . . .

It seemed hard for Brecht to sit through a meal with family
and guests. He would flee to his room before dessert. One
would discover at some point that he had run to his couch and
a detective novel. (He read them in English, his command of
the language being much greater than people thought who
heard him speak it.)

The rebelliousness of the Brecht children has its importance
for the student of Brecht: the children were the only channel
through which rebellion could come to Brecht and stay. He
would meet with someone like Ruth Fischer, née Eisler, rebel
against Stalinism, call her a swine and prescribe that she be
shot. One of his son's friends was a son of Viertel named Hans
who reports that Brecht would shout that *he* should be shot,
repeating the key word several times: shot, shot, shot! Hans
adds, however, that this was only when carried away and that
Brecht didn't really mean it: he was very friendly to Hans later.
That is the point. He would let the children rebel. He would
say he wouldn't, but still he did. About such as Fischer, there can
be little doubt that, if empowered, he *would* have condemned

her to death. Treason to the Soviet Union was treason *tout court*; only slowly, and at that incompletely, did BB come to see Stalin himself as traitor, "honored murderer of the people." Stefan Brecht and Hans Viertel were "Trotskyites" (perhaps the quotes are uncalled for) who had to be tolerated even in a home where tolerance was not preached. They helped to prevent Bertolt Brecht's mind from becoming entirely closed.

Strange how little has been said by memoirists and biographers about Brecht as a father.* Even I, who was not in the Brecht home often, have some vivid memories. *Item:* his daughter Barbara (this was in Zurich, and she was a young woman now) slamming the door of her room on both parents as she shrieked: "You can take your social significance and shove it!" *Item:* BB asking me to send money (this in Munich later still) to his son Stefan and adding rather savagely: "Why do I send it? He'll probably spend it on whores."

A "bad father," then, like many another writer? Yet a "correct," bourgeois father in the end, for, in his will, he did not order his estate on the *Chalk Circle* principle of "to those who can best use it," but left everything to his widow, the other women in his life (past and present), and the three surviving children. (The full story of the will—or rather, wills—is too long to tell here, and even now, in 1988, not all the facts are known.)

Helene Weigel held open house every Sunday evening. They were very nice occasions socially, unpretentious, warm, with beer and an item or two of Weigel's cooking. Hostess was a very good role for this actress, even if Host was not something her husband could bring himself to be. He would deposit himself in a corner where people had to come and seek him out, whereas she would flit about and make sure that any who felt unwelcome changed their minds. The guests were mainly German, and most of the conversation was in that language, but two types of people were present and no more: those for

---

*But in some cases this is explicable. My friend James K. Lyon was allowed to see certain material *on condition that* he say little or nothing about Brecht's offspring. When he asked me if I thought he was wrong to accept such a condition, I answered, no, not if he told his readers about it. However (in *Bertolt Brecht in America*), he did not tell his readers about it.

whom communism was the answer to everything, and unpolitical people from theater and film, like Charles Laughton. Peter Lorre was a necessary guest as being maybe the only one who comfortably straddled the two worlds, as well as being fluent both in German and English. In memory stays a moment when the words *Der Kommunismus* rang out loud and clear and was followed by a knock on the door. Conversation stopped. Had the FBI heard the word and sprung into action? In strides a round little man with a broad ironic smile and very keen eyes. "Der Kommunismus?" he asks loudly, "der Kommunismus?" It is Peter Lorre.

Brecht left America the year before Henry Wallace ran for president but the Wallace movement was under way and Brecht saw the imminent campaign as the Final Conflict. "It's Wallace or World War III!" he would exclaim and look you challengingly in the eye. The apocalyptic character of the man's vision relieved him of all liberal illusions about the Nazis: he was convinced from the outset that they would draw the line nowhere. In some of his moods he would describe all friends of capitalism as Nazis. When I told him I was flying to Europe by Youth Argosy, an outfit that arranged cheap chartered flights for students and was having difficulty getting recognition in the airports, Brecht was immediately certain that the major airlines would arrange for a Youth Argosy plane to sink in mid-Atlantic. He gravely advised that I make other arrangements.

And my own relation to this milieu? In Brecht's eyes at the time, I *had* to be seen as belonging, like his friend Laughton, to the unpolitical men, the uninstructed, the naïve. There was no alternative except to be "one of us." Because I saw no purpose in a pretense of argument (real argument being excluded, certainly), I allowed myself to be placed in this category, as far as BB himself was concerned. But I tried to get a point through to him that I thought might be of importance: my sense was that, if his allegiance to the Soviet Union was strong, his allegiance to his own literary career and destiny was even stronger. Though I knew I would not persuade him to admit as much, I felt that I might get through to him if I said: "Whatever the validity of Marxism or Stalinism, if we wish to make a future for your work in America, it must be through

your cogency as an artist, not your rightness as a philosopher."
I was able to tell Brecht that most of the ideas in his "Short
Organum" were not dependent on Marxism, let alone Stalin-
ism, for their validation.

Not that, even in those early years, I ever fully saw myself as
a champion of the "Organum" or of any of Brecht's theoreti-
cal writings. Even he never realized this but thanked me as late
as 1949 for being, apparently, not only *a* champion but *the*
champion of his "theory." His antipathy for individualism was
such, I suppose, that he could not conceive that anyone might
wish to champion, not a theory, or its philosophical background, but a practice, a person practicing. Am I saying that I
was impressed not by Marx and Stalin but by Brecht? Not that,
either. Marxism was important to me. I was and am deeply influenced by it. But I have never been a Marxist. On Stalin, like
some others, I had no consistent position, but this was a period when Winston Churchill himself could speak quite loudly
of "Stalin the Great" and, at a time when I abandoned paci-
fism for support of the Allied cause in World War II, I too did
some blathering of this sort. The curious can find a little such
blather in my first book, which came out in 1944, and which
caused me to be labeled a Stalinist by Philip Rahv, Sidney
Hook, and many others. I mention this here, however, only in
order to make, yes, "full disclosure," and not because my
short-lived approval of Stalin had much bearing on my continuing relation with Brecht. He never noticed my limited and
ephemeral support for Russia. What he noticed was that I was
never a Marxist; what he thought he noticed was that I championed his ideas about theater; and what he perhaps failed to
notice was that I was championing his work, his genius, and
therefore himself. The Communists in New York, like
Weiskopf, were telling me: "Brecht is good insofar he is Communist," but what I was privately concluding was that Brecht
was good insofar as he was Brecht. (And he was not Brecht
completely. Sometimes he was just Marxism or some other
ism. And then, according to me, he was less good.)

Though young and in many ways diffident, I even tried to
influence Brecht. I hoped to broaden his mind, though I knew
he held what the rest of us regard as breadth of mind in contempt. "Broadminded people," he said once, "see three points

for and three points against every proposition. The two sides cancel out. Three minus three is zero . . ." What I had read of the left-wing controversy over Realism rather bored me, and I realize now it should have bored me—or bothered me—utterly. Each of those wretched writers sought to take Realism and ram it down your throat. And while the "discussion" was null and void intellectually, it was dynamic politically: say the wrong thing and you went (if you lived in Russia anyway) straight to the Gulag or to the next world . . . Of course I did not know the political dimensions of the situation in the early 1940s, but, recognizing intellectual emptiness when I saw it, I (1) resolved to omit the word *Realism* entirely from my book-length account of modern drama (*The Playwright as Thinker*),* and (2) sent Brecht a copy of *Mimesis* by Erich Auerbach, a book which makes a supremely rational use of the word *Realism*. I'd be surprised to hear that he ever read one word of it. The critical works at hand, when I visited Brecht later, were by his old adversary, and longtime slave of Stalin, Georg Lukács, who probably did more than any other critic to empty the word *Realism* of meaning.

Charles Laughton

HE, of course, was the star of *Galileo* and the latest man of power who was supposed to give BB the status he felt he was entitled to. A very strong mutual admiration society was created. No praise for Mr. Laughton could be too high in the opinion of Mr. Brecht. No praise for Mr. Brecht could be too high in the opinion of Mr. Laughton. "I believe him to be the most important living dramatist," Laughton wrote me, adding in a postscript: "This is pretty strong and you could never print this but I believe there is Shakespeare and then Brecht."

That was in 1948. As yet Laughton could not believe Brecht and Eisler were really identified with the Communist movement. When FBI men haunted the Maxine Elliott Theatre in 1947, he couldn't "for the life of him" tell why. "Eisler, a Communist? Nonsense: his music is just like Mozart!" But the

---

*This fact is borne out by the edition in print in America in 1988. The word *Realism* crept back in—carefully defined, I trust—in some earlier editions.

times they were a-changin', and even such as Charles Laughton saw, if not the light, then the darkness. He *had* associated with Communists, but please teacher, he didn't mean to! What could he do to atone? Repent? What was Galileo's word: recant? He would do it. He would espouse the New Conservatism. He would direct a play with a different message indeed from what those rebels preached: *The Caine Mutiny Court Martial*. Even when the captain is a dangerous nut, a crew has no right to rebel because it's more important that authority should be respected than that justice should be done. Questioned about this by the press, Laughton simply declared, "Them's my sentiments." So when *Time* magazine ran a cover story on Laughton (March 31, 1952), and portraits were included of all the great men he had portrayed, there was an omission: Galileo Galilei. And if Laughton repudiated Brecht, Brecht repudiated Laughton in an epigram: "Speak now of the weather and bury that man for me deep in the earth who, before he'd spoken, took it back."

Actually, Laughton took nothing back: he hadn't been on the point of speaking. This friendship was all public relations, though not without its humanity. Laughton could get so tired of luxury that he'd forsake his gourmet cook and run over to the Brechts' where "Helli" would fix him a chop. But he was never accepted, chez Brecht, as what he was: a man trying to be honestly homosexual. (Honestly? Well, as much as was possible in those days without risking instant ruin. On a movie set, in front of the crew and a large crowd of extras, a director had shouted, "Charles, Charles, *must* you come on as a flaming queen?" and Charles had answered by extending his middle finger and shouting back, "Sometimes, my dear man, even in Hollywood, the truth will out!")

Charles had got his boyfriend cast as Andrea—the second-best part in *Galileo*. The boyfriend didn't deserve the part, as I pointed out to Ruth Berlau. She agreed. She told me everyone agreed, including the nominal director, Joseph Losey. "Then why isn't he replaced?" "Because," Ruth told me, "Brecht doesn't want to hear about such things." "But you—you could talk to him!" "No, no!" "Surely he wants the best actor for the part." "No. This is a subject that cannot be brought up in Brecht's presence." Curious: because, otherwise, Brecht was a single-minded champion of his own interests. (Soviet communism is homophobic, and even T. W. Adorno said "Totalitarianism and homosexuality belong together.")

The full text of Charles Laughton's letter quoted above reads as follows:

My dear Bentley:

I owe you many apologies for not replying to your appeals about Brecht before.

I believe him to be the most important living dramatist. At the same time, I have never been able to understand either yours or anybody else's translations of his plays. As far as I have got is to be able to dimly see the great architecture. I also understand that you didn't like my translation of *Galileo*, so the situation between us is not an easy one. If I allow you to say, "I believe Berthold Brecht to be the most important living dramatist," and if the general public is anything like myself, they will see my name stuck on something they cannot understand, which is somewhat of a black eye for me. At the same time I feel all kinds of a heel that I am not doing everything I possibly can for this great writer. I would certainly like to be a help, and not a hindrance.

Suggestions, please, and very warmest personal regards.

Sincerely yours,
Charles Laughton

P.S. I also feel that the actors as a whole failed this great man miserably in our production of *Galileo*. The demands he makes on actors are much the same as the demands that Shakespeare made on the actors in the Elizabethan days. This is pretty strong and you could never print this, but I believe there is Shakespeare, and then Brecht. To this end I have started a Shakespearean group, training a bunch of American actors and actresses in the business of verse speaking and prose speaking. We have been working together some 8 or 9 months, three evenings a week for three hours, and I believe that in another year (it will take no more, but will also take no less) we shall be the best team of speakers in the English language. I am doing this solely with the aim of getting a company together that can play Brecht's plays. I want to see *Galileo really* performed, and *Circle of Chalk* and *Mother Courage*, and the rest of them. I am devoting all my spare energies to that end.

1989

ARTHUR MILLER

With the productions of *All My Sons* (1947), *Death of a Salesman* (1949), *The Crucible* (1953), and *A View from the Bridge* (1955), Arthur Miller (1915–2005) was ranked as America's greatest living dramatist. (O'Neill had died in 1953.) In line with his acknowledged master Henrik Ibsen, these were morally earnest dramas showing individuals caught in ethical dilemmas, seeking, usually unsuccessfully, to preserve their integrity as human beings. The plays were suffused with Emersonian idealism and a Jewish liberal's outrage at injustice, but also with what Mary McCarthy identified as Miller's "thirst for universality." Enlisted as a spokesman for secular humanism, Miller began to write tendentious essays on tragedy and the common man (1949–58). Set texts for generations of undergraduates, they contain such obiter dicta as "The tragic feeling is evoked in us when we are in the presence of a character who is ready to lay down his life, if need be, to secure one thing—his sense of personal dignity." In an era of McCarthyite conformity, these sentiments had considerable resonance, but the solemnity of graven tablets is ever-present. More engaging is Miller's piece on the American theatre, commissioned by *Holiday* magazine in 1955, and described by George Oppenheimer as "a loving and discerning study of the trials, tribulations and defeats of the people, big and small, who populate Broadway." It also reflects the exuberance of a playwright who finds himself an undisputed success and, owing to his courtship of Marilyn Monroe, whom he married the following year, a media celebrity. New plays from his hand continued to be produced until 2004, by which time Miller professed a more modest and pragmatic view of writing for stage: "I have, I think, provided actors with some good things to do and say. Beyond that I cannot speak with any certainty."

The American Theater

THE American theater occupies five side streets, Forty-fourth to Forty-ninth, between Eighth Avenue and Broadway, with a few additional theaters to the north and south and across Broadway. In these thirty-two buildings every new play in the United States starts its life and ends it. There will undoubtedly be many objections to this statement—you cannot say anything about our theater without fear of contradiction—and demurrers will come from professors of drama, stock-company directors, and little-theater people in New York, Texas, California, and elsewhere who will claim that Broadway is not the United States and that much theatrical production is going on in other places. I agree, and repeat only that with practically no exceptions, the *new* American plays originate on Broadway. I would add that I wish they didn't, but they do. The American theater is five blocks long, by about one and a half blocks wide.

It would seem a simple matter to characterize so limited an area, but I write this with the certainty that whatever I say will appear not only new and strange to many theater people but utterly untrue. And this is because the man or woman whose tapping shoes you hear from the second-story dance studio over the delicatessen on Forty-sixth Street is in the theater, the ballet girl hurrying to rehearsal in her polo coat with a copy of Rimbaud in her pocket is in the theater, the peasant-faced Irish stagehand sunning himself on the sidewalk with a *Racing Form* in his hand is in the theater, the slow-staring, bald-headed ticket broker blinking out through his agency window is in the theater, the wealthy, Park-Avenue-born producer is in the theater, and his cigar-smoking colleague from the West Bronx is in the theater.

In the audience itself, though the bulk of it is of the middle class, there is no uniformity either. There will be the businessman in town from Duluth sitting beside Marlene Dietrich, whom he will probably not recognize, and behind them two esthetes from Harvard. The word theater means different things to different groups. To some its very pinnacle is *South Pacific*, which is despised by the esthetes, who in turn cherish a wispy fantasy whose meaning escapes the Duluth man. There is a vast group of people for whom the theater means nothing but amusement, and amusement means a musical or light comedy; and there are others who reserve their greatest enthusiasm for heavy dramas that they can chew on.

The actors, directors, and writers themselves are just as varied. There are playwrights who are as illiterate as high-school boys, and there are playwrights like Maxwell Anderson, who have spent a good deal of their lives studying the Elizabethan drama and attempting to recreate its mood and luxuriance on Broadway. There are fine actors who are universally admired but who have absolutely no theory of acting and there are other actors, equally good or equally bad, who have spent years studying the history of acting, taking voice lessons, and learning how to dance in order to walk more gracefully.

The theater, obviously, is an entirely different animal to each of these groups. As for myself, I cannot pretend to any Olympian viewpoint about it either. I believe there is a confusion in many minds between Show Business and the Theater. I belong to the Theater, which happens at the moment to be in a bad way, but since this word, when capitalized, usually implies something uplifting and boring, I must add that the rarely seen but very real Theater is the most engrossing theater of all; and when it isn't it is nothing. I make the distinction so that the reader will be warned where my prejudice lies and discount accordingly.

The "glamour of the theater," which is and always will be its most powerful attraction, is a subject of daily reporting by almost every newspaper, gossip columnist, and radio station. Every year, around the first cool days of fall, the illustrated sections of the press and the picture magazines and newsreels run the familiar photographs of the limousines gliding up to the lighted marquees, the taxis and cars pressing into Forty-fourth Street for the opening of some musical or drama, the inevitable montage of Sardi's restaurant at dinner time, and so on. For anyone who has made the slightest mark in this occupation there is a line of type waiting when he so much as pays his rent on time. Soon after *Death of a Salesman* opened, it was reported that I was a millionaire, which was pleasant news, if not true, and that despite my new affluence I still rode the subways. I keep wondering who was watching me going through the turnstiles. And the importance of this news still escapes me.

In fact, while everybody in the business is worried about its future—and if there is a heart of uncertainty in the country its loudest beat may be heard on these five blocks—to read the columns and the usual sources of theatrical information you would think it was all a continuous carnival of divorce, practical jokes, hilarious wit, elopements, and sudden acquisition of enormous wealth.

But there is evidently no way of glamourizing the often inspiring and heart-lifting experiences of the work itself, a kind of labor that began in the Western world about three thousand years ago, and which has provided some of the most powerful insights we possess into the way men think and feel.

The net result of this image of our theater, the carnival image, is that the out-of-towner strolling these streets may quickly sense that he has been bilked. He will discover, especially if he arrives in midday, that the theater buildings themselves are tawdry-looking, and may well be disillusioned when he sees that some of the marquees do not have even the electrically lit signs of his home movie house—only temporary cardboards painted with the title of the show within. When he ventures into the outer lobby he will perhaps be shocked to discover that a seat costs six—or even eight—dollars and, if the show is a hit, that he won't get a ticket for six months or a year unless he pays a scalper twenty-five to a hundred dollars. If it is not a hit, and he buys a ticket legitimately, he may learn that he could have bought two for the price of one; and by the time he gets inside for the performance, some of the glamour of it all may have worn a bit thin.

Once inside, however, our visitor may find certain compensations. He may recognize very important people, from statesmen to movie stars, sitting nearby, whom he would not see in the home-town movie house. He will notice a certain dressed-up air about people, a few even wearing evening clothes. There are ushers to show him to his seat, and there is a program, and possibly a little more surprising is the coat-check man waiting as he passes through the outer door. There is still a vestigial ceremony about playgoing from which one may derive a sense of self-importance if not careful, and it all may lead our visitor to feel that he is, indeed, among ladies and gentlemen.

Then, as the lights go down and the curtain rises, our visitor may feel a certain strange tension, an expectancy, and an intense curiosity that he never knew in a theater before. Instead of the enormity of the movie image before which he could sit back and relax, he is confronted by human beings in life-size, and since their voices do not roar out at him from a single point to which his ear may tune in once and then relax, he must pay more attention, his eyes must rove over a thirty-foot expanse; he must, in other words, *discover*. And if there happens to be something real up there, something human, something true, our visitor may come away with a new feeling in his heart, a sense of having been a part of something quite extraordinary and even beautiful. Unlike the movies, unlike television, he may feel he has been present at an *occasion*. For outside this theater, no one in the world heard what he heard or saw what he saw this night. I know that, for myself, there is nothing so immediate, so actual, as an excellent performance of an excellent play. I have never known the smell of sweat in a movie house. I have known it in the theater—and they are also air-conditioned. Nor have I known in a movie house the kind of audience unity that occasionally is created in the theater, an air of oneness among strangers that is possible in only one other gathering place—a church.

Nevertheless, by every account our theater is a vanishing institution. We have some thirty-two houses going today in New York as against forty or more ten years ago, and between seventy and eighty in the twenties. I could weave you such a tapestry of evil omens as to make it a closed case that we will have no theater in America in two decades. What I should like to do instead, however, is wonder aloud, as it were, why it is that each year thousands of aspiring actors, directors, and playwrights continue to press into these five blocks from every corner of the country when they know, or learn very quickly, that ninety percent of the professional actors are normally unemployed, that most of the producers are dead broke or within three cigars of being broke, and that to become a director of a Broadway show one must be prepared to gamble five to ten to fifteen years of one's life. And yet, on all the trains they keep coming, aspiring actors and eager audiences both.

As for the aspiring actors, I will not pretend to hunt for an answer, because I know it. It is simply that there are always certain persons who are born without all their marbles. Even so, the full-blown actors are merely the completed types of the secret actors who are called producers, backers, directors, yes, and playwrights. The rest of us would have been actors had we had the talent, or a left and right foot instead of two left ones, or straight teeth, or self-assurance. The actor himself is the lunacy in full profusion—the lunacy which in the others is partially concealed.

All over the country there are nine-year-old girls, for instance, who are walking around the house as my daughter is at this very moment, in high-heeled shoes with the lace tablecloth trailing from their shoulders. If mine doesn't recover before she is sixteen she will wake up one morning and something will click inside her head and she will go and hang around some producer's office, and if he talks to her, or just asks her what time it is, she may well be doomed for life.

The five blocks, therefore, are unlike any other five blocks in the United States, if only because here so many grown people are walking around trailing the old lace tablecloth from their shoulders.

If you know how to look you will find them waiting on you in Schrafft's, or behind the orange-drink counter at Nedick's. As a matter of fact, I have got so attuned to a certain look in their eyes that I can sometimes spot them on Sixth Avenue, which is not in the theater district. I was passing a truck being loaded there one day when I noticed a boy, unshaven, his hair uncombed, wearing paratroop boots; he was pitching boxes into the truck. And he looked at me, just a glance, and I thought to myself that he must be an actor. And about three days later I was sitting in my producer's office interviewing actors for *The Crucible*, when in he walked. Characteristically, he did not remember seeing me before—actors rarely do, since they are not looking at anyone but rather are being looked *at*. When asked the usual questions about his experience he just shrugged, and when asked if he wanted to read for us he shrugged again, quite as though the questions were impertinent when addressed to a great artist, and I knew then why I had tabbed him for an actor. It was the time when all the young actors were being Marlon Brando. He was being Marlon Brando even when loading the truck, for a real truck driver would never show up for work looking so unkempt.

The blessed blindness of actors to everything around them, their intense preoccupation with themselves, is the basic characteristic of all Broadway, and underlies most of its troubles, which, in another industry, would have been solved long ago. But since it is glamour which brings the young to Broadway, as well as the audience, it cannot be so quickly dismissed. The fact is, it exists. But it is not the glamour you are probably thinking of.

The time is gone when the Great Producer kept four or five Great Stars in ten-room apartments on Park Avenue, and they waited in their gilded cages for days and weeks for the Impresario to call for them—for without him they were forbidden to be seen in public lest they lose their "distance," their altitude above the common things of life. The time is gone when the leading lady dared not arrive at the theater in anything but a limousine with chauffeur and lap robe, while a line of stove-pipe-hatted men waited in the stage-door alley with flowers in their manicured hands. There are a few hangovers, of course, and I remember a show in Boston a few years ago whose leading lady, an hour before curtain time, phoned the producer to say she was ill and could not play. The poor man was desperate, but there was an old-time doorman in that theater who happened to be near the phone and he said, "Get a limousine and a chauffeur." The producer, a contemporary type who was as familiar with gallantry as any other businessman, mastered his uncertainty and hired a car and chauffeur and sent a mass of roses to the lady's hotel room. Her fever vanished in roughly four minutes and she played better than she ever had, and I must confess I couldn't blame her for wanting the glamour even if she had had to make it herself.

But leading ladies, nowadays, arrive in a taxi, and a lot of them come in by bus or subway.

I have been around only ten years or so and I never knew the kind of glamour that evidently existed. But a few years ago I had occasion to visit John Golden in his office, and I saw then that there was, in fact, a kind of bravado about being in the theater, a declaration of war against all ordinariness that I can find no more.

The average theatrical producer's office today consists mainly of a telephone, a girl to answer it, an outer room for actors to wait in, and an inner room with a window for the producer to stare out of when he has nothing to produce.

John Golden's office is different. It rests on top of the St. James Theatre; you rise in a private elevator, and come out in a dark, paper-cluttered reception room where an elderly and very wise lady bars you—with the help of a little gate—from entry. You know at once that behind her is not merely a man, but a Presence.

In his office the walls are painted with smoke. They are very dark and covered with hundreds of photographs, plaques, statuettes, hanging things, and jutting things of gold, silver, and shiny brass. There is an Oriental rug on the floor, an ornate desk at the distant end of the room, and there sits John Golden, who is now eighty years old. Behind him stands an imposing ascent of bookshelves filled with leather-bound plays he has produced. In a smaller adjoining room is a barber chair where his hair is cut, his beard shaved, and, I presume, his shoes shined. The windows are covered with drapes and obstructing statuary, because when this office was created, the man who worked in it had no time to look out into the street.

It was a time when the railroads were freighting out one after another of his productions, winter and summer, to all sections of the country. It was a time when, unlike now, important performers and even playwrights were kept on long-term contracts, when a producer owned his own theater and used his own money and was therefore not an accountant, nor even a businessman, but an impresario. In short, it was the time before the masses had left the theater for the new movies, and the theater was the main source of American popular entertainment. This office is now a kind of museum. There were once many like it, and many men like John Golden.

Their counterparts, the reflected images of Ziegfeld, Frohman, Belasco, and the others, appeared only later in Hollywood, for the masses are needed to create impresarios, or more precisely, a lucrative mass market. In Golden's office I saw the genesis of so much we have come to associate with Hollywood: the stars under long-term contract, the planning of one production after another instead of the present one-shot Broadway practice, the sense of permanence and even security. None of these are part of Broadway now, and they appear in their afterglow above the St. James; for it is not the masses we serve any more, not the "American People," but a fraction of one class—the more or less better-educated people, or the people aspiring to culture.

Golden's eyes blazed with pleasure as he talked of plays long since gone, like *Turn to the Right* and *Lightnin'* and others I remember my father raving about when I was a boy, and finally he sat back and mused about playwriting.

"You fellows have a much harder time," he said, "much harder than in the old days; nowadays every show has to seem new and original. But in the old days, you know, we had what you might call favorite scenes. There was the scene where the mother puts a candle on the window sill while she waits for her long-lost boy to come home. They loved that scene. We put that scene in one play after another. You can't do things like that any more. The audience is too smart now. They're more educated, I suppose, and sophisticated. Of course it was all sentimental, I guess, but they were good shows."

He was right, of course, except you *can* do that now; the movies have been doing it for thirty or forty years and now television is doing it all over again. I remember a friend who had worked in Hollywood writing a picture. The producer called him in with a bright new idea for a scene to be inserted in the script. My friend listened and was amazed. "But just last month you released a picture with that same scene in it," he reminded the producer.

"Sure," said the producer, "and didn't it go great?"

The Golden species of glamour is gone with the masses; it went with the big money to Hollywood, and now it is creating itself all over again in television. The present-day actors and directors would probably seem tame and dull to their counterparts of thirty and forty years ago. David Belasco, for instance, had even convinced himself that his was a glamorous profession, and took to dressing in black like a priest—the high priest of the theater—and turned his collar around to prove it. He carried on as no contemporary director would dare to do. Toward the last days of rehearsal, when he wanted some wooden but very beautiful leading lady to break down and weep, he would take out a watch, the watch he had been displaying for weeks as the one his mother gave him on her deathbed, and smash it on the floor in a high dudgeon, thus frightening the actress to tears and making her putty in his hands. It need hardly be added that he kept a large supply of these watches, each worth one dollar.

The traditional idea of the actor with his haughty stance, his peaked eyebrows, elegant speech, artistic temperament, and a necessary disdain for all that was common and plain, has long since disappeared. Now they are all trying to appear as ordinary as your Uncle Max. A group of actors sitting at a bar these days could easily be mistaken for delegates to a convention of white-collar people. They are more likely, upon landing in a hit show, to hurry over to the offices of a tax consultant than to rush out and buy a new Jaguar. For a few years after the war a certain amount of effort was put into aging their dungarees and wearing turtle-neck sweaters, and some of them stopped combing their hair, like the boy I noticed loading the truck. But you don't get Marlon Brando's talent by avoiding a bath, and gradually this fad has vanished. There are more "colorful" personalities up here in the tiny Connecticut village where I spend summers than you will find on all Broadway. The only real showman I know of is Joshua Logan, who can throw a party for a hundred people in his Park Avenue apartment and make it appear a normal evening. Logan is the only director I can name who would dare to knock a stage apart and build into it a real swimming pool, as he did for the musical *Wish You Were Here*, and can still talk about the theater with the open, full-blown excitement of one who has no reservations about it. The other directors, at least the half-dozen I know—and there are not many more—are more likely to be as deadly serious as any atomic physicist, and equally worried.

There is a special aura about the theater, nevertheless, a glamour, too, but it has little connection with the publicity that seeks to create it. There is undoubtedly as much sexual fooling around as there is in the refrigerator business, but I doubt if there is much more. The notion of theatrical immorality began when actors were socially inferior by common consent; but now a Winnifred Cushing (of the Boston Cushings), the loose woman in *Death of a Salesman*, hurries home to her mother after each show.

Not that it is an ordinary life. There is still nothing quite like it, if only because of the fanaticism with which so many respond to its lure. One cannot sit in a producer's office day after day interviewing actors for a play without being struck by their insistence that they belong in the theater and intend to make their lives in it. In the outer reception rooms of any producer's office at casting time is a cross section of a hundred small towns and big cities, the sons and daughters of the rich families and of the middle-class families and of families from the wrong side of the tracks. One feels, on meeting a youngster from a way-station town or a New Mexico ranch, that the spores of this poor theater must still possess vitality to have flown so far and rooted so deep. It is pathetic, it is saddening, but a thing is dead only when nobody wants it, and they do want it desperately. It is nothing unusual to tell a girl who has come to a casting office that she looks too respectable for the part, and to be greeted by her an hour later dressed in a slinky black dress, spike heels, outlandishly overdone make-up, and blond dye in her hair that has hardly had time to dry. One of our best-known actresses had her bowlegs broken in order to appear as she thought she must on the stage, and there is an actor who did the same to his knees in order to play Hamlet in tights.

There is, it must be admitted, an egotism in this that can be neither measured nor sometimes even stomached, but at casting time, when one spends hour after hour in the presence of human beings with so powerful a conviction and so great a desire to be heard and seen and judged as artists, the thing begins to surpass mere egotism and assumes the proportion of a cause, a belief, a mission. And when such sacrifices are made in its name one must begin to wonder at the circumstances that have reduced it to its present chaos. It might be helpful to take a look at how the whole thing is organized—or disorganized.

Everything begins with a script. I must add right off that in the old mass theater that came to an end somewhere in the late twenties, when the movies took over, the script was as often as not a botch of stolen scenes, off-the-cuff inventions of the producer or director, or simply pasted-together situations designed for some leading player. The audience today, however, demands more, and so the script has become the Holy Grail for which a producer dreams, prays, and lives every day of his life. Being so valuable, and so difficult to write, it is leased by the author on a royalty basis and never sold outright. He receives, I am happy to report, roughly ten percent of the gross receipts, or between two and three thousand dollars a week if he has a hit. (I would add that he resolves not to change his standard of living but he has a wife, and that is that.)

Three or four times a year the playwrights have a meeting of the Dramatists Guild, their union, in a private dining room of the St. Regis Hotel. Moss Hart, the author of *The Climate of Eden* and, with George Kaufman, of a string of successes like *The Man Who Came to Dinner* and *You Can't Take It With You*, is the current president of the Guild. There is probably more money represented here than at most union luncheons, the only trouble being that with a few exceptions none of the playwrights has any assets; that is, you can't write a hit every time so the three thousand a week begins to look smaller and smaller when it is averaged out over a period of unfruitful years. Oscar Hammerstein, another Guild member, put an ad in *Variety* after his *South Pacific* opened, listing a dozen or so of his failures that everyone had forgotten, and at the bottom of the page repeated the legend of show business, "I did it before and I can do it again."

Between the turtle soup and the veal scaloppine, various issues are discussed, all of which are usually impossible to solve, and the luncheons roll by and we know that our profession is on the edge of an abyss because the theater is contracting; and we all go home to write our plays. Occasionally we meet with a group of producers, and Max Gordon can usually be relied on to demand the floor; and red in the face, full of his wonderful fight, he will cut to the heart of the problem by shouting at the playwrights, "The producers are starving, you hear me? Starving!" Leland Hayward, who has scraped by on *South Pacific*, *Mister Roberts*, and other such titbits, will accuse me of making too much money, and Herman Shumlin, the producer of *The Little Foxes*, *The Children's Hour*, *Watch on the Rhine*, will solemnly avow that he is leaving the business forever unless we writers cut our royalties; and then we all go home. Once the late Lee Shubert came with the others to discuss the problems of the theater, and when he was asked if he would reduce the rentals of his many theaters, since the playwrights were willing to reduce their royalties, he looked as though the butter was, indeed, melting in his mouth, so he didn't open it. And we all went home again.

There are seemingly hundreds of producers, but actually only fifteen or twenty go on year after year. Few are wealthy, and money is usually promoted or lured out of any crack where it can be found. It is a common, although not universal, practice to hold a gathering of potential backers before whom either the playwright or the director reads the script. Established producers regard this as beneath their dignity, but some don't, or can't afford to. These readings usually take place either on Park Avenue or on swank Beekman Place, for some reason, and while I never attended one, I have known many playwrights who have, but never heard of one dollar being raised in that way.

Script in hand, then, and money either raised or on its way —usually in amounts under five hundred dollars per backer— the producer hires a director, also on a percentage with a fee in advance, and a scene designer; the set is sketched, approved, and ordered built. Casting begins. While the author sits home revising his script—for some reason no script can be produced as the author wrote it—agents are apprised of the kinds of parts to be filled, and in the producer's reception room next morning all hell breaks loose.

The basis upon which actors are hired or not hired is sometimes quite sound; for example, they may have been seen recently in a part which leads the director to believe they are right for the new role; but quite as often a horde of applicants is waiting beyond the door of the producer's private office and neither he nor the director nor the author has the slightest knowledge of any of them. It is at this point that things become painful, for the strange actor sits before them, so nervous and frightened that he either starts talking and can't stop, and sometimes *says* he can't stop, or is unable to say anything at all and says *that*. During the casting of one of my plays there entered a middle-aged woman who was so frightened she suddenly started to sing. The play being no musical, this was slightly beside the point, but the producer, the director, and myself, feeling so guilty ourselves, sat there and heard her through.

To further complicate matters there is each year the actor or actress who suddenly becomes what they call "hot." A hot performer is one not yet well-known, but who, for some mysterious reason, is generally conceded to be a coming star. It is possible, naturally, that a hot performer really has talent, but it is equally possible, and much more likely, that she or he is not a whit more attractive or more talented than a hundred others. Nevertheless, there comes a morning when every producer in these five blocks—some of them with parts the performer could never play—simply has to have him or her. Next season, of course, nobody hears about the new star and it starts all over again with somebody else.

All that is chancy in life, all that is fortuitous, is magnified to the bursting point at casting time; and that, I suspect, is one of the attractions of this whole affair, for it makes the ultimate winning of a part so much more zesty. It is also, to many actors, a most degrading process and more and more of them refuse to submit to these interviews until after the most delicate advances of friendship and hospitality are made to them. And their use of agents as intermediaries is often an attempt to soften the awkwardness of their applying for work.

The theatrical agents, in keeping with the unpredictable lunacy of the business, may be great corporations like the Music Corporation of America, which has an entire building on Madison Avenue, and will sell you anything from a tap dancer to a movie star, a symphony orchestra, saxophonists, crooners, scene designers, actors, and playwrights, to a movie script complete with cast; or they may be like Jane Broder, who works alone and can spread out her arms and touch both walls of her office. They may even be like Carl Cowl, who lives around the corner from me in Brooklyn. Carl is an ex-seaman who still ships out when he has no likely scripts on hand to sell, and when things get too nerve-racking he stays up all night playing Mozart on his flute. MCA has antique desks, English eighteenth-century prints, old broken clocks and inoperative antique barometers hanging on its paneled walls, but Carl Cowl had a hole in his floor that the cat got into, and when he finally got the landlord to repair it he was happy and sat down to play his flute again; but he heard meowing, and they had to rip the floor open again to let out the cat. Still, Carl is not incapable of landing a hit play and neither more nor less likely than MCA to get it produced, and that is another handicraft aspect of this much publicized small business, a quality of opportunity which keeps people coming into it. The fact is that theatrical agents do not sell anyone or anything in the way one sells merchandise. Their existence is mainly due to the need theater people have for a home, some semblance of order in their lives, some sense of being wanted during the long periods when they have nothing to do. To have an agent is to have a kind of reassurance that you exist. The actor is hired, however, mainly because he is wanted for the role.

By intuition, then, by rumor, on the recommendation of an agent—usually heartfelt; out of sheer exhaustion, and upsurge of sudden hope or what not, several candidates for each role are selected in the office of the producer, and are called for readings on the stage of a theater.

It is here that the still unsolved mystery begins, the mystery of what makes a stage performer. There are persons who, in an office, seem exciting candidates for a role, but as soon as they step onto a stage the observers out front—if they are experienced—know that the blessing was not given them. For myself, I know it when, regardless of how well the actor is reading, my eyes begin to wander up to the brick wall back of the stage. Conversely, there are many who make little impression in an office, but once on the stage it is impossible to take one's attention from them. It is a question neither of technique nor of ability, I think, but some quality of surprise inherent in the person.

For instance, when we were searching for a woman to play Linda, the mother in *Death of a Salesman*, a lady came in whom we all knew but could never imagine in the part. We needed a woman who looked as though she had lived in a house dress all her life, even somewhat coarse and certainly less than brilliant. Mildred Dunnock insisted she was that woman, but she was frail, delicate, not long ago a teacher in a girl's college, and a cultivated citizen who probably would not be out of place in a cabinet post. We told her this, in effect, and she understood, and left.

And the next day the line of women formed again in the wings, and suddenly there was Milly again. Now she had padded herself from neck to hem line to look a bit bigger, and for a moment none of us recognized her, and she read again. As soon as she spoke we started to laugh at her ruse; but we saw, too, that she *was* a little more worn now, and seemed less well-maintained, and while she was not quite ordinary, she reminded you of women who were. But we all agreed, when she was finished reading, that she was not right, and she left.

Next day she was there again in another getup, and the next and the next, and each day she agreed with us that she was wrong; and to make a long story short when it came time to make the final selection it had to be Milly, and she turned out to be magnificent. But in this case we had known her work; there was no doubt that she was an excellent actress. The number of talented applicants who are turned down because they are unknown is very large. Such is the crap-shooting chanciness of the business, its chaos, and part of its charm. In a world where one's fate so often seems machined and standardized, and unlikely to suddenly change, these five blocks are like a stockade inside which are people who insist that the unexpected, the sudden chance, must survive. And to experience it they keep coming on all the trains.

But to understand its apparently deathless lure for so many it is necessary, finally, to have participated in the first production of a new play. When a director takes his place at the beaten-up wooden table placed at the edge of the stage, and the cast for the first time sit before him in a semicircle, and he gives the nod to the actor who has the opening lines, the world seems to be filling with a kind of hope, a kind of regeneration that, at the time, anyway, makes all the sacrifices worth while.

The production of a new play, I have often thought, is like another chance in life, a chance to emerge cleansed of one's imperfections. Here, as when one was very young, it seems possible again to attain even greatness, or happiness, or some otherwise unattainable joy. And when production never loses that air of hope through all its three-and-a-half-week rehearsal period, one feels alive as at no other imaginable occasion. At such a time, it seems to all concerned that the very heart of life's mystery is what must be penetrated. They watch the director and each other and they listen with the avid attention of deaf mutes who have suddenly learned to speak and hear. Above their heads there begins to form a tantalizing sort of cloud, a question, a challenge to penetrate the mystery of why men move and speak and act.

It is a kind of glamour that can never be reported in a newspaper column, and yet it is the center of all the lure theater has. It is a kind of soul-testing that ordinary people rarely experience except in the greatest emergencies. The actor who has always regarded himself as a strong spirit discovers now that his vaunted power somehow sounds querulous, and he must look within himself to find his strength. The actress who has made her way on her charm discovers that she appears not charming so much as shallow now, and must evaluate herself all over again, and create anew what she always took for granted. And the great performers are merely those who have been able to face themselves without remorse.

In the production of a good play with a good cast and a knowing director a kind of banding together occurs; there is formed a fraternity whose members share a mutual sense of destiny. In these five blocks, where the rapping of the tap-dancer's feet and the bawling of the phonographs in the record-shop doorways mix with the roar of the Broadway traffic; where the lonely, the perverted, and the lost wander like the souls in Dante's hell and the life of the spirit seems impossible, there are still little circles of actors in the dead silence of empty theaters, with a director in their center, and a new creation of life taking place.

There are always certain moments in such rehearsals, moments of such wonder that the memory of them serves to further entrap all who witness them into this most insecure of all professions. Remembering such moments the resolution to leave and get a "real" job vanishes, and they are hooked again.

I think of Lee Cobb, the greatest dramatic actor I ever saw, when he was creating the role of Willy Loman in *Death of a Salesman*. When I hear people scoffing at actors as mere exhibitionists, when I hear them ask why there must be a theater if it cannot support itself as any business must, when I myself grow sick and weary of the endless waste and the many travesties of this most abused of all arts, I think then of Lee Cobb making that role and I know that the theater can yet be one of the chief glories of mankind.

He sat for days on the stage like a great lump, a sick seal, a mourning walrus. When it came his time to speak lines, he whispered meaninglessly. Kazan, the director, pretended certainty, but from where I sat he looked like an ant trying to prod an elephant off his haunches. Ten days went by. The other actors were by now much further advanced: Milly Dunnock, playing Linda, was already creating a role; Arthur Kennedy as Biff had long since begun to reach for his high notes; Cameron Mitchell had many scenes already perfected; but Cobb stared at them, heavy-eyed, morose, even persecuted, it seemed.

And then, one afternoon, there on the stage of the New Amsterdam way up on top of a movie theater on Forty-second Street (this roof theater had once been Ziegfeld's private playhouse in the gilded times, and now was barely heated and misty with dust), Lee rose from his chair and looked at Milly Dunnock and there was a silence. And then he said, "I was driving along, you understand, and then all of a sudden I'm going off the road. . . ."

And the theater vanished. The stage vanished. The chill of an age-old recognition shuddered my spine; a voice was sounding in the dimly lit air up front, a created spirit, an incarnation, a Godlike creation was taking place; a new human being was being formed before all our eyes, born for the first time on this earth, made real by an act of will, by an artist's summoning up of all his memories and his intelligence; a birth was taking place above the meaningless traffic below; a man was here transcending the limits of his body and his own history. Through the complete concentration of his mind he had even altered the stance of his body, which now was strangely not the body of Lee Cobb (he was thirty-seven then) but of a sixty-year-old salesman; a mere glance of his eye created a window beside him, with the gentle touch of his hand on this empty stage a bed appeared, and when he glanced up at the emptiness above him a ceiling was there, and there was even a crack in it where his stare rested.

I knew then that something astounding was being made

here. It would have been almost enough for me without even opening the play. The actors, like myself and Kazan and the producer, were happy, of course, that we might have a hit; but there was a good deal more. There was a new fact of life, there was an alteration of history for all of us that afternoon.

There is a certain immortality involved in theater, not created by monuments and books, but through the knowledge the actor keeps to his dying day that on a certain afternoon, in an empty and dusty theater, he cast a shadow of a being that was not himself but the distillation of all he had ever observed; all the unsingable heartsong the ordinary man may feel but never utter, he gave voice to. And by that he somehow joins the ages.

And that is the glamour that remains, but it will not be found in the gossip columns. And it is enough, once discovered, to make people stay with the theater, and others to come seeking it.

I think also that people keep coming into these five blocks because the theater is still so simple, so old-fashioned. And that is why, however often its obsequies are intoned, it somehow never really dies. Because underneath our shiny fronts of stone, our fascination with gadgets, and our new toys that can blow the earth into a million stars, we are still outside the doorway through which the great answers wait. Not all the cameras in Christendom nor all the tricky lights will move us one step closer to a better understanding of ourselves, but only, as it always was, the truly written word, the profoundly felt gesture, the naked and direct contemplation of man which is the enduring glamour of the stage.

1955

FRED ALLEN

The young Boston Irishman John Florence Sullivan worked for years in the stacks of the Boston Public Library. This may account for the extraordinary literacy of his patter when he went into show business under the name of Fred Allen (1894–1965). He entered vaudeville as a straight juggler, added gags, moved to comic monologues, and eventually rose from variety to *The Passing Show of 1922*, followed by *The Greenwich Village Follies* and similar intimate revues. In the 1930s he established himself as a popular radio comedian and his show, ultimately entitled *Town Hall Tonight*, became the longest-running hour-long variety program on the air. Its features included an opening topical monologue, the theatrics of "The Mighty Allen Art Players," the dialect comedy tradition perpetuated in *Allen's Alley*, and the ongoing (fictional) feud between Allen and his good friend Jack Benny. His inventions have been much imitated since, without acknowledgment, by a great many comedians, among them Johnny Carson, Rowan and Martin, and the *Saturday Night Live* crews. Partly because his wit was verbal, often ad-libbed, and his wizened face made for radio, partly because of running battles with censors, network executives, and sponsors in an attempt to preserve some vestige of intelligence in the scripts, Allen failed to make a successful transition to television. It was called a "medium," he said, "because nothing is well done." His own opinion of his career in broadcasting is summed up in the title of his 1954 retrospective *Treadmill to Oblivion*. On the other hand, the memoir *Much Ado About Me* (1956) contains one of the fondest, yet most clear-eyed, tributes to vaudeville left by one of its participants.

The Life and Death of Vaudeville

VAUDEVILLE is dead. The acrobats, the animal acts, the dancers, the singers, and the old-time comedians have taken their final bows and disappeared into the wings of obscurity. For fifty years—from 1875 to 1925—vaudeville was the popular entertainment of the masses. Nomadic tribes of nondescript players roamed the land. The vaudeville actor was part gypsy and part suitcase. With his brash manner, flashy clothes, capes and cane, and accompanied by his gaudy womenfolk, the vaudevillian brought happiness and excitement to the communities he visited. He spent his money freely and made friends easily. In the early days, the exact degree of prosperity the smalltimer was enjoying could be determined by taking inventory of the diamonds that adorned his person. If he was doing well, the smalltimer wore a large diamond horseshoe in his tie and two or three solitaires or clusters on his fingers; his wife, dripping with necklaces, rings, earrings, and bracelets, looked as though she had been pelted with ice cubes that had somehow stuck where they landed. The smalltimer's diamonds didn't have to be good. They just had to be big. What difference if the eight-karat ring was the color of a menthol cough drop as long as the stone sparkled in the spotlight during the act? To the smalltimer, a diamond represented security. It impressed the booker, the manager, and the audience, but, more important, the diamond was collateral. Confronted with a financial crisis in a strange community, the smalltimer didn't have to embarrass himself by attempting to convince a tradesman or a hotel manager that his credentials were valid. To obtain emergency funds, he merely stepped into the nearest pawnshop, slipped the ring from his finger, and consummated a legitimate routine business transaction. When his diamonds were temporarily on location, the smalltimer avoided his friends and his usual haunts, knowing that the absence of his Kimberley gravel was an admission that the panic was on. The instant his luck changed, the diamonds were redeemed and returned to their customary places. Back in the spotlight, with the horseshoe pin and the rings sparkling, the smalltimer's necktie and his ring fingers resumed strutting their stuff.

The herd instinct was a dominant impulse in the vaudeville actor's behavior pattern. When the season closed, the smalltimers congregated at vacation resorts to revel in each other's company. The smalltimer lived in another world. He thought and talked only about his act and about show business. Nothing else interested him. If you said to him, "Do you remember the Johnstown flood?" he would probably reply, "Remember the Johnstown flood? Are you kidding? I and the wife were playing Pittsburgh that week. Eva Tanguay was the star. Walter Kelly was next to closing. After the first show the manager comes running back and says, 'You kids is the hit of the bill!' He moves us down to next to closing for the rest of the week. Kelly is blowing his top. All week long I and the wife murder them!" Everybody in Johnstown could have been swept out of town: the smalltimer wouldn't know or care. He had nothing in common with anybody who was not in his profession.

The two vaudeville centers of the country were New York and Chicago. During the summer layoff season—theaters had no air conditioning then, and many closed during the hotter months—vaudeville colonies were formed. The Chicago acts rented or bought cottages near the lakes in Wisconsin or Michigan; the New York vaudevillians huddled together in Connecticut and down on Long Island. The most famous of the actors' colonies was founded at Freeport, Long Island. The stars first established summer homes at Freeport, and then the smalltimers precipitated a real-estate boom fighting to buy property and houses to make their home in Freeport to let the stars see how the other half lived.

The Long Island Good Hearted Thespians Society was formed. This was a social club whose members reduced the name to the Lights. The first president was Victor Moore. One of the traditional Lights Club functions was the celebration of Christmas on the Fourth of July. In December, most of the vaudeville actors were on the road, away from their homes, their families, and their friends. They spent their Christmas Days on trains, in dingy dressing rooms, or in drab hotels. Members of the Lights ignored the conventional Yule season and saved their Christmas greetings and presents until the return to Freeport. On July Fourth, though the temperature be in the nineties, the Lights' Christmas tree was decorated and lighted, Santa Claus was dressed in his heavy suit with the ermine trimmings, presents were placed under the tree, and the members and their children arrived in their furs, mittens, and earlaps, some even clattering into the club on snowshoes.

A vaudeville actor could relax and enjoy himself only in the company of another vaudeville actor. You could sit a vaudeville actor in front of a mirror and he would stay there contentedly for days on end. In cities on the road, the vaudeville performers congregated at the same boardinghouses or cheaper hotels. There was a time when the actor was *persona non grata* at the better inns, and this was especially true of vaudevillians, who were presumed to be irresponsible from the very fact that their profession was uncertain and their living precarious. It was generally understood that vaudeville performers went in for wild parties in their homes and that their domestic habits were rarely awarded the Good Housekeeping Seal of Approval. Accordingly it was deemed best for hotel clerks to smile blandly when they were asked for rooms and inform the vaudevillian that the hotel was "full up." Stage folk, except for those who had attained stellar rank, were pretty much pariahs around the decent hotels.

Duke Pohl, the manager of the Breevort Hotel in St. Louis, once told me that he was traveling in a special train to attend an annual convention of the Greeters of America, the official organization of the hotel men. Each man was asked to name his hotel and tell something about it. Duke later told me that when he announced that his Breevort catered to stage folks, "I could almost hear the gasp that went around the circle. I told them I considered stage people the most maligned persons on earth. I said that my experience with vaudevillians had been uniformly pleasant, that they paid their bills, were quiet in their rooms, were sober, sedate, and serious people trying to make a living."

Duke defended the profession at a time when many hotel and rooming-house owners were complaining that some vaudeville people were stealing towels. This practice was so common that jokes were being told about it. One joke was about the vaudeville actor who died and left an estate of eight hundred hotel and Pullman towels. Then there was the charge that actors checked into their hotels with heavy suitcases, stayed a week or two, then disappeared without paying their bills. Credit had been extended because the manager had seen the heavy suitcases; when, later, these were pried open, they were found to contain nothing but a collection of bricks and old telephone books. Indigent vaudeville actors were known to lower their suitcases out the window in the back of the hotel, then walk through the lobby empty handed, reclaim their cases, and leave town. An actor who had a trunk in his room received an extension of credit. When the bill mounted, the actor, anticipating that the manager would tip the trunk to ascertain its contents and to try to find out if clothing had been pawned, took the precaution of nailing the trunk to the floor. Ted Healy, a comedian, once owed a sizable bill at the Lincoln Hotel in New York. Ted brought the three stooges he used in his act up to his room and ordered each stooge to don two or three sets of his underwear, two complete suits of clothes, and an overcoat. Healy followed the stooges out of the Lincoln lobby wearing three suits and one topcoat, and carrying a raincoat with every pocket bulging. Healy left the Lincoln Hotel with two mementos of his stay: an empty room and an empty trunk. Things of this kind took place occasionally, and hotel owners were suspicious, but Duke Pohl believed in befriending actors, and they showed their appreciation. As Duke used to say, "I've never lost anything by it. They all paid me eventually."

Vaudeville could not vouch for the honesty, the integrity, or the mentality of the individuals who collectively made up the horde the medium embraced. All the human race demands of its members is that they be born. That is all vaudeville demanded. You just had to be born. You could be ignorant and be a star. You could be a moron and be wealthy. The elements that went to make up vaudeville were combed from the jungles, the four corners of the world, the intelligentsia and the subnormal. An endless, incongruous swarm crawled over the countryside dragging performing lions, bears, tigers, leopards, boxing kangaroos, horses, ponies, mules, dogs, cats, rats, seals, and monkeys in their wake. Others rode bicycles, did acrobatic and contortion tricks, walked wires, exhibited sharpshooting skills, played violins, trombones, cornets, pianos, concertinas, xylophones, harmonicas, and any other known instrument. There were hypnotists, iron-jawed ladies, one-legged dancers, one-armed cornetists, mind readers, female impersonators, male impersonators, Irish comedians, Jewish comedians, blackface, German, Swedish, Italian, and rube comedians, dramatic actors, Hindu conjurors, ventriloquists, bag punchers, singers and dancers of every description, clay modelers, and educated geese: all traveling from hamlet to town to city, presenting their shows. Vaudeville asked only that you own an animal or an instrument, or have a minimum of talent or a maximum of nerve. With these dubious assets vaudeville offered fame and riches. It was up to you.

Vaudeville families endured for generations. The female of the species foaled on trains, in dressing rooms, in tank towns, and in the big cities. The show must go on. At the theater the baby slept in the top of the trunk in the dressing room. At the hotel a crib was improvised by removing a large bureau drawer and placing it on the bed or between two chairs. A large blanket filled the drawer nicely; the baby, wrapped in its quilt, rested serene in his drawer bassinet. The vaudeville baby carried its own baggage. A small valise contained milk bottles, nipples, safety pins, and emergency diapers. On a sleeper jump, vaudeville couples with a baby always had the same routine: at 1 A.M., with the train thundering through the night, a tiny cry is heard. In two berths, an upper and a lower, lights snap on instantly. The husband jumps down from his upper berth into the aisle. The curtains of the lower berth part just a crack, muted voices are heard, the clasps on the miniature valise click open, and a nippled bottle, filled with milk, appears through the curtains. The husband steadies himself as he sways down the aisle on his way to arouse the porter to warm the precious quota of milk. In the lower berth, the sounds of the mother's soothing voice and the baby's cries persist until the husband returns. The warm milk bottle is passed in, the baby gurgles and stops crying, the curtains close, the husband crawls back up into his berth. The lights go off in both berths, and it is dark and silent once again; the train hurries ahead into the night.

Arriving in the next town, and safe in their room, the family goes to work. The husband removes a small drawer from the dresser, places a rubber sheet over the drawer, and pokes it snugly down into the four corners. Then he fills the drawer half full of tepid water. The mother lowers the baby gently into the drawer to enjoy its bath after the train trip.

The smalltime vaudeville mother had the endurance of a doorknob. She did three or four shows a day as part of the act. She cared for her baby on the road and prepared its food. She did the family washing: there was always a clothesline hanging and dripping away in the dressing room and the boarding-house, and the sinks were filled with diapers. As the family grew larger, the kids were packed like sardines into upper berths. (Midgets often traveled in clusters in upper berths; an actor in a lower berth once complained that he had been kept awake all night by a midget with insomnia who had been walking up and down in the upper berth.)

Many wives cooked the family meals in the dressing room; before electricity became promiscuous, vaudeville wives carried tin plates, cups, knives and forks, and prepared tasty meals over flaming gas jets and blazing Sterno cans in dressing and hotel rooms. Then there was a special theatrical trunk, made by the Herkert and Meisel Trunk Company of St. Louis, which was constantly adding new features to lighten the burden of the vaudeville wife. The H & M wardrobe trunk had such special innovations as a metal compartment in one drawer to hold an electric iron; a small rubber-lined compartment which enabled actors to pack wet sponges, washcloths, and soap on hurried closing nights; a hat compartment for man or woman; a flat drawer under the wardrobe section to hold shoes; a jewel box; an ironing board that could be attached securely to the trunk to enable women to iron in the theater. These, and many other features of this trunk, made life easier for the vaudeville mother.

Vaudeville families flourished. The babies teethed on greasepaint, and their sitters were other acts on the bill who watched the tots while the parents were on stage. When the babies were able to walk, they were led on stage to take their first bows. Later, they learned to imitate their parents and many other acts who played on the different bills. After completing their schooling, most of the children grew up and went into vaudeville, and had children who grew up and went into vaudeville.

The smalltimer plying his profession was exposed to many irritations. When his act laid an egg in one town, he couldn't wait to leave for the next town, where, he hoped, things would be better. When the audience was bad, the whole community was terrible; the hotel, the restaurants, the food, the newspapers, and the people all became impossible. When the smalltimer was a riot, his environment was perfect. Using the smalltimer's psychology, if his act went badly in Detroit, Detroit as a metropolis was a bust. If his act went big in Eureka, Eureka was Utopia.

Next to the audience, in its importance to the smalltimer, stood the theater orchestra. If the orchestra could not play his wife's ballad properly, if the tempo of his dance music was too fast or too slow, if the drummer didn't catch his pratfalls with a well-timed roll and crash or tear the cloth on cue as he pretended to rip his trousers, the actor fought with his wife and sulked in his dressing room until the next show. Vaudeville orchestras varied from one piece—a piano—to seven or eight pieces. The usual smalltime theater had piano, cornet, and drums. The drums were very important: they accentuated the falls and crashes of the comedians and played long rolls for the aerialists' sensational slides. For his music, the smalltimer carried eight or nine parts in cardboard or leather covers. Playing the cheaper theaters, which had only a piano and drum, only the piano and drum parts were used. After the smalltimer had played several weeks in dumps, and was then booked into a big theater, he would occasionally brag at rehearsal in order to leave the musicians with the impression that he was accustomed to playing good theaters. He couldn't fool the musicians, however, because the minute they saw the smalltimer's music they knew where the act had been playing. The violin, clarinet, cornet, and bass parts were brand-new; the piano and drum parts were filthy. At rehearsal in a new town, the smalltimer, sensing that the orchestra wasn't too friendly, examined his music. It explained everything. The drummer in the last town had written on the drum part, "This act is lousy." The clarinet player had written, "He died here." The cornet player had summed everything up by simply writing one word: "Stinks."

The smalltimer's billing was a matter of great concern. Before the opening show at each theater he examined the front of the theater to check on the size of his name and his position in the list of acts. The vaudeville headliner often had a clause in his contract assuring him of top billing. The smalltimer's billing depended on the whim of the local manager or the man who printed or painted the theater signs. Seeing his name in runt letters could catapult the smalltimer into a three-day funk. His position on the bill was of major importance. If his act had been next to closing and he suddenly found himself second on the bill, wires were dispatched to the booking office and his agent, and the theater manager was summoned to the dressing room before the smalltimer deigned to do the first show. Headliners had clauses in their contracts that entitled them to the best dressing rooms. The smalltimer dressed where he was told. If he used the same dressing room as his wife, the smalltimer immediately examined all walls and connecting doors for holes. A few depraved actors carried gimlets and bits around with them, and drilled holes in the walls to watch the sister act or the single woman in the next room undress. If holes were discovered, the stage manager was notified and the apertures were filled with shoemaker's wax. One worry less for the smalltimer.

The censoring of his act also upset the smalltimer. When Paul Keith, after running a museum on Washington Street in Boston, opened his first theater, the Bijou Dream, he insisted on clean entertainment. Mrs. Keith instigated the chaste policy, for she would tolerate no profanity, no suggestive allusions, *double-entendres*, or off-color monkey business. As the Keith circuit grew, every theater carried a sign on the bulletin board:

NOTICE
TO PERFORMERS

Don't say "slob" or "son-of-a-gun" or "hully gee" on this stage unless you want to be cancelled peremptorily. Do not address anyone in the audience in any manner. If you have not the ability to entertain Mr. Keith's audiences without risk of offending them, do the best you can. Lack of talent will be less open to censure than would be an insult to a patron. If you are in doubt as to the character of your act, consult the local manager before you go on the stage, for if you are guilty of uttering anything sacrilegious or even suggestive, you will be immediately closed and will never again be allowed in a theatre where Mr. Keith is in authority.

Long after Mr. Keith's death the circuit was still waging its campaign against suggestive material. For many months *Variety* published a column called "You Mustn't Say That" which featured deletions in stage material ("Hell" or "Lord Epsom, Secretary of the Interior," or "An old maid taking a tramp through the woods," and so on) made by the Keith censorship bureau. As most of the gamy lines and jokes were his biggest laughs, the smalltimer would fight to the death to keep them in his act.

Many smaller acts who used one or two jokes, or a few comedy lines, and could not buy special material subscribed to *Madison's Budget*. For twenty years—from 1898 to 1918—a man named James Madison published an annual collection of monologues, cross-fire jokes, sketches, minstrel-show afterpieces, and parodies. This assortment of humorous matter sold for one dollar and was known as *Madison's Budget*. If a comedian found six or eight jokes in the *Budget* that he could adapt to his act, his dollar investment had returned a hearty dividend.

Comedy acts were always the targets of the pirates. If a comedian was original and wrote his own material, or if he frequently bought new routines and songs to keep his act up to date, he soon found that other comedians were stealing parts of his act. For many years performers had no way to protect their gags, parodies, or bits of business. Copyright laws were ignored, and good gags spread like bad news. One blackface comedian on the big time stole so much material that he couldn't use it all in his act; he hired another blackface act and paid him a salary to play the smalltime using the stolen material he had left over. There was a young comedian whose father regularly attended the opening show at the Palace. If any of the acts had new lines, jokes, or song titles, the father copied them down and wired them to his son. The act continued convulsing the Palace audience in New York, little dreaming that its best jokes were being told in Omaha, San Francisco, or wherever the son happened to be playing.

Original material was spread around in many ways. For instance, when blackface acts and other comedy teams split up, many times the men or women took new partners, and both new acts continued to do the same routines. After a series of splittings it was not unusual to find four or five teams all doing the same act. Burlesque shows lifted scenes bodily from Broadway revues. Social directors at summer camps spent the winter copying down anything they found in the Broadway theaters which they thought they could use at the camps next summer. Johnny Neff, a monologist, used to explain to his audiences how crazy comedians were to buy jokes. Johnny would relate how Frank Tinney had paid a hundred dollars for a certain joke. Johnny would then tell the joke to prove that Tinney was insane. When Johnny had finished explaining how much money Raymond Hitchcock, Ed Wynn, Jack Donahue, Leon Errol, and Richard Carle had paid for their jokes, and after he had told all these jokes himself, Johnny had a hilarious monologue that hadn't cost him a penny. And Milton Berle for years has been bragging to audiences that he has stolen jokes from other comedians. There has been no reason to doubt his word.

When Mr. Albee founded the National Vaudeville Artists, Inc., after breaking the White Rats' strike (the White Rats had been the original vaudeville performers' association), one of the inducements to attract members was the new organization's Protected Material Department. Any member could protect his act. All he had to do was to enclose a copy of his material in a sealed envelope and deliver it to the N.V.A. office. The envelope was placed in the Protected Material files. Later, if a plagiarist was brought to bay, the act preferred charges, the sealed envelope was opened, and the N.V.A. officials dispensed justice. Hundreds of acts protected their material through this service. After Mr. Albee's death, vaudeville started over the hill and took the N.V.A. club with it. Before the members vacated the clubhouse on Forty-sixth Street, some official, by whose authority nobody will ever know, sold the entire contents of the N.V.A. Protected Material Department files to Olsen and Johnson.

Superstitions and irrational beliefs influenced the vaudevillian as he made his decisions and planned his daily activities. Many credulous omens the performer treated with respect. He thought bad luck ensued if he whistled in the dressing room, found peacock feathers anywhere in the theater, saw a bird on the window sill, threw away his old dancing shoes, and so forth. There were many other bad omens, but there were only two portents that assured the performer future happiness. Good luck was sure to follow if an actor put his undershirt on inside out, or if he touched a humpbacked person.

Vaudeville acts often assumed strange names to atract attention. An unusual name was easily remembered by bookers, managers, and audiences. A few uniquely named acts were: Fyne and Dandy (acrobats), Sharp and Flat (musicians), Willie Rolls (roller skater), Amazon and Nile (contortionists), Nip and Tuck (acrobats), North and South (musical act), Worth and While (sister act), Possum Welch (dancer), and Darn, Good, and Funny (comedy trio).

The early vaudeville performers were inventive; they had to create the unusual specialties they performed. Vaudeville grew, and new acts came along to help themselves to the ideas of the originators, and to elaborate on and embellish them. Many specialty artists, in constructing their acts, came up with some weird innovations. One of these was Orville Stamm. Not long ago I got a letter from Orville, asking if I remembered him. It was not easy to forget Orville. He billed himself as the "Strongest Boy in the World." To demonstrate his great strength, Orville played the violin; as he played, he had suspended from the crook of his bow arm an enormous English bulldog. The bulldog made graceful arcs in the air as Orville pizzicatoed and manipulated his bow. For the finish of his act, Orville lay flat on the stage and arched his back; in the better acrobat circles, this was known as "bending the crab." When Orville's chest and abdomen attained the correct altitude, a small upright piano was placed across his stomach. An assistant stood on Orville's thigh and played the piano accompaniment as Orville, in his "crab" position, sang "Ireland Must Be Heaven, 'Cause My Mother Came from There." This finish was a sensation, and I'm sure it was Orville's own idea.

Raymonde, a female impersonator, also originated an unusual finish. After doing his entire act as a girl, Raymonde took a bow and removed his wig. The audience, seeing man's hair, was amazed to find that the girl was a boy. As the applause continued, Raymonde removed the man's wig, and blond tresses tumbled down over his shoulders. The boy was now a girl again. The audience, again duped, was frantic. Raymonde took another bow or two to thunderous applause, then removed the girl's wig and was a boy again. Raymonde, emulating the manner of a female impersonator's conception of a truck driver, swaggered off the stage to absolute bedlam.

A man named Willard was billed as the "Man Who Grows." As he talked, he stretched his arms out a foot or more beyond their normal length. For his finish Willard grew four or five inches in height. I watched Willard many times backstage without being able to discover his secret. He must have been able to telescope his skin.

An inventive monologist in Chicago featured a singing goat. Following a dull fifteen minutes of talk, the monologist would introduce his partner, the Singing Goat. The orchestra would play "Mammy"; when the monologist finished the verse and started the chorus, the goat would join him in singing "Ma-a-a-my! Ma-a-a-my!" The act stopped the show. One matinee, a representative of the S.P.C.A. called at the theater and removed the goat from the premises. When the theater manager remonstrated, the S.P.C.A. man showed him the goat's lacerated buttocks; the monologist had been prodding his rump with a sharp-pointed nail.

This sort of thing often happened in animal acts. Trainers who exhibited lions and tigers could seemingly cause them to growl and snarl on cue. The audience little suspected that the beasts worked on metal flooring, and that the lions and tigers would naturally growl or snarl after this metal flooring had been charged with electricity. Similarly, dog acts often astounded audiences when the little white terrier climbed the ladder, rung by rung, hesitated on the top rung for a second, and then jumped into space, landing in its master's arms. Little did the audience know that the top rung of the high ladder was electrified. When the little white terrier hesitated on this top rung, he wasn't kidding; he was frightened. A short shock through the rung, however, and the dog jumped.

Another great inventive act was that of Will Mahoney, who danced to his own melodies by attaching xylophone hammers to the toes of his shoes, and then danced atop the xylophone. If Will had spent the same amount of effort in thinking that he did on his xylophone, he might have discovered penicillin. I am sure that if all the hours vaudeville performers spent trying to improve their acts had been donated to science, automation would have been here fifty years sooner.

Vaudeville old-timers may not be wallowing in affluence in later life, but each smalltimer has his store of memories that will help him to escape from the unhappy present into the happy past. When the time comes that I find myself confined to the rubbish heap of humanity, I can temper my plight by conjuring up random recollections from my smalltime years. I can recall . . .

The manager of the vaudeville theater at Sandusky, Ohio. The audience there was so bad that he felt sorry for the acts. He invented an applause machine and installed it in the back of the theater. The machine manufactured applause by slapping a series of wooden paddles together. When an act finished and the audience sat there in its customary silence, the manager turned on his applause machine. To the sound of the wooden clatter, the act returned, took one or two bows, and withdrew.

The manager at Sherbrooke, Ontario, who was in the raincoat business. I remember that on the last night of my stay there he tried to talk the actors into taking their salaries in raincoats.

The manager at Torrington, Connecticut, who, on closing night, was driving me and a contortionist back to New York. Speeding through one small Connecticut town at midnight, the car was overtaken and stopped by the local policeman. The manager stepped out of the car to explain. He said, "I'm sorry, officer. I'm the manager of the theater at Torrington."

"I don't know nothin' about that," said the rube. "You was doin' sixty-five."

"I've got to get to New York," pleaded the manager. "I've got a contortionist in the car. He has to catch a train."

"You got what in the car?"

"A contortionist."

"A *contortionist*?"

"Yes."

"What's a contortionist?"

The contortionist couldn't stand it any longer. He jumped out of the car in the dark, ran around in front of the headlights, and ripped his coat off. He did a handstand, twined his legs around his neck, and ran around in circles on his hands.

The rube watched him for a few minutes and said, "That's a contortionist, eh?"

"Yes," said the manager.

"I'll be damned," the policeman said. "Go ahead!"

I can remember, too, the little theater at Lancaster, Pennsylvania, that had the bowling alley upstairs. Just as I came to the punch line of my joke, somebody in the bowling alley made a strike and the audience heard nothing but the awful crash.

And then there was the butcher in the small Ohio town who converted his shop into a theater at night and showed pictures and Gus Sun smalltime vaudeville acts. In the window of the butcher shop he hung a sign:

> Hamburger—10¢ lb.
> Pork chops—20¢ lb.
> Veal—25¢ lb.
> Theater tonight—20¢

There was a theater at Bayonne, New Jersey, where, during my act, a cat came down the aisle, emitted a series of blood-curdling cries, and delivered a litter on the carpet. An usher rushed down the aisle with a coal shovel, scooped up the kittens, and returned, followed by the mother, to the back of the house. The audience was in a tumult. All I could do in feeble rebuttal was to coin the line "I thought my act was a monologue, not a catalogue."

The Jefferson Theatre, on Fourteenth Street in New York, had a mongrel audience: the theater was going to the dogs. Situated between Second and Third Avenues, it attracted patrons of all nationalities. Third Avenue at Fourteenth Street was an uptown Skid Row, and should have been renamed the Bowery-Plaza. Alcoholics of all sizes and in varying conditions frequented the neighborhood and used the Jefferson as a haven from the elements and a slumber sanctuary. At some performances the Jefferson took on the appearance of a flophouse that had put in vaudeville. At one supper show, during my monologue I heard a sort of "clunk!" noise that was repeated at regular intervals. It sounded like someone dropping wet wedges into a bathtub. I'd talk for thirty seconds—then a clunk. Another thirty seconds—and another clunk. Finally I located the source of the clunks. On the aisle, in the third row, sat a simian-faced specimen. Between his feet he was holding a wooden bucket; on the seat next to him he had a bag filled with oysters. As I was struggling through my monologue, this combination bivalve addict and theater patron was shucking his oysters and dropping the shells into the bucket.

I can remember, too, *l'affaire* midget at the depot at Quincy, Illinois. The headline act, a midget troupe, was leaving to open at Galesburg. One midget on the platform was berating the manager of the act, and demanding in squeaky words that he be given a raise in salary. The train started, but the midget refused to get aboard unless he was assured of more money. As the baggage car went by, the manager calmly picked up the midget and threw him in through the open door.

When I try to clamp the lid tightly on the past, names keep popping up. There was Eddie Borden, who did an English act with a partner called Sir James Dwyer. Eddie read a magazine ad for a preparation guaranteed to cure skin blemishes. The ad claimed that you could save the expense of a trip to Hot Springs by buying a bottle of the company's elixir and taking your own curative baths at home. Eddie, who was concerned about an acne condition, mailed in the coupon. At Minneapolis, the fluid arrived with full directions. To enjoy the Hot Springs bath at home, the patient had to close the bathroom door tightly, fill the tub with steaming hot water, pour in a given amount of the magic fluid, and lie in the tub to soak for an hour or more. Eddie followed the directions implicitly, finished his soaking, and went to bed. The next morning he opened the bathroom door, and instead of the pure white bathroom he had entered the night before, he now found a room with a brown ceiling, brown walls, brown tub, brown toilet seat and bowl, brown medicine cabinet, and a brown door. The Hot Springs elixir had contained sulfur, and the steam had transformed Eddie's suite into mahagany.

Jack Inglis was a funny nut comedian. One season, work was scarce. Jack lived in a rented house in Jersey with his wife and four children. A butcher friend of his knew that things were bad, and that the family wouldn't have a very happy Thanksgiving. Early in October, he gave Jack a live turkey. He told him he could keep it out in the yard in Jersey, and when the time came, he could kill the turkey for the family's Thanksgiving dinner. Jack took the turkey—a plump specimen—home, and turned it loose in the back yard. Every day for six weeks Jack's kids played with the turkey and chased it around. By the time Thanksgiving arrived, the turkey, after running away from the kids for six weeks, had lost some twenty pounds. For their Thanksgiving Day dinner that year the Inglis family had what looked like a tall sparrow.

The Billy Doss Revue was a smalltime girl act featuring Bill, a blackface comedian. I played on the bill with this act in Kansas City, Florence, Topeka, and Wichita in Kansas, and some dry oil wells in Oklahoma. The last chorus number of the revue was sung on a Southern dock with a river boat tied up in the background. On the dock there were bales of cotton, and on one of the bales sat a buxom mammy. For the act's finale the mammy jumped off the cotton bale and did an agile wooden-shoe dance to great applause. The mammy was really a boy in blackface wearing a bandana and a well-stuffed calico dress. The boy sat on his bale for three or four shows a day, looking at audiences, and with audiences looking at him. The only thing unusual about this is that the boy was wanted by the police. When they finally caught up with the blackface mammy, he was washed up for ten years, which he spent in the Ohio Penitentiary.

Nelson's Cats and Rats were a big-time act. The cats and rats, traditional enemies, performed together to the astonishment of audiences. One time, on a bill in Chicago, Fanny Brice was the headliner. As she arrived at the theater one evening and opened her dressing-room door, she shrieked. The stage manager rushed over to her and said, "What's wrong, Miss Brice?" Fanny gasped, "A rat! There's a big rat in my dressing room!" The stage manager, no fool, called Nelson, the cat and rat authority. Nelson rushed in, cornered the rat, caught him in a heavy towel, and took the rat out of the dressing room. A few weeks later, I was on the bill with Nelson's Cats and Rats. I asked Nelson what had happened to the rat he had caught in Fanny Brice's dressing room. He said, "The next show, watch the finish of my act." I watched the finish, and saw a big black rat walk across the tiny platform carrying an American flag. "That," said Nelson, "is the rat."

The smalltimer, as he trudged through the seasons, always felt that he was getting closer to his goal. Every vaudeville actor dreamed of his personal utopia. Weekly sums were banked or mailed home against the day the smalltimer "quit the business." Then he would open his restaurant, filling station,

real-estate office, chicken farm, dancing school, or other project that he had envisioned supporting him through his remaining years. Very few smalltimers saw their dreams take
dimension. As the vaudeville monologist would explain it, "A
funny thing happened to my savings on the way to my
utopia." Sickness, relatives, going into businesses he didn't
understand, meeting real-estate salesmen, joining collapsible
building and loan clubs, gambling, lending money to other actors who never repaid him, playing the stock market, and a
thousand other mishaps dissipated the smalltimer's savings and
shattered his hopes. The few that did realize their ambitions
found that after the travel and excitement of vaudeville, the
dull and sedentary routine imposed on them as they tried to
run some picayune enterprise in a small town was boring.

One vaudeville actor I knew couldn't wait to retire and start
his own chicken farm. After he had bought a farm in California
and tried to operate it for a few months, he was very unhappy.
I went out to visit him one afternoon and found him sitting
out in the yard under a tree, griping. Scampering around in a
large wire enclosure were hundreds of White Wyandottes. The
bottoms of these white hens had red circles on them; scooting
by, they looked like little Japanese flags with legs on them. I
asked the actor if his chickens had unusual markings. He said
no, that he had seen an ad for Lay or Bust Feed that would increase the size of any hen's eggs, and that he had been giving
his hens plenty of it. The hens started laying eggs that were
too large for their disposal equipment. Laying the big economy-
size eggs had sprung the hens' hips and split their sphincters.
"That accounts for the red circles on the bottoms of the
hens?" I asked. "Yes," he answered. "I had to catch every lousy
hen and dab her with mercurochrome!"

The smalltimer was never happy in retirement. Had it been
within his power, the vaudeville performer would have been a
timeless wanderer, spanning the generations by using the
bridge of his talents.

But vaudeville is dead. Vaudeville was more a matter of style
than of material. It was not so much what the two- and three-
a-day favorites said and did, as how they said and did it. For
fifty years vaudeville's minstrels found their way into all lands,
preaching their gospel of merriment and song, and rousing the

rest of the world to laughter and to tears. A few diehards who knew and enjoyed vaudeville hover over their television sets, hoping for a miracle. They believe that this electronic device is a modern oxygen tent that in some mysterious way can revive vaudeville and return its colorful performers of yesteryear to the current scene. The optimism of these day and night dreamers is wasted. Their vigils are futile. Vaudeville is dead. Period.

1956

WALTER KERR

If George Jean Nathan had the dubious honor of being impersonated by slippery George Sanders in *All About Eve*, Walter Kerr (1913–1996) had the purer pleasure of being portrayed by suave David Niven in *Please Don't Eat the Daisies*, a movie based on a best-selling book by his wife, Jean Kerr. A graduate of Northwestern, Kerr taught drama at Catholic University in Washington, D.C., while reviewing plays for the Catholic magazine *Commonweal*. In 1951 he became the dramatic critic for the *New York Herald Tribune* and, in 1959, described *Gypsy* as "the best damn musical I've seen in years," a line that appeared in the show's publicity for decades. When that newspaper folded in 1966, Kerr moved to *The New York Times* where he headed the drama desk until 1983. Most of his judgments were less exuberant than his verdict on *Gypsy*; with his academic background, he was unimpressed by what he considered intellectual pretension, so that the later works of Stephen Sondheim and Samuel Beckett often met with his disfavor. He fancied himself speaking for the middlebrow position and endorsing what his readers would approve. Kerr's essay on "Barns" is a reminder that, once the automobile ruled the roads and before air-conditioning became universal, summer stock provided an important hothouse for cultivating acting talent and new plays.

Barns

I

It seems to me that the pleasantest thing about summer theater—for the reviewer and paying customer alike—is that you don't have to go to it. This sounds like an insidious remark, and I hasten to add that it is intended as quite a compliment.

It just so happens that we live in an age when regular, or winter, playgoing involves a series of social, moral, and financial pressures. Our "smash hit" psychology decrees that there are a certain few shows we must see. It also decrees that we must see them while they are still suitable subject matter for cocktail conversation.

Furthermore, because seats for these lucky entertainments

are in such demand, we must see them at a time determined not by our own madcap impulse for a night on the town, but by the rigorous, impartial apportionment of the box-office man who handles mail orders.

When the appointed night finally rolls around, neither rain, hail, sleet, snow nor gastrointestinal embarrassment can keep us from our clear obligation. We know what it is we must do.

Summer theater reverses all this. Should a small hurricane be blowing up, you can shut the windows and go to bed in perfect composure; you haven't been holding onto a couple of hard-won pasteboards from time immemorial. Should a covey of house guests descend suddenly upon you, you can bid them welcome with an honest nonchalance; you don't have to tear up your tickets for *My Fair Lady* right in front of them, announcing with a kind of grisly gaiety that you didn't want to see the old thing anyway.

Better still, you can achieve a remarkable coup; you can get the house guest out of the house. Clapping him on the shoulder in idiot exuberance, you can suggest: "Say, why don't we all go over to the Old Black Barn? They've got quite an interesting show this week—Elmo Lincoln in his first stage appearance." And you can march him out the front door and over to that nearest strawhat with the confident expectation that you will be able to get seats and that you will have to play the hearty host for no more than two ten-minute intermissions.

The best thing about summer theater, I think, is that it puts play-going back on a whimsical basis. All urgencies disappear. Since the chances are better than three to one that you'll be seeing an old play, you don't have to spend much time worrying about whether or not you ought to like it. Your intellectual standing in the community isn't going to depend very heavily on your decision. In fact, you are really relieved of making any decision at all.

Since the new plays you do see (summer theaters are doing more and more of them) are still in the "tryout" stage, you can look right at them without fear or favor, taking or leaving them for precisely what they are. No one has hallowed or damned them yet. (It might be argued that this constitutes the only candid and direct author-audience relationship left to the contemporary theater.)

Since you haven't poured months of planning and preparation into the event, the entertainment doesn't have to work so hard to make things up to you. Even if the show isn't very good—which, it is whispered, is sometimes the case—you don't come out feeling cheated.

You've at least had a night out on the very night you wanted out, you've been able to indulge that secret yen for soda pop that embarrasses you in more formal circumstances, you've been able to fill your lungs with cigarette smoke and fresh air simultaneously, and you may even have been casually pleased. In the summer theaters, a nice little show is a nice little show, and what'll we do tomorrow night?

It's almost relaxing. I suspect that's how the actors find it, too. There is a canard in circulation to the effect that actors go to the country to make money. My own guess is that they do it to be near the Coke machines. Drop in on a summer-theater rehearsal and you will find a thriving social life centered around the dispenser on the patio; occasionally a performer or two will, when summoned, leave the socratic gathering to rush through a scene onstage, but his real objective is to get back to the clean-living world of the porch, his real mood that of the happy inland beachcomber.

Indeed, things were so relaxed at one barn rehearsal I attended that the director was able to guide the destinies of his players while lying flat on his back in the center aisle. He was sound of mind and body, too; he was just sparing himself the usual tensions of his profession.

And it must be pleasant to play an entire season without doom hanging over one's head. Even if the show isn't quite ready, even if the star and supporting company have barely met, the venture isn't in danger of closing in Philadelphia or at the end of its first Broadway week. Salaries are pretty certain to go right on into September. If they don't much like you this week, they may find you fascinating next. You can give the ulcers a rest, and pick up a tan.

On both sides of the footlights, summer theater—in a metaphorical sense, anyway—takes the heat off. Whatever its defects, it briefly restores theater to the kind of drop-in, come-as-you-are footing it once enjoyed all the year round and then lamentably lost to the movies.

2

As we've been saying, everyone supposes that the reason stars who have worked all winter go traipsing off to the summer theaters is money, and it is barely possible that money has something to do with it. There may be another lure, though—apart from the Coke machines. Actors may *like* to rehearse haphazardly, open insecurely, close at the precise moment they have begun to get the hang of a role, and wake every morning to the sound of apprentices' hammers knocking next week's scenery into deceptively sturdy shape, because it's the only way they can remember what the theater once meant to them.

One of the real penalties of being a professional is loss of glamour. (The more a player acquires it for other people, the less he is able to savor it for himself.) When a young enthusiast first arrives in New York, he is still faintly drunk with the smell of paint, the wobble of scenery sliding into place, the sheer pleasure of being in the company of other people who have typewritten "sides" stuffed in their pockets.

It's an aura that is quickly dispelled, not because the commercial theater doesn't have its own kind of excitement but because the commercial theater is essentially a place of urgent, efficient, common-sense work. Almost the first thing a tyro learns is to wipe that look of enthusiasm off his face; it marks him as a beginner. He doesn't burst into a manager's office with the light of love in his eyes. He strolls in, as indifferently as possible, with a knowing calm and—if he can manage it—a suggestion that he has been painfully lured away from pursuits that interest him a great deal more.

When he gets a part, he doesn't run through the streets waving his contract. He stubs out a cigarette in Sardi's and murmurs that, well, he does have to support his family somehow. At rehearsals, he is polite but matter-of-fact, adjusting his glasses and marking up his script with the philosophical despair of one who has seen playwrights come and go and is sure that they all will. While the play is coming together, he will spend as much time as is permissible in his dressing room silently trimming mustaches.

At the out-of-town opening, he doesn't bob around backstage wishing everyone luck at the top of his lungs and behaving like a happy firecracker that is about to explode; he confesses to opening-night nerves, all right, but in a dour and impatient fashion—as though he were extremely irritated with himself for not having got past these childish extravagances. When the opening-night curtain is down, he doesn't grab the leading lady and waltz her about the stage, amid hysterical cackles from the rest of the company. He immediately becomes soberer than ever, gets paper and pencil ready, and listens to the director's notes with alarming concentration and frequent shrewd nods to show that he knew *that* problem would be coming up.

As for the odor of glue and canvas, he doesn't even see the scenery until he gets to New Haven, and the thrill of the moment is somewhat modified by the squad of armed stagehands who are standing in front of it to make sure he doesn't accidentally help lift it.

Every once in a while, though, he must yearn for a whiff of the giddy, foolishly exhilarating, somewhat slapdash but much more comradely atmosphere that once made him want to become an actor. He needs to remember what he thought the theater was going to be like when he first talked a couple of friends into renting the YMCA auditorium for two risky nights, wrote Samuel French for a copy of *Grumpy*, and saw to the printing of tickets himself. He needs to have his efficiency relaxed and his love refreshed. And this, I think, is one reason why actors don't just lie down in an air-conditioned room and reread their notices all summer.

Not that the barns are going to let them get away with right-off-the-beach performances, or that audiences are going to invite them to turn a season's touring into something like Til Eulenspiegel's merry pranks. Standards in the country are getting higher all the time. But however professional the standards, and however cold the cash, that's still a different breeze blowing in under the rafters.

Instead of a cab ride from one city block to another, it's a walk across the lawn. Instead of a gray brick building arbitrarily set between a men's clothing store and a manufacturer of buntings, it's a theater standing all by itself. Instead of long, intense rehearsals with the death penalty waiting at the end of them, it's the best you can do in a week with a smile on your face and no great fear in your heart.

And if you'd got to feeling like a cog in a machine assembled in New Haven, you can stretch your limbs, stumble over lumber and get stuck to freshly painted fireplaces to your heart's content. You can even cheer the denim brigade on as they paint the second-act staircase during the first-act intermission.

It's like meeting a girl you haven't seen in years and discovering that your immature taste was a credit to you.

1957

TENNESSEE WILLIAMS

Tennessee Williams (1911–1983) made the critical establishment nervous. It had to acknowledge the raw emotional power and poetic imagination of *The Glass Menagerie* (1945), *A Streetcar Named Desire* (1947), *The Rose Tattoo* (1951), and *Cat on a Hot Tin Roof* (1955), but it was disturbed by the morbid obsessions and irrational violence indulged in by his souls in torment. It suspected that their weak wills and wayward desires hinted at even more outrageous passions lurking in the magnolia bushes. Still, the effect on audiences of the agonists' sensational confrontations, expressed in succulent dialogue, was undeniable, the effect on the imagination indelible. Williams refused to be pigeonholed as "Southern Gothic," arguing that his concerns were common to all humanity: "Desire is rooted in a longing for companionship, a release from the loneliness which haunts every individual." His 1957 essay on the director/playwright relationship points to an important development in the American theatre, the growing primacy of the creator of the *mise en scène*. The original productions of *Streetcar*, *Cat*, *Camino Real* (1953), and *Sweet Bird of Youth* (1959) had been staged by Elia Kazan in close collaboration with Williams; Kazan's casting and demands for rewrites (e.g., a whole new third act for *Cat*) often determined the emphases. There was a genuine affinity between the co-creators, but Williams occasionally chafed at the need to temper his vision to the exigencies of Broadway. Some would argue, however, that the emotional excesses and technical miscalculations of his last plays might have benefited from the strong editorial hand of a gifted director.

Author and Director: A Delicate Situation

WHETHER he likes it or not, a writer for the stage must face the fact that the making of a play is, finally, a collaborative venture, and plays have rarely achieved a full-scale success without being in some manner raised above their manuscript level by the brilliant gifts of actors, directors, designers, and frequently even the seasoned theatrical instincts of their producers. I often wonder, for personal instance, if *The Glass Menagerie* might not have been a mere *succès d'estime*, snobbishly remembered by a small coterie, if Laurette Taylor had not poured into it her startling light and power, or if, without the genius of Kazan, *A Streetcar Named Desire* could have been kept on the tracks in those dangerous, fast curves it made here and there, or if the same genius was not requisite to making *Cat on a Hot Tin Roof* acceptable to a theater public which is so squeamish about a naked study of life.

A playwright's attitude toward his fellow workers goes through a cycle of three main phases. When he is just beginning in his profession, he is submissive mostly out of intimidation, for he is "nobody" and almost everybody that he works with is "somebody." He is afraid to assert himself, even when demands are made on him which, complied with, might result in a distortion of his work. He will permit lines, speeches, sometimes even whole scenes to be cut from his script because a director has found them difficult to direct or an actor has found them difficult to act. He will put in or build up a scene for a star at the sacrifice of the play's just proportions and balance. A commercial producer can sometimes even bully him into softening the denouement of his play with the nearly always wrong idea that this will improve its chances at the box office. Or if he is suddenly driven to resistance, he is unable to offer it with a cool head and a tactful tongue. Intimidation having bottled him up until now, he now pops off with unnecessary violence, he flips his lid. That's the first phase of the cycle. The second is entered when the playwright has scored his first notable success. Then the dog has his day. From intimidation he passes into the opposite condition. All of a sudden he is the great, uncompromising Purist, feeling that all ideas but his own are threats to the integrity of his work. Being suddenly a "Name" playwright, explosions of fury are no longer necessary for him to get his way. Now that he has some weight, he throws it around with the assured nonchalance of a major league pitcher warming up by the dugout. When his script is submitted to a producer by his representatives, it is not unlike the bestowal of a crown in heaven, there is a sanctified solemnity and hush about the proceedings. The tacit

implication is: Here it is; take it or leave it; it will not be altered, since the slightest alteration would be nearly as sacrilegious as a revision of the Holy Scriptures.

Some playwrights are arrested at this second phase of the
cycle, which is really only an aggravated reaction to the first,
but sometimes the inevitable eventuality of an important failure after an important success or series of successes, will result
in a moderation of the playwright's embattled ego. The temple
or citadel of totally unsullied self-expression has not proven as
secure a refuge as it seemed to him when he first marched triumphantly into it. It may take only one failure, it may take two
or three, to persuade him that his single assessment of his work
is fallible, and meanwhile, if he is not hopelessly paranoiac, he
has come to learn of the existence of vitally creative minds in
other departments of theater than the writing department, and
that they have much to offer him, in the interpretation, the
clarification, and illumination of what he has to say; and even
if, sometimes, they wish him to express, or let him help them
express, certain ideas and feelings of their own, he has now
recognized that there are elements of the incomplete in his nature and in the work it produces. This is the third phase. There
is some danger in it. There is the danger that the playwright
may be as abruptly divested of confidence in his own convictions as that confidence was first born in him. He may suddenly become a sort of ventriloquist's dummy for ideas which
are not his own at all. But that is a danger to which only the
hack writer is exposed, and so it doesn't much matter. A serious playwright can only profit from passage into the third
phase, for what he will now do is this: he will listen; he will
consider; he will give a receptive attention to any creative mind
that he has the good fortune to work with. His own mind, and
its tastes, will open like the gates of a city no longer under
siege. He will then be willing to supplement his personal conceptions with outside conceptions which he will have learned
may be creative extensions of his own.

A mature playwright who has made this third and final step
in his relations to fellow workers has come to accept the collaborative nature of the theater: he knows now that each artist
in the theater is able to surpass his personal limits by respect
for and acceptance of the talent and vision of others. When a

gifted young actor rushes up to the playwright during rehearsals and cries out, I can't feel this, this doesn't ring true to me, the writer doesn't put on the austere mask of final authority. He moves over another seat from the aisle of a rehearsal hall, and bows his head in serious reflection while the actor tells him just what about the speech or the scene offends his sense of artistic justice, and usually the writer gets something from it. If he still disagrees with the actor, he says: "Let's get together with (whoever is directing) and talk this over at the bar next door. . . ." Maybe he won't sleep that night, but the chances are that in the morning he will reexamine the challenged segment with a sympathetic concern for an attitude which hasn't originated in his own brain and nerves, where sensibility is seated.

Now all of this that I've been rambling on about is my idea of the healthy course of development for a playwright *except*— I repeat, EXCEPT!—in those rare instances when the playwright's work is so highly individual that no one but the playwright is capable of discovering the right key for it. When this rare instance occurs, the playwright has just two alternatives. Either he must stage his play himself or he must find one particular director who has the very unusual combination of a truly creative imagination plus a true longing, or even just a true willingness, to devote his own gifts to the faithful projection of someone else's vision. This is a thing of rarity. There are very few directors who are imaginative and yet also willing to forego the willful imposition of their own ideas on a play. How can you blame them? It is all but impossibly hard for any artist to devote his gifts to the mere interpretation of the gifts of another. He wants to leave his own special signature on whatever he works on.

Here we encounter the sadly familiar conflict between playwright and director. And just as a playwright must recognize the value of conceptions outside his own, a director of serious plays must learn to accept the fact that nobody knows a play better than the man who wrote it. The director must know that the playwright has already produced his play on the stage of his own imagination, and just as it is important for a playwright to forget certain vanities in the interest of the total creation of the stage, so must the director. I must observe that certain directors are somewhat too dedicated to the principle that all playwrights must be "corrected." I don't think a director should accept a directorial assignment without feeling that, basically, the author of the play, if it's a serious work by a playwright of ability, has earned and deserves the right to speak out, more or less freely, during the rehearsal and tryout period of the production if this can be done in a way that will not disturb the actors. Yet it sometimes happens that the playwright is made to feel a helpless bystander while his work is being prepared for Broadway. It seems to me that the director is privileged to tell the author to "Shut up!" actually or tacitly, only when it is unmistakably evident that he, the director, is in total artistic command of the situation. Sometimes a director will go immediately from one very challenging and exhausting play production into another, being already committed by contract to do so. Then naturally he can't bring the same vitality to the second that he brought to the first. This becomes evident when the play has been blocked out, and after this blocking, little further progress is being made. The play remains at the stage of its initial blocking. The director may say, and quite honestly feel, that what he is doing is giving the public and critics a play precisely as it was written. However, this is evading the need and obligation that I mentioned first in this article, that a play must nearly always be raised above its manuscript level by the creative gifts and energies of its director, and all others involved in its production.

Perhaps it would be a good idea, sometimes, to have a good psychiatrist in attendance at the rehearsals and tryout of a difficult play, one who is used to working with highly charged creative people such as directors and actors and playwrights and producers, so that whenever there is a collision of nervous, frightened, and defensive egos, he can arbitrate among them, analyze their personal problems which have caused their professional problems, and "smooth things over" through the clearing house of a wise and objective observer.

Once in a while the exigencies and pressures of Broadway must step aside for another set of conditions which are too fragile and spiritually important to suffer violence through the silly but sadly human conflict of egos.

The theater *can* be a maker of great friendships!

1957

GORE VIDAL

To find someone writing in English who, like Gore Vidal (b. 1925), distinguished himself as a historical novelist, a commercial playwright, a political activist, and a dandy, attracting controversy and opprobrium along the way, one would have to go back to Edward Bulwer-Lytton. However, Vidal's waspish essays in the print media and his frequent appearances in the electronic media have made him familiar to a far wider public than the fustian baronet could aspire to. Conversant with backroom Washington politics from his boyhood (his grandfather was a senator), Vidal made a name at 19 with the war novel *Williwaw*, but then compromised his fame with *The City and the Pillar* (1948), whose homophilic core so outraged *The New York Times* that it placed an embargo on reviewing his fiction until 1964. Meanwhile, Vidal became a writer for the big screen, with the remake of *Ben Hur*, and the little, with *Visit to a Small Planet*, a parable about a time-traveling warmonger. It was successfully refashioned for Broadway (1957) and for the networks as a sitcom series and was followed by *The Best Man* (1960), an informed if jaundiced view of the presidential nomination process. Vidal's plays are influenced by his writing for television: they are intimate, unsparing in their closeups, a feature most obvious in *An Evening with Richard Nixon* (1972). Owing to his friendship with active playwrights such as Truman Capote and Tennessee Williams (Vidal fashioned the screenplay for *Suddenly Last Summer*), he rarely wrote theatre criticism. Consequently, the handful of pieces he published in 1958–59 are all the more valuable as the elegantly styled responses of a discriminating and intelligent insider.

Eugene O'Neill's "A Touch of the Poet"

SEVEN or perhaps eleven plays to encompass all things American from the Revolution to The Way We Live Now. Then after a number of false starts, the solemn burning of aborted fragments in a hotel room in Boston with only one completed play surviving, *A Touch of the Poet*, set in 1828. What could sound more unpromising? Especially in the wake of the self-indulgent

Long Day's Journey into Night, whose production and reception on Broadway resembled nothing so much as a state funeral, with black plumes waving and sonorous eulogies of the dead master from those who gave so little aid and comfort to the living master for his *The Iceman Cometh* in 1946.

I went to the theater expecting the worst. Even before the curtain went up, irritable phrases formed in my mind (how often, I wonder, does this happen to professional reviewers?). "Rhetoric is the attempt of the will to do the work of the imagination"—W. B. Yeats. . . . I would definitely use that one, for if there was ever a rhetorician it was O'Neill. Then I recalled my old resentment against his misuse of the *Oresteia* when, having crudely borrowed the relationships, the melodrama, the tension of Aeschylus, he blithely left out the whole idea of justice, which was the point to that trilogy. And, finally, the maddening urge of American primitives to include everything—to write cycles, tetralogies, epics—the whole hee-haw of the Thomas Wolfes as they list the rivers of America in alphabetical order, their minds innocent of civilization, their self-love filling the empty plains of a new continent which *ought* to have a tragedy, though just what it is no one has yet discovered.

The curtain rose. Two minor characters started talking. My heart sank as they explained at length necessary secrets. Then suddenly the stage was bathed in light. Helen Hayes and Kim Stanley were on; the drama had begun and O'Neill blazed.

A Touch of the Poet is a beautiful play, beautifully presented. It has but one fault (to which I shall come last), for which its virtues more than compensate. The play is *rose*, not *noire*, and it has a deliberate artifice that I prefer to the shapeless black melodramas O'Neill latterly preferred. Then, too, 1828 is just right: Andrew Jackson; the rise of the Democrats; the fall of J. Q. Adams and with him that oligarchical, gentlemanly society which began the nation. All this is symbolically right, and pleasing. It is time we used our bit of history, especially since the New York audience has no real sense of the United States before the First World War. Lincoln, of course, is recalled glumly; it is known that there was some sort of revolution at the beginning; and that's it—almost as if Van Wyck Brooks had never lived.

O'Neill reminds us of our past. He indicates the rise of the

Yankee merchants—busy, practical, contemptuous of the old aristocratic principle. With precision and uncharacteristic economy, O'Neill sets the scene for his moral action, which is the crushing of a man's false pride, his absorption into the main, his final realization that he has lived a bogus life, presuming to a position both worldly and moral to which he has no right but the one—and this is significant—of wanting.

Cornelius Melody (Eric Portman) was born of Irish peasants, served bravely in the Peninsular campaign, became a British officer, got a peasant girl pregnant, married her, came to America, opened a tavern and failed. He torments his wife (Helen Hayes) and his daughter (Kim Stanley). He quotes Byron to himself in a mirror. He assumes the manner of a king in exile. He is laughed at by the Yankees but adored by his wife, who understands him perhaps more profoundly in O'Neill-land than she would in life. She sees how lonely he is in his vanity (very Meredithian, this), and she loves him. He is alternately mocked and served by his daughter, a finely realized character; part dreamer, part materialist, veering this way and that, ambivalent and strange.

The story is simple. The daughter loves a Yankee of the new merchant class. He has escaped his family to write poetry but eventually he will go into business—happily. The girl must marry him to escape the world of unpaid bills and false pride. She also loves him and wants to cheat neither of them. His family deplores the match. They try to buy her off. Dressed in his British army uniform, Melody, drunk, goes to challenge the boy's father to a duel; he is beaten up by the police; he returns, pride gone, and in an incredible *volte-face* chooses reality to prideful illusion: he is only a Mick and a failure who loves his wife. The girl gets her Yankee, and all ends well.

What makes the play work thematically is the examination of Melody's dream world. It may well be that this is the most significant American theme of the twentieth century. Since reality did not please him, he chose to invent his own past. He told lies; he believed the lies and for various reasons was abetted in his fantasies by those about him. O'Neill has often dealt with this theme (*The Iceman Cometh*, for example) and so have many of our best writers, most notably Tennessee Williams in *A Streetcar Named Desire*.

Which brings us to an interesting question: What is it in modern American life (1828 is as good a date as any to start the "modern") which forces so many to prefer fantasy to reality? One observes the fantastifiers at every cocktail party: charming people, boring people, intelligent, dull—people of all sorts, telling lies, which no one much minds. It is all a game. Who shall I be? Who am I? And the person who drops the brick of truth is the only villain.

It is to this that the audience of *A Touch of the Poet* most responds. There is an element of Melody in all of us, and one watches with horrified fascination as he is brought at last to the truth about himself.

The production is good. Harold Clurman has taken the three most mannered actresses in our theater and imposed the play's manner on them with complete success. Miss Hayes is strong and direct and very moving, her usual cute pony-prancing severely curbed. Betty Field, whose old voice I always liked, has a new one which works admirably in her single scene. But the production's glory is Kim Stanley's performance. The old annoying tricks are still there, but now they glitter and she gets the character's ambivalence with such fairness that one is reminded of a character in Dostoevsky: light and shadow mysteriously fluctuating; the "yes" and the simultaneous "no." It is fine work.

The production's only flaw is the performance of Eric Portman. He is a fine technical actor whose attack here is unfortunately wrong. He belongs to what I call the "voice-music" school of English acting, whose honorary president is Sir Ralph Richardson. The voice-musicians hear some strange melody in the wings to which in counterpoint they sing their lines. Their songs are often fascinating but almost always irrelevant to the play's meaning. Mr. Portman is far better in the small neat plays of Terence Rattigan, because in the naturalistic idiom one can gobble and honk and sigh and mumble and the meaning will remain clear. Major Melody needs grandeur and thought, neither of which Mr. Portman provides. As I watched him strut about the stage on his spindly legs, his swollen body held tightly erect, like a pineapple on two sticks, I was haunted by *déjà vu*. Not until the final scene did I recall whom he reminded me of: a maleficent Mr. Micawber—and the moment one plays Melody like Micawber, O'Neill is brought down.

Happily, there are so many good things in this production—including the play—that the thing works, and one is pleased that Eugene O'Neill's final statement should be at once so human and so gently wise.

1958

The Commercialites

THE desire to give pleasure is a fundamental characteristic of the popular artist, nor is it necessarily a meretricious one: Shakespeare was an instinctive pleasure giver, and in our own time Tennessee Williams possesses in abundance (I nearly wrote "suffers from") this particular trait. The literary pleasure givers are happiest using the theater, loneliest in the novel. Even Charles Dickens, an archetypal pleasure giver, turned finally to the stage as performer. And it is understandable. A most tangible audience responds like a lover to pleasure given, and in his audience's response the artist is himself ravished by what he has done. The result is a beautiful circle of love which at its truest has been responsible for much good art in the theater along with most of the bad.

Opposed to the pleasure givers are the polemicist, the satirist, the nauseated, the reformer. In short, those writers whose primary objective is the criticism of a society which is in essential conflict with the writer's own sense of what life should be. Bernard Shaw is paradigmatic. His pleasure giving was deliberately calculated to disguise polemic intent as sugar does harsh medicine. (This was his own metaphor; to which a friend answered: "How clever of the public to lick off the sugar and leave your pill undigested!")

Americans of the mid-century, eager to be loved, have produced very few writers in the theater of this second kind—perhaps the odd George Kelly; Arthur Miller at moments . . .

and the list trails off. Even an "intellectual" like Thornton
Wilder is, finally, as pleasure-giving and mind-withholding as
all the other cocker spaniels who prance about Times Square,
tails wagging, eyes glowing with love—simulated or real: it
makes no difference as they go about demanding love for pleasure given.

Ultimately, of course, what matters is the work, not the motives of those who made it. But I suggest that when the work
accomplished exploits too crudely our prejudices and weaknesses, it is difficult not to ask: "*Why* are they doing this to us?
For what end?" Now to be commercial in the theater is, simply, to try to make money out of a basic investment of time,
money and talent. There is no other kind of theater in America, nor will there be as long as plays cost as much as they do to
mount. If we had a Bernard Shaw among us, and if he thought
it might be useful (and to him, if not to us, pleasurable) to
write a play showing that democracy is a disaster, or that Christianity is a bitter hoax, he would not be produced. That in itself is not necessarily the end of the matter. He could still use
the novel, the essay, the published play, which could make its
effect slowly upon readers and find peripheral production. But
the working dramatist must either not do what interests him the
most, or disguise it entirely, or—and here is the real tragedy of
commercialism—discard automatically any idea or theme
which he knows is not acceptable to the prejudices of an audience that must be won by flattery and charm. No American
dramatist in the last war would have written with such virulence against President Roosevelt as Aristophanes wrote
against the Athenian Establishment at a time of war and national disaster. Yet our dramatists cannot be scored for not attempting the impossible. Large societies are difficult to assault.
Novelists are let alone, for they have little public effect. The
Nation may attack J. Edgar Hoover until the hoods come
home, and the watchman will still cry "All's well!" But to use
the theater or television for stating ideas that do not give immediate pleasure to a large bland audience is to experience
harsh censorship; it is either not done at all or else so distorted
in the doing that the result is neither one thing nor the other.

The Crucible, by Arthur Miller, was much attacked when it
was first produced during the great days of the Wisconsin buf-

foon. Yet there is nothing in this good if rather glum little play which breaks new ground, which demonstrates anything but an old saw or two about bearing false witness and the panicky response of a weak-minded society to psychotics. I should think a playwright really daring if he were to show us dramatically that Communism or socialism or fascism is superior to democratic *laissez faire*. One might disagree, but at least we should have a new theme to consider. But this may not happen, for the inner censor is at work. To me that is the most terrible result of commercialism.

I remember how in the so-called Golden Age of television, writers were continually (and rightfully) chafing under network and advertising-agency censorship. To a man they wanted freedom. But when asked "Freedom to do what?" they would become evasive and tentative. Well, to be able to use four-letter words and naturalistic expletives the way the novelists do; to defend minority groups openly; to be allowed to call a Jew a Jew and not the weirdly generalized "He's one of *them*" (knowing wink) "and we know what *they* are!"—this much latitude would certainly be welcome, but it is not much to dream of. American popular writers (like their Russian counterparts) are prisoners of the state, sentenced for life. They want yard privileges and better food, but they shrink at the idea of choice, of life outside the familiar walls of superstition that we call the free world. I suspect, barring accident, that the next generation will prove both to the Soviet and to us how much alike great states are in the twentieth century, and how undesirable to those states true freedom is. The most dangerous and successful censorship is inner censorship. In this our Commercialites are anticipating the future.

Among the Commercialites, the team of Jerome Lawrence and Robert E. Lee is typical. I did not see their admired *Inherit the Wind*, but I did see something of theirs called *Auntie Mame*. Now they have run up a play about the Harding Administration. One wonders why. They have nothing to say about the political process in America, nothing to say about Harding and his associates. Sensing that they had no theme, they announced to the press shortly before the opening that their urgent message to the nation was "Beware government by crony!" But that is not an issue. Nowadays not even the vilest Presidential crony could steal as blithely as those in the play do. There are too many checks. Like the rest of our citizenry, politicians are congenitally inclined to dishonesty, but these days the dishonesty is intellectual and moral, not financial. In the glare of publicity at a national level there is little opportunity to steal anything except power.

Only one interesting thing happened in the theater the night I saw *The Gang's All Here*. When the Attorney General delivered an impassioned speech about the virtue of getting ahead and the obligation each individual has to himself to get all he can by any means, honest or dishonest, a section of the audience burst into spontaneous applause while the rest of us froze. It was an astonishing moment. Worship of the Golden Calf, though general in the free world, is ritually decried; yet here were worshipers flaunting their adoration of that brazen god.

The production is good enough. Melvyn Douglas is often touching as the bewildered President. (That is a real theme, by the way: the puzzled man thrust into a world he does not comprehend: "I'm not an expert in this but I think, uh, maybe . . ." After the last seven years any of us could make something out of that.) If I have any quarrel with Mr. Douglas's characterization, it is the laugh. One of the faults (or perhaps it is a virtue) of the Commercialites is that they do not take their characters from life but from other commercial plays. Fatuous politicians *always* smoke cigars and laugh genially. Therefore, since he is most fatuous of all, Mr. Douglas must chuckle like a hyena through nearly every phrase. I am sure that even our electorate with its passion for mediocrity would think twice before voting such a cretin into the Presidency.

At no point does the play betray any familiarity with politicians. Mr. Douglas at times seems more like a simpleminded movie star surrounded by conniving agents and producers, somewhat in the manner of *The Big Knife*. The dialogue is all wrong. "Has somebody got a number on Rutherford B. Hayes?" asks an ancient judge in a phrase that is pure 1950 show business—MCA, not the White House. Also, we have one pol address another pol as "*Mr.* Senator," and so on. The one distinguished thing about the production is E. G. Marshall as the Attorney General; he continues to be one of the

more satisfying actors of our time. The direction of George
Roy Hill, though vague as to milieu, is adequate despite a tendency to get actors in a long, sullen line with nothing to do.

And yet one is grateful to the Commercialites for dealing
with politics at all. Though they tell us nothing and though
the pleasure they give us is mechanical and calculated, at least
they have moved out of the world of small private relations informed by psychoanalysis which in recent years has made so
much of our theater boring. The Commercialites are shrewd
analysts, forever studying the audience, devising new ways of
exploiting the obvious, always on the lookout for a "property"
that will "go." The fact that Lawrence and Lee have taken
soundings and decided that the audience might accept a political cartoon, neutrally rendered, is a splendid bit of sleuthing
and a good omen, even pleasurable!*

1959

*Since Jerome Lawrence is an acquaintance of mine and a most amiable
man, I suffered real discomfort in giving him such a bad notice. And this, by
the way, is the most difficult part of being a critic. What do you do about
people you like whose work is not good? As the late President Harding would
say: "Don't knock; boost!" I do believe (perhaps wrongly) that I lack sadism.
I am positive I get no pleasure out of hurting others in print. Yet if one is not
scrupulously accurate in recording impressions there is no point to writing. I
was disturbed a few years ago when gossip columnists tried to create a "feud"
between Arthur Miller and me as a result of "Love Love Love." I don't know
Mr. Miller. I admire Mr. Miller. In a certain context I dealt with him severely
for his pretensions while praising his true talent. I had put, finally, the blame for
his failure (as well as for my own) on the society we live in. Beyond a point no
one can transcend the period to which he belongs (like that ninth-century
French bishop who at the end of a crude but oddly beautiful letter apologizes
for the poorness of his Latin, because "we have no longer civilization"). But in
the world of the Commercialites, all is personal. If you knock, it is either out
of revenge or envy. Good guys boost.

In any case, I was not happy at having dealt so harshly with *The Gang's All
Here*. To ease my conscience and to learn more about the subject, I started
reading biographies of Harding and I have a part-apology to make to
Lawrence and Lee. They did not exaggerate. Harding was, in many ways, even
more fatuous than the character shown us on the stage. He was also a near-
tragic figure in a completely American way. It was his madness to want to be
loved at any cost. He sacrificed everything to this one prevailing passion, and
nearly wrecked our government in the doing. He perished broken and puzzled, a Willy Loman, lusting only to be well-liked. Harding is a theme for
tragedy, and the fault of this now forgotten play is largely the absence of any

Bernard Shaw's "Heartbreak House"

"HEARTBREAK HOUSE . . . rhapsodized about love; but it believed in cruelty. It was afraid of the cruel people; and it saw that cruelty was at least effective. Cruelty did things that made money, whereas Love did nothing but prove the soundness of La Rochefoucauld's saying that very few people would fall in love if they had never read about it. Heartbreak House in short did not know how to live, at which point all that was left to it was the boast that at least it knew how to die: a melancholy accomplishment which the outbreak of war presently gave it practically unlimited opportunities of displaying. Thus were the first-born of Heartbreak House smitten; and the young, the innocent, the hopeful expiated the folly and worthlessness of their elders."

That is from Bernard Shaw's odd preface to his even odder play, now revived at the Billy Rose Theater. The preface is odd, among other things, because it is written with the wrong sort of hindsight. Shaw did not know when he began the play in 1913 that the first-born were going to be struck down. Nor is there any reference to war, actual or impending, in the first two acts. The third act, however, was completed after the first aerial bombardments in history, and Shaw, rather casually, uses this to drop a bomb and end the play. Yet it is not the residents of Heartbreak House or their first-born who get blown up; only a businessman and a burglar expiate the folly and worthlessness of . . . what? Not Heartbreak House certainly; capitalism, perhaps.

Everything about the play is queer, even its production history. Plans to put it on during the war went awry. Shaw finally published it, with preface, in 1919. Not until 1920 was the play produced, in New York. The next year it got to the West End. The preface is unique in Shaw for its bitterness and hysteria,

---

point of view about him. Lawrence and Lee are good craftsmen but too innocent of the real world to do more than make a chronicle without emphasis or . . . No! There I go again, and I meant to make it up to Mr. Lawrence by saying that the story he told was not as distorted as I said it was. The cartoon was accurate.

and the play . . . well, there are those who put it first among his work and there are those who don't know what to think of it. I'm afraid after seeing it performed for the first time the other day that I liked it a good deal less than I thought I did from having read it; parenthetically, I should put quite plainly here at the beginning that I regard Bernard Shaw as the best and most useful dramatist in English since the author of *Much Ado About Nothing* turned gentleman and let fall the feather.

What is Heartbreak House? In the context of the play it stands for the ruling class of England pre-1914: the "nice people," somewhat educated, somewhat sensitive, somewhat independent financially (their cousins the hearties lived over at Horseback Hall). They were devotees of laissez-faire; they rhapsodized about love—but I have already quoted Shaw's indictment. Heartbreak House, of course, is only another name for our new friend the Establishment, a protective association made up of public-school boys who come down from Oxbridge to take over Whitehall, the Church of England, the BBC, Fleet Street, the better-looking girls, and everything else that's fun, while (so young writers tell us) sneering at the newly articulate *Lumpenproletariat* who have gone to redbrick colleges where, if one reads the new novels accurately, the main course given is Opportunism: Don't reform, adapt. The jocose nihilism of many of the anti-Establishment novels and plays is no more than a love-hate acceptance of the Establishment; the Kingsley Amises approach it on its own terms in a way Shaw would have detested. Where he would have leveled Heartbreak House to make way for a carefully planned housing project, the new attackers of the Establishment merely want to move into some of those nice rooms at the top, an attitude ignoble to a socialist and hopelessly petty to an outsider who is aware that the rooms at the top of a diminished England are not much better than those directly under. The Establishment has only an island to tend, while Heartbreak House, with Asquith and Bonar Law and Ramsay Mac for weekend guests, governed much of the world. To put it plain, Shaw's target was important; and he knew what he wanted, which was not to adapt, or to make his own way, but to reform.

I think we know pretty much what Shaw intended to do in

Heartbreak House, yet what actually did he do in the play itself? For one thing, it is improvised work. Shaw admitted he
made it up as he went along, not knowing from day to day
what his characters would do or say or become. He always
tended to work this way, regarding a play essentially as an or-
ganism with a life of its own; one need only nurture it and let
it assume its own shape. He even used to keep a kind of
checkerboard at hand to remind him who was onstage and
who was off at any given moment in the writing. There is no
doubt this method served him as well as any other; his night
mind was not, to say the least, fantastic. I am sure deep in his
unconscious there lurked not the usual nightmare monsters of
the rest of us but yards of thesis, antithesis, and synthesis, all
neatly labeled and filed. Yet in *Heartbreak House* Shaw's improvisatory genius breaks down; he keeps marching into conversational culs-de-sac.

For example, in the second act the play comes to a grinding
halt after Boss Mangan, recovered from hypnotic trance, denounces and is denounced by those who happen to be onstage
at the moment, and exits. Then Captain Shotover tosses a Del-
phic phrase or two upon the night and paddles off. (Later the
Captain, while again trying for an exit, says, almost apologeti-
cally: "I must go in and out," a compulsion he shares with
everyone else in this play; they all go in and out at whim.) This
ill-madeness is often beguiling except on those occasions when
it defeats the author, who finds himself with nobody left onstage except a couple who don't have much of anything to say
to one another at the moment. It is then that Shaw invariably,
shamelessly, brings on the New Character, who is very often a
member of the lower classes with a colorful speech pattern
usually written out phonetically in the text. This time he is the
Burglar, a comic character right out of Dickens, where Shaw
claimed, not entirely facetiously, to have got most of his characters, at least those who are not himself. The Burglar is one of
Shaw's standbys, used in play after play; he is awful, but at least
he starts the second act moving again and gives it a certain vivacity. As usual, Shaw, delighted with his own cunning, starts
tying up ends; the Burglar is really the Captain's old bos'n, the
nurse's husband, etc., etc. And now let's have a long chat

about the poor and the exploited, the exploiters and the *rentiers*, and then end the act.

As a rule, Shaw's arbitrariness does not disturb. After all, he is conducting a seminar with enormous wit and style and we don't much mind his more casual contrivances. But in this play they don't come off. I think it has to do with a fundamental conflict between characters and settings. The characters, of course, are our old friends the Bernard Shaw Team of Fabian Debaters; we know each one of them already. But what are they doing in this peculiar Midsummer's Eve *ambiance*? They seem a bit puzzled, too. As they debate with their usual ease they tend nervously to eye the shrubbery: are there elves at the bottom of that garden? Have we been booked into an allegory? Are we going to find out we're all dead or something? Steady, chaps, the old boy's got us into one of *those* plays. They rattle on bravely but they are clearly ill at ease, and so is the audience. I think it was one of the New York daily critics who observed that the mood is not Chekhov but J. M. Barrie. Which is exactly right. We are led to expect magic, fey girls upon the heath, and revelation through fantasy. But we get none of it. Instead we are offered the old Debating Team in top form but in the wrong place and mood (oh, for that dentist's office!). As a result the debaters recede as characters; we grow indifferent to them; they are too humorous in the original sense of the word. Especially Ellie, Shaw's supergirl. In this version she is more than ever iron, ready to mother not heroes but heroines. Shaw dotes on Ellie; I found her purest drip-torture. Halfway through the play I had a startling *aperçu*: Shaw regarded himself not as a man or an artist or a social meliorist but as a kind of superwoman, a chaste spinster fiercely armed with the umbrella of dialectic, asexual limbs bluestockinged, and tongue wagging. Of all the debaters assembled, I liked only Captain Shotover, because his dottiness contrasted agreeably with the uneasy predictability of his teammates.

Finally, at the play's end, I found myself entirely confused as to what Shaw intended. Shaw is not, even when he would like to be, an impressionist, a Chekhov turning life before our eyes to no end but that life observed is sufficient. *Look, we live, we are*, says Chekhov. While Shaw declares briskly: *Pull up your socks!*

Fall in line there. Come along now. Double-quick march and we'll overtake the future by morning! One loves Shaw for his optimism, but moonlight is not a time for marching, and *Heartbreak House* is a moonlight play, suitable for recapturing the past; but moonlight is a hopeless time for making plans. Elegy and debate cancel one another out. Nor is the work really satiric, an attack on "folly and worthlessness." These people are splendid and unique, and Shaw knows it. He had no intention of blowing them up at the end.

Shaw's prefaces—no matter how proudly irrelevant their content may, at first, seem to the play that follows (sometimes a bit forlornly)—usually turn out to be apposite or at least complementary. But not this preface. In fact, it is misleading. Shaw talks about Chekhov. He finds the country-house mentality Chekhov *seems* to be writing about endemic to Europe, part of the sweet sickness of the bourgeoisie. Therefore Shaw will examine the same house in the same way, only in English terms. Ever since that preface, we have all dutifully considered this play in terms of Chekhov. Does it compare? Is it as good? Why is it *un*like? Brooks Atkinson recently remarked that Chekhov's dying fall does not suit Shaw, who never dies and never falls, who stands ready with a program for every need. This is certainly true, yet I have a hunch that if Shaw had not given us a false lead, none of us would have ever thought of comparing him to Chekhov. True, both are dealing with the same dying society of "nice people," but where Chekhov's interest was the "nice people," Shaw's interest was the dying society and the birth pains of the new.

Shaw once told Sir Cedric Hardwicke that he had no idea how to end the play until the first bombs fell. I suspect he had originally planned to allow Captain Shotover to attain "the Seventh Degree of concentration," thereby detonating the dynamite he had stored in the gravel pit and blowing up the enemy Mangan. As it was, at the last minute, the bomb from the Zeppelin did the trick even better, providing Shaw quite literally with a god from the machine. Then, almost as an afterthought, Shaw comes to the point:

HECTOR: Well, I don't mean to be drowned like a rat in a trap. I still have the will to live. What am I to do?

CAPTAIN SHOTOVER: Do? Nothing simpler. Learn your business as an
  Englishman.
HECTOR: And what may my business as an Englishman be, pray?
CAPTAIN SHOTOVER: Navigation. Learn it and live; or leave it and be
  damned.

And that's it. Captain Shotover, supposed to have sold his
soul to the devil, to have meddled with mysticism, to have
mastered the *non sequitur*, turns out to be a good Fabian
socialist after all. Obviously, Shotover was a humbug mystic,
excusably deranged by the setting Shaw put him in; not until
faced with his world's extinction does he throw off the mask of
dottiness to reveal the bright, hard, intelligent face of Bernard
Shaw, who to this day has a good deal to tell us about the danger of a society drifting as opposed to one which has learned
the virtue of setting a deliberate course by fixed stars. To navi-
gate is to plan. Laissez-faire, though always delightful for a
few, in crisis is disastrous for all. There is no alternative to a
planned society; that is the burden of the Shaw debate. Almost
as an afterthought he makes this familiar point as the bomb
drops near Heartbreak House.

The production now on view is ambitious, and at many
points successful. As usual, I found myself more attentive to
the audience than to the play. As they say in physics, there is no
action without reaction. I can think of no urgent reason for
writing about productions in the theater unless one also writes
about the audience, too. The play acts upon the audience,
which is society today; the audience reacts and in its reaction
one can get a sense of the superstitions and prejudices which
obtain. Theater can be revelatory. In fact, I wish sociologists
would spend more time in the theater and less in conducting
polls and drawing graphs. Any audience at *Tea and Sympathy*
or *Auntie Mame* will tell them more about the way we live
now than a house-to-house canvass from Morristown to White
Plains with pad and pencil.

In the case of an old play like *Heartbreak House* one may
also use it as a touchstone. In the 1920's it seemed one thing,
in the 1930's another, and so on. To those watching, the day I
saw it, *Heartbreak House* was a delightful place, menaced by
burglars, self-made men, and Zeppelins. The clothes were chic

yet quaint and every woman saw herself up there pouring tea for weak enamored men who tended to burst into tears while the ladies talked a bright blue streak. Whenever the debate really got going, 1959's attention flagged: Is that a rubber plant? Can they still get egret feathers or is that an imitation? Did you leave the keys in the car? . . . Bernard Shaw, I'm afraid, was being taken for Oscar Wilde, and afflicted with un-Wildean *longueurs*. To put it bluntly, we are not used to debate at any level. If Bernard Shaw, who made the act of argument as pleasurable as any writer who ever lived, cannot hold his audience except by predictable paradoxes and references to adultery and all the familiar junk of the Commercialites, we the audience are in a bad way. Although in fairness it must be admitted that talking about society and the better life and planning of any sort has never been a characteristic of the Anglo-American mind.

Nevertheless, Harold Clurman had directed this production just as though we were really awake out there and knew what was going on. He is enormously helped by Diana Wynyard and Pamela Brown, who are beautifully right for this kind of thing. Maurice Evans, an actor I seem to like only as Richard II no matter what else he plays, is unexpectedly fine as Captain Shotover. I'm not sure dressing up to look like Bernard Shaw was a wise idea; I suspect Shaw would have hated it; but it does help Mr. Evans to hide beneath whiskers and putty the self-pitying face of Richard II, and I could not have liked him more. Sam Levene of course was all wrong as Boss Mangan. He is a good *farceur*, but in another style, and his scenes tended to throw everyone else off: it was not unlike casting our own beloved Marjorie Main as Lady Bracknell. The other weak link is Diane Cilento as Ellie, the supergirl. Miss Cilento plays with a grinding monotony made worse because she has gone and got herself one of those Voices. Let me explain. Right after the war, Pamela Brown's most lovely strange diction was the ambition and despair of every English girl on the stage. We got Miss Brown's Voice in every possible key. Then there was heard in the land Joan Greenwood's hoarse, intimate rasp, to our delight and her peers' despair. Now Miss Cilento has distilled herself a voice which is two-parts Brown and one-part Greenwood, and I think she ought to give it up, right now. She is a beautiful girl with some talent; yet if Ellie is to be made less than revolting she must be played with as little artifice and as much "naturalness" as possible. I daresay Mr. Clurman was aware of this, but sooner get a bird to sing Mozart than force an actress to discard a Voice she has worked on. All in all, reservations about this particular play aside, I hope it runs forever and gives heart to those who expect the theater to be something more than a business for those who, in their calculated desire to please us, only make us more than ever absent of mind.

1959

LORRAINE HANSBERRY

Because of her premature death from cancer, Lorraine Hansberry (1930–1965) is known for one play, *A Raisin in the Sun* (1959). It has become so familiar, so iconic, so unavoidable a presence in African-American drama that, 30 years later, George C. Wolfe felt it necessary to exorcise it through parody. In his comic survey of black American culture, *The Colored Museum* (1986), it appears as "The Last Mama-on-the-Couch Play." Rooted in Hansberry's own experience as the daughter of a Chicago realtor who fought against redlining, the de facto racial segregation of neighborhoods, in form *Raisin* fits neatly into the tradition of one-setting, small-cast domestic dramas. In fact, it was revolutionary in its "firsts": the first play written by an African-American woman to be played on Broadway, the first Broadway production directed by an African-American (Lloyd Richards), the first award of the New York Drama Critics Circle to a woman under 30, the first play by a black author to capture a national audience and the longest-running (530 performances, outstripping Langston Hughes' *Mulatto*). Having worked with W.E.B. Du Bois, and on both Paul Robeson's newspaper *Freedom* and the lesbian magazine *The Ladder*, Hansberry intended her writings to ameliorate prevailing social conditions. In a prospectus of 1962, she envisaged an ideal theatre devoted to the African-American cultural heritage, repudiating both commercialism and the "impotent and obscurantist efforts of a mistaken avant garde." A play about the economics of slavery, *The Drinking Gourd* (1961), *The Sign in Sidney Brustein's Window* (1965), the posthumous *Les Blancs*, a riposte to Jean Genet, and the enthusiastically received assemblage of her writings *To Be Young, Gifted and Black* (1968–69) revealed how much promising talent had been abruptly cut short.

"Me tink me hear sounds in de night"

I WAS visited some weeks ago by a young actress, a member of the cast of a quite successful Broadway show, who had herself won considerable praise from critics and audiences. I also knew her to be among the truly serious students of her profession: one of those devoted actors who spend so many self-imposed extra hours per week in dance, acting and voice studios. She was twenty-four, deeply talented, profoundly dedicated to her work, possessed of a vigorous Broadway credit and—a Negro.

So we spoke at length of her career. Had she, for instance, had offers of other work when the current show closed? "Well," she told me between two sighs, "there is a fall-coming show that I was called in to read for. It turned out to be an opportunity to play Young Negro Problem again." She explained discerningly that an American author, on the incomplete, if desperately welcome, rebound from stereotypes, had written a part for someone who was to make an entrance as a Social Question and exit as a Social Question. And that swiftly.

"How," she asked, "can anybody study for *that*? How can you find shading and character in the absence of shading and character?" As an actress she wanted to know how it was possible to interpret humanly that which was simply devoid of human definition. When would contemporary dramatists not be afraid to invest Negro characters with ordinary human complication, now that, to some degree, more overtly obnoxious traditions had started to fade?

Thinking of her excellent notices in the current show, I asked if what she had described had *really* been the only sign of future work. She laughed and replied, "Oh, no. I had a television call to read for a *traditional*. Not a maid; the *other* category, the 'native girl' bit. And, thought I, a job is a job. So I got the script, studied the lines, and went to the reading. And I read: '*Me sit on me hummock and me tink me hear sounds in de night and den. . .*' I finally just choked up on it, and closed the book and thanked the people for hearing me, and left. I just can't make that scene any more, my dear. Dis here native is tired of sittin' on de hummock!"

When she departed I was left to reflect on the general situation of Negroes in the American theatre. The authors of the two plays we had discussed were not singularly stupid or untalented people; the question was larger and deeper than their mere inadequacy in dealing with certain kinds of characterization. They had been trapped creatively by an old, monumentally encompassing and deeply entrenched legacy from history.

The sixteenth-century spirit of mercantile expansionism that swept Europe, and gave rise to colonial conquest and the European slave trade, was also father of a modern concept of racism. The concept made it possible to render the African a "commodity" in the minds of white men, and to alienate the conscience of the rising European humanism from identification with the victims of that conquest and slave trade. In order to accommodate programs of commerce and empire on a scale never before known in history, the Negro had to be placed arbitrarily outside the pale of recognizable humanity in the psychology of Europeans and, eventually, of white America. Neither his soul nor his body was to be allowed to evoke empathy. He was to be—and, indeed, *became*, in a created mentality of white men—some grotesque expression of the mirth of nature; a fancied, static vestige of the primeval past; an eternal exotic who, unlike *men*, would not bleed when pricked nor revenge when wronged. Thus for three centuries in Europe and America alike, buffoonery or villainy was his only permissible role in the halls of entertainment or drama. And notwithstanding the few later exceptions in Europe (the most distinguished, of course, being the career of Ira Aldridge, an American-born Negro actor of the nineteenth century who toured Europe in Shakespearean companies and achieved considerable recognition), in America the sight or even the notion of a Negro gripped in the complex agonies of a Hamlet outraged a cultural legend as today it yet embarrasses it.

That is why, 140 years ago, local hoodlums descended on the African Repertory Theatre Company at Bleecker and Mercer Streets in New York City, and harassed its actors and audiences out of existence. And that is why Negroes are not integrated in our theatre today.

It is this old historical situation that confronts a theatre, some of whose dramatists are currently baffled by Negro character, and whose producers and their receptionists are reduced to rudeness or apologetic embarrassment as they face the miraculously stubborn and increasing battalion of dark, hopeful faces among the multitude of other hopeful faces in their famous outer offices.

Presumably talent, all talent, is as good for the theatre as democracy is for a democratic nation. But to say so is to ignore that breathlessness and perplexed expression in the countenance of our theatre as it asks, over and over again, "What can *realistically* be done about integrating the Negro in the theatre, given the present racial climate in the United States?"

The question implies that to integrate Negro actors in most dramatic situations is to perpetrate a social lie and invalidate the responsibility of art. It also has a way of starting at the point where artistic questions *are* relevant. It rather sneakily ignores a stupendous area where "art" has nothing to do with discrimination in the theatre. For instance, I have never had the experience of purchasing a ticket from a Negro in a Broadway box office; I cannot imagine it to be a matter of either art or qualification, since, I can testify from personal experience, short-temperedness is not limited to white people, and it is that trait, we have all come to assume, that is the prime qualification for those legendary posts. Nor have I ever purchased a box of mints, or received my program, from a Negro lobby vendor or usher. And, to proceed to more important areas, I have not, in my wanderings backstage, found my 10 per cent represented in the handling of flats, lights or properties, or calling time to the actors. Only on the rarest of occasions have I spotted Negroes in the orchestra pits (I believe only at New York's City Center does that phenomenon occur with even minimal regularity); and never, of course, wielding the baton, despite the lingering legend of a certain people's acute "musicalbility." Similar observations may be made of the chorus lines in our musical comedies.

As for the situation among other echelons of the theatre—the actors, writers and directors—I think only the first two deserve more concentrated thought than the categories already covered. Directors should be men or women who are sufficiently talented to have works of art put under their direction. I cannot believe that their height, diet, place of birth, or race will affect those talents. Naturally it is to be desired that a director have adequate cultural reference to his script, but intelligence dictates that we do not hesitate to appoint plays with Japanese settings to Americans, or American settings to decidedly English directors, and so on. When they are good directors they direct well; when they are poor ones they direct poorly. I have never been able to tell by the quality of a mounting what kind of accent a director has; only whether or not he has done a professional and imaginative piece of work. It would, indeed, take an imaginative piece or argument to show how or why it should be different for Negro directors.

The question of the employment of Negro actors, however, does raise interesting questions, which, it may be argued, in a different sociological atmosphere would be only minor questions of production techniques. But at the moment a fascinating and revealing dichotomy exists within the theatre's most literate circles with regard to the use of Negro actors. People who are most bored and outraged by what they call Ibsenesque or Shavian "boxes" on the imagination of the contemporary theatre, who long for fancy and illusion to take utter command, who can deliver whole sermons on the Philistinism of breaking "real eggs" on stage, very often are, astonishingly enough, among the first to shout betrayal of "realistic" attitudes if one speaks of putting a Negro actor into a non-Negro role. It is most curious. Whoever said, for instance, that Queen Titania was white—or anything else? Or the incidental postman, policeman, clerk or schoolmate in that contemporary play? Or *all* the people in that New York City crowd scene that is allegedly in Times Square. It takes rather more of a trick to imagine a good many urban American scenes without Negroes than with them.

But, above all, to defend a color barrier in the theatre is to ignore or argue against its essence, which has always been illusion. We do not get the blind to play the blind, or infants to play infants. Nor do we move Southern mansions or oceans on stage. It is not necessary. Our theatre must attain a sufficient degree of maturity and sophistication to put aside artificial barriers, to acknowledge that any truly qualified actor, Negro or white, who is made up properly, can do the job. I am speaking, of course, of roles that specify particular skin and hair coloring. When such matters are irrelevant rather than intrinsic, they should be viewed for what they are, and not be made the imagined basis for such barriers.

With regard to Negro writers, the theatre is yet saddled with the notion that their materials are necessarily parochial, and consequently without interest to the general theatregoing public. It is a difficult attitude to prove by looking back over the last six or seven years, when a fast total of *three* scripts by

Negro writers was allowed to reach the Broadway stage for judgment by *the public*. It is interesting to note that of the three, two were quite first-rate efforts. The first found a steady and appreciative audience off Broadway when its Broadway run came to a close, and a subsequent motion-picture sale made a rather tidy sum for its investors. The second not only copped a prize, and earned over a million and a half at last count; it ran more than a year (an excellent record, in view of the disturbingly poor showings made by dramas these days), and got itself scheduled for national tour this season; it received production and translation throughout the world, and only its motion-picture production schedule prevented the American company from being sent abroad, as requested by our government, *to represent our national drama*. That is a peculiar kind of parochialism. And even the third show, a dreadful little piece, lasted several weeks too long, in my opinion, before it was buried. Viewed from any point of view, it is hardly a ratio that the rest of Broadway could duplicate.

The above should not be confused, as it often is, with the production of "Negro shows" by non-Negro writers, a somewhat different field. Such shows can be produced more easily, and they are in an area that requires the most revolutionary transition. In the theatre it is our dramatists and musical-comedy book writers who have the largest responsibility for presenting our world to us with ever-increasing penetration and illumination. Sad to say, they have, with only a few fine and notable exceptions, an exceedingly poor tradition to draw on with regard to Negroes because of the scale of the old alienation.

The Negro, as primarily presented in the past, has never existed on land or sea. It has seldom been a portrait of men, only a portrait of a concept, and that concept has been a romance and no other thing. By its very nature white supremacy longed for the contentment of the Negro with "his place"; one is always eager to believe that *somebody else* is exhilarated by "plenty of nuttin'." Since real-life Negroes—with their history of insurrection, "underground railways," mass enlistments in the Union army, petitions, delegations, organizations, press and literature and even music of protest—have failed to oblige, the white writer, in the main, has not failed to people *his*

"Negro world" with Negroes who did not seem to know that slavery was intolerable, or that the subsequent and lingering oppression was a form of hell on earth. Thus in the make-believe domains of Porgy and Brutus Jones, only the foibles of *other Negroes* are assaulted; otherwise the heady passions of this particular happy breed are committed only to sex, liquor and mysteriously motivated ultra violence, usually over "dis or dat womans." A larger scale of dreams and anguish eluded their creators, and showed some otherwise great creative imaginations to be incapable of the recognition of the universal complexity of humankind.

This does not imply that malice has always been the intent. It would be as foolish to think that Mark Twain or Mrs. Stowe tried to defeat their own humanist protests as to suppose that Marc Connelly, in a different vein, ever dreamed that he was writing a racist document in "The Green Pastures." Rather, it is a matter of a partially innocent cultural heritage that, out of its own needs, was eager to believe in the colossal charm, among other things, of "childlike" peoples. From that notion, presumably, came the tendency to find non-Negro dramatic and musical materials rendered "quaint" when performed by "all-colored casts." From such an astonishing idea we have been treasured with the likes of "Carmen Jones" in the past, and will undoubtedly be treated to something like "Honey-chile Tosca" in the future before it is exhausted. It is also interesting to note, in view of the hoped-for transition, that these translations "to the Negro" have generally meant (aside from adding saxophones and red dresses) haphazardly assaulting the English language beyond recognition, as if the Negro people had not produced an idiom that has a real and specific character, which is not merely the random exclusion of verb endings.

That does not suggest a counterdesire to see Negroes talking (or behaving) just like "everybody else" because, by and large, Negroes do no such thing, as conscientious playwrights will swiftly discover. And neither does "everybody else." American speech is as varied as the wind, and few of our sophisticated writers would dream of putting the speech of Texans into the mouths of New Yorkers for any purpose save that of the broadest comedy. So there is nothing extraordinary in the expectation that Negro speech must eventually be presented with artistic respect for its true color, nuances and variations as they exist for each class and generation.

Finally, I think that American writers have already begun to believe what I suspect has always been one of the secrets of fine art: that there are no simple men. Chinese peasants and Congolese soldiers make drastic revolutions in the world while the obtuse and myth-accepting go on reflecting on the "inscrutability and eternal placidity" of those people. I believe that when the blinders are dropped, it will be discovered that while an excessively poignant Porgy was being instilled in generations of Americans, his truer-life counterpart was ravaged by longings that were, and are, in no way alien to those of the rest of mankind, and that bear within them the stuff of truly great art. He is waiting yet for those of us who will but look more carefully into his eyes, and listen more intently to his soliloquies. We must not be intimidated by the residue of the past; the world is paying too large a price for the deception of those centuries; each hour that flies teaches that Porgy is as much inclined to hymns of sedition as to lullabies and love songs; he is profoundly complicated and interesting; everywhere he is making his own sounds in the night. I believe that it is within the cultural descendants of Twain and Whitman and Melville and O'Neill to listen and absorb them, along with the totality of the American landscape, and give back their findings in new art to the great and vigorous institution that is the American theatre.

1960

EDWARD ALBEE

In 1961, the English critic Martin Esslin published *The Theatre of the Absurd*, in which he grouped a disparate set of playwrights (Ionesco, Adamov, Genet, Beckett, Pinter) under the umbrella "Absurdism." It came as godsend to theatrical journalists, who could now apply the term indiscriminately to any play that failed to fit accepted traditions of realism. Edward Albee (b. 1928) was the first American playwright to suffer from Esslin's taxonomy: his one-acts of 1959–60, *The Sandbox* and *The American Dream*, may be satiric cartoons, but *The Zoo Story* and *The Death of Bessie Smith* scrupulously keep within the bounds of lived experience. The critics' insistence on finding a pigeonhole for Albee has bedeviled his reception. *Who's Afraid of Virginia Woolf?* (1962) and *A Delicate Balance* (1966) differ from conventional drawing-room comedy chiefly in their extreme behavior and language and their failure to tie up existential loose ends. Now that Albee has become an honored gray eminence of the American theatre, one can see his career as an ingenious escape act from critical expectations and labels. His oeuvre alternates provocations—the enigmas of *Tiny Alice* (1964), the amphibians of *Seascape* (1974), the bestiality of *The Goat, or Who Is Sylvia?* (2005)—with genteel if equally indeterminate colloquies—*All Over* (1971), *The Lady from Dubuque* (1977–79), *Three Tall Women* (1991). Albee's skill lies in engaging and unsettling his audiences at the same time.

Which Theater Is the Absurd One?

A THEATER person of my acquaintance—a man whose judgment must be respected, though more for the infallibility of his intuition than for his reasoning—remarked just the other week, "The Theater of the Absurd has had it; it's on its way out; it's through."

Now this, on the surface of it, seems to be a pretty funny attitude to be taking toward a theater movement which has, only in the past couple of years, been impressing itself on the American public consciousness. Or is it? Must we judge that a theater of such plays as Samuel Beckett's *Krapp's Last Tape*, Jean

Genet's *The Balcony* (both long, long runners off-Broadway), and Eugene Ionesco's *Rhinoceros*—which, albeit in a hoked-up production, had a substantial season on Broadway—has been judged by the theater public and found wanting?

And shall we have to assume that the Theater of the Absurd Repertory Company, currently playing at New York's off-Broadway Cherry Lane Theater—presenting works by Beckett, Ionesco, Genet, Arrabal, Jack Richardson, Kenneth Koch, and myself—being the first such collective representation of the movement in the United States, is also a kind of farewell to the movement? For that matter, just what *is* the Theater of the Absurd?

Well, let me come at it obliquely. When I was told, about a year ago, that I was considered a member in good standing of the Theater of the Absurd I was deeply offended. I was deeply offended because I had never heard the term before and I immediately assumed that it applied to the theater uptown—Broadway.

What (I was reasoning to myself) could be more absurd than a theater in which the aesthetic criterion is something like this: A "good" play is one which makes money; a "bad" play (in the sense of "Naughty! Naughty!" I guess) is one which does not; a theater in which performers have plays rewritten to correspond to the public relations image of themselves; a theater in which playwrights are encouraged (what a funny word!) to think of themselves as little cogs in a great big wheel; a theater in which imitation has given way to imitation of imitation; a theater in which London "hits" are, willy-nilly, in a kind of reverse of chauvinism, greeted in a manner not unlike a colony's obeisance to the Crown; a theater in which real estate owners and theater party managements predetermine the success of unknown quantities; a theater in which everybody scratches and bites for billing as though it meant access to the last bomb shelter on earth; a theater in which, in a given season, there was not a single performance of a play by Beckett, Brecht, Chekhov, Genet, Ibsen, O'Casey, Pirandello, Shaw, Strindberg—or Shakespeare? What, indeed, I thought, could be more absurd than that? (My conclusions . . . obviously.)

For it emerged that the Theater of the Absurd, aside from

being the title of an excellent book by Martin Esslin on what is loosely called the avant-garde theater, was a somewhat less than fortunate catch-all phrase to describe the philosophical attitudes and theater methods of a number of Europe's finest and most adventurous playwrights and their followers.

I was less offended, but still a little dubious. Simply: I don't like labels; they can be facile and can lead to nonthink on the part of the public. And unless it is understood that the playwrights of the Theater of the Absurd represent a group only in the sense that they seem to be doing something of the same thing in vaguely similar ways at approximately the same time— unless this is understood, then the labeling itself will be more absurd than the label.

Playwrights, by nature, are grouchy, withdrawn, envious, greedy, suspicious and, in general, quite nice people—and the majority of them wouldn't be caught dead in a colloquy remotely resembling the following:

IONESCO: (*At a Left Bank café table, spying Beckett and Genet strolling past in animated conversation*) Hey! Sam! Jean!

GENET: Hey, it's Eugene! Sam, it's Eugene!

BECKETT: Well, I'll be damned. Hi there, Eugene boy.

IONESCO: Sit down, kids.

GENET: Sure thing.

IONESCO: (*Rubbing his hands together*) Well, what's new in the Theater of the Absurd?

BECKETT: Oh, less than a lot of people think. (*They all laugh.*)

Etc. No. Not very likely. Get a playwright alone sometime, get a few drinks in him, and maybe he'll be persuaded to sound off about his "intention" and the like—and hate himself for it the next day. But put a group of playwrights together in a room, and the conversation—if there is any—will, more likely than not, concern itself with sex, restaurants, and the movies.

Very briefly, then—and reluctantly, because I am a playwright and would much rather talk about sex, restaurants, and the movies—and stumblingly, because I do not pretend to understand it entirely, I will try to define the Theater of the Absurd. As I get it, the Theater of the Absurd is an absorption-in-art of certain existentialist and postexistentialist philosophical concepts having to do, in the main, with man's attempts to make sense for himself out of his senseless position in a world which makes no sense—which makes no sense because the moral, religious, political and social structures man has erected to "illusion" himself have collapsed.

Albert Camus put it this way: "A world that can be explained by reasoning, however faulty, is a familiar world. But in a universe that is suddenly deprived of illusions and of light, man feels a stranger. His is an irremediable exile, because he is deprived of memories of a lost homeland as much as he lacks the hope of a promised land to come. This divorce between man and his life, the actor and his setting, truly constitutes the feeling of Absurdity."

And Eugene Ionesco says this: "Absurd is that which is devoid of purpose . . . Cut off from his religious, metaphysical, and transcendental roots, man is lost; all his actions become senseless, absurd, useless."

And to sum up the movement, Martin Esslin writes, in his book *The Theater of the Absurd*: "Ultimately, a phenomenon like the Theater of the Absurd does not reflect despair or a return to dark irrational forces but expresses modern man's endeavor to come to terms with the world in which he lives. It attempts to make him face up to the human condition as it really is, to free him from illusions that are bound to cause constant maladjustment and disappointment . . . For the dignity of man lies in his ability to face reality in all its senselessness; to accept it freely, without fear, without illusions—and to laugh at it."

Amen.

(And while we're on the subject of Amen, one wearies of the complaint that the Theater of the Absurd playwrights alone are having at God these days. The notion that God is dead, indifferent, or insane—a notion blasphemous, premature, or academic depending on your persuasion—while surely a tenet of some of the playwrights under discussion, is, it seems to me, of a piece with Mr. Tennessee Williams's description of the Deity, in *The Night of the Iguana*, as "a senile delinquent.")

So much for the attempt to define terms. Now, what of this theater? What of this theater in which, for example, a legless old couple live out their lives in twin ashcans, surfacing occasionally for food or conversation (Samuel Beckett's *Endgame*); in which a man is seduced, and rather easily, by a girl with three well-formed and functioning noses (Eugene Ionesco's *Jack, or The Submission*); in which, on the same stage, one group of black actors is playing at pretending to be white and another group of black actors is playing at pretending to be black (Jean Genet's *The Blacks*)?

What of this theater? Is it, as it has been accused of being, obscure, sordid, destructive, antitheater, perverse, and absurd (in the sense of foolish)? Or is it merely, as I have so often heard it put, that, "This sort of stuff is too depressing, too . . . too mixed-up; I go to the theater to relax and have a good time."

I would submit that it is this latter attitude—that the theater is a place to relax and have a good time—in conflict with the purpose of the Theater of the Absurd—which is to make a man face up to the human condition as it really is—that has produced all the brouhaha and the dissent. I would submit that the Theater of the Absurd, in the sense that it is truly the contemporary theater, facing as it does man's condition as it is, is the Realistic theater of our time; and that the supposed Realistic theater—the term used here to mean most of what is done on Broadway—in the sense that it panders to the public need for self-congratulation and reassurance and presents a false picture of ourselves to ourselves is, with an occasional very lovely exception, really truly the Theater of the Absurd.

And I would submit further that the health of a nation, a society, can be determined by the art it demands. We have insisted of television and our movies that they not have anything to do with anything, that they be our never-never land; and if we demand this same function of our live theater, what will be left of the visual-auditory arts—save the dance (in which nobody talks) and music (to which nobody listens)?

It has been my fortune, the past two or three years, to travel around a good deal, in pursuit of my career—Berlin, London, Buenos Aires, for example; and I have discovered a couple of interesting things. I have discovered that audiences in these and other major cities demand of their commercial theater—and get—a season of plays in which the froth and junk are the exception and not the rule. To take a case: in Berlin, in 1959, Adamov, Genet, Beckett, and Brecht (naturally) were playing the big houses; this past fall, Beckett again, Genet again, Pinter twice, etc. To take another case: in Buenos Aires there are over a hundred experimental theaters.

These plays cannot be put on in Berlin over the head of a protesting or an indifferent audience; these experimental theaters cannot exist in Buenos Aires without subscription. In the end—and it must always come down to this, no matter what other failings a theater may have—in the end a public will get what it deserves, and no better.

I have also discovered, in my wanderings, that young people throng to what is new and fresh in the theater. Happily, this holds true in the United States as well. At the various colleges I have gone to to speak I have found an eager, friendly, and knowledgeable audience, an audience which is as dismayed by the Broadway scene as any proselytizer for the avant-garde. I have found among young people an audience which is not so preconditioned by pap as to have cut off half of its responses. (It is interesting to note, by the way, that if an off-Broadway play has a substantial run, its audiences will begin young and grow older as the run goes on, cloth coats give way to furs, walkers and subway riders to taxi-takers. Exactly the opposite is true on Broadway.)

The young, of course, are always questioning values, knocking the status quo about, considering shibboleths to see if they are pronounceable. In time, it is to be regretted, most of them —the kids—will settle down to their own version of the easy, the standard; but in the meanwhile . . . in the meanwhile they are a wonderful, alert, alive, accepting audience.

And I would go so far as to say that it is the responsibility of everyone who pretends any interest at all in the theater to get up off their overly-priced seats and find out what the theater is *really* about. For it is a lazy public which produces a slothful and irresponsible theater.

Now, I would suspect that my theater friend with the infallible intuition is probably right when he suggests that the Theater of the Absurd (or the avant-garde theater, or whatever you want to call it) as it now stands is on its way out. Or at least is undergoing change. All living organisms undergo constant change. And while it is certain that the nature of this theater will remain constant, its forms, its methods—its devices, if you will—most necessarily will undergo mutation.

This theater has no intention of running downhill; and the younger playwrights will make use of the immediate past and mould it to their own needs. (Harold Pinter, for example, could not have written *The Caretaker* had Samuel Beckett not existed, but Pinter is, nonetheless, moving in his own direction.) And it is my guess that the theater in the United States will always hew more closely to the post–Ibsen/Chekhov tradition than does the theater in France, let us say. It is our nature as a country, a society. But we will experiment, and we will expect your attention.

For just as it is true that our response to color and form was forever altered once the impressionist painters put their minds to canvas, it is just as true that the playwrights of the Theater of the Absurd have forever altered our response to the theater.

And one more point: The avant-garde theater is fun; it is free-swinging, bold, iconoclastic, and often wildly, wildly funny. If you will approach it with childlike innocence—putting your standard responses aside, for they do not apply—if you will approach it on its own terms, I think you will be in for a liberating surprise. I think you may no longer be content with plays that you can't remember halfway down the block. You will not only be doing yourself some good, but you will be having a great time, to boot. And even though it occurs to me that such a fine combination must be sinful, I still recommend it.

1962

CHARLES L. MEE, JR.

Before off-Broadway became a union-law designation for any house seating between 50 and 500, it meant an exciting venue for experimental theatre without concern for the box-office. In its program, the Living Theatre neatly summed up the aesthetic goals of the movement. The aim of Judith Malina and Julian Beck, who had studied at the New School for Social Research under the émigré director Erwin Piscator, was to introduce audiences to poetic drama that seldom got a hearing elsewhere. In 1959, with Jack Gelber's *The Connection*, a neo-realist play about drug-dealing, they moved into more dangerous territory, followed up by Kenneth Brown's *The Brig*, in which the physical abuse was not simulated but performed on the spot. Charles L. Mee, Jr. (b. 1938), an off-off-Broadway playwright, provided an overview of the theatre's status quo in a 1962 essay in the *Tulane Drama Review*, where he was contributing editor. Shortly thereafter Beck, in an article entitled "How to Close a Theatre," used the pages of *TDR* to advertise the Living Theatre's demise due to persecution by Manhattan landlords and the IRS. The company reconstituted itself in Europe as a nomadic tribe, putting on such physically elaborate spectacles as *Paradise Now* and *Frankenstein* in praise of personal freedom. In this avatar, with its public nudity and hallucinogenic imagery, it appealed to a younger, less literary audience and, as "Le Living," exercised an incalculable influence on both European and American artists.

As for Mee, after 20 years of history-writing and political activism, he returned to the performing arts in 1985, with the libretto for Martha Clarke's dance fantasia *Vienna Lusthaus*. Unconcerned with issues of originality or individuality, Mee usually works in collaboration, chiefly with the director Anne Bogart and her SITI company. "My plays are broken, jagged, filled with sharp edges, filled with things that take sudden turns, career into each other, smash up, veer off into sickening turns. . . . And I like to put this—with some sense of struggle remaining—into a classical form . . ." Ten of his plays are drastic reworkings of Greek tragedy, but more recently he has explored American history through the prism of visual artists (*bobrauschenbergamerica*; *Hotel Cassiopeia*, about Joseph Cornell; *Under Construction*, about Norman Rockwell) and played with comic romance, drawing on a plethora of cultural sources. Mee is perhaps America's most performed playwright because he posts his work on the Internet and, subsidized by a private patron, often charges no fees or royalties, especially if the plays are substantially refashioned.

The Becks' Living Theatre

In the opening scene of Jack Gelber's *The Apple* an action painter is flicking large globs of pigment at a piece of celluloid, commenting as he works, "No design is a grand design," and, "Art is precision." He takes a rolling pin and smears the paint over the celluloid, creating an arresting pastiche of brilliant colors, chaotic patterns, intriguing textures, and—if you look at it in just the right way—some sort of artistic expression. Then Julian Beck enters and asks, "Whose wet dream is that?" This jarring punch-line sets the tone of the Living Theatre's preoccupation with illusion and reality, a theatrical pair of dice that are constantly tumbled about and spilled into the audience. And the audience pays for it: the night I was there, the painting was auctioned off for $6.50.

The Living Theatre is New York's only true repertory company; consequently it is the only theatre in New York that has its own style. This style is the exclusive creation of Julian Beck and his wife Judith Malina, who founded the theatre, produce and direct it, act in it, sell tickets, design sets, read scripts, pull the curtain, sweep out and lock up. Now there's a difference between going to a play and going to a *theatre*. The Living Theatre's audiences don't come to see the four plays in the repertory; they come to attend the Becks' theatre. And that's a good thing, because the Becks don't produce plays; they run a theatre: the emphasis is on the style of the company, not on the styles of the plays. There's something wonderful in that—and something horrible, too.

Few theatres possess such an unusual and uncompromising personal vision, a vision which makes hard demands on its audience. The audience is part of every production, and it must hold up its half of the performance if the theatre is to succeed. Every kind of response is asked of the audience; actors walk through the aisles, speak to spectators, sit with them, direct business straight at them and, in *The Connection*, panhandle them. At one time the Becks could depend upon the right sort of audience, but more recently the enormous popularity of their theatre has begun to threaten them. They're worried about selling out, and Julian Beck has expressed a wistful desire to return one day to the small loft at Broadway and 100th Street. The Becks aren't selling out, but their popularity may be self-defeating. The critics have so lionized the company since the success of *The Connection* that the theatre is winning an audience largely composed of people who have come to watch a freak show, with no intention of becoming involved in what Beck calls "the free flow of feeling and thought" between actors and spectators. The question is: can a theatre from a small loft on the West Side find happiness and prosperity as the darling of Howard Taubman?

The Living Theatre was initially Judith Malina's idea. In the summer of 1946 she decided to start a theatre embodying ideas that later found their way into (what else?) a manifesto:

There is no final way of staging any play. That is one of the virtues of the theatre: its plasticity. And no play will be liked by all. We can only expect that our audience understand and enjoy our purpose, which is that of encouraging the modern poet to write for the theatre, and of bringing interest and stimulation to an art medium which tends to become repetitive in its form rather than creative.

Julian Beck, whom Miss Malina had known for some years, joined in the search for a soapbox. They married in 1948, and with many suggestions for their theatre incorporated into their own philosophy, they staged the first production in their own living room: a bill of one-acts by Brecht, Stein, Lorca, and Goodman, presented for three weeks to invited audiences of twenty persons.

Finally, in December, 1951, they opened in the Cherry Lane Theatre in Greenwich Village with Gertrude Stein's *Doctor Faustus Lights the Lights*, an appropriately extraordinary play in a personal idiom. This was quickly followed by an unsuccessful production of Kenneth Rexroth's *Beyond the Mountains*, a verse drama which retells the *Oresteia* in a somewhat baffling form, using elements of the Greek, Japanese, and Chinese theatres. Early in 1952 "An Evening of Bohemian Theatre" (Picasso's farce *Desire Trapped by the Tail*, T. S. Eliot's *Sweeney Agonistes*, and Stein's *Ladies' Voices*) was an immediate and sensational success. Off-Broadway had just begun to attract notice at this time, and so, fed on success, the Becks started their repertory system, placing Paul Goodman's *Faustina* on an alternating schedule with the other plays. With their vision well on the way to realization, another bill was mounted, comprising Alfred Jarry's *Ubu Roi* and John Ashbery's *The Heroes*. This program, too, was enthusiastically greeted, but it included some strong language and several clinical references to homosexuality. The Fire Department noticed a number of safety infractions in the auditorium and the theatre was closed.

It wasn't until two years later, in 1954, that another suitable place was found, an inexpensive third-floor loft at Broadway and 100th Street. The Becks' idea in opening this new house was the dream of most young theatre revolutionaries. They would charge no admission, rehearse a play until they felt it was ready to open, and pay the talent by dividing up contributions made at the door. Perhaps never before or since have the Becks had such independence, and certainty that they would play to precisely their kind of audience. The total cost of their first play in the loft was $136, an expenditure which caused much concern at the time. (Operating costs now run $3300 weekly, with maximum gross at $3800.) This premiere production was W. H. Auden's *The Age of Anxiety*, which boasted a twelve-tone score by Jackson MacLow, and James Agee in the role of the Radio Announcer. Then, in a paroxysm of activity, they mounted Strindberg's *Ghost Sonata*, Cocteau's *Orpheus*, a verse play called *The Idiot King*, the immensely popular *Tonight We Improvise* by Pirandello, Racine's *Phèdre*, Goodman's *The Young Disciple*, and a reading of William Carlos Williams' *Many Loves*.

In November, 1956 the Department of Buildings decided that the room in which the cast and sixty spectators were pursuing their poetic aspirations was fit for only eighteen occupants.

Undismayed, the Becks found a building on the corner of 14th Street and the Avenue of The Americas in June, 1957. Leaving the ground floor stores intact, one hundred volunteers followed the Becks into the former department store building, made an auditorium and lobby out of the second floor, and offices, dressing rooms, rehearsal studios, and classrooms of the third floor. They had room to store all the costumes and sets that a repertory company must keep (fortunately, Beck designs with a view to his limited storage area), space for a scene shop, and a little corner for what had now become very important (practically if not theoretically): the box office.

On January 13, 1959, Williams' *Many Loves* opened the Becks' new theatre. Later it was temporarily dropped from repertory, to be reinaugurated on May 15, 1961. The play was directed and designed by Julian Beck and is still part of the repertory. *Many Loves* is set in the framework of a dress rehearsal, and it is probably this that made it appealing to the Becks. The play's structure lets them throw lines to the audience and even have some of the actors sit with the audience, delivering their speeches from the auditorium. It is a poor man's Pirandello.

I walked into the theatre at about 8:20, sat down, and watched actors milling around the stage, presumably rehearsing bits of business, movement, lines, and light cues. At 8:45 all the lights in the theatre suddenly blacked out, someone called that a fuse had blown, and when the lights came back on I think the play started. I say "I think" because there was another ten or fifteen minutes of author, director, and actors arguing about little matters. Finally, though, a scene began and it developed that the play was a fairly standard collection of three scenes, each attempting to explore a different sort of love: homosexuality, lesbianism, several other perversions, and a few ordinary relationships. Dr. Williams analyzes love with the same tender care and unflinching compassion he must lavish on a urine specimen. His play resembles Plato's Symposium, though it has considerably less action and precious little justification for its metaphysical pap.

The production far surpassed its material. Beck's sets were rather dull (how else can you set dross?) and less imaginative than his other design work. His direction was static; although I had the impression that I saw a supremely rational mind at work, a mind of vast understanding, a mind that may lack the flair for lively direction, but one which presents a play without losing a single implication of the script. It is the mind, perhaps, of a theorist rather than a director. The acting was abysmal. Well, not altogether abysmal. There is certainly more talent at the Living Theatre than most critics have allowed. But, as a repertory company, they're incompetent. There are some fine actors, but they are not a smooth-working ensemble capable of executing the rhythms of the Becks' dream. In fact, Judith Malina herself is one of the worst in the company: dull, truthful to the point of fakery, occasionally bursting into a tantrum (never reaching tragic heights), and owning a very annoying voice. Julian Beck is the same sort of "amateur" actor, but far better than his wife. He is casual, with a grating voice, and he never loses sight of the fact that he is Beck playing a role. Most of the time he looks like a zombie. But he presents his character with the same intelligence with which he directs; every facet of the role is exposed, and the audience sees a full portrait. There is something of the *V-effekt* in Beck's (and consequently the company's) style, and there's a good deal of chance.

The perfect wedding of style and play came in the summer of 1959, when the Becks did *The Connection*. (They had, just before, won the Lola d'Annunzio Award for outstanding achievement in the off-Broadway theatre.) It's a commonplace to say that nothing happens in *The Connection*. Indeed the central point of the play is that nothing *can* happen in the world of drug addiction; literally you're "fixed." But there's another point to *The Connection* as well. The play has movement: verbal and physical fights, a mad scene, the continual interference of the author and producer, a jazz band which sporadically whips itself into a frenzy of activity, two cameramen filming the show (making the audience feel that it's watching a documentary with real addicts on stage) get involved with the addicts. Finally the fix arrives and turns on the junkies, and one of them nearly dies from an overdose. But all this motion does not disturb the basic feeling of ennui, sleepiness, and static desperation. The point is simple: all this movement is without purpose. Gelber says to his audience, whether we do nothing or whether we do everything, we're all hooked in one form or another and we all lead purposeless and self-annihilating lives.

Now this is a tremendously provocative statement, with a good measure of truth, and Gelber couldn't possibly have chosen a better metaphor than dope addiction to make his point.

Malina's directing, Beck's design, and Cernovich's lighting conspired perfectly to create a kaleidoscopic vision of reality and illusion breaking apart, jarring and insulting the audience, coming back together again to evoke a feeling of agonizing verisimilitude; a mating of the tawdriest naturalism and Brechtian acting bringing forth the Becks' vision of half-drama, half-ritual. It is, I think, the only complete success (well, almost complete) that the company currently has in its repertory. All of the Becks' rather puffed-up statements about their theatre are justified by *The Connection*:

> Life is not suspended in the theatre. The actor breathes, the spectator lives. In the theatre life is intensified. . . . We seek a style of acting that will produce revelation. . . . A performance is an act of love in which the playwright, actor, and theatre artist expose themselves, body and spirit, under ordeal, at great risk, to produce catharsis and enlightenment for an anonymous audience.

Miss Malina's direction catches every nuance, every subtle sleight-of-hand switch from reality to illusion and back again. She manages one of the most challenging directing jobs there is, to present boredom without boring. Lines are thrown away and swallowed, to great naturalistic effect. And, occasionally, all the actors talk or mumble at once, giving us a feeling of a chorus-like cry of anguish and confusion—again that beautiful blending of naturalism and poetry, creating the new form of theatre which the Becks seek. Eleven actors are on a small stage at once, and Miss Malina manages to keep them all visible while still conveying the feeling that they are piled on top of each other. (Why hasn't she succeeded in pulling off this same trick in her other shows?) There is calm, then restive motion; then there's a flurry of activity which subsides into calm again, purposeless, stultifying, exhausting. It is a play that could easily be banal with bad direction, but, despite its ugliness (including a scene where one of the addicts gives himself a fix on stage and then convulses, a moment that filled me with revulsion), *The Connection* emerges as a beautifully poetic work.

On November 5, 1959, Pirandello's *Tonight We Improvise* (one of the plays first done at the loft) was put into the repertory. Since it has been subsequently dropped, I shall not linger over it, except to note that it, along with *Many Loves*, shows that the Becks never consider one of their projects finished. Plays enter and leave the repertory, only to return again later. Both the Becks are objective about productions they consider failures, judging their work independent of critics and audiences. Beck said, "Twice I've really missed a play. They were *Beyond the Mountains* and *Women of Trachis*. *Trachis* is a great play. I would love to do it again sometime. A concept is formulating itself. It is not altogether clear yet. You know, once you do a thing it is hard to get rid of a notion." The Becks have a body of work which they can draw upon any time they care to.

In March, 1960, the Living Theatre received the Page One Award from the Newspaper Guild (ironic as that may seem) and in June, 1960, they won the *Village Voice*'s Obie for best new play, best production, and best actor (Warren Finnerty as Leach), all for *The Connection*.

After the box office failure of *Women of Trachis*, translated by Ezra Pound, and Jackson MacLow's *The Marrying Maiden* (they were kept in repertory for almost a year), Brecht's *In the Jungle of Cities* opened in December, 1960. It is still in the repertory. The play was written in 1921–23, considerably before Brecht's theories of Epic Theatre had evolved, but there are many indications of the qualities which were to become the staples of his later work. It is in many ways a fine play, but I find it diffuse, full of fireworks and distracting theatrical debris. My feelings about the play may have added to my distaste for the production. It was hampered by Gerhard Nellhaus' poor translation, very uneven performances, and some of the most inadequate direction I have ever seen. Julian Beck's set, however, although not suited to the play, made an interesting comment on it. The set was built of scrap lumber, nailed together overhead in a labyrinthian maze with sticks and stakes hanging from above which the actors often bumped into and set in motion. This was mounted on a platform raised a foot above the stage and rigged to appear like a fight ring, with a water bucket and towel in one corner.

Miss Malina seemed incapable of handling more than two people at the same time on stage. At one point she herself (playing Mary Garga as well as directing) managed to block both George Garga and Schlink while they were engaged in an important and animated exchange. This was no easy task, since Miss Malina weighs no more than a hundred pounds. Her crowd scenes had no force or drive; the actors milled around the stage, just the way they did (to such good effect) in *The Connection*. A play that demands effective and strong direction to keep it in motion and maintain its spirit was weakened and diffused to the point where it was difficult to know what sort of jungle Brecht intended. The production left me feeling that much of it had been improvised, left to chance. And if Brecht was talking about anything in *In the Jungle of Cities*, he was talking about necessities, not accidents.

The most recent addition to the Living Theatre repertory is Gelber's *The Apple*. After a few introductory remarks by one of the actors, the audience is faced with an action painter, a mannequin (department store, not Parisian kind), a drunk who wanders boisterously up from the audience, a spastic, and a collection of off-beat characters including an Oriental, a Negro, a Jew, and some others—all of whom, I assume, add up to cosmopolitan New York (in hip terms: "the apple"). The audience is bombarded with caustic remarks about Orientals, Negroes, and Jews. There is some casual talk, some violence, some "spontaneous" acting out of scenes, all of them, if only by virtue of an occasional remark, having to do with sex.

As I mentioned earlier, the popularity of the Living Theatre has added to the number of squares in its audience. In the lobby during the first intermission the audience was imposing order on Gelber's chaos. (Remember the old-guard playwrights who used to think that was their job?) "Are we dead and faceless like the mannequin," one young lady said to her escort, "or are we in a stupor like the drunk?" I refused to believe that Gelber was settling for anything so simple, but when I returned for the second act, I discovered that the lesson was even simpler: "Life is *so* apathetic," the audience was told; it shouldn't be that way because truly "life is change." We, the spectators, were urged "to come over to our side." I really wasn't certain what their side was; and I felt, too, that none of this "philosophizing," had arisen from the play. *The Apple* was quite a comedown from *The Connection*. I felt that much of the play came off the top of Gelber's head, fleeting observations that he might have made had he been standing looking at the apple of Manhattan on a street corner. Simple chaos, finally, amounts only to simple chaos; it all looks very much the same. Once this look has been dramatized, it has been said for all time; additional works on the same theme are superfluous.

Chance, accident, the refusal to formulate things too precisely, the insistence on maintaining some semblance of the "chaos" of the world is a thread which runs through all the productions at the Living Theatre, and is at once the source of its excitement and dangers. The performances always have a feeling of improvisation, and the actors are ready and eager to take advantage of any happenstance. In the middle of *The Connection* one night a fire engine siren screamed outside the theatre. One of the actors said: "Fire engine," and another answered, "I'm going to get some real hot chicks to come up here." Within the context of the play the interchange wasn't at all banal. It was hilarious and to the point. Modern art has made us very familiar with this matter of chance, but its application to the theatre is something else again.

It is harder to define the limits of theatrical improvisation, which are inextricably tied to the theatre of chance, of chaos. *The Connection* is a powerful example of what this sort of theatre can be. *The Apple* is an example of the dangers of carrying the disorganization too far; it reduces the potential of the method to a gimmick. Before I went into the auditorium to see *The Connection*, I spoke to Jonathan North, a young actor who plays small parts in the repertory. He was debating whether or not to take the night off, since he was entitled to it, but I convinced him to sit through the show with me. His job was to approach the addict who panhandled the audience in the lobby during intermission. When the time came North gave the actor five dollars so that he'd tell a story during the second act. ("I just got in from San Francisco, and I hear you tell good stories; so I want you to tell me one during the next part of the show.") Only two or three people who happened to be near the panhandler heard this exchange. But during the second act, North stood up in the audience and demanded his money's worth. The actor then told five dollars worth of story

(I would've paid about fifty cents for it) and for two or three people in the audience the play struck home a bit harder. It is an elaborate gesture for the benefit of only a few people, but it indicates the thoroughness with which the Becks approach their shows. Had North decided to take off that night, he told me, they'd have figured out another way to introduce the story. But I had the feeling that they might have just dropped it, and done something entirely different. In *The Connection* the blending of painstaking planning, improvisation, verisimilitude, the shattering of illusion by addressing quips to the audience, the Brechtian style of acting and the naturalism of sets, costumes, and dialogue, the moments of catharsis, the occasional pure accident, and the overall haphazard style of the production all *contradict* one another and yet all *combine* to produce an evening full of force that would not have been possible without the contradictions. (This is a technique that I'm sure the Becks learned from their modern poets, who, like Hart Crane, mixed their metaphors on purpose to create an inner tension.)

But these same contradictions brought the company to its knees in *Many Loves* and ruined *In the Jungle of Cities*. This is the limitation of the theatre of chance. It is, of course, frivolous to say that the Becks' style is "non-theatre" or that *The Connection* is a "non-play." The fact is simply that the style can encompass only so much and that, possibly, it is quickly exhausted (witness *The Apple*); it consumes its own possibilities and soon becomes repetitious and boring.

Quite obviously my attitude towards the Living Theatre is ambivalent. My own aesthetics are at odds with the Becks'. Yet there is such a great excitement at this place that it cannot be brushed aside. It is a perplexing theatre, a disturbing theatre, a theatre that will not be denied attention. There are no other theatres in America like it; and this preëminent fact is intriguing, and invites approval.

Whatever you say about the Becks can be only partially true. In one breath these people will deny all that Craig and Appia, all that Yeats, Brecht, and Strindberg have ever said; they will deny the validity of the carefully planned ritual, the thoroughly formed theatre, the old idea that an artist imposes form upon chaos. And yet, immediately, they will attempt to evoke ritual (only to break it with shattering jumps between illusion and reality), to shape chaos into a rational viewpoint, to make a Brechtian statement within a Brechtian aesthetic. The Becks are loaded with contradictions; therefore, their own style is not well defined, nor easily evaluated.

But, as I've indicated, we can extract (by force perhaps) one basic commitment, that made to the theatre of chance. The painter, composer, or writer who believes that an accident at a given time has a certain validity may justify his improvisation by saying that it reflects the form that unconsciously exists in his own mind. The underlying notion here is that all organisms, by the very nature of their existence, reflect form. The genius of the Becks lies in transplanting this idea to the theatre. Certainly art can be looked at in this way, as an unconscious expression of inner (or transcendental) form which is inherent in the human being without his being aware of it. But in the theatre this is a matter of degree. In the production of a play, the basic form has been traditionally that given by the playwright. The director and actors are translators, not full-fledged creators. If we violate this traditional assignment and assume that each actor projects his own notion of form, because it is more valid or closer to the audience than the playwright's, what we end up with is precisely what the Living Theatre too often offers us, many actors milling aimlessly about the stage. The theatre of chance is the theatre of utter chaos. This may or may not *reflect* in any intelligible way the actual chaos of the world; certainly in its own way it *duplicates* that chaos. Now I, for one, get plenty of the world in the world; I see no value in going to the theatre (and paying to get in at that) simply to perform an exercise in *my* ordering my world.

The artist who uses his unconscious mind as his "form" is refusing the responsibility of controlling his material. It is just one more contradiction in the life of the Becks to note that they are significantly among the pickets and protestors who are consciously attempting to control man's social and political destiny. It seems strange that they are unwilling to exercise the same attempt at control over their own artistic creations. While trying to change the flow of political currents (all to their credit), they leave their theatre to chance; in fact, they make a virtue out of accident and revel in chaos.

If this style is supposed to reflect or be a metaphor of the world, it is probably a falsehood. If it is meant to proselytize, it is a dangerous lie. I shudder to think that the twentieth century may be reflected, or its history prophesied, in the four plays currently at the Living Theatre. At first the greatness and experimentation, the drive, freedom, and power of *The Connection*. Then the indecisive, apologizing, soulless, static, haphazard *Many Loves*. After that the confusion and eventual destruction of *In the Jungle of Cities*. And finally the meaningless, fruitless, self-annihilating, unintelligent, incoherent, unreasoning, demoralizing chaos of *The Apple*.

The Living Theatre is an exciting, disturbing place. Its experimentation and innovation make us want to welcome it. But its underlying aesthetic is frightening. So the end is as ambivalent as the beginning; there's something wonderful in the Living Theatre—and something horrible, too.

ADDENDUM: Brecht's *Man Is Man* opened at the Living Theatre late in September. It brought no new dimension to the Becks' philosophy, nor did it offer any further clue toward understanding the contradictions in this philosophy.

1962

JOHN SIMON

Broadway legend has it that when Percy Hammond panned Orson Welles' all-black "voodoo" *Macbeth* in 1936, the Haitian witch doctors in the company cast a spell and Hammond died the next day. The worst John Simon (b. 1925) has had to endure from his negative reviews was an actress dumping a plate of food on his head in a restaurant. For 36 years (1968–2005), the Balkan-born Simon, who achieved a Ph.D. in comparative literature at Harvard, sniped at the American theatre from his column in *New York* magazine. Everything was grist for his grindstone: Maureen Stapleton's bulk, Barbra Streisand's nose, the grammatical errors of authors, cross-racial casting, what he saw as the pervasion of perversion. Returning tit for tat, David Mamet characterized his style as a "stunning amalgam of superciliousness and savagery" and his popularity with readers an "endorsement of proactive mediocrity." Simon's enthusiasms were so rare, if expressed with equal vigor, that actors and producers felt obliged to thank him personally. There is no question that Simon has genuinely high standards and is unwilling to compromise with the theatre's expediencies. His wholesale disfavor bespeaks the centuries-old American concern that the stage is a snare and a delusion, meretricious in its allure and unworthy of the high-minded. What keeps his diatribes from being merely the effusions of a common scold is his carefully crafted and elegant prose.

Boredom in the Theatre

THE theatre, though it is becoming harder and harder to believe it, still deals with people. And even though the playwright may not want them to be ordinary—any more than they themselves do—most people are precisely that, which is to say (kindly) of limited interest, or (unkindly) boring. The problem is how to render the conversation of such people without dishonesty creeping into the dialogue or audiences creeping out of the theatre.

People, and this often includes dramatists, are apt to forget that in a novel the ordinary person may emerge fascinating simply because of the author's brilliant analysis and comments;

but the playwright, who must rely on his character's actions and words exclusively, must make the ordinary seem extraordinary. Now there are always those who insist that people are infinitely absorbing creatures, or that, at the very least, they and their friends are quite unique, and that nature, having made them, threw away the mold. Yet it would seem to me that nature, tossing them out on the ant heap, threw *them* away, and kept the mold in order to produce their replicas ad infinitum. For if these optimists were to record on tape their words during work, cocktail parties, and love-making, I doubt that they could keep their best friends listening to more than a few minutes of it. Assuredly even these friends would not pay for sitting through two hours of it. They might, in a pinch, pay to get out. And so, to escape from themselves—or from themselves as reflected in their friends—people go out on the search for boredom-killers, which brings them, among other places, into the theatre.

That boredom has always been a very real disease in life and literature is demonstrated by the many terms for it that have become timeless and universal by-words: the *taedium vitae* of ancient Rome, the *vapours* of 18th-century England, the romantic *ennui* and symbolist *spleen* of 19th-century France. Perhaps nowhere did boredom become so crucial as in the drama of the Byronic-romantic tradition, which produced such colossal sufferers from it as Musset's Fantasio and Büchner's Leonce. But in their awareness of their malady there is something cathartic (now we would say, therapeutic) and a spur, ultimately, to unboring action. I am, therefore, chiefly concerned with plays whose characters are unable to recognize the boredom they endure or inflict, the boredom they personify. It is here that the dramatist is up against a real punching bag: the harder he hits his problem, the harder it is likely to bounce back in his face.

This is a comparatively recent danger in the theatre, for as long as most drama was larger than life-size, the heroic protagonist was, by definition, at odds with deities or destinies that took both action and diction out of the parenthesis of dullness. Not until the coming of realism and naturalism did the atmosphere of boredom materialize in all its unbreathableness around the unheroic heroes and heroines of our age.

The current Broadway season abounds in attempts at escaping from the problem. There are, first of all, musicals and more musicals, with which the theatre shirks not only the difficulty I am talking about but any and all difficulties that crop up when one faces reality. But there are also plays like Graham Greene's *The Complaisant Lover*, in which the entire action luxuriates in a warm bath of adulterous sex, and others, like Frederick Knott's *Write Me a Murder*, in which the ice-cold shower of murder is supposed to keep the nerves tingling. An item like *A Shot in the Dark* tries to be even more foolproof: sexual titillation and murder are sagaciously blended, and, amid all these hot and cold shivers, we are expected to be blissfully unaware of the presence—or absence—of anything else. Still another way of shirking responsibility is the flight into nonsense, currently exemplified by Harold Pinter's *The Caretaker*. But while these methods provide alternatives to facing squarely the ordinariness of plain, indeed dull, men and women, the result is spectacles of even greater boredom. For, as Alberto Moravia wisely observes in his newest novel, *The Empty Canvas*, boredom is not simply the opposite of amusement, but a lack of reality. Let us turn away, then, from the more or less fraudulent nostrums of the moment, and consider the prototypical answers with which some contemporary dramatists have parried, or failed to parry, the question of dramatizing our everyday dullness.

There is, to begin with, the playwright who makes an honest, foolish frontal attack on the problem. He picks the dreariest, most cluttered part of the home, the kitchen, and squeezes the big scene, if not the entire play, into it. His characters will have the commonest occupations: the father will be an insurance or dry-goods salesman, with dreams—not even delusions —of grandeur; the mother will be, of course, a housewife, and she will be doing homely chores while lecturing her two children (the perfect number for simple, basic differences or conflicts) on what a fine fellow their boring failure of a father is. If the play is the hit of the 1948–49 Broadway season, the mother's harangue runs:

> . . . I don't say he's a great man. Willy Loman never made a lot of money. His name was never in the paper. He's not the finest character

that ever lived. But he's a human being, and a terrible thing is happening to him. So attention must be paid. He's not to be allowed to fall into his grave like an old dog. Attention, attention must be finally paid to such a person. . . . And you tell me he has no character? The man who never worked a day but for your benefit? When does he get the medal for that? . . .

If, on the other hand, the play is the hit of the London season nine years later, the mother's homily will go:

. . . Your father wants to be a farmer. He hates [his] job; he's always wanted to be a farmer. You have no idea how much that means to him. He hates it and he's done it for you. For you, do you understand? He's a fine man. He's been through a great deal in all sorts of ways and you will treat him with respect. With respect! (*She sits.*) With respect! With respect! (*She puts her face in her hands and weeps.*)

It would be very nearly possible to transpose these speeches from Arthur Miller's *Death of a Salesman* and Robert Bolt's *Flowering Cherry* without in the least disturbing the insignificance and dullness of the respective scenes. And this is not to say that Miller is a hack or Bolt a plagiarist; only that both of them are dealing with a commonplace that neither Miller's fancier (though not necessarily better) language nor Bolt's naked simplicity is able to redeem. Significantly, *Flowering Cherry*, which Kenneth Tynan called "a remarkable new play," and which was both a critical and audience success in London, closed within a week in New York. *Death of a Salesman*, which was grovelingly worshiped in America by press and public alike, was accorded a barely lukewarm reception in London.

The point is that boredom—dullish characters in their everyday surroundings—is perishable indeed, and cannot readily be exported. We work up enthusiasm for our own, our recognizably national boredom, simply because it captures our personal blemishes and rut. In *The Picture of Dorian Grey*, Wilde spoke of Caliban's rage *at* seeing his face in the mirror; there is also, as Wilde knew, Caliban's rage *for* seeing his face there. Provided, of course, the lighting on the face is favorable, so that its dreariness has, if not grandeur, at least pathos. The important thing for the playwright is to portray the endemic boredom and frustration in which everyone recognizes himself or, preferably, his brother, and to spray the picture with a little human dignity for fixative. So it is that Willy Loman's greyness and monomania can be both deplored and sold, and Miller cashes in on his Picture of Boring Grey. But the moment that either Loman or Cherry is uprooted from the public out of which he sprouted, unwatered by audience tears and scathed by withering reviews, he perishes. Perishes, ultimately, of his own dullness.

Frontal attack, to be sure, is not the only way. There is the expressionists' manner of portraying boredom, as in the party scene of Elmer Rice's *The Adding Machine*. Seven couples, whose names range from Mr. and Mrs. Six to Mr. and Mrs. Zero, exchange disa and data:

> Mrs. Six: I like them little organdie dresses.
> Mrs. Five: Yeh, with a little lace trimmin' on the sleeves.
> Mrs. Four: Well, I like 'em plain myself.
> Mrs. Three: Yeh, what I always say is the plainer the more refined.
> Mrs. Two: Well, I don't think a little lace does any harm.
> Mrs. One: No, it kinda dresses it up.
> Mrs. Zero: Well, I always say it's all a matter of taste.

This is exaggeration: an enormous enlargement of boredom and also a caricature, but one that is more frightening than funny. It has the fascination of hyperbole, for the unit of conversation is no longer the word but the platitude. In this way boredom becomes interesting through sheer horror. But the difficulty with caricaturing boredom is that it requires almost superhuman skills to sustain it through a whole evening. This is why Eugène Ionesco, the current master of representing boredom by artful distortion, by suggestive nonsense and *reductio ad absurdum*, usually limits himself to short plays. His frenetic, surrealist humor is at times almost too successful in communicating blind, blustering boredom; in a play like *Rhinoceros*, his customarily perfect balance between excruciation and amusement swings a little too much toward the latter, and the barb turns into a barbiturate.

If Ionesco's plays tend to monumentalize the boredom in ordinary social situations, our other great master borer, Samuel Beckett, erects a more cosmic boredom, in some extraordinary, antisocial, mysteriously metaphysical ambience. In Beckett's *Endgame*, we meet the blind Hamm and his servant

Clov, apparently the last inhabitants of the universe—except for Nagg and Nell, Hamm's aged parents who live side by side in two ash bins. At one point Hamm says:

Hamm: Go and see is she dead. (*Clov goes to bins, raises the lid of Nell's, stoops, looks into it. Pause.*)
Clov: Looks like it. (*He closes the lid, straightens up. Hamm raises his toque. Pause. He puts it on again.*)
Hamm: (*with his hand to his toque*): And Nagg? (*Clov raises lid of Nagg's bin, stoops, looks into it. Pause.*)
Clov: Doesn't look like it. (*He closes the lid, straightens up.*)
Hamm: (*letting go his toque*): What's he doing? (*Clov raises lid of Nagg's bin, stoops, looks into it. Pause.*)
Clov: He's crying. (*He closes lid, straightens up.*)
Hamm: Then he's living. (*Pause.*)

But not many scenes of this short play are as eventful as that. One way or the other, however, such treatment of universal boredom makes its devastating point so quickly that it cannot last out three acts, no matter how great the wit and ingenuity. Beckett's longest plays are two-acters (and at that they may be too long); when Ionesco, in *Rhinoceros*, attempts a full-length play, proceedings begin to pall. So, too, the disciples of these two masters, Americans like Albee and Richardson, Britishers like Harold Pinter and N. F. Simpson, find it hard, or do not even try, to write three-act plays.*

As opposed to this travestying of boredom, there is the attempt by another school to idealize it: the endeavor to sell us insignificance, general human repetitiousness, and monotony of existence as supreme virtues. This is the approach of Thornton Wilder. Whether it is ninety Christmas dinners in the life of a family, fifteen years in the life of a town, or umpteen aeons in the life of the human race, Wilder reduces everything to a sweet suburban formula of familiar family felicities and infelicities couched in cultural slogans and homespun homiletics. Everything blurs into everything else—particularly evil into good, which always triumphs because it is really omnipresent —and everybody merges into everybody else because there are

---

*Since this writing, Albee has proved with *Who's Afraid of Virginia Woolf?* that he can sustain a full-length play, but only by making his dramaturgy more conventional, and his characters considerably less so.

no significant differences between bodies, and isn't that just wonderful? The most wonderful thing about it is its success, but even that isn't so extraordinary: it is merely Caliban, equally exasperated by seeing and not seeing his face in the glass, jumping with joy before a mirror that shows him Ariel's face as his own. Of course, Wilder uses every trick of the Pirandellian, expressionist, surrealist theatres to add zest to his litanies of dullness, and enjoyment of his technique and drolleries has reconciled people who should know better to his content. But he does not fool the shrewd observer; the German poet and critic Gottfried Benn writes about *The Skin of Our Teeth*: "Such datedness and such dullness . . . all this talking-into-the-audience, these narrators, this promiscuity with the orchestra pit is, eventually, utterly provincial. . . ." But Wilder is, at any rate, more honest than Saroyan, whose bores express their improbable magnanimity in impossible flights of sentimental prose poetry.

Another solution is to surround tiresome people in boring situations with so much authentic feeling for their plight and helplessness, reproducing their predicament with such genuine compassion or indignation, that we cannot but be moved. This can be the social thesis play as once written by Clifford Odets, and now by Arnold Wesker; or the plays with less or no clear-cut social purpose of John Osborne, William Inge, and various others, ranging to such a curious work as Marguerite Duras's *The Square*. In this interminable duologue between two idiot savants which at once repels and hypnotizes us, we experience the same spiritual equivalent of ingrown toenails from which Mlle Duras's characters, as well as her style, are suffering.

A more common approach to alleviating boredom is to set off one or two superior, or at least more sensitive, characters against a background of gaping dullness. Of course, if the superior figures can carry the whole play, as in Tennessee Williams's two or three true successes, the problem of boredom is automatically by-passed. But often the background characters preponderate. Thus Denis Donoghue recently criticized *Look Back in Anger* "because it allowed eloquence and energy only to one attitude, Jimmy Porter's; rival attitudes were assigned to nitwits." Such an objection seems more applicable to Osborne and Creighton's *Epitaph for George Dillon*: the second act, where the intelligent Ruth clashes with the complex Dillon, is totally absorbing; but the commonplaces, vulgarities, and squabbles of the Elliot family which make up the bulk of acts one and three are wearying.

Still another way of mitigating boredom is to put the dramatis personae into an unusual milieu, an extraordinary position. Jack Gelber's *The Connection* exploits to a large extent junkies, hypodermics, jazz, and hipster jargon; but for all its sensationalism, heightened by a fancy Pirandellian play-within-a-play and even movie-within-a-play, the painfully paralyzing boredom is there—for us, at times, as much as for the characters. Yet *The Connection* succeeds because Gelber's play has the benefit of language: the hip talk that blends with the more philosophical passages into a hallucinatory syncopation.

Indeed this is the fundamental way of making existential boredom theatrically valid: a language must be found that will turn tedium into poetry. Think of O'Neill: no playwright had a harder time finding his language, his style; but when, in some of his very last plays, he finds it, it is superb. Now, by poetry I do not mean the sort of thing that T. S. Eliot does in *The Cocktail Party*, where languorous pseudo-poetry is meant to express the ennui of high-class, highbrow bores. No, the poetry I have in mind is something other than the worrying of words and conceits into verse that is merely circumnavigating its navel.

Compare two speeches from two different plays in which two girls, one, to be sure, more promiscuous than the other, voice their none the less identical, unassuming happiness. Girl number one is talking to her girl friend:

> I think I'm happy, Marilyn. I can't tell you how I feel in so many words, but life seems very pleasant to me right now. I even get along with my mother. I think I'm in love. Seriously in love. I feel so full sometimes it just wells up in me, my feelings for him. He went away for three days on a business trip to Detroit, I thought I'd die before he came back.

Girl number two, in a garden, is talking to her baby:

> Me, Polly Garter, under the washing line, giving the breast to my bonny new baby. Nothing grows in our garden, only washing. And

babies. And where's their fathers live, my love? Over the hills and far away. You're looking up at me now. I know what you're thinking, you poor little milky creature. You're thinking, you're no better than you should be, Polly, and that's good enough for me. Oh, isn't life a terrible thing, thank God?

It is a stock situation, but the first girl, Paddy Chayefsky's Betty Preiss (in *Middle of the Night*), has only a stock way of expressing it. Dylan Thomas's Polly Garter (in *Under Milk Wood*) also utters banalities, but their happily slapdash juxtaposition, with just a sprinkling of poetic spice, makes them transcend their triviality. It is not easy to do, but a child can do it—if that eighteen-year-old child is called Shelagh Delaney. In *A Taste of Honey* we recently had a play in which humdrum people in standard grubby predicaments manage to be endearing, novel, and true—and, best of all, far more interesting than the characters our quotidian reviewers daily refer to as "endearing, novel, and true."

It does not matter whether our dull, ordinary life is conveyed in this manner or that, whether the boredom is physical or metaphysical, whether we are waiting for Lefty or for Godot, as long as a language is found to make us—not stand up and cheer, only sit up and take notice. This is where the dramatic imagination of the sixties might well busy itself. But, like the lover of Chayefsky's heroine, it seems to have gone on a business trip to Detroit. And we may be gone by the time it comes back.

1963

LUIS VALDÉZ

One of the effects of the counterculture of the 1960s, with its taste for street performance, colorful spontaneity, and political opposition, was to spur minorities to insist on a hearing for their voices, so far mute in the professional theatre. Luis Valdéz (b. 1940) claims that he first became aware of the power of make-believe at the age of six when he was taught to shape papier-mâché masks. While earning a degree in English at San Jose State, he wrote his first play, *The Shrunken Head of Pancho Villa* (1963); after graduation, he learned the concept of agitprop from the San Francisco Mime Troupe. His parents, migrant farm workers, were stupefied when, in 1965, he returned to his hometown of Delano, California, to form an acting group to support César Chávez and his National Farm Workers Association in their grape-picking strike. A self-styled "angry young man," Valdéz soon realized that his farmer-actors were illiterate and that improvisation, not declamation, had to be the basis of their dramas. "While we had the strength and urgency of the struggle," he recalled in an interview in 1985, "our artistry had to sustain our politics. Ultimately, it is the artistry that makes the point and cuts across barriers to understanding." El Teatro Campesino eventually developed into a more broadly based Chicano theatre, staging Valdéz's *actos* that drew on current events and Mexican folklore. Valdéz recognized the need to appeal to a mixed audience to escape one's own racism. The wildly successful *Zoot Suit* (1978), based on the Sleepy Lagoon riots of 1942, had its premiere in Los Angeles, and became the first play by a Chicano author to be staged on Broadway.

El Teatro Campesino

EL TEATRO CAMPESINO is somewhere between Brecht and Cantinflas. It is a farm workers' theater, a bi-lingual propaganda theater, but it borrows from Mexican folk humor to such an extent that its "propaganda" is salted with a wariness for human caprice. Linked by a cultural umbilical cord to the National Farm Workers Association, the Teatro lives in Delano as a part of a social movement. We perform for the grape strikers at our weekly meetings, seek to clarify strike aims, and go on tour throughout the state publicizing and raising funds for the Huelga.

Our most important aim is to reach the farm workers. All the actors are farm workers, and our single topic is the Huelga. We must create our own material, but this is hardly a limitation. Neither is our concentration on the strike. The hardest thing at first was finding limits, some kind of dramatic form, within which to work. Working together, we developed what we call "*actos*"—10 to 15 minute skits, sometimes with and sometimes without songs. We insist on calling them *actos* rather than *skits*, not only because we talk in Spanish most of the time, but because *skit* seems too light a word for the work we are trying to do.

Starting from scratch with a real life incident, character, or idea, everybody in the Teatro contributes to the development of an acto. Each is intended to make at least one specific point about the strike, but improvisations during each performance sharpen, alter or embellish the original idea. We use no scenery, no scripts, and no curtain. We use costumes and props only casually—an old pair of pants, a wine bottle, a pair of dark glasses, a mask, but mostly we like to show we are still strikers underneath, arm bands and all. This effect is very important to our aims. To simplify things, we hang signs around our necks, sometimes in black and white, sometimes in lively colors, indicating the characters portrayed.

Practicing our own brand of Commedia dell' arte, we improvise within the framework of traditional characters associated with the strike. Instead of Arlecchinos, Pantalones, and Brighellas, we have *Esquiroles* (scabs), *Contratistas* (contractors), *Patroncitos* (growers), and *Huelguistas* (strikers). We have experimented with these four types in dozens of combinations. Being free to act as they will, to infuse a character type with real thought and feeling, the farm workers of the Teatro have expressed the human complexity of the grape strike. This is where Brecht comes in. As propaganda, the Teatro is loyal to an *a priori* social end: i.e., the winning of the strike. We not only presume Our Cause is just; we know it.

Every member of the Teatro, however, *knows* it differently. We vary in age from 18 to 44, with drastically different degrees of education, but we are all drawn into the Teatro by a common enthusiasm to express what we *individually* know and feel. The freedom to do so lifts our propaganda into Brechtlike theater: Our Just Cause is many-faceted, like human nature.

The Teatro appeals to its actors for the same reason it appeals to its audience. It explores the meaning of a social movement without asking its participants to read or write. It is a learning experience with no formal prerequisites. This is all-important because most farm workers have never had a chance to go to school and are alienated by classrooms, blackboards and the formal teacher-student approach.

By contrast, our Cantinflas-inspired burlesque is familiar to the farm workers. It is in the family; it is *raza*; it is part of the Mexican people. They know that the Teatro discusses the Huelga, but the actors are fellow farm workers and strikers, not teachers. If the Teatro has a point to make, it is just a step ahead of the audience, and the audience takes the step easily.

In a Mexican way, we have discovered what Brecht is all about. If you want unbourgeois theater, find unbourgeois people to do it. Your head could burst open at the simplicity of the act, not the thought, but that's the way it is in Delano. Real theater lies in the excited laughter (or silence) of recognition *in the audience*, not in all the paraphernalia on the stage. Minus actors, the entire Teatro can be packed into one trunk, and when the Teatro goes on tour, the spirit of the Delano grape strike goes with it.

Last March and April, the Teatro toured with the pilgrimage from Delano to Sacramento. Part of the purpose of the *peregrinación* was to "turn on" the farm workers of the San Joaquin Valley, to expose them to our growing Huelga movement. The Teatro performed nightly at all the rallies we held in more than 20 farm worker towns. The response of the audience to the Teatro in all of these towns was a small triumph, within the greater triumph of the NFWA march.

Perhaps the best key to the "theater" of the Teatro Campesino is a description of our most successful performance on the pilgrimage. It occurred in Freeport, a small town just nine miles southwest of Sacramento. We were to arrive at the Capitol in two days, and Governor Brown had just refused to meet with us on Easter Sunday. He had previously promised he would meet the pilgrimage somewhere on the road, but that was off too.

The Teatro Campesino decided to bring the governor to the rally that same night. We revamped an old skit we had on Governor Brown, also involving the "DiGorgio Fruit Corp" and "Schunley." The "Schunley" character was dropped because Schenley Industries had recognized the NFWA as its workers' sole bargaining agent two days before. We replaced "Schunley" with another grower type, a "Mr. Zunavuvich," which—believe it or not—sounds incredibly like the name of a ranching family in Delano. To supplement Zunavuvich, and to hit at another DiGorgio interest, we introduced a new character, "Bank Amerika."

When the time for the Teatro came, the DiGorgio character —complete with sign, dark glasses, and cigar—leaped onto the one and a half ton truck used as a stage for the nightly rallies, and was quickly booed and reviled by the farm worker audience of over 300. Threatening them with loss of their jobs, blackballing, and deportation, DiGorgio blustered and guffawed his way through all the booing, and announced that his old high school buddy, the governor, was coming to speak to them that same night, and in Spanish. At this point, a car with a siren and a loudspeaker drove up behind the audience, honking and moving toward the platform. An authoritative voice commanded the workers to move out of the way, and the outside rally was momentarily halted as "Governor Brown" was pulled out of the car by his cronies and pushed onto the stage. The "governor" protested all the way that he couldn't speak Spanish, but DiGorgio, Zunavuvich and Bank Amerika convinced him to try:

" *No Huelga,*" they exhorted, "just say *no Huelga!*"

"And *no boycoteo,*" insisted DiGorgio.

The "governor"—played by long, thin, dark Augustin Lira wearing a huge fake paunch—not only spoke Spanish, though brokenly at first, he spoke so ardently that he turned into a Mexican. This is the turning point of the acto. DiGorgio and his friends were forced to drag the metamorphosed governor off the stage, as he shouted "Huelga! Huelga!" all the way down, to the laughter and applause of the farm worker audience.

It has never been easy to measure the actual effect of the Teatro as serious social propaganda, but we do receive indirect reports occasionally. After one Bakersfield performance we were told that two scabs vowed never to come to Delano as strike-breakers again, and they cited the Teatro's satire as the reason for their change of heart. More encouraging than any-thing is that farm workers on the march, as Delano strikers have been doing every week now for five months, kept asking, "Is there going to be a Teatro tonight?"

The first striker to join the Teatro was 21-year-old Augustin Lira. Irrepressible song-writer and guitar player, Augie was born in Torreon, Coahuila, Mexico. He has been a farm worker all his life, following the crops from Texas to California with his mother and seven brothers and sisters. He was picking grapes in the Fresno area when the strike started in Delano. He joined it in the second week. Proud and rebellious, he ex-presses a fierce loyalty to the "*raza*" through his gentle and sensitive songs.

Stage manager and mask-maker of the group is Errol Franklin, 28, a native of Cheyenne, Wyoming, who prefers to think of himself as a cowboy. He has traveled far and wide across the United States, and has worked as a horse breaker, fisherman, apple picker, tomato picker, short order cook, waiter, and longshoreman. Some months ago, he came to Delano to pick scab grapes, but joined the strike when the rov-ing picket line arrived at the vineyard where he was working. He is proud of his Indian blood and a good man with a tall tale. About two feet taller than the rest of us, he usually plays a rancher or a cop in the actos, lifting or pushing people as the situation demands.

Felipe Cantu, 44, is a comic genius. A family man and farm worker of practically no formal education, he was born and raised in Nuevo León, Mexico. He now lives in Delano with his wife and seven children. Felipe made his talents apparent on the picket line, where lively dialogues between pickets on the road and scabs in the field inspired his Mexican wit. He claims to have been everything from a "policeman to a clown" in Mexico, and resembles a Mexican version of Ben Turpin. Still, he can be a deeply serious man, especially when the well-being of his family is concerned. He speaks no English, but his wild, extravagant Cantinflas-like comic style needs no words. His *tour de force* is the role of a drunken scab who is needled by another character, his conscience, who reads him Jack London's "Definition of a Strike-Breaker" in Spanish.

Gilbert Rubio, 18, another valued member of the troupe, is third in a family of 13, born and raised in Lubbock, Texas. His family moved to California two years ago because there was no work in their home state, where many farm workers are still receiving 50 cents an hour for their labor. Always eager to learn, Gilbert got his chance to act as the rotten, smelly grape in the "Tres Uves" acto. He sings, too.

These men are only a few of the many farm workers who have participated in the Teatro. Unfortunately for the Teatro, the actors, encouraged to express themselves, often showed leadership potential and were put to work doing other things for the association. Some of our best natural talents have been sent to organize or boycott in Los Angeles, San Francisco and as far away as Texas.

The Teatro by its mere existence condemns the real loss of human talent, the deadening of the human spirit, the brutalization of mind and body caused by the callous, feudal exploitation that is farm labor today. Beyond that we can now afford to laugh as free men. The Teatro Campesino lives and grows in that laughter.

1966

SUSAN SONTAG

Theatre loomed large in the sensibility of Susan Sontag (1933–2004), from the time she was a child in Tucson. As a luminary of Manhattan's cultural elite from the 1960s on, she was in regular attendance at the latest thing and particularly stimulated by such innovative directors as Peter Brook, Patrice Chéreau, Lucien Pintilie, and Giorgio Strehler. However, Sontag avoided writing dramatic criticism, which she disdained as "consumer reporting," "monitoring productions and giving out grades." She believed that a surfeit of critical perspectives led to disenchantment with modernist high culture. Sontag's most extended analysis of a particular play is her essay on Peter Weiss's *Marat/Sade*, for Brook's visceral *mise-en-scène* had shaken intellectuals out of their complacent cerebrality and inaugurated a period of intense experimentation in the American theatre. Sontag's piece in *Partisan Review* received more attention when reprinted in *Against Interpretation* (1966), a collection that also contained her influential "Notes on Camp." Sontag preferred to comment on theatre in the abstract; in an essay for *The Drama Review* in 1966, comparing theatre and film, she refrained from taking sides, but pointed out that theatre in its liveness, continuous use of space, and deployment of artifice is unlike film in not being a "medium." Later, in an interview in 1977, she declared, "Theatre—and poetry and music—supply a lyricism not to be found in life." Her only produced play, *Alice in Bed*, about the sister of Henry and William James, was first directed in 1993 by Robert Wilson with the elaborate sound effects and projections that Sontag now found extraneous to the theatrical experience. Earlier that same year she had boldly traveled to a besieged Sarajevo and at the Youth Theatre staged *Waiting for Godot* in candlelight, to the accompaniment of Serb bombardments. Her last novel, *In America* (2000), was a fictional yet heavily documented biography of the Polish actress Helena Modjeska.

Marat/Sade/Artaud

> "The Primary and most beautiful of Nature's qualities is mo-
> tion, which agitates her at all times. But this motion is simply
> the perpetual consequence of crimes; and it is conserved by
> means of crimes alone."
>
> SADE

> "Everything that acts is a cruelty. It is upon this idea of extreme
> action, pushed beyond all limits, that theatre must be rebuilt."
>
> ARTAUD

THEATRICALITY and insanity—the two most potent subjects of the contemporary theater—are brilliantly fused in Peter Weiss' play, *The Persecution and Assassination of Marat as Performed by the Inmates of the Asylum at Charenton under the Direction of the Marquis de Sade*. The subject is a dramatic performance staged before the audience's eyes; the scene is a madhouse. The historical facts behind the play are that in the insane asylum just outside Paris where Sade was confined by order of Napoleon for the last eleven years of his life (1803–14), it was the enlightened policy of the director, M. Coulmier, to allow Charenton's inmates to stage theatrical productions of their own devising which were open to the Parisian public. In these circumstances Sade is known to have written and put on several plays (all lost), and Weiss' play ostensibly re-creates such a performance. The year is 1808 and the stage is the stark tiled bath-house of the asylum.

Theatricality permeates Weiss' cunning play in a peculiarly modern sense: most of *Marat/Sade* consists of a play-within-a-play. In Peter Brook's production, which opened in London last August, the aged, disheveled, flabby Sade (acted by Patrick Magee) sits quietly on the left side of the stage—prompting (with the aid of a fellow-patient who acts as stage manager and narrator), supervising, commenting. M. Coulmier, dressed formally and wearing some sort of honorific red sash, attended by his elegantly dressed wife and daughter, sits throughout the performance on the right side of the stage. There is also an abundance of theatricality in a more traditional sense: the emphatic appeal to the senses with spectacle and sound. A quartet of inmates with string hair and painted faces, wearing colored sacks and floppy hats, sing sardonic loony songs while the action described by the songs is mimed; their motley getup contrasts with the shapeless white tunics and straitjackets, the whey-colored faces of most of the rest of the inmates who act in Sade's passion play on the French Revolution. The verbal action, conducted by Sade, is repeatedly interrupted by brilliant bits of acting-out performed by the lunatics, the most forceful of which is a mass guillotining sequence, in which some inmates make metallic rasping noises, bang together parts of the ingenious set, and pour buckets of paint (blood) down drains, while other madmen gleefully jump into a pit in the center of the stage, leaving their heads piled above stage level, next to the guillotine.

In Brook's production, insanity proves the most authoritative and sensuous kind of theatricality. Insanity establishes the inflection, the intensity of *Marat/Sade*, from the opening image of the ghostly inmates who are to act in Sade's play, crouching in foetal postures or in a catatonic stupor or trembling or performing some obsessive ritual, then stumbling forward to greet the affable M. Coulmier and his family as they enter the stage and mount the platform where they will sit. Insanity is the register of the intensity of the individual performances as well: of Sade, who recites his long speeches with a painful clenched singsong deliberateness; of Marat (acted by Clive Revill), swathed in wet cloths (a treatment for his skin disease) and encased throughout the action in a portable metal bathtub, even in the midst of the most passionate declamation staring straight ahead as though he were already dead; of Charlotte Corday, Marat's assassin, who is played by a beautiful somnambule who periodically goes blank, forgets her lines, even lies down on the stage and has to be awakened by Sade; of Duperret, the Girondist deputy and lover of Corday, played by a lanky stiff-haired patient, an erotomaniac, who is constantly breaking down in his role of gentleman and lover and lunging lustfully toward the patient playing Corday (in the course of the play, he has to be put in a strait-jacket); of Simone Everard, Marat's mistress and nurse, played by an almost wholly disabled patient who can barely speak and is limited to jerky idiot movements as she changes Marat's dressings. Insanity becomes the privileged, most authentic metaphor for passion; or, what's the same thing in this case, the logical terminus of any strong emotion. Both dream (as in the "Marat's Nightmare" sequence) and dream-like states must end in violence. Being "calm" amounts to a failure to understand one's real situation. Thus, the slow-motion staging of Corday's murder of Marat (history, i.e. theater) is followed by the inmates shouting and singing of the fifteen bloody years since then, and ends with the "cast" assaulting the Coulmiers as they attempt to leave the stage.

It is through its depiction of theatricality and insanity that Weiss' play is also a play of ideas. The heart of the play is a running debate between Sade, in his chair, and Marat, in his bath, on the meaning of the French Revolution, that is, on the psychological and political premises of modern history, but seen through a very modern sensibility, one equipped with the hindsight afforded by the Nazi concentration camps. But *Marat/Sade* does not lend itself to being formulated as a particular theory about modern experience. Weiss' play seems to be more about the range of sensibility that concerns itself with, or is at stake in, the modern experience, than it is about an argument or an interpretation of that experience. Weiss does not present ideas as much as he immerses his audience in them. Intellectual debate is the material of the play, but it is not its subject or its end. The Charenton setting insures that this debate takes place in a constant atmosphere of barely suppressed violence: all ideas are volatile at this temperature. Again, insanity proves to be the most austere (even abstract) and drastic mode of expressing in theatrical terms the reenacting of ideas, as members of the cast reliving the Revolution run amuck and have to be restrained and the cries of the Parisian mob for liberty are suddenly metamorphosed into the cries of the patients howling to be let out of the asylum.

Such theater, whose fundamental action is the irrevocable careening toward extreme states of feeling, can end in only two ways. It can turn in on itself and become formal, and end in strict *da capo* fashion, with its own opening lines. Or it can turn outward, breaking the "frame," and assault the audience. Ionesco has admitted that he originally envisaged his first play, *The Bald Soprano*, ending with a massacre of the audience; in another version of the same play (which now ends *da capo*), the author was to leap on the stage, and shout imprecations at the audience till they fled the theater. Brook, or Weiss, or both, have devised for the end of *Marat/Sade* an equivalent of the same hostile gesture toward the audience. The inmates, that is, the "cast" of Sade's play, have gone berserk and assaulted the Coulmiers; but this riot—that is, the play—is broken off by the entry of the stage manager of the Aldwych Theater, in modern skirt, sweater, and gym shoes. She blows a whistle; the actors abruptly stop, turn, and face the audience; but when the audience applauds, the company responds with a slow ominous handclap, drowning out the "free" applause and leaving everyone pretty uncomfortable.

My own admiration for, and pleasure in, *Marat/Sade* is virtually unqualified. The play that opened in London last August, and will, it's rumored, soon be seen in New York, is one of the great experiences of anyone's theater-going lifetime. Yet almost everyone, from the daily reviewers to the most serious critics, have voiced serious reservations about, if not outright dislike for, Brook's production of Weiss' play. Why?

Three ready-made ideas seem to me to underlie most caviling at Weiss' play in Brook's production of it.

The connection between theater and literature. One ready-made idea: a work of theater is a branch of literature. The truth is, some works of theater may be judged primarily as works of literature, others not.

It is because this is not admitted, or generally understood, that one reads all too frequently the statement that while *Marat/Sade* is, theatrically, one of the most stunning things anyone has seen on the stage, it's a "director's play," meaning a first-rate production of a second-rate play. A well-known English poet told me he detested the play for this reason: because although he thought it marvelous when he saw it, he *knew* that if it hadn't had the benefit of Peter Brook's production, he wouldn't have liked it. It's also reported that the play in Konrad Swinarski's production last year in West Berlin made nowhere near the striking impression it does in the current production in London.

Granted, *Marat/Sade* is not the supreme masterpiece of

contemporary dramatic literature, but it is scarcely a second-rate play. Considered as a text alone, *Marat/Sade* is both sound and exciting. It is not the play which is at fault, but a narrow vision of theater which insists on one image of the director—as servant to the writer, bringing out meanings already resident in the text.

After all, to the extent that it is true that Weiss' text, in Adrian Mitchell's graceful translation, is enhanced greatly by being joined with Peter Brook's staging, what of it? Apart from a theater of dialogue (of language) in which the text is primary, there is also a theater of the senses. The first might be called "play," the second "theater work." In the case of a pure theater work, the writer who sets down words which are to be spoken by actors and staged by a director loses his primacy. In this case, the "author" or "creator" is, to quote Artaud, none other than "the person who controls the direct handling of the stage." The director's art is a material art—an art in which he deals with the bodies of actors, the props, the lights, the music. And what Brook has put together is particularly brilliant and inventive—the rhythm of the staging, the costumes, the ensemble mime scenes. In every detail of the production—one of the most remarkable elements of which is the clangorous tuneful music (by Richard Peaslee) featuring bells, cymbals, and the organ—there is an inexhaustible material inventiveness, a relentless address to the senses. Yet, something about Brook's sheer virtuosity in stage effects offends. It seems, to most people, to overwhelm the text. But perhaps that's just the point.

I'm not suggesting that *Marat/Sade* is simply theater of the senses. Weiss has supplied a complex and highly literate text which demands to be responded to. But *Marat/Sade* also demands to be taken on the sensory level as well, and only the sheerest prejudice about what theater must be (the prejudice, namely, that a work of theater is to be judged, in the last analysis, as a branch of literature) lies behind the demand that the written, and subsequently spoken, text of a theater work carry the whole play.

The connection between theater and psychology. Another ready-made idea: drama consists of the revelation of character, built on the conflict of realistically credible motives. But the most interesting modern theater is a theater which goes beyond psychology.

Again, to cite Artaud: "We need true action, but without practical consequences. It is not on the social level that the action of theater unfolds. Still less on the ethical and psychological levels. . . . This obstinacy in making characters talk about feelings, passions, desires, and impulses of a strictly psychological order, in which a single word is to compensate for innumerable gestures, is the reason . . . the theater has lost its true *raison d'être.*"

It's from this point of view, tendentiously formulated by Artaud, that one may properly approach the fact that Weiss has situated his argument in an insane asylum. The fact is that with the exception of the audience-figures on stage—M. Coulmier, who frequently interrupts the performance to remonstrate with Sade, and his wife and daughter, who have no lines—all the characters in the play are mad. But the setting of *Marat/Sade* does not amount to a statement that the world is insane. Nor is it an instance of a fashionable interest in the psychology of psychopathic behavior. On the contrary, the concern with insanity in art today usually reflects the desire to go beyond psychology. By representing characters with deranged behavior or deranged styles of speech, such dramatists as Pirandello, Genet, Beckett, and Ionesco make it unnecessary for their characters to embody in their acts or voice in their speech sequential and credible accounts of their motives. Freed from the limitations of what Artaud calls "psychological and dialogue painting of the individual," the dramatic representation is open to levels of experience which are more heroic, more rich in fantasy, more philosophical. The point applies, of course, not only to the drama. The choice of "insane" behavior as the subject-matter of art is, by now, the virtually classic strategy of modern artists who wish to transcend traditional "realism," that is, psychology.

Take the scene to which many people particularly objected, in which Sade persuades Charlotte Corday to whip him (Peter Brook has her do it with her hair)—while he, meanwhile, continues to recite, in agonized tones, some point about the Revolution, and the nature of human nature. The purpose of this scene is surely not to inform the audience that, as one critic put it, Sade is "sick, sick, sick"; nor is it fair to reproach Weiss' Sade, as the same critic does, with "using the theater less to advance an argument than to excite himself." (Anyway, why not both?) By combining rational or near-rational argument with irrational behavior, Weiss is not inviting the audience to make a judgment on Sade's character, mental competence, or state of mind. Rather, he is shifting to a kind of theater focused not on characters, but on intense transpersonal emotions borne by characters. He is providing a kind of vicarious emotional experience (in this case, frankly erotic) from which the theater has shied away too long.

Language is used in *Marat/Sade* primarily as a form of incantation, instead of being limited to the revelation of character and the exchange of ideas. This use of language as incantation is the point of another scene which many who saw the play have found objectionable, upsetting, and gratuitous— the bravura soliloquy of Sade, in which he illustrates the cruelty in the heart of man by relating in excruciating detail the public execution by slow dismemberment of Damiens, the would-be assassin of Louis XV.

The connection between theater and ideas. Another ready-made idea: a work of art is to be understood as being "about" or representing or arguing for an "idea." That being so, an implicit standard for a work of art is the value of the ideas it contains, and whether these are clearly and consistently expressed.

It is only to be expected that *Marat/Sade* would be subjected to these standards. Weiss' play, theatrical to its core, is also full of intelligence. It contains discussions of the deepest issues of contemporary morality and history and feeling that put to shame the banalities peddled by such would-be diagnosticians of these issues as Arthur Miller (see his current *After the Fall* and *Incident at Vichy*), Friedrich Duerrenmatt (*The Visit, The Physicists*), and Max Frisch (*The Firebugs, Andorra*). Yet, there is no doubt that *Marat/Sade* is intellectually puzzling. Argument is offered, only (seemingly) to be undermined by the context of the play—the insane asylum, and the avowed theatricality of the proceedings. People do seem to represent positions in Weiss' play. Roughly, Sade represents the claim of the permanence of human nature, in all its vileness, against Marat's revolutionary fervor and his belief that man can be changed by history. Sade thinks that "the world is made of bodies," Marat that it is made of forces. Secondary characters, too, have their moments of passionate advocacy: Duperret hails the eventual dawn of freedom, the priest Jacques Roux denounces Napoleon. But Sade and "Marat" are both madmen, each in a different style; "Charlotte Corday" is a sleepwalker, "Duperret" has satyriasis; "Roux" is hysterically ·violent. Doesn't this undercut their arguments? And, apart from the question of the context of insanity in which the ideas are presented, there is the device of the play-within-a-play. At one level, the running debate between Sade and Marat, in which the moral and social idealism attributed to Marat is countered by Sade's trans-moral advocacy of the claims of individual passion, seems a debate between equals. But, on another level, since the fiction of Weiss' play is that it is Sade's script which Marat is reciting, presumably Sade carries the argument. One critic goes so far as to say that because Marat has to double as a puppet in Sade's psychodrama, and as Sade's opponent in an evenly matched ideological contest, the debate between them is stillborn. And, lastly, some critics have attacked the play on the grounds of its lack of historical fidelity to the actual views of Marat, Sade, Duperret, and Roux.

These are some of the difficulties which have led people to charge *Marat/Sade* with being obscure or intellectually shallow. But most of these difficulties, and the objections made to them, are misunderstandings—misunderstandings of the connection between the drama and didacticism. Weiss' play cannot be treated like an argument of Arthur Miller, or even of Brecht. We have to do here with a kind of theater as different from these as Antonioni and Godard are from Eisenstein. Weiss' play contains an argument, or rather it employs the material of intellectual debate and historical reevaluation (the nature of human nature, the betrayal of the Revolution, etc.). But Weiss' play is only secondarily an argument. There is another use of ideas to be reckoned with in art: ideas as sensory stimulants. Antonioni has said of his films that he wants them to dispense with "the superannuated casuistry of positives and negatives." The same impulse discloses itself in a complex way in *Marat/Sade*. Such a position does not mean that these artists wish to dispense with ideas. What it does mean is that ideas, including moral ideas, are proffered in a new style. Ideas may function as décor, props, sensuous material.

One might perhaps compare the Weiss play with the long prose narratives of Genet. Genet is not really arguing that "cruelty is good" or "cruelty is holy" (a moral statement, albeit the opposite of traditional morality), but rather shifting the argument to another plane, from the moral to the aesthetic. But this is not quite the case with *Marat/Sade*. While the "cruelty" in *Marat/Sade* is not, ultimately, a moral issue, it is not an aesthetic one either. It is an ontological issue. While those who propose the aesthetic version of "cruelty" interest themselves in the richness of the surface of life, the proponents of the ontological version of "cruelty" want their art to act out the widest possible context for human action, at least a wider context than that provided by realistic art. That wider context is what Sade calls "nature" and what Artaud means when he says that "everything that acts is a cruelty." There is a moral vision in art like *Marat/Sade*, though clearly it cannot (and this has made its audience uncomfortable) be summed up with the slogans of "humanism." But "humanism" is not identical with morality. Precisely, art like *Marat/Sade* entails a rejection of "humanism," of the task of moralizing the world and thereby refusing to acknowledge the "crimes" of which Sade speaks.

I have repeatedly cited the writings of Artaud on the theater in discussing *Marat/Sade*. But Artaud—unlike Brecht, the other great theoretician of 20th century theater—did not create a body of work to illustrate his theory and sensibility.

Often, the sensibility (the theory, at a certain level of discourse) which governs certain works of art is formulated before there exist substantial works to embody that sensibility. Or, the theory may apply to works other than those for which they are developed. Thus, right now in France writers and critics such as Alain Robbe-Grillet (*Pour un Nouveau Roman*), Roland Barthes (*Essais Critiques*), and Michel Foucault (essays in *Tel Quel* and elsewhere) have worked out an elegant and persuasive anti-rhetorical aesthetic for the novel. But the novels produced by the *nouveau roman* writers and analyzed by them are in fact not as important or satisfying an illustration of this sensibility as certain films, and, moreover, films by directors, Italian as well as French, who have no connection with this school of new French writers, such as Bresson, Melville, Antonioni, Godard, and Bertolucci (*Before the Revolution*).

Similarly, it seems doubtful that the only stage production which Artaud personally supervised, of Shelley's *The Cenci*, or the 1948 radio broadcast *Pour en Finir avec le Jugement de Dieu*, came close to following the brilliant recipes for the theater in his writings, any more than did his public readings of Seneca's tragedies. We have up to now lacked a full-fledged example of Artaud's category, "the theater of cruelty." The closest thing to it are the theatrical events done in New York and elsewhere in the last five years, largely by painters (such as Alan Kaprow, Claes Oldenberg, Jim Dine, Bob Whitman, Red Grooms, Robert Watts) and without text or at least intelligible speech, called Happenings. Another example of work in a quasi-Artaudian spirit: the brilliant staging by Lawrence Kornfield and Al Carmines of Gertrude Stein's prose poem "What Happened," at the Judson Memorial Church last year. Another example: the final production of The Living Theater in New York, Kenneth H. Brown's *The Brig*, directed by Judith Malina.

All the works I have mentioned so far suffer, though, apart from all questions of individual execution, from smallness of scope and conception—as well as a narrowness of sensory means. Hence, the great interest of *Marat/Sade*, for it, more than any modern theater work I know of, comes near the scope, as well as the intent, of Artaud's theater. (I must reluctantly except, because I have never seen it, what sounds like the most interesting and ambitious theater group in the world today—the Theater Laboratory of Jerzy Grotowski in Opole, Poland. For an account of this work, which is an ambitious extension of Artaudian principles, see the *Tulane Drama Review*, Spring 1965.)

Yet Artaud's is not the only major influence reflected in the Weiss-Brook production. Weiss is reported to have said that in this play he wished—staggering ambition!—to combine Brecht and Artaud. And, to be sure, one can see what he means. Certain features of *Marat/Sade* are reminiscent of Brecht's theater —constructing the action around a debate on principles and reasons; the songs; the appeals to the audience through an M.C. And these blend well with the Artaudian texture of the situation and the staging. Yet the matter is not that simple. Indeed, the final question that Weiss' play raises is precisely the one of the ultimate compatibility of these two sensibilities and ideals. How *could* one reconcile Brecht's conception of a didactic theater, a theater of intelligence, with Artaud's theater of magic, of gesture, of "cruelty," of feeling?

The answer seems to be that, if one could effect such a reconciliation or synthesis, Weiss' play has taken a big step toward doing so. Hence the obtuseness of the critic who complained: "Useless ironies, insoluble conundrums, double meanings which could be multiplied indefinitely: Brecht's machinery without Brecht's incisiveness or firm commitment," forgetting about Artaud altogether. If one does put the two together, one sees that new perceptions must be allowed, new standards devised. For isn't an Artaudian theater of commitment, much less "firm commitment," a contradiction in terms? Or is it? The problem is not solved by ignoring the fact that Weiss in *Marat/Sade* means to employ ideas in a fugue form (rather than as literal assertions), and thereby necessarily refers beyond the arena of social material and didactic statement. A misunderstanding of the artistic aims implicit in *Marat/Sade* due to a narrow vision of the theater accounts for most of the critics' dissatisfaction with Weiss' play—an ungrateful dissatisfaction, considering the extraordinary richness of the text and of the Brook production. That the ideas taken up in *Marat/Sade* are not resolved, in an intellectual sense, is far less important than the extent to which they do work together in the sensory arena.

1966

ED BULLINS

The plays of Ed Bullins (b. 1935) share many of the characteristics of the Black Power movement: militancy, righteous rage, and a certain macho bravado (at one point Bullins was named minister of culture of the Black Panther party). He escaped the brutal Philadelphia ghetto in which he had grown up, first through the Navy, then by playwriting on the West Coast. *How Do You Do?* (1965), performed by the San Francisco Drama Circle, won a reputation for obscenity that prevented further efforts from being produced. Despite the play's surrealist elements, Bullins repudiated "absurdism" as an attempt "to perpetuate and adapt the white man's theatre, to extend western reality and finally to rescue his culture and have it benefit his needs." Bullins became the resident dramatist of the New Lafayette Theater in Harlem (1968–73), which banned white reviewers and devoted its efforts to the community struggle against racism. Although Bullins characterized the seven plays he wrote for it as "theatre of reality," he preferred the term "surnaturalism," because he structured them like jazz, orchestrated the speech patterns, and infused them with ritual, eventually composing four full-fledged rituals combining poetry, dance, and light shows. Long before August Wilson, he projected a Twentieth-Century Cycle, 20 short plays dealing with the everyday life of urban African-Americans. Comedy was integral to his scheme: the employment of stereotypes in *The Electronic Nigger* (1968) and the deployment of Aunt Jemima in *The Gentleman Caller* (1970) foretell the Wayans Brothers. However, the only one of Bullins' works to be officially recognized with awards by the white establishment was *The Taking of Miss Janie* (1975), perhaps because it is about an interracial relationship that devolves into a rape.

A Short Statement on Street Theatre

STREET THEATRE is the name given to the play or dramatic piece (i.e., skit, morality or political farce or black "commercial" that subliminally broadcasts blackness) written expressly to be presented upon the urban streets or adapted to that purpose.

When one envisions contemporary America one is compelled to think of faces moving, faces facing upwards, faces in crowds, faces in dynamic mobs—expanses of faces in the streets.

Faces in the streets and in the cities: Broadway, Main Street, Market Street, Broad Street, Grand Avenue, the thoroughfares of New York, Detroit, Providence, Chicago, San Francisco, Philadelphia, Atlanta, L.A.—BLACK FACES.

STREET PLAYS (Black Revolutionary Agit-Prop)

1. Purpose: communicating to masses of Black people. Contact with Black crowds. Communication with diverse classes of people, the Black working class, or with special groups (e.g., winos, pool hall brothers, prostitutes, pimps, hypes, etc.) who would not ordinarily come or be drawn into the theatre.

2. Method: first, draw a crowd. This can be done by use of drums, musicians, recording equipment, girls dancing, or by use of a barker or rallying cry which is familiar and revolutionary and nationalistic in connection (Burn Baby Burn). Or the crowd can be gotten spontaneously where masses of people are already assembled—the play done within the mob (Mob Action—Mob Act): immediacy—or done with a minimum of fanfare, in the street, upon a platform or a flat-bed truck. The truck can carry the equipment and be used as an object of interest if decorated attractively. Also, girls can ride atop the truck and aid in crowd-gathering (fishin'). Monitors can circulate throughout the crowd, distributing printed information, doing person-to-person verbal communicating and acting as guards for the performers and crew (The Black Guard).

3. Types of plays: short, sharp, incisive plays are best. Contemporary themes, satirical pieces on current counterrevolutionary figures or enemies of the people, humorous themes, also children's plays with revolutionary lessons are good street play material. Also, startling, unique material, something that gives the masses identifying images, symbols and challenging situations. Each individual in the crowd should have his sense of reality confronted, his consciousness assaulted.

1968

ELIZABETH HARDWICK

In many respects, the career of Elizabeth Hardwick (1916–2002) resembles those of Mary McCarthy and Susan Sontag: well-educated (Columbia University) and politicized, moving in New York circles, bohemian, liberal, and intellectual; married for a while to a challenging partner (the poet Robert Lowell from 1949 to 1972) and a contributor to *Partisan Review*. Like McCarthy, whose *The Group* she mercilessly parodied as *The Gang*, Hardwick created a stir with a hard-hitting polemic, "The Decline of Book Reviewing," in *Harper's* in 1959. It led to her co-founding *The New York Review of Books* during the newspaper strike of 1962. Hardwick, again like her counterparts, built a reputation for eloquently extolling those she admired and definitively damning those she did not. "I have always written essays as if they were examples of imaginative writing, as I believe them to be," she once said. Whenever the *New York Review* chose to discuss the theatre, as it did irregularly, Hardwick was its rational, skeptical commentator, particularly in the 1960s, when New York was throbbing with experimental work. She wrote discerningly about Sam Shepard and Edward Albee, Joe Chaikin and Jerzy Grotowski, and the new Lincoln Center repertory company. In an important essay of 1966, "The Theater of Sentimentality," she opined that "it is sentimentality that makes a single production in the American theater like every other production." Two years later, in "Notes on the New Theater," she offered a witty conspectus of the current scene, appreciative of the best but unsparing of mediocrity.

Notes on the New Theater

MOST of the plays have gone, the evenings in little downtown theaters dim in the memory. The most interesting works are not interesting to write about: they are bits and pieces of scene and action. Criticism lives on plot, character, and theme. In any case, the drama of real life, the far reaches of tragedy and farce, of noise and silence, seriously compete with the theater, particularly with the avant-garde theater that wants so much to be as interesting and unpredictable as life itself. There is a new style and it has just this minute become old and thus ready for a larger audience. In look and general tone, the new theater is rooted in Hippydom—innocent nudity, ingratiating obscenity, charming poverty . . . love and tolerance. Tom O'Horgan's successful Broadway production of *Hair* is an anthology of the acting and staging ideas developed downtown by groups and persons during the last few years. It is a series of quotations and deeply engrossing in this and every other way. . . .

A foreign journalist recently in conversation: "Yes, yes. I know de names. Amorica Horrah, Som Shopard, de Beard, de LaMama . . . but *describe* the work please, tell me what it is about!"

Well, *Futz* would rather lie with his pig than with Majorie Satz and we must not kill a man for that.

A new style will always be a critique of an old one. The theater of alienation is too austere and intellectual for Hippydom. The aim of the new theater is to *diminish* the distance between stage and audience. In the demonstrations of The Open Theatre, the actors go up and down the aisles, giving out flower petals, smiling and waving. In the end they applaud the audience, as the audience is (hopefully) applauding them. Reciprocal, unifying gestures, suitable to a peace-loving, radicalized mood. These same ideas are used in *Hair*, and also in Tom O'Horgan's brilliant production of *Tom Paine*, by Paul Foster.

The devices of audience participation, at least as we have them now in America, create a great resistance in me. In general I think one might say of The Open Theatre that it always seems to be having too good a time. False relaxation, genial improvisation, a belief in good intentions, youthfulness, verve—a new sentimentality threatens the revolution at its birth.

And participation, this evangelical urging of everyone to somehow take his own part in the theatrical event, is a substitution for a loss we are all trying to forget. An audience will not, perhaps cannot, stay in its seat without some kind of participation in the action on the stage. Since there is often neither character nor plot, in the usual sense, to which we can give the necessary inner attention and sympathy, we are invited to be one with the very vitality, noise and movement before us, to drown ourselves in the episodic. In Jacques Levy's new staging of Sam Shepard's *Red Cross*, he prepares the audience by meanly tormenting it with an excruciatingly loud and un-varied bit of recorded sound. There is no possible separation between you and the sound. No relief until the play begins. And perhaps you are to feel, by a subliminal suggestion, that there is no escape from the play, that you must surrender your-self, as to an engulfment.

It is also interesting that the actors in the La Mama Troupe and The Open Theatre do not look like theater people. They have their pimples and fat, their veins and bruises on display. It is almost a shock to see them assume their roles because we are used to the distance created by the extraordinary beauty of the men and women of the conventional theater. Except for char-acter parts, it was—and literally—unbearable for a heroine to have bad legs; in star roles, defects of skin and skeleton pre-vented belief. But if audience and actors are *together* creating theater, then the stage, like the public, must be open to every-one. It is astonishing, when one considers the exhausting ath-letics of the new stage, that the actors keep their fat, the same peanut-butter fat of the hippies and yippies. In any case, diet-ing is bourgeois and only for the most benighted flagellants of the jet set. The athleticism of the La Mama Troupe is muscle and sinew, not sleekness. It is the old, hefty, plebeian modern dance, somehow Scandinavian, as far as can be from the spi-dery thinness and mystery of the Balanchine ideal.

And yet why is it that the radical friendliness of the new the-ater, the concentration on the external, does not seem as promising this year as last year? Perhaps it has already been re-duced to a group of gestures, and gestures quickly become stale. After the applause and the greetings in the aisle and the not very shining efforts of the cast to break the text with im-provised conversation (*Tom Paine*), that is all. Participation, like alienation, must come from within. It cannot be imposed, demanded. It is a quality of style and of content.

Texts: 1. Tom O'Horgan's staging for La Mama of Sam Shepard's *Melodrama Play* was the most beautiful and inter-esting event of the New York season. The white vinyl set, dar-ingly simple and inspired, matched the ruthlessness of the text. As a playwright, Shepard is a sadist in a garden of masochists.

(How often in off-off Broadway productions one finds, there in the shadow of the obscene and daring, the sweetest little Tennessee Williams, mad at Mom, and on the brink of tears.)

Shepard's texts are images and arias, a harsh kind of pop art, cruel in their unrelieved dazzle and arrogance. The bleakness of his mood liberates the author from the need, felt by so many of the young playwrights, to prod an essentially harmless talent into scenes of violence and ugliness. Shepard's plays are hard to understand—not in the manner of Borges or of literature—but in the manner of Godard movies.

2. In The Open Theatre demonstrations the best scene was based on a text by Brecht and the second best on a tiresome bit of Ionesco that compulsively repeated the word "pig-headed." Still, this would seem to show the limits of improvisation and wordless style.

3. The new theater seldom tries to go beyond Act One. This is prudent. Striking images and sharp scenes have their formal boundaries. If pushed too far they may appear merely facile, as though the ability to create them were endless.

Memories: The Beard, triumphant cunnilingus. Jean Harlow and Billy the Kid are trapped in eternal light and life; they are being and symbol at once, monosyllabic, chained in repetition, their minds in eternity fixed on F . . king. If you cannot speak of *The Beard* as good or bad, you also cannot speak of it as boring. The text uses few words, but those, under the circumstances, fit. Unlike the dutifully fornicating pairs in Updike's *Couples*, Harlow and Billy are, as they say over and over, "divine." They suck their teeth, but needn't go to the dentist; they scream and fight, but never bring to mind domesticity. They are copulating essences, coarse, hoarse, solely occupied by cock and cunt in their blue velvet Heaven—or Hell. The Meaning? In the spare, croaking ugliness of *The Beard*, there is a spare, rasping, grating art. Most of the new theater is farce, and indeed this play is also, but prisons are always sad and eternity is death. In the play's prison of everlasting sex there is an appallingly genuine metaphysical conception. "If we don't do what we want, we're not divine," Billy the Kid says.

Camp: When Queens Collide! Conquest of the Universe! On the stage, exquisite drag queens shriek: Prepare for ramming! Tamberlaine cracks his (her) whip and calls for Bajazeth, a slithering boy in veils. The staging, acting and costuming of these shows, while modest in expense, are also brilliantly imaginative. (Less is more in the theater, too, as anyone who has been to Lincoln Center understands.) In these camp shows, the scenes rush by, mad, more like early silent films than anything else, or perverse, lewd, vaudeville and burlesque. They are a sort of cataract of fantasies—an anarchic energy released by the acceptance of endless play-acting and impersonation. The people—actors, writers, directors—seem to be outside society and, thereby, free to act out a childish theatricality. The texts are fantastic parodies of politics, drama, history, sex, films and the entertainments have, in the end, the profoundest authenticity. This homosexual theater is ritualized, ordered in its reversals, and able, in this way, to liberate a disordered psyche to frenzied creativity. The jokes are special—but then, I suppose, so are those of *Plaza Suite*. Each knows its man.

Old Theater: no relief in sight. *Summertree* by Rod Cowan, performed in the Forum at Lincoln Center. This is a desolating Kraft Music Hall script, badly written, miserably acted, all of it oiled over with a dated, false "seriousness," a hackneyed lyricism—its only excellence the reviews it received from our theater press. The author is a very young man, but his ideas and style are middle-aged. A great tacky tree dominates the stage; everyone, mother and father and son, naturally talks about roots. The play is antique in conception, echoing in every comma and cadence the commercial Broadway style of a few decades ago. It is *Our Town*, with death in Vietnam meretriciously added. To me this evening of shallow sentiments was more painful than any of the ugliness around.

Repertory: We went—up to Cincinnati I think it was—all those many years ago to see Helen Hayes in *Victoria Regina*. Her wrinkles and totters and quavers seemed the very heights of art. The little monarch was as strong, engaging, and enduring in her Power, as Mama in her apron . . . And Miss Cornell, her luscious vowels somewhat watery, round-faced, imposing and "classical."

When you go to the APA you are thrown back to those days of road tours, slapped in the face with the dead fish of memory. The audience is extraordinary, like a dream, days of the New Deal: polite couples, friendly secretaries, out-of-town school teachers. They never appear to have had cocktails or to be impatient for the water fountain at intermission . . . or a little chagrined and insecure as they are amidst the inescapable boredom at Lincoln Center. Instead there is a violent, insistent consensus, a sharing, a conviction. And their star is so aptly, perfectly Helen Hayes: plain, small, determined, a victory of unvarnished Americanism. When she appears on the stage there is a stopping ovation, matinee and evening. When she throws out a little shrug, or offers a funny, upward lift to a word, the audience almost rises to its feet with joy. Indeed, everyone is in such a condition of distraught receptivity that the play can hardly proceed. George Kelly's *The Show-Off*, a work of 1924—a sketch, roundly corny and squarely contrived, allows Helen Hayes to be one of those majorful, down-right, practical American mothers of the respectable lower class. It is difficult to imagine this enterprise if you have not seen it. . . . No more classics!

1968

WILLIAM GOLDMAN

Many people consider *The Season* (1969) to be the best book ever written about the Broadway theatre and its workings. Its author, William Goldman (b. 1931), knew whereof he spoke. After publishing a couple of novels, Goldman with his brother James wrote *Blood, Sweat, and Stanley Poole* (1961), a play that ran for about two months, and then the book and lyrics for the John Kander musical *Family Affair* (1962), which folded after 65 performances. He turned to doctoring scripts in Hollywood, eventually finding success with his own screenplays for *Harper* (1966) and the Oscar-winning *Butch Cassidy and the Sundance Kid* (1969). Buoyed by his new fame and income, Goldman returned to the East Coast to research the live entertainment industry: for one season he saw every show in New York and its immediate vicinity at least once. The resultant study is rich in aphorisms: "Nobody knows anything." "There are no rules on Broadway, and one of them this: Art must be both fresh and inevitable; you must surprise an audience in an unexpected way." Dinner tables and rehearsal rooms buzzed with Goldman's concepts of the snob-hit, the lazy theatre critic, the foolproof way to construct a one-man show, the fiscally inventive producer, the battling creative team. Mutatis mutandis, *The Season*'s findings hold true even now. The book had one unforeseen consequence. The show Goldman had visited most often was *Something Different* by Carl Reiner; the author introduced him to his son Rob Reiner, who offered to film Goldman's fairy-tale *The Princess Bride*. Ten years later it came to pass.

FROM

The Season

The First Week: Murphy's Law

THE Broadway season officially opened the last week in September with the arrival of three plays, *Dr. Cook's Garden*, *Keep It in the Family* and *Song of the Grasshopper*. Before going into the plays in some detail, I'd like to explain just what "the Broadway season" is, since that's what this book is about, one

Broadway season. I'd like to explain, but I can't quite, because I'm really not sure.

Actors' contracts expire on the last day in June, so that is the logical time to say that the season has ended. Only no one does. The season ends the last day in May, according to most theatrical records. No one quite knows why. Theoretically, then, anything that opens at a Broadway house after the first of June should be the start of the new season. But it doesn't work that way. Judy Garland opened at a Broadway house in July, and Hackett and Fisher in August, but they don't count officially, presumably because their shows were vaudeville and not plays. *The Unknown Soldier and His Wife* was a play, and it opened before the "official" opening, but it doesn't count either, presumably because it premièred at Lincoln Center.

At any rate, the bulk of openings takes place in a six-month period. Counting plays that have opened in the sixties, over 75% arrived between the first of October and the end of March. Producers don't much like coming in before October because their feeling is that the audience "isn't thinking theatre." (*Fiddler on the Roof* opened September 22.) And they don't like to open much later than March because business tapers off for the summer. (*Mame* opened May 24; *Wish You Were Here* opened June 25 and ran a year and a half, but that was a long time ago and doesn't count.) Whatever the season is, it began with *Dr. Cook's Garden*.

Broadway professionals instinctively gauge the potential success of an incoming production as soon as it has been assembled. They do this by weighing the skill and track record of the production's chief creative people. And although many September production staffs seem shaky, a pretty impressive bunch was involved in *Dr. Cook's Garden*.

The play was a melodrama by Ira Levin. Levin is the author of *A Kiss Before Dying*, an established classic in the mystery field, and *Rosemary's Baby*, already a best seller by the time rehearsals began. True, these were novels and not plays, but the point can be made that Levin is thoroughly expert at thrilling an audience. He was also not unfamiliar with Broadway success, having done the adaptation of *No Time for Sergeants*. His producer, Arnold Saint-Subber, universally known as "Saint," recently had produced *Barefoot in the Park* and *The Odd Couple*, and would certainly rate on anybody's ten-best list. Burl Ives, an Academy Award winner, was hired to play the title role, costarring with the up-and-coming Keir Dullea. As director: the famous George C. Scott.

Impressive as the names were, there were also worries. Scott is, of course, known as an actor, although he had directed before. However, his most recent Broadway shot at it had closed after two performances. Not only that, the author of the failure was the same Ira Levin, and, as Levin said of *General Seeger*, their earlier attempt at collaboration, "it wound up sort of unpleasantly." Another possible source of trouble was that Levin had never met Ives before Ives was cast.

Scott had met Ives, but only briefly, for an hour, before the play went into rehearsal. And Scott did not cast Ives. That had been arranged by Saint-Subber before Scott came on the scene. Scott was aware that Ives did not see the play the way he did, but he felt that Ives's appeal might make up for any difficulty. "He's bled into acting the last 15 years, and he has a wonderfully warm, folksy quality." Scott was also worried about the play itself, but before getting into that, an explanation of why a warm, folksy actor was needed in the title role.

The melodrama concerns a doctor who kills people instead of curing them. It is set in a small New England town where Dr. Cook is the lone medical man. It's a terrific place to live, and everybody in town is nice-looking. Because Dr. Cook kills all the uglies. Any time a cripple or a bad guy crops up, Dr. Cook sees to it that he mysteriously dies. That is the situation as the play opens.

In the first act, Jim (Keir Dullea), a young doctor who adores Dr. Cook, returns to his home town for a brief visit. The afternoon of his return, through a series of incidents chiefly having to do with an abbreviation system that Dr. Cook uses for both his garden and his patients, Jim comes to realize that the older man is killing people.

In the second act, that night, Jim confronts Cook with the charge. Cook eventually admits the murders, but explains that he's really doing good deeds by getting rid of the mean and the crippled. Jim makes Dr. Cook promise he'll stop with the murders. Dr. Cook agrees. Jim goes upstairs to unpack, and

Dr. Cook gets out a bottle of poison before preparing a little home-cooked dinner for the two of them.

In the last act, Cook poisons Jim, then gives him an antidote after Jim promises to leave Cook alone. Jim then tries to escape, he and Cook struggle, and Cook suffers a heart attack. Jim lets Cook die without trying to save him. The play ends with the possibility of Jim taking up where Cook left off as town doctor.

Scott was bothered that the play was superficial, that it didn't look deeply enough into the moral problems it inevitably raised. He talked about it while we had coffee in his office on East Fifty-fourth Street. Scott was about to turn forty at the time and was already, at least for me, one of the best actors in the world. There are a lot of unusual things about Scott but mainly it is his physical presence. Most male movie stars are stars from the neck up. Physically they are well enough put together, but what makes them magic is something in the face, usually the eyes. There are only two stars who are stars from the neck down, and they are Scott and Burt Lancaster. Both of them somehow give the feeling that if you say the wrong thing to them in an irritating enough way, they will kill you. Lancaster would kill you with grace and speed; Scott would brute-strength you to death. Understand, there is nothing in what Scott does to suggest this: it's just part of him. What he says is in no way menacing. The man is bright and well-read and funny and self-effacing; for someone in his position, the lack of ego is astonishing. He really seems like a marvelous man. You just don't want to mess with him, that's all.

He picked up a copy of *Dr. Cook's Garden*. "There's no scene in here where Cook has doubts about his killing, his gardening of the community. Without it we have a play about a suspicious young man who points the finger and a villain who rationalizes 21 years of killing. It's another Warner Brothers 1940 movie, and I don't want Sydney Greenstreet; I want Pasteur gone wrong. Someone told me Ives saw it as a morality play; I think he's reading in a depth that doesn't exist. I think Ira won't deepen the play because he's worried that it'll confuse what he's written. But how deep should we go? That's my problem."

Levin indeed did not want Dr. Cook wandering around,

wondering whether he'd been justified or not. "It would soften the character," Levin said. And as rehearsal time approached, he also said he wasn't worried. "I'm the eternal optimist; everything's going to be rosy, and not a line is going to be changed."

Saint-Subber was fatalistic before rehearsal. "I've never done a melodrama; that's why this appealed to me. By calling itself a melodrama it says it's not important. It's sleight of hand, a test for me. I've got to assemble just the right ingredients and then pray to God."

On September 11, *Dr. Cook's Garden* held its paid preview. At 8:05 that night, the Belasco lobby was completely empty except for a fat man with a poodle. The lack of activity was explained by a piece of paper taped to the inside of the door: "Preview Canceled." Now a canceled preview is not necessarily a sign of disaster. Trouble, yes; disaster, no. Four days later, more trouble: "George C. Scott quits job as Broadway director." This last from the New York *Times*. The article reported that Scott had bowed out as director because "a disagreement had arisen between Mr. Ives and Mr. Scott." Levin was to be the new director. (Levin had never directed before.) In the *Times* article, Levin praised Scott, saying, "Mr. Scott did 95% of the directorial job, and he did it beautifully too."

Clearly, things were going badly. But when previews finally did begin, things got worse: the audience was laughing in the wrong places. Warner Brothers, which had bought the film rights, was optimistic. A company man told me, "It's coming along, they're making it better; most of the laughs have been gotten rid of." There was a pause. "I never liked the play anyway. I always thought it had problems. But they say that Jimmy Stewart wants to do the picture." Another Warner's man confirmed that: "Stewart does want to do it, and we don't care that it's in trouble. We expected it would be in trouble. But it's going to make a marvelous movie from a not-so-marvelous play."

The critics agreed that it wasn't so marvelous. DR. COOK'S GARDEN IS PLANTED WITH STIFFS headlined Chapman in the *News*, while Clive Barnes, the *Times* man, termed it "ridiculous" and congratulated Scott for not being connected with it any more.

Scott, however, didn't feel much like being congratulated. What had worried him before rehearsals—the play's lack of depth—had never become a problem. What had become a problem was a good deal deeper: Scott could not communicate with Burl Ives. "I couldn't serve him. I refused to let him do those marvelous old vaudeville turns of his. He's got wonderful qualities: he looks great, speaks well, he's warm, easy to love, et cetera. What's working against him is this incredible lack of acting ability. He's a personality, and nothing I did seemed to help. Ira and Saint said, 'Lean on him,' but I'm not a taskmaster. I don't cope, I do what's worse; I turn my back on the situation.

"I just couldn't get through to him—that's not his fault, it's mine—and when I couldn't bear to sit out there and watch him any more, I wanted to fire him. But I didn't have the power. I said to Saint, 'Let me try for Eddie Robinson, Charles Boyer; let me get an actor so I can talk to him.' Saint said, 'Take him to dinner.' Take him to dinner? What the fuck am I gonna say to him? You can't work around a table drinking Bloody Marys.

"When I found I couldn't get rid of Ives, I got rid of myself. I didn't speak to Ira, simply to Saint. I said, 'I'm going,' and he said, 'I'll sue,' and I said, 'Lots of luck.' One of the things I feel worst about is that I didn't even speak to Ira. And that nice thing he said in the *Times* about me. I hadn't even told him good-bye, and he said that. I feel bad about not speaking to Ira. I bought the package, Ives included, and that was my mistake; I should have cast the part myself. Still, I agreed to do it, and the fact that I couldn't bring it off—I was there to serve and I couldn't find a way—I don't feel too fucking good about that either."

Dr. Cook's Garden closed the week it opened at a loss of approximately $100,000. "It's not the money," Saint-Subber said later. He was sitting on the sofa in his office on the fourth floor of his Sixty-fourth Street town house. "The money's not so painful, it's the time. What is it now, November, and I still haven't closed the books on the thing; I'm still burning the scenery and returning the props. The ingredients weren't right; the whole thing was utterly and completely my fault. Maybe I knew that." He shuffled some papers on the table before him. Then he put the papers down. "The most difficult thing to learn is to turn back, to forget the whole thing. Turning back; that's hard."

Months after the play closed, Levin was having a drink in the Algonquin Hotel. "I'm doing a book now," he said. "And after that, another book. And another book." He is a big man, bearded, and his movements are slow. "No, actually, it wasn't a bad experience with *Dr. Cook*. The problem with Scott and Ives only developed a week before Scott left. I thought we were going to be all right, I really did, though looking back now, I can see signs: all the people who didn't show up at the previews to give their reactions. Still, all in all, it wasn't so bad. Saint-Subber didn't come opening night. Anyway, I didn't see him. I don't think I saw him after the day Scott left, when he made a nice speech to the company. Then, of course, Ives got sick. That night we opened, Monday, he hadn't done the play since the Wednesday before. And, of course, I'd never directed. And then the previews being canceled, I'm not so sure that helped, but Ives had the right in his contract to an extra week of rehearsal by canceling the previews, and he exercised the right. And people began meddling—friends of his. Once— right here in the Algonquin—someone said that what the play really needed to work was for Ives to sing a hymn—*a hymn*— he and Keir should sing this hymn, and the other characters should join in. There was this big talk about that idea; they should all sing this hymn, and maybe if they did, it would save the play and . . ." Suddenly he was sitting up straight, staring out across the Algonquin. "Omigod—it was horrible— horrible—and it's all coming back to me now!"

On August 14, Bill Naughton's play *Spring and Port Wine* played its 750th performance in London's West End. That same day, Naughton's *Keep It in the Family* went into rehearsal in New York. Allan Davis directed both plays, and the similarities between the two do not end there: the London smash was about a North Country Englishman, living with his wife and four grown children, who becomes enmeshed in a family row when his youngest daughter refuses to eat a piece of herring. The American play was about a Massachusetts man, living with his wife and four grown children, who becomes enmeshed in a family row when his youngest daughter refuses to eat a piece of mackerel.

Obviously, you don't write two plays about fish fights, and Naughton didn't. The play entering rehearsal, *Keep It in the Family*, was an Americanization of *Spring and Port Wine*. The first question that comes to mind is: Since the play was a smash in London, and a smash is what everyone is after, why change it at all? The answer is that bringing a play over is an enormous gamble because there is little similarity in taste between London and New York. Of all the great hit plays, only one, *Arsenic and Old Lace*, managed to run 1,000 performances in both cities. *Boeing-Boeing*, which went into a fifth year in London, couldn't last three weeks here in 1965. And *The Mousetrap*, which has presently run more than 6,000 London performances, lived less than 200 here, and those at a smaller, off-Broadway house.

The problem of the transplant cannot be exaggerated in relation to Broadway: in the 1967–68 season, almost half of the straight plays were to have foreign origin, the great percentage English. Some plays are brought over unchanged; some are changed enormously but keep their original locale; some are Americanized, as was the case here. The decision of what to do with the transplant is usually left to the producer.

David Merrick, famed in song and story, was the producer of *Keep It in the Family*, and it was apparently his idea to Americanize Naughton's play. He explained why: "Naughton is deeply entrenched in North Country colloquialisms. Both his previous plays, good plays, failed in New York *and* in the West End too. If it's American, the audience can associate with it more."

To effect the transplant, Merrick went after N. Richard Nash, who was to suffer greatly this season. But Nash (best known for his wonderful romantic comedy, *The Rainmaker*) did not take much to the notion. "Merrick asked me to do it and I said 'No.' He said, 'At least go see it,' so I did, and I thought it was successful because of the monumental contribution of the director. I think that without the accumulation of telling detail he put into it, it would have failed in London." Merrick persisted. "Merrick called me in France, and I remember exactly what he said. He said, 'I'll make you two promises:

we'll have the same director, and you don't have to have your name on it. And since you don't, you're now in the position of doing me a favor or not with no harm to yourself. Which do you want to do?'" Later, Nash was to say, "David shouldn't have insisted, and I shouldn't have done it." But he did do it. He agreed to attempt the transplant, even though he hated the play.

Allan Davis, the director, was all in favor of Americanizing the play. "I was here in New York when one of Bill's [Naughton] plays came in; it seemed doomed from Princeton on. With Bill, it's all character. Simple plot. Character. And with North Country working-class people. Now, if the audience can't identify, you're in trouble. Before Merrick, I wanted to make it Manchester Jewish. Sam Levene, Molly Picon— their speech patterns would be close to Manchester Jewish. But Bill didn't like the idea of making them Jewish. Then I thought, 'They ought to be from your Midwest.'"

Nash thought they ought to be from Pennsylvania, and that is where he set it originally. But then one night in London, he and Merrick saw the Irish actor Patrick Magee in *Staircase*. When Merrick suggested Magee for the lead role of the tyrannical father, the family became Catholic and the setting jumped to Massachusetts.

The Americanized version of the play that eventually opened in New York was probably, academically speaking, a better play than the long-running London hit. Not only that, but, according to the director, "the Nash jokes went better than the Naughton jokes." In other words, *Keep It in the Family* was a better and funnier play than the original. It opened in New York on Wednesday, September 27, and closed three days later to a loss of approximately $95,000.

Why?

Before making an educated guess, a small briefing on the story. The English version, *Spring and Port Wine*, centers around a family war between a peculiar man who is a tyrant and his wife and four children. The man is a no-nonsense workingman—his wife has to account for every penny in her weekly accounts—and the four kids, though they may mock him in private, snap to when he is around. "Kids" is really the wrong word here. They are, more accurately, young men and

women, ranging from eighteen to their middle twenties. They
all live at home, and they all pay board to their father for the
privilege of doing so. Then the youngest daughter, nineteen,
and secretly pregnant, stands up to her father: she refuses to
eat a piece of herring. He insists. She will not budge. He decrees
that the same piece of herring will be served to her at every
meal until she does eat it, and until that time, nothing else will
be given her for sustenance. The battle goes on until the eighteen-year-old son feeds the herring to the family cat. The father
berates the boy, who collapses under the pressures. Eventually,
everyone rebels, and the family seems about to split apart. But
in the end, everyone is back together, sadder and wiser. In
other words, the revolt of the younger generation has taken
place in a small mill town outside Manchester, England.

But we've had that revolt in America. Looking around today, can anybody doubt that not only is the battle over, but the
young people won in a walk? So when you put that situation in
America, it all turns phony. What was real and compelling in
England becomes ludicrous in America of the late sixties. How
many families do you know where the four children, ranging
from eighteen to, say, twenty-five, still live at home? *And pay
rent?* What happened with the play here was that the reality,
crucial to the success in London, simply evaporated with the
anachronistic situation.

So, out of town, they set the play back 20 years. The idea of
changing the time had occurred to Merrick, Nash and Davis
while they were still in rehearsal. But the decision then was not
to do anything and hope that the anachronism would work
for the play; in other words, point up that the father was an
old-fashioned man behind the times, and this, theoretically,
would disarm the audience about the falseness of the general
situation.

They opened in Boston to mixed notices. Elliot Norton,
probably the most influential out-of-town reviewer, pointed
out that the play was anachronistic. So then they set it back 20
years, hoping that the audience would think that this was how
the revolt of the young people all started, because of situations
like this.

But though the program said it was 20 years ago, the feel of the play was still 1967, and they couldn't shake it. The whole situation of the children at home paying board just didn't wash. No one believed it, neither the audience nor the creative people. Nash said, "The kids paying board is ridiculous. But it could be made to work. I wanted to investigate it, to see what happens if you bring the problem into the open and have the oldest son complain and the father say to him, 'You're right. Now go find a room of your own.' Then you could see what would happen to the son when he is offered his freedom and is frightened. Then you could really get at what a tyrant is and what a weakling is." But this kind of scene, valid as it may be, would likely have ripped the fragile fabric of a play that was, at heart, pleasant family bickering. Nash was right to want to do the scene, and Merrick and Davis were right in not allowing it.

I talked to Nash the day that *Keep It in the Family* opened. He was at the Sovereign Apartments in Westwood, California, working on the Merrick musical *The Happy Time* and feeling very much like Cassandra. "I don't think the play's going to make it," he said. "I feel even more strongly about its problems now than when I began on it. There isn't a genuine conflict in the whole play—just squabbles. And if you're going to write a comedy, it has to be about something serious."

A few days after the play opened and closed, I spoke again with the director, Allan Davis. He was packing for the trip back home. "The characters just weren't as real as Americans. No one identified with them. We got the facts of American life right—coffee for tea, mackerel for herring—but it all seemed silly here, the fish business. And the audience wouldn't rise to the play . . . they just wouldn't rise."

Then was Americanizing the play a bad idea? Merrick himself wasn't sure. "Could be terrible," he said before the opening. Davis was positive, even after the opening, that they had done the right thing. "We never would have left Boston if the setting had stayed English, I'm sure of it. We absolutely would have closed out of town." No one's ever going to know how, just as no one will ever be able to state an accurate rule about how to effect successfully a transplant without rejection. Certainly the play was a failure here. And certainly a real play had been turned phony. But how much does it matter that it was phony—does anybody actually think *Cactus Flower* is real? And *Cactus Flower* is an Americanized version of a foreign play.

Is it fair to generalize about a phony play failing? Naughton's other plays failed here, including *Alfie*, and they were as real here as in England. Maybe the answer is not to bring over playwrights like Naughton, who seem particularly indigenous to their terrain. There is, after all, no law that states that *all* English hits must be given to us. But as long as English plays keep running, American producers are going to knife each other for the chance to bring them over. And God knows, *Spring and Port Wine* kept on running; it gave its 800th consecutive performance on the day director Davis returned to England. He seemed anxious to get back.

As has already been pointed out, Broadway professionals gauge the potential success of a production as soon as the creative elements have been contractually assembled. Some shows start out big and open big: *The Odd Couple*. Some start out big and open small: *Kean*. Some start out big and just don't open: *Breakfast at Tiffany's*.

On any rating system, the lowest rung is reserved for what is called the "Kiss of Death" production. This is the show that under no conceivable conditions can work. When a show feels like the Kiss of Death, it dies. "Feel" is really the operative word here. Louis Armstrong said of jazz that "if you can't feel it, I can't explain it to you," and the same holds true for the Kiss of Death. It's like Matthew Arnold's touchstone theory in reverse: no matter how talented the individual members of a production may be, the show is just going to lie there. Something in the combination presages disaster.

Song of the Grasshopper was the first Kiss of Death production of the season. Just why this was so cannot be definitively stated. But a brief study of the billing might prove at least a little instructive:

Gene Dingenary   Miranda d'Ancona   Nancy Levering
present
ALFRED DRAKE
in

SONG OF THE GRASSHOPPER
A New Comedy by
ALFONSO PASO
Adapted from the Spanish by
WILLIAM LAYTON and AUGUSTIN PENON
Directed by
CHARLES BOWDEN

Taking them in no particular order: the producers not only had never produced on Broadway before, they had never produced together as a trio before. Granted that everyone has to start somewhere; still, first producers tend to suffer more than experienced producers, who suffer greatly.

The adapters had never written a Broadway play before. They had, however, written a daily radio serial for the Quaker Oats Company, "Don Quakero," which for five years was broadcast to eight South American countries. So far, then, we have two new writers adapting a play for three new producers. The author of the original play, of course, was that incredibly successful figure, the author of 112 produced plays by the age of forty, the famous Alfonso Paso.

Who?

Now the feel is starting to come. If Paso is so famous, why hasn't anyone heard of him? Obviously because his plays haven't been done here. But if he's so successful, why haven't his plays been done here? Whatever the reasons, valid or not, it must be admitted that there hasn't exactly been a bull market for Spanish plays on Broadway lately. The last Spanish smash was _____ (fill in your own blank). There may never have been a Spanish blockbuster, which doesn't mean there couldn't be one, and if *Song of the Grasshopper* was going to make it, the director was going to be crucial. For director: Charles Bowden.

Who?

Charles Bowden, the producer. He produced Williams' *Night of the Iguana* and Camus's *Caligula*, and he worked for 14 years with the Lunts. But in the sixties, he had not been

credited with the staging of a single Broadway production. So
Song of the Grasshopper was going into production with three
untried producers, two untried adapters and one at least recently untried director. For star: Alfred Drake.

No "Who?" here. Alfred Drake is famous, gifted, dynamic,
intelligent, and he is a terrific musical-comedy performer, the
only man active in the theatre who has starred in three blockbuster musicals: *Oklahoma!*, *Kiss Me, Kate* and *Kismet*. But
Song of the Grasshopper wasn't a musical; it was a play. And in
the sixties Drake had appeared twice previously as the chief star
in Broadway plays: *Lorenzo*, boom, four performances and out,
and *Those That Play the Clowns*, boom, four performances and
out.

Total it up: producers who haven't produced, writers who
haven't written, a director who hasn't directed, and a star
whose selection of straight plays, though admittedly adventurous, has not been much in keeping with the public taste. All of
them turning their talents toward a seven-year-old Spanish play.

The Kiss of Death?

On August 9, *Song of the Grasshopper* went into rehearsal,
and nothing concrete was heard of it for a while, one way or
the other, which is standard: along the street, rehearsal period
is generally a time of meaningless gossip, and a play can range
from being a hit to a disaster and back on any given afternoon.
For close to a month, *Song of the Grasshopper* was just one of
any number of shows getting in shape.

Then, on September 6, it opened in Wilmington. There
were two reviews—one pan and one qualified negative. (No
one knew it then, but that was the high point, that qualified
negative.) Business in Wilmington was bad, less than 25% of capacity, which was damaging, but not nearly so damaging as the
troubles that were beginning to surface. By the time the show
opened in Philadelphia a week later, everyone around Broadway knew that there was terrible trouble with *Song of the
Grasshopper*: the authors weren't happy with the show, and the
director wasn't happy with the authors.

All three Philadelphia reviews were negative. Business
dropped to less than 15% of capacity. The producers waived
their third week out of town and came back to New York early.
By now a new writer had been brought in to doctor the script,

and the old writers contemplated not allowing the action. A representative of the Dramatists' Guild was sent in to try and settle things as amicably as possible. A decision was reached that allowed the new writer to work. But this kind of thing can never be amicable. When *Song of the Grasshopper* opened in New York on September 28, the old writers did not attend. "We could not evidence with our presence what was on stage," one of them told me.

The critics, however, did come. One of them thought that "*Song of the Grasshopper* has all the subtlety and charm of a bull stabbing." Another felt that "it is all dullness on the surface and, beneath that, more dullness." Still another: "At least now the season can only get better."

What was this play, and why did it die?

The main character, Aris (Alfred Drake), lives, separated from his wife, in a terrible pit of a house on the outskirts of Madrid. He has a lovely marriageable daughter, assorted younger children from assorted women, plus a crocodile in the bathroom. The latter, a recent addition, was found wandering on the property. He also has no money, the electricity is about to be turned off, the furniture taken away, and his last ten pesetas are invested in a raffle ticket.

He is also absolutely unperturbed about his situation. He knows that somehow everything is going to turn out all right. And the course of the play proves him right: he wins the raffle, returns the crocodile for a reward, etc. He is also reunited with his wife, who comes to see that his world view is the only one that really matters. So what if a grasshopper dies? You can never take away the singing it has done.

Clearly, this is a delicate play and must come across as such if it is to succeed. Said the authors: "The subject of the play was ignored in direction and interpretation; what we got was situation comedy, and the jokes aren't meant to carry it. Imagine *Harvey*, for example, being played as a situation comedy." Said the director: "What happened with us is what frequently happens when you have inexperienced writers: they become defensive; their ego becomes involved." Said Penon, one of the authors: "I had twelve conferences with the director. I thought he understood the play. I still don't know what happened; he talked so brilliantly about it." Said the director:

"The authors thought they should see the finished product at once. In rehearsals they would say, 'Oh, no, no, that's not right,' and I would say, 'Of course it isn't right yet, but it will be by the end of the afternoon.' They made everybody nervous." Said Penon: "He didn't want us at rehearsals; run-throughs we could go to, but rehearsals were something else." Said Bowden, the director: "We didn't really keep them out of the theatre." Said Layton, the other author: "They didn't go so far as to forbid our attending rehearsals—I would have asked to have that put in writing—but there was that trouble in the second week of rehearsal and . . ." (What happened, as closely as it can be reconstructed, is that one of the actresses had a line she didn't like: "I feel beastly as ever." She asked the writers for a new line. One of them gave it to her: "I feel as low as ever." But he didn't go through the director to do it, and one of the producers said he had committed a cardinal sin of the theatre. After that, the authors were isolated from the actors. As a general rule, authors should not do anything without first getting the permission of the director. But this infraction, though infraction it clearly was, seems so slight compared with the repercussions that an educated guess would be that there was a desire to get the authors out of rehearsals, and this was as convenient an excuse as any.)

Communication, already strained, snapped. The writers were kept away from the director. Any notes the writers had were sent to one of the producers, who then explained everything to the director. Naturally enough, there is a difference of opinion today about how the producers behaved throughout all this. The director said, "They were fantastically co-operative and well organized," while the writers felt, "They acted out of panic."

What the producers did, as has been noted, was to bring in a doctor. "The writers took it so personally," Bowden said. "They felt it was a personal affront. But you've got to learn to take criticism in this business. I had several dear friends of mine down to see the show, and they all agreed that the trouble was with the script, not my direction." After Bowden's friends had made their judgment, a new writer was sent for. The old writers said, "The new man was a friend of Bowden's.

He was brought in before we were consulted. He added jokes; we protested, vigorously, but . . ."

Now these are all men of good will, remember, and no one was setting about to sabotage anyone or anything. And remember, too, that this was a simple play, a play, as author Penon put it, "about a man who believes in Providence." He's got no money, he's deep in debt, there are mouths to feed, yet somehow it's all going to turn out. This is, naturally, a debatable notion, and during rehearsal period, Bowden and Alfred Drake wanted Aris to be given some kind of minor occupation for when Providence failed him—nothing big—maybe tutoring or doing small articles for the local papers. Bowden put it this way: "I feel he writes poems or takes in students. Occasionally. I don't think he does it for any set fee, but I think he does it."

At this point, I would like to talk briefly about the nature of Spanish and Portuguese comedy. (Ignore this paragraph; look at the one above.) Spanish comedy differs from Portuguese comedy in that . . . (Reread that paragraph above; do you see it?) . . . and, of course, one cannot estimate the effect of Franco and his consequent censorship . . . (You've got to have it by this time: the adapters were writing *a play about a man who believes in Providence*, while the director was directing *a play about a man who has an occupation for when Providence fails him*.)

That's the ball game. Right there. It's all over, and if you don't see why, the following is meant to put it in relief. We're writing a play about Columbus and Isabella. Scene: a great hall. Isabella on the throne at one end, Columbus kneeling before her. The room is lined with courtiers.

COLUMBUS
(*Rising*)
Your Majesty, I need three of your ships.

ISABELLA
(*Taken aback*)
Three . . . ? For what purpose, brave mariner?

COLUMBUS
(*He pauses, looks at the mocking courtiers. Then—a burst—*)
To sail around the world!

ISABELLA
Around the world? Fool, you'll sail clean off the edges.

COLUMBUS
(*Passionately*)
There aren't any edges, Your Majesty.

ISABELLA
How can there be no edges since the world is flat?

We have now arrived, as the hippies say, at the nitty-gritty. What can Columbus tell her? His existence is based on the lunatic notion that the world is round; and that is what makes him different from everybody else. (Just as Aris' thinking that Providence will take care of him *always* is what makes him different from everybody else.) Can Columbus say he's invented an edge rounder? No, he can't, because he's not a liar and because he hasn't invented one, and if he says he has, she'll sure ask to see the damn thing, and then where is he? Columbus could say that he isn't 100% sure: in other words, sometimes he thinks the world is round, but when he doesn't think it's round, he thinks it's flat. That is a perfectly valid line of reasoning, and you could write him that way, and if you did you would be writing about *a man who has doubts*. But that is exactly what the adapters of *Song of the Grasshopper* were *not* writing about. *Their man believed.* His entire existence is coupled with that mad belief: Providence will take care of me!

I know of no way of indicating the importance of this seemingly trivial disagreement between the writers and the director. It's like the Pentagon: no matter how big you're told it is, when you get there, it's bigger. The disagreement becomes reflected in every conceivable aspect of the production. Example: Aris, the believer, is a total innocent, and you get Alfred Drake to play him. Impossible. Drake is sophisticated, vital, a man who can't stand still. Aris is content to lie in his hovel with a crocodile in the head and wait for God to smile on him. Drake can't play that. Drake is Petruchio; he has to make things happen.

The breakdown of communication that began to surface in

rehearsal was present from the beginning. But the crucial questions between the creative personnel simply were not asked. Why weren't they? A guess would be because everybody probably thought that everybody else understood. This kind of communications problem happens constantly on Broadway, and not just to newcomers. Bob Fosse, the experienced and wonderfully gifted musical-comedy director, said, "I was doing a show once; we had opened out of town, and the reviews were terrible—*terrible*—and we were sitting around, and I was talking and the book writer was talking and the composer was talking, and it turned out we all saw three different shows. In our heads. We were all working on three completely different musical comedies. Now why didn't we find that out sooner? We just didn't—don't ask me why." One of Jerome Robbins' great strengths is his ability to ask anyone any question, no matter what. Sheldon Harnick, the lyricist for *Fiddler*, who worked with Robbins on that musical, says this: "Any show should be one man's vision. When Robbins takes over a show, it's his vision in every department. He drives the set designer crazy, he drives the orchestrater crazy, he has a total vision of what he wants. He presses you and presses you on every point, no matter how trivial, until it isn't trivial any more."

Song of the Grasshopper opened Thursday night, September 28, and closed two nights later, at a loss of its entire investment, about $100,000. Closings are generally sad; some become funereal. But the ending of *Song of the Grasshopper* was somehow angry; it was as if you were only there because you'd lost a bet. At 8:29 there was a total of 18 people in the lobby, counting the bartender. A woman with an eye patch walked by. At a hit she would have looked mysterious; here she just seemed wounded.

Inside, an usher was staring at the painfully empty orchestra. "Sit anywhere you want," she told me. "It's really a shame. No one walked out during the previews. It's just a shame 'cause it's not as bad as they say. It's no Pulitzer prize but . . ." She handed me my program, and then suddenly she was mad, her voice just the least out of control as she unloaded on Clive Barnes, who had cursed in his review of the play. "He said it was worse than *Dr. Cook's Garden*. He said 'goddam.' He used that word. In the *Times*."

She stopped then, confused, staring front, for Murphy's Law ("Everything that can go wrong will go wrong"), which had been operating all week long in the theatre, was still going full blast. Because right then, with the house lights still on bright, with a few ushers slowly leading a few people down the carpeted aisles, at 8:42 P.M., five minutes before the curtain went up, the curtain went up. Not all the way up. Probably no more than 15 feet. But there was old Alfred Drake on stage, not doing much of anything, just waiting for the curtain to go up, and he turned slowly front, and there we were, the audience—*the audience!*

And I think I'll always remember *Song of the Grasshopper* like that, caught with its curtain up, its numbed star staring around, the audience staring around, everybody staring around, all of us confused, a piece of Pirandello in the night.

1969

JOHN LAHR

Bert Lahr was one of America's great clowns. Tested in vaudeville and burlesque, his baggy-faced pugnacity and strangulated cry "Gnung-gnung-gnung" enlivened many a musical comedy and revue in the 1930s and '40s. The movies proved less congenial to his brand of broad buffoonery, but he won enduring affection as the Cowardly Lion in *The Wizard of Oz* (1938). Lahr's waning career took an upward turn in 1956, when he agreed to play Estragon in the U.S. premiere of Beckett's *Waiting for Godot*. Although the Miami opening was an unqualified disaster, the revival in New York turned into a personal triumph. Brooks Atkinson spoke for most of his colleagues when he wrote that "long experience as a bawling mountebank has equipped Mr. Lahr to represent eloquently the tragic comedy of one of the lost souls of the earth."

Lahr's son John (b. 1941) experienced a similar reversal of fortune. Educated at Yale and Oxford, serving as dramaturge at the Guthrie Theater (1968) and Lincoln Center (1969–71), he remained a minor player until he published a biography of his father, *Notes on a Cowardly Lion*, in 1970. The acclaim that greeted that book brought him to prominence: he published well-received studies of Joe Orton, "Dame Edna Everage," and Noël Coward and several volumes of his reviews from *Evergreen Review*, *The Nation*, and *The Village Voice*, frequently appeared as a talking head on television documentaries about popular entertainment, and in 1992 was appointed primary dramatic critic for *The New Yorker*. While stressing the importance of the review as a record of an ever-changing performance, Lahr also sees it as an act of creation. The "theater is psychology translated to behavior. It's all the psychology of individualism, the losing of the self." To capture this mercuriality, the critic must eschew taking notes and "bring the event to the reader" with prose that has "to pop, to empower, to get a lot of interest."

FROM

Notes on a Cowardly Lion

Waiting for Godot intrigued my father. No intellectual discussion intensified his appreciation. The play which would have a revolutionary effect on ideas and form in contemporary drama, was discussed, instead, with others whose advice he had always heeded in musical-comedy matters—with Jack O'Brian, the columnist and ex-drama critic, and Vaughn Deering, a friend and professor of drama at Fordham University who occasionally helped him rehearse. Both of them counseled Lahr to do it. However, the final and most forceful voice of approval came from Mildred, who had long advocated that her husband extend his talents into other areas of theater.

He was tough to convince. Without academic training he felt unsure of the play's complexities and of his ability to stamp it with his own personality. Even while deliberating whether to perform the play, he seemed to delight in its mystery and theatricality. "When I first read it, I realized that this was not stark tragedy. Beneath it was tremendous humor, two men trying to amuse themselves on earth by playing jokes and little games. And that was my conception."

Millions of critical words have been lavished on *Waiting for Godot*; Lahr conceived of it as a vision of action that reduced itself to a few simple sentences of explanation. While friends, and later the press, reacted to a low comic entering the intellectual arena with amusement, Lahr understood the play not from a literary point of view but strictly from a theatrical one. Once, while still undecided, he came into my room and read these lines:

Estragon:	In the meantime let us try and converse calmly, since we are incapable of keeping silent.
Vladimir:	You're right, we're inexhaustible.
Estragon:	It's so we won't think.
Vladimir:	We have that excuse.
Estragon:	It's so we won't hear.
Vladimir:	We have our reasons.
Estragon:	All the dead voices.
Vladimir:	They make a noise like wings.
Estragon:	Like leaves.
Vladimir:	Like sand.
Estragon:	Like leaves.
	Silence.

"He writes beautifully, doesn't he? His meter—he's a poet, isn't he? His rhythm is crisp; there's meter to it, same as in poetry. It's not cumbersome; it's in character. It flows."

That was all he ever said to indicate his appreciation of Beckett. If he had a reassuring sense of the play's poetry in private, he did not trust the weighty impact of its repetition so easily on stage. In the Miami tryout, he wanted to cut the lines he read to me so admiringly. Years later, talking to my Hunter College drama class, he recollected how sad and beautiful that dialogue was, adding, "And after the last repartee, there was a momentary silence in the audience and then laughter, as if they had held their breath and suddenly been allowed to relax."

As an actor, he understood the subtleties of the spoken word without ever having read poetry. He never read any other Beckett plays or novels. Lahr's simple words reflect an understanding of the pathos and meaning of the play that went beyond critical generalities. Lahr lived with silences; his understanding of language was commensurate with Beckett's precise, philosophical use of it. His appreciation of the playful potential of words went back to his burlesque days and his use of the malaprop; at the same time, Lahr was conscious of his own inability to make words convey his exact meaning. He didn't like to talk merely to pass time; he would rather remain silent—even with his family. Yet there were reasons why others talked—a motive that in his own shyness he understood. In a radio play, *Embers*, which Lahr would never read, Beckett gave an insight into the significance of his particular type of dramatic language. Talking about the sea, a man (Henry) remarks to his wife, Ada—

> . . Listen to it! . . . It's not so bad when you get out on it . . . Perhaps, I should have gone into the merchant navy.
>
> *Ada:* It's only the surface, you know. Underneath all is as quiet as the grave. Not a sound. All day, all night, not a sound.

The languid rhythm of Beckett's speakers, the endless gabble of trivialities between Vladimir and Estragon, creates precisely the surface activity that Beckett's characters refer to in the sea. The insight is also embedded in the laughter of Lahr's comedy scenes, from the inane blathering of the cop to cover his own embarrassment to the TV announcer's verbosity that reinterprets the baseball player's simple sentences. Lahr talked about playing Beckett "instinctively," a term by which he hints that Beckett spoke to his own immediate and intense private experience.

If he understood the play's poetry in a curiously unacademic way, his faith in Beckett as a craftsman came only after struggling through the play's interior structure on stage. "You never laugh at a blind man on stage or people with their legs cut off. But Beckett wrote in Pozzo and made such a heavy out of him that, by the second act, when he comes back blind, we play games with him. He falls down, he cries for help. Vladimir and Estragon are on the stage. We taunt him. We ask him how much he'll give us. We slide. We poke—you understand? The audience screams. If Beckett didn't know what he was doing, as so many people at the time claimed, he wouldn't have put the show in that running order. When I read it, and saw how deliberately he had placed Pozzo in the script, which was against all theatrical convention, I wasn't sure it would work. When I played it, I realized how brilliantly he had constructed the play. I always thought it was an important play—I just didn't realize how important."

Lahr decided to do the play, with the idea that if it worked well Myerberg would bring it to Broadway. On the surface, Lahr was pleased; but from the beginning his uneasiness with intellectual ideas, his fear of failure, the strange format of the show, and a young director bred anxiety. Myerberg had contracted with Alan Schneider to direct the production after Garson Kanin, his first choice, backed out at the last minute. Schneider, with only two Broadway credits—*Anastasia* and *The Remarkable Mrs. Pennypacker*—had been recommended to Myerberg by Thornton Wilder, who had seen Schneider's revival of *The Skin of Our Teeth*, which Myerberg had originally produced in 1943. Beckett's play extended Wilder's early fascination with the philosophical and dramatic consequences of the flux of time. Beckett was hard-headed where Wilder was sentimental, poetic where Wilder was folksy.

Schneider recounted his first introduction to Beckett's work and also his meeting with Beckett in an article for the *Chelsea Review* (Autumn 1958). As the director who later became Beckett's chief interpreter in the United States as well as the director of Edward Albee's major plays, Schneider's reactions are important. Beckett's significance in America at the time was limited to a small coterie of intellectuals; only after *Waiting for Godot* did he become the important literary and dramatic voice in America that he already was in Europe.

Schneider met Beckett; Lahr did not. Schneider saw the play in other countries; Lahr did not. Schneider's experience with Beckett is important because, as director, his vision of the play and how to convey Beckett's meaning were different from what finally evolved in Lahr's interpretation.

In 1954, Schneider saw *Waiting for Godot* in both its Zurich and Paris versions. Captivated by the play's strength of thought, he set about tracking down the seclusive Beckett. As he chronicles his exasperating search—

"Finally a friendly play-agent informed me that the English language rights had been acquired by a British director, Peter Glenville, who was planning to present the play in London with Alec Guinness as Vladimir and Ralph Richardson as Estragon. Besides, added the agent, the play was nothing an American audience would take—unless it could have a couple of topflight comedians like Bob Hope or Jack Benny kidding it, preferably with Laurel and Hardy in the other two roles. An American production under those circumstances seemed hopeless, and Mr. Beckett was as far removed as Mr. Godot himself. I came home to New York and went on to other matters.

"The next spring [1955] I had occasion to remember once more. *Godot* received its English language premiere in London, not with Guinness and Richardson at all, but with a non-star cast at London's charming Arts Theater Club. Damned without exception by daily critics, it was hailed in superlatives by both Harold Hobson and Kenneth Tynan (The Atkinson and Kerr of London) in their Sunday pieces, and soon became the top conversation piece of the English season. At the same time, the English translation was published by Grove Press in New York.

"I read and re-read the published version. Somehow on its closely spaced printed pages, it seemed cold and abstract, even harsh, after the remarkable ambience I had sensed at the Babylone. When a leading Broadway producer asked me what I thought of its chances, I responded only half-heartedly. Intrigued as I had been, I could not at the moment imagine a commercial production in Broadway terms.

"One day in the fall of that same year I was visiting my old Alma Mater, the University of Wisconsin, when to my utter amazement I received a long-distance phone call from producer Michael Myerberg asking if I would be interested in directing *Waiting for Godot* in New York. He had Bert Lahr and Tom Ewell signed for the two main roles . . . It was like Fate knocking at the door. After a desperate search in practically every bookshop in Chicago, I finally located a copy, stayed up all night on the train studying it with new eyes, and arrived back to New York to breathe a fervent 'yes' to Myerberg.

"Followed a series of conferences with Lahr and Ewell, both of whom confessed their complete bewilderment of the play; and with Myerberg, who insisted that no one could possibly be bewildered, least of all himself. He did think it might be a good idea, however, for me to see the English production, perhaps stopping off on the way to have a talk with Beckett himself. To say that I was pleased and excited would be a pale reflection of the reality. And my elation was tempered only by the fear that Beckett would continue to remain aloof—he had merely reluctantly consented to a brief meeting with 'the New York director.'

"At any rate, a week later, I found myself aboard the U.S.S. *Independence* bound for Paris and London—and by coincidence, the table companion and fellow conversationalist of Thornton Wilder, who was on his way to Rome and elsewhere. He greatly admired Beckett, considered *Godot* one of the two greatest modern plays (the other one, I believe, Cocteau's *Orpheus*), and openly contributed his ideas about an interpretation of the play which he had seen produced both in France and Germany. In fact, so detailed and regular were our daily meetings that a rumor circulated that Wilder was rewriting the script, something which later amused both authors considerably. What was true was that I was led to become increasingly familiar with the script, both in French and in translation and discovered what were the most important questions to ask Beckett in the limited time we were to have together. More specifically, I was now working in the frame of reference of an actual production situation—a three-week rehearsal period, a 'tryout' in a new theater in Miami, and, of course, Bert and Tommy. It wasn't Bob Hope and Jack Benny, but the Parisian agent of two summers before had been correct so far. Was she also going to prove correct in terms of the audience response?

"Beckett at that time had no phone—in fact, the only change I've noticed in him since his 'success' is the acquisition of one—so I sent him a message by pneumatique from the very plush hotel near the Etoile where Myerberg had lodged me. Within an hour, he rang up saying he'd meet me in the lobby—at the same time reminding me that he had only an hour or so to spare. Armed with a large bottle of Lacrima Christi as a present from both Wilder and myself, I stationed myself in the rather overdone lobby and waited for the elusive Mr. Beckett to appear. Promptly and very businesslike he strode in, his tall athletic figure ensconced in a worn raincoat; bespectacled in old-fashioned steel rims; his face was as long and sensitive as a greyhound's. Greetings exchanged, the biggest question became where we might drink our Lacrima Christi; we decided to walk a bit and see if we could come up with a solution. Walk we did, as we have done so many times since, and talk as we walked—about a variety of matters, including, occasionally, his play. Eventually, we took a taxi to his skylight apartment in the sixth arrondissement and wound up finishing most of the bottle. In between I plied him with all my studiously arrived-at questions as well as all the ones that came to me at the moment; and he tried to answer as directly and honestly as he could. The first one was 'Who or what does Godot mean?' and the answer was immediately forthcoming: 'If I knew I would have said so in the play.' Sam was perfectly willing to answer any questions of specific meaning or reference, but would not —as always—go into matters of larger or symbolic meanings, preferring his work to speak for itself and letting the supposed 'meanings' fall where they may.

"As it turned out, he did have an appointment; so we separated but not before we had made a date for dinner the next evening. On schedule, we had a leisurely meal at one of his favorite restaurants in Montparnasse, then I persuaded him to come along with me to a performance of *Anastasia* at the Theatre Antoine . . . it turned out to be very artificial and old-fashioned and Sam's suffering was acute. Immediately after the last curtain we retired to Fouquet's, once the favorite café of his friend and companion James Joyce . . . Shortly before dawn—since I had a plane to catch for London—we again separated. But not before Sam had asked me if it would be additionally helpful if he joined me in London at the performances of *Godot* there. He had not been to London in some years, had never liked it since his early days of poverty and struggle there, but he would be willing to come if I thought it helpful! I could hardly believe what I heard. Helpful!

"Two days later, Sam came into London incognito. . . . That night, and each night for the next five days, we went to see the production of *Godot*, which had been transferred by this time to the Criterion in Piccadilly Circus. The production was interesting, though scenically over-cluttered and missing many of the points which Sam had just cleared up for me. My fondest memories are of Sam's clutching my arm from time to time and in a clearly heard stage whisper saying, 'It's ahl wrahng! He's doing it ahul wrahng!' about a particular bit of stage business or the interpretation of a certain line. Every night after the performance, we would compare what we had seen to what he had intended, try to analyze why or how certain points were being lost, speak with the actors about their difficulties. Every night also, we would carefully watch the audience, a portion of which always left during the show. I always felt that Sam would have been disappointed if at least a few hadn't.

"Through all this, I discovered not only how clear and logical *Godot* was in its essences, but how much and how easy to know Sam was, how friendly beneath his basic shyness. I had met Sam, wanting primarily to latch on to anything which might help make *Godot* a success on Broadway. I left him, wanting nothing more than to please him. I came with respect; I left with a greater measure of devotion than I have ever felt for a writer whose work I was engaged in translating to the stage. . . ."

Myerberg's conception of *Waiting for Godot*, after seeing the London production, was more certain than Schneider's. Where Schneider had questioned its commercial nature, Myerberg was immediately impressed at the play's ability to hold an audience despite a production he considered, in general, to be mediocre. "Let's face it, *Waiting for Godot* is not everybody's cup of tea. It's a theatrical property; it might be called a great play. I call it a theater piece. I don't know what a play is myself. Everybody else seems to know, but I don't. I look for material that can be put on the stage and hold an audience for an evening. I don't know what a play is. . . ."

Schneider, in his article, registered little surprise at the suggestion of two stand-up comedians like Jack Benny or Bob Hope playing Vladimir and Estragon. Myerberg's first reaction was to envision Lahr in the role of Estragon. "Knowledge of performers is part of the producer's equipment. I have a kind of card index mind which riffles through them. I get one casting in my mind and that's the casting I go for. When I contracted for the play, I said 'I'll produce it only if I can get Bert Lahr to play in it. How I'll sell it to him, I don't know. If I don't get him, I won't produce it.'"

Myerberg's cunning led him to another important decision that had a bearing on the final performances. He would do *Waiting for Godot* on Broadway, not, as in London and Paris, in the experimental non-commercial theater clubs or off-Broadway houses. The choice, which astounded many, was not daring to a producer of Myerberg's frame of mind. "*Waiting for Godot* was a revolutionary play that had never been done here. Beckett had not really been introduced to the public. I regarded the problem of production this way: either you do it or you don't. I don't feel you can have the opportunity unless 1) you have the proper stage, 2) you attract the proper actors. I couldn't have gotten the final cast I got—E. G. Marshall, Kurt Kasznar, Alvin Epstein, and Lahr—for off-Broadway. It's just a question of professionalism. You couldn't have done the play off-Broadway on the scale it demanded. After it's established, then it can be done any place."

Myerberg's statement is an interesting backward glance; but

the initial tryout of *Waiting for Godot* was handled in such a myopic fashion as to suggest that even Myerberg, for all his assurance, did not quite know what he had on his hands.

Myerberg himself admits that mistakes were made. He had mounted the play on a highly stylized set that not only made it difficult for the actors to move, but also detracted from the words and action. As Myerberg later told *The New York Times*, "I went too far in my effort to give the play a base of popular acceptance. I accented the wrong things in trying to illuminate corners of the text I felt were left in shadow in the London production. For instance, I cast the play too close to type. In casting Bert Lahr and Tom Ewell I created the wrong impression about the play. Both actors were too well known in specific types of performance. The audience thought they were going to see Lahr and Ewell cut loose in a lot of capers. They expected a farcical comedy, which *Waiting for Godot*, of course, is not."

Myerberg had sold out the two-week Miami engagement a month in advance by advertising Beckett's play in the finest tradition of P. T. Barnum. The people who rushed to the box office had Myerberg's advance notice humming in their minds.

> Bert Lahr, the star of *Burlesque*, and Tom Ewell, the star of *The Seven Year Itch* in the laugh sensation of two continents—Samuel Beckett's *Waiting for Godot*.

(By the time Myerberg brought his controversial property to New York he had learned how to sell it. He ran an ad in *The New York Times* asking for seventy thousand intellectuals to support the play and warning audiences who wanted casual entertainment to stay away. His statement to the *Times* about going too far in giving "the play a popular base" is a ludicrous understatement.)

No one was pleased about opening at the Cocoanut Grove Playhouse in Miami except Myerberg, who had covered expenses with a large guarantee. Schneider, unhappy with the set and with Miami, liked the idea of doing *Waiting for Godot* with Lahr and Ewell in principle, but confesses "I was terrified of doing the play with stars. I was scared that ego problems would get in the way of the play."

Lahr has his own recollections. "Playing *Waiting for Godot* in Miami," he says, "was like doing *Giselle* at Roseland." He was skeptical about opening there, but never completely pessimistic. He brought his fishing tackle and his family to Florida, expecting to enjoy a little of both during the run.

Schneider is haunted by the anxiety of the first production. "We were all babes in the wood. We were groping around there with our shoes off." Even Lahr, riddled with doubts and petrified of public rejection, clung vehemently to comic simplicity that made sense out of (what seemed to him) intellectual confusion. His childlike recalcitrance caused more uneasiness than he would ever realize. Schneider sensed the problem that would materialize in Miami as he wound up his meeting with Beckett in Europe. "Bert was terrified of it from the beginning. I kept getting telegrams from Myerberg urging me to change my ship reservations and fly home":

LAHR AND EWELL NERVOUS AND DISTURBED URGE YOU
FLY BACK FRIDAY.   MYERBERG

LAHR SLOW STUDY STILL FEEL YOU SHOULD RETURN BY
AIR AT ONCE.   MYERBERG

Finally, Lahr himself tried to use his own powers of persuasion:

WE FEEL VERY NERVOUS ABOUT SHORT REHEARSAL
THINK IT URGENT BEGIN REHEARSAL MARCH 5TH
PLEASE MAKE EVERY EFFORT TO RETURN TO MAKE IT
POSSIBLE AS SO MUCH SCRIPT AND BUSINESS TO LEARN
APPRECIATE MUCHLY CABLE ARRIVAL   BERT LAHR

Lahr's relationship with Schneider is a study in misunderstanding, their association a wry commentary on Beckett's play. Like *Waiting for Godot*, it emphasized not only the limitations of language to convey experience but also the compulsive love-hate relationship of people engaged in a single enterprise. Vladimir and Estragon play a game to survive life. Lahr did not understand Schneider's language; and Schneider's inexperience and new conception of Beckett would not allow for the comic leeway that Lahr insisted would make the play "work." At the root of the problem was Schneider's understanding of the symbolic movement of the two main characters and Lahr's lack of it. Schneider's attitude, on one level, is accurate; but Lahr's intuition for play grated with Schneider's idea of its rhythm. "Estragon is rooted in the earth. Restless. Uncomfortable. Hungry. Rooted. Vladimir is the wanderer. He's curious. He's the Intellect. I would have to keep saying to Bert on stage 'Get back there. Stay on your mark.' Bert didn't like to do comedy standing still. I kept saying, 'Bert, you can't move around so much, remember Estragon's got sore feet.'"

In saying this, Schneider was not recognizing another symbolic movement, one closer to the rhythms of human relationships, which also clearly pervades Beckett's play. Beckett's stage directions indicate a flexibility and possibility for movement that Schneider did not see, but which Lahr suspected and could not verbalize.

(1)   They look at each other, recoiling, advancing, their heads on one side, as before a work of art, trembling towards each other more and more, then suddenly embrace, clasping each other on the back. End of embrace. Estragon no longer supported, almost falls.

(2)   They listen, huddled together. . . . They relax and separate.

(3)   . . . Exit Estragon left, precipitately. . . . He looks up, misses Estragon. . . . He moves wildly about the stage. Enter Estragon left, panting. He hastens to Vladimir, falls into his arms.

(4)   He draws Estragon after him. Estragon yields, then resists. They halt.

(5)   They turn, move apart, turn again and face each other.

Vladimir and Estragon come together out of necessity, yet the closer they get the more impossible it is for them to unite. They grope toward one another, then move away with the frantic momentum of burlesque comedians. Beckett's stage directions chronicle their friendship—a pantomime of loneliness and cowardice that Lahr had distilled in his own comic world through the lion, the prize fighter, the cop. The tramps' movement is never able to resolve itself and end in a lasting embrace. They bounce back from their pratfalls unaware of their plight.

Comedy without movement was impossible for Lahr. He balked at Schneider's dicta, at being asked to harness his energy. Lahr was suspicious and ignorant of the allegorical reasons at the basis of Schneider's demands. When the director would go on stage with masking tape and place strips where he was to stand, Lahr was shocked. "I began to think to myself—this is all wrong. It's stark. This is the wrong approach to the play. It's dire; it's slow. There isn't any movement."

Schneider's reverence for Beckett may have acounted for his inflexible direction. His intentions and Lahr's were at a Mexican standoff. Lahr felt stifled; Schneider felt hostile. Finally, Lahr confronted him: "'This is a comedy scene. These are music hall bits.' I could see it. I could see it because that was my basic training—burlesque. He said, 'I don't know anything about humor.'"

At that moment, the fate of the play seemed sealed in Lahr's imagination. "He was convinced it was his play from the beginning," says Schneider: "My problem working with him was to make him realize that there couldn't be a 'top banana' (a word he kept using) in a show of this kind. The play was a game of give and take, a partnership. Lahr kept insisting, 'There's a feed, and there's a joke.'"

The experience was painful, but Lahr would learn from his mistakes as would Schneider, who would go on to become one of the most successful directors of contemporary theater. However, in Miami the production of *Godot* met with conflicts at every turn.

Schneider was saddled with Myerberg's stylized set—a mound that faced the audience like a parabola. It hindered the actors' movements, and made the stage environment uncomfortable. Schneider was also disturbed by the fact that Lahr and he were staying in the same hotel, a tactical mistake for anyone who could not cope with Lahr's compulsive worry. Lahr would knock on Schneider's door at six a.m., already groomed and fretting over the day's work. "He wanted to discuss the play," Schneider recalls. "He didn't want to talk about meaning. He would ask me. 'Am I right for it?' 'Is it going to work?' 'Are we going to be a success?'"

Lahr's predictable perfectionism was matched by a predictable hypochondria. He was extremely difficult, beset nearly every day with a new ailment. A doctor was finally hired to sit in on rehearsals. Schneider felt Lahr's continual interruptions for medical reasons were symptomatic of something else. "We had more doctors around that rehearsal hall than I've ever seen. It was always something about his throat, his voice, an ache here or there. It all had to do with the fact that ultimately he didn't want to be there."

Schneider's insistence that he refrain from using old mannerisms made Lahr particularly nervous. The pressure was upsetting to him, but ultimately more creative than he acknowledges. Lahr originally wanted to substitute "gnong, gnong, gnong," for Beckett's pointed and pathetic "Ah!" He argued, but Schneider prevailed. "If he had inserted his old catch phrase, the tone would have been something else. It would have reminded everyone of *The Wizard of Oz*." Schneider, aware of the uniqueness of Beckett's play, did not want it filled with Lahr's famous musical-comedy mannerisms from the past. Lahr found new ones that matched his body's potential and the play's content.

Schneider's battles to preserve the text seemed incongruous to Lahr, who wanted to approach experimental theater on the only basis of experience he possessed—the musical-comedy stage. The ultimate arbiter of value was the audience. Anything that was not clear to the people out front or stymied their attention should be immediately disposed of. On that theory, Lahr's first instincts were to cut many of Pozzo's and Lucky's longer speeches. He was unable to relate the minor characters to the broader philosophical propositions of the play.

If Lahr's demands for textual changes were unreasonable, his instincts for the tragicomic had a potential that Schneider's own uncertainties kept him from exploring. While Schneider insisted that the play was a partnership, the melding of mind and body, privately he saw the mind dominating the belly ("The play is not about Estragon, but Vladimir"), a moot distinction that shades the comedy toward tragedy rather than vice versa.

Lahr's insight was from the gut. He knew that laughter would complement Beckett's poetry. Schneider leaned toward the poetry, but was afraid laughter would turn it into a romp. Lahr wanted to move away from the weight of philosophical statement as in Beckett's most beautiful passage, where the hobos try and distinguish the quality of sounds. The passage ends:

Vladimir:	They make a noise like feathers.
Estragon:	Like leaves.
Vladimir:	Like ashes.
Estragon:	Like leaves.
	Long silence.
Vladimir:	Say something!
Estragon:	I'm trying.
	Long silence.
Vladimir:	(*in anguish*). Say anything at all!
Estragon:	What do we do now?

The laughter highlights the poetry; by deflating the emotion, the sadness of the situation comes closer to the heart. Schneider appreciated the poetry of that particular passage, but felt that "if *that* dialogue gets laughs, it's over my dead body."

Lahr sensed laughter even at the height of the tramps' chaos. A messenger from Godot appears but cannot offer any information about his master or when he will arrive. The reaction of Vladimir and Estragon to the boy mirrors not only the blundering sadness of their interminable vigil, but also the laughable intensity of any zealot's commitment to values based on a faith not borne out by experience.

As Estragon shakes the Boy, trying to find out the truth, Vladimir intercedes—

Vladimir:	Will you let him alone! What's the matter with you? (*Estragon releases the Boy, moves away, covering his face with his hands. Vladimir and the Boy observe him. Estragon drops his hands. His face is convulsed.*) What's the matter with you?
Estragon:	I'm unhappy.
Vladimir:	Not really! Since when?
Estragon:	I'd forgotten.

The laughter in the situation is not ebullient burlesque laughter; but that of paradox which acknowledges a darker side of comedy, where pain treads the thin, ambiguous line between pleasure and sadness. Schneider disavowed the comic element here also. "When Estragon says 'I'm unhappy'—to me that's not a comic moment."

Lahr's disenchantment with Schneider made it difficult for the director and the rest of the cast. "He'd listen to me when he wanted to. I was a kid director." This lack of trust created conflicts over simple lines. Schneider recalls Lahr could not understand the line "boldly ignorant apes." "He wouldn't listen to the line. On stage he would throw it away."

At other times, Schneider tried to devise methods of communicating the intellectual intention of Beckett's play to Lahr's comic intuition. One of his most successful gambits was known to the cast as "the ping pong game." Schneider would say to Lahr, "Bert, the game is simply to bat the ball over the net." When Lahr would stumble on lines that involved this kind of playful repartee, Schneider would remind him, "Bert, that's a ping pong game." Once he understood the spirit of the tart return, he would leap into the lines with gusto. One of Lahr's fondest passages of the play is precisely one of Beckett's hilarious volleys:

Vladimir:	Moron!
Estragon:	Vermin!
Vladimir:	Abortion!
Estragon:	Morpion!
Vladimir:	Sewer-rat!
Estragon:	Curate!
Vladimir:	Cretin!
Estragon:	(*with finality*). Critic!
Vladimir:	Oh!
	He wilts, vanquished, and turns away.

Schneider recalls this moment of success with Lahr vividly. "He loved that. You're dealing with a child, in the best sense of the word."

No one knew what to expect. To Lahr, Schneider grew progressively more hostile and impatient as the older men had difficulty with their lines. To Schneider, Lahr became a *bête noire.* He found Lahr "elusive, evasive, constantly trying to get out of rehearsing the play." For Schneider, it was a conflict "to reach him either physically or mentally." He likens Lahr to his experience with Buster Keaton, whom he directed in Beckett's only movie, *Film.* "Lahr's reactions to Beckett were just like Buster's. He would do anything for you, but he didn't understand it. Buster always wanted to put in old bits. He'd say, 'Why don't you let me pick up a pencil the way I did in———.' Bert wanted to interpolate old business, too. Keaton was quieter, less persistent."

Lahr's insecurity mounted with each rehearsal. He wanted to help the material; but the content of the play was not easily within his grasp. His only moment of reassurance came when Tennessee Williams, an investor in the production and also in Florida for the opening of *Sweet Bird of Youth*, which followed *Waiting for Godot* into the Cocoanut Grove, introduced himself after a grueling afternoon of rehearsals. "Bert, you're the only one that feels this play." The moment was important for Lahr—"It gave me confidence."

The family hardly saw him. Even when he moved from the hotel near the theater to the house where we were staying, his cloth rehearsing cap was always on his head and his mind was on his work. He would return late in the day and immediately hand Mildred the script to go over his lines. Since he could not always see the logical progression of ideas, memorizing was painful. Sometimes he would ask me to help him. He worked furiously, but was secretive about how the show was going. Lester Shurr came down for the New Year's Eve Party a few days before the opening. Through all the festivities, Lahr remained somber. He went to bed at the same hour we did. The part, which we never saw him perform in Florida, seemed to sap his energy in a way that no other had done. We were sent home a few days before the opening—a gesture that should have told us what to expect.

The day of the opening, Schneider called a line rehearsal for six p.m. The cast was testy and anxious. During the rehearsal Lahr fell asleep. "Part of it was nerves," explains Schneider. "Part of it was trying to get away from the play." Neither the director nor the rest of the cast was pleased with Lahr's siesta.

Walter Winchell, who was in Florida for the premiere, came into Lahr's dressing room before the show. "What's this about, Bert?"

Lahr found himself saying, "I really don't know. It's very strange. We'll see."

The opening night was as gala as Miami could make it. Among the audience moving past the huge fountain, down the thickly carpeted aisles, were Tennessee Williams, Joseph Cotten, Joan Fontaine, Gloria de Haven, Winchell, and Myerberg.

The next day the Miami *Herald's* headline recounted the devastating effect of the occasion—

MINK CLAD AUDIENCE DISAPPOINTED IN WAITING FOR GODOT

The audience, gilt-edged and giddy with expectation at the "laugh-riot" the ads had promised, was completely dumbfounded by what it saw. As one local critic reported, "The audience was more in the mood for *Guys and Dolls.*" It was openly hostile to the event.

Lahr found himself living through a comedian's nightmare. He met a complete stone wall. "I have never experienced anything like this in the American theater. I don't think anybody has. Two thirds of the audience left after the first act."

Lahr's horror at the audience's reception sent him into a frenzy of activity. "He tried to do a one-man show," recalls Schneider. "He was trying to salvage the evening. There was nothing malicious in his gesture, but he would ride in on Tommy's laughs. I had to restrain Mrs. Ewell from going on the stage. Bert just couldn't believe that Vladimir could get laughs. The two of them ended up killing each other on the stage."

Lahr could never comprehend Ewell's reaction to him. In his mind, Estragon demanded the movement he brought to the part. "Tom thought I was moving on him; he'd wrap his arms around me on stage and hold me.

"I didn't do anything to him. I wasn't trying to hurt him. We'd been in this thing together—in fact, he'd finally convinced me to do the play. It was only a two-week run, and anyway, he was bigger than I was."

The next day there was a line in front of the Cocoanut Grove Theater, not to buy tickets, but to demand refunds. Lahr himself began receiving protest mail. One day soon after the opening, he approached Schneider and held out a letter for him to read.

Dear Mr. Lahr,

How can a man, who has charmed the youth of America as the lion in *The Wizard of Oz*, appear in a play which is communistic, atheistic and existential.

After Schneider glanced through the letter, Lahr asked, "What does existential mean?"

But Lahr's intuitions about the play changed gradually during the two-week run. He began to understand parts of the play that Schneider's careful words had not been able to convey.

Although he swore to Schneider that he would have nothing to do with another production, he could not deny that the play spoke to a vast, inarticulate region of his experience. Beckett's limbo would elicit similar responses from convicts in San Quentin who saw the San Francisco Actor's Workshop production in 1957. Middle-class audiences, however, found the experience unsettling and treated the production with an aggressive dislike. Walter Winchell wrote the first of a handful of notices that would characterize their typical arrogant obtuseness. While Lahr could not forget the caverns of emptiness the play dramatized, Winchell illustrated the antagonism of a class that refused to recognize it.

As one of the most influential of the old guard on the Broadway scene, his hostility, verging on hysteria, is pertinent. Some, like Walter Kerr, dismissed it ("an intellectual fruitbowl"), but Winchell wanted to destroy it as if it were subversive and those who took part in it insane.

Waiting for Godot will appear in Washington, Boston, and Philadelphia before it challenges New Yorkers at the Music Box. Lahr and Ewell are on stage throughout, trading double talk. The thing opens with Tom Ewell's trousers unzipped. . . . It ends with Lahr's pants falling to his ankles. In between there is considerable chatter about madness, boredom, human suffering and cruelty. . . . There are several profane utterances . . . some of which have never before been heard on the stage before. . . . Even the vulgarians who people the premiers found the dirty words vulgar. . . . "Unnecessary" exclaimed a hard boiled Broadwayite. George E. Engle, a multi-millionaire who loves theater people, renovated the Cocoanut Grove Playhouse and will play Broadway shows old and new. Mr. Engle is also the proprietor of 440 producing oil wells.

"What on earth possessed Myerberg to put on such a show," he asked John Shubert the Broadway showman. "Don't underestimate him," he said. "Myerberg was laughed at by experts when he put on Wilder's *Skin of Our Teeth*. He made so much money with it that he bought the Mansfield Theater!" . . . *Life* photographers "shot" the

elite audiences as the stars were taking alleged bows . . . If published, these pictures cannot help the new show since half the spectators fled after the opening stanza. . . .

The debacle was completed when Myerberg canceled the
out-of-town tryouts and folded the show. Much of the fault
lay with Myerberg himself. He had billed the production
falsely, mounted it outrageously, and brought it to a town with
no sympathetic audience to sustain an experimental play. But
Schneider had an even unhappier experience, for he was not
asked to direct the New York production, as he had expected.

For Schneider, however, the real sadness was in not having
done justice to the Beckett he understood. As he wrote in the
Chelsea Review,

The failure in Miami depressed me more than any experience I had
had in the theater, though I had for a time anticipated the probability
and done all in my power to avoid it. It is typical of Sam [Beckett]
that his response to Miami was concerned only with my feelings of
disappointment and never stressed or even mentioned his own. Nor
did he utter one word of blame for any mistakes I might have made
along the way. . . . We met several times. I told him the story of Miami as objectively as I could and he spoke to me of what he had heard
concerning both productions. Somehow he made me feel that what I
had at least tried to do in Miami was closer to what he wanted to
do—though he never criticized the efforts of anyone else. . . .

Schneider never saw the New York production.

The play's dismal reception in Miami never numbed Lahr's
faith in its fundamental theatricality. There were dimensions of
the play he felt his performance had not been able to tap
because of the director, the set, his own fear of the material.

"Everybody has their own interpretation of *Godot*. At one
point in the play, you thought the tramps were waiting for
God. But then Beckett would go off on another tangent. Then
you knew it wasn't God. At the finish, they were still waiting.
It was Waiting. Hopelessness. It was waiting for the best of
life; and it never came. I think he meant the two characters to
represent both sides of man. Estragon, my part, was the
animal: Sex, Hunger, Eating, Sleeping. The other, Vladimir,
was Suspicion, Inquiry, always examining everything. Intellect.

He had kind of an animal's love for the other. He cared for him almost like a baby."

Even Myerberg realized that "Lahr seemed to know the character better than anyone even from the beginning."

What did Lahr know? Questions of the Bible, of philosophy, and social organization that the play raised had never crossed his mind. His theatrical friends urged him to scrap the idea of playing *Godot*. Yet he found himself defending the play without being able to verbalize its special force. In 1964, when Beckett went to London to oversee another production of *Waiting for Godot*, he discussed approaches to the play that might have calmed those who scoffed at Lahr's persistence.

> This play is full of implications and every important statement can be taken three or four ways. But the actor has only to find the dominant one, because he does so, does not mean the other levels will be lost. . . .
> *Sunday Times*, December 20, 1964

Lahr found his approach to Beckett; the audience's violent reaction in Miami had solidified his idea. "When I saw them walking out, I knew, I knew." Many of Lahr's theatrical associates regarded his fascination with the play as childish. If he lacked the words to express his appreciation, his "instincts" would prove Beckett's statement correct, peeling layers of meaning and emotion from the play that neither actor nor author could have originally visualized.

1970

JOHN HOUSEMAN

Born in Bucharest as Jacques Haussmann, John Houseman (1902–1988) broke into the American theatre in 1934 as director of the Virgil Thomson/Gertrude Stein opera *Four Saints in Three Acts*. Partnered with Orson Welles, whose excesses he tried in vain to moderate, between 1935 and 1937 he organized the WPA Negro Theater Project and its "voodoo" *Macbeth*, the Classical Theatre with its revival of Elizabethan plays and its gypsy staging of *The Cradle Will Rock*, and the Mercury Theatre, with a modern-dress, fascism-inflected *Julius Caesar*. While continuing to direct on Broadway, he became a successful film producer, and in 1956 agreed to serve as artistic director of the new American Shakespeare Festival in Stratford, Connecticut, in hopes of nurturing an indigenous way of playing the Bard. As the Festival succumbed to the star system, Houseman left in 1959. Ten years later he formed the Drama Division of the Juilliard School and its acting company, based on the precepts of Michel Saint-Denis. The publication of *Run-Through*, the first volume of his memoirs, in 1972, reminded the world of the heady creativity of the American stage during the Depression and led to a re-examination of its achievements. Late in life, Houseman's aquiline profile and cut-glass accent became familiar to the mass public when he played an imperious law professor in the film and television series *The Paper Chase*.

FROM
Run-Through: A Memoir

The Cradle Will Rock, which its author, Marc Blitzstein, described as "a play with music" (while others, at various times, called it an opera, a labor opera, a social cartoon, a marching song and a propagandistic tour de force), had been written at white heat one year earlier—in the spring of 1936. I had known Marc slightly in the early thirties, soon after his return from Europe, where he had gone from a substantial, middle-class Philadelphia home and the Curtis Institute of Music to study composition, first with Schoenberg and then, in Paris, with the celebrated Nadia Boulanger. A musical sketch of his—*Triple*

Sec—had been admired in the last of the Theatre Guild's *Garrick Gaieties* but, generally, he was considered a sophisticated composer of "serious," "modern" music.

Blitzstein's father was a banker and a socialist of the old school, of whom his son once wrote that he was "as modern in social thinking as he was conservative in musical taste." Marc's own political conversion and its creative expression came late, after the advent of the New Deal. In the summer of 1934 he was swimming in the Mediterranean with his wife, the daughter of the former Viennese operetta star Lina Abarbanell. One afternoon, as they lay drying in the sun on a beach at Majorca, he said to her, "I don't think I want to stay here any more. I want to be working in my own country. There are things going on there I want to be part of." "I've already packed," Eva said.

The next year, at Provincetown, Marc wrote a dramatic sketch around the song "The Nickel Under the Foot" which, later, formed the basis of the streetwalker's scene in *The Cradle Will Rock*. He showed it to Bertolt Brecht, who was in New York and who approved but said it was not enough. "To literal prostitution you must add figurative prostitution—the sell-out of one's talent and dignity to the powers that be." Nine months later, soon after Eva's death, Blitzstein wrote *The Cradle Will Rock* in five weeks—partly in a friend's house in Connecticut, partly in his sister's home at Ventnor, New Jersey —and dedicated it to Brecht.

Among the directors and producers who heard Marc audition his work during 1936 were Herman Shumlin, Martin Gabel, Harold Clurman for the Group, Charles Freedman for the Theatre Union and members of the Actors' Repertory Company, a left-wing group which had successfully produced Irwin Shaw's *Bury the Dead* the previous spring and who now announced *The Cradle Will Rock* for the season of 1936–37. I was not present when Welles and Blitzstein met backstage, one night, during the run of *Horse Eats Hat*, to discuss the possibility of Orson's directing Marc's play with music. Apparently, it was love at first sight. Marc was entranced by Orson's brilliance and power; Orson was excited by the challenge of this, his first contact with musical theatre. I remember listening jealously, with an ill-concealed sense of rejection, to Orson's enthusiastic comments about the piece (which I had not heard) and to his ideas for casting and staging it, which he elaborated for my annoyance. *Hamlet* had opened and closed and *Faustus* was deep in rehearsal when the Actors' Repertory Company abandoned *The Cradle* for lack of funds.* Orson never spoke to me of his disappointment, but I gathered that he and Marc had parted with a mutual promise that if ever a producer was found for such a costly and difficult work, Welles would direct it.

So things stood in March 1937 when, in the midst of our doldrums and as part of the complicated game of one-upmanship that Orson and I were constantly playing together, I suggested one night in his dressing room that if I were ever invited to hear Marc's work, I might conceivably find it suitable for production at the Maxine Elliott by Project #891. I did. And soon after that Hallie Flanagan was invited one Sunday evening to a well-planned dinner at the apartment on East 55th Street which Virgil Thomson and I were occupying that spring. Afterwards—

Marc Blitzstein sat down at the piano and played, sang and acted with the hard, hypnotic drive which came to be familiar to audiences, his new opera. It took no wizardry to see that this was not just a play set to music, nor music illustrated by actors, but music and play equaling something new and better than either. This was in its percussive as well as its verbal beat Steeltown U.S.A.—America 1937.[†]

The next day *The Cradle Will Rock* was officially announced as the next production of Project #891. There was some feeling, later, in New York and Washington that Hallie had been irresponsible in allowing so controversial a piece to be produced at such a precarious time. I believe she knew exactly what she was doing. She had no way of guessing (none of us had) that a double accident of timing would project us all onto the front pages of the nation's press; but she did sense which way the political winds were blowing and realized, better than her more timid colleagues, that in the storm into which the

---

*It was a bad winter for theatrical troupes. That same month the Group Theatre disbanded for the year. "We shall go on," declared Harold Clurman on the eve of his departure to join Clifford Odets in Hollywood.

[†]*Arena* by Hallie Flanagan.

Arts Projects were headed, there was no safety in prudence and no virtue in caution. For my own part it was not entirely out of caprice or competitiveness that I had embarked on *The Cradle Will Rock*. The truth is that I was finding in Marc's opera a welcome release from the mounting tensions which were closing in on us that winter and spring.

Work on *The Cradle* started calmly enough. We had singers and dancers on the project, but Will Geer was brought in from the outside to play Mr. Mister, the lord of Steeltown, and Howard da Silva to be the proletarian hero—Larry Foreman. And to make up our chorus of thirty-two we borrowed or traded singers from other units. Rehearsals (which lasted for almost three months) were mostly musical at first and were conducted by Marc with help from Teddy Thomas, whom I promoted to associate producer. Lehman Engel, our conductor, came over daily from the Music Unit where he was working to sit in on rehearsals. Orson, between radio shows, spent hours learning the music and working with his designer on the sets, which, he informed me, were to be extremely elaborate and expensive.

Marc had created *The Cradle Will Rock* in haste, out of a burning conviction which he never quite recaptured in his subsequent work. As a result, it is free of those conflicts— between his wanting to be a serious composer, an artist with a social message and a Broadway winner—that confused so many of his other pieces. Its prime inspiration, admittedly, was *The Threepenny Opera* by Brecht and Weill, to which Marc added "whatever was indicated and at hand. There were recitatives, arias, revue patters, tap dances, suites, chorales, silly symphony, continuous incidental commentary music, lullaby music—all pitchforked into it without a great deal of initiative from me." There were also patches of Gilbert and Sullivan and echoes of the Agitprop experiments of the early thirties.

Like *Waiting for Lefty*, *The Cradle Will Rock* was both angry and sentimental. Like Odets (but more satirically), Marc used vignettes and flashbacks to develop his theme of corruption, then returned to the present with a direct appeal to the audience's emotions for his final climax. *Waiting for Lefty* was written for, and has always been played on, a bare stage. For America's first proletarian musical, Orson had devised an extravagant scenic scheme that called for a triple row of three-dimensional velour portals between which narrow, glass-bottomed, fluorescent platforms, loaded with scenery and props, slid smoothly past each other as the scene shifted back and forth from the night court to a street corner, a church, a drugstore, a hotel lobby, a faculty room, a doctor's office and the front lawn of the finest house in Steeltown U.S.A.

The style of the piece as it began to take form at rehearsals (before costumes and scenery came between the performers and their material) fell somewhere between realism, vaudeville and oratory: the singing ranged from *Sprechstimme* to arias, patter and blues. A few of our older, staider performers were vaguely uneasy in their satirical roles, but no more than they had been with the magic of *Faustus* or the bawdry of *Horse Eats Hat*. For the rest, the piece had the fascination that goes with the creation of something new and unusual in the theatre. And almost from the first day, there were strange, prophetic stirrings in the air—a turbulence that grew with the weeks as the harsh realities of the national crisis met the rising theatrical excitement that was being generated on our bare, worklit stage. As opening night approached, those winds reached tornado force. How they finally blew *The Cradle* right out of our theatre onto another stage nineteen blocks uptown has become part of American theatrical history.

It is not easy, with a world war, a cold war, Korea, Vietnam and some twenty years of inflation in between, to re-create the world we lived in during the mid-thirties. Nineteen thirty-seven was, in some ways, the most confused and disturbed of those difficult years—a time of transition between the end of the Great Depression and the beginning of the slowly gathering industrial boom that accompanied our preparations for World War II. It was the year in which the President of the United States, in his second inaugural address, referred to "those tens of millions of our citizens . . . who at this very moment are still denied the greater part of what the very lowest standards of today call the necessities of life." It was also the year in which labor violence vied for space with international news on the front pages of the nation's press.

* * *

It was in this tense but appropriate atmosphere that we concluded our rehearsals of *The Cradle Will Rock*. On May 27th most members of the project had taken a day off when the Federation of Architects, Engineers, Chemists and Technicians, the WPA branches of the Teachers' Union and Newspaper Guild, the Artists' Union, the City Projects Council and the Workers' Alliance called a one-day, city-wide strike of all WPA work in protest against threatened cuts. Seven thousand joined the stoppage. Some days later, after a performance by the Dance Unit of works by Tamiris and Charles Weidman at the Nora Bayes Theatre, audience and cast joined in an all-night sit-down while outside "44th Street was filled with marchers." This was the first major sit-down on the project. Asked to comment, the following day, at a convention of the American Theatre Council, Hallie Flanagan replied that the Federal Theatre workers had struck "for what was once described as life, liberty and the pursuit of happiness . . . If we object to that method, I feel that some word should come from this gathering as to a better one." *The New York Times* reported that no one in the audience had any suggestions.

Then, within a fortnight, came the announcement everyone had been dreading: a cut of thirty percent in the New York Theatre Project, involving the immediate dismissal of seventeen hundred workers. In protest, a number of sit-downs were called: in Harlem, at the Lafayette, three hundred members of the Negro Unit sat down at the close of a performance and four hundred members of the audience sat with them through the night while other sympathizers formed a picket line outside. That same night at the Federal Theatre of Music, where the first of a series of Brahms concerts was being presented, ticket holders rose and urged others in the theatre to remain all night in their seats. Three hundred and fifty responded.

Such action was not for us. Project #891 had a challenge of its own which I was determined to meet—to get Marc Blitzstein's play with music onto the stage of Maxine Elliott's Theatre against a variety of odds. These included all the hazards that normally went with the opening of Orson's productions.

By the end of May our three great portals were in place and our illuminated glass-bottomed floats were cruising across the stage, pursued by panting players, trailing yards of black, writhing cable in their wake. Dress rehearsals were as painful as usual: actors accustomed to an open stage and four months of piano accompaniment were startled to find themselves confronted by gliding platforms and a twenty-eight piece orchestra between themselves and the auditorium. Transitions had to be repeated interminably; there were the customary scenes of recrimination and reconciliation. But our real perils were not theatrical. What Hallie had taken, in mid-February, for a dynamic piece of Americana had turned, by early June (with the WPA in turmoil and steel strikers on the front page) into a time bomb that threatened to bring the entire project tumbling about her head. Already, some weeks earlier, following reports in Washington that the opera was "dangerous," a special envoy had arrived in New York, watched a run-through with Mrs. Flanagan and "pronounced it magnificent." Now, ten days before our opening, with more than eighteen thousand tickets sold, a new set of rumors began to fly. Unfamiliar faces were glimpsed around the theatre; inside dopesters assured us that the curtain would never rise on *The Cradle Will Rock*. We ignored them and continued rehearsing and selling tickets. Our first public preview was scheduled for June 16th, with our official premiere announced for two weeks after that. On June 12th the blow fell—in the insidious form of a routine memorandum received by all national directors prohibiting "because of impending cuts and reorganization, any new play, musical performance or art gallery to open before July 1st."

As producers, Orson and I were not noted for our punctuality. Our *Macbeth* opening had been postponed five times, *Horse Eats Hat* twice, *Doctor Faustus* three times. Normally, we would almost certainly have postponed the opening of *The Cradle*. But now, suddenly, we became demons of dependability, scrupulous to honor our public and artistic commitment. Hallie asked me how I felt about the delay. I told her that we refused to accept it. She called Washington and tried to get an exception to the ruling: she cited the quality of our show, its vast cost in materials and man hours, the size of our advance sale and the adverse publicity an enforced postponement was bound to provoke at such a time. When she failed, Orson and Archibald MacLeish, to whom we had turned for help, flew to Washington and visited the WPA administrators just as they were preparing to meet a Congressional committee on appropriations for the coming year. Hopkins was not available. In a sharp scene with David Niles, they were told that the show was postponed—not canceled. Welles said he did not believe this, and that if *The Cradle* failed to open as advertised under Government auspices, he and I would launch it privately. "In that case we would no longer be interested in it as a property," said Mr. Niles. The interview was brief and Orson was back in time for that night's dress rehearsal—the one before the last.

Early next morning we started telephoning; we called everyone we could think of—Right and Left, professionals and outsiders—and invited them to that night's final run-through which, we intimated, might be their last chance to see *The Cradle Will Rock*. There was no specific rule forbidding invited guests at rehearsals: several hundreds made their way past the guards at the doors, mostly theatre people, musicians and enthusiasts of the far Left. Among our audience that night, Marc was happy to identify such celebrities as Arthur Hopkins, George Kaufman, Moss Hart and V. J. Jerome. For my own part I remember little of the evening except that I felt it was not going too well. The glass wagons slid in and out—not too precisely; the actors, concerned with finding their places and lights, still lacked the fervor and energy of our earlier run-throughs; Lehman Engel, our conductor, was still struggling to establish a balance between their untrained voices and the twenty-eight not so subtly orchestrated instruments in our shallow pit. But near the end of the evening the piece came suddenly alive: I can still see Howard da Silva as Larry Foreman, with his dirty-blond toupee, his fist clenched and his jaw jutting out around his flashing teeth as he sang, with the chorus behind him, right over the blaring band into the faces of the cheering audience:

> That's thunder, that's lightning,
> And it's going to surround you!
> No wonder those stormbirds
> Seem to circle around you . . .

Well, you can't climb down, and you can't sit still;
That's a storm that's going to last until
The final wind blows . . . and when the wind blows . . .
The Cradle Will Rock!

(*Music, bugles, drums and fifes*)

CURTAIN

The audience which left the Maxine Elliott that night, filing out past the guards in the doorways and the Workers' Alliance handbill distributors on the sidewalk, was the only one that ever saw and heard Marc's work performed as he wrote it. After they had left, the lights were turned out and the doors of the theatre were locked. For us, they were never reopened.

The next day, June 15th, a dozen uniformed WPA guards took over the building in force. Project members arriving to sign in found their theatre sealed and dark. The Cossacks, as they came to be known, guarded the front of the house and the box office; they hovered in the alley outside the dressing rooms with orders to see that no Government property was used or removed. This included scenery, equipment, props and costumes: Howard da Silva, who attempted to retrieve his toupee (purchased with Federal funds) had it snatched from his head at the stage door and confiscated. But there was one place in the building from which the Cossacks were excluded —the pink powder room in the basement, which now became headquarters in the fight to save *The Cradle*. Here Orson, Marc, Lehman Engel, Feder, Teddy Thomas, George Zorn and I lived for the next thirty-six hours, sustained by Augusta Weissberger with coffee and sandwiches and by food and drink brought in by well-wishers from the outside, for we were afraid to leave the theatre lest the Cossacks prevent us from returning. Our telephones had not been cut off and we made the most of them.

Our strategy was as simple as it was unrealistic. WPA might have problems of its own, but these did not concern us: as artists and theatre men we felt obligated to honor our commitments. The authorities had notified the organizations which had bought our previews that these must be postponed or canceled. We called them back and urged them to show up in full force. They needed no urging, for they were all part of that new left-wing audience that had sprung up with the Depression—the crowds that filled the houses on *New Theatre* nights and made *Lefty* and *Bury the Dead* and *Stevedore* the thrilling theatrical events they became. The Federal Theatre, with its half-dollar top, had further expanded this audience. Fifty percent of our public came from organized theatre parties, mostly of the Left—prejudiced and semieducated but young and generous and eager to participate in the excitement which the stage alone seemed to offer them in those uncertain times. These were the audiences whose members had "sat in" with the WPA workers earlier in the month. We were determined to keep faith with them and the authorities were determined that we should not.

For by this time, after the trip to Washington and the arrival of the Cossacks, peace was no longer possible between us and the Works Progress Administration. Since we refused to appreciate their official dilemma (which was real and grievous), we must be silenced and disciplined as an example. We, on our part, convinced that Washington had no intention of letting us produce the piece (on July 2nd or at any other time), saw no point in passively conniving at its murder. Besides, I think we realized that our own days with the project were numbered: we had served it well and had, in the process, made reputations such as we could not possibly have achieved elsewhere. Having nothing further to gain, we might as well make our departure as explosive and dramatic as possible.

Throughout the day of June 15th we continued blithely announcing to the press—and to anyone else who called to inquire—that we would give our first public preview of *The Cradle Will Rock* on the following night, as announced, in this or some other theatre. At some time during the afternoon, MacLeish made a final, vain attempt to reach Harry Hopkins at the White House. Toward dusk Mina Curtiss, who liked crises and had driven down from the Berkshires, made her way past the guards in her black Bergdorf Goodman dress, bearing cherries, roast beef and a bottle of brandy. Later in the evening Helen Deutsch appeared and asked us bluntly but helpfully what we intended to do on the morrow. We said we would give the show. She asked us where and how. And we couldn't answer.

We had been so busy proclaiming our integrity that we had not given much thought to the problems of our performance. These were serious. The Administration, through the Cossacks, controlled our scenery, costumes and lights—not to mention our stage and our auditorium. That left the human element. We now discovered that we didn't control that either. Our orchestra, all craft union men, members of one of the most potent and cohesive organizations in the country (whose leaders never approved of *The Cradle*, which they regarded as straight CIO propaganda or worse), had been notified of their union's decision: if we moved to another theatre not only must the men be paid for full new rehearsal sessions at full Broadway salaries, but in view of the "operatic" nature of the work we must also increase the size of the orchestra. This was clearly impossible. Of our actors and singers less than half were Equity members; but they were the important ones, sufficient to make the performance impossible if they were refused permission to appear. We queried Equity and were promised an answer for the following day. Anxiously we awaited the Council's verdict, knowing that no matter how deeply and passionately involved our actors might be in the fate of *The Cradle*, they would not knowingly defy their own union's ruling.

The dawn of June 16th found us still in the powder room. The Downtown School of Music, main buyers of that night's theatre party, called early to know if there was any change in the situation. We assured them that the show would go on. Time? Eight-thirty. Place? To be determined later. In midsummer, with more than half of New York's theatres dark, this seemed the least of our problems. George Zorn, our house manager, in whom I had absolute confidence, was sent out to find a theatre broker and returned an hour later with a small, seedy man in a black felt hat—a specialist in distressed theatres. He had a long list of available houses.

Five hours later, their number had shrunk to zero. Every half-hour or so he would look up from the phone we had put at his disposal at Augusta's desk under the lavender mannequin and announce that we had a theatre. And each time, a few minutes later, it would turn out not to be so. Mostly, this failure was due to lack of time, an inability to reach the owner in midsummer or a reluctance on his part to reopen a dark house for such a brief and uncertain engagement. Once, early in the afternoon, we closed a deal for a house only to discover, as we were about to take possession, that its management was deep in a dispute with the Stagehands' Union and that we would have to cross a picket line to get in. After that the man in the black hat was ordered from the powder room in disgrace. He stayed on, unnoticed, making futile calls and, occasionally, trying to attract our attention. But by then we had other, more awful problems to occupy us.

Actors' Equity had reached its decision at two o'clock. Around three the company, assembled on stage between the glass-bottomed platforms, received from its deputy the Council's reasonable but catastrophic verdict. Actors who had been rehearsing a play for four months and who had been receiving pay during that time from one management (the Federal Theatre) could not perform that same play for another management (Houseman and Welles) without the permission of the first—which was, of course, not forthcoming. In consequence, Equity members in the cast of *The Cradle Will Rock* were enjoined from appearing in that piece on any stage or for any management other than their current employers—the Federal Theatre of the WPA. Our cast (Equity, non-Equity and chorus) heard the ruling in silence. One or two signed out and went home but the rest stayed around, waiting to see what would happen.

For fully an hour after this bomb burst in the basement of the Maxine Elliott Theatre, all activity ceased. The man in the black hat spoke once but no one heard him. We were defeated. We had nowhere to turn. We could give a show without scenery and without an orchestra—but not without actors. Marc's despair at this point was ghastly to behold. He who had come within a day of seeing his work presented by the director, the conductor and the performers of his choice, amid elegant settings, in a Broadway theatre, with a cast of sixty and an orchestra of twenty-eight, had seen these gifts snatched from him one by one, until, now, he was back where he had started a year ago. And the unkindest cut of all came with the realization that the final, fatal blows had been dealt him by those very unions in whose defense the piece had been written.*

Around five, members of the press summoned by Helen Deutsch began to arrive, including Lewis Nichols of the *Times* and Jack Gould of the *Tribune*. They had heard about Equity's ruling and wondered what our next step would be. They were invited to wait in the powder room while we held a meeting in the Ladies' toilet next door. Meantime, Jean Rosenthal, with a ten-dollar bill in her hand, had been sent out to rent a piano, before the stores closed, on the chance that we might need it. When we emerged, the man in the black hat tried to speak to us, but we thrust him aside. Jean was on the phone to say that she had located a piano (an upright) for five dollars a day and what should she do with it? I told her to hire a truck, load the piano onto it, then call for further instructions. After that we turned to face the press—Orson radiating confidence, I looking worried and Marc, recovered from his state of shock, looking pale but determined and eager for martyrdom. We told them that *The Cradle Will Rock* would be presented that night, as announced, even if Marc had to perform it alone on a piano and sing all the parts. When they inquired where this tour de force would take place we suggested they stay around and find out. Then we went up to talk to the actors who were still waiting, sitting and lying around in the darkened auditorium under the disapproving glare of the Cossacks. I told them of our decision and explained the fine legal point we had evolved in the Ladies' toilet: that while they were forbidden by their union to appear *on* the stage, there seemed to be no interdiction against their playing their parts from any other position in the theatre. "There is nothing to prevent you from entering whatever theatre we find, then getting up from your seats, as U.S. citizens, and speaking or singing your piece when your cue comes," we told them.

---

*Like most recent converts, Marc was surprisingly naive about the realities of union strife. It seems not to have occurred to him that by plugging the CIO he was risking the displeasure of its rival, the still powerful AFL, and that the spectacle of Larry Foreman clenching the fingers of his raised right fist was no more pleasing to an old-time craft-union official than it was to a member of the reactionary Liberty League.

Their reaction was mixed. The stalwarts, Will Geer, Howard da Silva and the rest of the non-relief ten percenters, were enthusiastic. Others—especially our older members and the predominantly Negro chorus—were understandably reluctant to risk the loss of the small weekly income that alone kept them and their dependents from total indigence through a quixotic gesture for a cause which they did not really understand or altogether approve. On these (on the chorus especially) we were careful to exert no pressure or moral suasion. Each had his own personal problems and each must do what seemed sensible or right, regardless of collective or personal loyalty. Amid applause and tears we returned to the powder room, where Archibald MacLeish in a white linen suit had now appeared. The press, in growing numbers, was being entertained by Helen Deutsch; the man in the black hat was still in his corner, looking glum and intimidated, and Jean Rosenthal was on the phone again. She reported success: after standing on the corner of Broadway and 37th Street, in the heart of the garment district, for forty minutes, propositioning New Jersey trucks headed home across the river, she had found one, hired it by the hour with its driver and loader and hoisted the piano aboard. Now, what should she do? "Keep riding around," I said, "and call in every fifteen minutes for orders."

It was now after six; the press was getting restless and we seemed no nearer to finding a theatre than we had been at noon. We tried ballrooms, night clubs and Turnvereins; Mina Curtis offered the living room of her apartment, but that was useless for it was clear by now that no matter what form the performance of *The Cradle* would take that night, it would be given before a considerable audience.

Already, two hours before curtain time, officials of the Downtown School of Music, who had bought the preview and refused to cancel it, were standing before the locked doors of the Maxine Elliott Theatre on which a handwritten sign had been tacked: NO SHOW TONIGHT. Around seven Orson and I came out through the stage door and gave our personal assurance that the show would go on—"Somewhere! Somehow!" By now, sensing excitement, a considerable crowd had assembled on 39th Street; they formed little indignant knots,

between which members of the City Projects Council circulated, distributing handbills:

YOUR FRIENDS HAVE BEEN DISMISSED!
YOU MAY BE NEXT!

June 30th marks the End of all W.P.A. Projects.
42,000 W.P.A. Workers are being dismissed in
preparation for the dismantling of W.P.A.
The <u>City Projects Council</u> is your organization!
Join NOW! Save Your Job!
Fight for an American Standard of Living in
the W.P.A.!

At seven-twenty, as the swelling crowd began to get restless,
several of our actors appeared on the sidewalk and offered a
brief preview of the show to come. With their shadows lengthening in the early summer twilight, Hiram Sherman sang "I
Wanna Go ter Honolulu" and Will Geer (veteran of many a
union picnic and hootenanny) enacted one of Mr. Mister's
more repulsive scenes.

Meanwhile, inside the theatre, the gloom deepened. In the
pink powder room a hopeless silence had fallen, broken only
by the uneven whir of a single fan that barely stirred the stale
air of the overcrowded basement. It was now seven-forty—an
hour from curtain time; our piano, with Jean Rosenthal on top
of it, had been circling the block for almost two hours and the
driver was theatening to quit. Clearly, this was the end. After
all our big talk, for lack of a theatre, *The Cradle* would not be
performed—on this or any other night.

It was then that the miracle occurred. The man in the black
felt hat, the down-at-heel theatrical real estate agent, rose from
his corner and moved toward the stair. In the doorway he
paused, turned and spoke. It was an exit speech, uttered in a
weak, despondent tone. No one, later, could remember exactly what he said, but the gist of it seemed to be that since
there was nothing more he could do, he might as well go home.
Only he still couldn't understand what was wrong with the
Venice Theatre. With a sigh he turned and started up the
stairs. He was already halfway up when he was seized, turned,
dragged down, shaken and howled at. What was he talking
about? What Venice Theatre? He then explained in a flat, ag-

grieved voice that for three hours he had been offering us a theatre that was open, empty, available, reasonable, unpicketed and in every way suitable to our requirements—but that none had listened to him.

Within one minute, five twenty-dollar bills had been thrust into his hand: the Venice Theatre was ours and Feder, Teddy Thomas and Marc were in a cab headed north. Two minutes later Jean Rosenthal, reporting for orders for the sixth time, was told to route her truck at full speed up Seventh Avenue to the block between 58th and 59th. She got there first and her men from New Jersey dumped the piano on the sidewalk and drove off. Four firemen from the hook and ladder station next door were carrying it into the theatre for her when Feder arrived (with a spotlight he had picked up en route) and broke open the stage door for them. Back on 39th Street, the moment we had word of their safe arrival, announcements were made—inside and outside the theatre. From the Maxine Elliott to the Venice is a distance of twenty-one city blocks. To cover possible delays in transit, our curtain time was changed to 9 P.M.; and since our adopted theatre was more than twice as large as our own, everyone was urged to invite one or more friends. There was cheering as the voyage began—by bus, subway, taxi and (it being a fine June evening) on foot.

In this unique migration, the largest single element was the preview audience from the Downtown Music School benefit, numbering six or seven hundred. Rumors and phone calls must have sent another thousand scurrying uptown, singly and in groups, not counting the press and a number of WPA official observers—friendly and unfriendly. Finally there were our own people—members of the staff, company and chorus. Not all of them arrived. It was one thing to make resolutions of solidarity, another for them to appear in open defiance of the authority on which they depended for a living. Now, as the move north began, a few stayed behind in the theatre, signed out and went quietly to their homes. Others who remained in doubt were willing to risk the voyage; they entered the Venice Theatre and took their seats, not knowing whether they would take part in the performance as spectators or performers. Howard da Silva made a final attempt to recapture his Government toupee, failed, rushed home to get his own, could not find it, and still managed to be one of the first to arrive on 58th Street. Lehman Engel, our conductor, was among the last to evacuate the Maxine Elliott. Two of the Cossacks, sweating gently in the early summer heat, must have been surprised to see him leaving the building in a large overcoat, but failed to search him. If they had, they would have found, clasped against his stomach, the piano and vocal score of *The Cradle Will Rock*.

By seven-fifty the Maxine Elliott was dark. Only a few guards and workmen remained to patrol its emptiness. Orson and I left with Archie MacLeish in someone's white Nash roadster with never a look back at the building in which we had prepared three shows together and opened two. Driving up Broadway through the light summer traffic, MacLeish seemed troubled; he was afraid we were going too far in our insubordination, yet he was reluctant to abandon us. Besides, there was a strong smell of history in the air which he was unwilling to miss.

The Venice Theatre, the scene of our first venture in independent management, was variously known, before it was finally torn down, as the Century, the Jolson, the Venice, the New Century and the New York Video Tape Center. In the forties it knew temporary prosperity as the home of *Kiss Me Kate* and *Up in Central Park*. But in the summer of 1937, it was run-down and dark save for occasional weekend performances by a local Italian stock company. This explained the stained and fading Neapolitian backdrop which Feder and his cohorts found hanging "in one" when they forced their way, with their spotlight and piano, past a sleepy, protesting watchman, onto the stage. The piano, a battered upright, was placed in front of the drop, and Feder immediately set about "lighting" it. One minute later, with a sharp flash of bright-blue flame, a whole bank of dimmers on the rusted switchboard blew out and Feder, his right arm bleeding and burned, was taken by Teddy Thomas to a doctor on 58th Street for emergency treatment. Marc's hand was blackened but unhurt; by the time we arrived he was sitting at the piano, trying it out and demanding that its front be pulled out ("so that the guts showed") for greater volume in such a vast house.

By this time, the audience had begun to arrive from downtown and was milling around the front of the house with

Cokes, hot dogs and preview tickets* in their hands. As soon as the house crew appeared (obligatory under union rules), puzzled and disgruntled, the sleazy front curtain was lowered, the house lights turned on and the doors opened. There were no ticket takers that night, no ushers and no programs. By eight-thirty the main floor was more than half-filled except for the front two rows, which we had hopefully reserved for the cast. Upstairs, his arm in a sling, Feder was howling at his single electrician as the follow spot was hurriedly installed on the balcony rail. While they were testing its focus, the light beam fell accidentally on a large Italian flag draped over the edge of the upper right stage box. Instantly the crowd began to protest (Mussolini's activities first in Ethiopia and then in Spain had not endeared him to the Left) till, amid loud booing, someone climbed up and hauled it down. This gave the crowd a release: they laughed and applauded. Orson and I were backstage by that time but there were rents in the drapes through which we could peer out at the rapidly filling house. By eight-fifty there was not an empty seat; standees were beginning to accumulate at the back of the theatre and along the walls of the side aisles. Marc, seated stiffly at his piano, ready for his great moment, could hear the excited buzzing behind the thin curtain. At nine-five, they began to clap. We decided it was time to begin. We shook hands with Marc. Then, like partners in a vaudeville act, Orson and I made our entrance together from the wings onto the stage.

As supervisor of Project #891 I spoke first—sincerely but disingenuously. I made it clear that ours was a gesture of artistic, not political, defiance. I traced the history of *The Cradle Will Rock* and the circumstances leading up to this night's crisis. I expressed the gratitude we all felt to Mrs. Flanagan† and the Federal Theatre for allowing us to undertake a new

---

*One way in which we raised money on this and subsequent nights was to collect these preview tickets at the door and cash them in the next day at the Maxine Elliott box office.

†Hallie, herself, was torn between her loyalty to Harry Hopkins, her pride in what we were doing and her duties as head of the Federal Theatre. Later, in her book, she rationalized: "Probably it is worth a case of censorship to launch a group of our most brilliant directors and actors with a play for which the cast had been provided as well as an audience and a springboard for publicity."

American work which no private management had been willing or able to produce and which we had been preparing for
months, with dedication and love, till it had reached that stage
of readiness when it must be shared with an audience. Now,
suddenly, for no good reason, we were being denied permission to open. As artists and theatre men, we had no choice but
to defy this arbitrary and unjust order. That is why we were
here tonight, in this unfamiliar place—keeping our word to
ourselves and to our public in the only way that was left open
to us. (Since we still did not know exactly what this way would
be, I left this part vague.) Then I introduced our director—
Orson Welles. Looking tall and boyish, Orson thanked them
in a deep voice for making the long voyage uptown; he told
them of his feeling for Marc's work and of the performance
they would have witnessed if our theatre had not been taken
over by the Cossacks of the WPA (boos and laughter). While
he set the scene and described the characters of Steeltown, I
had a chance to look around at what, till then, had been
nothing but a dark, frightening blur before my eyes: the huge
house packed to the roof, the aisles crowded and, in among
this mass, down toward the front, a few familiar faces: Lehman
Engel in the second row, without his overcoat, the score
propped up against the arm of the seat beside him and, in the
boxes, calm, fierce and confident, Geer, da Silva, Blanche
Collins and the other stalwarts. "We have the honor to present
—with the composer at the piano—*The Cradle Will Rock*!"
Orson concluded.

Amid applause we withdrew as gracefully as we could into
the wings, then raced through the fire door into the front of
the house just in time to see the curtain rise and Marc, in his
shirt-sleeves, with his suspenders showing, sitting pale and
tense at his eviscerated piano before a washed-out view of the
Bay of Naples with Vesuvius smoking in the distance. Feder
caught him in the spotlight. "And there I was alone on a bare
stage—myself produced by John Houseman, directed by Orson Welles, lit by Feder and conducted by Lehman Engel. I
started, ready to do the whole show myself."*

*Marc Blitzstein: "As He Remembered It," reprinted posthumously in *The
New York Times* from the Spoken Arts recording—"Marc Blitzstein Presents."

The Cradle Will Rock started cold, without an overture. A short vamp that sounded harsh and tinny on Jean Rosenthal's rented, untuned upright, and Marc's voice, clipped, precise and high-pitched: "A Street corner—Steeltown, U.S.A." Then, the Moll's opening lyrics:

> I'm checking home now, call it a night.
> Going up to my room, turn on the light—
> Jesus, turn off the light!

It was a few seconds before we realized that to Marc's strained tenor another voice—a faint, wavering soprano—had been added. It was not clear at first where it came from, as the two voices continued together for a few lines—

> I ain't in Steeltown long;
> I work two days a week;
> The other five my efforts ain't required.

Then, hearing the words taken out of his mouth, Marc paused, and at that moment the spotlight moved off the stage, past the proscenium arch into the house, and came to rest on the lower left box where a thin girl in a green dress with dyed red hair was standing, glassy-eyed, stiff with fear, only half audible at first in the huge theatre but gathering strength with every note:

> For two days out of seven
> Two dollar bills I'm given . . .

It was almost impossible, at this distance in time, to convey the throat-catching, sickeningly exciting quality of that moment or to describe the emotions of gratitude and love with which we saw and heard that slim green figure. Years later, Hiram Sherman wrote to me: "If Olive Stanton had not risen on cue in the box, I doubt if the rest of us would have had the courage to stand up and carry on. But once that thin, incredibly clear voice came out, we all fell in line." On technical grounds alone, it must have taken almost superhuman courage for an inexperienced performer (whom we had cast in the part only because we had already exceeded our non-relief quota) to stand up before two thousand people, in an ill-placed and terribly exposed location, and start a show with a difficult song to the accompaniment of a piano that was more than fifty feet away. Add to this that she was a relief worker, wholly dependent on her weekly WPA check, and that she held no political views whatsoever.

> So I'm just searchin' along the street
> For on those days it's nice to eat.
> Jesus, Jesus, who said let's eat?

That was the end of her song. A flash-bulb went off. The audience began to clap—not sure what they were applauding—the girl, the song, Marc or the occasion. And, immediately, with no musical transition—

"Enter Gent."

said Marc at the piano and was prepared to speak the next line, but again it was taken out of his mouth, as a young man with a long nose rose from a seat somewhere in the front section of the orchestra and addressed the girl in green in the stage box.

GENT
Hello, baby!

MOLL
Hello, big boy!

GENT
Busy, baby?

MOLL
Not so very.

So a scene which, three nights before, had been acted in atmospheric blue light, around a prop lamppost, downstage right, was now played in the middle of a half-lit auditorium by two frightened relief workers thirty yards apart.

From then on, it was a breeze. Nothing surprised the audience or Marc or any of us after that, as scenes and numbers followed each other in fantastic sequence from one part of the house to another. Blitzstein played half a dozen roles that night, to cover for those who "had not wished to take their lives, or rather, their living wage, into their hands." Other replacements were made spontaneously, on the spot: Hiram Sherman, word perfect, took over for the Reverend Salvation, whose unctuous part he had never rehearsed, and later repeated this achievement, from an upper box, in the role of Professor Scoot, an "academic prostitute." Scenes were played, at first, wherever the actors happened to be sitting, so that the audience found itself "turning, as at a tennis match" from one character to another, and from one part of the house to the other. Then, as the act progressed and their confidence grew, the actors began to move around, selecting their own locations, improvising their actions, while instinctively communicating with each other from a distance. No one later remembered all that happened. But I do recall that Mr. Mister and Mrs. Mister sang and danced "I Wanna Go ter Honolulu" in the same center aisle in which Mr. Mister and his stooges later played their big bribery scene. Mrs. Mister did both her scenes upstairs in a balcony loge (directly above the Moll), from which she wafted down imaginary "donations" to the Reverend Salvation, who stood on the orchestra floor at the head of the aisle with his back to the stage facing the audience, as did Ella Hammer later for her "Joe Worker" number. The chorus were clustered in the third and fourth rows, surrounding Lehman Engel, where they presently provided another of that evening's memorable moments.

Just before leaving 39th Street I had made a last round of the theatre, thanked the members of the chorus for their loyalty and urged them not to take any unnecessary chances. It was all the more startling, therefore, in Scene Three, to hear the Reverend Salvation's booming pieties:

> Righteousness conquers! Iniquity perishes!
> Peace is a wonderful thing!

answered by an "Amen" reverently intoned by two-dozen rich Negro voices. On their own, without consulting anyone, they had traveled uptown and found their places behind their conductor. Now, as their first cue came up, without rising, taking their beat from Lehman Engel, they sang like angels. Melting into the half-darkness of the crowd, they were not individually distinguishable, and this gave their responses a particularly moving quality. A moment later they were on their feet savagely clamoring:

> CHORUS
> WAR! WAR! Kill all the dirty Huns!
> and those Austrungarians!
> WAR! War! We're entering the War!
> The Lusitania's an unpaid debt.
> Remember Troy! Remember Lafayette!
> Remember the Alamo! Remember our womanhood!
> Remember those innocent unborn babies!

To which the Reverend Salvation suavely responded—

> REV. SALVATION
> Of course, it's peace we're for—
> This is war to end all war!

And the Chorus sang—

> CHORUS
> (*reverently*)
> Amen. . . .

Another surprise came when Marc suddenly became aware that, instrumentally, he was no longer performing alone. Of the twenty-eight members of Musicians' Local 802, not one was to be seen that night at the Venice—but one was clearly heard. Somewhere, high up in the balcony, Rudy, the accordionist, sat hidden among the audience with his instrument open on his knees, playing along with his composer in passages where he felt it would help.

The Cradle, at the Maxine Elliott, was to have been performed without an intermission.* This night, at the Venice, we improvised an act break after Scene Six. Scene Five shows the planting of a bomb by company thugs, the death of the young Polish couple and the druggist's son. This is followed immediately by a scene in the hotel lobby where Yasha and Dauber, the kept artists, in a comic vaudeville routine, first insist that "There's something so damned low about the rich!," then ser-

---

*Which is how Leonard Bernstein played it in his concert performance at City Center in November 1947.

enade their patroness, Mrs. Mister, before leaving with her for the weekend to Beethoven's *Egmont* motif played on her limousine horns outside. The curtain fell to laughter and applause as the houselights came up full. Then somebody, probably George Zorn, began calling out that there would be a fifteen-minute intermission and please not to smoke in the theatre.

The "inflammatory" scenes of *The Cradle Will Rock* occur cumulatively, toward the end. During the intermission the crowd milling around the jammed lobby and spilling out into Seventh Avenue was agitated and happy but not overexcited. They kept meeting friends and inquiring how they got there and telling each other how splendid it all was. It took a long time to get them back inside—which was just as well, for Marc was limp with exhaustion. We were backstage with him when MacLeish appeared, his fears now entirely dispelled, and said he would like to say a few words before Act Two. Orson conducted him before the curtain in his crumpled white suit, looked down on the hundreds who were still making their way back to their seats and announced: "When you have all sat down, the one man still standing will be the poet—Archibald MacLeish."

It was a warm speech—a revised and augmented version of the one he had delivered on the last night of *Panic* two years before. He praised the creative forces in the Federal Theatre, with particular reference to Project #891 and its directors. He lauded Marc Blitzstein. But above all he hailed the "new" audience that he saw before him as opposed to the "supine" audience of the commercial theatre. In his introduction to the published version of *The Cradle*, the following winter, he wrote of that evening—

There was no audience. There was instead a room full of men and women as eager in the play as any actor. As actors rose in one part and another of the auditorium the faces of these men and women made new and changing circles around them. They were well-wishing faces: human faces such as man may sometimes see among partisans of the same cause or friends who hope for good things for one another.

The second act went like a house afire. It opens with The Moll's "Nickel Under the Foot" blues, followed by the long-retarded entrance of the labor hero, Larry Foreman, and the first hearing of the title song. Mr. Mister is seen again in his doctor's office, increasingly scared and malignant, corrupting the medical profession as he has the Church, the University and the Press. After that comes the angriest number in the show—"Joe Worker":

> One big question inside me cries
> How many frame-ups, how many shake-downs,
> Lock-outs, sell-outs,
> How many toiling, ailing, dying, piled-up bodies
> Brother, does it take to make you wise?

And then, finally, the showdown: Larry Foreman confronting Mr. Mister and his Liberty Committee in the crowded night court. Only this night they were all on their feet, singing and shouting from all over the theatre as they built to the final, triumphal release—

> That's STEEL marching out in front! but one day there's
>   gonna be
> Wheat . . . and sidewalks . . .
> Cows . . . and music . . .
> Shops . . . houses . . .
> Poems . . . bridges . . . drugstores . . .

MR. MISTER

(*the surrender to fear*)

> My God! What do they want with me?

LARRY

> Don't worry, that's not for you . . .
> That's thunder, that's lightning,
> And it's going to surround you!
> No wonder those stormbirds
> Seem to circle around you . . .

He sang it without his toupee, his scalp gleaming under the strong spotlight:

> When you can't climb down, and you can't sit still;
> That's a storm that's going to last until
> The final wind blows . . . and when the wind blows . . .
> *The Cradle Will Rock!*

There were no "bugles, drums and fifes" that night—only Marc's pounding of an untuned piano before a wrinkled backdrop of the Bay of Naples. As the curtain fell and the actors started to go back to their seats, there was a second's silence— then all hell broke loose. It was past midnight before we could clear the theatre. We had rented it till eleven and had to pay twenty dollars extra, but it was worth it.

1972

SPALDING GRAY

The phenomenon of Off-Off-Broadway began around 1958 with impromptu, roughhewn performances at Caffé Cino in Greenwich
Village, La MaMa E.T.C. under Ellen Stewart, and Judson Poets' Theater under Al Carmines. Influenced by the methods of the Polish
director Jerzy Grotowski and the antinomian attitudes of the Flower-
Power generation, experimental troupes proliferated throughout the
1960s. When Spalding Gray (1941–2004) came to New York from San
Francisco's Esalen Institute in 1967, he immersed himself in the current. He was a member of Richard Schechner's Performance Group
from 1970 to 1980 and then helped to found the Wooster Group in
1975. With Elizabeth LeCompte he devised an autobiographical trilogy and then launched what would become a series of 18 monologues.
Sitting behind a simple table, a glass of water, and a spiral notebook,
Gray would spin yarns about his past experiences, remembrances, fantasies. He took on the persona of a bewildered secondary character, a
neurotic version of T. S. Eliot's "attendant lord, one that will do to
swell a progress." In such narratives as *Swimming to Cambodia* (1985),
In Search of the Monkey Girl (1987), and *Monster in a Box* (1992), he
distilled his melancholia into mirth. "Anecdotage is a defense and it's
dangerous," Gray acknowledged, alert to the perils of delving into
memory to amuse an audience. Prey to depression ("my mind is a
painful place"), Gray jumped off the Staten Island Ferry to commit
what he had predicted would be a "dramatic and creative suicide."

FROM
A Personal History of the American Theatre

The Curious Savage
The Curious Savage was the first play that I was in. It was done
at my boarding school. I think that certain people decide to
become professional actors, just like certain people decide
to become doctors and dentists. Somewhere along the line,
they say "I guess I'll go into acting." And they study it and
become an actor. It's an act of will.

But with other people, it's an ontological condition. There
is no way out. They are born into it. They find that they are

"acting out" all the time, and they don't know what to do about it. They have these inappropriate responses to reality, and they are trying to find a nice place to "act out" other than in an insane asylum.

Now for me, I think it was the ontological condition. I was bored with life, actually. I know I shouldn't have been. I know I should have been thankful. But it was all so flat. It was just a flat thing. And I would keep hyping it up with this kind of "acting out."

For instance, Fourth of July, some fireworks go off outside. I'm just a kid. Pop-pop-pop-pop-pop-pop! I run to the window, and say, "Mom! Come quick! Russ Davis, our neighbor, is up on the roof shooting his kids!" This was in the old days when that wasn't done so often. And my mother, believing it, would rush to the window, and then she would say, "Oh Spuddy dear . . . No, no, no. Now WHY did you have to do that?"

So I was looking for a place to take refuge, and I thought it might be the theatre. But I was too nervous to read, my junior year, for the role, because I had a kind of dyslexia, and also th-th-th-th-the book sh-shook so much in my hand I couldn't read it, so I didn't get the role.

So, in my senior year, *The Curious Savage* was the senior play, and I was determined to hold the book down. I thought, I'll read it one word at a time, and they can do what they want with that. So I held the book down and read, "Because . . . they . . . eat . . . their . . . own . . . weight . . . in . . . worms . . . every . . . day . . . and . . . they . . . starve . . . to . . . death . . . in . . . a . . . half . . . hour." I got the role. Because it takes place in an insane asylum.

And they thought I was perfect for the role of Hannibal. The man thinks he's Hannibal, he has delusions of grandeur. He also thinks he can play the violin, and the play ends with wonderful violin music, and I'm sawing away as though I was finally able to have my fantasy come true.

Opening night, they put down a rug that was not there for dress rehearsal, and it had squares on it. And I was to make a downstage left cross, and I decided to all of a sudden just—I did it, I improvised, and did a hopscotch on the squares to get downstage left, and everyone laughed. Everyone. And I was hooked.

It just went through me, just like a drug. There was no way out. They had me—it had me. I went directly to my guidance counsellor and said, "I don't want to go to college. I've decided, I want to go directly to New York City and become an actor." He said, "What do you know about acting? You've been in one play! You've got to go to a liberal arts college!"

*   *   *

Commune

This was directed by Richard Schechner here in the Performing Garage, in 1970. It was a very risky play in this sense, that he started using people's actual personalities as material. First of all, it was a collaborative hodgepodge soup of a work that was based on the killing of Sharon Tate supposedly by Charles Manson. It hadn't been proven yet, it had just come out in *Life* magazine, and was based on that material. Also the Bible, *Moby Dick*, *Walden*, *The Tempest*, other Shakespeare plays—it was a real soup. And Richard asked the performers, in the middle of one of these scenes, to begin talking about themselves and their own feelings. So it got like an *8½* situation where some people were playing just themselves, or a character, or both, and it was never resolved in their head. He used a lot of typecasting. For instance, the person who played the Charles Manson figure was an actual redneck from Oklahoma, so there was some confusion. For instance, at a party, someone said, "Oh, I just loved that stinky old redneck you played in that play!" and he'd reply, "What redneck?"

And then Bruce White, who was a white magician from Minneapolis, was playing the Christ figure. And he in fact lived in a Jesus commune on 4th Avenue, which was a cracked house, a cracked loft, in a way—they had no heat, they were paying no rent, they were living in tents. And at the time, for the Holy Eucharist, they were taking blotter acid, blotter LSD. It would be, if you can imagine, a piece of paper this big, with dots of acid all the way across it, this would be shoved under their door about once a month for the whole commune, no one would ask for any money at all. Blue would be the spirit, brown the body, and red would be the blood. After taking it, they would go to God. Bruce would spend sometimes two evenings with God, and come in the next day and rehearse. He hadn't slept all night.

I wanted in, I wanted some of it. I didn't know what was going on, but I really was curious. And so what they had planned was, they had this divinely inspired music group called The Trees in which they played music that was divinely inspired. For instance, a perfect example was, I would go over there for one of their jam sessions. We'd have brown rice and vegetables, and then after the Red Zinger tea, out would come the instruments: penny whistles, some recorders, tambourine, even an Irish harp. And we would jam.

And I can remember getting into a jam session with Bruce's wife. The two penny whistles went beautifully, we were just kind of soaring in and out of each other. And when we finished I said, "Hey Jody that was great." And she said, "I didn't do anything . . . It was just coming through me . . . just coming through me . . ."

Well, they had a plan. Bruce was trying to gradually convert the Performance Group to Christianity through giving them the Holy Eucharist, and then reading to them from the Bible, and people in the group were all rather reluctant to take the LSD. I was particularly upset about it. I didn't want to take it. I had read that if you had any schizophrenic tendencies, it could be disastrous. Later on I found that I was only schizoid and a Gemini, which is quite a different thing from being schizophrenic. But at the time I was staying clear of it.

But their major plan was to convert Richard Schechner from Judaism to Christianity. A noble project, but it would take more energy than—well, that's another play in itself. You couldn't make *Commune* and do that as well. But they were going for broke. And one of the reasons they wanted to convert him was, that they felt Richard was floundering. They felt he was going to the devil. *Commune* was a very dark play, and Richard was looking for a way to end it on an up note, called "symbols of possibility." And no one could figure out what symbols of possibility were, in 1970, in New York City. But The Trees, they had an idea. And that idea was that at the end of the play, they would all assemble with their instruments, on a float out on Wooster Street, and they would play divinely inspired music as the garage door went up, and they would roll in and that would be IT. They would be the symbols of possibility.

So they were working on that, and they were working on trying to convert Richard. Around this time we went to CUNY New Paltz for a summer residency. So I thought, "Hmmm! This is a good time to try the LSD!" It was very countrified up there, and I was alone with Bruce, and I thought, "Why not?" And in keeping with the idea of being a schizophrenic, I would start with half a tab.

So I took it, and then I said to Bruce, "Now I'd like to go up to the woods." And he said, "Well, uh, you sure you don't want to stay down here?"

And then I thought, "Uh-oh, this is something we should have discussed before I took the LSD. Because I think he's going to want to read to me from the Bible." And I was deeply resisting inside.

So, finally, he did take me up to the woods. There was no problem. We got up there, and I decided to go off on my own. And I walked down to this stream, and stepped out onto a rock, and this rushing water was pouring around the rock, and I stood there, and just looked straight ahead, and said: "I am." Nothing happened, so I thought I'd try it a little louder. "I am." The water kept rushing. "I AM!" And then I thought, "Oh God, maybe I'm upsetting the campers here, the woods were filled with them." So I went back looking for Bruce, and the sun was going down, and I saw a bat fly over.

And then I looked up and I saw a thousand bats, with peacock feathers a yard long coming off their tails. And then I went up to Bruce, and I said, "Bruce, this is incredible. This is fantastic, but what if—what if . . ." (I was always there with the "what-ifs") "what if we were on 8th Street tripping now with all the hippies?" And just as I asked that, out of the bushes, as though it had been choreographed by Bruce or someone, came about fifteen hippies from 8th Street.

And they came down, and they saw that we were tripping (I don't know how they knew, I guess because our faces were blue), and they started attacking the exposed tree roots with their hatchets. And they cried out "Aaaah! Argh! AAAh! That's the fifth poisonous snake we've killed tonight!"

But it wasn't bothering me at all. I was so high that I saw them as tree roots. Tree roots after the image of tree roots: real tree roots. But my friend Steven Snow—he was still a little in the old guilt circle, and he saw them as poisonous snakes, because he thought that Susan Belinda Moonshine had drowned. You see, we were all asked while making *Commune* to change our names, just like in the real communes, and Bruce White and I kept our names, but everyone else changed theirs. Patrick Epstein changed hers to Susan Belinda Moonshine. And she was tripping on acid at the time we were, and was down swimming in the stream, and Steven Snow was watching her. And she disappeared. And he thought that Susan Belinda Patrick Epstein Moonshine had drowned.

And that's when I just knew . . . it doesn't matter! But he didn't understand what I was talking about and so we were lost, and it was dark, and these hippies led us out of the woods. And I came out and there was this road, this highway. And the moon wasn't out, just the stars, so the stars were very vivid. And I couldn't believe it. I just saw the stars were very vivid. And I couldn't believe it. I just saw the stars for the first time in my life. No thoughts in between, no mediation, just stars . . . and I went down on my knees, and said, "Oh my God, the stars! Take me to the edge of the cliff, Bruce!"

And we drove down a little way in the car, and he let me out on the edge of that cliff, on the way down to New Paltz, where you can look over the entire valley. And the entire valley was just breathing. And my body was an outline, like a Matisse drawing, that the valley was floating through. The whole landscape was floating through the outline of my body. And I like that very much. Nothing was left but a little pyramid in the top of my head. And I got back in the car, and we started down the mountain road toward New Paltz, and I started in again on the "What-ifs."

"What if . . . what if, Bruce, what if . . . what if we were in Vietnam tripping now?" And then I saw it, just coming up, clearly, like this big Ferris wheel. The gondolas on the wheel were thoughts—mine—and I could look at them go by or stop it, read it a little bit, and let it go by. We got down into New Paltz, and Bruce said, "NOW I'm going to read to you from the Bible." And it didn't matter! The pages were blowing like in a wind, but there was no wind. And Susan Belinda Moon-shine had come back from the dead and was there. And everything was fine.

Now shortly after that, Bruce organized a seance on the anniversary of the murder of Sharon Tate. And he had everyone come to his room. We all sat at a big table and held hands and he asked us to empty our bodies out, empty our minds out, and he asked for the spirit of Sharon Tate be allowed to enter.

Now I knew how to do that—how to empty the body out—cause of the Matisse outline experience on the cliff. All of a sudden, my body and mind started going up just like a thermometer. Just like the Red Feather Tuberculosis Drive—going up and stopping just between my eyes. And it was empty except for this little pyramid just between my eyes.

And then the question came: "Wait a minute. Do I really want the spirit of Sharon Tate to enter me?" Up until then I'd considered it a privilege. And then Bruce said, "Well, we have a lot of resistance here tonight, I'm afraid we'll have to stop"; And then he said, "Well, anyway, I have to tell you all: I was calling Christ. And I thought I would call Him in the name of Sharon Tate because none of you guys would let Christ in but you might let Sharon Tate in." Ah, he was a trickster.

Those were cryptic days of LSD. Our audience thought that we were tripping all the time, and they claimed that they were peaking at the same time we were. But we weren't tripping, they were. We were down at Goucher College and at the end of the show a woman came and touched my feet, we were barefoot during the performance, and she said, "You KNOW, don't you? Oh you KNOW! You KNOW! You KNOW!"

So we opened *Commune* at the Performing Garage in the Fall of '71. It was an audience-participation piece in many ways: people were asked to come and sit in the middle of that wave and represent the villagers of My Lai while we shot them with our hands. You can imagine, some of the people resisted, and some didn't want to come out at all. It was directed that the play would not go on until they all came out.

Once the play stopped for two hours, and a woman went to the phone and called her lawyer. She refused to leave the Garage, she was going to sue for breach of ticket contract, some of the company started leaving, and people came out of the audience and read in the roles to finish the play. Finally it was completed.

We toured *Commune* in Poland. They went wild for it in Poland. They wanted to see the American spectacle. They didn't care what it was about. They just called it the "American Spectacle." In Breslau we had five guards at the gate trying to control people. The students would get a running jump and run right over the top of the people like a football game, come down on the other side, and shinny up those long curtains that they have to keep the cold air out, and hang there like monkeys for the entire production. You could throw hammers at them, wrenches, screwdrivers—it wouldn't do any good.

When we played in Warsaw there was a riot of a thousand people in the street and the police were called. Finally the people came around the outside and started bending the bars in the men's room to get through. After Poland we toured *Commune* to France, and we were playing in one of Napoleon's mistresses' chalets in Strasbourg. And we had big problems with the French. Not only are they style conscious, but they are very perverse. Someone would steal one boot (because everyone had to take off their shoes). One night it would be one right boot, then another night, one left boot. We were spending about two to three hundred dollars a night on buying new boots.

The Tower of Babel

This was directed by Tony Abeson at The Ensemble Theater Repertory Company. Tony was very dedicated to Grotowski.

A very dedicated director. Very thin, wiry. He did all the Grotowski plastiques and body work, and only wore black. I think he had one black outfit: a black turtleneck, black chinos and black boots. He only drank the purest Polish vodka. I don't remember what he ate, actually. I don't remember ever seeing him eating. I mean, what comes to mind is a box of Hartz Mountain birdseed. I never saw him eat that, but that's what I had in my mind.

Anyway, he was very dedicated, and the way that we were working was that we would come in in the morning and lie on the floor in the dark, in this little basement hole-in-the-wall on West 19th Street. And we would just lie there, in the dark, for an hour, listening to the trash trucks on West 19th Street. Then Tony would bring the lights up just a little bit on a dimmer. And that was our cue to begin rolling and thrashing. And we'd all begin rolling and thrashing and screaming. If you didn't have the impetus to do that, all you'd have to do was wait just a little bit until you got hit by a thrashing body. Then that would set you off. It would be a chain reaction, bouncing off the walls.

Then Tony would bring the lights up a little bit more, as a signal for "Encounter Time." And we'd all go to each other and look into each other's eyes, and touch certain selective body parts. This went on for about an hour.

Now, we did this for about six months. And then we started working on *The Tower of Babel*. Keeping with the Grotowski idea of a simple theme from the Bible, Tony chose this, the idea being the simple story of all mankind having one common language, and deciding to build this great tower up to God, taller than God, even. And God is so angry with this presumption and pride that God knocks it down, and mankind and womankind are spread out all over the world, all speaking different languages.

So basically, that's how it went. We would all come out from different parts of the room in our leotards, all with a common language: "AH AH AH AH AH AH AH AH AH." That was the common language. We would commonly begin to build this big body pile, God, because the ceiling was only about ten feet high. So we would just build this body pile up until something happened where someone lost balance and the whole thing would go "KLUMP" into a big sweaty heap. And then we'd all go off, with our own different languages. "OWEE-BA!" "LEAKAKA!" "LEAKAKA" and that was the play.

Now somehow, and I don't know how, we were invited to play this at grade schools in Missouri. I don't know how it came to pass, but we made it out there, and the first location was beautiful. It was like a Hopper painting. Dirt, schoolyard, swings, clapboard school, and all the kids were in the window, crying . . . "Oh My God, The New York Actors! OOOOHHH!" So we were performing in the cafeteria and we're completely surrounded by kids, probably from other schools as well, it looked like hundreds of kids. And we came out with our common language, "AH AH AH AH AH AH AH AH AH." And as soon as we started to build the body pile, the children went mad. They picked up on our energy and began spinning like dervishes and screaming. And the teachers were shouting, "Back! Back!" "Clear the Stage!" "Clear the Stage!"

One teacher rushed forward blowing a gym whistle and the show was stopped, and we were taken immediately back to St. Louis and put on trail by a Cultural Committee of women, and we were banned from the state. We were sent directly back to New York and our contract was not honored.

We were making little enough money as it was, and we came back to New York in a total state of shame, which is a difficult state to maintain in New York City, but we did it. We were so ashamed we never opened the play.

1984

THOMAS M. DISCH

In an age when most writers make a living by teaching or some form of journalism, the career of Thomas Disch (1940–2008) hearkens back to a more rough-and-ready time. To support his "nocturnal writing habit," he worked as a door-to-door salesman in Minneapolis, cloakroom attendant at the Majestic Theatre in New York, spear carrier at the Metropolitan Opera, bookstore and office clerk, insurance agent, bank teller, mortuary assistant, professional wrestler, and advertising copywriter. These variegated activities are reflected in the diversity of the genres he exercised, under a number of pseudonyms. Best known for his award-winning science fiction and horror novels, he also published prolific collections of short stories, essays, and poetry, even devising interactive computer adventure narratives. He contributed book and opera reviews to a number of publications (William Gibson said that his review of *The Difference Engine* in *The New York Times* was "perhaps the high point, for me, of the book's publication"); his theatre criticism for *The Nation* was relished for its hilarious retelling of bad nights on the aisle. Besides the libretto for an opera of *Frankenstein* and the original treatment of *The Lion King*, Disch wrote plays that he described as "as far off-off-Broadway as Broadway can get." In 1990, when his one-act monologue *The Cardinal Detoxes* was staged at the RAPP Arts Center on the Lower East Side, the Roman Catholic Archdiocese, the theater's landlord, tried to get the Buildings Department to bar the front door. Depressed by deteriorating health, the death of his longtime partner, the flooding of his country house, and eviction from his Manhattan apartment, the man once praised as "the American Borges" shot himself on the Fourth of July, 2008.

The Death of Broadway

A CITY is a machine that works by inertia. By virtue of their solidity and expense, large buildings act as a brake on social change. Each one, from the most squalid tenement to the ritziest hotel, represents a way of life that has jelled into just this form and is jealous of its right to continue as is. Thus neighborhoods in the process of gentrification acquire graffiti

threatening death to yuppie invaders, and all bastions of privilege hire doormen to defend them from riffraff. Finally, however, no single building, no street, no neighborhood, can hold
its own against the glacial advance of larger social forces.

Right now such a social glacier is poised at the edge of New
York City's already much eroded theater district. For many
decades inertial real-estate values, abetted by landmark-desig-
nation legislation, have earned Broadway the dubious epithet
"Fabulous Invalid." In the nineties the Fabulous Invalid is destined to become the Inglorious Corpse, and the Great White
Way to become a graveyard for great white elephants, as, one
by one, the thirty-six theaters left in the Broadway area find
themselves unable to attract either shows or audiences.

Those who feel a professional obligation to contradict the
handwriting on the wall—theater owners, producers, and press
agents—can cite cheery statistics. The League of American
Theatres and Producers announced last June that for the third
year in a row Broadway set box-office records, with $283 mil-
lion in ticket sales. However, this record reflects not dramatically increased attendance but only higher ticket prices—as
high as $55 or $60 for musicals. Actual attendance for the past
four seasons was, in millions, 6.97, 8.14, 7.97, and 8.04. Ten
seasons ago attendance totaled 10.82 million. Twenty-two
years ago William Goldman noted in *The Season*, the best book
about the Broadway theater ever written, that the 1967–1968
season had set an all-time high for ticket sales, $59 million;
then, too, the reason was higher ticket prices—soon to be as
high as $15.

The most revealing and dismaying contrast between Goldman's season and the one just past is in the number of plays
produced. In the 1967–1968 season fifty-eight shows opened
on Broadway: forty-four nonmusical plays (twenty-five dramas, nineteen comedies) and fourteen musicals. The 1989–
1990 season yielded thirty-five shows: twenty-one nonmusical
plays (six of them revivals) and twelve musicals (four of them
revivals), plus two "special attractions." Musicals seem to be
holding their own, but clearly "legit" drama (to use *Variety*'s
parlance) is an endangered species. In 1967–1968 there were
new plays by Harold Pinter, Tennessee Williams, Arthur Miller,
Tom Stoppard, Gore Vidal, Eugene O'Neill, Joe Orton,

Edward Albee, Neil Simon, Peter Nichols, Lillian Hellman, Ira Levin, Peter Ustinov (two plays), and some twenty-seven other playwrights, not counting those who wrote books for musicals. Last season the "name" playwrights presenting new work were Larry Gelbart, David Hare, Tom Stoppard (with a radio play from 1972 on stage for the first time), August Wilson, A. R. Gurney, and Peter Shaffer. As of January 1, a time when the season is usually at its peak, only five legit dramas were playing on Broadway—three held over from last season and two survivors from among the scant four that opened last fall, one of them at Lincoln Center, which is a "Broadway" theater only by a legal fiction.

The steep decline since 1967–1968 represents but a portion of a longer-term downward trend. Throughout his book Goldman lamented the diminished state of the theater in *his* time. There were 264 new productions in the 1927–1928 season and 187 three years later, after the double whammy of the Depression and talkies; there were sixty in 1940–1941. The sixties brought a mild upsurge, but, as Brooks Atkinson lamented in his historical account *Broadway* (1970), "in the seventies there was a surplus of theaters all through the year. Most theaters were dark during long periods. . . . Herman Levin, producer of the legendary *My Fair Lady*, believes that the day is not too distant when ten theaters will be enough." Levin may prove to have been an optimist.

There are many reasons for this situation, but the main one has nothing directly to do with the theater. Manhattan, long regarded as a nice place to visit but not to live, is becoming useless for either purpose. On September 3 of last year this was dramatized with a vividness that no Broadway playwright has achieved in the past many seasons, when a "gang of ritualistic muggers" (to quote a headline in *The New York Times*) killed a twenty-two-year-old Utah tourist, Brian Watkins, as he tried to defend his mother from their attack. And why do you suppose the gang (called FTS, an acronym for Fuck That Shit) was down in the subway mugging tourists? Not to get money for crack, no. They wanted to go dancing at Roseland, where many of them were later arrested as they exited at closing time.

The story is a natural for a full-scale Broadway musical. It would open at FTS headquarters, in Flushing, where the gang leader, Rocstar, is explaining in a rap song to two new recruits that to be initiated into FTS they must mug someone that night. Cut to the Watkins family in front of a traditional bright-lights-along-the-Great-White-Way backdrop as they sing a medley of standards in praise of Broadway. Then the mugging, performed as a slow-motion duet for Rocstar and Brian. Finally the big Hip-Hop Ballet in Roseland, as the gang members, exhilarated by their kill, vie to see who is the most spectacular dancer. The young murderer's friends told the *Times* that Rocstar had a special talent for graffiti, so there is the possibility of a dance solo for Rocstar in which he would declare his love for the ingenue (another Big-Apple-loving Utahan, whom he's met only that night, at Roseland) in tragic eight-foot letters just before the cops arrive.

Some may object that such a scenario is in questionable taste, offensive to victims and assaulters alike. One of the more refined cruelties of living in New York City is that it is considered bad form openly to excoriate minority public enemies like the members of FTS. Yet it is impossible to speak of the problems of the Broadway neighborhood without mentioning what all visitors immediately notice: its streets have become a gauntlet of sinister and sleazy pushers, hookers, panhandlers, mad derelicts, wristwatch con artists, and small, silent clusters of youths who look like recruiting material for FTS. Where there were once nightclubs and restaurants catering to theatergoers, there are head shops and pizza parlors of surpassing grunginess. The very Roseland where FTS members held their victory celebration was for decades a ballroom frequented by the same fuddy-duddies who could be counted on to fill the now darkened theaters.

I came to New York City in 1957, after daydreaming about Gotham all through my high school years in Minnesota, and landed a job checking hats and selling orange juice at the Majestic Theater through most of the runs of *The Music Man* and *Camelot*. I had no theatrical ambitions myself; I just wanted an address at the center of the universe. The Broadway I became acquainted with corresponded at most points with the myth that had brought me there. My boss at the Majestic, Arthur Gross, might have stepped out of a Damon Runyon story, with his gravelly dese-dem-dose accent and a belief in his destined luck at the racetrack which no losses could dampen. My fellow orange-juice vendors had a similarly quixotic faith that they were Broadway bound, and a few did eventually land jobs in the chorus lines of musicals.

The neighborhood was filled with such now vanished lower-middle-class amenities as cafeterias and automats and bars that actually provided a free lunch of sorts for the price (fifteen cents) of a glass of beer. Forty-second Street, whose scuzziness has by now proved so intractable that it is slated for bulldozing as a last cosmetic resort, was then a benign honky-tonk of movie houses that played second-run double features until the wee hours. The teenage gangs of that era had made only a symbolic beachhead on Broadway, as the Jets and Sharks in the Bernstein and Sondheim *West Side Story* of 1957. Homelessness, similarly, was the theme of a musical comedy, *Subways Are for Sleeping*, in 1961, long before it became a permanent feature of the landscape. (In fact, the cheapest movie houses on Forty-second Street specialized in movies so old and dull that only winos would pay the thirty-five-cent admission charge, and thus provided the city with large de facto dormitories.)

The Times Square venues that I knew as a checkroom attendant earning $32 a week were, needless to say, the very meanest socio-economic niche. The audiences whose coats and hats I checked set the general tone of the area, which was one of middle-class mass-market glitz: Schrafft's, Howard Johnson's, Childs. A rung up from those were Sardi's, Gallagher's, the Stork Club. Now, in the era of $60 tickets (more if you buy from scalpers), it is only the upper end of the spectrum that still, tenuously, survives. As with housing in New York City, there is little provision for middle-class, middle-income needs. In the fifties and early sixties Broadway shows were one of the city's basic amenities, available even to those (and they were a majority in the Majestic balcony) who hesitated before they splurged on a thirty-five-cent half-pint carton of orange juice. Now, except among the rich, a night on the town has become a once-a-year extravagance, a fact reflected in the strength of Broadway musicals relative to plays. Last season musicals accounted for 67 percent of attendance and 75 percent of gross receipts. After all, people can see actors on TV any night of the week; they can read a good story. When they go to the theater, they want a lavish production, visible millions, their money's worth.

As a latter-day Irving Berlin might observe, there's no industry like the entertainment industry. None, certainly, likely to yield such a small return on the money invested. Consider the fate of *Jerome Robbins' Broadway*, the most expensive show in Broadway history and the winner of six Tony awards. After a run of less than two years, and while it was still playing to 90 percent capacity (more than 10,000 people a week), it closed, having earned only $4.8 million of its $8.8 million cost. Its weekly expenses were so high and its profit margin so slim that its producers decided to take a scaled-down version on the road and to Japan while the show was still relatively fresh. The Robbins show epitomizes the current desperate situation of Broadway not just in terms of profit and loss but in its essence as well. It's an anthology of show-stopping moments of the kind that just don't happen on Broadway anymore, except in revivals. Three of the excerpted shows—*Gypsy*, *Fiddler on the Roof*, and *Peter Pan*—were also revived last year; two have already closed.

How do theater people themselves account for the quick failure of many shows and the probability that the rest will be unprofitable? Usually they blame the messenger—that is, the *New York Times* theater critic, Frank Rich, who reviews almost all Broadway shows and most other major theatrical events in the city. When Rich pans a show and it flops, he is always ready to hand as a scapegoat. Last November the English playwright David Hare's fulminations against Rich's review of Hare's *The Secret Rapture* earned banner headlines in *Variety*. Hare kvetched, "There is an unmistakable personal nastiness in what [Rich] writes, a series of *ad hominem* attacks that seem unmotivated by what he has seen on the stage but by some personal bitterness about artists." Hare's outrage strikes me as a classic instance of denial and of the sense of entitlement common to artists who have waxed fat on subsidies. I thought Rich was too kind to the play.

But Rich does in fact exercise a life-or-death power over

most plays, despite his disingenuous insistence that it is producers who close shows, not his reviews. His raves have helped
such minor-league works as *Eastern Standard*, *Mastergate*, and
Once on This Island win transfers out of pre-Broadway venues,
while his pans in just this past season sank not only Hare's play
but also *Accomplice*, *The Cemetery Club*, and a revival of Paddy
Chayefsky's *The Tenth Man*. These three victims were all, on
the face of it, likely survivors, filling niches (thriller, sentimental comedy, Jewish high-minded drama) otherwise unoccupied
at the time they opened. *Accomplice* was an ingeniously plot-
ted comic murder mystery in the vein of *Deathtrap*, which
Rich found "incomprehensible." Rich dismissed *The Cemetery
Club*, a benign, formulaic comedy about Jewish widows in
Queens, as " 'Golden Girls' at four times the length but with at
most one-fourth the star wattage," and "one of the best arguments yet advanced for cremation." He was acerbic about the
Lincoln Center production of *The Tenth Man*, Chayefsky's
most successful play, and dismissive of Somerset Maugham as a
playwright in reviewing a revival of *The Circle*, but that show
survived by sheer star power, in the shape of Rex Harrison,
Glynis Johns, and Stewart Granger. One would have to be an
intrepid producer to mount further revivals of Maugham while
Rich remains the *Times*'s sole Broadway critic. As for the living
playwrights Rich has hexed, what can they do but bewail their
fate, like Hare, and resign themselves to writing for Off Broadway and regional theaters?

As *The Nation*'s reviewer, I have seen the same plays that
Rich has seen for the past three seasons, and while I have usually been better disposed toward the "well-made" plays Rich
tends to pan, I think Rich's tastes are more congruent with the
expectations of actual Broadway audiences than are my own.
His slighting comparison of *The Cemetery Club* to *The Golden
Girls* isn't off target. The latter is one of the best-scripted TV
sitcoms since *Taxi*, and few sentimental comedies on stage in
recent years have been as amusing. If audiences insist that what
they see in the theater must be of another magnitude altogether than the best things available on TV, then Broadway had
better just scrap the genre of sentimental comedy altogether.
And so, by and large, it has. The most notable successes in that
vein—*Steel Magnolias* and *Driving Miss Daisy*—had long runs

Off Broadway, where a show can survive if it sells in a week what most Broadway houses have to pull in every night. Both shows went on to become popular movies. Yet they would probably have fared no better than *The Cemetery Club* on Broadway, where sitcom wholesomeness has little box-office appeal, even among those who enjoy it in other contexts. Who goes to the Four Seasons for a hot dog?

It is the same with a thriller like *Accomplice* (despite a set—incorporating an operational mill wheel—that offered the kind of conspicuous expense unavailable in smaller theaters), with a "serious" or writerly drama like last season's *The Lisbon Traviata*, and with most revivals, from Shakespeare to Arthur Miller. For such plays Off Broadway is a more natural venue. A larger set in exchange for being three times as far away from the actors is a poor trade-off. The chance to see Dustin Hoffman play Shylock or Kathleen Turner play Maggie the Cat is not worth double the price of admission to see a noncelebrity actor in a more freewheeling performance any night of the week.

Broadway has become a tourist attraction, New York City's dilapidated and inadequate response to Disney World. Most native New Yorkers have come to regard it as they do the Empire State Building or the Statue of Liberty—a place one goes to, if at all, only with out-of-town visitors. A friend of mine who works in the city courts and used to take in three or four Broadway shows a year with his wife is typical of many: he has decided that two hours of live entertainment simply isn't worth the price of tickets and a risky subway ride into the heart of the city's darkness. And this is a man who used to be a Transit Authority cop.

The reason that Broadway appeals less to New Yorkers these days isn't just that Broadway has changed: so have New Yorkers. Middle-class flight to the suburbs and subsequent inner-city decay have not yet reached the proportions in Manhattan that they have in Detroit or Philadelphia (or in Brooklyn or the Bronx, for that matter), but even so these are basic demographic facts of life. Some of the émigrés to the suburbs still work in the city and constitute, probably, a moiety of the vanishing breed of "regular" theatergoers. But a glance around the lobby at any Broadway show reveals who *isn't* there: any of the city's readily identifiable minorities—blacks, Hispanics, Asians, and the young.

It isn't just the expense; it's the fact that New Yorkers no longer have a common culture. The melting pot has been replaced by a mosaic, the separate components of which regard one another with apathy or contempt. Allegories of neighborliness like *Abie's Irish Rose* and *West Side Story* are passé. When blacks appear on Broadway, as they have recently in August Wilson's dramas or musicals like *Black and Blue* and *Once on This Island*, it is usually in an all-black production performed for predominantly white audiences (though *Black and Blue* is the particular favorite of Japanese tourists). Only one play now on Broadway proper, *Prelude to a Kiss*, and another at Lincoln Center, *Six Degrees of Separation*, can be said to mirror contemporary urban reality—or fantasy, for that matter.

In his recent comedy, *The Cocktail Hour*, A. R. Gurney drew a vivid portrait of a middle-class couple from the older generation, who loved to go to the kind of Broadway plays that Lunt and Fontanne starred in—plays about smart, sophisticated tipplers having romantic adventures amid nice furniture. No American playwright in our time has a better handle on the WASP milieu; few are as funny, none more skilled in basic carpentry. Yet *The Cocktail Hour*, like most of Gurney's plays, had an Off-Broadway run. A significant exception was *Love Letters*, a play requiring only two actors and no set. An additional selling point was that since the actors *read* their lines, anyone could perform the play with a week's rehearsal or less, and so it was a play that any currently unemployed pair of actors could perform in any currently darkened theater.

More and more, Broadway theaters have tried to keep their marquees lit by offering evening-long monologues (*Tru*) and solo recitals, as well as two-handers like *Love Letters*. This trend has not been limited to Broadway. Two- and three-character plays have abounded at resident theater companies across the country in the past season. Regional theaters have also become uncommonly attentive to that part of theatrical heritage that is in the public domain. In Minneapolis the Guthrie Theater offered a season of five plays by Shakespeare, one by Euripides, *The Front Page* (1928), *The Skin of Our Teeth* (1942), and, inevitably, *A Christmas Carol.* At the Actors Theatre of Louisville, long noted for its premieres of new plays, five of seven forthcoming productions are of works more than twenty-five years old. Since Broadway has become accustomed to having regional theaters do much of the work of development, this trend will represent a significant rupture in the pipeline in the years ahead.

Supply and demand does not operate in the theater as it does in classical economic theory. Writers, perceiving an abundance of dark theaters, will not consider this an opportunity to write new plays to augment a dwindling supply. Universities— and the world at large—are filled with people aspiring to be writers, and for almost all of them that means writing novels, since the likelihood of publishing one's first novel is many times greater than that of having a first play produced. The likelihood of earning a living as a novelist, slim as it is, is also much greater than that of doing so as a playwright. Accordingly, apprentice writers with a shred of sense try to develop their novel-writing muscles first. Some writers, of course, lack that much sense, or have a natural flair for the theater, and a few are able to buck the odds and get produced.

But even for those few there is Hollywood and the vast talent-gobbling maw of television. In the TV era it has come to be understood that the stage is only a stepping-stone to Hollywood. Playwriting has become the larval stage of a screenwriter's career, the mere grubby precondition of butterfly success. And rarely do those who have gone west continue to write for the Broadway stage, Neil Simon and David Mamet being notable exceptions.

Who, then, does write plays nowadays? A canny few playwrights like Israel Horovitz and the late Charles Ludlam have managed to create their own little Bayreuths, where they have been able to produce and direct their work without constantly seeking new or renewed funding. The luckiest have a comfortable relationship with one of the established regional or Off-Broadway venues that can serve (when fueled by a rave from Frank Rich) as a launching pad to Broadway: Lanford Wilson at Circle Rep, August Wilson at Yale, David Rabe at the Public Theater. More commonly, however, playwrights of a literary bent produce work with no expectation of a Broadway production. Often they represent a minority sensibility—gay, feminist, black—in a combative mood: Christopher Durang, Megan Terry, and Charles Fuller are examples.

Indeed, what most non-Broadway playwrights have in common is contentiousness. They remain children of the counter-culture, with the bad manners and chip-bearing shoulders common to that breed. They don't attend the Broadway theater, they don't write for it, and they are almost unanimous in seeing Broadway as facing extinction—even those who, by a fluke, have been produced there. Marsha Norman, who wrote 'night, Mother, declares Broadway to be "virtually closed for serious drama." Stephen Sondheim observes that "a whole generation and a half has grown up without the theatregoing habit," and that "much of the middle class that used to support the theater can't afford it anymore." Lanford Wilson grouses, "I don't think there have been more than two good plays on Broadway since '62."

Equally dire pronouncements about Broadway and the future of theater in general have been made by Christopher Durang, John Guare, Michael Weller, and, indeed, virtually all the other seventeen contributors to *In Their Own Words*, the anthology of interviews with American playwrights from which the quotations above were extracted. The only cheery view of the situation comes from David Mamet, who declares,

I think it's a great time to be a young person in the theatre. All bets are off, as in such times of social upheaval as the twenties in Germany, the sixties in Chicago, the period from 1898 to 1920 in Russia. . . . I think we're going to start putting people in jail again for what they write. People have been subconsciously afraid of expressing themselves because the times are so tenuous. And the reality will follow that feeling. So that will be exciting.

Maybe, but one thing is sure—the excitement won't be on Broadway.

It isn't only cautious, pandering producers who are the enemies of playwrights, however. In their own way, directors and actors have an ageless and unassuageable grudge against the tyranny of the text. In the film industry the director has long been considered the No. 1 Artist, the *auteur*, while the star has the most box-office clout. In Hollywood, notoriously, the script has always been a mutable thing. But in the theater authors once had more authority. Even dead authors' printed texts were too famous to be seriously tampered with. Directors were in charge of the actors' performances and coordinated the decorative aspects of a production—sets, costumes, music. But they were bound to follow the story line as a train must follow its tracks.

Gradually that changed. The examples both of Hollywood and of musical comedy (where the book has usually been a negligible part of the production) emboldened directors to assert their own artistic claims. Elia Kazan forced rewrites from Tennessee Williams that turned his plots around 180 degrees. Bob Fosse managed to turn Stephen Schwartz's *Pippin* from the sentimental celebration of innocence and idealism that the author thought he had written into a glitzkrieg that reflected his own obsessed hedonism—and audiences loved it. The show ran four and a half years. Finally, Fosse's *auteur* instincts produced the film *All That Jazz*, the story of his life coauthored by an obscure writer willing to stroke Fosse's ego.

Actors resent the authority of writers no less than directors do. They have special cause, having to mouth the same words night after night until they must feel like puppets. They know that a scene's success, even a play's, often depends on their delivery rather than on what is being delivered. In retrospect it seems almost inevitable that actors and directors would band together to subvert the tyranny of the text. Plays under the baton of Judith Malina, of the Living Theater, or Jean-Claude van Itallie, of the Open Theater, or Richard Schechner, of the Performance Group, became communal creations in which each actor did his own thing. At first, during the sixties and early seventies, the results were often exciting. But as the novelty wore off, the excitement diminished and jelled into a new avant-garde orthodoxy that dispenses not only with authorship but also with narrative, coherence, linearity, and anything like human interest. Richard Foreman and the Wooster Group have been the chief exponents of this style, but it recently reached its apotheosis in Martha Clarke's million-dollar fiasco, *Endangered Species*, a spectacle that sought to make a large statement about animal oppression, racial domination, the

Holocaust, the Civil War, and the tyranny of love, using no text but lines cobbled together from Whitman's *Leaves of Grass*. This state of affairs was dictated not by Clarke's artistic vision but by a dispute over whether the intended author, Charles Mee, would receive equal billing with her. Clarke refused, Mee stood his ground, and the result was a mishmash of grandiose good intentions that starred a circus elephant. Elephants are impressive animals, but in the theater writers may still be more essential.

Martha Clarke is not a Broadway impresario, though her budgets tend to make her look like one. Nor is there any threat that Off Broadway's war against the written word will establish a beachhead on Times Square anytime soon. But if the largest budgets are reserved for the inchoate visions of the most ambitious directors, that is one more reason for playwrights to write plays on a small scale or not at all.

Let us suppose that legitimate theater is a lost cause on Broadway, except for a few ever-more-retro revivals each season. Doesn't that still leave the musical as a living art form? I think not, and for parallel reasons—the dwindling supply of talent and the disparity between what producers can offer and what consumers want.

To begin with the supply side of the equation, a paucity of opportunities dictates fewer apprenticeship positions. The entertainment industry has, however, been aware of the need to provide some seed money for research and development, and so there are a few institutions that encourage fledgling composers and lyricists to learn their craft. In the course of three years of reviewing I have seen a fair number of the resulting musical comedies, both in New York and out of town, one of which, *Once on This Island*, recently graduated to Broadway (thanks to a rave from Frank Rich). I thought that this "calypso" musical was bologna on white bread, an innocuous minstrel show put on by an all-black cast and an all-white creative team. It was subsidized by AT&T and showcased at Playwrights Horizons. At about the same time, *A Change in the Heir*, by another team of hopefuls, opened on Broadway, having been developed at the New Tuners Theatre, in

Chicago. It fell just short of legendary awfulness. And those two were probably the best of the neophyte musicals I've seen.

The talent isn't there anymore, or isn't visible, and the only musicals that have lately made any sort of mark on Broadway bear this out. Last season's musical successes were a revival of *Gypsy*, *City of Angels*, with a score by Cy Coleman, who has been writing hit musicals for thirty years; *Grand Hotel*, with a resuscitated score from Robert Wright and George Forrest, who did *Song of Norway* and *Kismet* (the score was fortified by a few solid songs by Maury Yeston); and *Aspects of Love*, by Andrew Lloyd Webber, the English composer, who has two other musicals currently running. This season brought revivals of *Oh, Kay!* (1926), *Fiddler on the Roof* (1964), and *Peter Pan* (1954); a revue of Yiddish musical-theater favorites; and an homage to Buddy Holly.

If Broadway's musical menu is beginning to be almost as antiquarian as the Metropolitan Opera's, the reasons are no further away than your radio and your cable-TV screen. Broadway style, however broadly defined, no longer represents the consensus preference in matters of song and dance. While a few efforts have been made to come to terms with rock-and-roll (the best, *Grease* and *Little Shop of Horrors*, were Off-Broadway shows), by and large Broadway composers go for wit, romance, schmaltz, and the tempos of ballroom dancing. The current Tommy Tune hit *Grand Hotel* is a state-of-the-art example of what can still be done, but surely it is significant that the show is set in 1928, and that its two best dance numbers are a Charleston and a bolero, which are, respectively, show-stopping and heart-stopping.

Or so they seemed to this fifty-year-old, who started seeing musicals at movie theaters in the early 1950s, when the movies regularly reproduced Broadway hits. However, when I talked recently to a class of college freshmen at the School of Visual Arts, twelve of whom had just seen *Grand Hotel*, I was pained to discover that only one student would admit to having liked it. The others thought the songs "dull" or "phony," and found the alternation between speech and song off-putting. In short, they disliked the *idea* of musical comedy, and indeed, when I asked them to name a musical that they had liked, I got mostly blank looks. I might as well have asked them who was their favorite Puritan divine.

The one transformation that musicals have made to adapt to these changing tastes is represented by the work of Andrew Lloyd Webber and of the French team of Boublil and Schönberg, the creators of *Les Miserables* and the forthcoming *Miss Saigon*. Their recipe is to move musical comedy in the direction of opera by reducing the comedy component to near zero, replacing ordinary speech with recitative, so as to promote a continuous musical flow, and providing large dollops of spectacle. It also helps to have elements of religious (*Jesus Christ Superstar*) or political (*Evita*, *Les Miserables*) uplift, in order to reassure audiences that they're not frittering away their money on mere entertainment.

So far, no Americans have managed to produce musicals in this new vein. The one edge that Broadway still has on the English and French invaders is dancing, and the best indigenous hits of the past ten years have been revues and revivals that showcase great dancing, such as *Black and Blue*, *42nd Street*, and *Jerome Robbins' Broadway*. But the days of great dancing are also numbered, because choreographers are, literally, a dying breed. Gower Champion died the day his *42nd Street* opened; Bob Fosse died in 1987, having already choreographed the occasion in *All That Jazz*; Michael Bennett, of *A Chorus Line* and *Dreamgirls*, died the same year. Jerome Robbins has semi-retired. Of all the choreographer-directors of the first rank, only Tommy Tune is still active.

Bennett died of AIDS. No single group in the New York art world has been harder hit by the AIDS epidemic than dancers and choreographers, and this cannot help having an effect on what producers are able to produce. There are not so very many first-class talents in the field that we can expect the gaps in the ranks to continue to be filled by new recruits year after year, as in a Civil War army. There is no way to measure what will never happen, or what might have been had so many not died or become too ill or despairing to work. Lesley Farlow, a dance specialist in New York City, has initiated an oral-history project for the dance collection of the New York Public Library, taping the testimony of dancers and choreographers stricken with AIDS. Probably no one has a better grasp of the overall situation than Farlow, and she says that hundreds and hundreds of prominent dance-world figures have died AIDS-related deaths.

Few of the problems facing Broadway are within the scope of the entertainment industry to remedy. Ticket prices might be scaled back, and in fact there is a new scheme afoot to supplement the existing last-minute-discount TKTS office in Times Square with a more extensive operation, called STAR*TIX, in Grand Central Terminal. Another scheme is the Broadway Alliance, an agreement among producers, unions, and theater owners to make three Broadway theaters available for plays with budgets of less than $400,000 (that is, not musicals), for which ticket prices can be reduced to $24, $19, and $10, thanks to financial concessions by all parties. If the scheme succeeds, perhaps it could be extended to more than three theaters; at least a dozen are dark most of the time.

The problem of Times Square's squalor is of another magnitude, one that requires solutions on the scale on which Robert Moses worked. Indeed, bulldozers are poised to begin a Moses-style effort that will entail leveling Forty-second Street and several blocks around, and replacing all the local low-life with high-rise office towers and a convention center. Already, new hotels have gone up in the area, their acres of lobbies and restaurants serving as a kind of middle-class bastion from which tourist-hunting muggers can legally be excluded, as they cannot be from the streets. The imminent battle between developers who would like to create protected environments and civil libertarians who fear the creation of a two-tiered city with high-safety precincts accessed by credit cards will probably eventually be fought in court—assuming that the urban engineers have the funding to begin building such a safe new world.

The city's latest budget crunch makes this seem a less likely assumption than that the slide into old-fashioned urban decay will continue. Perhaps the middle class will abandon Manhattan altogether, and the Great White Way can repeat the history of Forty-second Street on a larger scale, converting to the MTV generation's equivalent of burlesque and vaudeville—raunchy popular entertainment at low prices for mass audiences.

Out-of-towners could come in busloads and see it on chaper-
oned tours, the way the French and the Japanese now tour
Harlem. But probably the future holds a combination of the
two—a state-financed last bastion in a sea of picturesque, life-
threatening sleaze. Which is to say, just what we've got now,
only more so.

1991

CHARLES LUDLAM

Charles Ludlam (1943–1987) took part in the late-night Manhattan theatre scene of the Warhol era, with its competing street transvestites, would-be "superstars," and resale-shop glamour; but, more ambitious and better trained, in 1967 he founded the Ridiculous Theatre Company, housed in Sheridan Square. His first plays there, *When Queens Collide* and *Turds in Hell*, were in a similarly anarchic, sexually exhibitionist mode; but with *Bluebeard* (1970), Ludlam discovered the value of a strong plot. The breakthrough came when *Camille* (1973), both a camp exercise in drag performance and an illuminating interpretation of a classic, and *Stage Blood* (1975), an ingenious riff on *Hamlet*, were noticed and praised by the uptown critics. Ludlam's plays are palimpsests: a thick layer of allusions to B movies, comic books, and pop music laid over erudite inscriptions drawn from literature, opera, and mythology. As Martin Gottfried pointed out early on, Ludlam was a superb comic playwright excluded from the mainstream because his work was too zany (and exuberantly homosexual) and from the underground theatre because it was too recondite. Ludlam rejected the term "avant-garde," seeing himself as the guardian of histrionic tradition, naming Molière and Ibsen as his models. Since his death from AIDS, only his two-man quick-change farce *The Mystery of Irma Vep* (1984) is regularly revived, but his inspiration can be traced throughout the tidal wave of gay performance art that came in his wake.

Gay Theatre

IN the theatre there has always been a high percentage of homosexuals because—for one thing—to pursue a life in the theatre it's better not to have a family. Gay people have always found a refuge in the arts, and the Ridiculous Theatre is notable for admitting it. The people in it—and it is a very sophisticated theatre, culturally—never dream of hiding anything about themselves that they feel is honest and true and the best part of themselves. *Nothing* is concealed in the Ridiculous.

But proselytizing lifestyles is a Brechtian thing—in the tradition of advertising and propaganda work—which doesn't have anything to do with the absolutely rigorous individualism that goes into our work.

When people were saying there was gay theatre, I think a lot of that was about me, because my theatre was being taken that way, as it should have been. There was nothing wrong with that. However, later, people wanted gay theatre to be a political theatre that catered to gay people's needs for group reinforcement and self-respect, dignifying the gay image. My theatre is terrible for dignifying anybody's image.

The people who wanted to show the respectable gay image—La Coste shorts and pleats—were horrified that in my plays they were always disreputable drag queens, and that monstrosities were being committed. In my plays, people exhibit terrible behavior because it's showing the ridiculous side of life.

My art is not based on showing a positive image for any one group. I think that would be a terrible cop-out. That kind of theatre, the preachy type, has less to do with the gay sensibility than with showing how gay people could be just like straight people.

Once I was on a panel of gay artists at the Old Firehouse of the Gay Activists Alliance with Jill Johnston, Merle Miller and a bunch of others. They were saying that gay people could be just as straight as straight people and I said, "No. Gay people should be more *queer*. We shouldn't give up our difference. We're a different force."

I think the real liberating effect is to have something that dares to be defiant, not to show that we can be normal and married with joint bank accounts and holding down respectable jobs. I know for a lot of people that's very important, but I'm an artist. I can be more bohemian. I don't have to pass for anything. It's not that way in computer programming and teaching grammar school, but my value is to throw things open, let air in on forbidden subject matter. Rather than saying, "Oh, it's all so respectable," I say, "What's so respectable about being respectable?"

My work is very much for people who might not approve of the gayness. I take them over the bumps, make them draw certain conclusions about sexism through parody, hold sexism up to ridicule. The same techniques that other playwrights use to maneuver their audience into a sexist position can also be used to make them accept something they wouldn't ordinarily accept.

In a sense, I think I had a big influence on there being such a thing as gay theatre, but at the same time I wouldn't play at all the way they wanted me to. The rage that might have been in some of my plays could never be transmuted into that kind of comfy-cozy thing.

When we played in San Francisco in 1980, everyone thought, "This is going to be the biggest smash in history." But the gays did not come out, the gay papers panned us, people were saying to me, "Nobody says this to your face, but they don't think you're good for their image."

I felt let down in a way. But I also realized that the straight press was misrepresenting the plays as being more gay even than they were in an attempt to discredit them, and the gay people were playing right into their hands by wanting to be so straight about it.

Also, I think it's very dangerous to create an all-gay community because there's no influence from the outside world.

Everybody but a couple of people in my company are gay, but what we do is political in a different way from gay theatre. It's just entertainment, not agit-prop. It isn't preachy and it's for everybody. Politics is a subsidiary function. My own natural, liberated nature has made it that on a very high level.

I think the distinction between gay theatre and what I do, which some people call "queer theatre," is that gay theatre is really a political movement to show that gay people can be admirable, responsible members of the community. It shows their problems. I don't do that. "Queer theatre" embraces more variation, and the possibility of something being odd or peculiar rather than just simply homosexuality.

Homosexuals, just as women, are not politically one group. They are communists and they are extreme right wing, they are fascists, there is every kind of opinion. Gay becomes an ineffective category, whereas "queer" is a little more of a splash of cold water. There is more room for more people in the queer category.

It's the theatre that is queer. This theatre is weird, it is odd, it's peculiar, it's eccentric, it's different. That is also implied, you see, aside from the slightly smarmy little sexual reference in it.

I've written plays that have had gay characters. When I did *Caprice*, I portrayed a gay character. But I got the feeling they wanted Richard Chamberlain playing that particular gay guy. They didn't want to see me as representing gay.

Not that I was representing gay politically in that work. What I was trying to do was to explain the relationship between a homosexual artist—in this case, a fashion designer —and his view of the world.

Because I'm a satirist and inherently try to show what's wrong with the world, some groups become picky, overly sensitive. These people feel that you're being negative and critical to them, which may not be so.

I think that it's ghettoization. It's the same as black theatre.

My theatre does use certain elements of this deviant, deserted point of view to interpret to the world, but it's not gay writing about gay. Because I am homosexual, it becomes significant to homosexuals, I suppose. But I don't think it's me trying to prove that gay people are these remarkable members of society who are going to be bourgeois, because I don't think that's necessarily right. If they want to, fine. I don't doubt that they can be teachers and office workers who are reliable, but maybe depicting them as dangerous characters would be more interesting. Maybe we're not as housebroken as those plays want to make it seem.

Plays have to be archetypical human situations that everybody's involved in. The weakness of gay plays is that because the character is gay everybody isn't involved, so the gay person, to make it universal, has to be involved in something that could happen to anybody.

It comes down to the question of, "Is it gay theatre if gay people do it?"

We all know that there are a lot of gay people who write, direct, act, produce plays, and are hush-hush about their sexual identity. Their works aren't particularly gay. Some even pretend to be heterosexual.

The avant-garde is largely dominated by gays who are more

or less in the closet, whose abstract works and concepts don't relate to their sexuality. Is that gay theatre or is it just abstract?

Should a play proselytize, try to preach a lesson about gay liberation? For me, my sexuality has always been right out there—sometimes in question and sometimes *the* issue.

Some artists I know are gay writers writing so-called "normal" plays, year in and year out, and nobody ever mentions what their sexuality is. Nobody cares. Major choreographers, dance theatre, theatre of images, abstract conceptual artists— no one ever brings up *their* sexuality. But from the first day I set foot onstage, my sexuality was a major subject of discussion. It always comes up. I may be exuding my own brand of sexuality, thus making a statement about it, but it's always been there as an issue.

If homosexuality has had an influence on me, it has made me feel a greater understanding of both sexes rather than a limitation.

It's a crazy situation. I think it is an invalid artistic judgment to try to oppress art and turn it into an advertisement tool for a political point of view, which is not even a profound point of view, because a political point of view could change like that! Meanwhile they want you to devote your life to putting out slogans, which is what they do in the press to a large extent. The critics—I think—are very slogan oriented.

Their prejudice creeps in. They're dealing with the fact that to them there's something disreputable about it.

They call you female impersonator if you play a woman. But why don't they call the heterosexual men who play gay characters homosexual impersonators? Or heterosexual impersonators. Or male impersonators.

They don't write about it as gay theatre though! They have never, really. A few have tried. But now they have code words. They say that it is camp or put it into a different category I don't think really applies.

Being pigeonholed or put into a category, you can be dismissed, rendered less effective in your interaction with culture. Because what they are really trying to say is, "This is for one audience—a small segment—and it is not for everybody," thereby depriving the majority of people of this work which I think they need!

A company that was all male or female would immediately lower the level of artistic consciousness. It would turn into a social club, become political. Women are essential in Ridiculous theatre. If they weren't here, it would be a partial view of the world.

Women fare very well in my plays—they come out on top. Women have traditionally been considered sacred. That's something that had to go out the window if women were to become people.

Obviously, in a Ridiculous play everything is ridiculous, but the women in my company feel that they get a fair shake. Homosexuality is not a sexist phenomenon—so it's not homosexuals against women. It's not so much being against women as being skeptical of them and not taking a kind of blanket sentimental attitude towards them.

Just the idea that women are equal to men doesn't mean anything. Specific women have to be compared to specific men, and even then—how can you compare two people?

Even the idea of liberating women makes no sense to great women. It only appeals to women who have accepted rather conventional and erroneous ideas about their own existence because of economic factors and the like.

My work has something to say for everybody that has nothing to do with sexuality. And I think the company, by not being exclusively a homosexual or a heterosexual company, is a model for social organization, enables people to work together in harmony. They don't have to work with people that have just their own predilections.

The conversations are much more interesting having people of different sexualities call each other on certain preconceptions. There is a lot of that in this theatre, which you wouldn't get in a theatre where everybody is the same.

In theatre where everyone is different, where there are gay men and gay women, heterosexual men, heterosexual women, and other permutations, you find them calling each other on things. It's much the same with race: with racial mix in a company—it becomes much clearer.

At some point you have to embrace the terms of oppression. The Ridiculous is a theatre that is not ashamed. It doesn't try to conceal the homosexuality of some of its actors, as others do.

What's happened really is that we reach a much wider audience. What we are doing isn't considered gay art.

I never thought of it as gay art.

1992

FRANK RICH

Frank Rich (b. 1949) was still a Harvard undergraduate writing for *The Crimson* when a piece of his on the out-of-town tryout of the musical *Follies* attracted the favorable attention of its director, Harold Prince, and its composer, Stephen Sondheim. His first professional reviews for the New York *Post* and *Time* were, however, of film and television. In 1980, he was made primary dramatic critic of *The New York Times* and, in short order, branded "the Butcher of Broadway" because, it was asserted, a negative report from him could close a show overnight. The nickname was unfair; other critics were more programmatically venomous and there was no hard evidence to prove a connection between a critique and a fiasco. Rich genuinely enjoyed the theatre, but insisted on talent and intelligence, always giving reasons for his opinions. His Sunday essays were entertaining accounts of how to take pleasure from flops or how to see through plays that pretend to be serious. Rich was particularly astute about the musical, which had become the dominant form in American theatre. His short piece on Carol Channing's withdrawal from *Hello, Dolly!* displays his virtues: a personal response and attention to detail framed by reference to wider social issues. In 1993, Rich gave up the theatre desk to return to full-time editorial writing and outspoken political commentary, deploring, in particular, the replacement of truth by "truthiness." He has now become a bête noire of the radical right and has been dubbed by them as "the Beast of the Beltway."

"Dolly" Goes Away

Until her closing performance in New York last Sunday, I hadn't seen Carol Channing in "Hello, Dolly!" since I was 14 and the show was in Washington, trying out on its way to Broadway. On that night, the audience roared at a newly added Act I finale in which Dolly, a widow, sang of how she must stop mourning and reclaim her life "before the parade passes by." Only weeks earlier President Kennedy's funeral cortege had passed by the theater on its way down Pennsylvania Avenue. Miss Channing was our own irrational incitement to throw off grief and start living again.

It's a memory I didn't want to mess with. So when Miss Channing returned to New York in "Hello, Dolly!" yet again last fall after yet another national tour, I elected not to see it. If she wasn't 32 years older, I was—and so was a musical some found old-fashioned the first time around. Those who did go described a freak show in which an elderly, self-caricaturing star plodded through her paces for the 4,000th-odd time. But a few persistent others—like my friend Suzanne, who finally shamed me into going—said it was the end of an era, more uplifting than grotesque, and could not be missed.

The truth is that Miss Channing's era—in which larger-than-life Broadway stars disseminated carefree mass entertainment to a bedazzled America—was over even before the original production of "Hello, Dolly!" ended its nearly seven-year run in 1970. As I arrived on Sunday for Miss Channing's last matinee at the Lunt-Fontanne Theater—and who remembers anymore who Lunt and Fontanne were?—19 of Broadway's 34 other playhouses were dark. Though "Dolly" in this incarnation had received great reviews in New York, it had not drawn great houses; this run was petering out after merely 14 weeks.

On Sunday, though, the theater *was* full, with Broadway die-hards on hand to pay their respects. When Miss Channing made her first entrance, she acknowledged the crowd's ovation with eyes as hungry as I've ever seen; she tilted her broad face upward to take in the balcony and bask in the lights, as if only an audience's adoration could sustain her. And then she gave a performance that, while an octave lower in pitch, seemed line by line the same I had seen in January 1964.

Miss Channing doesn't look the same. Her official biography says she turns 75 today, and her efforts to preserve Dolly in aspic are hard labor. The Looney Tunes accent, the thick and garish rouge, the cotton-candy wigs and the painted eyelashes are the paraphernalia of a clown. And in the noble, professional sense, that's what she is. Her fastidiously polished rituals of comic or balletic business—a lengthy eating scene, her descent down a staircase for the title song—are vaudeville shtick of another age.

The other great stage clowns of Miss Channing's Broadway heyday are all retired or dead. So is the whole idea of theater in which a single musical-comedy performer, carrying a show on the back of her own invented and idiosyncratic personality, must hand-deliver a vehicle from town to town, without benefit of electronic pyrotechnics, sex, violence or even fresh material.

Such is Miss Channing's belief in her craft and her drive to maintain its illusion that she has spent nearly half a century barnstorming the country in essentially two roles (Lorelei Lee of "Gentlemen Prefer Blondes" is the other). She never made the transition to film or TV, and, unlike today's stars, always put her work ahead of a private life, to the point of trotting out her meticulously scripted stage persona for each interview and public appearance. She is famous for never missing a performance and for having no real home, only the hotel rooms of the road.

As she was pelted with roses from the balcony at her last curtain call, she bravely assured the audience that "Hello, Dolly!" will tour again next fall. But as far as Broadway goes, this was the implicit farewell of a star whose intensity remained undimmed but whose cultural cosmos had disappeared, taking most of her audience with it. It was only too fitting that Carol Channing took her final bows on Sunday just as the rest of the country was gathering at its TV sets to enjoy a totemic spectacle of today's impersonal, bone-crunching mass culture—the Super Bowl. As the curtain fell, you could feel a parade pass by.

1996

WENDY WASSERSTEIN

Like her classmate and occasional collaborator Chris Durang, Wendy Wasserstein (1950–2006) responded to the weight of literary tradition learned at the Yale School of Drama with irreverence. Her thesis play *Uncommon Women and Others* (1977) comes across as Mary McCarthy's *The Group* rewritten by Woody Allen; a later comedy *The Sisters Rosensweig* (1992) views Chekhov through a similar New York Jewish neurotic filter. Her most performed and honored work, *The Heidi Chronicles* (1988), resonated with women of the baby-boomer generation, who were instructed by Hollywood to seek romance and sexual fulfillment, yet indoctrinated by feminism to maintain their independence and not succumb to the lure of the nuclear family. Wasserstein regarded herself as a political playwright, but often found herself in hot water with doctrinaire feminists; she was too funny, too ambivalent, too willing to see both sides of a question. Although each of her 11 plays is about "relationships," the most enduring ones tend to be friendships, often between a young woman and a gay man. Lymphoma prevented her from finishing a libretto for a musical version of Clare Booth Luce's *The Women*, to be named, typically, *Best Friends*. It has been claimed that without her example and the ambience she pioneered, the television series *Sex and the City* would have been unthinkable.

Heidi Chronicled

DURING my years in the mid-sixties at the Calhoun School in New York, the greatest hits of female preparatory-school drama departments were largely of the convent and weeping-widow genre: *Cradle Song* and García Lorca's *The House of Bernarda Alba*. Also popular were the abbreviated *Trojan Women* and the mini *Lysistrata*. At Calhoun, during the *gaudeamus igitur* curtain call of the annual Latin-class Saturnalia show, the Velcro hooks on our Fieldcrest twin-sheet togas came unfastened, proving for all the parent body the true value of a classical education: *Nulla res melior spectaculo est*— or, very roughly, there's no business like show business.

In the late 1960s, when junior-year women were admitted to

the male bastions of ivy, the walls of single-sex education came tumbling down. Amherst College, for instance, experimented with the very balanced ratio of 23 in-house females, of which I made up a twenty-third, to 1,200 males. Rather than in convent plays, I was suddenly appearing nightly in leather as Beryl the Dominatrix in a dormitory-basement production of Terrence McNally's one-act, *Noon*. For my senior year, I returned to Mount Holyoke and the comfort of an all-female audience.

Twenty-five years later, and a month after Jamie Lee Curtis wrapped her film portrayal as Heidi Holland in my play *The Heidi Chronicles*, Anna Cash made her ninth-grade debut in the Brearley School all-female production. The entire upper school was present for the performance. Sitting in the balcony were the proud parents, mostly in their forties and looking suspiciously like academics, doctors, and assorted serious good people. Indeed, Anna Cash's mother is the novelist Mary Gordon.

If "The Rime of the Ancient Mariner" is about a man who shot a bird, *The Heidi Chronicles* is about a feminist art historian who gets sad. The play follows the life of Heidi—not the goat girl or the Beverly Hills matchmaker—from a Miss Crain's school dance in 1965 to her choice to adopt a baby alone in 1989. In the Brearley interpretation, Anna Cash appeared and began the play's opening monologue—an art history lecture about ignored women artists—in front of a slide painting by Sofonisba Anguissola (circa 1559). The upper school at Brearley is apparently big on irony: Miss Cash got a house laugh on "This portrait can be perceived as a meditation on the brevity of youth, beauty, and light—but what can't?" On Broadway, the line often didn't even get an educated smirk.

The girls giggled through the Miss Crain's dance scene. Tenley Laserson was very hip as Chip Boxer, the cool boy in Weejuns and a tweed jacket, still a familiar type at first-rate female prep schools. When Rachel Grand as Scoop Rosenbaum asked Heidi to go to bed with him in the 1968 Eugene McCarthy mixer scene, I noted the first bit of revisionism. In *The Heidi Chronicles* for grown-ups, Scoop says he can't promise Heidi "equal orgasms." At Brearley, Scoop couldn't promise Heidi an "equal relationship." The most interesting bit of nineties invention came in the women's-rap-group scene. Fran, a physicist, was described in an Ann Arbor women's-consciousness-raising rap group in 1970 as an "open" lesbian. In my original text, she is merely a lesbian. Clearly, the Brearley ninth grade has had discussions on open and closed sexual preference. Anna Cash, like Jamie Lee Curtis, ended the rap-group scene singing and dancing Aretha Franklin's "Respect" as the women celebrated feminism and all that it promised for their future. When, after the performance, I asked the cast if the play seemed pertinent to them, Rebecca Mancuso, who played Fran, smiled through her braces. "The women's-movement stuff was the most fun," she said. "We all loved that."

I remember returning to Mount Holyoke on Sunday nights in the late sixties after a weekend in New Haven or Hanover. (You never revealed the name of the college you were dating if you had any savvy.) Finally, the stress of a weekend away pretending not to be who we really were was over, and we'd sit for hours in flannel shirts and jeans, smart women just talking. As I left the Brearley School a few weeks ago, I passed through the lunchroom, and there was a new generation of smart women talking about life, men, Heidegger, and *The Heidi Chronicles. Nulla res melior feminae re*—or, very roughly, there's no business like women's business.

1995

HENRY LOUIS GATES, JR.

A native of West Virginia, Henry Louis Gates, Jr., (b. 1950) enjoyed an exceptional education, with degrees in history from Yale and in English literature from Clare College, Cambridge. At Cambridge, he befriended the Nigerian playwright and novelist Wole Soyinka and devoted several studies to his works. On his return to the U.S., Gates taught in newly founded Afro-American (as they were then called) Studies programs at Yale (1976–84), Cornell (1985–89) and Duke (1989–91), before going to Harvard where he heads the W.E.B. Du Bois Institute for African and African American Research. It co-sponsored the short-lived Institute on Arts and Civic Dialogue (1997–2000), which invited Anna Deavere Smith to campus with her one-woman, multi-character explorations of racial politics. Opposed to a separatist view of African-American culture, Gates has been prominent as a "public intellectual," popularizing his findings and viewpoints through articles and interviews in widely read newspapers and magazines, television series, and even lawsuits. Gates' interest in vernacular tradition led him to an overlooked phenomenon, a grass-roots black theatre that escaped the attention of the critics and the ideologues. Because the term "Chitlin Circuit" is borrowed from the all-black vaudeville wheel of the early 20th century, some scholars prefer "the Urban Circuit." Whatever the name, this money-making form, which exploits gospel singing, celebrities, audience participation, church venues, all topped by a happy ending, reveals the class differences in African-American taste. Audiences that cannot be persuaded to buy a ticket to an August Wilson play throng to such shows as *He Say, She Say, But What Does God Say?*

The Chitlin Circuit

THE setting was the McCarter Theatre, a brick-and-stone edifice on the outskirts of the Princeton University campus. On a hot, sticky evening last June, five hundred members of the Theatre Communications Group—all representatives of serious, which is to say nonprofit, theatre—had gathered for their eleventh biennial national conference. The keynote speech was being delivered by August Wilson, who, at fifty-one, is probably the most celebrated American playwright now writing and is certainly the most accomplished black playwright in this nation's history. Before he said a word, the largely white audience greeted him with a standing ovation.

That was the conference's last moment of unanimity. For here, at this gathering of saints, the dean of American dramatists had come to deliver an unexpected and disturbing polemic. American theatre, Wilson declared, was an instrument of white cultural hegemony, and the recent campaign to integrate and diversify it only made things worse. The spiritual and moral survival of black Americans demanded that they be given a stage of their own. They needed their very own theatres the way they needed sunlight and oxygen. They needed integration the way they needed acid rain.

"There are and have always been two distinct and parallel traditions in black art: that is, art that is conceived and designed to entertain white society, and art that feeds the spirit and celebrates the life of black America," Wilson told his Princeton audience, in a quietly impassioned voice. "The second tradition occurred when the African in the confines of the slave quarters sought to invest his spirit with the strength of his ancestors by conceiving in his art, in his song and dance, a world in which he was the spiritual center." That was the tradition Wilson found to be exemplified by the Black Power movement of the sixties and its cultural arm, the Black Arts scene. Revolutionary Black Arts dramatists such as Ed Bullins and Amiri Baraka were models for authentic black creativity, Wilson maintained, and he placed himself in their direct line of descent.

"His speech was shocking and it was thrilling," recalled Ricardo Khan, the president of the Theatre Communications Group and the artistic director of the country's premier black repertory company, the Crossroads Theatre, in New Brunswick. Wilson is light-skinned, with sparse hair and a close-cropped beard: to some in the audience, he brought to mind Maulana Karenga ("Black art must expose the enemy, praise the people and support the revolution"); to others, Ernst Blofeld ("Hot enough for you, Mr. Bond?"). The black members of the audience started glancing at one another: heads bobbed, a black-power sign was flashed, encouragement was murmured—"Go ahead, brother," "Tell it." Many white audience members, meanwhile, began to shift uneasily, gradually acquiring an expression compounded of pain and puzzlement: *After all we've done for him, this is how he thanks us?* The world of nonprofit theatre is tiny but intense, and, as soon became clear, Wilson's oration was its version of the Simpson verdict.

In the conversational ferment that ensued, almost every conceivable question was given a full airing: Did Wilson's call for an autonomous black theatre amount to separatism? Did race matter to culture, and if so, how much? Was Wilson's salvific notion of the theatre—and his dream of a theatre that would address ordinary black folk—mere romantic delusion? In the course of much high-minded hand-wringing, practically the only possibility not broached was that a black theatre for the masses *already* existed—just not of an order that anybody in the world of serious theatre had in mind.

What attracted the greatest immediate attention was Wilson's unqualified denunciation of color-blind casting. To cast black actors in "white" plays was, he said, "to cast us in the role of mimics." Worse, for a black actor to walk the stage of Western drama was to collaborate with the culture of racism, "to be in league with a thousand naysayers who wish to corrupt the vigor and spirit of his heart." An all-black production of "Death of a Salesman," say, would "deny us our own humanity."

Not surprisingly, Wilson's stand on this issue has found little acceptance among working black actors, dramatists, and directors. Lloyd Richards—Wilson's longtime director and creative partner—has never thought twice about casting James Earl Jones as Timon of Athens or as Judge Brack in "Hedda Gabler." Wole Soyinka, the Nigerian playwright and Nobel Laureate, staunchly declares, "I can assure you that if 'Death of a Salesman' were performed in Nigeria by an all-Eskimo cast it would have resonances totally outside the mediation of color." What's more surprising is that many stars of the Black Arts firmament are equally dismissive. "If O.J. can play a black man, I don't see any problem with Olivier playing Othello," Amiri Baraka says, with a mordant laugh. And the legendary black playwright and director Douglas Turner Ward claims that many of Sean O'Casey's plays, with their ethos of alienation, actually work better with black actors.

But the dissent on color-blind casting was almost something of a footnote to Wilson's larger brief—that of encouraging the creation of an authentic black theatre. As he saw it, the stakes couldn't be greater. Black theatre could help change the world: it could be "the spearhead of a movement to reignite and reunite our people's positive energy for a political and social change that is reflective of our spiritual truths rather than economic fallacies." The urgency of this creed led to a seemingly self-divided rhetoric. On the one hand, Wilson maintained that "we cannot depend on others," that we must be a "self-determining, self-respecting people." On the other hand, this self-sufficiency was to be subsidized by foundations and government agencies.

If Wilson's rhetoric struck many of his listeners as contradictory—seeming to alternate the balled fist and the outstretched palm—the contradictions only multiplied upon further investigation. August Wilson, born Frederick August Kittel, is in some respects an unlikely spokesman for a new Black Arts movement. He neither looks nor sounds typically black—had he the desire, he could easily pass—and that makes him black first and foremost by self-identification. (His father was a German-American baker in Pittsburgh, where he grew up.) Some see significance in this. The estimable black playwright OyamO, né Charles Gordon, says, "Within our history, many people who are lighter—including the very lightest of us, who can really pass—are sometimes the most angry."

Nor has it escaped comment that Wilson failed to acknowledge his own power and stature within the world of mainstream theatre: his works début at major Broadway theatres, and the white critical establishment has honored them with a cascade of Pulitzer, Drama Desk, and Tony awards. The experimental black playwright Suzan-Lori Parks, whose works include "Venus" and "The Death of the Last Black Man in the Whole Entire World," says, "August can start by having his own acclaimed plays première in black theatres, instead of where they première now. I'm sorry, but he should examine his own house." One historical luminary of black theatre

charges that Wilson himself is the problem of which he pur-
ports to hold the solution: "Once the white mainstream
theatre found a black artistic spokesman, the one playwright
who could do no wrong, the money that used to go to autonomous black theatre started to dry up."

And yet, on closer examination, sharply drawn lines of battle
begin to blur. Wilson's oration provoked a swingeing rebuttal
in *American Theatre* by Robert Brustein, who is the artistic director of the American Repertory Theatre, the drama critic for
The New Republic, and a longtime sparring partner of Wilson's. Brustein charged Wilson with promoting subsidized
separatism: "What next?" he asked. "Separate schools? Separate washrooms? Separate drinking fountains?" With Anna
Deavere Smith—herself a paradigm of casting beyond color—
serving as the moderator, the men are to continue their debate
this Monday, in New York's Town Hall. The critic Paul Gold-
berger, writing in the *Times* last week, went so far as to declare
that "this is shaping up to be the sharpest cultural debate"
since the Mapplethorpe controversy. You'd never guess that
Brustein and Wilson are in complete agreement on the one
subject that agitates them most: the disastrous nature of the
donor-driven trend to diversify regional theatres. Brustein
dislikes the trend because he believes that it supplants aesthetic considerations with sociological ones. Wilson dislikes it
because, as is true of all movement toward integration, it
undermines the integrity and strength of autonomous black
institutions.

He has a point. George Wolfe, the producer of the Public
Theatre, singles out the Lila Wallace–Reader's Digest Fund as
having been "incredibly irresponsible" in this regard. He goes
on to explain, "It has created a peculiar dynamic where, you
know, there was a struggling black theatre that had been nurturing a series of artists and all of a sudden this predominantly
white theatre next door is getting a couple of million dollars to
invite artists of color into its fold." (To be sure, the officials at
the Lila Wallace Fund have also given money to black companies like the Crossroads.) But Wilson wants to take things another step, and create black theatres where they do not
currently exist. He believes that any theatre situated in a city
with a black population of more than sixty per cent should be

converted into a black theatre. White board members and staff would be largely retired in order to insure what he believes to be a cultural and moral imperative: art by, of, and for black people.

Unquestionably, Wilson remains in the grip of a sentimental separatism. (I'll own that it has an emotional grip on me, too, just a rather attenuated one.) He says he has a lot of respect for the "do for self" philosophy of the Nation of Islam; in the early seventies, he was briefly a convert, though mostly in order to keep his Muslim wife company. He's a man who views integration primarily as a destructive force—one that ruined once vital black institutions. He thinks back fondly to an era when we had our own dress shops and businesses, our own Negro Baseball League. This segregated, pre-Brown v. Board of Education era was, he'll tell you, "black America at its strongest and most culturally self-sufficient." From his perspective, separate-but-equal, far from being a perversion of social justice, is an ideal that we should aspire to.

Now, it's one thing to hear this view espoused by Minister Louis Farrakhan and quite another to hear it advanced by August Wilson, a man as lionized as any writer of his generation. It represents a romantic attempt to retrieve an imaginary community in the wake of what seems to be a disintegration of the real one. One of the functions of literature is to bring back the dead, the absent, the train gone by; you might say that cultural nationalism is what happens when the genre of the elegy devolves into ideology, the way furniture might be kilned into charcoal.

Certainly the brutal reductionism of August Wilson's polemics is in stark contrast to his richly textured dramatic oeuvre. Wilson first came to prominence in the mid-eighties, with his fourth play, "Ma Rainey's Black Bottom," which the director Lloyd Richards was able to move from the Yale Repertory Theatre to the Cort Theatre on Broadway. There, his dramatic and verbal imagination galvanized critics, who heralded a major new presence on the American stage. With "Ma Rainey," an ambitious, and still ongoing, cycle of plays came to public notice. Wilson's aim is to explore black American life through plays set during each of the decades of the century; most are situated in a black working-class neighborhood of

Pittsburgh. "Joe Turner's Come and Gone" (1986), for example, takes place in 1911, and deals with the sense of cultural loss that accompanied the Great Migration; "The Piano Lesson" (which received the Pulitzer in 1987), set during the Depression, uses a dispute over an inherited piano—once the possession of a slave owner—to show that the past is never quite past. In "Fences" (a 1990 Pulitzer), which opens in the year 1957, the grandiloquently embittered Troy Maxson is a former Negro League baseball player who now works as a garbage man; the trajectory of his own life has made a mockery of the supposed glories of integration.

Wilson's 1990 play "Two Trains Running" takes place in a Pittsburgh luncheonette in the late sixties:

> WOLF: I thought [the jukebox] was just fixed. Memphis, I thought you was gonna get you a new jukebox.
> MEMPHIS: I told Zanelli to bring me a new one. That what he say he gonna do. He been saying that for the last year.

If you're black, you can't rely on the Zanellis of the world, as the characters in the play learn to their detriment. But a great deal more than race politics is going on here. An unruly luxuriance of language—an ability to ease between trash talk and near-choral transport—is Wilson's great gift; sometimes you wish he were less generous with that gift, for it can come at the expense of conventional dramaturgic virtues like pacing and the sense of closure. Even when he falters, however, Wilson's work is demanding and complex—at the furthest remove from a cultural manifesto.

But if Wilson's avowed cultural politics is difficult to square with his art, it comes with a venerable history of its own. In 1926, W. E. B. Du Bois, writing in his magazine *The Crisis*, took a dim view of "colored" productions of mainstream plays (they "miss the real path," he warned) and called for a new Negro theatre, for which he laid down "four fundamental principles":

> The plays of a real Negro theatre must be: 1. *About us.* That is, they must have plots which reveal Negro life as it is. 2. *By us.* That is, they must be written by Negro authors who understand from birth and continual association just what it means to be a Negro today. 3. *For us.* That is, the theatre must cater primarily to Negro audiences and be supported and sustained by their entertainment and approval.

4. *Near us.* The theatre must be in a Negro neighborhood near the mass of ordinary Negro people.

What would such a theatre look like? Wilson, of course, directs us to what may seem the most plausible candidate: the dramatic art of the Black Power era. That moment and milieu bring to mind a radicalized, leather-clad generation forging its art in the streets, writing plays fuelled by the masses' righteous rage: revolutionary art by the people and for the people. That's certainly how the illuminati liked to represent their project. Baraka's manifesto for "The Revolutionary Theatre" provides a representative précis: "What we show must cause the blood to rush, so that prerevolutionary temperaments will be bathed in this blood, and it will cause their deepest souls to move, and they will find themselves tensed and clenched, even ready to die. . . . We will scream and cry, murder, run through the streets in agony, if it means some soul will be moved."

Theatre, precisely because of its supposed potential to mobilize the masses, was always at the forefront of the Black Arts movement. Still, it's a funny thing about cultural movements: as a rule, they consist of a handful of people. (The Aesthetic, the Constructivist, the Futurist movements were devoted largely to declaring themselves, self-consciously, to *be* movements.) And by the late sixties, it was clear that the vitality of Black Arts drama had come to center upon two New York-based theatres: the Negro Ensemble Company (N.E.C.), based downtown, under the direction of Douglas Turner Ward; and the New Lafayette Theatre, based in Harlem, under the direction of Robert Macbeth. Here was the full flowering of genuine black theatre in this country—the kind that would raise consciousness and temperatures, that promised to make us whole.

"Populist modernism," in a phrase coined by the literary scholar Werner Sollors, characterized the regnant ethos of that time and place—its aspiration to an art of high seriousness that would engage the energies of the masses. But between the ideals of modernism and those of populism, one or the other had to give. OyamO—who, like many more senior luminaries of the Black Arts scene (Baraka and Ed Bullins among them),

was affiliated with the blacker and artier New Lafayette—
recalls that the Harlem theatre's high-flown airs were accompanied by paltry audiences. "There was a condescending attitude toward this community, buttressed by the fact that it was
getting five hundred grand from the Ford Foundation every
year," he recalls. And the N.E.C. was similarly provided for.
This isn't to say that worthy and important work wasn't created in these theatres; it was. But these companies do provide
a textbook example of how quickly beneficence becomes entitlement, and patronage a paycheck.

And so the dirty little secret of the Black Arts movement was
that it was a project promoted and sustained largely by the
Ford Foundation. Liberal-minded Medicis made it; in the fullness of time, they left it to unmake itself. Ed Bullins, one of the
principals of the New Lafayette, remembers how that particular temple—a magnificent structure on 137th Street, which the
Ford had converted from a movie house with the help of some
tony theatrical architects—was destroyed. He describes a
meeting between a visiting program officer from the Ford
Foundation and the theatre's board. The visitor noticed that
there were no women on the board, and he asked about their
absence. Bullins both laughs and groans when he recalls, "And
then some great mind from Harlem, an actor, spoke up and
said, 'Oh, no, we don't need any women on the board,
because every thirty days women go through their period and
they get evil.' Then and there, I saw one million dollars start
sprouting wings and flapping away through the door."

These days, of course, *all* nonprofit theatre is starved for
cash. And yet black theatres are already out there, as someone
like Larry Leon Hamlin could tell you. Hamlin is the artistic
director of the National Black Theatre Festival, and by his
count there are perhaps two hundred and fifty regional black
theatres in this country, about forty of which are reasonably
active. Of course, most of Wilson's own plays gestated at
places like the Huntington Theatre Company or the Yale Rep
before they were launched on the Great White Way. I asked
Wilson about this apparent contradiction. He explained that
the Negro Ensemble Company had fallen into decline by the
early eighties: "It was not doing work of the quality that we

deserve, and there's no theatre that's since stepped into the breach." Wilson can sound as if he were boycotting black theatres for artistic reasons, which is why some people in the black-theatre world can't decide whether he's their savior or their slayer. "I do good work," he says, his point being that his plays deserve the best conditions he can secure for them. And among white theatres, he says, "the rush is now on to do anything that's black. Largely through my plays, what the theatres have found out is that they had this white audience that was starving to get a little understanding of what was happening with the black population, because they very seldom come into contact with them, so they're curious. The white theatres have discovered that there is a market for that."

The fact that part of Wilson's success owes to the appeal of ethnography is precisely what disturbs some black critics: they suspect that Wilson's work is systematically overrated along those lines. "August is genuinely very gifted," Margo Jefferson, one of those critics, says. "Whites who don't know the world whereof he writes get a sense of vast, existential melodramas, sweeping pageants, and it's very exciting, with his insistence always that these people onstage are the real and genuine black people. What happens with whites is that the race element is signalling them every minute, 'You know nothing about this, you're lucky to be here.'"

So if you're looking for a theatre of black folk, by black folk, and for black folk—a genuinely sequestered cultural preserve —you'll have to cross the extraordinary dramas of August Wilson off your list. Nor would the Black Arts scene, for all its grand aspirations, qualify: the revolution, it's safe to say, will not be subsidized. You could be forgiven for wondering whether such a black popular theatre really exists. But it does, and, if populist modernism is your creed, it will probably turn your stomach. It's called the Chitlin Circuit, and nobody says you have to like it. But everything in God's creation has a reason, and the Chitlin Circuit is no exception. Perhaps OyamO brings us closest to comprehension when he despairingly observes an uncomfortable truth: "A lot of what they call highbrow, progressive, avant-garde theatre is *boring the shit out of people*." Not to put too fine a point on it.

*

The setting now is the Sarah Vaughan Concert Hall—built in
1925 as a Masonic temple—on Broad Street, in downtown
Newark. It's a chilly, overcast Sunday afternoon, closing in on
three o'clock, which is when the matinée performance of
Adrian Williamson's play "My Grandmother Prayed for Me" is
supposed to begin. In every sense, we're a long way from the
Princeton campus, the site of the despond-drenched T.C.G.
conference. On the sidewalk, patrons are eating grilled sau-
sages and hot dogs. Older people make their way inside with
the assistance of wheelchairs or walkers; younger ones strut
about and survey one another appraisingly. There is much to
appraise. These people are styling out, many of them having
come from church: you see cloudlike tulle, hatbands of the
finest grosgrain ribbon, wool suits and pants in neon shades.
Women have taken care to match their shoes and handbags;
men sport Stetson and Dobbs hats, Kente-cloth cummerbunds
and scarves. There's a blue velvet fedora here, electric-blue
trousers there, a Superfly hat and overcoat on a man escorting
his magenta-clad wife. Bodies are gleaming, moisturized and
fragrant; cheeks are lightly powdered, eyes mascaraed. Broad
Street is a poor substitute for a models' runway, but it will have
to do until the theatre doors open and swallow up this impromptu village. There are nearly three thousand seats in the
hall; within several minutes, most of them are occupied.

The Chitlin Circuit dates back to the nineteen-twenties,
when the Theater Owners Booking Association brought plays
and other forms of entertainment to black audiences throughout the South and the Midwest. Though it had a reputation
for lousy pay and demanding scheduling—its acronym, TOBA,
was sometimes said to stand for "Tough on Black Asses"—it
was the spawning ground for a good number of accomplished
black actors, comics, and musicians. TOBA proper had gone
into eclipse by the decade's end, yet the tradition it began—
that disparagingly named Chitlin Circuit—never entirely died
out. Touring black companies would play anywhere—in a
theatre if there was one (sometimes they booked space on
weekends or late at night, when the boards would otherwise
be vacant) or in a school auditorium if there wasn't. Criss-
crossing black America, the circuit established an empire of

comedy and pathos, the sublime and the ridiculous: a movable feast that enabled blacks to patronize black entertainers. On the whole, these productions were for the moment, not for the ages. They were the kind of melodrama or farce—or as often both—in which nothing succeeded like excess. But the productions were for, by, and about black folks; and their audience wasn't much inclined to check them against their Stanislavsky anyway.

You don't expect anything very fancy from something called the Chitlin Circuit. Wilson—by way of emphasizing the irreducible differences between blacks and whites—had told the T.C.G. members that "in our culinary history we had to make do with the . . . intestines of the pig rather than the loin and the ham and the bacon." The intestines of the pig are the source of the delicacy known as chitlins; it's a good example of how something that was originally eaten of necessity became, as is the way with acquired tastes, a thing actively enjoyed. The same might be said of the Chitlin Circuit, for the circuit is back in full flush, and has been for several years. Black audiences throughout the country flock to halls like the Beacon Theatre in New York, the Strand Theatre in Boston, and the Fox Theatre in Atlanta. Those audiences are basically blue-collar and pink-collar, and not the type to attend traditional theatre, Larry Leon Hamlin adjudges. But, as the saying has it, they know what they like.

The people behind the shows tend not to vaporize about the "emancipatory potentialities" of their work, or about "forging organic links to the community": they'd be out of business if black folks stopped turning up. Instead, they like to talk numbers. Terryl Calloway, who has worked as a New England promoter for some Chitlin Circuit productions, tells me about plays that have grossed twenty million dollars or more. "It's no joke," he says gravely.

"Good afternoon! Are you ready to have a good time?" This is the master of ceremonies warming up the Newark crowd. The play that ensues is a now standard combination of elements; that is, it's basically a melodrama, with abundant comic relief and a handful of gospel songs interspersed.

So what have we turned out to see? It seems that Grandmother—stout of body and of spirit—is doing her best to raise her two grandsons, their mother, Samantha, having fallen into crack addiction and prostitution. (When we first see Samantha, she is trying to steal her mother's television in order to pay for her habit.) The elder boy, Rashad, is devout and studious, but the younger one, Ein, has taken up with bad company; in fact, today is the day that he and his best friend, Stickey, are to be inducted into the Big Guns, a local gang headed by Slow Pimp. When Stickey is killed on the street by a member of a rival gang, Ein sets out, gun in hand, to avenge his death. What's a grandmother to do? Well, pray, for one thing.

Artistically speaking, "My Grandmother Prayed for Me" makes "Good Times" look like Strindberg. The performances are loud and large; most of the gospel is blared by said grandmother with all the interpretative nuance of a car horn. So broad, so coarse, so over-the-top is this production that to render an aesthetic evaluation would seem a sort of category mistake, like asking Julia Child to taste-test chewing tobacco. But it deals with matters that are of immediate concern to the Newark audience, working-class and middle-class alike: gang violence, crack addiction, teen-age pregnancy, deadbeat dads. For this audience, these issues are not *Times* Op-Ed-page fodder; they're the problems of everyday life, as real and close at hand as parking tickets and head colds. It's also true that black America remains disproportionately religious. (Count on a black rap artist—"gangsta" or no—to thank Jesus in his liner notes.) So that's part of it, too.

On my way to the Sarah Vaughan Concert Hall, I bumped into Amiri Baraka, who, when he learned my destination, gave me a gleaming smile and some brotherly advice: "You're about to step into some deep doo-doo." Maybe he's right, and yet I find myself enjoying the spectacle as much as everybody else here. "You lost faith in the church, abandoned your kids, and I even heard you were prostituting," the grandmother tells her daughter. "Let me tell you something. Them drugs ain't nothing but a demon." Samantha's response: "Well, if they a demon, then I'm gon' love hell." People laugh, but they recognize the sound of a lost soul. So the two fabled institutions of the inner city, the pusher and the preacher, must battle for Samantha's soul. There's a similar exchange between the good son and the one going to the bad:

RASHAD: Those boys you hang with ain't nothing but a bunch of punks. All y'all do is run around these streets beating up on people, robbing people, our black folks at that. . . .

EIN: If we so-called punks, why we got everybody scared of us? I'll tell you why—because we hardcore. We'll smoke anybody that get in our way.

RASHAD: Hardcore? . . . Ain't a thing you out there doing hardcore. Let me tell you what hardcore is: hardcore is going to school, putting your nose in a book getting an education. Hardcore is going to church trying to live your life right for the Lord. Hardcore is going to work every day, busting your behind providing for a family. Look around you. Grandma provided all of this for us, and she pray for us every day. Now *that's* hardcore.

This doubtless isn't what Wilson has in mind when he speaks of the spiritual fortification and survival that black drama can provide. All the same, the audience is audibly stirred by Rashad's peroration, crying out "Hallelujah!" and "Testify!" The subject of racism—or, for that matter, white people— simply never arises: in the all-black world depicted onstage, the risks and remedies are all much closer to hand.

That's one puzzle. Here's another: If theatre is dying, what do we make of these nearly three thousand black folks gathered in downtown Newark? The phenomenon I'm witnessing has nothing in common with "Tony n' Tina's Wedding," say, or dinner theatre in Westchester, offering "Damn Yankees" over a steak and two veg. It's true that black audiences have always had a predilection for talking back at performances. But more than that is going on in this theatre: the intensity of engagement is palpable. During some of the gospel numbers, there are members of the audience who stand up and do the Holy Dance by their seats. However crude the script and the production, they're generating the kind of audience communion that most playwrights can only dream of.

In "My Grandmother Prayed for Me," the deus ex machina is pretty literal. When Ein sets off to seek vengeance, his grandma and brother go in search of him, joined by Samantha, who—having been visited by an angel in the shape of a little boy—has seen the light. ("It was this voice, Mama, this voice from Heaven. It told me that Ein and Rashad need a good mama.") The curtain rises on a gang-infested project. It appears that Ein, too, has seen the light and laid down his gun. "I know I haven't had the best things in life," he tells Slow Pimp defiantly, "but God gave me the best grandmother in the world." Slow Pimp doesn't take his defection well, but it's Rashad who catches the first bullet. Next, Slow Pimp turns his gat on the meddling grandmother. She prays for divine intervention and gets it: the gun jams; Slow Pimp is struck by lightning; the angel raises Rashad from the ground. The audience goes wild.

Nobody said it was high culture, but historically this is what a lot of American theatre, particularly before the First World War, was like. Other "ghettoized" theatres, for all their vibrancy, also ignored many of the criteria for serious art—not least the Yiddish theatre, a center of immigrant Jewish life in New York at the end of the nineteenth century and the beginning of the twentieth. The former *Times* theatre critic Frank Rich says, "What we think of as the Yiddish theatre today was essentially popular entertainment for immigrants. There were what we'd now think of as hilarious versions of, say, 'King Lear,' in which King Lear lives. Or there were fairy tales, about an impoverished family arriving on the Lower East Side and ending up on Riverside Drive living high on the hog." (There was also, as he notes, an avant-garde Yiddish theatre, based largely in the Bronx, but that's a different, and more elevated, story.)

The fact that the audience at the Sarah Vaughan Concert Hall is entirely black creates an essential dynamic. I mentioned elements of comic relief: they include a black preacher greedy for Grandma's chicken wings; a randy old man trailing toilet paper from a split seam in the back of his pants; the grandmother herself, whose churchiness is outlandishly caricatured; endless references to Stickey's lapses of personal hygiene. All the very worst stereotypes of the race are on display, larger than life. Here, in this racially sequestered space, a black audience laughs uninhibitedly, whereas the presence of white folks would have engendered a familiar anxiety: *Will they think that's what we're really like?* If this drama were shown on television—on any integrated forum—Jesse Jackson would probably denounce it, the N.A.A.C.P. would demand a boycott, and every soul here would swap his or her finery for sandwich boards in order to picket it. You don't want white people to see this kind of spectacle; you want them to see the noble dramas of August Wilson, where the injuries and injustices perpetrated by the white man are never far from our consciousness. (It should be mentioned that there are far more respectable and well-groomed versions of gospel drama—most notably Vy Higgenson's "Mama I Want to Sing" and its progeny—that have achieved a measure of crossover success, serving mainly as vehicles for some very impressive singing. But they're better regarded as pageants, or revues, than stage plays.) By contrast, these Chitlin Circuit plays carry an invisible racial warning sticker: For domestic consumption only—export strictly prohibited.

For the creators of this theatre, there are other gratifications to be had. "I've never made so much money in my life as I made when I did the forty or so cities we did on the Chitlin Circuit," James Chapmyn, one veteran of the circuit, tells me. And Chapmyn wasn't even one of the top grossers. "The guy that did 'Beauty Shop' probably grossed fifteen to twenty-five million dollars in the Chitlin Circuit," he says. "These plays make enormous money."

Chapmyn is a blunt-featured, odd-shaped man, with a bullet head and a Buddha belly. He's thirty-six, and he grew up in Kansas, the son of a Baptist minister. He tells me that he fell out with his father in his early twenties. "He was adamant in teaching us to stand up for who we are, and who I am happens to be a black gay man. He taught me to tell the truth," Chapmyn says, but adds that his father changed his mind when his son came out. "I just wish you had lied," the minister told his son. A resulting disaffection with the church—and a spell as a homeless person—impelled him to write a play for which he has become widely known: "Our Young Black Men Are Dying and Nobody Seems to Care." His experience with the Chitlin Circuit was decidedly mixed but still memorable.

Chapmyn, like everyone else who has succeeded on the Chitlin Circuit, had to master the dark arts of marketing and promotion; and to do so while bypassing the major media. He genially explains the ground rules: "What has happened in America is that you have a very active African-American theatre audience that doesn't get their information from the arts section in the newspaper; that doesn't read reviews but listens to the radio, gets things stuffed in their bulletins in church, has flyers put on their car when they're nightclubbing. That's how people get to know about black theatre. Buying the arts section ain't going to cut it for us. That audience is not interested in the 'black theatre,' and the black-theatre audience is not interested in reading that information. We use radio quite extensively, because in our community and places we've gone African-Americans listen to radio. In fact, there's kind of an unspoken rule on the Chitlin Circuit: if a city doesn't have a black radio station, then the Chitlin Circuit won't perform there."

But the Chitlin Circuit has a less amiable side; indeed, to judge from some of the tales you hear, many of its most dramatic events occur offstage. The inner-city version of foundation program officers are drug dealers with money to burn, and their influence is unmistakable. "They do everything in cash," Chapmyn says. "At our highest point, I know that after we all got our money, we were still collecting in the neighborhood of a hundred thousand dollars a week. That was cash being given to us, usually in envelopes, by people we didn't know. It was scary." He continues, "When I was in that circuit, I dealt with a lot of people who didn't have anything but beeper numbers, who would call me with hotel numbers, who operated through post-office boxes, who would show up at the time of the show—and most of the time take care of me and my people very well."

Not always, though. "In one city, I think we did three shows, and the receipts after expenses were a hundred and forty thousand dollars," Chapmyn recounts. "My percentage of that was to be sixty-five thousand dollars. I remember the people gave me five thousand and told me that if I wanted the rest I'd have to sue them." He ended up spending the night in jail. "I was so mad I was ready to hurt somebody," he explains. "Somebody is going to tell me that they got my sixty thousand dollars and they ain't going to give it to me? I think I flipped a table over and hit somebody in the face."

Larry Leon Hamlin, too, becomes animated when he talks about the sleazy world of popular theatre. "Contracts have been put out on people," he tells me. "If you are a big-time drug dealer, it's like, 'These plays are making money, and I've got money. I'm going to put out a play.' That drug dealer will write a play who has never written a play before, will direct the play, who has never directed a play before. They get deep with guns." James Chapmyn says he dropped out of the circuit because of the criminal element: "Here I am doing a play about all the things killing African-American men, chief among those things being the violence and the drugs, and I'm doing business with people who are probably using the money they make from drugs to promote my play. I had a fundamental problem with that." Chapmyn, plainly, is a man with a mission of uplift. By contrast, many other stars of the Chitlin Circuit have the more single-minded intent of pleasing an audience: they stoop to conquer.

That might be said, certainly, of the most successful impresario of the Chitlin Circuit, a man named Shelly Garrett. Garrett maintains that his play "Beauty Shop" has been seen by more than twenty million people; that it's the most successful black stage play in American history; and that he himself is "America's No. 1 black theatrical producer, director, and playwright." Shelly Garrett has never met August Wilson; August Wilson has never heard of Shelly Garrett. They are as unacquainted with each other as art and commerce are said to be. (Except for "Fences" and "The Piano Lesson," both of which were profitable, all of August Wilson's plays have lost money.)

Garrett is a handsome man in his early fifties, given to bright-colored sports coats and heavy gold jewelry, and there is about him the unquiet air of a gambler. He was born in Dallas, worked there as a disk jockey, and later moved to Los Angeles to begin an acting career; he didn't make his début as a dramatist until 1986, with "Snuff and Miniskirts." It played in the Ebony Showcase Theatre, in Los Angeles, for about six weeks. The following year, he staged "Beauty Shop." After running on and off in Los Angeles, that show went on tour, and, as Garrett likes to say, "the rest is history." Garrett had his audience in the palm of his hand and his formula at his fingertips; all that was left was for him to repeat it with slight variation, in plays like "Beauty Shop Part 2," "Living Room," "Barber Shop," and "Laundromat."

"It reminds you of the old commedia-dell'arte stuff," OyamO says of Garrett's approach to theatre. "But it's black, and it's today, and it's loud." He also makes the obvious remark that "if a white man was producing 'Beauty Shop,' they would be lynching it." Still, what Shelly Garrett does has a far better claim to be "community theatre" than what we normally refer to by that name.

Garrett's dramatis personae are as uniform as restaurant place settings: the parts invariably include a mouthy fat woman, a beautiful vamp, a sharp-tongued and swishy gay man, and a handsome black stud, who will ultimately be coupled with the fat woman. Much of the dialogue consists of insults and trash talk. Other options and accessories may be added, to taste; but typically there's a striptease scene, and lots of Teddy Pendergrass on the mixing board. The gay man and the fat woman swap gibes—"play the dozens"—during lulls in the action.

Although Garrett's plays adhere to pretty much the same situational and narrative template, they are not dashed off. "I take so much time in rehearsals and writing these shows," Garrett tells me. "I might rewrite a show forty times, and I take so much time with them and the rehearsals and the delivery of the lines that I just run actors crazy. I run them nuts. But then, at the end, when they get their standing ovation, they love me." A strained chuckle: "Takes them a long time to love me, but finally they do." Garrett prides himself on his professionalism, which lifts him far above the cheesier theatrical realm where drug-pusher auteurs and shakedown artists might freelance. And there's something disarming about his buoyant, show-me-the-money brand of dramaturgy.

Garrett is not the product of anyone's drama workshop; he comes from a world in which the Method refers to a birth-control technique. He has seen almost no "legitimate" theatre, even in its low-end form: "I'm embarrassed to tell people that I've never even seen 'The Wiz.' On Broadway, I've seen 'Les Miz,' 'Cats,' and— What was that black show that had Gregory Hines in it?" His shows play to ordinary black people—the "people on the avenue," as Wilson wistfully puts it—and if these shows are essentially invisible to the white mainstream, so much the better. "But I have things in my show that black people can relate to," Garrett declares. "If you're sitting in that audience and something is happening on that stage that you can absolutely not relate to, why are you even there?"

In "Beauty Shop," Terry (conservative, pretty) is the proprietor of the hair salon; Sylvia (sexy), Margaret (fat), and Chris (gay) are stylists; and Rachel (tall, well dressed) is a customer.

TERRY: Barbara Dell! Is that man still beating on her?

SYLVIA: Punching her lights out! It must have been a humdinger 'cause her glasses were *real* dark!

TERRY: Well, if she's stupid enough to stay there with him, she deserves it!

RACHEL: I have never understood why a woman just takes that kind of stuff off of a man.

MARGARET: I can't understand a man raising his hand to *hit* a woman!

CHRIS: I guess you wouldn't. What man would be *brave* enough to hit *you*?

Despite outrageous caricature, it doesn't seem quite right to call these plays homophobic. The gay characters may be stereotyped, but the bigots aren't treated charitably, either; the queen is always given the last word. "You are an embarrassment to the male gender, to the Y.M.C.A., the Cub Scouts, Boy Scouts, U.S. Army, and . . . Old Spice!" a customer tells Chris in the course of a steadily escalating argument. Chris replies, "Now what you *need* to do is go home and have a little talk with you *mother*! I wasn't *always* gay, I *might* be your *daddy*!" Politically correct it isn't, but neither is it mean-spirited. At the end, the fat woman is rewarded with a desirable man. And occasionally there are even monologues with morals, in which philandering males are put in their place by right-on women.

First and foremost, though, Garrett is a businessman. His production company moves along with him; he refuses to fly, but has a bus that's fully equipped with fax and phone. He's known for his skill in saturating the black press and radio stations. He's also known for the money he makes selling merchandise like T-shirts and programs. He can tell you that his average ticket price is twenty-seven dollars and fifty cents, that he rarely plays a venue with fewer than two thousand seats, that a show he did in Atlanta netted about six hundred thousand dollars a week. (For purposes of comparison, the weekly net of hit "straight" plays—like "Master Class," "Taking Sides," and so forth—is typically between one and two hundred thousand dollars; the weekly net of hit musicals like "Miss Saigon," "Les Misérables," and "Sunset Boulevard" is usually in the neighborhood of five hundred thousand.) In New York, Garrett's "Beauty Shop" had weekly revenues of more than eight hundred thousand, and that was for an eleven-week run, during which the show sold out every week but one. Garrett remembers the time fondly: "They put me up at the Plaza in New York. First black to ever stay at the penthouse of the Plaza. And I was there for three weeks—the penthouse of the Plaza!"

To most people who both take the theatrical arts seriously and aspire to an "organic connection" with the black community, Garrett is a cultural candy man, and his plays the equivalent of caries. Woodie King, Jr., of New York's New Federal Theatre (which has had unusual success in attracting black audiences for black theatre), expresses a widespread sentiment in the world of political theatre when he describes Garrett as "an individual going after our personal riches." He says, "It's not doing anything for any kind of black community. It's not like he's going to make money, then find five deserving women writers and put on their work. It's always going to be about him." It's clear that for dramatists who view themselves as producing work for their community, but depend for their existence on foundation and government support, Garrett is an embarrassment in more ways than one.

"Artistically, I think they're horrible," the Crossroads' Ricardo Khan says of the Chitlin Circuit's carnivalesque productions. "I don't think the acting is good, I don't think the direction is good, I don't think the level of production is good. But I don't put them down for being able to speak to something that people are feeling. I think the reason it's working is that it's making people laugh at themselves, making them feel good, and they're tired of heavy stuff." But his political consciousness rebels at the easy anodyne, the theatregoer's opiate. His own work, he says, aspires to raise consciousness and transform society. He sounds almost discouraged when he adds, "But people don't always want that. Sometimes they just want to have fun."

Nobody wants to see the Chitlin Circuit and the Crossroads converge. But there's something heartening about the spectacle of black drama that pays its own way—even if aficionados of serious theatre find something disheartening about the nature of that drama. So maybe we shouldn't worry so much about those Du Boisian yardsticks of blackness. That way lies heartbreak, or confusion. Wilson and his supporters, to listen to them, would divvy up American culture along the color line, sorting out possessions like an amicably divorcing couple. But, as I insist, Wilson's polemics disserve his poetics.

Indeed, his work is a tribute to a hybrid vigor, as an amalgam of black vernacular, American naturalism, and high modernist influences. (In the history of black drama, perhaps only Baraka's 1964 play "Dutchman" represents as formidable an achievement, and that was explicitly a drama of interracial conflict. By contrast, one of Wilson's accomplishments is to register the ambiguous presence of white folks in a segregated black world—the way you see them nowhere and feel them everywhere.) There's no contradiction in the fact that Wilson revels in the black cadences of the barbershop and the barbecue, on the one hand, and pledges fealty to Aristotle's Poetics, on the other. Wilson may talk about cultural autarky, but, to his credit, he doesn't practice it. Inevitably, the audience for serious plays in this mostly white country is mostly white. Wilson writes serious plays. His audience is mostly white. What's to apologize for?

By all means, let there be "political" art and formalist art, populism and modernism, Baraka and Beckett, but let them jostle and collide in the cultural agora. There will be theatres that are black, and also Latino and Asian, and what you will; but, all told, it's better that they not arise from the edicts of cultural commissioners. Despite all the rhetoric about inclusion, I was struck by the fact that many black playwrights told me they felt that their kind of work—usually more "experimental" than realist—was distinctly unwelcome in most black regional theatres. Suzan-Lori Parks reminds me that she didn't grow up in the 'hood: "I'm not black according to a nationalist definition of black womanhood. . . . We discriminate in our own family." As a working dramatist and director, George Wolfe—who, in the spirit of pluralism, says he welcomes all kinds of theatres, ethnically specific and otherwise—admits unease about the neatly color-coded cultural landscape that Wilson conjures up. "I don't live in the world of absolutes," Wolfe says. "I don't think it's a matter of a black theatre versus an American theatre, a black theatre versus a white theatre. I think we need an American theatre that is of, for, and by us—*all* of us."

You may wonder, then, what happens to that self-divided creed of populist modernism: the dream of an art that combines aesthetic vanguardism with popular engagement—which is to say the elevated black theatre for which Wilson seeks patronage. "People are not busting their ass to go and see this stuff," OyamO says bluntly, "and I keep thinking, if this stuff is so significant, why can't it touch ordinary people?" There's reason to believe that such impatience is beginning to spread. Indeed, maybe the most transgressive move for such black theatre would be to explore that sordid, sullying world of the truly demotic. Ed Bullins, the doyen of black revolutionary theatre, regales me with stories he's heard about Chitlin Circuit entrepreneurs "rolling away at night with suitcases of money"—about the shadowy realm of cash-only transactions. But the challenge appeals to him, all the same.

So brace yourself: the Ed Bullins to whom Wilson paid tribute—as one whose dramatic art was hallowed with the blood of proud black warriors—now tells me he's been thinking about entering the Chitlin Circuit himself. Call it populist postmodernism. Somehow, he relishes the idea of a theatre that would be self-supporting, one that didn't just glorify the masses but actually appealed to them. Naturally, though, he'd try to do it a little better. "The idea is to upgrade the production a bit, but go after the same market," he says eagerly. Now, that's a radical thought.

1997

DAVID MAMET

In line with Carl Sandburg's image of Chicago as the city of big shoulders, bursting out of its blue collar, David Mamet (b. 1947) luxuriated in the persona of a cigar-smoking, poker-playing guy from the Windy City. He spent some time in New York, acting at the Neighborhood Playhouse while working as an usher and house manager at the Sullivan Street Playhouse during the long run of *The Fantasticks*, but his journeyman plays got their first real hearing in Chicago. From the first, they dealt with mendacious relationships and failed scams: the lies of *Sexual Perversity in Chicago* (1976) were succeeded by the sleazy schemes of *American Buffalo* (1977) which expanded into the testosterone-driven competition of *Glengarry Glen Ross* (1984). For a while Mamet suggested that his sinewy, foul-mouthed dialogue replicated what could be heard on the street, because ordinary people "don't institutionalize thought"; in fact, its staccato rhythms and baroque convolutions are as carefully wrought as its equivalent in Odets. Because the rare female characters he created in *Speed-the-Plow* (1988) and *Oleanna* (1992) came across as devious and stupid, Mamet has been accused of misogyny, but the charge ought to be misanthropy: "People, in circumstances of stress, can behave like swine, and this, indeed, is not only a fit subject, but the only subject of drama." Despite the importance to his success of Gregory Mosher of the Goodman Theatre and players like William H. Macy, Mamet disdains directors as interfering middlemen and believes actors should simply "speak the words." Mamet has declared an affinity with Chekhov, but with his fondness for the machinations of knaves and fools, his ear for intricately foul language, and his recent turn to satiric comedy in *Romance* (2005) and *November* (2007), he most closely resembles Ben Jonson.

The Problem Play

THE problem play is a melodrama cleansed of invention.

Its stated question, "How do we cure spousal abuse, AIDS, deafness, religious or racial intolerance?" allows the viewer to indulge in a fantasy of power: "I see the options presented, and I decide (with the author) which is correct. Were *I* in the place of those upon the stage, *I* would make the correct choice. And I would vote with the hero or heroine, rather than with the villain."

When (either through the triumph or the ennobling failure of the protagonist), the correct choice is vouchsafed to the audience, its members can, and will, say smugly, "And did I not know it all the time? I *knew* that homosexuals, blacks, Jews, women were people too. And, lo, my perceptions have been proved correct."

That is the reward offered by attendance at the problem play. The reward offered by the traditional melodrama is somewhat different. That melodrama offers anxiety undergone in safety, the problem play offers indignation. (Television news offers both.) In these false dramas we indulge a desire to feel superior to events, to history, in short, to the natural order.

Myth, religion, and tragedy approach our insecurity somewhat differently. They awaken awe. They do not deny our powerlessness, but through its avowal they free us of the burden of its repression.

(The merely ignorant may enjoy Shakespeare's plays. But I would imagine that the anti-Stratfordian's experience of them is never completely untainted by annoyance at their false attribution.)

Romance celebrates the inevitable salvation/triumph of the individual over (or through the actions of) the gods—such triumph due, finally, not even to exertion, but to some inherent (if unsuspected) excellence on the part of the protagonist.

Tragedy celebrates the individual's subjugation and thus his or her release from the burden of repression and its attendant anxiety ("when remedy is exhausted, so is grief").

The theater is about the hero journey, the hero and the heroine are those people who do not give in to temptation. The hero story is about a person undergoing a test that he or she didn't choose.

Heroes or heroines in the problem play, however, undergo a test over which they have complete control. They have chosen the test and they are going to succeed. It's a melodrama, and we go along because it makes us feel, to a certain extent, good about ourselves; it's the fulfillment of an adolescent fantasy, like the science fiction film.

We know that at the end of this fantasy good will prevail. We know the Martians will be conquered. We know the hero will discover, in the problem play, that deaf people are also people, that blind people are also people. The villain will be vanquished. The hero will come in and save the girl on the railroad track. And so our enjoyment evaporates the instant we leave the theater. We wanted, like the adolescent, to indulge ourselves in a fantasy of power over the adult world—we did so, and, for the brief moment of the adventure (the stealing of the stop sign) it made us feel powerful.

On the other hand, the hero of a tragedy has to fight the world, though powerless—and with no tools whatever except his will. Like Hamlet or Odysseus or Oedipus or Othello. All hands are turned against these heroes, and they are unfit for the journey they must take. The strength of these heroes comes from the power to resist. They resist the desire to manipulate, the desire to "help." The writer of the Superman comic book, or, for that matter, the government economist can "help" us get to the solution by proclaiming they have suspended natural laws, but finally Hamlet, Othello, and you and I and the rest of the audience have to live in a real world, and the "help" of repression of this knowledge is poor help indeed.

Somebody said (Reagan said it, and I'm sure it was said before him), "The worst nine words in the language are: 'I'm from the government and I'm here to help.'" It means, "I'm going to suggest solutions to a problem in which I'm not only uninvolved but to which I feel superior." It's done by politicians. It's done by teachers and parents.

The children, the voters, the viewers, on hearing of this forthcoming aid, feel hostile but suppress their hostility. They say: "Wait a second, this person is giving me a gift; it's not the gift I wanted, but how dare I feel rage?"

The process of "helping," in the theater, is not participating in the hero journey. It's a process of infantilizing, of manipulating the audience.

The leader, the great man or woman, does not say, "The end justifies the means." The great person says, "There is no end, and even though it may *cost* me (as it cost Saint Joan her life; as it may cost X, Y, or Z the election; as it may cost the actor the audition), I'm not going to give them what they want, if what they want is a lie."

It's the power to resist that affects us. It's the power of someone like Dr. King saying, "I have no tools, you can kill me if you want to, but you will have to kill me."

It's the power of Theodor Herzl, who said, "If you will it, it's not a dream."

Herzl went to the Dreyfus trial and said, "Jews need a homeland, this persecution has got to stop, I'm sorry." And none of the rich would give him money. So he went to the poor and asked them for a dime and a nickel. And everyone said he was a fool. But fifty years later, there's the state of Israel.

The power to resist makes the hero journey affective. And for the audience to undergo that journey, it's essential that the writer undergo the journey. That's why writing never gets any easier.

The people who subject themselves to the hero journey come up with the poems of Wallace Stevens or the music of Charles Ives or the novels of Virginia Woolf; or, to put it differently, you can't sing the blues if you haven't had the blues.

Theater is a communal art. One of the best things I know about community is what Saint Paul said: "What I am for you frightens me, but what I am *with* you comforts me. For you, I am a bishop; with you, I am a Christian."

When you come into the theater, you have to be willing to say, "We're all here to undergo a communion, to find out what the hell is going on in this world." If you're not willing to say that, what you get is entertainment instead of art, and poor entertainment at that.

In the problem play, the evening news, the romance, of the *uber*-individual, the eventual triumph is assigned a courtesy position as "in doubt" (the possibility of U.S. victory in the Gulf war; the fate of Sherlock Holmes) to allow us, again, to savor—and overcome—anxiety. But as soon as that installment or that particular war is complete, as soon as "our" victory is proclaimed, the anxiety reasserts itself. We knew it was a false struggle, and we now must cast about for another opponent/

another villain/another action film/another oppressed people to "free," so we can reassure ourselves, again, of what we know to be untrue: that we are superior to circumstance (that we are, in effect, God).

In these—the problem play, the evening news, the romance, the political drama—we have conquered not our nature but our terror, the one specific proposition: we have championed the romantic, which is to say the specious, the fictional, the untrue; and our victory leaves us more anxious than before. If others accept our proclamation of godhead, things in the world must be worse than we imagined, and our anxiety grows. The dictator looks for even less probable ideas to assert, and enforces obedience to them more and more cruelly; the United States searches ludicrously for some just cause in which to triumph; Conan Doyle is forced back to Sherlock Holmes and must rescue him from the Reichenbach Falls.

Our anxious quest for superiority cannot be allayed by momentary triumph. For we know, in the end, we must succumb.

Western European romance gave us Hitler, the novels of Trollope, and the American musical. In each the sometimes hidden but always emerging excellence of the hero wins over all. These dramas may be diverting, but they are false, and have a cumulatively debilitating effect.

We live in an extraordinarily debauched, interesting, savage world, where things really don't come out even. The purpose of true drama is to help remind us of that. Perhaps this does have an accidental, a cumulative social effect—to remind us to be a little more humble or a little more grateful or a little more ruminative.

Stanislavsky says there are two kinds of plays. There are plays that you leave, and you say to yourself, "By God, I just, I never, gosh, I want to, *now* I understand! *What* a masterpiece! Let's get a cup of coffee," and by the time you get home, you can't remember the name of the play, you can't remember what the play was about.

And there are plays—and books and songs and poems and dances—that are perhaps upsetting or intricate or unusual, that you leave unsure, but which you think about perhaps the next day, and perhaps for a week, and perhaps for the rest of your life.

Because they aren't clean, they aren't neat, but there's something in them that comes from the heart, and, so, goes to the heart.

What comes from the head is perceived by the audience, the child, the electorate, as manipulative. And we may succumb to the manipulative for a moment because it makes us feel good to side with the powerful. But finally we understand we're being manipulated. And we resent it.

Tragedy is a celebration not of our eventual triumph but of the truth—it is not a victory but a resignation. Much of its calmative power comes, again, from that operation described by Shakespeare: when remedy is exhausted, so is grief.

1998

ANNE BOGART

When Joseph Papp, the powerful head of the New York Public Theatre, stepped down in 1990 and named as his successor JoAnne Akalaitis of the experimental troupe Mabou Mines, it sent tremors through the theatre world. Although Akalaitis's tenure turned out to be brief, it proclaimed that women were a force to be reckoned with as artistic directors. Lynne Meadow at the Manhattan Theatre Club, Tanya Berezin at the Circle Repertory Company, Carey Perloff at the Classic Repertory Company and then the American Conservatory Theatre in San Francisco, Mary Zimmerman at the Goodman Theatre and Tina Landau at Steppenwolf in Chicago, Emily Mann at the Princeton Rep, and Julie Taymor all over the place. Although Anne Bogart (b. 1951) has been more of a freelance (her reign at the Trinity Rep lasted only one season), she must be reckoned one of the most influential of this sorority. She first attracted attention with reinterpretations of American classics: *South Pacific* set in a mental ward for veterans (1984); *A Streetcar Named Desire* with 8 Stanleys and 12 Blanches, one of them male; an invigoratingly physical *Picnic*. Like many postmodern directors, she often prefers to forge a show from a writer's entire oeuvre or to explore ideas through the medium of the actor's body. "Most of the truly remarkable experiences I've had in the theatre have filled me with uncertainty and disorientation . . . And yet I am somehow changed when the journey is completed." Her creativity is enriched by collaboration: with Landau, she played variations on traditional popular entertainment (*American Vaudeville, Marathon Dancing, The Birth of a Nation*, 1992–94) and with Tadashi Suzuki she founded the Saratoga International Theatre Institute (SITI, 1994). There she developed The Viewpoints, a non-verbal, highly physical method that forces actors to function within clearly established spatial and temporal boundaries. It has become a popular technique in university acting programs.

FROM
A Director Prepares

Terror

A large part of our excessive, unnecessary manifestations come
from a terror that if we are not somehow signaling all the time
that we exist, we will in fact no longer be there.

(Peter Brook)

My first encounters with theatre were startling and exposed
me to art alive with an unnameable mystery and danger. These
early experiences have made it difficult for me to relate to art
that is not rooted in some form of terror. The energy of individuals who face and incorporate their own terror is genuine,
palpable and contagious. In combination with the artist's deep
sense of play, terror makes for compelling theatre both in the
creative process and in the experience of an audience.

I grew up in a Navy family and we moved every year or two
to a new naval base in another part of the country or another
part of the world. My cultural references were Disney movies,
cocktail parties, and aircraft carriers. My first brush with terror
in art happened in a park in Tokyo, Japan, when I was six years
old. A huge white painted face leered down at me from an
immense multicoloured body. I hid, terrified, behind my
mother's skirt. This horrendous and beautiful vision was my
first exposure to an actor in costume wearing a mask. A few
months later, in the same city, I watched, terrified, as huge
wooden altars borne high by drunken Japanese men charged
down the streets of Tokyo on a holy day. The drunken men
and the altars sporadically smashed into shopwindows. The
men seemed out of control, out of their minds and utterly
unforgettable.

At fifteen, when my father was stationed in Newport, Rhode
Island, I saw my first professional theatre production at Trinity
Repertory Company, in Providence, Rhode Island. The National Endowment for the Arts (NEA) had granted the company enough money to bring every high school student in the
state into the theatre to see their plays. I was one of those stu-

dents and travelled to Providence in a big yellow school bus to see Shakespeare's *Macbeth*. The production terrified, disorientated and bewildered me. I couldn't figure out my orientation to the action. The witches dropped unexpectedly out of the ceiling, the action surrounded us on big runways and I didn't understand the words. The unfamiliar English sounded like a foreign language and the fantastic visual language, also strange to me, made my first encounter with Shakespeare extraordinary. This production of *Macbeth* constituted my first encounter with the disorientating poetic language of the stage where size and scale could be altered by the artist to create unforgettable journeys for the audience. The experience was frightening but compelling. I didn't *understand* the play, but I knew instantly that I would spend my life in pursuit of this remarkable universe. On that day in 1967, I received my first lesson as a director: *never talk down to an audience*. It was immediately clear to me that the experience of theatre was not about us understanding the meaning of the play or the significance of the staging. We were invited into a unique world, an arena that changed everything previously defined. The Trinity Company could have easily used their big grant to present facile children's theatre and fulfil their requirements to the NEA. Instead, they presented a complex, highly personal vision in a compelling, rough fashion. The production and the artists involved spoke to me directly in a visceral and fantastic manner.

Most of the truly remarkable experiences I've had in the theatre have filled me with uncertainty and disorientation. I may suddenly not recognize a building that was once familiar or I cannot tell up from down, close from far, big from little. Actors I thought that I knew are entirely unrecognizable. I often don't know if I hate or love what I am experiencing. I notice that I am sitting forward, not leaning back. These milestone productions are often long and difficult; I feel disjointed and a little out of my element. And yet I am somehow changed when the journey is completed.

We are born in terror and trembling. In the face of our terror before the uncontrollable chaos of the universe, we label as much as we can with language in the hope that once we have named something we need no longer fear it. This labelling enables us to feel safer but also kills the mystery in what has been labelled, removing the life and danger from what has been defined. The artist's responsibility is to bring the potential, the mystery and terror, the trembling, back. James Baldwin wrote, 'The purpose of art is to lay bare the questions which have been hidden by the answers.' The artist attempts to undefine, to present the moment, the word, the gesture as new and full of uncontrolled potential.

I became a theatre director knowing unconsciously that I was going to have to use my own terror in my life as an artist. I had to learn to work in trust and not in fear of that terror. I was relieved to find that the theatre is a useful place to concentrate that energy. Out of the almost uncontrollable chaos of life, I could create a place of beauty and a sense of community. In the most terrible depths of doubt and difficulty, I found encouragement and inspiration in collaborating with others. We have been able to create an atmosphere of grace, intensity and love. I have created a refuge for myself, for actors and for audiences through the metaphor that is theatre.

I believe that theatre's function is to remind us of the big human issues to remind us of our terror and our humanity. In our quotidian lives, we live in constant repetitions of habitual patterns. Many of us sleep through our lives. Art should offer experiences that alter these patterns, awaken what is asleep, and remind us of our original terror. Humans first created theatre in response to the everyday terror of life. From cave drawings to ecstatic dances around numberless fires; from Hedda Gabler raising her pistol, to the disintegration of Blanche Dubois, we create shapes that deal with our distress. I have found that theatre that does not channel terror has no energy. We create out of fear, not from a place of security and safety. According to the physicist Werner Heisenberg, artists and scientists share a common approach. They enter into their work with one hand firmly grasping the specific and the other hand on the unknown. We must trust ourselves to enter this abyss with openness, with trust in ourselves, despite the unbalance and vulnerability. How do we trust ourselves, our collaborators and our abilities enough to work within the terror we experience in the moment of entering?

In an interview with *The New York Times*, one actor, William

Hurt, said, 'Those who function out of fear, seek security, those who function out of trust, seek freedom.' These two possible agendas dramatically influence the creative process. The atmosphere in the rehearsal hall, therefore, can be imbued with either fear or trust. Are the choices made in rehearsal based on a desire for security or a search for freedom? I am convinced that the most dynamic and thrilling choices are made when there is a trust in the process, in the artists and in the material. The saving grace in one's work is love, trust and a sense of humour—trust in collaborators and the creative act in rehearsal, love for the art and a sense of humour about the impossible task. These are the elements that bring grace into a rehearsal situation and onto the stage. In the face of terror, beauty is created and hence, grace.

I want to create theatre that is full of terror, beauty, love and belief in the innate human potential for change. Delmore Schwarz said, 'In dreams begin responsibilities.' How can I begin to work with this spirit and this responsibility? How can I endeavour not to conquer but to embrace terror, disorientation and difficulty?

Every time I begin work on a new production I feel as though I am out of my league; that I know nothing and have no notion how to begin and I'm sure that someone else should be doing my job, someone assured, who knows what to do, someone who is really a professional. I feel unbalanced, uncomfortable and out of place. I feel like a sham. In short, I am terrified.

Normally, I find a way to make it through the research and table-work stage of rehearsal, where the necessary dramaturgical discussions, analysis and readings happen. But then, always, the dreaded moment arrives when it is time to put something on to the stage. How can anything be right, true or appropriate? I desperately try to find an excuse to do anything else, to procrastinate further. When we do finally have to begin work on the stage, everything feels artificial, arbitrary and affected to me. And I am convinced that the actors think that I am out of my mind. Every time the dramaturge steps into the rehearsal hall, I am sure that they are distressed that nothing we are doing reflects the previous dramaturgical discussions. I feel unsophisticated and superficial. Fortunately, after a while in this dance of insecurity, I start to notice that the actors are actually beginning to transform the senseless staging into something I can get enthused about and respond to.

I have spoken with a number of theatre directors and found that I am not alone in this sensation of being out of my league at the beginning of rehearsals. We all tremble in terror before the impossibility of beginning. It is important to remember that a director's work, as with any artist, is intuitive. Many young directors make the big mistake of assuming that directing is about being in control, telling others what to do, having ideas and getting what you ask for. I do not believe that these abilities are the qualities that make a good director or exciting theatre. Directing is about feeling, about being in the room with other people; with actors, with designers, with an audience. It is about having a feel for time and space, about breathing, and responding fully to the situation at hand, being able to plunge and encourage a plunge into the unknown at the right moment. David Salle, the painter, said in an interview:

I feel that the only thing that really matters in art and life is to go against the tidal wave of literalism and literal-mindedness to insist on and *live* the life of the imagination. A painting has to be the experience instead of pointing to it. I want to have and give *access to feeling*. That is the riskiest and only important way to connect art to the world—to make it alive. The rest is just current events.

I know that I cannot sit down when work is happening on the stage. If I sit, a deadness sets in. I direct from impulses in my body responding to the stage, the actors' bodies, their inclinations. If I sit down I lose my spontaneity, my connection to myself, to the stage and to the actors. I try to soften my eyes, that is, not to look too hard or with too much desire, because vision is dominant and eviscerates the other senses.

When I am lost in rehearsal, when I am stymied and have no idea what to do next or how to solve a problem, I know that this is the moment to make a leap. Because directing is intuitive, it involves walking with trembling and terror into the unknown. Right there, in that moment, in that rehearsal, I have to say, 'I know!' and start walking towards the stage. During the crisis of the walk, something *must* happen; some insight, some idea. The sensation of this walk to the stage, to the actors, feels like falling into a treacherous abyss. The walk creates a crisis in which innovation must happen, invention must transpire. I create the crisis in rehearsal to get out of my own way. I create despite myself and my limitations, my private terror and my hesitancy. In unbalance and falling lie the potential to create. When things start to fall apart in rehearsal, the possibility of creation exists. What we have planned before, our dramaturgical decisions, what we have previously decided to do, in that moment is not interesting or productive. Rollo May wrote that all artists and scientists, when they are doing their best work, feel as though they are not doing the creating; they feel as though they are being spoken through. This suggests that the constant problem we face in our rehearsals is *how do we get out of our own way?* How can we become a vessel through which we are spoken? I believe that part of the answer is the acceptance of terror as primal motivation and then a full body-listening to what develops out of it.

For me, the essential aspect of a given work is its vitality. This vitality, or energy, is a reflection of the artist's courageousness in the face of her or his own terror. The creation of art is not an escape from life but a penetration into it. I saw a retrospective of Martha Graham's early dance works before the company's unfortunate demise. I was astonished that pieces such as *Primitive Mysteries*, which are now over fifty years old, were *still* risky and exposed. Graham once wrote to Agnes DeMille:

There is a vitality, a life-force, a quickening that is translated through you into action, and because there is only one of you in all time, this expression is unique. And if you block it, it will never exist through any other medium and be lost. The world will not have it. It is not your business to determine how good it is; nor how valuable it is; nor how it compares with other expressions. It is your business to keep it yours clearly and directly, to keep the channel open. You do not have to believe in yourself or your work. You have to keep open and aware directly to the urges that motivate you.

Vitality in art is a result of articulation, energy and differentiation. All great art is differentiated art. Our awareness of the differences between things around us touches upon the source of our terror. It is more comfortable to feel similarities; yet we have to accept the terror of differences in order to create vital art. The terrible truth is that no two people are alike, no two snowflakes are alike, no two moments are alike. Quantum physicists say that nothing touches, nothing in the universe has contact; there is only movement and change. This is a terrifying notion given our attempt to make contact with one another. The ability to see, experience and articulate the differences between things is called *differentiation*. Great artworks are differentiated. An exceptional painting is one in which, for example, colours are highly and visibly differentiated from one another, in which we see the differences in textures, shapes, spatial relationships. What made Glenn Gould a brilliant musician was his openness to high differentiation in music, which created the ecstatic intensity of his playing. In the best theatre, moments are highly differentiated. An actor's craft lies in the differentiation of one moment from the next. A great actor appears dangerous, unpredictable, full of life and differentiation.

We not only need to use our terror of differentiation but also our terror of conflict. Americans are plagued with the disease of agreement. In the theatre, we often presume that collaboration means agreement. I believe that too much agreement creates productions with no vitality, no dialectic, no truth. Unreflected agreement deadens the energy in a rehearsal. I do not believe that collaboration means mechanically doing what the director dictates. Without resistance there is no fire. The Germans have a useful word that has no suitable English equivalent: *Auseinandersetzung*. The word, literally 'to set oneself apart from another', is usually translated into English as 'argument', a word with generally negative connotations. As much as I would be happier with a congenial and easygoing environment in rehearsal, my best work emanates from *Auseinandersetzung* which means to me that to create we must set ourselves apart from others. This does not mean 'No, I don't like your approach, or your ideas.' It does not mean 'No, I won't do what you are asking me to do.' It means 'Yes, I will include your suggestion, but I will come at it from another angle and add these new notions.' It means that we attack one another, that we may collide; it means that we may argue, doubt each other, offer alternatives. It means that feisty doubt and a lively atmosphere will exist between us. It means that I will probably feel foolish and unprepared as a result. It means that rather than blindly fulfilling instructions, we examine choices in the heat of rehearsal, through repetition and trial and error. I have found that German theatre artists tend to work with too much *Auseinandersetzung*, which becomes debilitating and can create static, heady productions. Americans tend towards too much agreement, which can create superficial, unexamined, facile art.

These words are easier to write than to practise in rehearsal. In moments of confrontation with terror, disorientation and difficulty, most of us want to call it a night and go home. These thoughts are meant to be reflections and notions to help give us some perspective, to help us to work with more faith and courage. I'd like to close with a quote from Brian Swimme.

How else can we express feelings but by entering deeply into them? How can we capture the mystery of anguish unless we become one with anguish? Shakespeare lived his life, stunned by its majesty, and in his writing attempted to seize what he felt, to capture this passion in symbolic form. Lured into the intensity of living, he re-presented this intensity in language. And why? Because beauty stunned him. Because the soul can not confine such feelings.

2001

TONY KUSHNER

Angels in America is the seminal play of the 1990s. Because Tony Kushner subtitled it "A Gay Fantasia on National Themes" and its action pivots on cases of AIDS, he is often labeled a gay playwright. He would prefer to be known as a political playwright, and, regularly addressing problems of individual conscience in the face of cataclysm, rarely repeats himself in his themes or treatments. *A Bright Room Called Day* (1985), a verse play set in Weimar Berlin, offered directors a series of alternative texts and has been periodically revised. *Slavs!* (1994) constitutes an ironic 80-minute meditation on the Russian Revolution, the prose one-acts *Homebody/Kabul* (2001) presciently address the crisis in the Middle East, and *Caroline, or Change* (2002) is a musical that deals with racism. *Angels* (1991–92) is as ambitious in its historical and thematic scope as Dos Passos' *U.S.A.* and in its apocalyptic disquisitions as Shaw's *Back to Methuselah*, interweaving real people, fictional characters, and supernatural beings. When original inspiration flags, Kushner turns his hand to adaptations of the classics, among them Corneille's *L'Illusion comique*, S. Anski's *Dybbuk* and Brecht's *The Good Person of Szechwan* and *Mother Courage*. He has spoken in favor of "difficult plays," "demands for a better world, a world that can understand them . . . A world of audiences hungry for the Difficult is the sort of world I want." His tribute to Arthur Miller on the occasion of his death is, in some respects, a mirror reflecting Kushner's own sense of responsibility as a playwright. Recently he has returned to address Shaw and gay identity, as well as his personal interest in Judaism, in *The Intelligent Homosexual's Guide to Capitalism and Socialism with a Key to the Scriptures* (2009).

Kushner on Miller

ARTHUR MILLER died on Bertolt Brecht's birthday. There are two ways in which this means nothing at all: I'm sure Arthur didn't plan it, and the two playwrights, apart from being universally described, and self-identified, as "political writers," don't have all that much in common. But their difference is interesting. Arthur Miller's was a great voice, one of the principal voices, raised in opposition, calling for resistance, offering critical scrutiny and lamentation—in other words, he was politically progressive, as politically progressive is best defined in these dark times. He demanded that we must be able to answer, on behalf of our plays, our endeavors, our lives, a really tough question, one that Arthur wrote was the chief and, in a sense, only reason for writing and speaking: "What is its relevancy," he asks, "to the survival of the race? Not," he stipulates, "the American race, or the Jewish race, or the German race, but the human race." He demanded that our work and our lives have some relevance to human survival. The question implies anxiety about that survival, a refusal of complacency, an acknowledgment that there is a human community for which each of us bears responsibility and a warning that we are in danger. Miller tells us that what we do, the things we choose to struggle with in art and elsewhere, can have some effect on the outcome. There is, in other words, reason to hope, and change is possible. Arthur was a grieving pessimist, but what truly progressive person isn't?

He was one of those political people who refused an identification with a specific race or nation or movement or party. He certainly wasn't a communist, and he wasn't a socialist. During the Depression, his grandfather, whom Arthur described as "a Republican all his life . . . [with] bags under his eyes like von Hindenburg," shocked the family by turning to his unemployed grandson one night after dinner and saying, "You know what you ought to do? You ought to go to Russia."

"The silence that fell" in the dining room, Arthur wrote, "is better described as a vacuum so powerful it threatened to suck the walls in. Even my father woke up on the couch. I asked [my grandfather] why I should go to Russia.

"'Because [he answered] in Russia they haven't got anything. Here they got too much. You can't sell anything anymore. You go to Russia and open a chain of clothing stores; you could do a big business. That's a new country, Russia.'"

"'But,' I said, 'you can't do that there.'

"'Why not?' he said, disbelieving.

"'The government owns the stores there.' His face would have put fears into Karl Marx himself. 'Them bastards,' he said, and went back to his paper."

The grandson was a great believer in democracy and self-reliance and in anything conducive to and supportive of individual human dignity and integrity. His drama was the drama of individual integrity, individual wholeness or completeness or repleteness versus unaccountable power—or perhaps one could say of the individual versus history. And one way Arthur Miller's theater and politics differ from a writer like Brecht's is that Arthur focused his critical gaze, and located his sense of political struggle, within the arena of an individual consciousness, in an important sense his own individual consciousness. Would it be correct to say that he was not a joiner of parties or group identities because, a loyalist only to the human race, he manifested that loyalty by being true to himself? Though he was clearly interested in history, he was uncomfortable writing about it. *The Crucible* and *Incident at Vichy* are not, finally, historical plays. Each sets its scene in the midst of a historical crime in progress, but soon the great dramatist that Arthur Miller was has turned his unsparing, unblinking, loving intelligence away from the grand-scale horror to demand of a single human being: Never mind all that out there, as overwhelming as it is. Even in the face of horror you must still ask yourself, and hard as it is, you are capable of asking it: What do you mean to yourself, what do you know yourself to be? What, in other words, is your relevance to the survival of the race?

He wasn't interested in the examination of history as the opportunity to illuminate metatheories about the ultimate direction the human community was taking. Arthur Miller was one of those very rare people whose politics were inseparable from the drama of his personal integrity. He was his own proving ground; he felt his successes and his failures as a human being were consequential to something greater than himself, and so they were publicly examined and, in a sense, the only thing worth talking about. He wasn't certain that a single individual has relevance to our collective survival, but he saw no other question worth pursuing.

He once wrote that he stopped studying economics as an undergraduate because economics, as it was and is taught, can "measure the giant's footsteps but not look into his eyes." His observation reflects his indebtedness to left political analysis—a central tenet of which is the critical consideration of the human, ethical and political meanings of money, rather than the mere prognostication of its tides and currents—and it also reflects his conviction, or perhaps predilection, or natural inclination, even when considering the giant, to look for truth by looking into his eyes, the windows of the soul. Arthur Miller had the curse of empathy, even for the enemy. Humans justify themselves to themselves, even bad humans, and Arthur the playwright always wanted to know how and why. Look into his eyes.

He made it clear in his plays and his essays that his critical thinking and social consciousness had their genesis in the red politics that were pervasive when he was growing up, a politics catalyzed by the suffering he witnessed and experienced in the Great Depression, a politics shaped in response to the toxic, obnoxious valorization of greed always, always re-emerging in American history as a bedrock tenet of the political right. Although he refused the mechanical determinism of the unthinking Marxist left, he created in his greatest play a drama in which it is impossible to avoid thinking about economics—money—in any attempt to render coherent the human tragedy unfolding before you. Consider the Lomans: What has brought darkness down upon this family? Their flaws are part of their tragedy, but only a part—every flaw is magnified, distorted, made fatal by, well, alienation, by the market, where the pressure is inhuman and the human is expendable. Consider the moment when the Nothing of tragedy is enunciated, and annunciated, in *Death of a Salesman*, Biff and Willy's final fight ("Pop, I'm nothing! I'm nothing, Pop! Can't you understand that? There's no spite in it anymore. I'm just what I am, that's all. Will you let me go, for Christ's sake?"). It's tragic negation, vast and shatteringly intimate; everything is annihilated, and at the same time something new is being born. It's "nothing" of the tragedies of Euripides and Shakespeare, and in Miller's postwar, marketplace masterpiece, one hears an echo of another "nothing," tragic but also political—namely, "You have nothing to lose but your chains."

If Arthur's Emersonian temperament saved him from the terrible mistakes of the doctrinaire left of his time, if his habits of scrupulousness and independence carried him into a healthy, immensely vital skepticism, if he refused partisanship, he also never ceased reminding us of his indebtedness to, indeed his affinity with, the left, with progressive thought. He never became a cynic, or a nihilist, or an ego-anarchist, or a despoiler of humanist utopian dreams, or a neocon. His great personal courage and his graceful confidence in his stature and talents made it unnecessary for him to cuddle up to power elites, allowed him to retain his sympathy, his affinity for the disinherited, the marginal and the powerless. He never wanted us to forget that without economic justice, the concept of social justice is an absurdity and, worse, a lie.

I first saw Arthur Miller in person at the 1994 Tony Awards, when I sat behind him, too unnerved to introduce myself; for the whole evening I stared at the back of his head, which was far, far more interesting to me than anything transpiring onstage. Inside this impressive cranium, inside this dome, I thought to myself, Willy Loman was conceived—for an American playwright, a place comparable in sacrosanctity to the Ark of the Covenant or the Bodhi Tree or the Manger in Bethlehem. I wanted to touch the head, but I worried its owner might object. The ceremonies ended, and I'd missed my opportunity to make contact with the quarry whence came one of the postwar pillars upon which the stature of serious American playwriting rests.

Thanks to my friend Oskar Eustis I got to meet Arthur several years later, in Providence, Rhode Island, when I presented him with an award. On that occasion I had the chance to thank him personally. I said, "Mr. Miller, yours is a career and a body of work every playwright envies and wishes were her or his own; yours is the difficult standard against which we are measured and measure ourselves. For many sleepless nights and days of despair, I want to say thanks a lot; and for making my heart break, and burst into flames, time and time again, since the night, when I was 6 years old, I saw my mother play Linda Loman in a Louisiana community theater production of *Salesman*, and I think at that moment secretly deciding I wanted to be a playwright. Seeing *Incident at Vichy* on TV a few years later, I admitted to myself the decision I'd made. Watching splendid recent revivals of *View From the Bridge*, *Salesman*,

The Crucible, I have gone home, chastened, to re-question all my assumptions about what playwriting is and how one ought to do it. And for always being there, on my bookshelf, when people say that real art can't be political, or that a real artist can't also be a political activist; your life and work are there to remind me what preposterous canards those are—for all this, I want to say thanks a lot."

For American playwrights who come after Arthur Miller, there is of course an unpayable debt. Those of us who seek mastery of dramatic realist narrative have his plays to try to emulate. Scene after scene, they are perhaps our best constructed plays, works of a master carpenter/builder. Those of us who seek not mastery but new ways of making theater have to emulate his refusal to sit comfortably where *Salesman* enthroned him. Arthur once praised Tennessee Williams for a "restless inconsolability with his solutions which is inevitable in a genuine writer," for making "an assault upon his own viewpoint in an attempt to break it up and reform it on a wider circumference."

American playwrights have most to learn from the sound of Arthur Miller's voice: Humility, decency, generosity are its trademarks. Turn down the braying of ego, it says to us, turn down the chatter of entertainment, the whine of pornographic sensuality and prurience, abandon the practice of rendering judgment as an expression of isolation, superstition and terror, and reach for a deeper judgment, the kind of judgment that pulls a person beyond his expected reach toward something more than any single human animal ought to be capable of— toward something shared, communal, maybe even toward something universal, maybe even toward God. It's a path to knowing that is the birthright of dramatists and "genuine writers." It seems to me difficult because it's a lonely path, and Jewish in its demanding interiority. It's Jewish also in its faith that words have an awesome, almost sacred, power, force, weight. God, or the world, is listening, Arthur Miller reminds us, and when you speak, when you write, God, or the world, is also speaking and writing. "A great drama is a great jurisprudence," Arthur wrote. "Balance is all. It will evade us until we can once again see man as a whole, until sensitivity and power, justice and necessity are utterly face to face, until authority's justifications and rebellion's too are tracked even to those heights where the breath fails, where—because the largest point of view as well as the smaller has spoken—truly, the rest is silence."

2005

SOURCES & ACKNOWLEDGMENTS

INDEX

Sources and Acknowledgments

Great care has been taken to locate and acknowledge all owners of copyrighted material included in this book. If any owner has inadvertently been omitted, acknowledgment will gladly be made in future printings.

Edward Albee. Which Theater Is the Absurd One?: *Stretching My Mind* (New York: Avalon, 2005), pp. 5–13. Originally published in *New York Times Magazine,* February 25, 1962. Copyright © 1966 by Edward Albee. Reprinted by permission.

Fred Allen. The Life and Death of Vaudeville: *Much Ado About Me* (Boston: Little Brown, 1956), pp. 236–57.

Brooks Atkinson. Our Town: *New York Times,* February 2, 1938. Standards in Drama Criticism: *New York Times,* March 13, 1938. Copyright © 1938 The New York Times. All rights reserved. Used by permission and protected by the Copyright Laws of the United States. The printing, copying, redistribution, or retransmission of the Material without express written permission is prohibited.

Djuna Barnes. The Days of Jig Cook: *Theatre Guild Magazine,* January, 1929, pp. 31–43. Alla Nazimova: *Theatre Guild Magazine,* June 1930, pp. 32, 34, 61.

Robert Benchley. *Abie's Irish Rose* Review and Bulletins: *Life,* 1922–26. Reprinted by permission of The Estate of Robert Benchley.

Eric Bentley. Folklore on Forty-Seventh Street: *What Is Theatre?* (New York: Hill and Wang, 2000), pp. 107–10. Originally published in *The New Republic,* October 19, 1953. Copyright © 2000 by Eric Bentley. Reprinted by permission of Hill & Wang, a division of Farrar, Straus and Giroux, LLC. *From* Bentley on Brecht: *Bentley on Brecht* (Evanston, Il.: Northwestern University Press, 2008), pp. 393–401. Copyright © 1985 by Eric Bentley. Reprinted by permission of Northwestern University Press.

Anne Bogart. *From* A Director Prepares: *A Director Prepares* (London: Routledge, 2001), pp. 79–90. Copyright © 2001 by Anne Bogart. Reproduced by permission of Taylor & Francis Books UK.

John Mason Brown. Even as You and I: *Still Seeing Things* (New York: McGraw-Hill, 1950), pp. 195–204. Originally published in *Saturday Review of Literature,* February 26, 1949. Copyright © 1949 by John Mason Brown. Reprinted by permission of the Estate of John Mason Brown.

Ed Bullins. A Short Statement on Street Theatre: *The Drama Review,*

Summer 1968. Copyright © 1968 by Ed Bullins. Reprinted by permission of the author.

Willa Cather. *Uncle Tom's Cabin*: *Nebraska State Journal*, September 30, 1894. *Antony and Cleopatra* (1): *Nebraska State Journal*, October 23, 1895, p. 6; *Antony and Cleopatra* (2): *Lincoln Courier*, October 26, 1895, pp. 6–7.

Harold Clurman. Tennessee Williams: *The Divine Pastime: Theatre Essays* (New York: Macmillan, 1974), pp. 11–18. Originally published in *Tomorrow*, 1948. The Famous "Method": *The Divine Pastime: Theatre Essays* (New York: Macmillan, 1974), pp. 74–81. Originally published in *Encore*, March–April 1958, pp. 17–23. *From* The Theatre of the Thirties: *Famous American Plays of the 1930s* (New York: Dell Pub. Co., 1959), pp. 7–17. Copyright © 1994 Applause Theatre Books. All rights reserved. Reprinted by permission of Hal Leonard Corporation on behalf of Applause Theatre & Cinema Books.

Alan Dale (Alfred J. Cohen). Clara Morris: *Familiar Chats with the Queens of the Stage* (New York: G. W. Dillingham, 1890), pp. 353–73.

Thomas Disch. The Death of Broadway: *The Atlantic Monthly*, March 1991, pp. 92–104. Copyright © 1991 by Thomas Disch. All rights reserved by the Estate of Thomas Disch c/o Writer's Representative LLC, New York, NY.

William Dunlap. *From* History of the American Theatre: *History of the American Theatre* (London: Richard Bentley, 1833), pp. 242–52.

Morton Eustis. George Kaufman Directs *The Man Who Came to Dinner*: *Theatre Arts*, November 1939, pp. 789–98.

Hallie Flanagan. *From* Arena: *Arena* (New York: Duell, Sloan and Pearce, 1940), pp. 340–46.

Hamlin Garland. James A. and Katharine Herne: *Roadside Meetings* (New York: The Macmillan Company, 1930), pp. 65–89.

Henry Louis Gates, Jr. The Chitlin Circuit: *The New Yorker*, February 3, 1997. Copyright ©1997 by Henry Louis Gates, Jr. Reprinted by permission of the author.

William Gillette. "The Illusion of the First Time" in Drama: *Proceedings of the American Academy of Arts and Letters and of the National Institute of Arts and Letters*, August 1, 1914, pp. 16–24.

William Goldman. *From* The Season: *The Season* (New York: Harcourt, Brace & Co., 1969), pp. 23–39. Copyright © 1969 by William Goldman. Reprinted by permission of Houghton Mifflin Harcourt Publishing Company.

Spalding Gray. *From* A Personal History of the American Theatre: *Performing Arts Journal*, 1984. Copyright © Spalding Gray. Reprinted by permission of the Estate of Spalding Gray.

Lorraine Hansberry. Me tink me hear sounds in de night: *Theatre Arts*, October 1960. Copyright © 1960 by Lorraine Hansberry.

Hutchins Hapgood. *From* The Spirit of the Ghetto: *The Spirit of the Ghetto* (New York: Funk and Wagnalls, 1902), pp. 113–35.

Elizabeth Hardwick. Notes on the New Theater: *The New York Review of Books*, June 20, 1968. Copyright © 1968 by Elizabeth Hardwick. Reprinted by permission of The Wylie Agency, LLC.

Rollin Lynde Hartt. Melodrama: *The People at Play* (Boston and New York: Houghton Mifflin Company, 1909), pp. 155–91.

Edward P. Hingston. *From* The Genial Showman: The Church in the Theatre and the Theatre in the Church: *The Genial Showman* (London: Chatto and Windus, 1881), p. 464–76.

Philip Hone.The Astor Place Riot: *The Diary of Philip Hone, 1828–1851*, ed. Bayard Tuckerman, vol. 2 (New York: Dodd, Mead, 1889), May 8–12, 1849.

John Houseman. *From* Run-Through: *Run-Through* (New York: Simon and Schuster, 1972), pp. 245–75. Copyright © 1972 by John Houseman.

Langston Hughes. Trouble with the Angels: *New Theatre*, July, 1935, pp. 6–7. Copyright © 1996 by Ramona Bass and Arnold Rampersad. Reprinted by permission of Hill and Wang, a division of Farrar, Straus and Giroux, LLC.

James Huneker. Frank Wedekind: *Ivory Apes and Peacocks* (New York: Charles Scribner's Sons, 1917), pp. 121–40.

Henry James. Notes on the Theatres: *The Nation*, March 11, 1875. *From* A Small Boy and Others: *A Small Boy and Others* (New York: Charles Scribner's Sons, 1913), pp. 154–71.

Washington Irving. *From* Letters of Jonathan Oldstyle, Gent.: *Washington Irving: History, Tales & Sketches*, James W. Tuttleton, ed. (New York: Library of America, 1983), pp. 10–18. Originally published in New York *Morning Chronicle*. Letter III, December 1, 1802; Letter IV, December 4, 1802.

Elia Kazan. Audience Tomorrow: Preview in New Guinea: *Theatre Arts*, October 1945, pp. 568–77.

Walter Kerr. Barns: *Pieces at Eight* (New York: Simon and Schuster, 1957), pp. 239–44. Copyright © 1957 by Walter Kerr. Reprinted by permission of the Author's Estate.

Frances Parkinson Keyes. Terry Helburn: *Atlantic Monthly*, April, 1953, pp. 35–40.

Tony Kushner. On Arthur Miller: *The Nation*, June 13, 2005. Copyright © 2005 by Tony Kushner. Reprinted by permission of the author.

John Lahr. *From* Notes on a Cowardly Lion: *Notes on a Cowardly Lion* (New York: Ballantine Books, 1970), pp. 294–314. Copyright © 1969, 2000 by John Lahr. Reprinted with permission.

Ring Lardner. I Gaspiri—"The Upholsterers": A Drama in Three Acts. *First and Last* (New York: Charles Scribner's Sons, 1934), pp. 401–3. Copyright © Ring Lardner. Reprinted by permission of the Estate of Ring Lardner.

Ludwig Lewisohn. Mr. Belasco Explains: *The Drama and the Stage* (New York: Harcourt, Brace and Company, 1919), pp. 47–52. Susan Glaspell: *The Drama and the Stage* (New York: Harcourt, Brace and Company, 1919), pp. 102–10.

Alain Locke. The Negro and the American Stage: *Theatre Arts Monthly*, February 1926, pp. 112–20.

Olive Logan. About Nudity in Theatres: *Apropos of Women and The-atres*, (New York, Carleton, 1869), pp. 123–53.

Charles Ludlam. Gay Theatre: *Ridiculous Theatre* (New York: The-atre Communications Group, 1992), pp. 228–33. Copyright © 1992 by the Estate of Charles Ludlam. Used by permission of Theatre Communications Group.

David Mamet. The Problem Play: *3 Uses of the Knife* (New York: Co-lumbia University Press, 1998), pp. 14–22. Copyright © 1998 by David Mamet. Reprinted by permission of International Cre-ative Management, Inc.

Don Marquis. the old trouper: *the lives and times of archie and mehitabel* (Garden City, New York: Doubleday and Company, 1927), pp. 109–13. Copyright © 1927, 1930, 1933, 1935, 1950 by Doubleday, a division of Random House, Inc. Used by permis-sion of Doubleday, a division of Random House, Inc.

Mary McCarthy. A Streetcar Called Success: *Mary McCarthy's The-atre Chronicles* (New York: Farrar, Straus and Company, 1963), pp. 131–35. Originally published in *Partisan Review*, March 1948. Copyright © 1948 by Mary McCarthy. Reprinted by permission of the Mary McCarthy Literary Trust.

Charles L. Mee, Jr. The Becks' Living Theatre: *Tulane Drama Re-view*, Winter 1962, pp. 194–205.

Arthur Miller. The American Theater: *The Theater Essays of Arthur Miller* (New York: The Viking Press, 1978), pp. 31–50. Originally published in *Holiday*, January 1955, 90–104. Copyright © 1954 by Arthur Miller. Used by permission of Viking Penguin, a di-vision of Penguin Group (USA) Inc.

Anna Cora Mowatt. *From* Mimic Life; or Before and Behind the Curtain: *Mimic Life; or Before and Behind the Curtain* (Boston: Ticknor and Fields, 1856), pp. 65–92.

George Jean Nathan. The Audience Emotion: *The World of George Jean Nathan* (New York: Alfred A. Knopf, 1952), pp. 386–90. Originally published in *The American Mercury*, June 1927. On Vaudeville: *The World of George Jean Nathan* (New York: Alfred A. Knopf, 1952), 464–65. Originally published in *Testament of a Critic* (New York: Alfred A. Knopf, 1931), pp. 245–47. Eugene O'Neill: *The World of George Jean Nathan* (New York: Alfred A.

Knopf, 1952), pp. 395–411. Originally published in *Theatre Book of the Year 1946–47*, pp. 93–111. Copyright © George Jean Nathan Estate. Reprinted by permission of Patricia Angelin, Literary Executrix, George Jean Nathan Estate.

Charles King Newcomb. *From* The Journals: *The Journals of Charles King Newcomb*, Judith Kennedy Johnson, ed. (Providence, R.I.: Brown University Press, 1946), pp. 120–31, 139–47, 219, 227.

Dorothy Parker. *The Jest*: *Vanity Fair*, June 1919, p. 41.

Lottie Blair Parker. My Most Successful Play: *The Green Book Album*, October 1911, pp. 879–84.

S. J. Perelman. Waiting for Santy: *Crazy Like a Fox* (New York: Random House, 1944), pp. 15–18. Originally published in *The New Yorker*, December 26, 1936, p. 17. Copyright © 1936 by S. J. Perelman. Reprinted by permission of Harold Ober Associates Incorporated.

Edgar Allan Poe. On Anna Cora Mowatt's *Fashion*: *Broadway Journal*, March 29, 1845; April 5, 1845, pp. 203–5; 219–20.

Channing Pollock. Stage Struck: *The Footlights Fore and Aft* (Boston: The Gorham Press, 1911), pp. 164–91.

Ezra Pound. Mr. James Joyce and the Modern Stage: *The Drama* (February 1916), pp. 122–32.

Frank Rich. "Dolly" Goes Away: *New York Times*, January 31, 1996. Copyright © 1996 The New York Times. All rights reserved. Used by permission and protected by the Copyright Laws of the United States. The printing, copying, redistribution, or retransmission of the Material without express written permission is prohibited.

Gilbert Seldes. The Daemonic in the American Theatre: *The Seven Lively Arts*, (New York: Harper and Brothers, 1924), pp. 191–200. Copyright © 1924 by Gilbert Seldes, renewed in 1952 by Gilbert Seldes. Reprinted by permission of Russell & Volkening as agents for the author.

John Simon. Boredom in the Theatre: *Acid Test* (New York: Stein and Day, 1963), pp. 94–101. Copyright © 1963 by John Simon. Reprinted by permission of the author.

Lee Simonson. The Painter and the Stage: *Theatre Arts Magazine*, December 1917, pp. 4–12.

Sidney Skolsky. Cain's Warehouse: *Times Square Tintypes*, (New York: Ives Washburn, 1930), pp. 251–55.

Susan Sontag. Marat/Sade/Artaud: *Against Interpretation* (New York: Farrar, Straus and Giroux, 1966), pp. 163–74. Copyright © 1964, 1966, renewed 1994 by Susan Sontag. Reprinted by permission of Farrar, Straus and Giroux, LLC.

Charles Sprague. Prologue for the Opening of the Chestnut Street Theatre, Philadelphia: *The Rejected Addresses, presented for the*

Cup offered for the best Address on the opening of the New Theatre, Philadelphia. To which is prefixed, The Prize Address (Philadelphia: H. C. Carey & Lea, 1823).

Alexis de Tocqueville. Some Observations on the Theater of Democratic Peoples: *Democracy in America*, Arthur Goldhammer, trans.; Olivier Zunz, ed. (New York: Library of America, 2004), pp. 563–68. Originally published in *De la démocratie en Amérique*, 1840. Translation copyright © 2004 by The Library of America.

Frances Trollope. *From* Domestic Manners of the Americans: *Domestic Manners of the Americans* (London, Whittaker, Treachers & Co., 1832), pp. 114–17.

Mark Twain. The Menken: *Mark Twain of the* Enterprise, Henry Nash Smith, ed. (Berkeley, CA: University of California Press, 1957), pp. 78–80. Originally published in Virginia City *Territorial Enterprise*, September 17, 1863. The Model Artists: San Francisco *Daily Alta*, March 28, 1867. The Minstrel Show: *Mark Twain in Eruption*, Bernard DeVoto, ed. (New York: Harper & Brothers, 1940), pp. 110–18. Copyright © The Mark Twain Foundation. Reprinted by permission of Richard A. Watson and JP Morgan Chase Bank, N.A., trustees of the Mark Twain Foundation.

Luis Valdéz. El Teatro Campesino: *Ramparts*, July, 1966, pp. 55–56. Copyright © 1966. Reprinted with permission of the author.

Carl Van Vechten. Mimi Aguglia as Salome: *In the Garret* (New York: Alfred A. Knopf, 1920), pp. 287–301.

Gore Vidal. Eugene O'Neill's "A Touch of the Poet": *Rocking the Boat* (Boston: Little, Brown & Co., 1962), pp. 88–93. Originally published in *The Nation*, October 25, 1958. Copyright © 1958 by Gore Vidal. Reprinted by permission of the author. Bernard Shaw's "Heartbreak House": *Rocking the Boat* (Boston: Little, Brown & Co., 1962), pp. 94–105. Originally published in the *The Reporter*, November 26, 1959. Copyright © 1959 by Gore Vidal. Reprinted by permission of the author. The Commercialites: *Rocking the Boat* (Boston: Little, Brown & Co., 1962), pp. 106–12, 286–87. Originally published in *The Reporter*, November 12, 1959. Copyright © 1959 by Gore Vidal. Reprinted by permission of the author.

Wendy Wasserstein. Heidi Chronicled: *Shiksa Goddess* (New York: Vintage, 2001), pp. 128–30. Originally published in *The New Yorker*, March 6, 1995. Copyright © 2001 by Wendy Wasserstein. Used by permission of Alfred A. Knopf, a division of Random House, Inc.

Walt Whitman. The Gladiator—Mr. Forrest—Acting: *Brooklyn Daily Eagle*, December 26, 1846. Miserable State of the Stage: *Brooklyn Daily Eagle*, February 8, 1847. The Old Bowery: *Walt Whit-*

man: Poetry and Prose, Justin Kaplan, ed. (New York: Library of America, 1982), pp. 1185–92. Originally published in New York *Tribune*, August 16, 1885. Collected in *Complete Prose* (1902).

Thornton Wilder. Some Thoughts on Playwriting: *Thornton Wilder: Collected Plays and Writings on Theater*, J. D. McClatchy, ed. (New York: Library of America, 2007) pp. 694–703. Originally published in *The Intent of the Artist* (1941). Copyright © 1941 by The Wilder Family, LLC. Reprinted by permission of The Wilder Family, LLC c/o The Barbara Hogenson Agency, Inc.

Tennessee Williams. Author and Director: A Delicate Situation: *Where I Live* (New York: New Directions, 1978) pp. 93–99. Originally published in *Playbill*, September 30, 1957. Copyright © 1957 by The University of the South. Reprinted by permission of New Directions Publishing Corp.

Edmund Wilson. Burlesque Shows: *Edmund Wilson: Literary Essays and Reviews of the 1920s and 30s*, Lewis M. Dabney, ed. (New York: Library of America, 2007), pp. 228–33. Originally published in *The New Republic*: National Winter Garden (July 8, 1925); Peaches—A Humdinger (August 18, 1926). Collected in *The Shores of Light* (1952). Copyright © 1952 by Edmund Wilson. Copyright renewed © 1980 by Helen Miranda Wilson. Reprinted by permission of Farrar, Straus and Giroux, LLC.

William Winter: Edwin Booth as Hamlet, *The Life and Art of Edwin Booth*, (London: T. Fisher Unwin, 1893), pp. 161–77.

Thomas Wolfe. *From* Of Time and the River: *Of Time and the River* (New York: Charles Scribner's Sons, 1935), pp. 167–75. Copyright © 1935 by Charles Scribner's Sons. Copyright renewed © 1963 by Fred Gitlin, Administrator, C.T.A. Reprinted with the permission of Scribner, a Division of Simon & Schuster, Inc. All rights reserved.

Alexander Woollcott: Mrs. Fiske on Ibsen the Popular, *Mrs. Fiske: Her Views on the Stage, Recorded by Alexander Woollcott*, (New York: The Century Co., 1917), pp. 41–74.

Stark Young. Some American Dramatic Material: *The Drama*, May, 1912, pp. 210–21. Hamlet: *Immortal Shadows*, (New York: Hill and Wang, 1948), pp. 18–14. Originally published in *The Nation*, December 16, 1922, pp. 45–46.

This volume presents the texts of the original printings and manuscripts chosen for inclusion here, but it does not attempt to reproduce features of their typographic design, such as the display capitalization of chapter openings. The texts are presented without change, except for the correction of typographical errors. Spelling, punctuation, and capitalization are often expressive features, and they are not altered, even when inconsistent or irregular. The following is a list of typographical errors corrected, cited by page and line number: 32.10, withold; 38.7, Bourcicault; 38.31, Tennison; 38.32, Fog; 43.12, forgot say; 45.26, ocasion; 46.38, charletans; 50.7, *pere*; 82.25, Spectular; 83.29–30, arrayed . . . tableau [line transposed]; 103.30, Ellsler; 104.23, inuendoes; 114.11, JUST.'; 144.25, city; 158.24, symmetery; 164.32, topsy; 165.30, Shakespearian; 166.1, Enorbarbus; 166.5, Cyndus; 166.11, Actum; 166.22, Marsh; 166.26, exactl; 166.30, 200 hundred; 168.14, just good; 175.6, Tomashevsky; 206.25, choose; 215.1, innoculated; 215.15, manger; 222.37, impressario; 238.24, graduel; 247.5, Its; 268.26, Isben; 270.23, unversities; 277.2, pistols—; 283.31, Stephan; 288.6, to tragic; 301.25, mahogony; 305.17, Eleanora; 340.2, *affetuoso;*; 340.29, it; 386.12, produce; 389.9, sigh by; 389.11, drunkeness; 399.25, Hearts of Oak; 400.27, Shore Acres; 404.25, The Country Circus; 410.4, Fall River; 411.37, Shore Acres; 437.12, do?"; 457.12, Dies, rangy; 489.28, woks; 493.16, in in; 546.36, the"; 616.17–18, permissable; 632.4, Ashberry; 636.33, labyrinthean; 647.37, *Virgina*; 654.5, on old; 655.6, Dealno; 668.13, multipled; 670.15, ralling; 700.4, verbocity; 701.39, times; 713.7, come; 747.25, schzoid; 748.12, 'Well,; 771.29, theatre; 817.17, responsibility; 820.12, Glen; 823.31–34, "Because . . . Russia."; 823.36, 'Why; 832.37, 'The;

Index

Plays are indexed by author's name if known; otherwise they are indexed under the title. Operas are indexed under the composer's name; musicals, however, are listed by title. Films are indexed by title.

THE LIBRARY OF AMERICA SERIES

The Library of America fosters appreciation and pride in America's literary heritage by publishing, and keeping permanently in print, authoritative editions of America's best and most significant writing. An independent nonprofit organization, it was founded in 1979 with seed money from the National Endowment for the Humanities and the Ford Foundation.

To subscribe to the series or to order individual copies,
please visit www.loa.org or call (800) 964.5778.

This book is set in 10 point Linotron Galliard,
a face designed for photocomposition by Matthew Carter
and based on the sixteenth-century face Granjon. The paper
is acid-free lightweight opaque and meets the requirements
for permanence of the American National Standards Institute.
The binding material is Brillianta, a woven rayon cloth made
by Van Heek-Scholco Textielfabrieken, Holland. Composition by Dedicated Business Services. Printing by
Malloy Incorporated. Binding by Dekker Book-
binding. Designed by Bruce Campbell.